UNDERSTANDING AND USING

English Grammar

FOURTH EDITION

Betty S. Azar
Stacy A. Hagen

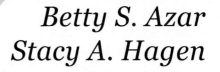

PEARSON
Longman

Understanding and Using English Grammar, Fourth Edition

Azar Associates: Shelley Hartle, Editor, and Sue Van Etten, Manager

Pearson Education, 10 Bank Street, White Plains, NY 10606

Staff credits: The people who made up the *Understanding and Using English Grammar Fourth Edition* team, representing editorial, production, design, and manufacturing, are Janice Baillie, Dave Dickey, Ann France, Amy McCormick, Robert Ruvo, and Ruth Voetmann.

Text composition: S4Carlisle Publishing Services
Text font: 10/12.5 Plantin
Illustrations: Don Martinetti, pages 2, 3, 4, 5, 14, 16, 17, 18, 23, 26, 27, 31, 36, 37, 47, 50, 51, 65, 72, 73, 81, 84, 88, 91, 99, 103, 107, 109, 115, 119, 120, 121, 123, 127, 131, 135, 139, 143, 145, 148, 152, 161, 169, 183, 185, 188, 190, 194, 201, 213, 220, 223, 232, 236, 238, 247, 255, 256, 259, 260 (top), 275, 278, 280, 286, 287, 292, 301, 303, 308, 316, 319, 321, 328, 340, 342, 347, 353, 355, 357, 362, 371, 373, 389, 396, 408, 413, 420, 424, 425, 432, 441, 446; Chris Pavely, pages 8, 41, 43, 45, 47, 54, 56, 60, 68, 70, 71, 74, 75, 77, 79, 86, 98, 100, 113, 116, 138, 142, 146, 153, 158, 170, 174, 175, 178, 181, 196, 198, 206, 211, 228, 235, 251, 257, 260 (bottom), 265, 272, 284, 289, 293, 309, 315, 331, 345, 349, 360, 363, 367, 378, 385, 393, 394, 403, 414, 422, 428; Kris Wiltse, pages 17, 19, 28, 29

Library of Congress Cataloging-in-Publication Data

Azar, Betty Schrampfer, 1941-
    Understanding and using English grammar. -- 4th ed. / Betty S. Azar,
Stacy A. Hagen.
        p. cm.
    ISBN-13: 978-0-13-233333-7 (with audio)
    ISBN-10: 0-13-233333-3 (with audio)
    ISBN-13: 978-0-13-233331-3 (with audio and answer key)
    ISBN-10: 0-13-233331-7 (with audio and answer key)
    [etc.]
    1. English language--Textbooks for foreign speakers. 2. English
language--Grammar--Problems, exercises, etc. I. Hagen, Stacy A., 1956-
II. Title.
    PE1128.A97 2009
    428.2'4--dc22   2008050357

Printed in the United States of America
ISBN 13: 978-0-13-233333-7
ISBN 10: 0-13-233333-3
5 6 7 8 9 10—V011—14 13 12 11 10

ISBN 13: 978-0-13-246448-2 (International Edition)
ISBN 10: 0-13-246448-9 (International Edition)
5 6 7 8 9 10—V011—14 13 12 11

For Larry
B.S.A.

For Andy and Julianna
S.H.

Contents

Preface to the Fourth Edition

Understanding and Using English Grammar is a developmental skills text for intermediate to advanced English language learners. It uses a grammar-based approach integrated with communicative methodologies to promote the development of all language skills in a variety of ways. Starting from a foundation of understanding form and meaning, students engage in meaningful communication about real actions, real things, and their own real lives in the classroom context. *Understanding and Using English Grammar* functions principally as a classroom teaching text but also serves as a comprehensive reference text for students and teachers.

The eclectic approach and abundant variety of exercise material remain the same as in the earlier editions, but each new edition incorporates new ways and means. In particular:

- **WARM-UP EXERCISES FOR THE GRAMMAR CHARTS**
  Newly created for the fourth edition, these innovative exercises precede the grammar charts and introduce the point(s) to be taught. They have been carefully crafted to help students *discover* the target grammar as they progress through each warm-up exercise.

- **LISTENING PRACTICE**
  Numerous listening exercises help students interact with the spoken language in a variety of settings that range from the relaxed, casual speech of everyday conversation to the academic content of classroom lectures. An audio CD accompanies the student text, and a full audio script can be found in the back of the book.

- **ACADEMIC READINGS**
  Students can read and respond to a wide selection of carefully crafted readings that focus on the target grammar structure.

- **EXPANDED SPEAKING ACTIVITIES**
  Students have even more opportunities in this fourth edition to share their experiences, express their opinions, and relate the target grammar to their personal lives. The text often uses the students' own life experiences as context and regularly introduces topics of interest to stimulate the free expression of ideas in structured as well as open discussions.

- **CORPUS-INFORMED CONTENT**
  Based on the findings of our corpus researcher, Gena Bennett, grammar content has been added, deleted, or modified to reflect the discourse patterns of spoken and written English.

Understanding and Using English Grammar is accompanied by

- A comprehensive **Workbook**, consisting of self-study exercises for independent work.
- An all-new **Teacher's Guide**, with step-by-step teaching suggestions for each chart, notes to the teacher on key grammar structures, vocabulary lists, and expansion activities and *PowerPoint* presentations for key chapters.
- An expanded **Test Bank**, with additional quizzes, chapter tests, and mid-term and final exams.
- **Test-Generator** software that allows teachers to customize their own tests using quizzes and tests from the *Test Bank*.
- **Azar Interactive**, a computer-based program keyed to the text, provides easily understood content, all-new exercises, readings, listening and speaking activities, and comprehensive tests.
- **PowerPoint** presentations for key chapters. Based on real-world readings, these lessons are designed for use in the classroom as "beyond-the-book" activities. They can be found in the new *Teacher's Guide* or downloaded from AzarGrammar.com.
- A **Chartbook**, a reference book consisting only of the grammar charts.
- **AzarGrammar.com**. This Web site provides a variety of supplementary classroom materials and is a place where teachers can support each other by sharing their knowledge and experience.
- **Fun with Grammar**, a teacher resource text by Suzanne Woodward with communicative activities correlated with the Azar-Hagen Grammar Series. It is available as a text or as a download on *AzarGrammar.com*.

The Azar-Hagen Grammar Series consists of

- *Understanding and Using English Grammar* (blue cover), for upper-level students.
- *Fundamentals of English Grammar* (black), for mid-level students.
- *Basic English Grammar* (red), for lower or beginning levels.

Acknowledgments

A revision of this scope could not have been done without the skills of top-notch professionals. We began with a group of outstanding reviewers whose detailed comments guided our writing. We wish to express our gratitude for their thoughtful reviews. They are Tonie Badillo, El Paso Community College; Edina Bagley, Nassau Community College; Michael Berman, Montgomery College; Elizabeth Bottcher, Columbia University; Eric Clinkscales, Teikyo Loretto Heights University; Cathy Costa, Edmonds Community College; Ms. Carlin Good, Columbia University; Deanna Cecil Ferreira, English Language Institute; Linda Gossard, DPT Business School ESL Program; Dr. Sheila Hakner, St. John's University; Martha Hall, New England School of English; Jennifer Hannon, Massachusetts Community College; Alyson Hanson, Gateway Community College; Joan Heiman, Community College of Denver; Steven Lasswell, Santa Barbara City College; Linda Leary, Albany Education; Louis Lucca, LaGuardia Community College; Kate Masterson, Boston Center for Adult Education; Phyllis McCollum, DPT Business School ESL Program; David Moody, El Paso Community College; Jan Peterson, Edmonds Community College; Antonina Rodgers, Northern Virginia Community College; Lenka Rohls, LaGuardia Community College; Rebecca Suarez, The University of Texas at El Paso; Ann Marie Tamayo, Queens Community College; and Kelly Roberts Weibel, Edmonds Community College.

We would like to thank a terrific support team that allows us to do what we do with enjoyment and ease: Shelley Hartle, managing editor par excellence, who worked magic on every page; Amy McCormick, Azar product manager, who oversaw our project and handled our myriad requests with unfailing grace, humor, and skill; Ruth Voetmann, development editor, whose attention to detail helped polish each chart and exercise; Janice Baillie, expert production editor and copy editor; Sue Van Etten, our skilled and multi-talented business and Web site manager; Gena Bennett, corpus researcher, whose findings helped keep us abreast of the nuances and changes in spoken and written discourse; and Robert Ruvo, our invaluable production liaison at Pearson Education.

Finally, we'd like to thank the dedicated leadership team from Pearson Education that guided this project: JoAnn Dresner, Anne Boynton-Trigg, Rhea Banker, and Sherry Preiss.

For the new design of this fourth edition we were lucky to have had the combined talents of Michael Cimilluca from Lindsay Communications, Ann France from Pearson Education, and freelance artist Kris Wiltse.

Our appreciation also goes to illustrators Don Martinetti and Chris Pavely for their humor and inspired artwork.

Finally, we would like to thank our families for their unflagging patience and encouragement throughout this extensive revision. Their insights and support are a continual source of inspiration.

Betty S. Azar
Stacy A. Hagen

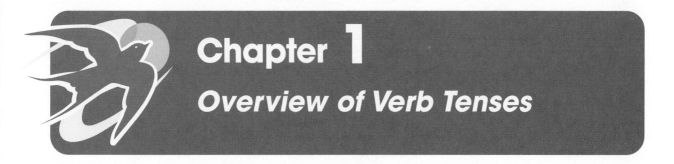

❏ **Exercise 1. Let's talk: interviews and introductions.**
Interview a classmate, and then introduce this person to the rest of the class or to a small group of classmates. Use the given topics or topics of your own choosing.

1. name
2. spelling of name
3. country of origin
4. birthplace
5. current residence

6. reason for coming here
7. length of time, both past and future, in this city/country
8. field of study or work
9. activities in free time
10. comments on living here

❏ **Exercise 2. Let's talk: preview of verb tenses.** (Chapters 1 → 5)
Work with a partner. Take turns asking questions with ***what*** + *a form of **do***. Help each other decide which verb tense should be used. When you finish asking and answering the questions, discuss your use of verb forms with the rest of the class.

Example: every morning
PARTNER A: What do you do every morning?
PARTNER B: I (go to classes / eat breakfast / etc.) every morning. What do you do every morning?
PARTNER A: I (eat breakfast / do my homework / etc.).

Partner A	Partner B
1. every day before you leave home	1. last night
2. since you got up this morning	2. tomorrow
3. right now	3. for the past five minutes
4. at (this exact time) yesterday	4. at (this exact time) tomorrow
5. by the time you got here today	5. by the time you go to bed tonight

❏ **Exercise 3. Warm-up.** (Chart 1-1)
Do you agree or disagree with each sentence? Circle *yes* or *no*. Discuss the verbs in blue. What information do the verb tenses provide?

1. Warm air rises.   yes   no
2. I talk on the phone a lot.   yes   no
3. I sent an email today.   yes   no
4. I'm going to make a phone call today.   yes   no

1

1-1 The Simple Tenses

This basic diagram will be used in all tense descriptions.

```
                              now
                               ↑
              past ←───────────┼───────────→ future
```

Tense	Examples	Meaning
Simple Present ✗✗✗✗✗✗✗✗✗✗✗	(a) It *snows* in Alaska. (b) Tom *watches* TV every day.	In general, the simple present expresses events or situations that exist *always, usually, habitually;* they exist now, have existed in the past, and probably will exist in the future.
Simple Past ✗	(c) It *snowed* yesterday. (d) Tom *watched* TV last night.	*At one particular time in the past,* this happened. It began and ended in the past.
Simple Future ✗	(e) It *will snow* tomorrow. It *is going to snow* tomorrow. (f) Tom *will watch* TV tonight. Tom *is going to watch* TV tonight.	*At one particular time in the future,* this will happen.

❑ **Exercise 4. Let's listen and talk.** (Chart 1-1)

CD 1
Track 2

Listen to the sentences and write the words you hear. Are the sentences true for you? Choose *yes* or *no.* Share your answers with the class, adding information if you like.

Example: You will hear: I wore jeans to class yesterday.

You will write: I _____*wore*_____ jeans to class yesterday.   yes   (no)

You might say: I didn't wear jeans to class yesterday.

I wore a skirt.

1. I _____ my own dinner last night.   yes   no

2. I _____ a textbook yesterday.   yes   no

3. I _____ on the internet every day.   yes   no

4. I _____ home tonight.   yes   no

5. I _____ a movie this weekend.   yes   no

❏ **Exercise 5. Warm-up.** (Chart 1-2)
Answer the questions.

1. What are you doing right now? Look around the room. What are your classmates doing right now? What is happening outside the classroom right now?
2. Where were you at two o'clock this morning? What were you doing?
3. Where will you be at two o'clock tomorrow? What will you be doing?

1-2 The Progressive Tenses

Form: **be** + **-ing** (present participle)

Meaning: The progressive tenses* give the idea that an action is in progress during a particular time. The tenses say that an action *begins before, is in progress during, and continues after* another time or action.

Present Progressive	(a) Tom *is sleeping* right now.	It is now 11:00. Tom went to sleep at 10:00 tonight, and he is still asleep. His sleep began in the past, *is in progress at the present time,* and probably will continue.
Past Progressive	(b) Tom *was sleeping* when I arrived.	Tom went to sleep at 10:00 last night. I arrived at 11:00. He was still asleep. His sleep began before and *was in progress at a particular time in the past.* It continued after I arrived.
Future Progressive	(c) Tom *will be sleeping* when we arrive.	Tom will go to sleep at 10:00 tomorrow night. We will arrive at 11:00. The action of sleeping will begin before we arrive, and it *will be in progress at a particular time in the future.* Probably his sleep will continue.

*The progressive tenses are also called the "continuous" tenses: present continuous, past continuous, and future continuous.

❏ **Exercise 6. Let's listen and talk.** (Chart 1-2)

CD 1
Track 3

Listen to the sentences and write the words you hear. Are the sentences true for you? Choose *yes* or *no*. Share your answers with the class, adding information if you like.

1. At midnight last night, I _____.   yes   no

2. Right now I _____ about grammar.   yes   no

3. Tomorrow I _____ in class at this time.   yes   no

4. Tonight at 9:00, I _____ TV.   yes   no

5. Last night at 9:00, I _____ TV.   yes   no

□ **Exercise 7. Warm-up.** (Chart 1-3)
Answer the questions.

1. Have you eaten today? When did you eat?
2. Had you eaten before you went to bed last night?
3. Will you have eaten by the time you go to bed tonight?

1-3 The Perfect Tenses

Form: **have** + *past participle*
Meaning: The perfect tenses all give the idea that one thing *happens before* another time or event.

Present Perfect	(a) Tom *has* already *eaten*.	Tom *finished* eating *sometime before now.* The exact time is not important.
Past Perfect	(b) Tom *had* already *eaten* when his friend arrived.	First Tom finished eating. Later his friend arrived. Tom's eating was completely *finished before another time in the past.*
Future Perfect	(c) Tom *will* already *have eaten* when his friend arrives.	First Tom will finish eating. Later his friend will arrive. Tom's eating will be completely *finished before another time in the future.*

□ **Exercise 8. Let's listen and talk.** (Chart 1-3)
Listen to the sentences and write the words you hear. Are the sentences true for you? Choose *yes* or *no.* Share your answers with the class, adding information if you like.

CD 1
Track 4

1. I _____ my homework already.   yes   no

2. Before I went to bed last night, I _____ all
   my homework.   yes   no

3. By the time I finish this chapter, I _____
   several verb exercises.   yes   no

4. I _____ all the English verb tenses.   yes   no

5. Before I began this class, I _____
   all the English verb tenses.   yes   no

Answer the questions.

1. What are you doing right now? How long have you been (doing it)?
2. What were you doing last night at nine o'clock? What time did you stop (doing it)? Why did you stop (doing it)? How long had you been (doing it) before you stopped?
3. What are you going to be doing at nine o'clock tomorrow night? What time are you going to stop (doing it)? Why? How long will you have been (doing it) before you stop?

1-4 The Perfect Progressive Tenses

Form: **have** + **been** + **-ing** (present participle)
Meaning: The perfect progressive tenses give the idea that one event is *in progress immediately before, up to, until another time or event.* The tenses are used to express the *duration* of the first event.

Present Perfect Progressive 2 hrs.	(a) Tom *has been studying* for two hours.	Event in progress: studying. When? *Before now, up to now.* How long? For two hours.
Past Perfect Progressive 2 hrs.	(b) Tom *had been studying* for two hours before his friend came.	Event in progress: studying. When? *Before another event in the past.* How long? For two hours.
Future Perfect Progressive 2 hrs.	(c) Tom *will have been studying* for two hours by the time his friend arrives.	Event in progress: studying. When? *Before another event in the future.* How long? For two hours.

❏ **Exercise 10. Looking at grammar.** (Chart 1-4)
Complete the sentences with your own words.

1. I'm in class right now. I arrived in class today and sat down at _____

   (*time*). Right now the time is _____. That means that I **have been sitting**

   in this seat for _____ minutes.

2. I **had been sitting** here for _____ minutes before class started.

3. By the time class finishes at _____, I **will have been sitting** here for

   _____ minutes.

1-5 Summary Chart of Verb Tenses

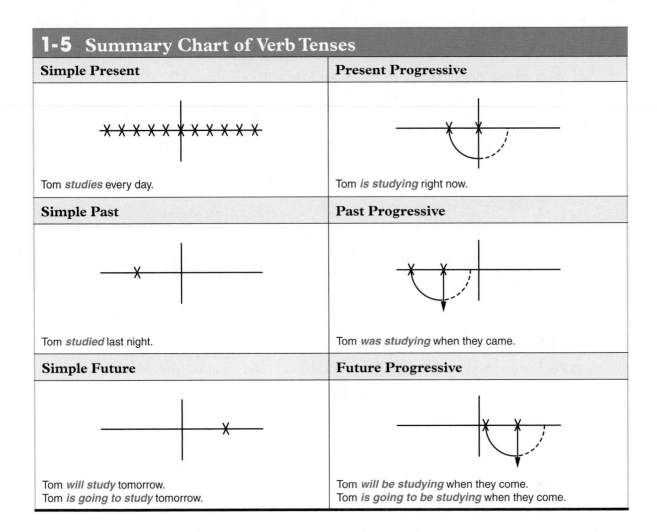

Simple Present	Present Progressive
Tom *studies* every day.	Tom *is studying* right now.

Simple Past	Past Progressive
Tom *studied* last night.	Tom *was studying* when they came.

Simple Future	Future Progressive
Tom *will study* tomorrow. Tom *is going to study* tomorrow.	Tom *will be studying* when they come. Tom *is going to be studying* when they come.

❑ **Exercise 11. Looking at grammar.** (Charts 1-1 → 1-5)
Complete the sentences with a form of ***study*** and any words in parentheses. Then compare your completions with the sentences in Chart 1-5.

1. Tom is a student. He _____*studies*_____ every day.

2. Tom is at his desk. He _____ right now.

3. Tom had some homework to do, so he _____ last night.

4. Tom began studying at 7:00 last night. His friends came over around 7:30. Tom was still at his desk when they arrived. In other words, Tom _____ last night when his friends came over.

5. Tom _____ tomorrow.

6. Tom is going to begin studying at 7:00 tomorrow. His friends are going to come over at 7:30. Tom _____ when they arrive.

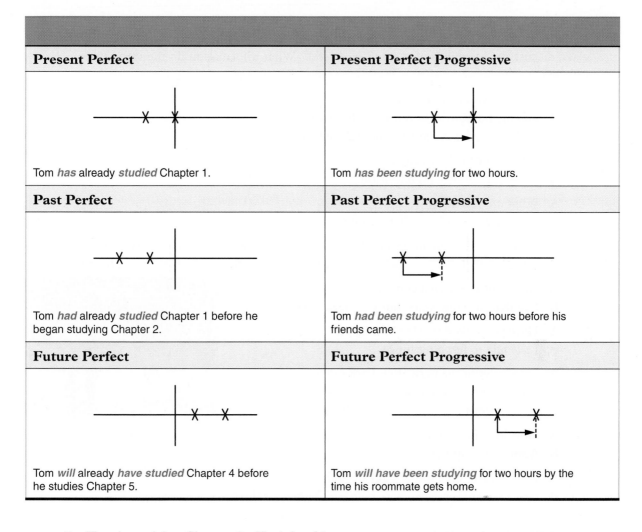

Present Perfect	Present Perfect Progressive
Tom *has* already *studied* Chapter 1.	Tom *has been studying* for two hours.
Past Perfect	**Past Perfect Progressive**
Tom *had* already *studied* Chapter 1 before he began studying Chapter 2.	Tom *had been studying* for two hours before his friends came.
Future Perfect	**Future Perfect Progressive**
Tom *will* already *have studied* Chapter 4 before he studies Chapter 5.	Tom *will have been studying* for two hours by the time his roommate gets home.

7. Tom is studying Chapter 2. He (*already*) _____ Chapter 1.

8. Last week Tom finished studying Chapter 1. This week he's studying Chapter 2. He (*already*) _____ Chapter 1 when he started Chapter 2.

9. Next week Tom will finish Chapters 4 and 5. Before Tom studies Chapter 5, he (*already*) _____ Chapter 4.

10. Today Tom began studying at 8:00. Now it is 10:00. Tom _____ _____ for two hours.

11. Yesterday Tom began studying at 8:00. Tom's friends came over at 10:00. Before his friends came, Tom _____ for two hours.

12. It's 8:00. Tom's roommate gets home at 10:00. By the time Tom's roommate gets home, Tom _____ for two hours.

□ **Exercise 12. Let's talk.** (Charts 1-1 → 1-5)
In the following dialogues, many of the verbs are in *italics*.* In pairs, in small groups, or as a class, discuss the meanings of the *italicized* verbs. What information do the verb tenses provide?

1. A: What *do* you *do* in the evening?
   B: I *do* my homework and *watch* a little TV.
      → *The speakers are talking about daily habits.*

2. A: What *did* you *do* last night?
   B: I *watched* a movie on television.

3. A: What *are* you *doing*?
   B: I *am working* on English grammar.

4. A: I called you last night around 9:00, but no one answered. Where were you?
   B: I was home, but I *was studying.* I always turn my phone off when I want to study.

5. A: *Have* you ever *seen* a comet?
   B: I*'ve seen* shooting stars, but I*'ve* never *seen* a comet.

6. A: Have you talked to Mrs. Chang yet?
   B: I *will talk* to her after lunch.

7. A: Let's meet at the park after work today.
   B: Okay. I *will be sitting* on a bench near the Forest Avenue entrance. Look for me there.

8. A: How long *have* you *been working* on this grammar exercise?
   B: About ten minutes.

9. A: Did you like the food at Paul's Café?
   B: Yes. I *had* never *eaten* there before. Thanks for the recommendation.

□ **Exercise 13. Let's talk.** (Charts 1-1 → 1-5)
Answer the questions in complete sentences. If you work in pairs, alternate asking and answering the sets of questions. You may want to take notes and later share a few of the answers with the rest of the class.
   If you work in small groups, select a leader who will ask the questions and elicit two or three responses to each. You may wish to rotate the role of leader.
   If you work as a class, close your book and answer the teacher's questions.

1. a. What do you do every day?
   b. What are you doing now?

2. a. What did you do last week?
   b. What had you done before that?

3. a. What will you do next week?
   b. What will you be doing at this time next week?
   c. What will you have done by this time next year?

---

*Words that are "italicized" or "in italics" have slanted print. Regular print looks like this. *Italic print looks like this.*

4. a. What were you doing at this time yesterday?
   b. What will you be doing at this time tomorrow?

5. a. What have you done since you got up this morning?
   b. What are you doing right now? How long have you been doing that?

6. a. What were you doing before you walked into the classroom today?
      How long had you been doing that?
   b. What will you be doing before our teacher walks into the classroom tomorrow? How
      long will you have been doing that?

❑ **Exercise 14. What do I already know?** (Appendix Charts B-1, B-2, and D-1)
This exercise covers question and negative verb forms you will use in the following chapters.
Check your understanding of these forms by correcting the errors in these sentences.*

1. Does Pedro walks to work every morning?

2. What you are talking about?

3. Did you finished your work?

4. My friend doesn't liking her apartment.

5. Do you are working for this company?

6. What time your plane did it arrive?

7. How long have you are living in this city?

8. Ali won't to be in class tomorrow.

❑ **Exercise 15. Warm-up: listening.** (Chart 1-6)
You will be using many verbs in their *-ing* and *-ed* forms in the following chapters. Use this
pretest to check your spelling.

Example: You will hear: Listened. We listened to music. Listened.
   You will write: _____listened_____

1. _____   6. _____

2. _____   7. _____

3. _____   8. _____

4. _____   9. _____

5. _____   10. _____

---

*For information about forming questions and negatives, see these self-study charts in the Appendix: B-1 (Forms of Yes/No
and Information Questions), B-2 (Question Words), and D-1 (Using *Not* and Other Negative Words).

1-6 Spelling of *-ing* and *-ed* Forms

(1)	VERBS THAT END IN A CONSONANT AND *-e*	(a)	hope date injure	hoping dating injuring	hoped dated injured	*-ING* FORM: If the word ends in *-e*, drop the *-e* and add *-ing*.* *-ED* FORM: If the word ends in a consonant and *-e*, just add *-d*.

(2) VERBS THAT END IN A VOWEL AND A CONSONANT	**ONE-SYLLABLE VERBS**

		(b)	stop rob	stopping robbing	stopped robbed	1 vowel → 2 consonants**
		(c)	rain fool	raining fooling	rained fooled	2 vowels → 1 consonant

TWO-SYLLABLE VERBS

		(d)	listen offer	listening offering	listened offered	1st syllable stressed → 1 consonant
		(e)	begin prefer	beginning preferring	(began) preferred	2nd syllable stressed → 2 consonants
(3)	VERBS THAT END IN TWO CONSONANTS	(f)	start fold demand	starting folding demanding	started folded demanded	If the word ends in two consonants, just add the ending.
(4)	VERBS THAT END IN *-y*	(g)	enjoy pray	enjoying praying	enjoyed prayed	If *-y* is preceded by a vowel, keep the *-y*.
		(h)	study try reply	studying trying replying	studied tried replied	If *-y* is preceded by a consonant: *-ING* FORM: keep the *-y*; add *-ing*. *-ED* FORM: change *-y* to *-i*; add *-ed*.
(5)	VERBS THAT END IN *-ie*	(i)	die lie	dying lying	died lied	*-ING* FORM: Change *-ie* to *-y*; add *-ing*. *-ED* FORM: Add *-d*.

*Exception: If a verb ends in *-ee*, the final *-e* is not dropped: *seeing, agreeing, freeing*.

**Exception: *-w* and *-x* are not doubled: *plow → plowed; fix → fixed*.

❑ **Exercise 16. Looking at spelling.** (Chart 1-6)
Write the correct forms of the given verbs.

Part I. Write the *-ing* form of these verbs in the correct columns.

✓date	grade	stay
dine	happen	stop
enjoy	put	win

Drop the *-e*.	Double the consonant.	Just add *-ing*.
dating		

Part II. Write the **-ed** form of these verbs in the correct columns.

✓answer	listen	open	plan
control	offer	permit	prefer

Do not double the consonant.	Double the consonant.
answered	

❏ **Exercise 17. Looking at spelling.** (Chart 1-6)
Practice spelling verb forms.

Part I. Write the correct **-ing** form of the given verbs.

1. hold _____holding_____   7. eat _____

2. hide _____   8. pat _____

3. run _____   9. lie _____

4. ruin _____   10. begin _____

5. come _____   11. earn _____

6. write _____   12. fly _____

Part II. Write the correct **-ing** and **-ed** forms of the given verbs.

1. boil _____boiling, boiled_____

2. plan _____

3. rain _____

4. tape _____

5. tap _____

6. enter _____

7. prefer _____

8. translate _____

9. die _____

10. employ _____

11. bury   _____

12. admit   _____

13. visit   _____

14. wait   _____

❏ **Exercise 18. Listening.** (Chart 1-6)

Listen to the sentences and write the words you hear.

CD 1
Track 6

Example: You will hear: We are visiting family this weekend.

          You will write: We _____*are visiting*_____ family this weekend.

1. We _____ an apartment in the city.

2. We _____ to rent and see how we liked city life.

3. The earthquake _____ the town.

4. Our children _____ their grandparents.

5. We _____ a little weight on our vacation.

6. I _____ a short trip this summer.

7. I _____ a few weeks off from work.

8. Right now I _____ to several emails.

9. I'm done. I _____ to all of them.

❏ **Exercise 19. Let's talk and write.** (Chapter 1)

Do one or more of these activities.

Activities:

1. Interview a classmate outside of class and write a story of his/her life.

2. Interview a native speaker of English and write a story of his/her life.

3. With a classmate, take a trip to a particular place, such as a museum, a park, or a restaurant. Write a report of your trip, or give an oral report to your classmates.

4. Write a brief paragraph about yourself, telling who you are, what you have done in the past two years, and what your plans are for the next two years. Then exchange papers with a classmate. Read your classmate's paragraph and ask questions if you need more information or clarification. Next, join two other students to form a group of four. Tell the others in the group about your classmate. Use the information from the paragraph he/she wrote.

12 CHAPTER 1

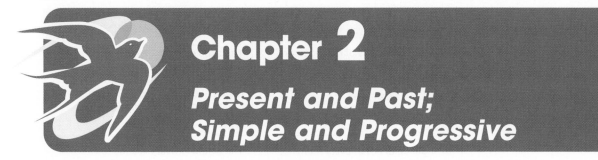

Chapter 2
Present and Past;
Simple and Progressive

❏ **Exercise 1. What do I already know?** (Chapter 2)
Correct the errors in verb forms.

        do
1. I ~~am~~ not agree with your opinion.

2. I'm not knowing Sam's wife.

3. My roommate usually watch television, listen to music, or going out in the evening.

4. When I turned the key, the car was starting.

5. Air is consisting of oxygen, nitrogen, and other gases.

6. The children drawed some pictures in school this morning.

7. Right now Sally in the kitchen eating breakfast.

8. While I'm driving home last night, I heared a strange noise in the engine.

9. A: What you are talking about?

    B: I talking about the political situation in my country.

❏ **Exercise 2. Warm-up.** (Charts 2-1 and 2-2)
Work individually and then as a class.

Part I. Read each sentence and circle *yes* or *no*. If the information is not true, restate it.

1. I read a newspaper every day.   yes   no
2. I am sitting next to someone from Asia.   yes   no
3. The sun revolves around the earth.   yes   no

Part II. Answer the questions.

4. Which sentence discusses a general truth?
5. Which sentence talks about a daily habit?
6. Which sentence talks about something that is happening right now?

2-1 Simple Present

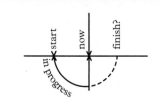

(a) Water *consists* of hydrogen and oxygen. (b) The average person *breathes* 21,600 times a day. (c) The world *is* round.	The simple present says that something was true in the past, is true in the present, and will be true in the future. It expresses *general statements of fact and general truths.*
(d) I *get* up at seven *every morning.* (e) I *always eat* a salad for lunch.	The simple present is used to express *habitual or everyday activities.*

2-2 Present Progressive

(f) The students *are sitting* at their desks right now. (g) I need an umbrella because it *is raining.* (h) I *am taking* five courses this semester.	The present progressive expresses an activity that is *in progress at the moment of speaking.* It is a temporary activity that began in the past, is continuing at present, and will probably end at some point in the future.

❑ **Exercise 3. Let's talk.** (Charts 2-1 and 2-2)
Work in small groups.

Part I. Discuss the given topics. Each member of the group should contribute one sentence for each topic. Share some of your sentences with the class.

Topics:
Tell your group one daily habit you have.
Look around the room. Describe one activity that is happening right now.
Describe something that is happening in the world right now.

Part II. Use the simple present to make generalizations about some of the given topics. Use your own verbs or those in the list.

beat	consist	eat	make	save
breathe	contain	have	produce	sleep
cause	drink	live	revolve	use

Topics:

the earth	snowflakes
air	the average person
trees	hybrid cars★
the human heart	mammals

snowflakes

★*hybrid cars* = cars that use both gasoline and electricity for power.

❏ **Exercise 4. Looking at grammar.** (Charts 2-1 and 2-2)
Complete the sentences with the simple present or the present progressive form of the verbs in parentheses.

1. Kristin can't come to the phone because she (*wash*) _____ is washing _____ her hair.

2. Kristin (*wash*) _____ her hair every other day or so.

3. Tony (*sit, usually*) _____ in the front row during class, but today

   he (*sit*) _____ in the last row.

4. Please be quiet. I (*try*) _____ to concentrate.

5. (*you, lock, always*) _____ the door to your apartment when

   you leave?

6. I wrote to my friend last week. She hasn't answered my letter yet. I (*wait, still*)

   _____ for a reply.

7. After six days of rain, I'm glad that the sun (*shine*) _____ today.

8. Every morning, the sun (*shine*) _____ in my bedroom window and

   (*wake*) _____ me up.

❏ **Exercise 5. Listening.** (Charts 2-1 and 2-2)
CD 1
Track 7
Listen to the sentences. Circle the correct completion(s). More than one completion may be possible.

1. right now.   every day.   in the summer.

2. today.   in the winter.   every April.

3. every year.   right now.   this week.

4. right now.   today.   every winter.

5. every summer.   right now.   in the spring.

6. this week.   every January.   every winter.

❏ **Exercise 6. Let's talk: class activity.** (Charts 2-1 and 2-2)
On a piece of paper, write an action that a classmate can demonstrate (e.g., stand up, smile, open the door, sneeze, write on the board). Give your paper to the teacher, who will redistribute the papers at random to the class. Everyone will take turns performing these actions for the entire class. Describe the actions using the present progressive.

❏ **Exercise 7. Warm-up.** (Chart 2-3)
Choose the correct completions.

1. The chef is in his kitchen right now. He _____.
   a. cooks   b. is cooking

2. He _____ some soup.
   a. tastes   b. is tasting

3. It _____ too salty.
   a. tastes   b. is tasting

4. He _____ it.
   a. doesn't like   b. isn't liking

2-3 Non-Progressive Verbs

(a) I *know* your cousin. (b) INCORRECT: I ~~am knowing~~ your cousin.	Some verbs, like ***know***, are *non-progressive;** i.e., they are rarely used in progressive tenses. They describe states, not actions. ("States" are conditions or situations that exist.)

Common Verbs That Are Usually Non-Progressive (like *know*)

know	like	dislike	belong	consist of	hear	agree
believe	appreciate	fear	possess	contain	sound	disagree
doubt	care about	hate	own			mean
recognize	please	mind		exist	seem	promise
remember	prefer		desire	matter	look like	amaze
suppose			need		resemble	surprise
understand			want			
			wish			

(c) I *think* that your cousin is very nice. (d) I *'m thinking* about my trip to Rome.	Some verbs, like ***think***, have both *non-progressive* meanings and *progressive* meanings. In (c): ***think*** means "believe." In (d): ***am thinking*** means "thoughts are going around in my mind right now."

Common Verbs with Both Non-Progressive and Progressive Meanings (like *think*)

	NON-PROGRESSIVE	PROGRESSIVE
look	It *looks* cold outside.	Olga *is looking* out the window.
appear	Jack *appears* to be tired today.	She *'s appearing* on a TV show today.
think	I *think* that Mr. Liu is a good teacher.	I *'m thinking* about my family right now.
feel	I *feel* that Mr. Liu is a good teacher.	I *'m feeling* a little tired today.
have	I *have* a bicycle.	I *'m having* a good time.
see	*Do* you *see* that bird?	The doctor *is seeing* a patient right now.
taste	The soup *tastes* salty.	The chef *is tasting* the soup.
smell	Something *smells* bad. What is it?	Ann *is smelling* the perfume to see if she wants to buy it.
love	Ken *loves* his baby daughter.	Ken is enjoying parenthood. In fact, he *'s loving* it!
be	Mary *is* old and wise.	Al is ill but won't see a doctor. He *is being foolish.***

*Non-progressive verbs are also called "stative verbs" or non-action verbs.

***Am/is/are being* + *an adjective* describes temporary behavior. In the example, Al is usually not foolish, but right now he is acting that way.

❑ **Exercise 8. Let's talk.** (Chart 2-3)

Discuss the differences in meaning of the *italicized* verbs in each group of sentences. Work in pairs, in small groups, or as a class.

1. a. These flowers *smell* good.
   b. James *is smelling* the flowers.

2. a. I *think* Roberto is a kind man.
   b. I *am thinking* about this exercise.

3. a. I *see* a butterfly. Do you *see* it too?
   b. Alex *is seeing* a doctor about his headaches.
   c. Jack and Ann *are seeing* each other. They go out together every weekend.

4. a. Astrid *looks* cold. I'll lend her my coat.
   b. Tina *is looking* out the window. She sees a butterfly.

5. a. Sue *is feeling* the cat's fur.
   b. The cat's fur *feels* soft.
   c. I'*m not feeling* well today.
   d. I *feel* that it is important to respect other people's opinions.

6. a. I *remember* my first teacher. *Do* you *remember* yours?
   b. Aunt Sara is looking through an old picture album.
      She *is remembering* the wonderful days of her childhood.

7. a. The children want a snack. They'*re* hungry.
   b. Like many kids, our children are often quite noisy when they
      play. They're playing right now in the next room. Hmmm.
      They'*re being* awfully quiet. What do you suppose they're doing?

8. a. Our son *is appearing* in a school play this week.
   b. The grocer is weighing the bananas. He *appears* to be busy.

□ **Exercise 9. Looking at grammar.** (Chart 2-3)
Choose the correct completions.

1. This isn't my notebook. It _____ to Mai.
   (a.) belongs   b. is belonging

2. Ask Ahmed for your notebook. He _____ it.
   a. has   b. is having

3. Your notebook is over there. Ahmed _____ it.
   a. holds   b. is holding

4. Look at Olga. She's smiling and dancing. She _____ a good time.
   a. has   b. is having

5. Relax. You don't have to tell me any more about it. I _____ you.
   a. believe   b. am believing

6. Dinosaurs became extinct a long time ago. They _____ anymore.
   a. don't exist   b. aren't existing

□ **Exercise 10. Looking at grammar.** (Charts 2-1 → 2-3)
Complete the sentences. Use the simple present or the present progressive of the verbs in parentheses.

1. Look. It (*begin*) __is beginning__ to rain. Unfortunately, I (*have, not*[*])

   _____ my umbrella with me. I (*own, not*) _____

   an umbrella. Spiro is lucky. He (*wear*) _____ a raincoat. I (*wear*)

   _____ a waterproof hat on rainy days.

2. Right now Martha is in the science building.

   The chemistry experiment she (*do*)

   _____ is dangerous, so she (*be*)

   _____ very careful. She

   (*want, not*) _____ to spill

   any of the acid. She (*be, always*)

   _____ careful when

   she does a chemistry experiment.

---

[*]A form of **do** is usually used in the negative when the main verb is **have**, especially in American English (AmE) but also commonly in British English (BrE): *I don't have a car.* Using **have** without a form of **do** is also possible but less common: *I haven't a car.*

3. Right now I (*look*) _____ at Nicole. She (*look*) _____

angry. I wonder what's the matter. She (*have*) _____ a frown on her face.

She certainly (*have, not*) _____ any fun right now.

4. A: How (*you, like*) _____ the soup? (*it, need*) _____

_____ more garlic?

B: No, it (*taste*) _____ delicious. It (*remind*) _____ me of

my grandmother's soup.

5. A: What (*you, look*) _____ at?

B: You! You (*look*) _____ like your father.

A: (*you, think*) _____ so? Many people tell me I (*resemble*)

_____ my mother.

B: I (*see*) _____ your father's face when I look at you.

6. Right now I (*look*) _____ around the classroom. Yoko (*write*)

_____ in her book. Carlos (*bite*) _____ his pencil.

Wan-Ning (*scratch*) _____ his head. Ali (*stare*) _____

out the window. He (*seem*) _____ to be daydreaming, but perhaps he

(*think*) _____ hard about verb tenses. What (*you, think*) _____

_____ Ali (*do*) _____?

❑ **Exercise 11. Let's write.** (Charts 2-1 → 2-3)
Go to a place where there are many people (such as a zoo, a hotel lobby, a street corner) or imagine yourself to be there. Describe what you see. Let your reader "see" what you see by drawing a picture in words. Use present tenses. Write one paragraph. Begin with a description of what you are doing: *I am sitting on a bench at the zoo.*

2-4 Regular and Irregular Verbs

Regular Verbs: The simple past and past participle end in *-ed*.

SIMPLE FORM	SIMPLE PAST	PAST PARTICIPLE	PRESENT PARTICIPLE
hope	hoped	hoped	hoping
stop	stopped	stopped	stopping
listen	listened	listened	listening
study	studied	studied	studying
start	started	started	starting

English verbs have four principal parts:
(1) simple form
(2) simple past
(3) past participle
(4) present participle

Irregular Verbs: The simple past and past participle do not end in *-ed*.

SIMPLE FORM	SIMPLE PAST	PAST PARTICIPLE	PRESENT PARTICIPLE
hit	hit	hit	hitting
find	found	found	finding
swim	swam	swum	swimming
break	broke	broken	breaking

Some verbs have irregular past forms.

Most of the irregular verbs in English are given in the alphabetical list on the inside front and back covers.

2-5 Irregular Verb List

Group 1: All three forms are the same.

SIMPLE FORM	SIMPLE PAST	PAST PARTICIPLE	SIMPLE FORM	SIMPLE PAST	PAST PARTICIPLE
bet	bet	bet	let	let	let
burst	burst	burst	put	put	put
cost	cost	cost	quit	quit	quit
cut	cut	cut	shut	shut	shut
fit	fit/fitted	fit/fitted	split	split	split
hit	hit	hit	spread	spread	spread
hurt	hurt	hurt	upset	upset	upset

Group 2: Past participle ends in *-en*.

awake	awoke	awoken	hide	hid	hidden
bite	bit	bitten	prove	proved	proven/proved
break	broke	broken	ride	rode	ridden
choose	chose	chosen	rise	rose	risen
drive	drove	driven	shake	shook	shaken
eat	ate	eaten	speak	spoke	spoken
fall	fell	fallen	steal	stole	stolen
forget	forgot	forgotten	swell	swelled	swollen/swelled
forgive	forgave	forgiven	take	took	taken
freeze	froze	frozen	wake	woke/waked	woken
get	got	gotten/got*	write	wrote	written
give	gave	given			

* In BrE: *get-got-got*.

Group 3: Vowel changes from *a* in the simple past to *u* in the past participle.

begin	began	begun	shrink	shrank	shrunk
drink	drank	drunk	sing	sang	sung
ring	rang	rung	sink	sank	sunk
run	ran	run	swim	swam	swum

Group 4: Past tense and past participle forms are the same.

bend	bent	bent	mislay	mislaid	mislaid
bleed	bled	bled	pay	paid	paid
bring	brought	brought	read	read	read
build	built	built	say	said	said
burn	burnt	burnt	seek	sought	sought
buy	bought	bought	sell	sold	sold
catch	caught	caught	send	sent	sent
dig	dug	dug	shoot	shot	shot
feed	fed	fed	sit	sat	sat
feel	felt	felt	sleep	slept	slept
fight	fought	fought	slide	slid	slid
find	found	found	sneak	snuck/sneaked	snuck/sneaked
flee	fled	fled	speed	sped/speeded	sped/speeded
grind	ground	ground	spend	spent	spent
hang	hung	hung	spin	spun	spun
have	had	had	stand	stood	stood
hear	heard	heard	stick	stuck	stuck
hold	held	held	sting	stung	stung
keep	kept	kept	strike	struck	struck
lay	laid	laid	sweep	swept	swept
lead	led	led	swing	swung	swung
leave	left	left	teach	taught	taught
lend	lent	lent	tell	told	told
light	lit/lighted	lit/lighted	think	thought	thought
lose	lost	lost	understand	understood	understood
make	made	made	weep	wept	wept
mean	meant	meant	win	won	won
meet	met	met			

Group 5: Past participle adds -*n* to the simple form, with or without a spelling change.

blow	blew	blown	see	saw	seen
do	did	done	swear	swore	sworn
draw	drew	drawn	tear	tore	torn
fly	flew	flown	throw	threw	thrown
grow	grew	grown	wear	wore	worn
know	knew	known	withdraw	withdrew	withdrawn
lie	lay	lain			

Group 6: The first and third forms are the same.

become	became	become
come	came	come
run	ran	run

Group 7: One of the three forms is very different.

be	was, were	been
go	went	gone

Group 8: Both regular and irregular forms are used. (The regular form is more common in AmE, and the irregular form is more common in BrE.)

burn	burned/burnt	burned/burnt	learn	learned/learnt	learned/learnt
dream	dreamed/dreamt	dreamed/dreamt	smell	smelled/smelt	smelled/smelt
kneel	kneeled/knelt	kneeled/knelt	spill	spilled/spilt	spilled/spilt
lean	leaned/leant	leaned/leant	spoil	spoiled/spoilt	spoiled/spoilt

NOTE: See the inside front and back covers for an alphabetical list of these verbs as well as some additional irregular verbs that occur less frequently. Also included are definitions of the lesser-known verbs.

❏ **Exercise 12. Listening.** (Charts 2-4 and 2-5)

Listen to the questions. Complete each answer with the correct form of the verb you hear.

NOTE: Exercises 12 through 19 are quick reviews of the simple past of irregular verbs. Which irregular verbs are easy for you? Which ones are more troublesome? Which ones don't you know? Make a note of the verbs that are difficult for you and review them.

CD 1
Track 8

Example: You will hear: Did Sara go to class yesterday?

You will write: Yes, she _____*went*_____ to class yesterday.

SITUATION 1: Sara is a lazy student. She doesn't care about studying. She was at school yesterday.

1. Yes, she _____ her notebook.

2. Yes, she _____ her homework.

3. Yes, she _____ a lot of mistakes on the writing test.

4. Yes, she _____ several words incorrectly.

5. Yes, she _____ another student's homework to copy.

SITUATION 2: Jim is a serious student. He loves to learn. He was at school yesterday.

6. Yes, he _____ his homework.

7. Yes, he _____ the homework.

8. Yes, he _____ his homework to class.

9. Yes, he _____ a good grade on the test.

10. Yes, he _____ all the answers on the test.

SITUATION 3: Ms. Brooks is a good English teacher. She's also friendly. She taught yesterday.

11. Yes, she _____ class on time.

12. Yes, she _____ clearly.

13. Yes, she _____ a fair test.

14. Yes, she _____ extra time helping her students.

15. Yes, she _____ her students jokes.

16. Yes, she _____ her students a song.

17. Yes, she _____ with her students.

❏ **Exercise 13. Let's talk: pairwork.** (Charts 2-4 and 2-5)
Work with a partner. Partner A asks the questions. Partner B answers the questions with **Yes** and a complete sentence. NOTE: Although a short answer is usually given to a yes/no question (*Did you sit down? Yes, I did.*), practice the long answer in these exercises.

SITUATION: Imagine that you came to class today with a big bandage on your finger. You were in a pet store yesterday. You were thinking of buying a parrot, but it bit you.

Example:
PARTNER A (*book open*):   Did you go somewhere?
PARTNER B (*book closed*): Yes, I went somewhere. OR Yes, I did. I went somewhere.

Change roles.

1. Did you find a pet store?
2. Did you buy a parrot?
3. Did you take it out of its cage?
4. Did you have some trouble with it?
5. Did it bite you?

6. Did you leave the pet store?
7. Did you go to a doctor?
8. Did you drive to the doctor's office?
9. Did she put a bandage on your finger?
10. Did you pay her?

❏ **Exercise 14. Listening.** (Charts 2-4 and 2-5)
Listen to the questions. Complete each answer with the correct form of the verb you hear.

CD 1
Track 9

SITUATION: A group of friends was at the beach yesterday.

1. Yes, they _____ in the water.

2. Yes, they _____ in the waves.

3. Yes, they _____ down in the waves.

4. Yes, they _____ barefoot on the sand.

5. Yes, they _____ in the sun.

6. Yes, they _____ sunscreen.

7. Yes, they _____ in the sand.

8. Yes, they _____ giant sandcastles.

9. Yes, they _____ their names in the sand.

10. Yes, they _____ pictures in the sand.

11. Yes, they _____ their feet in the sand.

12. Yes, they _____ songs.

13. Yes, some bees _____ them.

14. Yes, they _____ the sunset.

❏ **Exercise 15. Let's talk: pairwork.** (Charts 2-4 and 2-5)
Work with a partner. Partner A asks the questions. Partner B answers the questions with **Yes** and a complete sentence.

SITUATION: You just came back from a vacation in Greece.

Example: Did you fly back last night?
PARTNER A (*book open*): Did you fly back last night?
PARTNER B (*book closed*): Yes, I flew back last night.

Change roles.

1. Did you have a great trip?
2. Did you come back feeling rested?
3. Did you meet many people?
4. Did you hang out with* local people?
5. Did you do a lot of tourist activities?
6. Did you stand on the Acropolis?
7. Did you spend time in museums?

8. Did you buy some Greek sandals?
9. Did you speak a little Greek?
10. Did you eat in typical Greek restaurants?
11. Did you get my emails?
12. Did you bring me a present?
13. Did you send me a postcard?
14. Were you sad to leave Greece?

❏ **Exercise 16. Listening.** (Charts 2-4 and 2-5)
Listen to the questions. Complete each answer with the correct form of the verb you hear.

CD 1
Track 10

SITUATION: Maria was sick yesterday.

1. Yes, she _____ up sick.

2. Yes, she _____ a cold.

3. Yes, her head _____ .

4. Yes, she _____ her temperature.

5. Yes, she _____ a fever.

6. Yes, she _____ bad.

7. Yes, she _____ her pajamas on.

8. Yes, she _____ on the couch.

9. Yes, she _____ for several hours.

10. Yes, she _____ about scary things.

11. Yes, she _____ some chicken soup.

12. Yes, she _____ to the doctor.

13. Yes, she _____ some medicine.

14. Yes, she _____ the instructions on the label.

---

* *hang out with* = spend time with.

Exercise 17. Let's talk: pairwork. (Charts 2-4 and 2-5)
Work with a partner. Partner A asks the questions. Partner B answers the questions with **Yes** and a complete sentence. NOTE: Use the appropriate pronoun (**he/she**) in the questions.

SITUATION: You come to class very, very tired. You live with a noisy roommate and didn't get much sleep. NOTE: Tell your partner if you have a male or female roommate.

Example: Did you have a bad night?
PARTNER A (*book open*):   Did you have a bad night?
PARTNER B (*book closed*): Yes, I had a bad night.

Change roles.

1. Did your roommate wake you up a lot?
2. Did you hear a lot of noise?
3. Did your roommate's cell phone ring many times?
4. Did she/he fight with someone?
5. Did she/he put on a CD?
6. Did she/he sing loudly?
7. Did she/he make breakfast at midnight?

8. Did she/he grind some coffee beans first?
9. Did she/he feed the neighbor's cats?
10. Did she/he sweep the floor afterwards?
11. Did she/he know you were awake?
12. Did she/he mean to wake you up?
13. Did she/he upset you?
14. Were you upset?

❏ **Exercise 18. Listening.** (Charts 2-4 and 2-5)
CD 1
Track 11
Listen to the beginning of each sentence. Circle the correct completion(s). More than one completion may be possible.

1. happy.   good about my decision.   on some ice.

2. two classes.   about his wife.   at night.

3. the car with gas?   sick?   okay?

4. with colored pencils.   several faces.   for several hours.

5. in the woods.   some money.   the rain.

6. a picture.   from the math class.   some money from the bank.

7. my hand.   some rice.   was cooking.

8. the washing machine?   these jeans?   my shirt?

9. at the sad ending.   the actors.   when the play finished.

10. over the fence.   very quickly.   in a sunny spot.

❏ **Exercise 19. Listening.** (Charts 2-4 and 2-5)
CD 1
Track 12
Part I. Anna had a bad experience last night. Listen to her story with your book closed. Then open your book and listen to the statements. Circle "T" for true and "F" for false.

1. T   F   4. T   F

2. T   F   5. T   F

3. T   F   6. T   F

Part II. Listen again. Complete the sentences with the verbs you hear.

I _____ a terrible experience last night. You won't believe

        1

what happened! A thief _____ into my apartment

               2

while I was asleep. There I was, just sleeping peacefully when

someone _____ the glass in the sliding door!

         3

    The sound _____ me up. I _____

             4   5

the sliding door open, so I reached for the phone by the bed and

called the police. My voice _____ as I told the

                         6

operator there was an intruder in my home.

    I _____ in my bedroom closet while the thief was sneaking around my office. Soon

       7

I _____ sirens as the police _____ to my building. From the crack in

    8   9

the closet door, I _____ the thief as he _____ outside with my computer.

               10   11

    The police jumped out of their cars and followed the thief, but he managed to get away in a

car that was waiting for him. The police _____ back in their cars and drove after

                             12

him. Later I learned that they _____ the thief a few miles from my building.

                         13

    I _____ really frightened by all this. It really _____ me, as you

        14   15

can imagine. I think I'll stay at my sister's house tonight.

❏ **Exercise 20. Warm-up: listening.** (Chart 2-6)

CD 1

Track 13

Listen to each pair of verbs. Decide if the verb endings have the same sound or a different
sound.

Examples: You will hear: talked, pushed

                You will choose: (same)   different

                You will hear: rented, called

                You will choose: same   (different)

1. same	different	4. same	different	7. same	different
2. same	different	5. same	different	8. same	different
3. same	different	6. same	different	9. same	different

2-6 Regular Verbs: Pronunciation of -ed Endings

Final **-ed** has three different pronunciations: /t/, /d/, and /əd/. The schwa /ə/ is an unstressed vowel sound. It is pronounced like *a* in *alone* in normal, rapid speech (e.g., *She lives alone.*).

(a) looked → look/t/ clapped → clap/t/ missed → miss/t/ watched → watch/t/ finished → finish/t/ laughed → laugh/t/	Final **-ed** is pronounced /t/ after voiceless sounds. Voiceless sounds are made by pushing air through your mouth; no sound comes from your throat. Examples of voiceless sounds: "k," "p," "s," "ch," "sh," "f."
(b) smelled → smell/d/ saved → save/d/ cleaned → clean/d/ robbed → rob/d/ played → play/d/	Final **-ed** is pronounced /d/ after voiced sounds. Voiced sounds come from your throat. If you touch your neck when you make a voiced sound, you can feel your voice box vibrate. Examples of voiced sounds: "l," "v," "n," "b," and all vowel sounds.

(c) decided → decide/əd/
needed → need/əd/
wanted → want/əd/
invited → invite/əd/
	Final **-ed** is pronounced /əd/ after "t" and "d" sounds. The sound /əd/ adds a whole syllable to a word.
	COMPARE: looked = one syllable → look/t/
	                smelled = one syllable → smell/d/
	                needed = two syllables → need/əd/

Exercise 21. Listening. (Chart 2-6)
CD 1 Track 14

Listen to each word. Circle the pronunciation of the **-ed** ending you hear.

1. /t/	/d/	/əd/	4. /t/	/d/	/əd/	7. /t/	/d/	/əd/
2. /t/	/d/	/əd/	5. /t/	/d/	/əd/	8. /t/	/d/	/əd/
3. /t/	/d/	/əd/	6. /t/	/d/	/əd/	9. /t/	/d/	/əd/

Exercise 22. Listening and pronunciation. (Chart 2-6)
CD 1 Track 15

Listen to the sentences. Practice saying them aloud. Write the pronunciations of the **-ed** endings you hear.

1. Olga blinked /t/, yawned /　/, and stretched /　/.

2. Mrs. Olsen mopped /　/ the kitchen floor, vacuumed /　/ the carpet, and dusted /　/ the furniture.

3. The meeting started /　/ late and ended /　/ early.

4. My friend jumped /　/ up and down and yelled /　/ when she got the news.

5. The airplane departed /　/ at six and landed /　/ at eight.

6. When I asked /　/ the doctor about some medication, he suggested /　/ a new one.

❑ **Exercise 23. Let's talk: small groups.** (Chart 2-6)

Work in small groups. Take turns choosing a verb from the list in any order you wish. Say the simple past. Your classmates will write that word in the correct column.

accept	complain	miss	push	thank
believe	die	need	rain	work
chase	fix	play	request	worry

/t/	/d/	/əd/

❑ **Exercise 24. Let's talk: pairwork.** (Chart 2-6)

Practice pronouncing the **-ed** endings.

Part I. Check (✓) all the activities you did yesterday. Tell your partner about them.

___ combed my hair	___ washed clothes	___ surfed the internet
___ brushed my teeth	___ typed an email	___ translated some words
___ cooked breakfast	___ worked on a computer	___ added some numbers
___ waited for a bus	___ exercised	___ cleaned my room
___ walked to school	___ talked on the phone	___ listened to music

Part II. Choose four to six activities your partner talked about. Tell the class about them.

❑ **Exercise 25. Warm-up.** (Charts 2-7 and 2-8)

Write the complete sentence (a. or b.) that correctly describes each scene.

  a. Rita was standing under a tree when it began to rain.
  b. Rita stood under a tree when it began to rain.

1st: It began to rain.

2nd: Rita stood under a tree.

SCENE 1: _____

1st: Rita stood under a tree.　　　　　　　　**2nd:** It began to rain.

SCENE 2: _____

2-7 Simple Past

✕ (timeline)	(a) I *walked* to school yesterday. (b) John *lived* in Paris for ten years, but now he lives in Rome. (c) I *bought* a new car three days ago.	The simple past indicates that an activity or situation *began and ended at a particular time in the past.*
	(d) Rita *stood* under a tree *when it began to rain.* (e) *When Mrs. Chu heard* a strange noise, she *got* up to investigate. (f) *When I dropped* my cup, the coffee *spilled* on my lap.	If a sentence contains **when** and has the simple past in both clauses, the action in the *when*-clause happens first. In (d): 1st: The rain began. 　　　　2nd: Rita stood under a tree.

2-8 Past Progressive

(timeline)	(g) I *was walking* down the street when it began to rain. (h) While I *was walking* down the street, it began to rain. (i) Rita *was standing* under a tree when it began to rain. (j) At eight o'clock last night, I *was studying*.	In (g): 1st: I was walking down the street. 2nd: It began to rain. Both actions occurred at the same time, but *one action began earlier and was in progress when the other action occurred.* In (j): My studying began before 8:00, was in progress at that time, and probably continued.
	(k) While I *was studying* in one room of our apartment, my roommate *was having* a party in the other room.	Sometimes the past progressive is used in both parts of a sentence when two actions are in progress simultaneously.

❑ **Exercise 26. Let's talk.** (Charts 2-7 and 2-8)
Choose the question or statement you would expect the speaker to say. Discuss your answers. Work in pairs, in small groups, or as a class.

1. When I went to bed late last night, I noticed that the light was on in your bedroom.

　　a. Were you reading?　　　　　　b. Did you read?

2. Jane's cousin was at the party last night.

    a. Were you meeting him?   b. Did you meet him?

3. A small airplane flew over our house several times last night.

    a. We were sitting out on the patio, and it made us nervous.

    b. We sat out on the patio, and it made us nervous.

4. I'm not sure if I met Carol Jones at the party last night. Describe her for me.

    a. What was she wearing?   b. What did she wear?

❏ **Exercise 27. Looking at grammar.** (Charts 2-7 and 2-8)
Complete the sentences. Use the simple past or the past progressive of the verbs in parentheses.

1. I am sitting in class right now. I (*sit*) _____*was sitting*_____ in class at this exact same time yesterday.

2. I (*call*) _____ Roger at nine last night, but he (*be, not*) _____ at home. He (*study*) _____ at the library.

3. I (*hear, not*) _____ the thunder during the storm last night because I (*sleep*) _____ .

4. It was beautiful yesterday when we went for a walk in the park. The sun (*shine*) _____ . A cool breeze (*blow*) _____ . The birds (*sing*) _____ .

5. My brother and sister (*argue*) _____ about something when I (*walk*) _____ into the room.

6. I got a package in the mail. When I (*open*) _____ it, I (*find*) _____ a surprise.

7. While Mrs. Emerson (*read*) _____ the little boy a story, he (*fall*) _____ asleep, so she (*close*) _____ the book and quietly (*sneak*) _____ out of the room.

8. A: (*you, hear*) _____ what the teacher just said?

    B: No, I (*listen, not*) _____ . I (*think*) _____ about something else.

9. I really enjoyed my last vacation. While it (*snow*) _____ in Iowa, the sun (*shine*) _____ in Florida. While you (*shovel*) _____ snow in Iowa all last week, I (*lie*) _____ on a beach in Florida.

❏ **Exercise 28. Let's talk: pairwork.** (Charts 2-7 and 2-8)
Work with a partner. Complete the sentences with the given verbs and the words in parentheses. Use the simple past or the past progressive. Role-play one of the dialogues for the rest of the class or a small group of classmates. Try not to look at your book when you perform the dialogue.

1. *call, wait*

   A: Why weren't you at the meeting?

   B: I _____ for an overseas call from my family.

   A: (*they*) _____?

   B: Yes. It was wonderful to hear from them.

2. *break, cross, slip*

   A: How (*you*) _____
   your arm?

   B: I _____ on the ice while
   I _____ the street in
   front of the dorm.

3. *find, look, park*

   A: You're late again! You were supposed to be here ten minutes ago. Where were you?

   B: I _____ for a place to park.

   A: (*you*) _____ one?

   B: Well, yes and no. I _____ my car illegally.

4. *ask, decide, look, see, work*

   A: How did it go? (*you*) _____ the manager for a raise when
   you _____ her yesterday?

   B: No, she _____ on a big presentation for next week. She
   _____ pretty busy. I _____ to wait until later.

5. *drive, get, happen, keep, pay, see*

   A: I had a bad day yesterday.

   B: Oh? What _____?

   A: I _____ a traffic ticket.

   B: Really? That's too bad. What was it for?

   A: For running a red light. I _____ home and (*not*)
   _____ attention to the road. I (*not*) _____
   the red light and just _____ driving.

□ **Exercise 29. Grammar and listening.** (Charts 2-7 and 2-8)

CD 1
Track 16

Complete the sentences. Use the simple past or the past progressive form of the verbs in the list. Then listen to the passage to check your completions. Use each verb only one time.

be	find	look	sit	speak	stop	walk

It was my first day of class. I finally _____ the right room. The room
                                                        1
_____ already full of students.
          2

On one side of the room, students were talking to each other in Japanese or Arabic. On the

other side, students _____ in Spanish or Portuguese. It sounded like
                                        3

the United Nations. Some of the students, however, _____ quietly by
                                                                          4

themselves, not talking to anyone.

I _____ for an empty seat in the last row and sat down. In a few
          5

minutes, the teacher _____ into the room, and all the multilingual
                                    6

conversation suddenly _____.
                                      7

□ **Exercise 30. Let's talk.** (Charts 2-7 and 2-8)

Watch a classmate perform a pantomime. Then in pairs, in small groups, or as a class, describe the actions in the pantomime step by step. Pay special attention to the use of past verb forms in the descriptions. SUGGESTION: Watch and describe a few pantomimes in each class period for the next week or two in order to keep practicing past verbs.

Example: washing one's hands

→ She was standing at a sink. She turned on the faucet. Then she picked up some soap. While she was washing her hands, the soap slipped out of her hands and dropped to the floor. She bent over to pick it up. Then she finished washing her hands and turned off the faucet. At the end, she wiped her hands on a towel.

Possible pantomime subjects:
   opening a door with a key   reading a newspaper while drinking a cup of coffee
   taking a picture with a camera   being unable to start a car; looking under the hood

□ **Exercise 31. Let's write.** (Charts 2-7 and 2-8)

In writing, describe one or more of your classmates' pantomimes. Give a title to the pantomime and identify the pantomimist. Use a few time words to show the order in which the actions were performed: *first, next, then, after that, before, when, while, etc.*

□ **Exercise 32. Let's write.** (Charts 2-1 → 2-8)

First, write about your first day or two in this country or city. Use past tense verbs. What did you do? What did you think? What did you see? Who did you meet? Did you have any interesting experiences? How did you feel about this place?

    Second, write about how you feel about this place now. In what ways are your present experiences here different from your earlier experiences?

❑ **Exercise 33. Warm-up.** (Chart 2-9)
Check (✓) the sentences that are correct. What do you notice about the use of *always* with verb tenses in these sentences?

1. __ Nadia is always talking on the phone when I'm trying to study.
2. __ Frank always studies in the library after school.
3. __ My friends always do their homework together.
4. __ Our math teacher is always giving us surprise quizzes.

2-9 Using Progressive Verbs with *Always*	
(a) Mary *always leaves* for school at 7:45.	In sentences referring to present time, usually the simple present is used with *always* to describe habitual or everyday activities, as in (a).
(b) Mary *is always leaving* her dirty socks on the floor for me to pick up! Who does she think I am? Her maid?	In special circumstances, a speaker may use the present progressive with *always* to express annoyance, as in (b).
(c) I am *always/forever/constantly picking* up Mary's dirty socks!	In addition to *always*, the words *forever* and *constantly* are used with progressive verbs to express annoyance.

❑ **Exercise 34. Let's talk.** (Chart 2-9)
Your roommate, Jack, has many bad habits. These bad habits annoy you. Pretend you are speaking to a friend and complaining about Jack. Use the present progressive of a verb in Column A and complete the sentence with a phrase from Column B. Use *always, constantly,* or *forever* in each sentence. Say your sentence aloud with annoyance in your voice.

Example: He's always messing up the kitchen!

Column A	Column B
1. mess up	a. about himself
2. leave	✓ b. the kitchen
3. borrow	c. my clothes without asking me
4. try	d. to give me my phone messages
5. brag	e. his dirty dishes on the table
6. crack	f. to show me he's smarter than me★
7. forget	g. his knuckles while I'm trying to study

❑ **Exercise 35. In your own words.** (Chart 2-9)
Complete the sentences with your own words.

A: I don't know if I can stand Sue as a roommate one more day. She's driving me crazy.

B: Oh? What's wrong?

A: Well, for one thing she's always _____ !
₁

★In formal English, a subject pronoun follows *than*: *He's older than I (am).* In everyday informal English, an object pronoun is frequently used after *than*: *He's older than me.*

B: Really?

A: And not only that. She's forever _____ !
                                                    2

B: That must be a hassle for you.

A: It is. And what's more, she's constantly _____ !
                                                            3
   Can you believe that? And she's always _____ !
                                                            4

B: I think you're right. You need to find a new roommate.

❏ **Exercise 36. Warm-up.** (Chart 2-10)
Read the two short dialogues. What do you notice about the word order? How is the focus different?

1. A: What was Hans doing when you arrived?
   B: He was reading a book in bed.

2. A: Where was Hans when you arrived?
   B: He was in bed reading a book.

2-10	Using Expressions of Place with Progressive Verbs
(a) — What is Kay doing? — She*'s studying **in her room**.*	In usual word order, an expression of place follows a verb. In (a): *is studying* + ***in her room*** = the focus is on Kay's activity.
(b) — Where's Kay? — She*'s **in her room** studying.*	An expression of place can sometimes come between the auxiliary ***be*** and the ***-ing*** verb in a progressive verb form. In (b): *was* + ***in her room*** + *studying* = the focus is on Kay's location.

❏ **Exercise 37. Looking at grammar.** (Chart 2-10)
Work individually, in small groups, or as a class. Use the given verbs and expressions of place to complete the dialogues. Use usual word order if the focus is on an activity in progress. If the focus is on the person's location, put the expression of place between ***be*** and the ***-ing*** verb.

1. *listen to music \ in her room*

   A: Where's Sally?

   B: _____*She's in her room listening to music.*_____

2. *listen to music \ in the living room*

   A: What's Soon doing?

   B: He's _____*listening to music in the living room.*_____

3. *watch TV \ in his bedroom*

   A: Where was Jim when you got home?

   B: He was _____

4. *watch TV \ in his bedroom*

   A: What was Jim doing when you got home?

   B: He was _____

5. *take a nap \ on the couch in the living room*

   A: What's Kurt doing?

   B: He's _____

6. *take a nap \ on the couch in the living room*

   A: Where's Kurt?

   B: He's _____

7. *attend a conference \ in Singapore*

   A: Where's Ms. Chang this week?

   B: She's _____

❑ **Exercise 38. Check your knowledge.** (Chapter 2)
Correct the errors.

1. Breakfast is an important meal. I'm always eating breakfast.

2. While I was working in my office yesterday, my cousin stops by to visit me.

3. Yuki staied home because she catched a bad cold.

4. My brother is looks like our father, but I am resembling my mother.

5. Jun, are you listen to me? I am talk to you!

6. While I was surfing the internet yesterday, I was finding a really interesting Web site.

7. Did you spoke English before you were come here?

8. Yesterday, while I was working at my computer, Shelley was suddenly coming into the room. I wasn't knowing she was there. I was concentrate hard on my work. When she suddenly speak, I am jump. She startle me.

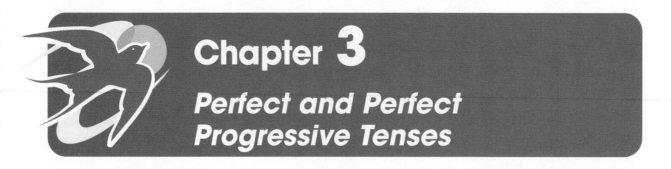

Chapter **3**

Perfect and Perfect Progressive Tenses

❏ **Exercise 1. Let's talk: pairwork.** (Charts 2-4 and 2-5)
Work with a partner to review past participles. Partner A asks questions beginning with ***Have you ever***. Partner B answers the questions with ***No, I haven't. I've never . . . .***

Example: see a silent film
PARTNER A (*book open*):   Have you ever seen a silent film?
PARTNER B (*book closed*): No, I haven't. I've never seen a silent film.

1. buy a boat
2. break a window
3. hide from the police
4. teach English
5. make ice cream
6. win a contest
7. ride an elephant
8. fly an airplane
9. catch a butterfly
10. leave your umbrella at a restaurant
11. dig a hole to plant a tree
12. drive a school bus
13. draw a picture of yourself

Change roles.
14. build a house
15. forget your own name
16. fall off a ladder
17. hold a poisonous snake
18. steal anything
19. eat a duck egg
20. swing a baseball bat
21. feed a lion
22. split wood with an axe
23. hit a baseball
24. read a play by Shakespeare
25. grow tomatoes from seed
26. tear a page out of a library book

❏ **Exercise 2. Let's listen and talk.** (Charts 1-6 and 2-4)

🎧
CD 1
Track 17
You will hear a sentence and the beginning of a question. Complete the question with the past participle of the verb you heard in the first sentence. Have you ever done these things? Circle *yes* or *no*. Tell another student some of the things you have and haven't done.

Example: You will hear: I took an English test. Have you ever . . . ?

You will write: Have you ever _____*taken*_____ an English test?   (yes)   no

1. Have you ever _____ a book? yes no

2. Have you ever _____ your wallet? yes no

3. Have you ever _____ a mountain? yes no

4. Have you ever _____ a speech to a large audience? yes no

5. Have you ever _____ a lie? yes no

6. Have you ever _____ in public? yes no

7. Have you ever _____ on a motorcycle? yes no

8. Have you ever _____ Turkish coffee? yes no

9. Have you ever _____ a cooking class? yes no

10. Have you ever _____ hands with a famous person? yes no

11. Have you ever _____ another person with English? yes no

12. Have you ever _____ in a tent? yes no

13. Have you ever _____ a truck? yes no

14. Have you ever _____ a car accident? yes no

15. Have you ever _____ biology? yes no

16. Have you ever _____ a violin? yes no

❏ **Exercise 3. Warm-up.** (Chart 3-1)
Complete the sentences with your own words. What do you notice about the verb tenses in blue? In which sentences do the situations continue from the past until now?

1. I got up at _____ (*time*) today.

2. I have been awake since _____ (*time*).

3. I am studying English grammar in this class. I have come to this class

   _____ (*number*) times so far this month.

4. I took my first English class in _____ (*year*).

3-1 Present Perfect

(a)		
(a) 2002 — now — up to now	(a) Mrs. Oh **has been** a teacher *since* 2002. (b) I **have been** in this city *since* last May. (c) We **have been** here *since* nine o'clock.	The present perfect is often used with *since* and *for* to talk about *situations that began in the past and continue up to now.* In (a): SITUATION = being a teacher TIME FRAME = from 2002 up to now
	(d) Rita knows Rob. They met two months ago. She **has known** him *for* two months. I met him three years ago. I **have known** him *for* three years. (e) I **have known** Rob *since* I was in high school.	Notice the use of *since* vs. *for* in the examples: **since** + *a specific point in time* (e.g., 2002, last May, nine o'clock) **for** + *a length of time* (e.g., two months, three years) In (e): **since** + *a time clause* (i.e., a subject and verb may follow *since*).*
(f) time? — now	(f) — **Have** you *ever* **seen** snow? — No, I **haven't**. I've *never* **seen** snow. But Anna has **seen** snow. (g) **Have** you **finished** your homework *yet*? I *still* **haven't finished** mine. Jack **has** *already* **finished** his.	The present perfect can talk about *events that have (or haven't) happened before now.* The exact time of the event is unspecified. The adverbs *ever, never, yet, still,* and *already* are often used with the present perfect. In (f): EVENT = seeing snow TIME FRAME = from the beginning of their lives up to now In (g): EVENT = doing homework TIME FRAME = from the time the people started up to now
(h) beginning of term — now — up to now — test 1 test 2 test 3	(h) We **have had** three tests *so far* this term. (i) I**'ve met** many people *since* I came here.	The present perfect can also express *an event that has occurred repeatedly from a point in the past up to the present time. The event may happen again.* In (h): REPEATED EVENT = taking tests TIME FRAME = from the beginning of the term up to now In (i): REPEATED EVENT = meeting people TIME FRAME = from the time I came here up to now
CONTRACTIONS: (j) *I've* been there. *You've* been there. *We've* been there. *They've* been there. *He's* been there. *She's* been there. *It's* been interesting.		**Have** and **has** are usually contracted with personal pronouns in informal writing, as in (j). NOTE: **He's** there. **He's** = **He is** **He's** been there. **He's** = **He has**

*See Chart 18-2, p. 388, for more information about time clauses.

❑ **Exercise 4. Looking at grammar.** (Chart 3-1)
    Complete the sentences with *since* or *for*.

1. There has been snow on the ground _____ New Year's Day.

2. The weather has been cold _____ a long time.

3. Maria has studied English _____ less than a year.

4. Mr. and Mrs. Roberts have been together _____ they were in college.

5. They have known each other _____ more than fifty years.

6. We haven't seen Aziz _____ last month.

7. I've had a cold _____ over a week.

8. I haven't heard from my sister _____ the beginning of March.

❑ **Exercise 5. Let's talk.** (Chart 3-1)
    Complete the sentences with any appropriate time expression. Work in pairs, in small groups, or as a class.

1. Today is ____*the 14th of June*____. I bought this book ____*two weeks*____ ago.
   I have had this book since ____*the first of June*____.
   I have had this book for ____*two weeks*____.

2. I moved to this city _____.
   I have been in this city since _____.
   I have been here for _____.

3. It is the year _____.
   I started going to school in the year _____.
   I've been a student for _____.
   I've been a student since _____.

4. I first met our teacher _____.
   I've known her/him for _____.
   I've known her/him since _____.

5. I have (*a/an*) _____ that I bought _____ ago.
   I have had it since _____.
   I have had it for _____.

❏ **Exercise 6. Let's talk.** (Chart 3-1)
Answer the questions in complete sentences. Student B will use *for*. Student C will use *since*. Close your book.

Example: To A: When did you come here? To B: Use *for*. To C: Or, using *since*?
TEACHER: When did you come here?
STUDENT A: I came here on June 2nd.
TEACHER: How long has (*Student A*) been here? Use *for*.
STUDENT B: He/She has been here for two weeks.
TEACHER: Or, using *since*?
STUDENT C: He's/She's been here since June 2nd.

1. To A: When did you get to class today?

    To B: How long has (_____) been in class? Use *for*. To C: Or, using *since*?

2. To A: What time did you get up this morning?

    To B: How long has (_____) been up? Use *for*. To C: Or, using *since*?

3. To A: Who in this class owns a car/bicycle? When did you buy it?

    To B: How long has (_____) had a car/bicycle? Use *for*. To C: Or, using *since*?

4. To A: Who is wearing a watch? When did you get it?

    To B: How long has (_____) had his/her watch? Use *for*. To C: Or, using *since*?

5. To A: Who is married? When did you get married?

    To B: How long has (_____) been married? Use *for*. To C: Or, using *since*?

6. To A: Do you know (_____)? When did you meet him/her?

    To B: How long has (_____) known (_____)? Use *for*. To C: Or, using *since*?

❏ **Exercise 7. Looking at grammar.** (Chart 3-1)
Underline the present perfect verbs. What is the time frame in each situation?

Example: I <u>haven't attended</u> any parties since I came to this city. I don't know anyone here.
    → *Present perfect verb: haven't attended*
    → *Time frame: from the time the speaker arrived in this city to the present time*

1. So far this week, I've had two tests and a quiz. And it's only Wednesday!

2. Try not to be absent from class again for the rest of the term. You've already missed too many classes.

3. I'm really hungry. I haven't eaten since I got up.

4. Nadia started her homework right after dinner, but she still hasn't finished it. She probably won't be able to go to bed until after midnight.

5. A: Hi, Judy. Welcome to the party. Have you ever met my cousin?
    B: No, I haven't.

6. A: Do you like lobster?

   B: I don't know. I've never eaten it.

7. A: How did you like the book I lent you?

   B: Gosh, I'm sorry, but I haven't read it yet. I haven't had time.

❏ **Exercise 8. Let's talk.** (Chart 3-1)
Answer the questions. Work in pairs, in small groups, or as a class.

Example:
SPEAKER A (*book open*): How many tests have you taken since you started coming to this class?
SPEAKER B (*book closed*): I have taken (*three, several, many*) tests since I started coming to this class. OR I haven't taken any tests since I started coming to this class.

1. How many textbooks have you bought since the beginning of the year?
2. How many emails have you gotten so far this week/month?
3. How many emails have you written since the beginning of the week/month?
4. How many questions have I asked so far?
5. How many times have you flown in an airplane?

(*Change roles if working in pairs.*)
6. How many people have you met since you came here?
7. How many classes have you missed since the beginning of the semester?
8. How many cups of coffee have you had since you got up this morning?
9. How many classes have you had so far today?
10. How many times have you eaten your native food at a restaurant this month?

❏ **Exercise 9. Let's write and talk.** (Chart 3-1)
What are some interesting and unusual things you have done in your lifetime? Answer this question by writing four to six sentences, some of them true and some of them false. Then share your sentences with a partner, a small group, or the class, who will guess whether your statement is true or false.

Example:
SPEAKER A: I have jumped from an airplane.
SPEAKER B: I think that's false.
SPEAKER A: You're right. I've never jumped from an airplane, but I've thought about going skydiving sometime.

❏ **Exercise 10. Warm-up: listening.** (Chart 3-2)
Listen for reduced speech in these sentences. How are **have** and **has** pronounced?

CD 1
Track 18

1. The Browns have decided to grow their own vegetables.
2. It's past midnight. Where have you been?
3. Laura has offered to help us move into our new apartment.
4. Is Nick in trouble again? What has he done this time?
5. Janet has traveled all over the world.
6. Her parents have traveled a lot too.

3-2 *Have* and *Has* in Spoken English

(a) **How have** you been?
   Spoken: How/v/ you been? OR
         How/əv/ you been?
	In spoken English, the present perfect helping verbs **has** and **have** are often reduced following nouns and question words.*
	In (a): **have** can sound like /v/ or /əv/.

(b) **Jane has** already eaten lunch.
   Spoken: Jane/z/ already eaten lunch. OR
         Jane/əz/ already eaten lunch.
	In (b): **has** can sound like /z/ or /əz/.
	In (c): **has** can sound like /s/ or /əs/.**

(c) **Mike has** already left.
   Spoken: Mike/s/ already left. OR
         Mike/əs/ already left.
	NOTE: Jane/z/ eaten. **Jane's = Jane has**
	       Jane/z/ here. **Jane's = Jane is**
	
	       Mike/s/ left. **Mike's = Mike has**
	       Mike/s/ here. **Mike's = Mike is**

*In very informal writing, **has** is sometimes contracted with nouns (e.g., **Jane's** *already eaten.*) and question words (e.g., **Where's** *he gone?*). **Have** is rarely contracted in writing except with pronouns (e.g., *I've*). See Chart 3-1 for written contractions of **have** and **has** with pronouns. See Appendix Chart C for more information about contractions in general.

**See Chart 6-1, p. 85, for the pronunciation of final *-s* after voiced and voiceless sounds.

❑ **Exercise 11. Listening.** (Chart 3-2)

CD 1
Track 19

Listen to the sentences. You will hear reduced forms for **have, has,** and **is,** but you will write their full (non-reduced) forms and any other words you hear.

Example: You will hear: Sorry I'm late. How long have you been here?

        You will write: How long _____*have you been*_____ here?

1. My teacher _____ in the classroom.

2. Your teacher _____.

3. All of the other teachers _____ too.

4. You're late! Where _____?

5. Susan has a guilty look on her face. What _____?

6. Finally! The mail _____.

7. My neighbors _____ in the same apartment for over thirty years.

8. Vicky _____ a trip to Brazil.

9. It's great to see you. How _____?

10. India _____ an independent country since 1947.

11. The weather _____ very nice.

12. The weather _____ warm lately.

13. The children _____ their drawings.

14. Ruth _____ four novels so far this month.

❑ **Exercise 12. Warm-up.** (Chart 3-3)
What do you notice about the verb tenses in blue? Discuss the differences.

3-3 Present Perfect vs. Simple Past

Present Perfect		
time? / now / up to now	(a) I*'ve met* Linda, but I *haven't met* her husband. *Have* you *met* them?	The PRESENT PERFECT is used to talk about *past events when there is no specific mention of time.* In (a): The speaker is talking about *some unspecified time before now.*
Simple Past		
yesterday	(b) I *met* Helen *yesterday* at a party. Her husband *was* there too, but I *didn't meet* him. *Did* you *meet* them at the party?	The SIMPLE PAST is used when there is *a specific mention of time.* In (b): The speaker is thinking of a specific time: yesterday.
Present Perfect		
10 years ago / up to now	(c) Sam *has been* a teacher *for* ten years. He loves teaching.	The PRESENT PERFECT is used for *situations that began in the past and continue to the present.* In (c): The present perfect tells us that Sam is still a teacher now.
Simple Past		
1995–2005	(d) Jim *was* a teacher *for* ten years, from 1995 to 2005. Now he is a salesman.	The SIMPLE PAST is used for *situations that began and ended in the past.* In (d): The simple past tells us that Jim is not a teacher now.

❏ **Exercise 13. Looking at grammar.** (Charts 2-6 and 3-3)
Complete the sentences. Use the simple past or the present perfect form of the verbs in parentheses.

1. Fatima is from a hot, arid part of her country. She (*see, never*) _____

   _____ snow.

2. Last January, I (*see*) _____ snow for the first time in my life.

3. Last night my friend and I (*have*) _____ some free time, so we (*go*)

   _____ to a show.

4. Since classes began, I (*have, not*) _____ much free time. My

   classes keep me really busy.

5. Ming Won (*be*) _____ in this class for three months. His English is

   getting better and better. He plans to take this class until the end of May.

6. Mrs. Perez (*be*) _____ in our class for three months, but then she left

   school to get a job.

7. Late-breaking news! A major earthquake (*occur, just*) _____

   in southern California. It (*occur*) _____ at 9:25 A.M. Pacific Standard

   Time.

8. I admit that I (*get★*) _____ older since I last (*see*) _____

   you, but with any luck at all, I (*get, also*) _____ wiser.

9. A: Are you taking Chemistry 101 this semester?

   B: No, I (*take, already★★*) _____ it. I (*take*)

   _____ it last semester. This semester I'm in 102.

10. Greg Adams? Yes, I know him. I (*know*) _____ him since college.

11. Joe North passed away? I'm sorry to hear that. I (*know*) _____ him

    well when we were in college together.

★COMPARE:
(a) *I have gotten* OR *have got* four letters so far this week. In this sentence, *have gotten / have got* is present perfect. (NOTE: *Got* is used as the past participle of *get* in both American English and British English. *Gotten* occurs only in American English.)
(b) *I have got* a problem. In this sentence, *have got* is NOT present perfect. *I've got a problem = I have a problem.* The expression *have got* means "have" and is common in informal spoken English. Its meaning is present; it has no past form.

★★Typically, the present perfect is used in sentences with *already, yet,* and *just,* but in some situations the simple past is also commonly used with these adverbs in informal English, especially American English, with no difference in meaning.

❏ **Exercise 14. Let's talk: find someone who . . . .** (Charts 3-1 and 3-3)

Walk around the room. Ask a complete question for each item using the present perfect of the given verb. Begin your questions with ***Have you ever.*** When you find someone who answers "yes," ask a follow-up question using the *wh*-word and the simple past.

Example: see a bear? Where?
SPEAKER A: (Hassan), have you ever seen a bear?
SPEAKER B: No, I haven't.
SPEAKER A: Okay. Thanks.
  (Maria), have you ever seen a bear?
SPEAKER C: Yes, I have.
SPEAKER A: Really? Where did you see it?
SPEAKER C: In a zoo.

Have you ever . . .

1. break something valuable? What . . . ?
2. lose something important? What . . . ?
3. stay up all night? Why . . . ?
4. travel to an interesting place? Where . . . ?
5. be in a car accident? When . . . ?
6. play a team sport? Which . . . ?

❏ **Exercise 15. Warm-up.** (Chart 3-4)

Check (✓) each correct sentence. NOTE: One sentence in each group is incorrect.

1. Anita is at the bus stop.
   a. ____ She is waiting for the bus.
   b. ____ She is waiting for the bus for fifteen minutes.
   c. ____ She has been waiting for the bus for fifteen minutes.

2. Tarik is at the bus stop too.
   a. ____ He is standing beside Anita.
   b. ____ He is standing there since five o'clock.
   c. ____ He has been standing there since five o'clock.

3-4 Present Perfect Progressive

how long
up to now?

(a) Right now I **am sitting** at my desk.

(b) I **have been sitting** at my desk *since* seven o'clock. I **have been sitting** here *for* two hours.

(c) It*'s been raining* all day. It's still raining right now.

COMPARE:

In (a): The PRESENT PROGRESSIVE expresses *an activity in progress right now.* (See Chart 2-2, p. 14.)

In (b): The PRESENT PERFECT PROGRESSIVE expresses *how long* an activity has been in progress. In other words, it expresses *the duration of an activity that began in the past and continues to the present.*

Time expressions often used with this tense are
- *since* and *for,* as in (b).
- *all day/all morning/all week,* as in (c).

NOTE: In (c): **It's** *been raining.* **It's** = **It has**
It's *still raining.* **It's** = **It is**

(d) I **'ve known** Alex *since* he was a child.

INCORRECT: ~~I've been knowing~~ Alex since he was a child.

For non-progressive verbs such as *know,* the present perfect (not the present perfect progressive) is used to express the *duration* of a situation that began in the past and continues to the present.

(See Charts 2-3, p. 16, and 3-1, p. 38.)

(e) How long **have** you **been living** here?

(f) How long **have** you **lived** here?

(g) Al **has been wearing** glasses since he was ten.

(h) Al **has worn** glasses since he was ten.

For some (not all) verbs, the idea of *how long* can be expressed by either tense — the present perfect progressive or the present perfect.

NOTE: (e) and (f) have the same meaning; (g) and (h) have the same meaning.

Either tense can be used only when the verb expresses the duration of present activities or situations that happen regularly, usually, habitually: e.g., *live, work, teach, study, wear glasses, play chess, etc.*

recently

(i) I*'ve been thinking* about looking for a different job. This one doesn't pay enough.

(j) All of the students *have been studying* hard. Final exams start next week.

When the tense is used without any mention of time, it expresses a general activity in progress recently, lately. For example, (i) means *I've been thinking about this recently, lately.*

❑ **Exercise 16. Looking at grammar.** (Chart 3-4)
Complete the sentences. Use the present progressive or the present perfect progressive form of the verbs in parentheses.

1. Mr. and Mrs. Jones (*sit*) _____*are sitting*_____ outside on their porch right

   now. They (*sit*) _____*have been sitting*_____ there since after dinner.

2. The test begins at 1:00. Right now it's 11:00. Sara is at the library. She (*review*)

   _____ her notes right now. She (*review*) _____

   _____ her notes all morning.

3. Marco is in a store. He (*stand*) _____ at a checkout

   counter right now. He (*stand*) _____ there for over five

   minutes. He wishes he could find a salesperson. He wants to buy a pair of jeans.

4. The little girl is dirty from head to foot because she (*play*)

   _____ in the mud.

5. The children are excited about the concert. They (*practice*)

   _____ a lot in the last few weeks.

   They're going to sing for their parents.

6. My back hurts, so I (*sleep*) _____ on

   a pad on the floor lately. The bed is too soft.

❑ **Exercise 17. Let's write.** (Charts 2-6, 3-1, and 3-4)
Write about the picture using the verbs in the list and the verb form given in each item.

| cook | fix | memorize | plant | vacuum | wash |

1. Tom has had a busy day so far. Right now, he's taking a break. What has Tom been doing? Write at least four sentences on another piece of paper. Use the present perfect progressive.
2. Rewrite your sentences using *yesterday*. Use the simple past.
3. Rewrite your sentences using *just*. Use the present perfect.

□ **Exercise 18. Listening.** (Charts 3-1 and 3-4)

Listen to the dialogue one time with your book closed. Then, with your book open, listen again and write the words you hear.

CD 1
Track 20

A: Good to see you! So what _____ 1 _____ up to lately?

B: Not too much. _____ 2 _____ it easy.

A: How nice! Glad to hear you _____ 3 _____ too hard.

By the way, _____ 4 _____ your parents? I _____ 5 _____ them

for a while.

B: _____ 6 _____ great. _____ 7 _____ now

that they're retired.

A: How long _____ 8 _____ retired?

B: Gosh, I don't know. _____ 9 _____ a couple of years now.

A: So _____ 10 _____ a lot*?

B: Yeah. _____ 11 _____ in warm, sunny places in the winter and

_____ 12 _____ summers here.

A: What a great way to spend retirement! I'm glad to hear _____ 13 _____

themselves.

□ **Exercise 19. Looking at grammar.** (Charts 3-1 and 3-4)

Complete the sentences. Use the verb in *italics* in the first sentence of each item to complete the remaining sentence(s). Use the present perfect or the present perfect progressive. In some sentences, either verb form is correct.

1. I'm *trying* to study. I ____*have been trying*____ to study **for** the last hour, but something always seems to interrupt me. I think I'd better go to the library.

2. Joe *has* an old bicycle. He ____*has had*____ the same bicycle **for** twenty years.

3. Matt *works* at the ABC Company. He ____*has worked / has been working*____ there **since** 2005.

4. Toshi *is waiting* for his friend. He _____ for her **since** five o'clock. She's late for their date.

5. I *like* cowboy movies. I _____ cowboy movies ever **since** I was a child.

---

*Notice: A statement form (not a question form) can sometimes be used to ask a question by using a rising intonation at the end of a sentence.

6. Susie *is watching* a cowboy movie. She _____ it **for** over two hours without a break.

7. Dr. Chang *teaches* math. He is an excellent teacher. He _____ _____ math at this school **for** more than 25 years.

8. Sue and Rick *are playing* tennis right now and they're getting tired. They _____ **since** nine o'clock this morning. Sue's winning. She's the better tennis player. She _____ tennis **since** she was ten. Rick started playing only last year.

❑ **Exercise 20. Listening.** (Charts 3-1 and 3-4)

CD 1
Track 21
Listen to the description of each item and complete the sentence that follows it. Use the present perfect and the present perfect progressive.

Example: You will hear: Manuel has called Eva five times in the last hour, but her line is busy. He'll keep trying until he reaches her.

You will write: Manuel (*try*) __has been trying__ to reach Eva for __an hour__ to talk about their plans for the weekend.

1. Susan (*wait*) _____ in the doctor's office since _____. She hopes she doesn't have to wait much longer.

2. Alexi (*own*) _____ his motorcycle for _____.

3. Joe (*decide, not*) _____ which job to take yet. He'll decide soon.

4. Mika is frustrated. She (*sit*) _____ in rush-hour traffic since _____. She's going to be very late for work.

5. Andrew and Donna (*play*) _____ chess for _____ hours.

❑ **Exercise 21. Let's write.** (Charts 3-1, 3-3, and 3-4)
Choose one topic to write about.

Topics:
1. Write about your first day in this class. What did you see, hear, feel, think? Then write about what you have done and have been doing in this class since the first day.
2. Describe your last week at home before you came to this city/country. Then describe what you have done and have been doing since you arrived here.

❑ **Exercise 22. Warm-up.** (Chart 3-5)
Each of the following talks about two events. Which event happened first?

1. The teacher stood up. Someone had knocked on the classroom door.
2. I looked at the chalkboard. The teacher had written my name there.

3-5 Past Perfect

	(a) Sam arrived at 10:00. Ann left at 9:30. In other words, Ann **had** already **left** when Sam arrived.	The past perfect expresses *an activity that was complete before another activity or time in the past.*

(b) *By the time* Sam got there, Ann **had** already **left**.	In (a): 1st: Ann left. 2nd: Sam arrived. Adverb clauses with *by the time* are frequently used with the past perfect in the main clause, as in (b).★

(c) Sam **had left** before Ann got there. (d) Sam **left** before Ann got there. (e) *After* the guests **had left,** I went to bed. (f) *After* the guests **left,** I went to bed.	If either *before* or *after* is used in the sentence, the past perfect is often not necessary because the time relationship is already clear. The simple past may be used, as in (d) and (f). NOTE: (c) and (d) have the same meaning; (e) and (f) have the same meaning.

(g) *Actual spoken words:* I **lost** my keys. (h) *Reported words:* Jenny **said that** she **had lost** her keys.	The past perfect is commonly used in reported speech.★★ If the actual spoken words use the simple past, the past perfect is often used in reporting those words, as in (h). Common reporting verbs include *tell (someone), say, find out, learn,* and *discover.*

(i) *Written:* Bill *felt* great that evening. Earlier in the day, Annie **had caught** one fish, and he **had caught** three. They **had had** a delicious picnic near the lake and then **had gone** swimming again. It **had been** a nearly perfect vacation day.	The past perfect is often found in more formal writing such as fiction. In (i), the fiction writer uses the simple past to say that an event happened (*Bill felt great*), and then uses the past perfect to explain what had happened before that event.

(j) *I'd* finished. *You'd* finished. *We'd* finished. *They'd* finished. *She'd* finished. *He'd* finished. *It'd* finished.	**Had** is often contracted with personal pronouns in informal writing. NOTE: *I'd* finished. *I'd* = *I had* *I'd* like to go. *I'd* = *I would*

★For more information about *by the time,* see Chart 17-2, p. 368.

★★For more information about verb form usage in reported speech, see Chart 12-7, p. 261.

❑ **Exercise 23. Looking at grammar.** (Charts 2-6 and 3-5)
Use the simple past or the past perfect form of the verbs in parentheses to complete the sentences. In some cases, either tense is correct.

1. Samir (*be*) _____was / had been_____ a newspaper reporter before he (*become*)

   _____became_____ a businessman.

2. I (*feel*) _____ a little better after I (*take*) _____

   the medicine.

3. I was late. The teacher (*give, already*) _____ a quiz when I

   (*get*) _____ to class.

4. It was raining hard, but by the time class (*be*) _____ over, the

   rain (*stop*) _____.

5. Millions of years ago, dinosaurs (*roam*) _____ the earth, but they

   (*become*) _____ extinct by the time people first (*appear*)

   _____.

6. I (*see, never*) _____ any of Picasso's paintings before I (*visit*)

   _____ the art museum.

7. After work, I went to Rosa's office to give her a ride home, but I couldn't find her. She

   (*leave*) _____ with someone else.

8. I got ready to pay the bill, but when I (*look*) _____ in my pocket, I

   discovered that I (*leave*) _____ my wallet at home. With some

   embarrassment, I told my friend that I (*forget*) _____ my wallet.

   She kindly (*offer*) _____ to pay my part of the bill for me.

9. Yesterday at a meeting, I (*see*) _____ Rick Collins, an old friend of mine. I (*see, not*) _____ him in years. At first, I (*recognize, not*) _____ him because he (*lose*) _____ a great deal of weight.

10. In 1980, my parents (*emigrate*) _____ to the United States from China. They (*travel, never*) _____ outside of China and were, of course, excited by the challenge of relocating to a foreign country. Eventually, they (*settle*) _____ in California. My sister and I were born there and (*grow*) _____ up there. Last year, I (*go*) _____ to China for the first time to study at Beijing University. I (*want, always*) _____ to visit China and learn more about my own family background. My dreams finally came true.

□ **Exercise 24. Looking at grammar.** (Chart 3-5)
Underline the past perfect verbs. Which of the passages is typical of fiction writing? Which of the passages is typical of spoken English? What are the differences in verb form usage?

1. The thief simply walked in. Mrs. Garcia had forgotten to lock the door. Her son's school had called to say that he was ill, so she had rushed out the door without thinking to lock it.

2. Hey, Anna! Did you hear? A thief got into Mrs. Garcia's house. Yeah. She forgot to lock the door. The school called and told her that her son was sick, so she rushed out the door without locking it.

3. Sometime in 1995, Mr. Parvaz took a long, hard look at his life. He had had the same job for almost three decades. His dear wife had passed away. His children had grown and moved away. So he quit his job, packed everything he owned, and moved to London. That was the beginning of his adventure.

□ **Exercise 25. Warm-up: listening.** (Chart 3-6)
Listen for reduced speech in these sentences. How is ***had*** pronounced?

CD 1
Track 22

1. I'm sorry we missed the meeting. We had forgotten about it.
2. The movie had already begun by the time we got there.
3. I couldn't change my schedule. I had already planned my day.
4. I got home late. My roommate had already gone to bed.

3-6 *Had* in Spoken English

(a) **Joe had** already heard the story. 　*Spoken:* *Joe*/d/ already heard the story. OR 　　　　 *Joe*/əd/ already heard the story. (b) **Who had** been there before you? 　*Spoken:* *Who*/d/ been there before you? OR 　　　　 *Who*/əd/ been there before you?	In spoken English, the helping verb **had** in the past perfect is often reduced following nouns and question words. It can be pronounced as /d/ or as /əd/.*
(c) The dog **had** a bone. 　*Spoken:* The dog *had* a bone.	**Had** is not reduced when it is a main verb, as in (c).

*See Chart 3-5 for written contractions of **had** with pronouns.

☐ **Exercise 26. Listening.** (Chart 3-6)

CD 1
Track 23

Listen for reduced forms of **had**. If you hear a reduced form, <u>underline</u> **had** and the word it is combined with. Practice saying the reduced forms.

Examples: You will hear:　　Anna had missed the bus.
　　　　　　 You will underline:　<u>Anna had</u> missed the bus.

　　　　　　 You will hear:　　She had a headache.
　　　　　　 You will underline:　(*nothing*)

1. We had never seen it. He had never seen it. They had never seen it.
2. We got home late. The children had already fallen asleep.
3. My roommates had finished dinner by the time I got home.
4. My roommates had dinner early.
5. We couldn't drive across the river. The flood had washed away the bridge.
6. You were at Jim's at 8:00. Where had you been before that?
7. I had never visited there before. I'd like to go again. I had a good time.

☐ **Exercise 27. Listening.** (Charts 3-2 and 3-6)

CD 1
Track 24

Listen to the sentences. You will hear reduced forms for **have**, **had**, **is**, and **would**, but you will write their non-reduced forms.

1. You're a new student, aren't you? How long ____*have*____ you been in this country?

2. You must miss your old neighbor. How long _____ you known Mr. Kim before he moved away?

3. You're looking for Jack? Jack _____ left. He isn't here.

4. We were late, and Natasha _____ left by the time we got there.

5. Unfortunately, I didn't have my cell phone with me when we got lost. I _____ left it at home.

6. Since we're teachers, we have the summers off and do a lot of traveling. We

_____ like to travel to Africa next.

7. Talk about long marriages! Can you believe that Mr. and Mrs. Cho _____

been married for 65 years?

8. Serena _____ an amazing chef. She _____ created so many

new and popular dishes that it's almost impossible to get a reservation at her restaurant.

□ **Exercise 28. Listening.** (Charts 3-5 and 3-6)

First listen to the whole passage. Then listen again, and write the words that you hear.

CD 1
Track 25

A Pleasant Surprise

Last night, Amy got home from work two hours late. Usually she's home by 7:30, but last

night she didn't get there until almost 9:30.

When she got home, her husband, Jamal, _____ dinner
                                                                    1

and was washing the dishes. With a worried tone in his voice, he **asked** her where

_____. She **told** him _____ to work late,
            2   3

and then, on her way home, _____ a big accident that had
                                        4

slowed traffic to a crawl. He **asked** her why she _____. She **said**
                                                                5

_____ to recharge her cell phone, so she couldn't call him.
            6

Jamal smiled warmly and said that he was just glad that she was safely home. Then he

offered to make her dinner — which she gratefully accepted. A home–cooked meal sounded

wonderful. _____ a long day!
                        7

❏ **Exercise 29. Warm-up.** (Chart 3-7)
Which sentence (a. or b.) logically follows each statement? Discuss the meanings of the verbs in blue.

1. I have been working outside for almost an hour. _____

2. I had been working outside for almost an hour. _____

    a. It's hot. I think I'll go inside.

    b. But I got too hot and came inside.

3. I have been waiting for Jack since 5:00. _____

4. I had been waiting for Jack since 5:00. _____

    a. Then I left.

    b. And I'm still here.

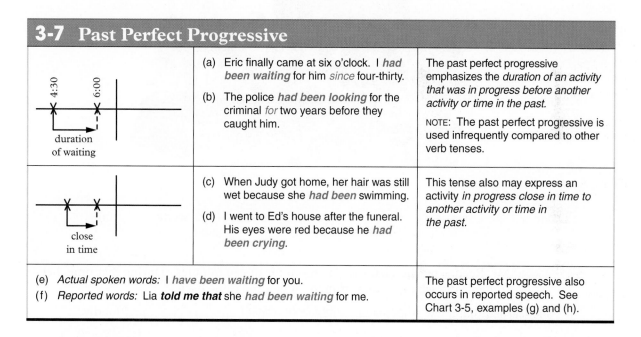

3-7	**Past Perfect Progressive**	
4:30 6:00 duration of waiting	(a) Eric finally came at six o'clock. I *had been waiting* for him *since* four-thirty. (b) The police *had been looking* for the criminal *for* two years before they caught him.	The past perfect progressive emphasizes the *duration of an activity that was in progress before another activity or time in the past.* NOTE: The past perfect progressive is used infrequently compared to other verb tenses.
close in time	(c) When Judy got home, her hair was still wet because she *had been* swimming. (d) I went to Ed's house after the funeral. His eyes were red because he *had been crying*.	This tense also may express an activity *in progress close in time to* another activity or time in the past.
(e) *Actual spoken words:* I *have been waiting* for you. (f) *Reported words:* Lia **told me that** she *had been waiting* for me.		The past perfect progressive also occurs in reported speech. See Chart 3-5, examples (g) and (h).

❏ **Exercise 30. Looking at grammar.** (Charts 3-4 and 3-7)
Complete the sentences. Use the present perfect progressive or the past perfect progressive form of the verbs in parentheses.

1. We (*wait*) _____*have been waiting*_____ for Nancy for the last two hours, but she still hasn't arrived.

2. We (*wait*) _____*had been waiting*_____ for Nancy for over three hours before she finally arrived yesterday.

3. It is midnight. I (*study*) _____ for five straight hours. No wonder I'm getting tired.

4. It was midnight. I (*study*) _____ for five straight hours. No wonder I was getting tired.

5. Jack suddenly realized that the teacher was asking him a question. He couldn't answer because he (*daydream*) _____ for the last ten minutes.

6. Wake up! You (*sleep*) _____ long enough. It's time to get up.

❏ **Exercise 31. Looking at grammar.** (Chart 3-7)
Complete the sentences. Use the past perfect progressive form of the verbs in the list (or your own words).

dance	draw	look	play	✓sing	study	talk

SITUATION: Ms. Reed, a teacher, left the classroom for fifteen minutes. During that time, her students did whatever they wanted. When she came back, ...

1. She learned that a few students ___*had been singing*___ loudly.

2. She found out that a couple of students _____ on cell phones.

3. Someone told her that one student _____ loud music.

4. She heard that several students _____ in the aisles.

5. She found out that a group of students _____ in her grade book.

6. She saw that a couple of students _____ pictures on the board.

7. She happily discovered that a few students _____ the whole time.

❏ **Exercise 32. Let's talk: class activity.** (Chapters 1 → 3)
Discuss the meaning of the verb forms and answer the questions about each pair of sentences.
Work in pairs, in small groups, or as a class.

1. a. When the rain stopped, Gloria was riding her bicycle to work.
   b. When the rain stopped, Paul jumped on his bicycle and rode to work.

   QUESTION: Who got wet on the way to work?

   ANSWER: Gloria.

2. a. Ms. Lincoln taught at this school for nine years.
   b. Mr. Sanchez has taught at this school for nine years.

   QUESTION: Who is teaching at this school now?

3. a. Alice was opening the door when the doorbell rang.
   b. George walked to the door after the doorbell rang.

   QUESTION: Who had been expecting a visitor?

4. a. Donna lived in Chicago for five years.
   b. Carlos has been living in Chicago for five years.

   QUESTION: Who still lives in Chicago?

5. a. Jane put some lotion on her face because she had been lying in the sun.
   b. Sue put some lotion on her face because she was lying in the sun.

   QUESTION: Who put lotion on her face after she finished sunbathing?

6. a. I looked across the street. Mr. Fox was waving at me.
   b. I looked across the street. Mrs. Cook waved at me.

   QUESTION: Who began to wave at me before I looked across the street?

7. a. Dan was leaving the room when I walked in.
   b. Sam had left the room when I walked in.

   QUESTION: Who did I see when I came into the room?

8. a. Ken went to the store because he was running out of food.
   b. Ann went to the store because she had run out of food.

   QUESTION: Who is better at planning ahead?

9. a. Jack had been studying Spanish since he was in elementary school. He spoke it very well by the time he moved to Peru.
   b. Robert has been studying Spanish since he was in elementary school. His Spanish is getting quite good.

   QUESTION: Who is studying Spanish in school?

❑ **Exercise 33. Listening.** (Chapters 1→ 3)

🎧
CD 1
Track 26

Listen to each situation. Choose the sentence (a. or b.) that correctly describes it.

Example: You will hear: Haven't you finished your term paper yet? You've been working on it for three days. It's due tomorrow, you know, Alice.

You will circle: ⓐ. Alice has been working on her term paper.
    b. Alice finished her term paper three days ago.

1. a. Yoko knows how to ski now.

   b. Yoko is learning to ski.

2. a. Yoko knows how to ski now.

   b. Yoko is learning to ski.

3. a. Mia is working as an auto mechanic right now.

   b. Mia has experience as an auto mechanic.

4. a. Jon is traveling now.

   b. Jon has traveled in the past, but he isn't traveling now.

5. a. Jon is currently working in sales.

   b. Jon no longer works in sales.

❑ **Exercise 34. Check your knowledge.** (Chapters 1→ 3)

Correct the errors.

1. Since I came to this country, I am learning a lot about the way of life here.

2. I arrive here only a short time ago. I am here since last Friday.

3. How long you been living here? I been here for almost two years.

4. Why you no have been in class for the last couple of days?

5. I am coaching a soccer team for the last two months.

6. My grandfather had lived in a small village in Italy when he was a child. At nineteen, he had moved to Rome, where he had met and had married my grandmother in 1957. My father had been born in Rome in 1960. I am born in Rome in 1989.

7. I'm living in my cousin's apartment since I have arrived here. It very small, and we are sharing the bedroom. I am needing my own place, but I don't find one so far.

8. When I was a child, I had lived with my grandmother instead of my parents. Grandpa has die before I am born, so I never knew him. Grandma raised me alone.

❏ **Exercise 35. Let's talk.** (Chapters 1 → 3)

From the given situation, make up a "chain story." One person begins the story; then others continue the story in turn, using cue words from the list. The cue words may be used in any order and may be used more than once. Work in small groups or as a class.

Example: (Pierre) had a terrible day yesterday. The trouble began early in the morning. His alarm clock rang at 7:00.

SPEAKER A: **When** his alarm clock rang, he got out of bed and stepped on a snake. He was nearly frightened to death, but the snake got away without biting him.

SPEAKER B: **After** the snake left, Pierre got dressed in a hurry and ran downstairs to have breakfast.

SPEAKER C: **While** he was running downstairs, he fell and broke his arm. Etc.

after	as soon as	by the time	never	then
after that	before	for (a length of time)	next	when
already	because	later	since	while

Possible beginning sentences:

1. (_____) had a terrible day yesterday.
2. (_____) had a great vacation last summer.
3. (_____) got into a lot of trouble a couple of days ago.
4. (_____) had an interesting experience last week.
5. (*Make up your own beginning sentence.*)

❏ **Exercise 36. Let's write and talk: small groups.** (Chapters 1 → 3)

Form a group and sit in a circle. On a separate sheet of paper, write the following sentence, using the name of the person sitting to your right: (. . .) *had a strange experience yesterday.*

Then write two or three additional sentences and pass your paper to the person sitting to your left, who will continue the story. Continue to pass the papers to the left until everyone in the group has had a chance to write part of each story.

Then decide which story in your group is the most entertaining or the most interesting. As a group, make any necessary corrections in grammar or spelling. Read the story aloud to the rest of the class. NOTE: You may wish to establish a time limit for each contribution to the story. (Use a buzzer or bell, or appoint someone to say "pass.") When the time limit is up, each person must pass his/her paper to the left even if it contains an unfinished sentence. The next person will then have to finish the sentence and continue writing the story.

❏ **Exercise 37. Let's write.** (Chapters 1 → 3)

Choose one to write about.

1. Describe the state of the world in the year of your birth. What significant or historical events occurred or were occurring at that time? Who were the leaders of your country? Then describe the changes that have occurred since that time and discuss the state of the world today.

2. Describe your family in the year you were born. Where were they living and working? Were they in a good situation? Who did your family consist of? Who in your family hadn't been born yet? Then describe the changes in your family that have occurred since the year of your birth and your family's current situation.

Chapter **4**
Future Time

❑ **Exercise 1. What do I already know?** (Chapter 4)
Look at the verbs in *italics*. Do the sentences express present or future time?

1.	The students *are going to give* oral reports today.	present	(future)
2.	I*'m beginning* a new job next week.	present	future
3.	Look. It*'s beginning* to rain.	present	future
4.	The teacher *will be* in her office after class today.	present	future
5.	When class *is* over, the teacher will be in her office.	present	future
6.	Finally, class *is* over. Let's get a cup of coffee.	present	future
7.	Oh no! We *have* only five minutes to make our train!	present	future
8.	Our train *leaves* from Track 37 in five minutes.	present	future
9.	The soccer team *is playing* in Barcelona next week.	present	future
10.	The soccer team *is playing* well today. They're winning.	present	future

❑ **Exercise 2. Warm-up.** (Chart 4-1)
Correct the errors.

1. Marie will cooks some chicken and rice for dinner tonight.

2. Where you will be tomorrow morning?

3. I no will ride the bus to work tomorrow.

4. Marco will probably to call us this evening.

5. I going to look for a new apartment.

60

4-1 Simple Future: *Will* and *Be Going To*

(graph with X mark)	(a) Jack *will finish* his work tomorrow. (b) Jack *is going to finish* his work tomorrow.	*Will* and ***be going to*** express future time and often have essentially the same meaning. Examples (a) and (b) have the same meaning. See Chart 4-2 for differences in meaning between the two forms.

Will

(c) Anna *will come* tomorrow around 5:00. INCORRECT: Anna ~~wills~~ come. INCORRECT: Anna ~~will~~ comes. INCORRECT: Anna ~~will~~ to come.	*Will* typically expresses predictions about the future, as in (c). *Will* does not take a final *-s*. *Will* is followed immediately by the simple form of a verb.
(d) Alex *will not be* here tomorrow. Peter *won't be* here either.	NEGATIVE: *will* + *not* = *won't*
(e) *Will you be* here tomorrow? How *will you get* here?	QUESTION: *will* + *subject* + *main verb* In (e): The speaker is asking for information about a future event.*
(f) *Spoken* or *written:* I'll be there. (g) *Spoken:* Tom'll be there too. *Written:* Tom *will* be there too. (h) *Spoken* or *very informal writing:* Nobody'll notice. That'll be fun. There'll be a test tomorrow.	CONTRACTIONS WITH PRONOUNS AND NOUNS: *Will* is often contracted with pronouns in both speaking and informal writing: *I'll, you'll, she'll, he'll, it'll, we'll, they'll.* *Will* is also often contracted with nouns in speaking but usually not in writing, as in (g). In very informal writing, ***will*** may be contracted with other kinds of pronouns and *there,* as in (h).

Be Going To

(i) Anna *is going to come* tomorrow around 5:00. (j) *Informally spoken:* Anna*'s gonna come* tomorrow around 5:00. (k) Tom *isn't going to come*. (l) *Are you going to come*?	***Be going to*** also commonly expresses predictions about the future. In informal speech, *going to* is often pronounced "gonna." NEGATIVE: *be* + *not* + *going to*, as in (k) QUESTION: *be* + *subject* + *going to*, as in (l)

*****Will*** can also be used in questions to make polite requests: ***Will*** *you **open** the door for me, please?* See Chart 9-3, p. 159.

☐ **Exercise 3. Listening.** (Chart 4-1)
If you hear a form of ***will***, choose *yes*. If not, choose *no*.

CD 1
Track 27

Example: I'll have time to see you tomorrow.   (yes)   no
            I have time to see you tomorrow.   yes   (no)

1. yes   no   5. yes   no
2. yes   no   6. yes   no
3. yes   no   7. yes   no
4. yes   no   8. yes   no

□ **Exercise 4. Pronunciation.** (Chart 4-1)
Practice pronouncing contractions with *will*.

1. Bob will be here soon.
   → *Bob'll be here soon.*
2. I'll come. He'll come. You'll come.
3. She'll help us. They'll help us too.
4. I'm sure we'll do well on the test.
5. It'll probably rain tomorrow.
6. The weather will be hot in August.
7. Mary will come tomorrow.
8. Bill will be here too.
9. The children will be home at 3:00.
10. Who will be at the meeting?
11. Where will you be around five?
12. How long will Tom be here?
13. Nobody will recognize you in that wig.
14. That will be interesting.
15. What will you do?

□ **Exercise 5. Listening.** (Chart 4-1)

CD 1
Track 28

Complete the sentences with the words you hear. Write the non-contracted forms of the verbs you hear.

1. _____ to turn in all your assignments by tomorrow.

2. _____ for the final exam on Monday.

3. The _____ 50 questions.

4. _____ 50 questions on the exam.

5. _____ the whole hour to complete the test.

6. It's a long exam. Sorry, but _____ early.

7. _____ a lot of work. Study hard!

8. The _____ available in my office the next day.

□ **Exercise 6. Listening.** (Chart 4-1)

CD 1
Track 29

Listen to the sentences. Circle whether you hear "going to" or "gonna."

1. going to   gonna   3. going to   gonna

2. going to   gonna   4. going to   gonna

□ **Exercise 7. Let's talk: small groups.** (Chart 4-1)
Choose a leader for your group. Practice using *be going to*. Follow these steps:
   (1) Every person in the group, including the leader, will hand the leader a slip of paper on which is written the name of an occupation or any kind of work adults do. *Examples:* movie star, teacher, plumber, peace activist, artist, stay-at-home dad, civil engineer, architect, politician.
   (2) The leader will redistribute the slips of paper to the group.
   (3) Each member of the group will then explain what he/she is going to be or do according to what is written on the slip of paper. *Example:* "I'm going to be a famous movie star."
   (4) The group will ask the speaker questions about his/her future career. *Example:* "What kind of movies are you going to be in? Where will you live?" Etc.

❑ **Exercise 8. Warm-up.** (Chart 4-2)
Read the sentences and answer the questions.

   a. It's going to rain tomorrow.
   b. I'm going to paint the house next week.
   c. Here. I'll help you carry that box. It looks heavy.
   d. It will be cloudy this weekend.

1. Which sentence expresses a prior plan?   _____
2. Which sentences are predictions?   _____ and _____
3. Which sentence expresses willingness?   _____

4-2 *Will* vs. *Be Going To*

Prediction

(a) According to the weather report, it *will be* cloudy tomorrow. (b) According to the weather report, it *is going to* be cloudy tomorrow.	*Will* and *be going to* mean the same when they make *predictions* about the future (*prediction* = a statement about something the speaker thinks will be true or will occur in the future). Examples (a) and (b) have the same meaning.

Prior Plan

(c) —Why did you buy this paint? 　　—I'm going to *paint* my bedroom tomorrow.	*Be going to* (but not *will*) is used to express a *prior plan* (i.e., a plan made before the moment of speaking).* In (c): The speaker already has a plan to paint his/her bedroom.

Willingness

(d) —The phone's ringing. 　　—I'll *get* it. (e) —How old is Aunt Agnes? 　　—I don't know. She *won't tell* me. (f) The car *won't start*. Maybe the battery is dead.	*Will* (but not *be going to*) is used to express *willingness*. In this case, *will* expresses a decision the speaker makes at the moment of speaking. In (d): The speaker decides to answer the phone at the immediate present moment; she/he does not have a prior plan. *Will not / won't* can express *refusal*, as in (e) with a person or in (f) with an inanimate object.

*COMPARE:
Situation 1: A: *Are you busy this evening?*
　　　　　　　B: *Yes.* **I'm going to meet** *Jack at the library at seven.* **We're going to study** *together.*
In Situation 1, only **be going to** is possible. The speaker has a prior plan, so he uses **be going to**.
Situation 2: A: *Are you busy this evening?*
　　　　　　　B: *Well, I really haven't made any plans.* **I'll eat** (OR **I'm going to eat**) *dinner, of course. And then* **I'll probably**
　　　　　　　　　watch (OR **I'm probably going to watch**) *TV for a little while.*
In Situation 2, either **will** or **be going to** is possible. Speaker B has not planned his evening. He is "predicting" his evening (rather than stating any prior plans), so he may use either **will** or **be going to**.

❏ **Exercise 9. Looking at grammar.** (Chart 4-2)
Discuss the *italicized* verbs in these short conversations. Decide if the speakers are expressing
    (a) predictions,
    (b) decisions they are making at the moment of speaking (willingness), or
    (c) plans they made before the moment of speaking.

1. A: Are you busy Saturday night? I've got front-row seats for the baseball game.
    B: Oh, I wish I could, but I can't. I*'m going to be* at my niece's wedding on Saturday.

2. A: Masako's such a creative artist. And she's so patient with children.
    B: She*'ll be* very successful as an elementary art teacher.

3. A: We*'re going to go* out to dinner in a few minutes. Do you want to join us?
    B: Sure. Give me just a minute. I*'ll grab* my coat.

4. A: I heard Sue and David are engaged for the third time!
    B: They *won't* ever *get married*. They fight too much.

5. A: How do you spell "accustomed"?
    B: I'm not sure. I*'ll look* it up for you.

6. A: That's great news about your new job.
    B: Well, actually, I've changed my mind about it. I*'m not going to take* it after all. I've
       decided to stay with my old job.

❏ **Exercise 10. Looking at grammar.** (Chart 4-2)
Decide if each *italicized* verb expresses a prediction, a prior plan, or willingness.

1. Dinner's almost ready. I*'ll set* the table.	prediction	plan	(willingness)
2. Ivan has some vacation time. He *is going to take* next week off.	prediction	plan	willingness
3. Heidi *will love* her birthday present. It's just what she wants.	prediction	plan	willingness
4. I don't like my job. I*'m going to quit* when I get back from vacation.	prediction	plan	willingness
5. That's okay. Don't worry about the spilled coffee. I*'ll clean* it up.	prediction	plan	willingness
6. Someday, there *are going to be* computers in every classroom in the world.	prediction	plan	willingness
7. The light bulb is burned out. I*'ll get* a new one from the supply room.	prediction	plan	willingness
8. I*'m going* to the bookstore. Do you want to go with me?	prediction	plan	willingness

❏ **Exercise 11. Looking at grammar.** (Chart 4-2)
Complete the sentences with **be going to** if you think the speaker is expressing a prior plan. If you think she/he has no prior plan, use **will**. Use **won't** if the speaker is expressing refusal.

1. A: This letter is in French, and I don't speak French. Can you help me?

   B: Sure. I (*translate*) _____will translate_____ it for you.

2. A: Do you want to go shopping with me? I (*go*) _____am going to go_____ to the shopping mall downtown.

   B: Sure. What time do you want to leave?

   A: How about 1:00?

   B: Great! See you then.

3. A: Who wants to erase the board? Are there any volunteers?

   B: I (*do*) _____ it!

   C: I (*do*) _____ it!

4. A: Why does he have an eraser in his hand?

   B: He (*erase*) _____ the board.

5. A: How about getting together for dinner tonight?

   B: Sounds good. Where?

   A: How about Alice's Restaurant or the Gateway Café? You decide.

   B: Alice's Restaurant. I (*meet*) _____ you there around six.

   A: Great. I (*see*) _____ you then.

   B: It's a date.

6. A: Do you have plans for dinner?

   B: Yes. I (*meet**) _____ a co-worker for dinner at Alice's

   Restaurant. Want to join us?

7. A: Why is that little boy crying?

   B: I don't know. He (*tell, not*) _____ me. I wonder where his parents are.

8. A: What's wrong?

   B: The door (*open, not*) _____.

   A: Well, of course not. It's locked.

☐ **Exercise 12. Listening.** (Chart 4-2)
Listen to the sentences and choose the expected response (a. or b.).

CD 1
Track 30

1. a. I'm going to work at a summer resort in the mountains.

   b. I'll work at a summer resort in the mountains.

2. a. Sure. I'm going to drop it off on my way to work.

   b. Sure. I'll drop it off on my way to work.

3. a. I'm going to attend my cousin's funeral.

   b. I'll attend my cousin's funeral.

4. a. Here, give it to me. I'm going to fix it for you.

   b. Here, give it to me. I'll fix it for you.

5. a. I'm going to sweep the front steps.

   b. I'll sweep the front steps.

☐ **Exercise 13. Warm-up.** (Chart 4-3)
Complete the sentences with your own words. All the sentences talk about future time. What
do you notice about the verbs in blue?

1. After I leave this class, I'm going to _____.

2. As soon as I get home tonight, I'll _____.

3. When I finish my English studies, I'm going to _____.

---

*When **be going to** expresses a prior plan, it is often also possible to use the present progressive with no change in meaning.
See Chart 4-2, p. 63. There is no difference in meaning between these sentences:

   I am going to meet Larry at Alice's Restaurant at six.

   I am meeting Larry at Alice's Restaurant at six.

4-3 Expressing the Future in Time Clauses

(a) Bob will come soon. *When Bob **comes**, we will see him.*	In (a): ***When Bob comes*** is a time clause.* ***when*** + *subject* + *verb* = *a time clause* When the meaning of the time clause is future, the SIMPLE PRESENT tense is used. *Will* or *be going to* is not used in the time clause.
(b) Linda is going to leave soon. *Before she **leaves**, she is going to finish her work.*	
(c) I will get home at 5:30. *After I **get** home, I will eat dinner.*	A time clause begins with such words as *when, before, after, as soon as, until,* and *while* and includes a subject and a verb. The time clause can come either at the beginning of the sentence or in the second part of the sentence: 　*When he comes,* we'll see him. OR 　We'll see him *when he comes.* Notice: A comma is used when the time clause comes first in a sentence.
(d) The taxi will arrive soon. *As soon as it **arrives**, we'll be able to leave for the airport.*	
(e) They are going to come soon. I'll wait here *until they **come**.*	
(f) *While I **am traveling** in Europe next year,* I'm going to save money by staying in youth hostels.	Sometimes the PRESENT PROGRESSIVE is used in a time clause to express an activity that will be in progress in the future, as in (f).
(g) I will go to bed *after I **finish** my work.* (h) I will go to bed *after I **have finished** my work.*	Occasionally, the PRESENT PERFECT is used in a time clause, as in (h). Examples (g) and (h) have the same meaning. The present perfect in the time clause emphasizes the completion of one act before a second act occurs in the future.

*A *time clause* is an adverb clause. See Charts 17-1 (p. 365) and 17-2 (p. 368) for more information.

❑ **Exercise 14. Looking at grammar.** (Chart 4-3)
Draw brackets around the time clause in each sentence and underline its verb. Identify and discuss the use of verb tenses.

1. We'll be here [when you <u>arrive</u> tomorrow.]

2. After the rain stops, I'm going to sweep the front porch.

3. I'm going to start making dinner before my wife gets home from work today.

4. I'm going to wait right here until Sonya comes.

5. As soon as the war is over, there will be new elections.

6. Right now the tide is low, but when the tide comes in, the ship will leave the harbor.

7. While I'm driving to work tomorrow, I'm going to listen to my Greek language CD.

❑ **Exercise 15. Looking at grammar.** (Chart 4-3)
Use ***will***/***be going to*** or the simple present. (In this exercise, both ***will*** and ***be going to*** are possible when a future verb is necessary, with little or no difference in meaning.)

1. Pete is going to leave in half an hour. He (*finish*) _____*will finish / is going to finish*_____ all of his work before he (*leave*) _____*leaves*_____.

2. I'm going to eat lunch at 12:30. After I (*eat*) _____,
   I (*take, probably*) _____ a nap.

3. I'll get home around six. When I (*get*) _____ home, I (*give*)
   _____ Sharon a call.

4. I'm going to watch a TV program at nine, but before I (*watch*) _____
   the program, I (*call*) _____ my parents.

5. Bakir will come soon. I (*wait*) _____ here until he (*come*)
   _____.

6. I'm sure it will stop raining soon. As soon as the rain (*stop*) _____,
   I (*walk*) _____ to the store to get some film.

7. I'm a junior in college this year. After I (*graduate*) _____ with a B.A.
   next year, I (*intend*) _____ to enter
   graduate school and work for an M.A. Perhaps I
   (*go*) _____ on for a Ph.D. after
   I (*get*) _____ my master's degree.

8. I (*listen*) _____ to
   an English language course while I (*sleep*)
   _____ tonight. Do you
   think it will help me learn English faster?

❏ **Exercise 16. Let's talk: interview.** (Chart 4-3)
Make questions using the given words. Ask two students each question. Share some of their
answers with the class. Use **be going to** for the future verb.

   1. What \ you \ do \ after \ you \ wake up \ tomorrow?
   2. What \ you \ do \ as soon as \ class \ end \ today?
   3. Before \ you \ go \ to bed \ tonight \ what \ you \ do?
   4. What \ you \ do \ when \ you \ have \ free time \ this weekend?
   5. When \ you \ finish \ school \ what \ you \ do?

❏ **Exercise 17. Warm-up.** (Chart 4-4)
Decide if each sentence has a present or future meaning. What do you notice about the verb
tense in each sentence?

   1. I'm meeting a friend for dinner tonight.   present meaning   future meaning
   2. We're taking a flight at midnight.   present meaning   future meaning
   3. Class starts in ten minutes.   present meaning   future meaning

4-4 Using the Present Progressive and the Simple Present to Express Future Time

Present Progressive

(a) My wife has an appointment with a doctor. She *is seeing* Dr. North *next Tuesday*.	The PRESENT PROGRESSIVE may be used to *express future time when the idea of the sentence concerns a planned event or definite intention.*
(b) Sam has already made his plans. He *is leaving* at noon tomorrow.	COMPARE: A verb such as *rain* is not used in the present progressive to indicate future time because rain is not a planned event.
(c) — What are you going to do this afternoon? — *After lunch*, I *am meeting* a friend of mine. We *are going* shopping. Would you like to come along?	A future meaning for the present progressive tense is indicated either by future time words in the sentence or by the context.

Simple Present

(d) The museum *opens* at 10:00 tomorrow morning.	The SIMPLE PRESENT can also be used to *express future time in a sentence concerning events that are on a definite schedule or timetable.* These sentences usually contain future time words. Only a few verbs are used in this way: e.g., *open, close, begin, end, start, finish, arrive, leave, come, return.*
(e) Classes *begin* next week.	
(f) John's plane *arrives* at 6:05 P.M. next Monday.	

❏ **Exercise 18. Looking at grammar.** (Chart 4-4)
Decide the meaning of each *italicized* verb. Write *in the future*, *now*, or *habitually*.

1. I *am taking* four courses next semester.   <u>in the future</u>

2. I *am taking* four courses this semester.   <u>now</u>

3. Students usually *take* four courses every semester.   <u>habitually</u>

4. I'll mail this letter at the corner when I *take* Susan home.   _____

5. My brother's birthday is next week. I *am giving* him a sweater.   _____

6. Shhh. The broadcaster *is giving* the latest news about the crisis overseas. I want to hear what she's saying.   _____

7. When I *graduate*, I'm going to return home.   _____

8. When students *graduate*, they receive diplomas.   _____

9. I'm tired. I *am going* to bed early tonight.   _____

10. When I *am* in New York, I'm going to visit the Museum of Modern Art.   _____

11. When I *am* home alone in the evening, I like to read or watch television.   _____

12. A: Are you busy?

    B: Not really.

    A: What *are* you *doing?*   A: _____

    B: I'*m writing* a letter to my folks.   B: _____

    A: When you *finish* your letter, do you want to play a
        game of chess?   A: _____

13. A: What *are* you *doing* after work today?   A: _____

    B: I'*m playing* tennis with Brown at the health club.
        And you?   B: _____

    A: I'*m meeting* Smith for a round of golf.   A: _____

❏ **Exercise 19. Looking at grammar.** (Chart 4-4)
Complete each sentence with any present progressive verb.

   1. A: How about going across the street for a cup of coffee?

       B: I can't. I ____*am meeting*____ Jennifer at the library at 5:00.

   2. A: Why are you in such a hurry?

       B: I have to be at the airport in an hour. I _____ the four

          o'clock plane to New York. I have an important meeting there tomorrow.

   3. A: I see you're smoking. I thought you stopped last month.

       B: I did. I don't know why I started again. I _____ tomorrow,

          and this time I mean it.

4. A: Your cough sounds terrible! You should see a doctor.

B: I know. It just won't go away. I _____

Dr. Murray later this afternoon.

5. A: Where are you and your family going for your vacation this summer?

B: Ontario, Canada.

A: Are you planning to fly?

B: No, we _____ so we can take our time and enjoy the scenery.

A: That sounds wonderful.

❏ **Exercise 20. Let's write.** (Chart 4-4)
Pretend that you are going to take your ideal vacation next week. All of your plans are made, and your itinerary is in front of you. Write your travel plans. Use present tenses where appropriate.

Example: This coming Saturday, I am beginning my "vacation of a lifetime." The first place I'm going to is Bali. My plane leaves at six-thirty Saturday morning. I arrive in Bali late that afternoon. I'm staying at the Nusa Dua Beach Hotel. I leave Bali on the fifteenth and travel to the Philippines. While I'm there, I'm staying with some friends. Etc.

❏ **Exercise 21. Warm-up.** (Chart 4-5)
Notice the verbs in blue. What do they have in common?

1. Right now, I'm sitting in class.
2. Yesterday at this time, I was sitting in class.
3. Tomorrow at this time, I will be sitting in class.

4-5 Future Progressive

	(a) I will begin to study at seven. You will come at eight. I *will be studying* when you come.	The future progressive expresses an activity that *will be in progress at a time in the future.*
	(b) Don't call me at nine because I won't be home. I *am going to be studying* at the library.	The progressive form of *be going to*: *be going to* + *be* + *-ing*, as in (b)
	(c) Don't worry. She *will be coming* soon. (d) Don't worry. She *will come* soon.	Sometimes there is little or no difference between the future progressive and the simple future, especially when the future event will occur at an indefinite time in the future, as in (c) and (d).

❑ **Exercise 22. Looking at grammar.** (Chart 4-5)
Complete the sentences. Use the future progressive form of the given verbs.

1. *finish, sleep, study*

   Please don't call our house after 9:00 tonight. The baby _____*is going to be sleeping*_____

   _____OR *will be sleeping*_____. My husband _____

   for a test. I _____ a project for work.

2. *talk, do, see*

   Dr. Roberts is the town's only medical doctor and works long hours. Tomorrow she has an

   especially busy schedule. From early in the morning until lunch, she _____

   _____ patients at her clinic. After lunch, she _____

   research at the hospital. In the evening, she _____ to

   medical students about rural health care.

❑ **Exercise 23. Looking at grammar.** (Chart 4-5)
Complete the sentences. Use the future progressive or the simple present form of the verbs in
parentheses.

1. Tomorrow I'm going to leave for home. When I (*arrive*) _____ at the

   airport, my whole family (*wait*) _____ for me.

2. When I (*get*) _____ up tomorrow morning, the sun (*shine*)

   _____, the birds (*sing*) _____, and my

   roommate (*lie, still*) _____ in bed fast asleep.

3. A: When do you leave for Florida?

   B: Tomorrow. Just think! Two days from now

      I (*enjoy*) _____

      my vacation in the sun.

   A: Sounds great! I (*think*) _____

      _____ about you.

4. A: Are you going to be in town next Saturday?

   B: No. I (*visit, in Chicago**) _____

      _____ my aunt.

5. A: Where are you going to be this evening?

   B: I (*work, at the library*) _____

      on my research paper.

---

*Expressions of place can often be used between the helping verb and the main verb in progressive tenses. See Chart 2-10, p. 34.

❑ **Exercise 24. Warm-up.** (Chart 4-6)
Notice the verbs in blue. What do they have in common?

1. Eric isn't here. He has left.
2. Eric wasn't there. He had left by the time we got there.
3. Eric won't be there. He will have left by the time we get there.

4-6 Future Perfect and Future Perfect Progressive

NOTE: These two tenses are rarely used compared to the other verb tenses.

Future Perfect	(a) I will graduate in June. I will see you in July. By the time I see you, I *will have graduated.*	The FUTURE PERFECT expresses an activity that will be *completed before another time or event in the future.*
Future Perfect Progressive	(b) I will go to bed at 10:00 P.M. Ed will get home at midnight. At midnight I will be sleeping. I *will have been sleeping* for two hours by the time Ed gets home.	The FUTURE PERFECT PROGRESSIVE emphasizes the *duration* of an activity that will be *in progress before another time or event in the future.*
	(c) When Professor Jones retires next month, he *will have taught* OR *will have been teaching* for 45 years.	Sometimes the future perfect and the future perfect progressive have the same meaning, as in (c). Also, notice that the activity expressed by either of these two tenses may begin in the past.

❑ **Exercise 25. Looking at grammar.** (Chapter 3; Charts 4-5 and 4-6)
Complete the sentences. Use any appropriate tense of the verbs in parentheses.

1. Ann and Andy got married on June 1st.
   Today is June 15th. They (*be*) _____
   married for two weeks.

   By June 8th, they (*be*) _____
   married for one week.

   By June 29th, they (*be*) _____
   married for four weeks.

June

Sun	Mon	Tues	Wed	Thurs	Fri	Sat
						1
2	3	4	5	6	7	8
9	10	11	12	13	14	15
16	17	18	19	20	21	22
23	24	25	26	27	28	29
30						

2. This traffic is terrible. We're going to be late. By the time we

   (*get*) _____ to the airport, Yuri's plane (*arrive, already**)

   _____, and he'll be wondering where we are.

---

*With the future perfect, *already* has two possible midsentence positions: *I will **already** have finished.*
*I will have **already** finished.*

❏ **Exercise 3. Let's talk.** (Chapters 1→4)
Practice verb tenses by answering the questions in complete sentences. Work in pairs, in small groups, or as a class. Only the questioner's book is open.

1. What have we been studying? What is one tense we have studied since the beginning of the term? When, as best as you can remember, did we study it?
2. What else will we have studied in this class by the time the term ends?
3. This class began on (*date*). Had you studied verb tenses before that?
4. We're going to finish studying Chapter 5 on (*day or date*). How long will we have been studying Chapter 5 by that time?
5. Where are you going to be living in five years?
6. Think about recent news. What's happening in world affairs? What's happened recently?

(*Change roles if working in pairs.*)
7. What are you doing right now? How long have you been doing that?
8. What were you doing at this time yesterday? What did you do after that?
9. What will you be doing tonight at midnight? What were you doing last night at midnight?
10. What places have you been to since you came to (*this city*)?
11. What are some of the things you have done in your lifetime? When did you do them?
12. What countries/cities have you visited? When did you visit (_____)? Why did you go there? What did you like about (_____)? What did you dislike about (_____)? Are you planning to go there again someday?

❏ **Exercise 4. Listening.** (Chapters 1→4)

Part I. Listen to the story with your book closed. Then open your book and read the statements. Circle "T" for true and "F" for false.

CD 1
Track 31

1. The man broke the lock on the door.   T   F
2. The man thought a stranger was in his apartment.   T   F
3. The man's wife opened the door.   T   F
4. The man felt he had done something stupid.   T   F

Part II. Listen again. Complete the sentences with the verbs you hear.

When I _____(1)_____ home to my apartment last night, I _____(2)_____ out my key to open the door as usual. As always, I _____(3)_____ it in the lock, but the door _____(4)_____. I _____(5)_____ my key again and again with no luck. So I _____(6)_____ on the door for my wife to let me in. Finally the door _____(7)_____, but I _____(8)_____ my wife on the other side. I _____(9)_____ a stranger. I _____(10)_____ to get into the wrong apartment! I quickly _____(11)_____ and _____(12)_____ to my own. I _____(13)_____ very stupid about what I _____(14)_____.

❑ **Exercise 5. Let's talk and write.** (Chapters 1→4)
Before you come to class, think of an interesting, dangerous, or amusing experience you have had. Tell the story to a classmate, who will report your experience in a composition.

❑ **Exercise 6. Looking at grammar.** (Chapters 1→4)
Complete the sentences with any appropriate tense of the verbs in parentheses.

Dear Anna,

I (*get*) _____ your long email about two
                    1
weeks ago and (*try*) _____
                              2
to find time to write you back ever since. I (*be*)

_____ very busy lately. In the past
             3
two weeks, I (*have*) _____ four tests, and
                            4
I have another one next week. In addition, a friend (*stay*)

_____ with me since last Thursday. She wanted to see the
             5
city, so we (*spend*) _____ a lot of time visiting some of the
                              6
interesting places here. We (*be*) _____ to the zoo, the art museum,
                                            7
and the botanical gardens.

Yesterday we (*go*) _____ to the park and (*watch*) _____ a
                          8   9
balloon race. Between showing her the city and studying for my exams, I (*have, barely*)

_____ enough time to breathe.
             10
Right now it (*be*) _____ 3:00 A.M., and I (*sit*) _____ at my
                          11   12
desk. I (*sit*) _____ here for five hours doing my studying. My
                      13
friend's plane (*leave*) _____ in a few hours, so I (*decide*)
                                14
_____ not to go to bed. That's why I (*write*) _____ to
       15   16
you at such an early hour in the day. I (*get*) _____ a little sleepy, but I
                                                      17
would rather stay up. I (*take*) _____ a nap after I (*get*) _____
                                      18   19
back from taking her to the airport.

How (*you, get*) _____ along? How
                          20
(*your classes, go*) _____? Please write soon.
                            21
Yours,
Yoko

❑ **Exercise 7. Let's write.** (Chapters 1 → 4)
Write a letter to a friend or family member. Discuss your activities, thoughts, feelings, and adventures in the present, past, and future.

Use as many different tenses as seems natural. For example, in the course of your letter, tell your reader what you *are doing, do every day, have done since a certain time, have been doing lately, did at some particular time, had done before you did something else, are going to do*, etc.

❑ **Exercise 8. Listening.** (Chapters 1 → 4)

CD 1
Track 32

Listen to each situation and choose the sentence that comes next (a. or b.).

1. a. Now the passengers are waiting in the baggage claim area.
   b. After the plane lands, the passengers will be waiting in the baggage claim area.

2. a. Then his boss called.
   b. He's finding it very relaxing.

3. a. When did it stop?
   b. When's it going to stop?

4. a. Some people in the audience said "Shhh" as we sat down.
   b. We missed the first half hour.

5. a. She's glad that she's finished her training.
   b. She's going to take another one next month.

6. a. They never caught him.
   b. They'll never catch him.

❑ **Exercise 9. Looking at grammar.** (Chapters 1 → 4)
Complete the sentences with the words in parentheses. Use any appropriate tense.

Almost every part of the world (*experience*) _____ an

earthquake in recent years, and almost every part of the world (*experience*)

_____ earthquakes in the years to come. Since the ancient
          2

Chinese (*begin*) _____ to keep records several thousand years ago, more than 13
          3

million earthquakes (*occur*) _____ worldwide by some estimates.
          4

What (*cause*) _____ earthquakes? Throughout time, different cultures
          5

(*develop*) _____ myths to explain these violent earth movements.
          6

From India comes the story of six strong elephants who (*hold*) _____ up the
          7

earth on their heads. Whenever one elephant (*move*) _____ its head, the earth
          8

trembles.

According to a Japanese myth, a playful catfish lives in the mud under the earth. Whenever it feels like playing, it (wave) _____ its fat tail around in the mud. The result? Earthquakes.

Nowadays, although scientists (know) _____ more about the causes of earthquakes, they still cannot prevent the terrible damage. One of the strongest quakes in the last hundred years (happen) _____ in Anchorage, Alaska, on March 24, 1964, at about six o'clock in the evening. When the earthquake (strike) _____ that evening, many families (sit) _____ down to eat dinner. People in the city (find, suddenly) _____ themselves in the dark because most of the lights in the city went out when the earthquake occurred. Many people (die) _____ instantly when tall buildings (collapse) _____ and (send) _____ tons of brick and concrete crashing into the streets. When (the next earthquake, occur) _____? No one really knows for sure.

Interestingly enough, throughout history animals (help, often) _____ people predict earthquakes shortly before they happen. At present, some scientists (study) _____ catfish because catfish swim excitedly just before an earthquake.

According to some studies, snakes, monkeys, and rodents (appear, also) _____ to be sensitive to the approach of violent movement in the earth's surface. Some animals (seem) _____ to know a great deal more than humans about when an earthquake will occur.

In recent years, scientists (develop) _____ many extremely sensitive instruments. Perhaps someday the instruments (be) _____ able to give us a sufficiently early warning so that we can be waiting calmly in a safe place when the next earthquake (strike) _____.

❑ **Exercise 10. Let's talk: pairwork.** (Chapters 1 → 4)
Work with a partner.

PARTNER A: Pretend to be a famous living person. Agree to an interview by a nosy newspaper reporter (Partner B). Tell the reporter all about yourself. Invent answers. Use your imagination. Begin with *I* . . . .

PARTNER B: You're the reporter. Ask the famous person (Partner A) all sorts of questions about his/her past, present, and future.

After the interview, write an article with your partner about this person.

❑ **Exercise 11. Let's talk: small groups.** (Chapters 1 → 4)
Divide up the tasks within your group. Put together a news release about your class. It should contain the following:
  • a few sentences about each class member and the teacher
  • activities you have done in this class
  • a description of the classroom, the building it's in, and the surrounding area
  • some information about the school you're attending
  • other interesting information about your class

❑ **Exercise 12. Let's talk and write.** (Chapters 1 → 4)
In a short talk (two or three minutes), summarize a recent news event. Present your talk to a small group or to the class. If necessary, you may speak from brief notes (an outline of only the most important points). Listeners can write short summaries of each presentation.

❑ **Exercise 13. Check your knowledge.** (Chapters 1 → 4)
Correct the errors in verb tense usage.

1. I haven't been in this town very long. I come here just two weeks ago.

2. Dormitory life is not quiet. Everyone shouted and make a lot of noise in the halls.

3. My friends will meet me when I will arrive at the airport.

4. Hasn't anyone ever tell you to knock on the door before you enter someone else's room? Didn't your parents taught you that?

5. The phone rung while I doing the dishes. I dry my hands and answer it. When I am hear my husband's voice, I very happy.

6. I am in the United States for the last four months. During this time, I had done many things and saw many places.

7. When the old man started to walk back to his hut, the sun has already hided itself behind the mountain.

8. While I am writing my composition last night, someone knocks on the door.

9. Why did you writing a children's book?

10. I'm really glad you to visit my hometown next year.

11. While I was visitting my cousin in Los Angeles, we went to a restaurant and eat Thai food.

12. When I was a child, I viewed things from a much lower height. Many physical objects around me appear very large. When I want to move something such as a chair, I need help.

13. When I was in my country, I am afraid to come to the United States. I thought I couldn't walk outside at night because of the terrible crime. But now I am having a different opinion. I live in this small town for three months and learn that there is very little crime here.

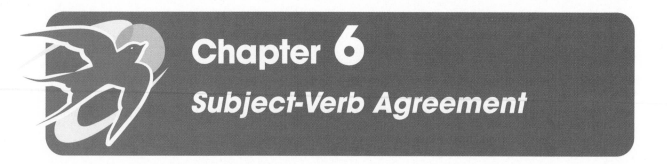

Chapter **6**
Subject-Verb Agreement

❏ **Exercise 1. What do I already know?** (Chart 6-1)
Add *-s* or *-es* where necessary. Do not change or omit any other words. All of the sentences are simple present. Discuss the use, spelling, and pronunciation of final *-s/-es*.

1. Erica miss_∧ her mother and father.
   es

2. My parent visit many countries when they travel in Europe.

3. Robert sing when he take a shower.

4. Chicken, duck, and turkey lay egg.

5. Anna wear glove on her hand when she work in

   her garden.

6. She scratch her chin when it itch.

❏ **Exercise 2. Warm-up.** (Chart 6-1)
Look at the words that end in *-s*. Are they singular or plural? Are they nouns or verbs?

	Singular	Plural	Noun	Verb
1. A new car *costs* a lot of money.	x			x
2. New *cars* cost a lot of money.				
3. My neighbor *makes* a lot of noise.				
4. My *neighbors* make a lot of noise.				
5. Bill *drinks* tea for breakfast.				
6. Cold *drinks* taste good on a hot day.				

6-1 Final -s/-es: Use, Pronunciation, and Spelling

Use

(a)	*Noun + -s:* Friends are important. *Noun + -es:* I like my classes.	A final **-s** or **-es** is added to a noun to make the noun plural. **Friend** and **class** = singular nouns **Friends** and **classes** = plural nouns
(b)	*Verb + -s:* Mary works at the bank. *Verb + -es:* John watches birds.	A final **-s** or **-es** is added to a simple present verb when the subject is a singular noun (e.g., *Mary, my father, the machine*) or third person singular pronoun (*she, he, it*). **Mary works** = singular **She works** = singular **The students work** = plural **They work** = plural

Pronunciation

(c)	seats ropes backs	→ seat/s/ → rope/s/ → back/s/	Final **-s** is pronounced /s/ after voiceless sounds, as in (c): "t," "p," and "k" are examples of voiceless sounds.*
(d)	seeds robes bags sees	→ seed/z/ → robe/z/ → bag/z/ → see/z/	Final **-s** is pronounced /z/ after voiced sounds, as in (d): "d," "b," "g," and "ee" are examples of voiced sounds.*
(e)	dishes catches kisses mixes prizes edges	→ dish/əz/ → catch/əz/ → kiss/əz/ → mix/əz/ → prize/əz/ → edge/əz/	Final **-s** and **-es** are pronounced /əz/ after "sh," "ch," "s," "x," "z," and "ge"/"dge" sounds. The /əz/ ending adds a syllable. All of the words in (e) are pronounced with two syllables. COMPARE: All of the words in (c) and (d) are pronounced with one syllable.

Spelling

(f)	sing song	→ sings → songs	For most words (whether a verb or a noun), simply add a final **-s** to spell the word correctly.
(g)	wash watch class buzz box	→ washes → watches → classes → buzzes → boxes	Final **-es** is added to words that end in **-sh**, **-ch**, **-s**, **-z**, and **-x**.
(h) (i)	toy buy baby cry	→ toys → buys → babies → cries	For words that end in **-y**: In (h): If **-y** is preceded by a vowel, only **-s** is added. In (i): If **-y** is preceded by a consonant, the **-y** is changed to **-i** and **-es** is added.

*See Chart 2-6, p. 27, for an explanation of voiced vs. voiceless sounds.

❑ **Exercise 3. Listening and pronunciation.** (Chart 6-1)

Listen to the words. Practice saying them aloud. Write the pronunciation of final **-s/-es** after each word.

CD 1
Track 33

1. rides   __/z/__
2. writes   _____
3. robs   _____

4. rugs   _____
5. sleeps   _____
6. locks   _____

7. wishes   _____
8. pages   _____
9. months   _____

❏ **Exercise 4. Spelling and pronunciation.** (Chart 6-1)
Add **-s** or **-es** to the given words to make them plural. Practice saying them aloud. Write the pronunciation for each ending.

1. floor _s_   _/z/_   7. season _____   _____

2. tax _es_   _/əz/_   8. develop _____   _____

3. talk _s_   _/s/_   9. touch _____   _____

4. bush _____   _____   10. cough _____   _____

5. hat _____   _____   11. method _____   _____

6. rise _____   _____   12. language _____   _____

❏ **Exercise 5. Listening and pronunciation.** (Chart 6-1)
CD 1
Track 34
Complete the sentences with the words you hear. Practice pronouncing final **-s/-es** by reading the sentences aloud.

1. _____ _____ eighteen _____ a day.

2. People come in many _____ and _____.

3. Maria _____ pronunciation by reading _____ aloud.

4. The _____ _____ good _____.

5. Our _____ _____ us to speak English outside of class.

6. When Jack has a cold, he _____ and _____.

❏ **Exercise 6. Let's talk: pairwork.** (Chart 6-1)
Work with a partner. Each item contains a subject and a verb. Make two sentences for each item. Help each other with the use of final **-s/-es** if necessary. Partner A uses a <u>plural</u> subject. Partner B uses a <u>singular</u> subject and begins with **A/An**.

Example: alarm clock \ ring
PARTNER A: Alarm clocks ring.
PARTNER B: An alarm clock rings.

1. opera singer \ sing
2. teacher \ teach
3. butterfly \ fly
4. ball \ bounce
5. door \ open and close

Change roles.
6. mosquito bite \ itch
7. hungry baby \ cry
8. student \ ask questions
9. snake \ hiss
10. dog \ say "arf-arf" in English

□ **Exercise 7. Warm-up.** (Chart 6-2)
Look at the verbs in blue in each pair of sentences. How do you know when to use a singular or a plural verb?

1. a. A girl is in the classroom.
   b. Some girls are in the classroom.

2. a. A girl and a boy are in the classroom.
   b. Every girl and boy is in the classroom.

3. a. The fruit at those markets is cheap.
   b. The apples at that market are cheap.

4. a. Vegetables are good for you.
   b. Eating vegetables is good for you.

6-2 Basic Subject-Verb Agreement

Singular Verb	Plural Verb	
(a) My *friend lives* in Boston.	(b) My *friends live* in Boston.	*Verb* + *-s/-es* = third person singular in the simple present tense *Noun* + *-s/-es* = plural
	(c) My *brother and sister live* in Boston. (d) My *brother, sister, and cousin live* in Boston.	Two or more subjects connected by *and* require a plural verb.
(e) *Every* man, woman, *and* child *needs* love. (f) *Each* book *and* magazine *is* listed in the bibliography.		EXCEPTION: *Every* and *each* are always followed immediately by singular nouns. (See Chart 7-11, p. 129.) In this case, even when there are two (or more) nouns connected by *and*, the verb is singular.
(g) That *book* on political parties *is* interesting. (i) The *book* that I got from my parents *was* very interesting.	(h) The *ideas* in that book *are* interesting. (j) The *books* I bought at the bookstore *were* expensive.	Sometimes a phrase or clause separates a subject from its verb. These interrupting structures do not affect basic agreement. For example, in (g) the interrupting prepositional phrase *on political parties* does not change the fact that the verb *is* must agree with the subject *book*. In (i) and (j): The subject and verb are separated by an adjective clause. (See Chapter 13.)
(k) *Watching* old movies *is* fun.		A gerund (e.g., *watching*) used as the subject of the sentence requires a singular verb. (See Chart 14-8, p. 322.)

□ **Exercise 8. Looking at grammar.** (Chart 6-2)
Choose the correct completions.

1. Lettuce (*is*, *are*) good for you.

2. The subjects you will be studying in this course (*is*, *are*) listed in the syllabus.

3. The extent of Fatima's knowledge on various subjects (*astounds*, *astound*) me.

4. Oranges, tomatoes, fresh strawberries, cabbage, and lettuce (*is*, *are*) rich in vitamin C.

5. Every man, woman, and child (*is, are*) protected under the law.

6. The professor and the student (*agrees, agree*) on that point.

7. Almost every professor and student at the university (*approves, approve*) of the choice of Dr. Brown as the new president.

8. Each girl and boy in the sixth-grade class (*has, have*) to do a science project.

9. Tomatoes (*is, are*) easy to grow. Growing tomatoes (*is, are*) especially easy in hot climates.

10. Getting to know students from all over the world (*is, are*) one of the best parts of my job.

11. Where (*does, do*) your parents live?

12. Annie had a hard time when she was coming home from the store because the bag of groceries (*was, were*) too heavy for her to carry.

13. Why (*was, were*) Yoko and Alex late for the meeting?

14. (*Is, Are*) having the responsibility for taking care of pets good for young children?

15. I like to go shopping when I'm on vacation, but I don't buy many things. A lot of the stuff* in tourist shops (*is, are*) cheaply made and overpriced.

❏ **Exercise 9. Listening.** (Chart 6-2)

Listen to the beginning of each sentence. Choose the correct verb.

CD 1
Track 35

Example: You will hear: The student . . .
          You will choose: (*know,* (*knows*)) the assignment.

1. (*know, knows*)   basic math calculations.

2. (*know, knows*)   when the assignments are due.

3. (*know, knows*)   how to use a thesaurus.

4. (*know, knows*)   the classroom routine.

5. (*know, knows*)   her expectations.

6. (*know, knows*)   how to use the internet.

7. (*know, knows*)   how to use sign language.

8. (*know, knows*)   where to go in case of fire.

❏ **Exercise 10. Warm-up.** (Chart 6-3)

Look at the verbs in blue. How do you know when to use a singular or a plural verb?

1. Some of this book is interesting.
2. Some of those books are interesting.
3. Most of those books are interesting.

4. Most of the book is interesting.
5. One of those books is Linda's.
6. Each of those books is yours.

---

*stuff = a noun used in informal English to refer to a group of things. For example: *My stuff is in my backpack.* My stuff = my books, pens, gym clothes, etc.

6-3 Subject-Verb Agreement: Using Expressions of Quantity

Singular Verb	Plural Verb	

(a) *Some of the **book is** good.*
(c) *A lot of the **equipment is** new.*
(e) *Two-thirds of the **money is** mine.*
(g) *Most of our **homework is** easy.*
	(b) *Some of the **books are** good.*
	(d) *A lot of my **friends are** here.*
	(f) *Two-thirds of the **boys are** here.*
	(h) *Most of our **assignments are** easy.*
		In most expressions of quantity, the verb is determined by the noun (or pronoun) that follows ***of**.
		
		For example, in (a) and (b):
		    some of + *singular noun = singular verb*
		    some of + *plural noun = plural verb*

(i) ***One** of my friends **is** here.* (j) ***Each** of my friends **is** here.* (k) ***Every one** of my friends **is** here.*		EXCEPTIONS: ***One of**, **each of**, and **every one of*** take singular verbs. ***one of*** ***each of*** } + *plural noun = singular verb* ***every one of***
(l) ***None** of the boys **is** here.*	(m) ***None** of the boys **are** here.*	Subjects with ***none of*** used to be considered singular in very formal English, but plural verbs are often used in informal English and sometimes even in formal writing.
(n) ***The number** of students in the class **is** fifteen.*	(o) *A number of **students were** late for class.*	COMPARE: In (n): ***The number*** is the subject. In (o): ***A number of*** is an expression of quantity meaning "a lot of." It is followed by a plural noun and a plural verb.

❑ **Exercise 11. Looking at grammar.** (Chart 6-3)
Choose the correct completions. <u>Underline</u> the word(s) that determine whether the verb is singular or plural.

1. Some of the <u>fruit</u> in this bowl (*is,* *are*) rotten.

2. Some of the apples in that bowl (*is, are*) rotten.

3. Most of the movie (*is, are*) funny.

4. Most of the movies (*is, are*) funny.

5. Half of the students in the class (*is, are*) from Arabic-speaking countries.

6. Half of this money (*is, are*) yours.

7. A lot of the students in the class (*is, are*) from Southeast Asia.

8. A lot of clothing in those stores (*is, are*) on sale this week.

9. One of my best friends (*is, are*) coming to visit me next month.

10. Each boy in the class (*has, have*) his own notebook.

11. Each of the boys in the class (*has, have*) his own notebook.

12. Every one of the students (*is, are*) required to take the final test.

13. None of the animals at the zoo (*is, are*) free to roam. All of them (*is, are*) in enclosures.

14. A number of students (*is, are*) absent today.

15. The number of employees in my company (*is, are*) approximately ten thousand.

16. One of the chief materials in bones and teeth (*is, are*) calcium.

17. (*Does, Do*) all of the students have their books?

18. (*Does, Do*) all of this homework have to be finished by tomorrow?

19. Why (*was, were*) some of the students excused from the examination?

20. Why (*was, were*) one of the students excused from the examination?

❑ **Exercise 12. Looking at grammar.** (Chart 6-3)
Take turns making sentences. Work with a partner or in small groups.

. . . is/are unusual.

1. The story → *The story is unusual.*
2. The stories
3. Some of the story
4. Some of the stories
5. Two-thirds of the story
6. One of the stories
7. Each of the stories
8. None of the story
9. None of the stories
10. A number of stories

. . . is/are secondhand.

11. The furniture
12. A lot of the furniture
13. A lot of the chairs
14. Some of the furniture
15. Half of the furniture
16. None of the furniture
17. Some of the chairs
18. Three-fourths of the furniture
19. Seventy-five percent of the furniture
20. Half of the chairs

❑ **Exercise 13. Warm-up.** (Chart 6-4)
Complete the sentences with your own words.

1. Think about (or look around) your classroom.

   There are _____ in my classroom.

   There is _____ in my classroom.

2. Think about (or look around) your bedroom.

   There are _____ in my bedroom.

   There is _____ in my bedroom.

6-4 Subject-Verb Agreement: Using *There* + *Be*

(a) **There is** *a fly* in the room. (b) **There are** *three windows* in this room.	**There** + **be** introduces the idea that something exists in a particular place. **There** + **be** + *subject* + *expression of place** The subject follows **be** when **there** is used. In (a): The subject is *a fly.* (singular) In (b): The subject is *three windows.* (plural)
(c) INFORMAL: There*'s two sides* to every story.	In informal spoken English, some native speakers use a singular verb even when the subject is plural, as in (c). The use of this form is fairly frequent but is not generally considered to be grammatically correct.

*Sometimes the expression of place is omitted when the meaning is clear. For example, *There are seven continents.* The implied expression of place is clearly *in the world.*

❏ **Exercise 14. Looking at grammar.** (Chart 6-4)
Choose the correct completions.

1. There (*isn't, aren't*) any letters in the mail for you today.

2. There (*isn't, aren't*) any mail for you today.

3. There (*is, are*) a lot of problems in the world.

4. There (*is, are*) a hole in his sock.

5. How many kinds of birds (*is, are*) there in the world?

6. Why (*isn't, aren't*) there a hospital close to those villages?

7. There (*was, were*) a terrible earthquake in Iran last year.

8. Why (*is, are*) there a shortage of available apartments for rent in this city at present?

9. There (*is, are*) more women than men in my office.

10. There (*has been, have been*) a line in front of that theater every night for the past two weeks.

11. How many wars do you suppose there (*has been, have been*) in the history of the world?

❏ **Exercise 15. Listening.** (Chart 6-4)
Choose the words you hear. For many of the sentences, you will hear reductions of the given words. NOTE: **Is** + **there** can sound like "ih-zehr." For example, **Is there** ("ih-zehr") *a doctor in the house?*

CD 1
Track 36

Example: You will hear: There's a spider on the wall.
You will choose: (There is) There are

1.	There is	There are	5. Is there	Are there
2.	there is	there are	6. Is there	Are there
3.	There is	There are	7. there is	there are
4.	There is	There are	8. Is there	Are there

❑ **Exercise 16. Let's talk.** (Chart 6-4)
Using *there* and *be*, name four or five things that exist in the given places. Work in small groups or as a class.

Example: in this book
SPEAKER A: There are exercises in this book.
SPEAKER B: There's an index in this book.
SPEAKER C: There are illustrations in this book.

1. on this page
2. in this room
3. in this city
4. on an airplane
5. in the world
6. in outer space

❑ **Exercise 17. Let's talk and write.** (Chart 6-4)
Choose the correct verb in each sentence. Based on the city/town you're in now, do you agree or disagree with each statement? Circle *yes* or *no*. Afterward, write four more true sentences about this city/town. Begin your sentences with **There is**/**There are**. Share some of them with the class.

1. There (*is, are*) good public transportation.   yes   no

2. There (*is, are*) clean air.   yes   no

3. There (*is, are*) enough recreation areas.   yes   no

4. There (*is, are*) good restaurants.   yes   no

5. There (*is, are*) excellent medical facilities.   yes   no

❑ **Exercise 18. Warm-up.** (Chart 6-5)
Look at the subjects and verbs (in blue) in each pair of sentences. Some of them are "exceptions to the rule." For example, nouns that end in *-s* usually take a plural verb, but sometimes not. Look for these irregularities.

1. a. Nations are groups of people who share a common identity.
   b. The United Nations is an international organization.

2. a. Kilometers are measures of distance.
   b. Seven kilometers is too far for me to run.

3. a. *Mix* and *fix* are verbs.
   b. Six and six is twelve.

4. a. Whales are mammals.
   b. People are mammals.

5. a. English is a language.
   b. The English are concerned about global warming.

6-5 Subject–Verb Agreement: Some Irregularities

Singular Verb

(a) *The United States is* big. (b) *The Philippines consists* of more than 7,000 islands. (c) *The United Nations has* its headquarters in New York City. (d) *Harrods is* a department store.	Sometimes a proper noun that ends in *-s* is singular. In the examples, if the noun is changed to a pronoun, the singular pronoun *it* is used (not the plural pronoun *they*) because the noun is singular. In (a): *The United States* = *it* (not *they*)
(e) The *news is* interesting.	*News* is singular.
(f) *Mathematics is* easy for her. *Physics is* easy for her too.	Fields of study that end in *-ics* require singular verbs.
(g) *Diabetes is* an illness.	Certain illnesses that end in *-s* are singular: *diabetes, measles, mumps, rabies, rickets, shingles.*
(h) *Eight hours* of sleep *is* enough. (i) *Ten dollars is* too much to pay. (j) *Five thousand miles is* too far to travel.	Expressions of time, money, and distance usually require a singular verb.
(k) *Two and two is* four. *Two and two equals* four. *Two plus two is/equals* four. (l) *Five times five is* twenty-five.	Arithmetic expressions require singular verbs.

Plural Verb

(m) *Those people are* from Canada. (n) *The police have* been called. (o) *Cattle are* domestic animals. (p) *Fish live* under water.	*People,* police, cattle,* and *fish* do not end in *-s*, but they are plural nouns in the example sentences and require plural verbs.

Singular Verb	Plural Verb	
(q) *English is* spoken in many countries. (s) *Chinese is* his native language.	(r) *The English drink* tea. (t) *The Chinese have* an interesting history.	In (q): *English* = language In (r): *The English* = people from England Some nouns of nationality that end in *-sh*, *-ese*, and *-ch* can mean either language or people, e.g., *English, Spanish, Chinese, Japanese, Vietnamese, Portuguese, French.*
	(u) *The poor have* many problems. (v) *The rich get* richer.	A few adjectives can be preceded by *the* and used as a plural noun (without final *-s*) to refer to people who have that quality. Other examples: *the young, the elderly, the living, the dead, the blind, the deaf, the disabled.*

*The word *people* has a final *-s* (*peoples*) only when it is used to refer to ethnic or national groups: *All the **peoples** of the world desire peace.*

Exercise 19. Looking at grammar. (Chart 6-5)
Choose the correct completions.

1. The United States ((has,) have) a population of around 300 million.

2. The news about Mr. Gonzalez (*is*, *are*) surprising.

3. The *New York Times* (*is*, *are*) an established and respected newspaper.

4. Physics (*seek*, *seeks*) to understand the mysteries of the physical world.

5. Statistics (*is*, *are*) a branch of mathematics.

6. The statistics in that report on oil production (*is*, *are*) incorrect.★

7. Fifty minutes (*is*, *are*) the maximum length of time allowed for the exam.

8. Twenty dollars (*is*, *are*) an unreasonable price for the necklace.

9. Many people in the world (*does*, *do*) not have enough to eat.

10. The police (*is*, *are*) prepared in case there is a riot.

11. Rabies (*is*, *are*) an infectious and often fatal disease.

12. The French (*is*, *are*) proud, independent people.

13. French (*is*, *are*) not my native language.

14. Many Japanese (*commutes*, *commute*) to their places of work.

15. Portuguese (*is*, *are*) somewhat similar to Spanish, (*isn't it*, *aren't they*)?

16. The poor (*is*, *are*) helped by government programs.

17. The blind (*want*, *wants*) the rest of us to treat them the same way we treat everyone else.

18. The effect of a honeybee's sting on a human being (*depends*, *depend*) on that person's susceptibility to the bee's venom. Most people (*is*, *are*) not in danger if they are stung, but there (*has*, *have*) been instances of allergic deaths from a single honeybee sting.

❑   **Exercise 20. Game.** (Chart 6-5)
Check your knowledge by choosing the correct words (or numbers) in parentheses. Then complete the sentences with **is** or **are**. Work in pairs or small groups. (The correct answers can be found on page 476.)

1. (*The Scots, The Irish,* (*The English*)) __are__ famous for educational institutions like Oxford and Cambridge.

2. (*Statistics, Linguistics, Physics*) _____ the study of the structure and nature of language.

3. (*Diabetes, Measles, Rabies*) _____ a blood-sugar illness.

4. (*English, French, Afrikaans*) _____ the official language of Namibia.

★*Statistics* is singular when it refers to a field of study (e.g., ***Statistics is*** *an interesting field of study.*). When it refers to particular numbers, it is used as a count noun: *singular = one statistic* (no final *-s*); *plural = two statistics.* For example, ***This statistic is*** *correct.* ***Those statistics are*** *incorrect.*

5. People from Canada _____ called (*Canadas, Canadians, Canadese*).

6. Approximately (*60 percent, 70 percent, 80 percent*) of the earth _____ covered by water, but only (*one percent, ten percent, twenty percent*) of the earth's water _____ drinkable.

7. $312 \times .5 + 100$ _____ (*227, 275, 256*).

8. (*The United Arab Emirates, The Netherlands, The Philippines*) _____ in the Northern Hemisphere (i.e., north of the equator).

9. (*Fish, Whales, Cattle*) _____ not mammals.

❑ **Exercise 21. Let's talk.** (Chart 6-5)
Work in small groups. Take turns giving answers.

1. How many hours of sleep is enough for you? How are you affected if you don't get that amount of sleep?

2. Write one math equation for each answer: 250, 75, 700, and 1,000. Use addition, subtraction, multiplication, or division. Read the equations aloud for others to answer.

3. What do you think is a reasonable amount of money to pay for school supplies and textbooks for one term?

4. What do you think is a manageable distance for a person to commute to and from a job? Give your answer in miles or kilometers.

5. In your opinion, what advantages do the old have over the young? The young over the old?

6. Consider various school subjects: science (biology, chemistry, etc.), mathematics (algebra, geometry, etc.), languages, etc. Which class is easy for you to understand? Which is difficult for you? Which is the most enjoyable?

7. Think of a country that has a history you're familiar with. Share some information about the people (the Chinese, the French, the Egyptians, etc.) of this country. Which country has a history you'd like to know more about?

❑ **Exercise 22. Looking at grammar.** (Charts 6-2 → 6-5)
Your teacher will give you phrases to complete with *is* or *are*. Close your book for this activity.

Example:
TEACHER (*book open*):   Women
SPEAKER A: (*book closed*): are
TEACHER (*book open*)   Every man, woman, and child
SPEAKER B (*book closed*): is

1. A woman and her child
2. One of the countries I would like to visit
3. Some of the cities I would like to visit
4. A number of students
5. Ten minutes
6. Most people
7. Chinese
8. The Chinese
9. The poor in my country
10. Washing the dishes
11. The United States
12. This exercise on subject-verb agreement

Exercise 23. Looking at grammar. (Charts 6-2 → 6-5)
Your teacher will give you phrases to complete with *is* or *are*. Close your book for this activity.

Example:
TEACHER (*book open*):   His idea \ interesting
STUDENT A (*book closed*): His idea is interesting.

1. His ideas \ interesting
2. Some of the people \ friendly
3. One of the girls \ absent
4. Italian \ a Romance language
5. Two-thirds of the food \ gone
6. The clothes in that store \ expensive
7. The clothing in those stores \ inexpensive
8. Most of the stores in tourist towns \ overpriced

❏ **Exercise 24. Let's talk.** (Charts 6-2 → 6-5)
Choose the correct verb in each sentence. Are the sentences true in your opinion? Circle *yes* or *no*. Share some of your answers with the class.

1. The United Nations (*has, have*) an important role in today's world.   yes   no

2. Mathematics (*is, are*) an interesting subject.   yes   no

3. Both boys and girls (*needs, need*) to learn how to do housecleaning.   yes   no

4. Every girl and boy in my country (*needs, need*) to have
   immunizations for certain diseases before entering public school.   yes   no

5. Two hours of homework per day (*is, are*) too much for elementary
   school children.   yes   no

6. Having good computer skills (*is, are*) necessary if you want to get a
   high-paying job.   yes   no

7. One of the biggest problems in the world today (*is, are*) the lack of
   clean, fresh drinking water for significant numbers of people.   yes   no

8. We may come from different cultures and have different customs,
   but I believe that people across the world (*is, are*) more alike than
   different.   yes   no

❏ **Exercise 25. Game.** (Charts 6-2 → 6-5)
Work in teams. Decide if the sentences are correct (C) or incorrect (I). If incorrect, make the necessary changes. Your teacher will give you a time limit. The team with the most correct answers wins.

C   I
                                         was
___ ✓   1. The news about the economy ~~were~~ disappointing.

✓ ___   2. The economy is not doing well.

___ ___   3. Economists is worried.

___ ___   4. Economics is a field of study.

C   I

__ __   5. Where's Kenya on the map?

__ __   6. Where's my gloves? I can't find them.

__ __   7. More men than women are left-handed.

__ __   8. Chinese have more than fifty thousand written characters.

__ __   9. About two-thirds of the Vietnamese works in agriculture.

__ __   10. Two hours is too long to wait, don't you think?

__ __   11. How many people is there in Canada?

__ __   12. What is the population of Canada?

__ __   13. Everybody in my family enjoys music and reading.

__ __   14. Some of the movies these days contains too much violence.

❏ **Exercise 26. Looking at grammar.** (Chapter 6)
Complete the sentences. Use the simple present form of the verbs in parentheses.

1. My alarm clock (*ring*) ___*rings*___ at seven every morning.

2. There (*be*) _____ a lot of sheep in the field.

3. One of my friends (*keep*) _____ a goldfish bowl on her kitchen table.

4. Sensitivity to other people's feelings (*make*) _____ Giorgio a kind person.

5. Each car, truck, and motorcycle (*be*) _____ stopped at the border by customs officials.

6. My driver's license (*be*) _____ in my wallet.

7. (*Do*) _____ Sergei's uncle live in the suburbs?

8. (*Do*) _____ most of the students live in the dormitories?

9. An orange and black bird (*be*) _____ sitting in that tree.

10. An orange bird and a black bird (*be*) _____ sitting in that tree.

11. The insurance rates on our car (*be*) _____ high because we live in a city.

12. (*Be*) _____ January and February the coldest months of the year in the Northern Hemisphere?

13. Almost two-thirds of the land in the southwestern areas of the country (*be*) _____ unsuitable for farming.

14. A car with poor brakes and no brake lights (*be*) _____ dangerous.

15. Almost all the information in those texts on the Aztec Indians and their civilization (*appear*) _____ to be well researched.

16. Every day there (*be*) _____ more than a dozen traffic accidents in the city.

17. No news (*be*) _____ good news.

18. Four hours of skiing (*provide*)

    _____ plenty

of exercise.

❏ **Exercise 27. Check your knowledge.** (Chapter 6)
Correct the errors in subject-verb agreement. Some sentences contain no errors.

   are
1. The books in my office ~~is~~ very valuable to me.

2. All of the windows in our house were broken in the earthquake. (*no errors*)

3. A lot of the people in my class works during the day and attends class in the evening.

4. Many of the satellites orbiting the earth is used for communications.

5. The news about the long-range effects of air pollution on the development of children's

   lungs is disturbing.

6. Studying a foreign language often lead students to learn about the culture of the countries

   where it is spoken.

7. One of the most common names for dogs in the United States are "Rover."

8. A number of planes were delayed due to the snowstorm in Denver.

9. Most of the mountain peaks in the Himalayan Range is covered with snow the year round.

10. The number of passengers affected by the delays was great.

11. Seventy-five percent of the people in New York City lives in upstairs apartments, not on

    the ground floor.

12. Approximately 76 percent of all the data in computers around the world is in English.

13. Unless there are a profound and extensive reform of government policies in the near future, the economic conditions in that country will continue to deteriorate.

14. While I was in Paris, some of the best food I found were not at the well-known eating places but in small out-of-the-way cafés.

❑ **Exercise 28. Let's talk.** (Chapter 6)
Work in small groups. Share your experiences as second language learners. Discuss the following questions and any other thoughts that occur to you. Summarize some of your group's conclusions for the rest of the class. Listen to each other for subject-verb agreement.

1. How much English do you speak and read outside the classroom? Is using English in class sufficient for you to meet your language-learning goals? What are some good ways to get practice with English outside the classroom?
2. Do you avoid certain situations if you have to speak English? For example, speaking on the phone? Attending a party? Participating in class discussion?
3. Are you afraid of making mistakes when you speak? Everyone who is learning a second language makes mistakes. It's part of the process. Do mistakes matter?

❑ **Exercise 29. Let's talk and write.** (Chapter 6)
Tell a fairy/folk tale from your country or from your imagination. Present your story to a small group or to the class in five minutes or less. Begin your tale with ***Once upon a time, there was/were***. Listeners can write short summaries of each story.

Example: *Once upon a time, there was* a mother duck who was sitting on her nest of eggs. Suddenly they began to hatch. Six cute, yellow ducklings popped out of their shells, but the seventh had gray feathers and looked very strange. The ugly duckling struggled to fit in, but he felt that nobody wanted him because he looked so different from all the others.* Etc.

---

*Adapted from *The Ugly Duckling* by Hans Christian Andersen.

Chapter 7
Nouns

❏ **Exercise 1. What do I already know?** (Chart 7-1)
Write the plural forms of the given nouns.

1. one child, two _____children_____

2. one branch, two _____

3. one mouse, two _____

4. one enemy, two _____

5. one valley, two _____

6. one shelf, two _____

7. one belief, two _____

8. one woman, two _____

9. one echo, two _____

10. one photo, two _____

11. one zero, two _____

12. one crisis, two _____

13. one curriculum, two _____

14. one offspring, two _____

❏ **Exercise 2. Warm-up.** (Chart 7-1)
Complete the sentences with the plural forms of the given nouns.

Last night I ate a lot of ____.

1. tomato _____tomatoes_____

2. potato _____

3. fish _____

4. sandwich _____

5. carrot _____

6. vegetable _____

Did you see any ____ at the zoo?

7. kangaroo _____

8. goose _____

9. donkey _____

10. deer _____

11. wolf _____

12. sheep _____

7-1 Regular and Irregular Plural Nouns

(a) song—*songs*	The plural of most nouns is formed by adding final **-s**.*
(b) box—*boxes*	Final **-es** is added to nouns that end in **-sh**, **-ch**, **-s**, **-z**, and **-x**.*
(c) baby—*babies*	The plural of words that end in a consonant + **-y** is spelled **-ies**.*
(d) man—*men* ox—*oxen* tooth—*teeth* woman—*women* foot—*feet* mouse—*mice* child—*children* goose—*geese* louse—*lice*	The nouns in (d) have irregular plural forms that do not end in **-s**.
(e) echo—*echoes* potato—*potatoes* hero—*heroes* tomato—*tomatoes*	Some nouns that end in **-o** add **-es** to form the plural.
(f) auto—*autos* photo—*photos* studio—*studios* ghetto—*ghettos* piano—*pianos* tatoo—*tatoos* kangaroo—*kangaroos* radio—*radios* video—*videos* kilo—*kilos* solo—*solos* zoo—*zoos* memo—*memos* soprano—*sopranos*	Some nouns that end in **-o** add only **-s** to form the plural. NOTE: When in doubt, use your dictionary or spellcheck.
(g) memento—*mementoes/mementos* volcano—*volcanoes/volcanos* mosquito—*mosquitoes/mosquitos* zero—*zeroes/zeros* tornado—*tornadoes/tornados*	Some nouns that end in **-o** add either **-es** or **-s** to form the plural (with **-es** being the more usual plural form).
(h) calf—*calves* life—*lives* thief—*thieves* half—*halves* loaf—*loaves* wolf—*wolves* knife—*knives* self—*selves* scarf—*scarves/scarfs* leaf—*leaves* shelf—*shelves*	Some nouns that end in **-f** or **-fe** are changed to **-ves** to form the plural.
(i) belief—*beliefs* cliff—*cliffs* chief—*chiefs* roof—*roofs*	Some nouns that end in **-f** simply add **-s** to form the plural.

(j) one deer—*two deer*   one series—*two series*
one fish—*two fish***   one sheep—*two sheep*
one means—*two means*   one shrimp—*two shrimp****
one offspring—*two offspring*   one species—*two species*
	Some nouns have the same singular and plural form: e.g.,
	   One deer is . . . .
	   Two deer are . . . .

(k) criterion—*criteria* (m) analysis—*analyses* phenomenon—*phenomena* basis—*bases* crisis—*crises* (l) bacterium—*bacteria* hypothesis—*hypotheses* curriculum—*curricula* parenthesis—*parentheses* datum—*data* thesis—*theses* medium—*media* memorandum—*memoranda*	Some nouns that English has borrowed from other languages have foreign plurals.

*For information about the pronunciation and spelling of words ending in **-s/-es**, see Chart 6-1, p. 85.

**Fishes* is also possible but rarely used.

***Especially in British English, but also occasionally in American English, the plural of *shrimp* can be *shrimps*.

❏ **Exercise 3. Game.** (Chart 7-1)
Divide into teams of three to five members. The leader has paper and a pen. Use Chart 7-1 to list plural nouns that fit the given categories.

     The team that comes up with the most words within the given time limit wins. Be ready to explain a choice if another team questions it. Your teacher will decide if the word belongs on the list.

Example: things that cause people physical problems
TEAM A LEADER writes: *mosquitoes, lice, tornadoes, autos,* etc.
TEAM B: How do autos cause physical problems?
TEAM A: They hit people.
TEACHER: We'll accept *autos* on the list.

Make a list of:
  1. things that you find in nature
  2. things that you see every day
  3. things in life that can be dangerous
  4. things that you can hear

❏ **Exercise 4. Looking at spelling.** (Chart 7-1)
Write the plural form of each word in the correct column. Some forms have two possible spellings.

✓belief	✓deer	leaf	photo	tomato
box	fish	life	potato	video
chief	✓hero	loaf	scarf	wolf
class	kilo	match	sheep	zoo
cloud	✓knife	memo	shelf	

-s	*-es*	*-ves*	no change
beliefs	*heroes*	*knives*	*deer*

❑ **Exercise 5. Looking at grammar.** (Chart 7-1)
Write the correct forms of the given nouns. Use each noun only one time.

attorney	discovery	✓match	piano
beach	laboratory	medium	phenomenon
box	man	ox	✓tooth
cliff			

1. The baby has been crying and not sleeping well at night because she is getting her first
   _____teeth_____ .

2. I need some _____matches_____ to light the fire.

3. Studies are showing that _____ process information differently from
   women.

4. Maria needed some legal advice for her businesses, so she contacted two
   _____ .

5. New scientific _____ are made every day in _____
   throughout the world.

6. The farmer loaded his cart with _____ of fresh vegetables to take to market.
   His cart was pulled by two _____ .

7. The north side of the island has no _____ for people to walk on. There are
   only steep _____ . No one can climb these steep walls of rock.

8. The music building at the university has 27 _____ for students to play on.
   Students need to sign up for practice times.

9. Thunder and lightning are _____ of nature.

10. People get most of their news about the world through the mass _____ , that
    is, through radio, television, the internet, newspapers, and magazines.

❑ **Exercise 6. Looking at grammar.** (Chart 7-1)
Change the nouns to plural as necessary. Do not change any other words.

    Bacteria
(1) ~~Bacterium~~ are the smallest living thing. They are simple organism that consist of

one cell.

(2) Bacterium exist almost everywhere. They are in the air, water, and soil* as well as in the

body of all living creature.

(3) There are thousand of kind of bacterium. Most of them are harmless to human being,

but some cause diseases such as tuberculosis and pneumonia.

(4) Virus are also microscopic organism, but virus live in the cell of other living thing. By

themselves, they are lifeless particle that cannot reproduce, but inside a living cell they become

active and can multiply hundred of time.

(5) Virus cause many disease. They infect human being with such illness as influenza, the

common cold, measles, and AIDS (Acquired Immune Deficiency Syndrome).

(6) Virus are tiny. The virus that causes AIDS is 230 million** times smaller than the period

at the end of this sentence. Some viral infection are difficult or impossible to treat.

❑ **Exercise 7. Warm-up.** (Chart 7-2)
Decide if the words in blue refer to one person or more than one person. If the meaning is
one, write **1**. If the meaning is more than one, write **2**.

1. his sisters' opinions ___
2. his sister's opinions ___
3. my son's school ___

4. my sons' school ___
5. the men's hats ___
6. the man's hats ___

Air, water, and *soil* are used as noncount nouns and thus have no plural form. See Chart 7-4 for information about noncount nouns.

When the words *hundred thousand, million,* and *billion* are used with numerals, they remain in their singular form: ***Six hundred* employees will attend the company picnic this year. There are ***three thousand*** entrants in the photo contest. When they are used without numerals to indicate an indefinite but large number of something, they are used in their plural form: ***Hundreds*** of people came to the concert. There are ***thousands*** of earthquakes in the world every year. ***Millions*** of people in the world are starving.

7-2 Possessive Nouns

Singular Noun	Possessive Form	
(a) the girl	*the girl's*	To show possession, add an apostrophe (') and **-s** to a singular noun: *The **girl's** book is on the table.*
(b) Tom	*Tom's*	
(c) my wife	*my wife's*	If a singular noun ends in **-s**, there are two possible forms:
(d) a lady	*a lady's*	1. Add an apostrophe and **-s**: **Thomas's** book.
(e) Thomas	*Thomas's/Thomas'*	2. Add only an apostrophe: **Thomas'** book.

Plural Noun	Possessive Form	
(f) the girls	*the girls'*	Add only an apostrophe to a plural noun that ends in **-s**: *The **girls'** books are on the table.*
(g) their wives	*their wives'*	
(h) the ladies	*the ladies'*	Add an apostrophe and **-s** to plural nouns that do not end in **-s**: *The **men's** books are on the table.*
(i) the men	*the men's*	
(j) my children	*my children's*	

(k) ***Alan and Lisa's** apartment is on the third floor.*	When two (or more) names are connected by **and**, only the final name shows possession.

❏ **Exercise 8. Looking at grammar.** (Chart 7-2)
Complete the sentences. Use the possessive form of the nouns in parentheses.

1. (*Mrs. Smith*) _____Mrs. Smith's_____ husband often gives her flowers.

2. The (*boy*) _____ hat is red.

3. The (*boys*) _____ hats are red.

4. The (*children*) _____ toys are all over the floor.

5. I fixed the (*child*) _____ bicycle.

6. (*Sally*) _____ last name is White.

7. (*Bess*) _____ last name is Young.

8. There are many problems in (*today*) _____ world.

9. It would cost me a (*month*) _____ salary to buy that refrigerator.

10. We went to (*Jack and Larry*) _____ house for dinner.

❏ **Exercise 9. Looking at grammar.** (Chart 7-2)
Correct the errors. Use the possessive nouns by adding apostrophes and final **-s/-es** as necessary.

                   friends'
1. I enjoy visiting ~~friend~~ houses.

                                  friend's
2. When I was in Chicago, I stayed at a ~~friend~~ house.

3. My uncle is my father brother.

4. I have four aunts. All of my aunt homes are within walking distance of my mother apartment.

5. Esteban's aunt oldest son is a violinist.

6. Bill wife is a factory worker.

7. I walked into my boss office.

8. I borrowed the secretary pen to fill out the application form.

9. Five astronauts were aboard the space shuttle. The astronaut safe return to earth was a welcome sight to millions of television viewers.

10. It is the people right to know what the city is going to do about the housing problem.

11. Quite a few diplomats are assigned to our city. Almost all of the diplomat children attend a special school.

12. A diplomat work invariably involves numerous meetings.

❑ **Exercise 10. Looking at grammar.** (Chart 7-2)
Correct the errors in the use of possessive nouns by adding apostrophes as necessary.

1. Texas is a leading producer of petroleum and natural gas. It is one of the world's largest storage areas for petroleum.

2. Psychologists have developed many different kinds of tests. A "personality test" is used to evaluate an individuals personal characteristics, such as friendliness or trustworthiness.

3. Many mythological stories tell of heroes encounters with giants or dangerous animals. In one story, the heros encounter with a dragon saves a village from destruction.

4. Childrens play is an important part of their lives. It teaches them about their environment while they are having fun. For instance, they can learn that boats float and can practice ways to make boats move across water. Toys are not limited to children. Adults have their own toys, such as pleasure boats, and children have theirs, such as miniature boats. Adults toys are usually much more expensive than childrens toys.

❑ **Exercise 11. Warm-up.** (Chart 7-3)
Which nouns in the list commonly follow the nouns *computer* and *airplane*?

error	passenger	pilot	screen	skills	ticket

1. computer _____   2. airplane _____

   computer _____   airplane _____

   computer _____   airplane _____

7-3 Nouns as Adjectives

(a) The soup has vegetables in it. It is **vegetable** soup.	When a noun is used as an adjective, it is in its singular form.* *INCORRECT:* vegetable -s̶ soup
(b) The building has offices in it. It is an **office** building.	
(c) The test lasted two hours. It was a **two-hour** test.	When a noun used as a modifier is combined with a number expression, the noun is singular and a hyphen (-) is used. *INCORRECT:* She has a five year -s̶ old son.
(d) Her son is five years old. She has a **five-year-old** son.	

*Adjectives never take a final -**s** (*INCORRECT:* beautiful -s̶ pictures). See Appendix Chart A-2.

❏ **Exercise 12. Looking at grammar.** (Chart 7-3)
Complete the sentences with the words in *italics*. Use the singular or plural form as appropriate. Include hyphens (-) as necessary.

1. *shoe*   They sell ____shoes____ at that store. It is a ____shoe____ store.

2. *flower*   My garden has _____ in it. It is a _____ garden.

3. *bean*   This soup is made from black _____. It is black _____ soup.

4. *baby*   People can buy special food in small jars for _____. It is called _____ food.

5. *child*   Dr. Adams is trained as a psychologist for _____. She is a _____ psychologist.

6. *salad*   At a formal dinner, there are usually two forks on the table. The smaller fork is for _____. It is a _____ fork.

7. *mosquito* In tropical climates, sometimes it is necessary to hang a net over a bed to protect the sleeper from _____.

   It is called a _____ net.

8. *two + hour*   The plane was late. We had a _____ wait.

We had to wait for _____ .

9. *ten + year + old*   My brother is _____ . I have a

_____ brother.

10. *three + letter*   *Arm* and *dog* are _____ words. Each

word has _____ .

❑ **Exercise 13. Game.** (Chart 7-3)
Work in teams. Think of common expressions in which the given nouns are used to modify other nouns. The team that comes up with the most expressions in the given time wins.

Example: flower → *a flower vase, a flower garden, a flower shop, etc.*

1. cotton	5. telephone	9. morning	13. kitchen
2. grammar	6. mountain	10. street	14. baby
3. birthday	7. government	11. newspaper	15. vegetable
4. chicken	8. football	12. hotel	16. bicycle

❑ **Exercise 14. Listening.** (Chart 7-3)
Listen to the sentences. Choose the words you hear.

CD 1
Track 37

Examples: You will hear: Ted is a professor at two well-known colleges.

You will choose: (professor)   professors   college   (colleges)

You will hear: Ted is a highly respected college professor.

You will choose: (college)   colleges   (professor)   professors

1. taxi	taxis	driver	drivers
2. driver	drivers	taxi	taxis
3. office	offices	manager	managers
4. manager	managers	office	offices
5. airplane	airplanes	seat	seats
6. airplane	airplanes	seat	seats
7. school	schools	activity	activities
8. school	schools	activity	activities

❑ **Exercise 15. Warm-up.** (Chart 7-4)
Choose all the correct completions.

1. I got one _____.
   a. letter   b. postcard   c. package   d. mail

2. My room has one _____.
   a. chair   b. furniture   c. table   d. bed

7-4 Count and Noncount Nouns

(a) I bought *a chair*. Sam bought *three chairs*.			***Chair*** is called a "count noun." This means you can count chairs: *one chair, two chairs,* etc.
(b) We bought *some furniture*. INCORRECT: We bought some furniture~~s~~. INCORRECT: We bought ~~a~~ furniture.			***Furniture*** is called a "noncount noun." In grammar, you cannot use numbers (*one, two,* etc.) with the word ***furniture***.

	Singular	**Plural**	
Count Noun	*a* chair *one* chair	*two* chairs *some* chairs *a lot of* chairs *many* chairs Ø chairs★	A count noun: (1) may be preceded by ***a/an*** or ***one*** in the singular. (2) takes a final ***-s/-es*** in the plural.
Noncount Noun	*some* furniture *a lot of* furniture *much* furniture Ø furniture★		A noncount noun: (1) is not immediately preceded by ***a/an*** or ***one***. (2) has no plural form, so does not add a final ***-s/-es***.

★Ø = nothing (i.e., no article or other determiner).

❏ **Exercise 16. Looking at grammar.** (Chart 7-4)
Look at the *italicized* nouns. Write "C" above the count nouns and "NC" above the noncount nouns.

1. I bought some *chairs, tables,* and *desks*. In other words, I bought some *furniture*.

(C C C ... NC)

2. Michiko likes to wear *jewelry*. Today she is wearing four *rings,* six *bracelets,* and a *necklace*.

3. We saw beautiful *mountains, fields,* and *lakes* on our trip. We saw beautiful *scenery*.

4. *Gold* and *iron* are *metals*.

5. I used an *iron* to press my wrinkled shirt.

6. They have a rusty *car* without an *engine,* broken *furniture,* and

   an old *refrigerator* in their front yard. Their yard is full of *junk*.

7-5 Noncount Nouns

(a) I bought some chairs, tables, and desks. In other words, I bought some *furniture*.	Many noncount nouns refer to a "whole" that is made up of different parts. In (a): *furniture* represents a whole group of things that is made up of similar but separate items.
(b) I put some *sugar* in my *coffee*.	In (b): *sugar* and *coffee* represent whole masses made up of individual particles or elements.*
(c) I wish you *luck*.	Many noncount nouns are abstractions. In (c): *luck* is an abstract concept, an abstract "whole." It has no physical form; you can't touch it; you can't count it.
(d) *Sunshine* is warm and cheerful.	A phenomenon of nature, such as *sunshine*, is frequently used as a noncount noun, as in (d).

(e) NONCOUNT: Ann has brown *hair*.
     COUNT: Tom has a *hair* on his jacket.
 	
(f) NONCOUNT: I opened the curtains to let in some *light*.
     COUNT: Don't forget to turn off the *light* before you go to bed.
	Many nouns can be used as either noncount or count nouns, but the meaning is different, e.g., *hair* in (e) and *light* in (f).
	(Dictionaries written especially for learners of English as a second language are a good source of information on count/noncount usage of nouns.)

*To express a particular quantity, some noncount nouns may be preceded by unit expressions: *a spoonful of sugar, a glass of water, a cup of coffee, a quart of milk, a loaf of bread, a grain of rice, a bowl of soup, a bag of flour, a pound of meat, a piece of furniture, a piece of paper, a piece of jewelry.*

7-6 Some Common Noncount Nouns

This list is a sample of nouns that are commonly used as noncount nouns. Many other nouns can also be used as noncount nouns.

(a) WHOLE GROUPS MADE UP OF SIMILAR ITEMS: baggage, clothing, equipment, food, fruit, furniture, garbage, hardware, jewelry, junk, luggage, machinery, mail, makeup, money/cash/change, postage, scenery, stuff, traffic, etc.

(b) FLUIDS: water, coffee, tea, milk, oil, soup, gasoline, blood, etc.
(c) SOLIDS: ice, bread, butter, cheese, meat, gold, iron, silver, glass, paper, wood, cotton, wool, etc.
(d) GASES: steam, air, oxygen, nitrogen, smoke, smog, pollution, etc.
(e) PARTICLES: rice, chalk, corn, dirt, dust, flour, grass, hair, pepper, salt, sand, sugar, wheat, etc.

(f) ABSTRACTIONS:
—beauty, confidence, courage, education, enjoyment, fun, happiness, health, help, honesty, hospitality, importance, intelligence, justice, knowledge, laughter, luck, music, patience, peace, pride, progress, recreation, significance, sleep, truth, violence, wealth, etc.
—advice, information, news, evidence, proof, etc.
—time, space, energy, etc.
—homework, work, etc.
—grammar, slang, vocabulary, etc.
(g) LANGUAGES: Arabic, Chinese, English, Spanish, etc.
(h) FIELDS OF STUDY: chemistry, engineering, history, literature, mathematics, psychology, etc.
(i) RECREATION: baseball, soccer, tennis, chess, bridge, poker, etc.
(j) ACTIVITIES: driving, studying, swimming, traveling, walking (and other gerunds)

(k) NATURAL PHENOMENA: weather, dew, fog, hail, heat, humidity, lightning, rain, sleet, snow, thunder, wind, darkness, light, sunshine, electricity, fire, gravity, etc.

❑ **Exercise 17. Looking at grammar.** (Charts 7-3, 7-5, and 7-6)
Add final *-s/-es* to the nouns in *italics* if necessary. Do not add or change any other words.

1. Isabel always has fresh *egg*ₛ available because she raises *chicken*ₛ in her yard.

2. I had *chicken* and *rice* for dinner last night. (*no change*)

3. Outside my window, I can see a lot of *tree, bush, grass, dirt,* and *flower*.

4. Abdullah gave me some good *advice*. Nadia also gave me some good *suggestion*.

5. Yoko learned several new *word* today. She increased her *vocabulary* today.

6. I drank two *glass* of *water*.

7. *Window* are made of *glass*.

8. Mr. Chu wears *glass* because he has poor *eyesight*.

9. It took me a lot of *time* to finish my *homework*. I had a lot of *assignment*.

10. I have been in Mexico three *time*. I've spent a lot of *time* there.

11. The air is full of *smoke, dust,* carbon *monoxide,* and many other harmful *substance*. We must try to reduce air *pollution*.

12. I like to read good *literature*. I especially like to read *novel, poetry,* and *essay*. My favorite *poet* are Longfellow and Wordsworth. I have always liked their *poem*.

13. I like to experience different *season*. I like both hot and cold *weather*.

14. Being a parent has brought me a lot of *happiness*. Parenting requires a lot of *patience,* but it provides many *reward*.

15. There are more *star* in the universe than there are *grain* of *sand* on all the beaches on earth.

16. The true sign of *intelligence* is not *knowledge* but *imagination*.★

❑ **Exercise 18. Game.** (Chart 7-6)
Work in teams. The leader has paper and a pen. The teacher will say a noncount noun. Working together, make a list of things that belong to this category until the teacher says "Stop." The team with the most nouns in a list is the winner of that list.

Example:
TEACHER (*book open*): mail
LEADER writes (*book closed*): *mail*
TEAM to LEADER (*book closed*): letters, postcards, packages, etc.

1. fruit   4. garbage
2. jewelry   5. traffic
3. clothing   6. office equipment

★This is a quote from Albert Einstein, Nobel Prize winner in physics.

❑ **Exercise 19. Looking at grammar.** (Charts 7-5 and 7-6)
Complete the sentences with the given nouns. Add final *-s/-es* if necessary. Use each noun only one time. In one sentence, you will need to choose the correct word in parentheses.

advice	definition	music	symphony
✓change	equipment	problem	traffic
✓coin	homework	progress	truck
computer	information	river	vocabulary

1. Yes, I have some money. I have a few _____*coins*_____ in my pocket. In other words, I have some _____*change*_____ in my pocket.

2. The Mississippi, the Amazon, and the Nile are well-known _____.

3. I like to listen to operas, _____, and folk songs. I enjoy _____ and listen to it often on my iPod.

4. The street is full of cars, _____, and buses. In other words, it is full of _____.

5. There are _____ , copiers, telephones, and staplers in a typical business office. A business office needs a lot of _____.

6. Tonight I have to read 20 pages in my history book, do 30 algebra _____, and write a composition. In other words, I have a lot of _____ to do tonight.

7. Antonio is studying the meaning of English words. He learned some new _____ today. For example, he learned that the word *fly* has at least two _____.

8. Toronto is 365 feet/109 meters above sea level. The average annual precipitation in Toronto is 32 inches/81 centimeters. The population of the metropolitan area is over 3,000,000. I found (*this / these*) _____ on the internet.

9. I didn't feel good. Ann said, "You should see a doctor." Nick said, "You should go home and go to bed." Martha said, "You should drink fruit juice and rest." I got _____ from three people.

10. My English is slowly getting better. My vocabulary is increasing. It's getting easier for me to write, and I make fewer mistakes. I can often understand people even when they talk fast. I'm satisfied with the _____ I've made in learning English.

❏ **Exercise 20. Warm-up.** (Chart 7-7)
Read the dialogues. Notice the words in blue, and notice whether or not the speaker and the
listener are thinking of the same specific cats. Then answer the questions.

Dialogue 1

TOM: Sally will take care of
the cat while we're away.
ANNA: Good.

Dialogue 2

TOM: Our new neighbor has a cat.
It's very friendly.
ANNA: Oh? What does it look like?

Dialogue 3

TOM: A cat has an independent nature.
ANNA: That's true. But cats can also
express a lot of affection when
they want to.

Questions:
1. In dialogue 1, why do you think Tom uses **the?**
2. In dialogue 2, Tom is thinking of a particular cat, but he uses **a** (not **the**) when he is
talking to Anna. Why?
3. In dialogue 3, Tom and Anna do not use **the.** Are they talking about specific cats, or are
they talking about any and all cats in general?

7-7 Basic Article Usage

I. Using *A* or Ø: Generic Nouns

Singular Count Noun	(a) *A banana* is yellow.*	A speaker uses generic nouns to make generalizations. A generic noun represents a whole class of things; it is not a specific, real, concrete thing, but rather a symbol of a whole group.
Plural Count Noun	(b) Ø *Bananas* are yellow.	In (a) and (b): The speaker is talking about any banana, all bananas, bananas in general. In (c): The speaker is talking about any and all fruit, fruit in general.
Noncount Noun	(c) Ø *Fruit* is good for you.	Notice that no article (Ø) is used to make generalizations with plural count nouns, as in (b), and with noncount nouns, as in (c).

II. Using *A* or *Some:* Indefinite Nouns

Singular Count Noun	(d) I ate *a banana*.	Indefinite nouns are actual things (not symbols), but they are not specifically identified. In (d): The speaker is not referring to "this banana" or "that banana" or "the banana you gave me." The speaker is simply saying that she/he ate one banana. The listener does not know or need to know which specific banana was eaten; it was simply one banana out of all bananas.
Plural Count Noun	(e) I ate **some** bananas.	
Noncount Noun	(f) I ate **some** fruit.	In (e) and (f): **Some** is often used with indefinite plural count nouns and indefinite noncount nouns. In addition to **some**, a speaker might use *two, a few, several, a lot of, etc.,* with plural count nouns, or *a little, a lot of, etc.,* with noncount nouns. (See Chart 7-4.)

III. Using *The:* Definite Nouns

Singular Count Noun	(g) Thank you for *the* banana.	A noun is definite when both the speaker and the listener are thinking about the same specific thing. In (g): The speaker uses **the** because the listener knows which specific banana the speaker is talking about, i.e., that particular banana which the listener gave to the speaker.
Plural Count Noun	(h) Thank you for *the* bananas.	
Noncount Noun	(i) Thank you for *the* fruit.	Notice that **the** is used with both singular and plural count nouns and with noncount nouns.

*Usually *a/an* is used with a singular generic count noun. Examples: *A window is made of glass.* *A doctor heals sick people.* *Parents must give **a** child love.* *A box has six sides.* *An apple can be red, green, or yellow.*

However, **the** is sometimes used with a singular generic count noun (not a plural generic count noun, not a generic noncount noun). "Generic **the**" is commonly used with, in particular:

(1) species of animals: *The blue whale is the largest mammal on earth.* *The elephant is the largest land mammal.*

(2) inventions: *Who invented **the telephone**? **the wheel**? **the refrigerator**? **the airplane**? **The computer** will play an increasingly large role in all of our lives.*

(3) instruments: *I'd like to learn to play **the piano**. Do you play **the guitar**?*

❑ **Exercise 21. Looking at grammar.** (Chart 7-7)
Add *a/an* if necessary. Write Ø if the noun is noncount. Capitalize as necessary.

1. _A_ bird has wings.

2. _An_ animal needs a regular supply of food.

3. _Ø_ F̶food is a necessity of life.

4. _____ tennis is a sport.

5. _____ tennis player has to practice long hours.

6. _____ island is a piece of land surrounded by water.

7. _____ gold is a metal.

8. _____ bridge is a structure that spans a river.

9. _____ health is one of the most important things in life.

10. _____ adjective is a word that modifies a noun.

11. _____ tree needs water to survive.

12. _____ water is composed of oxygen and hydrogen.

13. _____ knowledge is a source of power.

14. _____ homework is a necessary part of a course of study.

15. _____ grammar is interesting and fun.

16. _____ sentence usually contains a subject and a verb.

17. _____ English is used in airports throughout much of the world.

18. _____ air is free.

19. _____ fruit is good for you.

20. _____ orange is green until it ripens.

21. _____ iron is a metal.

22. _____ iron is an appliance used to take wrinkles out of cloth.

23. _____ basketball is round.

24. _____ basketball is a sport.

❑ **Exercise 22. Looking at grammar.** (Chart 7-7)
Complete the sentences with *a, an,* or *some*.

1. The teacher made _____*an*_____ announcement.

2. I saw _____*a*_____ bird.

3. I saw _____*some*_____ birds.

4. Rosa borrowed _____*some*_____ money from her uncle.

5. I had _____ accident.

6. I have _____ homework to do tonight.

7. There is _____ table in the room.

8. There is _____ furniture in the room.

9. There are _____ chairs in the room.

10. My father gave me _____ advice.

11. Sonya is carrying _____ bag.

12. Sonya is pulling _____ luggage.

13. There was _____ earthquake in California.

14. I got _____ letters in the mail.

15. Helen got _____ letter from her mother.

16. Mr. Alvarez got _____ mail yesterday.

17. A computer is _____ machine that can solve problems.

18. The factory bought _____ new machinery.

19. _____ machines are powered by electricity. Some use other sources of energy.

20. I threw away _____ junk.

21. I threw away _____ old basket that was falling apart.

22. I threw away _____ old boots that had holes in them.

❑ **Exercise 23. Listening.** (Chart 7-7)

A and *an* can be hard to hear. Listen to each sentence and choose the word you hear. If you do not hear *a* or *an*, circle **Ø**.

CD 1
Track 38

Example: You will hear: That's an excellent idea.
You will choose: a ⟨an⟩ Ø

1.	a	an	Ø		5.	a	an	Ø
2.	a	an	Ø		6.	a	an	Ø
3.	a	an	Ø		7.	a	an	Ø
4.	a	an	Ø		8.	a	an	Ø

❑ **Exercise 24. Game.** (Charts 7-4 → 7-7)

A favorite game played with a group of people is called "My Grandfather's Store." Each person begins his/her turn by saying "I went to my grandfather's store and bought . . . ." The first person names something that begins with the letter "A." The second person repeats what the first person said, and then names something that begins with the letter "B." The game continues to the letter "Z," the end of the alphabet. The people in the group have to listen carefully and remember all the items previously named.

Assume that "grandfather's store" sells just about anything anyone would ever think of. Pay special attention to the use of *a/an* and *some*.

Example:
SPEAKER A: I went to my grandfather's store and bought **an apple**.
SPEAKER B: I went to my grandfather's store and bought **an apple** and **some bread**.
SPEAKER C: I went to my grandfather's store and bought **an apple**, **some bread**, and **a camel**.
SPEAKER D: I went to my grandfather's store and bought **an apple**, **some bread**, **a camel**, and **some dark socks**.
Etc.

Alternative beginnings:
Tomorrow I'm going to (*name of a place*). In my suitcase, I will pack . . . .
My friends are having a party. I'm going to bring . . . .

❑ **Exercise 25. Warm-up.** (Chart 7-8)
Correct the errors.

1. Oh, look at moon! It's beautiful tonight.

2. I saw a cat and a bird outside my window. Cat was trying to catch a bird, but it didn't succeed. Bird flew away.

3. The birds have the wings. Many insects have wings too.

4. We all look for the happiness.

5. I have book.

7-8 General Guidelines for Article Usage

(a) *The sun* is bright today. Please hand this book to *the teacher*. Please open *the door*. Omar is in *the kitchen*.	GUIDELINE: Use *the* when you know or assume that your listener is familiar with and thinking about the same specific thing or person you are talking about.
(b) Yesterday I saw *some dogs*. *The dogs* were chasing *a cat*. *The cat* was chasing *a mouse*. *The mouse* ran into *a hole*. *The hole* was very small.	GUIDELINE: Use *the* for the second mention of an indefinite noun.* In (b): first mention = *some dogs, a cat, a mouse, a hole*; second mention = *the dogs, the cat, the mouse, the hole*
(c) CORRECT: *Apples* are my favorite fruit. INCORRECT: ~~The~~ apples are my favorite fruit. (d) CORRECT: *Gold* is a metal. INCORRECT: ~~The~~ gold is a metal.	GUIDELINE: Do NOT use *the* with a plural count noun (e.g., *apples*) or a noncount noun (e.g., *gold*) when you are making a generalization.
(e) CORRECT: (1) I drove *a car*. / I drove *the car*. (2) I drove *that car*. (3) I drove *his car*. INCORRECT: I drove car.	GUIDELINE: A singular count noun (e.g., *car*) is always preceded by: (1) an article (*a/an* or *the*); OR (2) *this/that*; OR (3) a possessive pronoun.

The is NOT used for the second mention of a generic noun. COMPARE:
(1) *What color is a banana* (generic noun)*? A banana* (generic noun) *is yellow.*
(2) *Joe offered me a banana* (indefinite noun) *or an apple.* I chose *the banana* (definite noun).

❑ **Exercise 26. Looking at grammar.** (Charts 7-7 and 7-8)
Complete the dialogues with *a, an,* or *the*. Capitalize as necessary.

1. A: I have __*an*__ idea. Let's go on __*a*__ picnic Saturday.

   B: Okay.

2. A: Did you have fun at __*the*__ picnic yesterday?

   B: Sure did. And you?

3. A: You'd better have _____ good reason for being late!

   B: I do.

4. A: Did you think _____ reason Mike gave for being late was believable?

   B: Not really.

5. A: Where's my blue shirt?

   B: It's in _____ washing machine.

   A: That's okay. I can wear _____ different shirt.

6. A: I wish we had _____ washing machine.

   B: So do I. It would make it a lot easier to do our laundry.

7. A: Have you seen my boots?

   B: They're in _____ closet in _____ front hallway.

8. A: Can you repair my car for me?

   B: What's wrong with it?

   A: _____ radiator has _____ leak, and one of _____ windshield wipers doesn't work.

   B: Can you show me where _____ leak is?

9. A: What happened to your bicycle? _____ front wheel is bent.

   B: I ran into _____ parked car when I swerved to avoid _____ big pothole.

   A: Did you damage _____ car?

   B: A little.

   A: What did you do?

   B: I left _____ note for _____ owner of _____ car.

   A: What did you write on _____ note?

   B: My name and address. I also wrote _____ apology.

❑ **Exercise 27. Looking at grammar.** (Charts 7-7 and 7-8)
Complete the sentences with *a, an, the,* or **Ø**. Capitalize as necessary.

1. ___Ø___ ᴮbeef is a kind of ___Ø___ meat.

2. ___The___ beef we had for dinner last night was excellent.

3. Lucy is wearing ___a___ straw hat today.

4. Lucy likes to wear _____ hats.

5. _____ hat is _____ article of clothing.

6. _____ hats are _____ articles of clothing.

7. _____ brown hat on that hook over there belongs to Mark.

8. Everyone has _____ problems in _____ life.

9. That book is about _____ life of Helen Keller.*

10. The Brooklyn Bridge was designed by _____ engineer.

11. John Roebling is _____ name of _____ engineer who designed the Brooklyn Bridge. He died in 1869 from _____ infection before _____ bridge was completed.

---

*The first blind and deaf person to graduate from college, Helen Keller (1880–1968) overcame her double handicap to become a noted American author, activist, and lecturer.

Exercise 28. Grammar and speaking. (Charts 7-7 and 7-8)

Complete the sentences with *a, an, the,* or Ø. Do you agree or disagree with the statements?
Circle *yes* or *no*. Share some of your answers with the class. Capitalize as necessary.

1. Everyone needs to have _____ cell phone.   yes   no

2. If you have a cell phone, you don't need to wear _____ watch.   yes   no

3. _____ cell phones are replacing _____ watches.   yes   no

4. One key to _____ healthy life is daily physical exercise.   yes   no

5. You'd like to read a book about _____ life and art of Pablo Picasso.   yes   no

6. _____ jewelry looks good on both _____ men and _____ women.   yes   no

7. English is _____ easy language to learn.   yes   no

8. _____ beings similar to human beings exist somewhere in _____ universe.   yes   no

9. Listening to _____ loud rock music is fun.   yes   no

10. _____ music you like best is rock 'n roll.   yes   no

11. _____ vocabulary in this exercise is easy.   yes   no

Exercise 29. Looking at grammar. (Charts 7-7 and 7-8)

Complete the sentences with *a, an, the,* or Ø. Capitalize as necessary.

1. We need to get _____ new phone.

2. Alex, would you please answer _____ phone?

3. _____ people use _____ plants in _____ many different ways. Plants supply us with
   oxygen. They are a source of _____ lifesaving medicines. We use plant products to build
   _____ houses and to make _____ paper and _____ textiles.

4. The biggest bird in the world is the ostrich. It eats just about
   anything it can reach, including _____ stones, _____ glass,
   and _____ keys. It can kill _____ person with one kick.

5. In _____ recent newspaper article, I read about _____
   Australian swimmer who was saved from _____ shark by
   _____ group of dolphins. When _____ shark attacked _____
   swimmer, _____ dolphins chased it away. They saved _____
   swimmer's life.

6. I heard on the radio that there is _____ evidence that _____ dolphins suffer in captivity. Dolphins that are free in _____ nature live around 40 years. Captive dolphins live _____ average of 12 years. It is believed that some captive dolphins commit _____ suicide.

7. Look. There's _____ fly walking on _____ ceiling. It's upside down. Do you suppose _____ fly was flying rightside up and flipped over at the last second, or was it flying upside down when it landed on _____ ceiling?

❏ **Exercise 30. Listening.** (Charts 7-7 and 7-8)

CD 1
Track 39

Listen to this informal talk with your book closed. Then open your book and listen again. Complete the sentences with *a*, *an*, or *the*.

Computer Bugs

When there is _____ problem with _____ computer, we often say we have _____
              1   2   3
"computer bug." Of course, it's not _____ real insect. It refers to _____ technical difficulty
                                     4   5
we are having. _____ expression actually goes back to Thomas Edison, who was _____
               6   7
famous inventor. When he was working on his first phonograph, he had a lot of problems. He

attributed _____ problems to _____ imaginary insect that had hidden inside _____
           8   9   10
machine. He was quoted in _____ newspaper as saying there was "_____ bug" in his
                          11   12
phonograph. This was in 1889, and it is _____ first recorded use of _____ word *bug* in such
                                         13   14
_____ context.
15

❏ **Exercise 31. Warm-up.** (Chart 7-9)

Before you look at the next chart, try this exercise. Draw a line through the words/expressions that <u>cannot</u> be used to complete the sentences.

Example: I bought _____ furniture.
  1. some
  2. ~~a couple of~~
  3. ~~several~~
  4. too much
  5. ~~too many~~

6. I can't go with you because I have too _____ work to do.

7. A: How _____ side does a pentagon have?

   B: Five.

8. I couldn't find _____ information in that book.

9. I haven't met _____ people since I came here.

10. How _____ postage does this letter need?

11. I think there (*is*, *are*) too _____ violence on television.

12. I don't have _____ patience with incompetence.

13. The doctor has so _____ patient that she has to work at least twelve hours a day.

14. A: How _____ tooth does the average person have?

    B: Thirty-two.

15. There (*isn't*, *aren't*) _____ international news in the local paper.

❏ **Exercise 34. Looking at grammar.** (Chart 7-9)
If the given noun can be used to complete the sentence, write it in its correct form (singular or plural). If the given noun cannot be used to complete the sentence, write **Ø**.

1. *Helen bought several _____.*

   lamp   _____lamps_____

   furniture   _____Ø_____

   jewelry   _____Ø_____

   necklace   _____necklaces_____

2. *Sam bought a lot of _____.*

   stamp   _____

   rice   _____

   stuff   _____

   thing   _____

3. *Jack bought too much _____.*

   shoe   _____

   salt   _____

   equipment   _____

   tool   _____

4. *Alice bought a couple of _____.*

   bread   _____

   loaf of bread _____

   honey   _____

   jar of honey   _____

5. I read a few _____ .

novel   _____

literature   _____

poem   _____

poetry   _____

6. I bought some _____ .

orange juice   _____

light bulb   _____

hardware   _____

computer
    software   _____

7. We need plenty of _____ .

sleep   _____

information   _____

fact   _____

help   _____

8. I saw both _____ .

woman   _____

movie   _____

scene   _____

scenery   _____

9. Nick has a number of _____ .

shirt   _____

homework   _____

pen   _____

chalk   _____

10. I don't have a great deal of _____ .

patience   _____

wealth   _____

friend   _____

pencil   _____

11. I need a little _____ .

money   _____

advice   _____

time   _____

minute   _____

12. The author has many _____ .

idea   _____

theory   _____

hypothesis   _____

knowledge   _____

❏ **Exercise 35. Let's talk: interview.** (Chart 7-9)
Interview two other students. Ask them to complete the given sentences. Share some of their answers with the class.

1. I have a number of . . . .
2. I need to have a lot of . . . .
3. Teachers need to have a great deal of . . . .
4. People in (*name of a country*) have too much / too many . . . .

□ **Exercise 36. Warm-up.** (Chart 7-10)
Choose the correct answers.

1. Which sentence gives a negative meaning of "not many people"?
   a. Deserts are largely uninhabited. *Very few people* live in the middle of a desert.
   b. We had a good time. We met *a few people* and had some nice conversations.

2. Which sentence gives a negative meaning of "not much water"?
   a. It's hot today. You should drink *a little water.*
   b. A desert is a dry place. There is *little water* in a desert.

7-10	Using *A Few* and *Few; A Little* and *Little*	
COUNT: (a) We sang *a few* songs. NONCOUNT: (b) We listened to *a little* music.		*A few* and *few* are used with plural count nouns, as in (a). *A little* and *little* are used with noncount nouns, as in (b).
(c) She has been here only two weeks, but she has already made *a few friends.* *(Positive idea: She has made some friends.)* (d) I'm very pleased. I've been able to save *a little* money this month. *(Positive idea: I have saved some money instead of spending all of it.)*		*A few* and *a little* give a positive idea; they indicate that something exists, is present, as in (c) and (d).
(e) I feel sorry for her. She has *(very) few* friends. *(Negative idea: She does not have many friends; she has almost no friends.)* (f) I have *(very) little* money. I don't even have enough money to buy food for dinner. *(Negative idea: I do not have much money; I have almost no money.)*		*Few* and *little* (without *a*) give a negative idea; they indicate that something is largely absent, as in (e). *Very* (+ *few/little*) makes the negative stronger, the number/amount smaller, as in (f).

□ **Exercise 37. Looking at grammar.** (Chart 7-10)
Without changing the meaning of the sentence, replace the *italicized* words with *a few*, (*very*) *few*, *a little*, or (*very*) *little*.

        a little
1. I think that ~~some~~ lemon juice on fish makes it taste better.
                   (very) few
2. Many people are multilingual, but ~~not many~~ people speak more than ten languages.

3. *Some* sunshine is better than none.

4. January is a cold and dreary month in the northern states. There is *not much* sunshine
   during that month.

5. My parents like to watch TV. Every evening they watch *two or three* programs on TV before
   they go to bed.

6. I don't watch TV very much because there are *hardly any* television programs that I enjoy.

7. If a door squeaks, *several* drops of oil in the right places can prevent future trouble.

8. If your door squeaks, put *some* oil on the hinges.

9. Mr. Adams doesn't like to wear rings on his fingers. He wears *almost no* jewelry.

❑ **Exercise 38. Looking at grammar.** (Chart 7-10)
Complete the sentences with *a few*, *(very) few*, *a little*, or *(very) little*.

1. Do you have _____*a few*_____ minutes? I'd like to ask you _____*a few*_____ questions. I need _____*a little*_____ more information.

2. Diana's previous employer gave her a good recommendation because she makes _____*(very) few*_____ mistakes in her work.

3. Ben is having a lot of trouble adjusting to high school. He seems to be unpopular. Unfortunately, he has _____ friends.

4. We're looking forward to our vacation. We're planning to spend _____ days with my folks and then _____ days with my husband's folks. After that, we're going to go to a fishing resort in Canada.

5. I was hungry, so I ate _____ nuts.

6. Because the family is very poor, the children have _____ toys. And the parents have to work two jobs, so they have _____ time to spend with their children.

7. Into each life, _____ rain must fall.★

8. Natasha likes sweet tea. She usually adds _____ honey to her tea. Sometimes she adds _____ milk too.

_____

★This is a common English saying that means "no life is perfect."

❑ **Exercise 39. Listening.** (Chart 7-10)

Choose the sentence (a. or b.) that best describes the situation you hear.

CD 1
Track 40

Example: You will hear: Rosie was still hungry. She wanted some more rice.
You will choose: (a.) Rosie wanted a little rice.
b. Rosie wanted little rice.

1. a. I add a little salt to my food.
   b. I add little salt to my food.

2. a. I packed a few sandwiches
   b. I packed few sandwiches.

3. a. Mr. Hong knows a little English.
   b. Mr. Hong knows little English.

4. a. His daughter knows a little English.
   b. His daughter knows little English.

5. a. Linda has a few problems, I'd say.
   b. Linda has few problems in her life.

6. a. Billy has a few problems, I'd say.
   b. Billy has very few problems, I'd say.

7. a. A few people like working for him.
   b. Few people like working for him.

❑ **Exercise 40. Let's talk.** (Charts 7-9 and 7-10)

Read the list of the food in Dan and Eva's kitchen. Do they have enough food for the next week? Give your opinion using the given expressions of quantity. Work in pairs, in small groups, or as a class.

Example: 36 eggs
→ They have too many eggs.

too much*	too little	(not) enough	just the right amount of
too many	too few	(not) nearly enough	just the right number of

The food in Dan and Eva's kitchen:

40 apples	10 bags of rice	1 kilo of coffee
1 banana	20 cans of tomatoes	2 teabags
6 oranges	0 fresh vegetables	1 box of breakfast cereal
1 quart of orange juice	1 bottle of olive oil	2 slices of bread
4 gallons of ice cream	1 cup of sugar	5 pounds of cheese

❑ **Exercise 41. Warm-up.** (Chart 7-11)

Notice the words in blue. Complete the sentences with *country* or *countries*.

1. One _____ I would like to visit is Malaysia.

2. One of the _____ my wife would like to visit is Brazil.

3. I'd like to visit every _____ in the world before I die.

   Each _____ is special.

4. I've had wonderful experiences in each of the _____ I've visited

   during my travels.

---

*In spoken English, **too** is often modified by *way* or *far: They have **way/far** too many eggs. They have **way/far** too few teabags.*

7-11 Singular Expressions of Quantity: *One, Each, Every*

(a) *One student* was late to class. (b) *Each student* has a schedule. (c) *Every student* has a schedule.	*One*, *each*, and *every* are followed immediately by singular count nouns (never plural nouns, never noncount nouns).
(d) *One of the students* was late to class. (e) *Each (one) of the students* has a schedule (f) *Every one of the students* has a schedule.	*One of*, *each of*, and *every one of** are followed by specific plural count nouns (never singular nouns; never noncount nouns).

*COMPARE:

Every one (two words) is an expression of quantity (e.g., *I have read* ***every one*** *of those books*).

Everyone (one word) is an indefinite pronoun. It has the same meaning as *everybody* (e.g., ***Everyone/Everybody*** *has a schedule*).

NOTE: *Each* and *every* have essentially the same meaning.

Each is used when the speaker is thinking of one person/thing at a time: ***Each*** *student has a schedule.* = *Mary has a schedule. Hiroshi has a schedule. Carlos has a schedule. Sabrina has a schedule. Etc.*

Every is used when the speaker means ***all***: ***Every*** *student has a schedule.* = ***All of the*** *students have schedules.*

❑ **Exercise 42. Looking at grammar.** (Chart 7-11)
Complete the sentences. Use the singular or plural form of the nouns in parentheses.

1. There is only one (*girl*) _____girl_____ on the sixth-grade soccer team.

2. Only one of the (*girl*) _____ in the sixth grade is on the soccer team.

3. Each of the (*child*) _____ got a present.

4. Mr. Hoover gave a present to each (*child*) _____.

5. We invited every (*member*) _____ of the club.

6. Every one of the (*member*) _____ came.

7. One (*student*) _____ stayed after class to ask a question.

8. One of the (*student*) _____ stayed after class.

9. All of the students enjoyed the debate. The teacher was very excited when every (*student*) _____ in the class participated in the discussion.

10. Each of the (*student*) _____ joined the conversation.

❑ **Exercise 43. Check your knowledge.** (Chart 7-11)
Correct the errors. Some of the sentences do not contain any errors.

1. It's important for every ~~students~~ *student* to have a book.

2. Each of the students in my class has a book. (*no change*)

3. The teacher gave each of students a test paper.

4. Every student in the class did well on the test.

5. Spain is one of the country I want to visit.

6. Every furniture in that room is made of wood.

7. One of the equipment in our office is broken.

8. I gave a present to each of the woman in the room.

9. One of my favorite place in the world is an island in the Caribbean Sea.

10. Each one of your suitcases will be checked when you go through customs.

11. It's impossible for one human being to know every languages in the world.

12. I found each of the error in this exercise.

□ **Exercise 44. Warm-up.** (Chart 7-11)
Complete the sentences with *of* or **Ø**. How do you know when to use *of* in expressions of quantity?

I saw _____.

1. some ___*Ø*___ students.

2. some ___*of*___ the students.

3. several _____ students.

4. several _____ the students.

5. several _____ your students.

6. most _____ your students.

7. most _____ them.

I know _____.

8. many _____ students.

9. many _____ those students.

10. many _____ them.

11. a lot _____ students.

12. a lot _____ those students.

13. none _____ those students.

14. none _____ them.

7-12 Using *Of* in Expressions of Quantity

(a) I bought *one book*. (b) I bought *many books*.	With some expressions of quantity, **of** is not used when the noun is nonspecific, as in (a) and (b).
(c) *One of **those*** books is mine. (d) *Some of **the*** books are yours. (e) *Many of **my*** books are in Spanish. (f) *Most of **them*** are paperbacks.	**Of** is used with: • specific nouns, as in (c), (d), and (e). • pronouns, as in (f).
(g) I have *a lot of books*. (h) I've read *a lot of **those*** books.	Some expressions of quantity, like **a lot of**, always include **of**, whether the noun is nonspecific, as in (g), or specific, as in (h).

Expressions of quantity

one (of)	all (of)	some (of)
two (of)	each (of)	several (of)
half of	every	(a) few (of)
50 percent of	almost all (of)	(a) little (of)
three-fourths of	most (of)	hardly any (of)
a majority of	many (of)	none of
hundreds of	much (of)	no
thousands of	a number of	
millions of	a great deal of	
	a lot of	

❑ **Exercise 45. Looking at grammar.** (Chart 7-12)
Complete the sentences with **of** or **Ø**.

1. I know several ___of___ Jack's friends.

2. I've made several ___Ø___ friends lately.

3. Some _____ students are lazy. Most _____ students are hard-working.

4. Some _____ the students in Mrs. Gray's class are a little lazy.

5. I usually get a lot _____ mail.

6. A lot _____ the mail I get is junk mail.

7. Most _____ books have an index.

8. Most _____ Ali's books are written in Arabic.

mailbox

9. I bought a few _____ books yesterday.

10. I've read a few _____ those books.

11. I'm new here. I don't know many _____ people yet.

12. I've just moved into a new apartment. I don't know many _____ my neighbors yet.

13. Millions _____ people watch World Cup soccer.

❑ **Exercise 46. Let's talk.** (Charts 7-11 and 7-12)
Use the expressions of quantity in the list to make sentences about the given situation. Work in pairs, in small groups, or as a class.

all of	the majority of	several of	a couple of
almost all of	some of	a few of	hardly any of
most of	about half of	very few of	one of

SITUATION: There are 15 students taking a basic Chinese language class.

Example: Three have studied Chinese before.
SPEAKER A: Several of them have studied Chinese before.
SPEAKER B: Most of them have never studied Chinese before.

1. Thirteen speak English as their native language.
2. One speaks Thai, and one speaks Arabic.
3. No one speaks Spanish.
4. Two have studied several languages already.
5. Fifteen think Chinese is very difficult.
6. Fourteen are enjoying the class.
7. Five have already bought the textbook.
8. Four are men; eleven are women.

❑ **Exercise 47. Let's talk: interview.** (Charts 7-9 → 7-12)
Conduct a poll among your classmates and report your findings.

Part I. Prepare five yes/no questions that ask for opinions or information about your classmates' likes, dislikes, habits, or experiences. Record their responses.

Sample questions:
Do you read an English-language newspaper every day?
Do you like living in this city?
Do you have a car?
Have you ever ridden a horse?
Are you going to be in bed before midnight tonight?

Part II. Report your findings to the class using expressions of quantity to make generalizations about what you learned.

Sample report:
Only a few of the people in this class read an English newspaper every day.
Most of them like living in this city.
Three of the people in this class have cars.
About half of them have ridden a horse at some time in their lives.
Almost all of them are going to be in bed before midnight tonight.

☐ **Exercise 48. Let's talk.** (Charts 7-9 → 7-12)
Most of the statements are overgeneralizations. Make each statement clearer or more accurate by adding an expression of quantity. Add other words to the sentences or make any other changes you wish. Work in pairs, in small groups, or as a class.

Example: My classmates are from Japan.
→ Most of my classmates are from Japan.
→ All (of) my classmates are from Japan.★
→ One of my classmates is from Japan.
→ Hardly any of my classmates are from Japan.
→ None of my classmates is from Japan.

1. My classmates speak Arabic.
2. People are friendly.
3. The pages in this book contain illustrations.
4. Babies are born bald.
5. The students in my class are from South America.
6. People like to live alone.
7. The people I know like to live alone.
8. The countries in the world are in the Northern Hemisphere.
9. The citizens of the United States speak English.
10. Children like to read scary stories.
11. The children in my country go to school.
12. Airplanes depart and arrive precisely on time.
13. The rivers in the world are polluted.
14. The pollution in the world today is caused by human beings.

☐ **Exercise 49. Let's talk.** (Charts 7-9 → 7-12)
As a class, make a list of controversial topics (i.e., topics that generate opinions not everyone agrees with) that you think are interesting. From this list, choose topics that you would like to discuss with your classmates; then, divide into groups to talk about them.

At the end of the discussion time, the leader of each group will report on the opinions of his or her group using expressions of quantity to make generalizations (e.g., *Most of us believe that* . . . OR *Only a few of us think that* . . .). The number of topics you choose to discuss depends on the time available.

Sample topics:
physician-assisted suicide for terminally ill patients
birth control education in public schools
a current war or other political crisis
the dangers posed by global warming

★Using *of* after *all* is optional with a specific noun.
CORRECT: *All of* my classmates . . . .
CORRECT: *All* my classmates are . . . .

□   **Exercise 50. Check your knowledge.** (Chapter 7)
Correct the errors.

1. That book contain many different kind of story and article.

2. In my country, there is alot of schools.

3. She is always willing to help her friends in every possible ways.

4. In the past, horses was the principal mean of transportation.

5. He succeeded in creating one of the best army in the world.

6. There are a lot of equipments in the research laboratory, but undergraduates are not allowed to use them.

7. I have a five years old daughter and a three years old son.

8. Most of people in my apartment's building is friendly.

9. Everyone seek the happiness in the life.

10. Writing compositions are very hard for me.

11. Almost of the student in my class are from Asia.

12. It's difficult for me to understand English when people uses a lot of slangs.

Chapter 8
Pronouns

❑ **Exercise 1. What do I already know?** (Chart 8-1)
Correct the errors in pronoun usage.

1. My friends and I ordered Indian food at the restaurant. I wasn't very hungry, but I ate most of them.

2. When we were in school, my sister and me used to play tennis after school every day.

3. If you want to pass you're exams, you had better study very hard for it.

4. A hippopotamus spends most of it's time in the water of rivers and lakes.

5. After work, Mr. Gray asked to speak to Mona and I about the company's new policies. He explained it to us and asked for ours opinions.

6. My friends asked to borrow my car because their's was in the garage for repairs.

❑ **Exercise 2. Warm-up.** (Chart 8-1)
Talk about names, paying special attention to pronouns.

Part I. Use personal pronouns to refer to people in the classroom. Begin your sentence with the given pronoun.

Examples: She → *She is Marika.*
     Their → *Their names are Marika, Carlos, and Talal.*

1. He   5. Their   9. Her
2. They   6. Our   10. His
3. I   7. You (singular) 11. She
4. We   8. You (plural) 12. Your

Part II. Discuss these topics. Listen for pronouns.

1. In many cultures, first names have special meanings. For example, in Japanese, *Akira* means "intelligent." In Spanish, *Amanda* means "loveable." In Chinese, *Liang* means "kindhearted." Does your name have a special meaning?

2. What kind of names do people in your culture give pets? What are some common names?

8-1 Personal Pronouns

	Subject Pronoun	Object Pronoun	Possessive Pronoun	Possessive Adjective
Singular	*I* *you* *she, he, it*	*me* *you* *her, him, it*	*mine* *yours* *hers, his, its*	*my* (name) *your* (name) *her, his, its* (name)
Plural	*we* *you* *they*	*us* *you* *them*	*ours* *yours* *theirs*	*our* (names) *your* (names) *their* (names)

(a) I read *a book. It* was good.	A PRONOUN is used in place of a noun. The noun it refers to is called the "antecedent." In (a): The pronoun *it* refers to the antecedent noun **book**. A singular pronoun is used to refer to a singular noun, as in (a). A plural pronoun is used to refer to a plural noun, as in (b).
(b) I read *some books. They* were good.	
(c) *I* like tea. Do *you* like tea too?	Sometimes the antecedent noun is understood, not explicitly stated. In (c): *I* refers to the speaker, and *you* refers to the person the speaker is talking to.
(d) John has a car. *He drives* to work.	SUBJECT PRONOUNS are used as subjects of sentences, as *he* in (d).
(e) John works in my office. I *know him* well. (f) I talk *to him* every day.	OBJECT PRONOUNS are used as the objects of verbs, as *him* in (e), or as the objects of prepositions, as *him* in (f).
(g) That book is *hers.* *Yours* is over there.	POSSESSIVE PRONOUNS are not followed immediately by a noun; they stand alone, as in (g). Possessive pronouns DO NOT take apostrophes, as in (h). (See Chart 7-2, p. 105, for the use of apostrophes with possessive nouns.)
(h) *INCORRECT:* That book is ~~her's~~. ~~Your's~~ is over there.	
(i) *Her* book is here. *Your* book is over there.	POSSESSIVE ADJECTIVES are followed immediately by a noun; they do not stand alone.
(j) A bird uses *its* wings to fly. (k) *INCORRECT:* A bird uses ~~it's~~ wings to fly. (l) *It's* cold today. (m) The Harbour Inn is my favorite old hotel. *It's been* in business since 1933.	COMPARE: **Its** has NO APOSTROPHE when it is used as a possessive, as in (j). **It's** has an apostrophe when it is used as a contraction of *it is*, as in (l), or *it has* when **has** is part of the present perfect tense, as in (m). NOTE: **It's** vs. **its** is a common source of error for native speakers of English.

□ **Exercise 3. Looking at grammar.** (Chart 8-1)
Identify the personal pronouns and their antecedents.

1. Jack has a part-time job. He works at a fast-food restaurant.
   → (***he*** = *a pronoun;* ***Jack*** = *the antecedent*)
2. Most monkeys don't like water, but they can swim well when they have to.
3. The teacher graded the students' papers last night. She returned them during class today.
4. Nancy took an apple with her to work. She ate it at lunchtime.
5. A dog makes a good pet if it is properly trained.
6. Yuri's cat is named Maybelle Alice. She* is very independent. She never obeys Yuri. His dogs, on the other hand, obey him gladly. They like to please him.

□ **Exercise 4. Looking at grammar.** (Chart 8-1)
Choose the words in *italics* that are grammatically correct. NOTE: A number of native English speakers commonly use subject pronouns after ***and***, even when the grammatically correct choice is an object pronoun.

1. My parents always read bedtime stories to my sister and *I / me*.
2. Just between you and *I / me*, I think Ms. Lucas is going to lose her job.
3. There's Kevin. Let's go talk to him. I need to tell you and *he / him* something.
4. Mrs. Minski needs to know the truth. I'm going to tell Mr. Chang and *she / her* the truth, and you can't stop me.
5. Alex introduced Sally and *I / me* to his cousin from Mexico City.

□ **Exercise 5. Looking at grammar.** (Chart 8-1)
Complete the sentences in each situation with pronouns for the word in *italics*.

SITUATION 1: There's *Sarah*.

1. I need to go talk to ___*her*___ .

2. _____ and I have been friends since high school.

3. I went to elementary school with _____ brother and _____ .

4. _____ parents are best friends with my parents.

5. _____ is getting married next month. Another friend and I are taking _____ on a

   short trip before _____ marriage.

6. Being with _____ is a lot of fun. We laugh a lot.

7. _____ always has a good time with _____ friends.

---

*If the sex of a particular animal is known, usually ***she*** or ***he*** is used instead of ***it***.

SITUATION 2: *I'm not feeling well.* I think I'd better stay home today.

8. My friends and _____ were planning to volunteer at our local food bank* today.

9. The food bank often asks my friends and _____ to help them with various projects.

10. But my friends will have to go without _____.

11. I'd better call _____ friend Sami to tell him I can't come today.

12. Could I use your cell phone? I don't have _____ with _____.

❏ **Exercise 6. Looking at grammar.** (Chart 8-1)
Choose the correct words in *italics*.

1. This is (*my*) / *mine* umbrella. (*Your*) / *Yours* umbrella is over there.

2. This umbrella is *my* / *mine*. The other one is *your* / *yours*.

3. Mary and Bob have *their* / *theirs* books. In other words, Mary has *her* / *hers*, and Bob has *his* / *him*.

4. *Our* / *Ours* house is almost the same as *our* / *ours* neighbors' house. The only difference in appearance is that *our* / *ours* is gray and *their* / *theirs* is white.

❏ **Exercise 7. Let's talk.** (Chart 8-1)
Place a pen or pencil on your desk. Your teacher will say a sentence. One student will repeat the sentence, indicating the person(s) the sentence refers to. Close your book for this activity.

Example:
TEACHER: This one is mine, and that one is hers. Ahmed?
AHMED: (*Ahmed points to his pen and gestures toward himself*): This one is mine. (*Ahmed points to another pen and gestures toward Anita*): And that one is hers.

1. This pen is mine, and that pen is yours.
2. This pen is hers, and that pen is his.
3. These are ours, and those are theirs.
4. This one is yours, and that one is his.
5. Their pens are there, and her pen is here.
6. This isn't hers. It's his.

❏ **Exercise 8. Looking at grammar.** (Chart 8-1)
Complete the sentences with *its* or *it's*.

1. Are you looking for the olive oil? _____It's_____ on the top shelf.

2. A honeybee has two wings on each side of _____ body.

food bank = a place that receives donations of food and gives them away to needy people.

3. Tom has a pet. _____ name is Squeak. _____ a turtle. _____ been his pet for several years.

4. A nation that does not educate _____ children has no future.

5. All of us can help create peace in the world. Indeed, _____ our responsibility to do so.

❑ **Exercise 9. Looking at grammar.** (Chart 8-1)
Choose the correct words in *italics*.

When I was in Florida, I observed an interesting bird called an anhinga. (*It's*) / *Its* a fish eater. *It / They   dives / dive* into the water and *spears/spear   its / it's* prey on *its / it's* long, pointed bill. After emerging from the water, *it / they tosses / toss* the fish into the air and *catches / catch it / them* in mid-air, and then *swallows / swallow it / them* headfirst. *Its / It's* interesting to watch anhingas in action. I enjoy watching *it / them* a lot.

❑ **Exercise 10. Listening.** (Chart 8-1)
Pronouns can be hard to hear in spoken English because they are usually unstressed. Additionally, if the pronoun begins with "h," the /h/ sound is often dropped in rapid, relaxed speech. Complete each conversation with the words you hear.

CD 1
Track 41

1. Where's Kim?

A: I don't know. I haven't seen _____ this morning.

B: I think _____ in the restroom.

C: I'm looking for _____ too.

D: Ask _____ assistant. He'll know.

E: Have you tried looking in _____ office? I know _____ not there much, but maybe _____ surprise you.

2. The Nelsons are giving their daughter a motorcycle for graduation.

A: Hmmm. _____ like motorcycles that much?

B: Really? _____ a motorcycle rider?

C: That's an odd gift. I wonder what _____ were thinking.

D: That's what the Smiths gave _____ son. I think _____ already had an accident.

E: I'm not a fan of motorcycles. Cars just don't see _____ in traffic.

F: I think _____ a wonderful gift! I've had _____ for years, and _____ been great.

Exercise 11. Warm-up. (Chart 8-2)
Pretend you are writing an article about seat belts. Which sentence would you choose to include? Why? NOTE: All the sentences are correct.

1. A driver should put on his seat belt as soon as he gets in his car.
2. A driver should put on her seat belt as soon as she gets in her car.
3. A driver should put on his or her seat belt as soon as he or she gets in his or her car.
4. Drivers should put on their seat belts as soon as they get in their cars.

8-2 Personal Pronouns: Agreement with Generic Nouns and Indefinite Pronouns

(a) *A student* walked into the room. *She* was looking for the teacher.	In (a) and (b): The pronouns refer to particular individuals whose gender is known. The nouns are not generic.
(b) *A student* walked into the room. *He* was looking for the teacher.	
(c) *A student* should always do *his* assignments.	A GENERIC NOUN* does not refer to any person or thing in particular; rather, it represents a whole group.
(d) *A student* should always do *his or her* assignments.	In (c): *A student* is a generic noun; it refers to *anyone who is a student*. With a generic noun, a singular masculine pronoun has been used traditionally, but many English speakers now use both masculine and feminine pronouns to refer to a singular generic noun, as in (d).
(e) *Students* should always do *their* assignments.	Problems with choosing masculine and/or feminine pronouns can often be avoided by using a plural rather than a singular generic noun, as in (e).

Indefinite pronouns

everyone	someone	anyone	no one**
everybody	somebody	anybody	nobody
everything	something	anything	nothing

(f) *Somebody* left *his* book on the desk. (g) *Everyone* has *his or her* own ideas.	In formal English, the use of a singular pronoun to refer to an INDEFINITE PRONOUN is generally considered to be grammatically correct, as in (f) and (g).
(h) *INFORMAL:* *Somebody* left *their* book on the desk. *Everyone* has *their* own ideas.	In everyday, informal English (and sometimes even in more formal English), a plural personal pronoun is usually used to refer to an indefinite pronoun, as in (h).

*See Chart 7-7, p. 114, for basic article usage.
**No one* can also be written with a hyphen in British English: *No-one heard me.*

❏ **Exercise 12. Looking at grammar.** (Chart 8-2)
Change the sentences by using plural instead of singular generic nouns where possible. Change pronouns and verbs as necessary. Discuss the advantages of using plural rather than singular generic nouns.

1. When a student wants to study, he or she should find a quiet place.
   → *When students want to study, they should find a quiet place.*

2. I talked to a student in my chemistry class. I asked to borrow her notes from the class I missed. She gave them to me gladly. (*no change*)

3. Each student in Biology 101 has to spend three hours per week in the laboratory where he or she does various experiments by following the directions in his or her lab manual.

4. A citizen has two primary responsibilities. He should vote in every election, and he should serve willingly on a jury.

5. We listened to a really interesting lecturer last night. She discussed her experiences as an archeologist in Argentina.

❏ **Exercise 13. Looking at grammar.** (Chart 8-2)
Complete each sentence with the pronoun(s) that seems appropriate to the given situation. Choose the correct verbs in parentheses as necessary. Discuss formal vs. informal pronoun usage.

1. *One classmate to another:* Look. Somebody left ___their*___ book on my desk. Is it yours?

2. *One friend to another:* Of course you can learn to dance! Anyone can learn how to dance if _____ (*wants, want*) to.

3. *Business textbook:* An effective corporate manager must be able to motivate _____ employees.

4. *One roommate to another:* If anyone asks where I am, tell _____ you don't know. I want to keep my meeting with Jim a secret.

5. *Son to his mother:* Gosh, Mom, everyone who came to the class picnic was supposed to bring _____ own food. I didn't know that, so I didn't have anything to eat. I'm really hungry!

6. *A university lecture:* I will end my lecture today by saying that I believe a teacher needs to work in partnership with _____ students.

7. *A magazine article:* People do not always see things the same way. Each person has _____ own way of understanding a situation.

❏ **Exercise 14. Warm-up.** (Chart 8-3)
All the pronouns in blue refer to the noun **team**. Discuss how the pronouns in the two sentences are different. NOTE: Both sentences are correct.

1. When the soccer **team** won in the closing moments of the game, they ran to the player who had scored the winning goal and lifted him on their shoulders.

2. A basketball **team** is relatively small. It doesn't have as many members as a baseball team.

_____

*also possible: *his; his or her; her or his.*

8-3 Personal Pronouns: Agreement with Collective Nouns

(a) My *family* is large. *It* is composed of nine members.	When a collective noun refers to a single impersonal unit, a singular gender-neutral pronoun (*it, its*) is used, as in (a).
(b) My *family* is loving and supportive. *They* are always ready to help me.	When a collective noun refers to a collection of various individuals, a plural pronoun (*they, them, their*) is used, as in (b).*

Examples of collective nouns			
audience	couple	family	public
class	crowd	government	staff
committee	faculty	group	team

*NOTE: When the collective noun refers to a collection of individuals, the verb may be either singular or plural: *My family is* OR *are loving and supportive.* A singular verb is generally preferred in American English. A plural verb is used more frequently in British English, especially with the words *government* or *public.* (American: ***The government is** planning many changes.* British: ***The government are** planning many changes.*)

❑ **Exercise 15. Looking at grammar.** (Chart 8-3)
Complete the sentences with pronouns. In some of the sentences, there is more than one possibility. Choose the correct singular or plural verb in parentheses as necessary.

1. I have a wonderful family. I love _____*them*_____ very much, and _____*they*_____
   (*loves, love*) me.

2. I looked up some information about the average American family. I found out that
   _____ (*consists, consist*) of 2.3 children.

3. The audience clapped enthusiastically. Obviously _____ had enjoyed the
   concert.

4. The crowd at the soccer game was huge. _____ exceeded 100,000 people.

5. The crowd became more and more excited as the premier's motorcade approached.
   _____ began to shout and wave flags in the air.

6. The audience filled the room to overflowing. _____ (*was, were*) larger than I had expected.

7. The class is planning a party for the last day of school. _____ (*is, are*) going to bring many different kinds of food and invite some of _____ friends to celebrate with _____ .

8. The class is too small. _____ (*is, are*) going to be canceled.

❏ **Exercise 16. Warm-up.** (Chart 8-4)
Draw a picture of yourself. Show it to the rest of the class. Answer the questions in complete sentences. Your teacher will supply student names in items 1 and 5.

1. (_____), what did you draw?
2. Who drew a picture of herself? Name someone.
3. Who drew a picture of himself? Name someone.
4. Who drew pictures of themselves? Name them.
5. (_____), did you and (_____) draw pictures of yourselves?

SELF-PORTRAIT

8-4 Reflexive Pronouns

Singular	**Plural**
myself	*ourselves*
yourself	*yourselves*
herself, himself, itself, oneself	*themselves*

(a) Larry was in the theater. *I saw him.* I talked *to him.*	Compare (a) and (b): Usually an object pronoun is used as the object of a verb or preposition, as *him* in (a). (See Chart 8-1.)
(b) *I saw myself* in the mirror. *I looked at myself* for a long time.	A reflexive pronoun is used as the object of a verb or preposition when the subject of the sentence and the object are the same person, as in (b).* *I* and *myself* are the same person.
(c) INCORRECT: I saw ~~me~~ in the mirror.	
— Did someone email the report to Mr. Lee? — Yes. — Are you sure? (d) — Yes. *I myself* emailed the report to him. (e) — *I* emailed the report to him *myself*.	Reflexive pronouns are also used for emphasis. In (d): The speaker would say "I myself" strongly, with emphasis. The emphatic reflexive pronoun can immediately follow a noun or pronoun, as in (d), or come at the end of the clause, as in (e).
(f) Anna lives *by herself.*	The expression *by* + *a reflexive pronoun* means "alone."

*Sometimes an object pronoun is used as the object of a preposition even when the subject and object pronoun are the same person. Examples: *I took my books with me. Bob brought his books with him. I looked around me. She kept her son close to her.*

❑ **Exercise 17. Looking at grammar.** (Chart 8-4)

Complete the sentences with appropriate reflexive pronouns.

1. Everyone drew self-portraits. I drew a picture of _____ *myself* _____ .

2. Rosa drew a picture of _____ .

3. Yusef drew a picture of _____ .

4. The children drew pictures of _____ .

5. We drew pictures of _____ .

6. Olga, you drew a picture of _____ , didn't you?

7. All of you drew pictures of _____ , didn't you?

8. When one draws a picture of _____ , it is called a self-portrait.

❑ **Exercise 18. Looking at grammar.** (Chart 8-4)

Complete the sentences with appropriate reflexive pronouns.

1. Tommy told a lie. He was ashamed of _____ *himself* _____ .

2. Masako cut _____ while she was chopping vegetables.

3. People surround _____ with friends and family during holidays.

4. Omar thinks Oscar is telling the truth. So does Ricardo. I _____ don't believe Oscar's story for a minute!

5. Now that their children are grown, Mr. and Mrs. Grayson live by _____ .

6. A: Should I marry Steve?

   B: No one can make that decision for you, Ann. Only you _____ can make such an important decision about your own life.

7. Emily and Ryan, be careful! You're going to hurt _____ !

8. A: I hate my job.

   B: Me too. I envy Jacob. He's self-employed.

   A: Yeah. I'd like to work for _____ too.

9. Jason, you need to eat better and get more exercise. You should take better care of _____ . Your father takes care of _____ , and I take care of _____ . Your father and I are healthy because we take good care of _____ . People who take care of _____ have a better chance of staying healthy than those who don't.

❑ **Exercise 19. Looking at grammar.** (Chart 8-4)
Complete each sentence with a word or expression from the list and an appropriate reflexive pronoun. Use each word/expression only one time.

angry at	introduced	promised
enjoy	killed	proud of
entertained	laugh at	talking to
feeling sorry for	pat	✓taught

1. Karen Williams never took lessons. She ___taught herself___ how to play the piano.

2. Did Roberto have a good time at the party? Did he _____?

3. All of you did a good job. You should be _____.

4. You did a good job, Barbara. You should _____ on the back.

5. A man down the street committed suicide. We were all shocked by the news that he had _____.

6. The children played very well without adult supervision. They _____ _____ by playing school.

7. I had always wanted to meet Hong Tran. When I saw her at a party last night, I walked over and _____ to her.

8. Nothing good ever comes from self-pity. You should stop _____ _____, George, and start doing something to solve your problems.

9. People might think you're a little crazy, but _____ is one way to practice using English.

10. Humor can ease the problems we encounter in life. Sometimes we have to be able to _____.

11. Carol made several careless mistakes at work last week, and her boss is getting impatient with her. Carol has _____ to do better work in the future.

12. Yesterday Fred's car ran out of gas. He had to walk a long way to a gas station. He is still _____ for forgetting to fill the tank.

❏ **Exercise 20. Listening.** (Chart 8-4)

Listen to the beginning of each sentence. Choose the correct completion.

CD 1
Track 42

Example: You will hear: We wanted to save money, so we painted the inside of our

apartment _____.

You will circle: myself (ourselves) yourselves

1. himself	herself	yourself
2. yourself	myself	ourselves
3. ourselves	themselves	myself
4. themselves	himself	herself
5. ourselves	yourselves	themselves
6. himself	herself	myself

❏ **Exercise 21. Looking at grammar.** (Chapters 6 → 8)

Choose the correct words in *italics*.

1. (*Penguin*, (*Penguins*)) are interesting (*creature*, (*creatures*)). They are (*bird*, *birds*), but (*it*, *they*) cannot fly.

2. (*Million*, *Millions*) of (*year*, *years*) ago, they had (*wing*, *wings*). (*This*, *These*) wings changed as the birds adapted to (*its*, *their*) environment.

3. (*Penguin's*, *Penguins'*) principal food (*was*, *were*) (*fish*, *fishes*). Penguins needed to be able to swim to find their food, so eventually their (*wing*, *wings*) evolved into (*flipper*, *flippers*) that enabled (*it*, *them*) to swim through water with speed and ease.

4. Penguins (*spends*, *spend*) most of their lives in (*water*, *waters*). However, they lay their (*egg*, *eggs*) on (*land*, *lands*).

5. Emperor penguins have interesting egg-laying (*habit*, *habits*).

6. The female (*lays*, *lay*) one (*egg*, *eggs*) on the (*ice*, *ices*) in Antarctic regions and then immediately (*returns*, *return*) to the ocean.

7. After the female lays the egg, the male (*takes*, *take*) over. (*He*, *They*) (*covers*, *cover*) the egg with (*his*, *their*) body until (*she*, *he*, *it*, *they*) (*hatches*, *hatch*).

8. (*This*, *These*) process (*takes*, *take*) seven to eight (*week*, *weeks*). During (*this*, *these*) time, the male (*doesn't*, *don't*) eat.

9. After the egg (*hatches*, *hatch*), the female returns to take care of the chick, and the male (*goes*, *go*) to the ocean to find food for (*himself*, *herself*), his mate, and their (*offspring*, *offsprings*).

10. (*Penguin*, *Penguins*) live in a harsh (*environment*, *environments*). (*He*, *They*) (*need*, *needs*) endurance to survive.

Exercise 22. Warm-up. (Chart 8-5)
Read the dialogue. Discuss the pronouns in blue. Who or what do they refer to?

MRS. COOK: Jack Woods bought a used car. Did *you* hear?

MR. COOK: Yes, I heard all about his car. *He* paid next to nothing for *it*.

MRS. COOK: Right. And now *it* doesn't run.

MR. COOK: Well, as *they* say, *you* get what *you* pay for.

MRS. COOK: That's certainly true. *One* gets what *one* pays for.

8-5 Using *You, One,* and *They* as Impersonal Pronouns

(a) *One* should always be polite.	In (a) and (b): *One* means "any person, people in general."
(b) How does *one* get to Fifth Avenue from here?	In (c) and (d): *You* means "any person, people in general."
(c) *You* should always be polite.	*One* is much more formal than *you*. Impersonal *you*, rather than *one*, is used more frequently in everyday English.
(d) How do *you* get to Fifth Avenue from here?	
(e) Iowa is an agricultural state. *They* grow a lot of corn there.	*They* is used as an impersonal pronoun in spoken or very informal English to mean "people in general" or "an undefined group of people."
	They has no stated antecedent. Often the antecedent is implied.
	In (e): *They* = farmers in Iowa

❑ **Exercise 23. Looking at grammar.** (Chart 8-5)
Discuss the meanings of the pronouns in *italics*.

1. I agree with Kyung's decision to quit his corporate job and go to art school. I think *you* need to follow *your* dreams.
   → *The pronouns refer to everyone, anyone, people in general, all of us.*
2. Jake, if *you* really want my advice, I think *you* should find a new job.
   → *The pronouns refer to Jake, a specific person.*
3. Wool requires special care. If *you* wash wool in hot water, it will shrink. *You* shouldn't throw a wool sweater into a washing machine with *your* cottons.
4. Alex, I told *you* not to wash *your* sweater in hot water. Now look at it. It's ruined!
5. Generosity is its own reward. *You* always get back more than *you* give.
6. Sonya, let's make a deal. If *you* wash the dishes, I'll take out the garbage.
7. The earth's environmental problems are getting worse all the time. *They* say that the ozone layer is being depleted more and more every year.
8. Memory is selective. Often *you* remember only what *you* want to remember. If *you* ask two people to tell *you* about an experience they shared, they might tell *you* two different stories.
9. I would have loved to have gone to the concert last night. *They* played Beethoven's Seventh Symphony. I heard it was wonderful.
10. I've grown to dislike airplane travel. *They* never give *you* enough room for *your* legs. And if the person in front of *you* puts his seat back, *you* can barely move. *You* can't even reach down to pick up something from the floor.

❏ **Exercise 24. Let's talk.** (Chart 8-5)

Discuss the meanings of these common English sayings. Work in pairs, in small groups, or as a class.

1. "You can't teach an old dog new tricks."
2. "You are what you eat."
3. "If you're not part of the solution, you're part of the problem."
4. "You can fool some of the people all of the time, and you can fool all of the people some of the time, but you can't fool all of the people all of the time." —*Abraham Lincoln*

❏ **Exercise 25. Warm-up.** (Chart 8-6)

Match each sentence to the picture it describes.

1. Some of the crows are flying. The others are sitting on a fence.
2. Some of the crows are flying. Others are sitting on a fence.

Picture A

Picture B

8-6 Forms of *Other*

	Adjective	**Pronoun**	
Singular Plural	*another* book (is) *other* books (are)	*another* (is) *others* (are)	Forms of ***other*** are used as either adjectives or pronouns. Notice: • ***Another*** is always singular. • A final ***-s*** is used only for a plural pronoun (***others***).
Singular Plural	*the other* book (is) *the other* books (are)	*the other* (is) *the others* (are)	

(a) The students in the class come from many countries. One of the students is from Mexico. ***Another student is*** from Iraq. ***Another is*** from Japan. ***Other students are*** from Brazil. ***Others are*** from Algeria.	The meaning of ***another***: "one more in addition to or different from the one(s) already mentioned." The meaning of ***other/others*** (without ***the***): "several more in addition to or different from the one(s) already mentioned."
(b) I have three books. Two are mine. ***The other book*** is yours. (***The other*** is yours.) (c) I have three books. One is mine. ***The other books*** are yours. (***The others*** are yours.)	The meaning of ***the other***(s): "all that remains from a given number; the rest of a specific group."
(d) I will be here for ***another three years***. (e) I need ***another five dollars***. (f) We drove ***another ten miles***.	***Another*** is used as an adjective with expressions of time, money, and distance, even if these expressions contain plural nouns. ***Another*** means "an additional" in these expressions.

❑ **Exercise 26. Looking at grammar.** (Chart 8-6)
Complete the sentences with a form of *other*.

1. I got three letters. One was from my father. _____*Another*_____ one was from my
   sister. _____*The other*_____ letter was from my girlfriend.

2. Look at your hand. You have five fingers. One is your thumb. _____ is
   your index finger. _____ is your middle finger. _____
   finger is your ring finger. And _____ finger (the last of the five) is your
   little finger.

3. Look at your hands. One is your right hand. _____ is your left hand.

4. I lost my dictionary, so I bought _____.

5. Some people have red hair. _____ have brown hair.

6. Some people have red hair. _____ people have brown hair.

7. I have four children. One of them has red hair. _____ children have
   brown hair.

8. I have four children. One of them has red hair. _____ have brown hair.

❑ **Exercise 27. Looking at grammar.** (Chart 8-6)
Read each pair of sentences and answer the question that follows.

1. a. One North African country Helen plans to visit is Algeria. Another is Morocco.
   b. One North African country Alex plans to visit is Tunisia. The other is Algeria.
      QUESTION: Who is planning to visit more than two countries in North Africa?

2. a. Purple is one of Mai's favorite colors. The others she likes are blue and green.
   b. Purple is one of Elaine's favorite colors. Others she likes are blue and green.
      QUESTION: Who has only three favorite colors?

3. a. Kazuo took a cookie from the cookie jar and ate it. Then he took another one and
      ate it too.
   b. Susie took a cookie from the cookie jar and ate it. Then she took the other one and
      ate it too.
      QUESTION: Whose cookie jar had only two cookies?

4. a. Some of the men at the business meeting on Thursday wore dark blue suits. Others
      wore black suits.
   b. Some of the men at the business meeting on Friday wore dark blue suits. The others
      wore black suits.
      QUESTION: Mr. Anton wore a gray suit to the business meeting. Which day did he
      attend the meeting, Thursday or Friday?

❏ **Exercise 28. Looking at grammar.** (Chart 8-6)
Complete the sentences with a form of *other*.

1. There are two women standing on the corner. One is Helen Jansen, and
   _____the other_____ is Pat Hendricks.

2. They have three children. One has graduated from college and has a job.
   _____ is at Yale University. _____ is still living at home.

3. I would like some more books on this subject. Do you have any _____
   that you could lend me?

4. I would like to read more about this subject. Do you have any _____
   books that you could lend me?

5. Marina reads the *New York Times* every day. She doesn't read any _____
   newspapers.

6. Some people prefer classical music, but _____ prefer rock music.

7. I'm almost finished. I just need _____ five minutes.

8. One of the most important inventions in the history of the world was the printing press.
   _____ was the electric light. _____ were the telephone,
   the television, and the computer.

9. Some babies begin talking as early as six months; _____ don't speak until
   they are more than two years old.

10. One common preposition is *from.* _____ common one is *in.*
    _____ are *by, for,* and *of.* The most frequently used prepositions in
    English are *at, by, for, from, in, of, to,* and *with.* What are some _____
    prepositions?

11. That country has two basic problems. One is inflation, and _____ is the
    instability of the government.

12. I have been in only three cities since I came to the United States. One is New York, and
    _____ are Washington, D.C., and Chicago.

13. When his alarm went off this morning, Toshi shut it off, rolled over, and slept for
    _____ hour.

14. Individual differences in children must be recognized. Whereas one child might have a
    strong interest in mathematics and science, _____ child might be more
    artistic.

□ **Exercise 29. Let's talk.** (Chart 8-6)

Complete the sentences, using an appropriate form of ***other***. Work in pairs, in small groups, or as a class.

Example:
SPEAKER A (*book open*):   There are two books on my desk. One is . . . .
SPEAKER B (*book closed*): One is red. The other is blue.

1. I speak two languages. One is . . . .
2. I speak three languages. One is . . . .
3. I lost my textbook, so I had to buy . . . .
4. Some people have brown hair, but . . . .
5. Hawaii is a popular tourist destination. Italy is . . . .
6. I have two books. One is . . . .

(*Change roles if working in pairs.*)

7. Some TV programs are excellent, but . . . .
8. Some people need at least eight hours of sleep each night, but . . . .
9. Only two of the students failed the quiz. All of . . . .
10. There are three colors that I especially like. One is . . . .
11. I have two candy bars. I want only one of them. Would you like . . . ?
12. There are three places in particular I would like to see when I visit (*a city/country*).
    One is . . . .

□ **Exercise 30. Listening.** (Chart 8-6)

CD 1
Track 43

Complete each sentence with the form of ***other*** you hear.

1. This coffee is delicious. Could I please have _____ cup?

2. The coffee isn't in this grocery bag, so I'll look in _____ one.

3. There are supposed to be ten chairs in the room, but I count only five. Where are
   _____?

4. No, let's not use this printer. Let's use _____ one.

5. Bob is a nickname for Robert. _____ are Rob and Robbie.

6. The sky is clearing. It's going to be _____ beautiful day.

□ **Exercise 31. Warm-up.** (Chart 8-7)

Read about Kate and Lisa. Are the statements about them true? Circle "T" for true and "F" for false.

SITUATION: Lisa and Kate talk to each other every other day. Kate saw Lisa the other day at the park. Lisa was with her five children. They were walking behind her, one after the other.

1. Kate talks to Lisa often.	T	F
2. Kate talked to Lisa today. She'll talk to her again tomorrow.	T	F
3. Kate last saw Lisa a few weeks ago.	T	F
4. Lisa's children were walking in a line.	T	F

8-7 Common Expressions with *Other*

(a) Mike and I write to **each other** every week. We write to **one another** every week.	**Each other** and **one another** indicate a reciprocal relationship.* In (a): I write to him every week, and he writes to me every week.
(b) Please write on **every other** line.	**Every other** can give the idea of "alternate." The meaning in (b) means: Write on the first line. Do not write on the second line. Write on the third line. Do not write on the fourth line. (Etc.)
(c) — Have you seen Ali recently? — Yes. I saw him just **the other day**.	**The other** is used in time expressions such as *the other day, the other morning, the other week, etc.,* to refer to the recent past. In (c): **the other day** means "a few days ago, not long ago."
(d) The ducklings walked in a line behind the mother duck. Then the mother duck slipped into the pond. The ducklings followed her. They slipped into the water **one after the other**. (e) They slipped into the water **one after another**.	In (d): **one after the other** expresses the idea that separate actions occurred very close in time. In (e): **one after another** has the same meaning as **one after the other**.

(f) No one knows my secret **other than** Rosa. (g) No one knows my secret **except** (*for*) Rosa.	**Other than** is usually used after a negative to mean "except," as in (f). Example (g) has the same meaning as (f).
(h) Fruit and vegetables are full of vitamins and minerals. **In other words**, they are good for you.	In (h): **In other words** is used to explain, usually in simpler or clearer terms, the meaning of the preceding sentence(s).

*In typical usage, *each other* and *one another* are interchangeable; there is no difference between them. Some native speakers, however, use *each other* when they are talking about only two persons or things, and *one another* when there are more than two.

❑ **Exercise 32. Looking at grammar.** (Charts 8-6 and 8-7)
Complete the sentences with a form of *other*.

1. Two countries border on the United States. One is Canada. _____*The other*_____ is Mexico.

2. One of the countries I would like to visit is Sweden. _____ is Malaysia. Of course, besides these two countries, there are many _____ places I would like to see.

3. Louis and I have been friends for a long time. We've known _____ since we were children.

4. A: I talked to Sam _____ day.

   B: Oh? How is he? I haven't seen him for ages.

5. In the Southwest there is a large area of land that has little or no rainfall, no trees, and very few plants _____ than cactuses. In _____ words, this area of the country is a desert.

6. Thank you for inviting me to the picnic. I'd like to go with you, but I've already made _____ plans.

7. Some people are tall; _____ are short. Some people are fat; _____ are thin. Some people are nearsighted; _____ people are farsighted.

8. Mr. and Mrs. Jay love _____ . They support _____ . They like _____ . In _____ words, they are a happily married couple.

9. A: How often do you travel to Portland?

   B: Every _____ month I go there to visit my grandmother in a nursing home.

10. Could I borrow your pen? I need to write a check, but I have nothing to write with _____ than this pencil.

11. My niece, Kathy, ate one cookie after _____ until she finished the whole box. That's why she had a bad stomachache.

❑ **Exercise 33. Looking at grammar.** (Charts 8-6 and 8-7)
Complete the sentences with your own words. Use a form of ***other*** where indicated.

Example: Some people like ____ while (*other*) ____ prefer ____.
  → *Some people like coffee while others prefer tea.*

1. I have two ____. One is ____, and (*other*) ____ is ____.
2. One of the longest rivers in the world is ____. (*other*) ____ is ____.
3. Some people like to ____ in their free time. (*other*) ____ prefer ____.
4. There are three ____ that I especially like. One is ____. (*other*) ____ is ____. (*other*)
   ____ is ____.
5. There are many kinds of ____. Some are ____, (*other*) ____ are ____, and (*other*) ____
   are ____.

❑ **Exercise 34. Listening.** (Chart 8-7)
Listen to the way ***other*** and ***except*** are used. Choose the sentence that is closest in meaning
to the one you hear.

CD 1
Track 44

Example: You will hear: I spend a lot of time with my grandmother. We enjoy each other's
                 company.
         You will choose: a. My grandmother and I like to spend time with others.
                 (b.) I enjoy spending time with my grandmother.

1. a. All of the students had the wrong answer.
    b. Some students had the wrong answer.

2. a. The Clarks each see others on weekends.
    b. The Clarks spend time together on weekends.

3. a. Susan spoke with him a while ago.
    b. Susan spoke with him recently.

4. a. Three people know about the engagement.
    b. Four people know about the engagement.

5. a. Jan knows about the party.
    b. Jan doesn't know about the party.

❑ **Exercise 35. Check your knowledge.** (Chapters 6 → 8)
Correct the errors.

1. There ~~is~~ *are* many different kind*s* of animal*s* in the world.

2. My cousin and her husband moved to other city because they don't like a cold weather.

3. I like to travel because I like to learn about other country and custom.

4. Collecting stamps is one of my hobby.

5. I came here three and a half month ago. I think I have made a good progress in English.

6. When I lost my passport, I had to apply for the another one.

7. When I got to class, all of the others students were already in their seats.

8. English has borrowed quite a few of word from another languages.

9. There is many student from differents countries in this class.

10. Thousand of athlete take part in the Olympics.

11. Education is one of the most important aspect of life. Knowledges about many different things allow us to live fuller lives.

12. All of the students names were on the list.

13. I live in a two rooms apartment. Its too small for my family.

14. Many of people prefer to live in small towns. Their attachment to their communities prevent them from moving from place to place in search of works.

15. Todays news is just as bad as yesterdays news.

16. Almost of the students in our class speaks English well.

17. The teacher gave us several homework to hand in next Tuesday.

18. In today's world, womans work as doctor, pilot, archeologist, and many other thing. Both my mother and father are teacher's.

19. Every employees in our company respect Mr. Ward.

20. A child needs to learn how to get along with another people, how to spend their time wisely, and how to depend on yourself.

❏ **Exercise 36. Let's write.** (Chapters 6 → 8)
Write a paragraph on one of the given topics. Write as quickly as you can. Write whatever comes into your mind. Try to write 100 words in ten minutes.

When you finish your paragraph, exchange it with a classmate. Correct each other's errors before giving it to your teacher.

Topics:

food	computers
English	families
this room	movies
animals	holidays

❏ **Exercise 37. Let's write and talk.** (Chapters 6 → 8)

Choose an object and write a short paragraph about it. Do NOT include the name of the object in your writing; always use a pronoun to refer to it, not the noun itself.

Describe the object (What does it look like? What is it made of? What does it feel like? Does it make a noise? Does it have a smell? Etc.), and explain why people use it or how it is used. Begin with its general characteristics; then gradually get more specific.

Finally, read your paragraph aloud to the class or to a small group of classmates. They will try to guess what the object is.

Example: It is usually made of metal. It is hollow. It is round on one end. It can be very small — small enough to fit in your pocket — or large, but not as large as a car. It is used to make noise. It can be used to give a signal. Sometimes it's part of an orchestra. Sometimes it is electric and you push a button to make it ring. What is it?

❏ **Exercise 38. Let's talk.** (Chapters 6 → 8)

Think of the best present you have ever been given. Maybe it was something for your birthday, maybe for an anniversary, or maybe it wasn't for any special occasion at all. It could be an object, an activity, or perhaps something someone did for you. Describe it to the class or a small group. Include what it looked like, how it made you feel, and why it was special. The class or group will try to guess what it was.

Example: The best present I ever received was something my son gave me. He had to work hard in order to be able to give me this gift. When he was 18, he decided to go to college. That made me very happy. Many times he didn't think he could finish, but I told him that a good education would be his key to success in life. He studied very hard and never quit. This present took place on one day. I was there and watched him with tears in my eyes. What was this gift?

Answer: Your son's graduation from college.

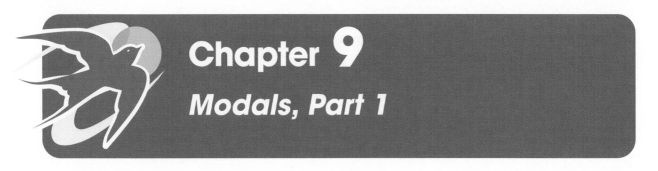

Chapter 9
Modals, Part 1

❑ **Exercise 1. Warm-up.** (Chart 9-1)
Correct the errors in verb forms.

see
1. She can ~~saw~~ it.
2. She can to see it.
3. She cans see it.
4. She can sees it.

5. Can pass you the rice, please?
6. Do you can see it?★
7. They don't can go there.★★
8. They aren't able pay their rent.

9-1 Basic Modal Introduction

Modal auxiliaries generally express speakers' attitudes. For example, modals can express that a speaker feels something is necessary, advisable, permissible, possible, or probable; and, in addition, they can convey the strength of those attitudes. Each modal has more than one meaning or use. See Chart 10-10, p. 204–205, for a summary overview of modals.

Modal auxiliaries in English

can	had better	might	ought (to)	should	would
could	may	must	shall	will	

Modal Auxiliaries

I You He She It We You They + *can* do it. *could* do it. *had better* do it. *may* do it. *might* do it. *must* do it. *ought to* do it. *shall* do it. *should* do it. *will* do it. *would* do it.

Modals do not take a final **-s**, even when the subject is *she, he,* or *it.*
CORRECT: **She can do it.**
INCORRECT: She ~~cans~~ do it.

Modals are followed immediately by the simple form of a verb.
CORRECT: **She can do it.**
INCORRECT: She can ~~to~~ do it. / She can ~~does~~ it. / She can ~~did~~ it.

The only exception is *ought*, which is followed by an infinitive (*to + the simple form of a verb*).
CORRECT: He **ought to go** to the meeting.

Phrasal Modals

be able to do it
be going to do it
be supposed to do it
have to do it
have got to do it

Phrasal modals are common expressions whose meanings are similar to those of some of the modal auxiliaries. For example: *be able to* is similar to *can*; *be going to* is similar to *will*.

An infinitive (*to + the simple form of a verb*) is used in these similar expressions.

★See Appendix Chart B-1 for question forms with modals.
★★See Appendix Chart D-1 for negative forms with modals.

❏ **Exercise 2. Warm-up.** (Charts 9-2 and 9-3)
Complete the requests with *I* or *you*. Which sentences have essentially the same meaning?

1. Could _____ see that book? Thanks.

2. Could _____ hand me that book? Thanks.

3. May _____ see that book? Thanks.

4. Can _____ hand me that book? Thanks.

5. Can _____ see that book? Thanks.

6. Would _____ hand me that book? Thanks.

7. Will _____ please hand me that book? Thanks.

9-2 Polite Requests with *"I"* as the Subject

May I *Could I*	(a) ***May I borrow*** your pen (please)? (b) ***Could I*** (please) ***borrow*** your pen?	***May I*** and ***could I*** are used to request permission. They are equally polite, but ***may I*** sounds more formal.* NOTE in (b): In a polite request, ***could*** has a present or future meaning, not a past meaning.
Can I	(c) ***Can I borrow*** your pen?	***Can I*** is used informally to request permission, especially if the speaker is talking to someone she/he knows fairly well. ***Can I*** is usually considered a little less polite than ***may I*** or ***could I***.
	TYPICAL RESPONSES Certainly. Yes, certainly. Of course. Yes, of course. *INFORMAL:* Sure.	Often the response to a polite request is an action, such as a nod or shake of the head, or a simple "uh-huh," meaning "yes."

*****Might*** is also possible: ***Might I borrow*** *your pen?* ***Might I*** is quite formal and polite; it is used much less frequently than ***may I*** or ***could I***.

9-3 Polite Requests with "*You*" as the Subject

Would you *Will you*	(a) ***Would you pass*** the salt (please)? (b) ***Will you*** (please) ***pass*** the salt?	The meaning of ***would you*** and ***will you*** in a polite request is the same. ***Would you*** is more common and is often considered more polite. The degree of politeness, however, is often determined by the speaker's tone of voice.
Could you	(c) ***Could you pass*** the salt (please)?	Basically, ***could you*** and ***would you*** have the same meaning. The difference is slight. ***Would you*** = *Do you want to do this please?* ***Could you*** = *Do you want to do this please, and is it possible for you to do this?* ***Could you*** and ***would you*** are equally polite.
Can you	(d) ***Can you*** (please) ***pass*** the salt?	***Can you*** is often used informally. It usually sounds a little less polite than ***could you*** or ***would you***.
	TYPICAL RESPONSES Yes, I'd (I would) be happy to / be glad to. Certainly. INFORMAL: Sure.	A person usually responds in the affirmative to a polite request. If a negative response is necessary, a person might begin by saying, "I'd like to, but . . ." (e.g., "I'd like to pass the salt, but I can't reach it.").
	(e) INCORRECT: May ~~you~~ pass the salt?	***May*** is used only with *I* or *we* in polite requests.

❏ **Exercise 3. Let's talk.** (Charts 9-2 and 9-3)
Ask and answer polite questions. Speaker A presents the situation to Speaker B. Speaker B makes a polite request using ***Would*/*Could you*,** and Speaker A gives a typical response. Work in pairs or as a class.

Example:
SPEAKER A (*book open*):　You and I are co-workers. We don't know each other well.
　　　　　　　　　　　　We're at a lunch table in a cafeteria. You want the pepper.
SPEAKER B (*book closed*):　*Would/Could* you please pass me the pepper? (*Will* is also possible
　　　　　　　　　　　　because the speaker uses *please*, but *can* is probably not appropriate in
　　　　　　　　　　　　this situation.)
SPEAKER A (*book open*):　Certainly. I'd be glad to. Here you are.

1. You and I are good friends. We're in my apartment. You want to use the phone.
2. I'm your instructor. You want to leave class early.
3. I'm a student in your class. You hand me some papers. You want me to pass them out to the class.

(*Change roles if working in pairs.*)

4. I'm your supervisor at work. You knock on my half-open office door. I'm sitting at my desk. You want to come in.
5. I'm Dr. North's assistant. You want to make an appointment to see Dr. North.
6. You are running toward the elevator. I'm already inside. The door is closing. You ask me to hold it open.

❏ **Exercise 4. Warm-up.** (Chart 9-4)
In each dialogue, choose the speaker (A or B) who is going to turn down the heat.

1. A: Would you mind turning down the heat?

    B: No, not at all.

2. A: Would you mind if I turned down the heat?

    B: No, not at all.

9-4 Polite Requests with *Would You Mind*

Asking Permission

(a) *Would you mind **if I closed** the window?* (b) *Would you mind **if I used** the phone?* TYPICAL RESPONSES No, not at all. No, of course not. No, that would be fine.	Notice in (a): ***Would you mind if I*** is followed by the simple past.* The meaning in (a): *May I close the window? Is it all right if I close the window? Will it cause you any trouble or discomfort if I close the window?* Notice that the typical response is "no." "Yes" means *Yes, I mind.* In other words: *It is a problem for me.* Another typical response might be "unh-uh," meaning "no."

Asking Someone to Do Something

(c) *Would you mind **closing** the window?* (d) Excuse me. *Would you mind **repeating** that?* TYPICAL RESPONSES No. I'd be happy to. Not at all. I'd be glad to. *INFORMAL:* No problem. / Sure. / Okay.	Notice in (c): ***Would you mind*** is followed by the *-ing* form of a verb (a gerund). The meaning in (c): *I don't want to cause you any trouble, but would you please close the window? Would that cause you any inconvenience?* The informal responses "Sure" and "Okay" are common but not logical. The speaker means *No, I wouldn't mind* but seems to be saying the opposite: *Yes, I would mind.* Native speakers understand that the response "Sure" or "Okay" in this situation means that the speaker agrees to the request.

*Sometimes, in informal spoken English, the simple present is used: *Would you mind if I **close** the window?*

NOTE: The simple past does not refer to past time after ***would you mind***; it refers to present or future time. See Chart 20-3, p. 419, for more information.

❏ **Exercise 5. Looking at grammar.** (Chart 9-4)
Make sentences using ***Would you mind***.

1. a. I want to leave early. → *Would you mind if I left early?*
   b. I want you to leave early. → *Would you mind leaving early?*

2. a. I want you to speak with John.
   b. I want to speak with John.

3. a. I want to turn on the air conditioner.
   b. I want you to turn on the air conditioner.

❑ **Exercise 6. Looking at grammar.** (Chart 9-4)
Complete the sentences with the verbs in parentheses. Use *if I* + *the past tense* OR the *-ing form of the verb*. In some of the sentences, either response is possible, but the meaning is different.

1. A: I'm very tired and need to sleep. Would you mind (*go*) _____*if I went*_____ to bed?

   B: I'm sorry. I didn't understand what you said. Would you mind (*repeat*)
   _____*repeating*_____ that?

2. A: Are you coming with us?

   B: I know I promised to go with you, but I'm not feeling very good. Would you mind
   (*stay*) _____ home?

   A: Of course not.

3. A: It's getting hot in here. Would you mind (*open*) _____ the window?

   B: No.

4. A: This is probably none of my business, but would you mind (*ask*) _____
   you a personal question?

   B: It depends.

5. A: Would you mind (*smoke*) _____?

   B: I'd really rather you didn't.

6. A: Excuse me. Would you mind (*speak*)

   _____ a little more slowly? I didn't catch what you said.

   B: Oh, of course. I'm sorry.

7. A: I don't like this TV program. Would you mind (*change*) _____ the
   channel?

   B: Unh-uh.

❑ **Exercise 7. Listening.** (Chart 9-4)
Listen to each request. Choose the expected response (a. or b.). In relaxed speech, the *you* in **would you** may sound like "ju" or "juh."

CD 1
Track 45

Example: You will hear: This room is stuffy. Would you mind if I opened the door?
You will choose: (a.) No, of course not.   b. Yes.

1. a. Yes.   b. Not at all. I'd be glad to.

2. a. Yes.   b. No, that would be fine.

3. a. Yes.   b. No, I'd be happy to.

4. a. Sure.   b. Yes.

5. a. Yes.   b. No problem.

❑ **Exercise 8. Let's talk: pairwork.** (Chart 9-4)
Work with a partner. Read each situation and create a dialogue. Partner A makes a polite request using **Would you mind**. Partner B gives a typical response.

Example: You have a library book. You want the other person to take it back to the library
for you.
PARTNER A: Are you going to the library?
PARTNER B: Yes.
PARTNER A: This book is due. Would you mind taking it back to the library for me?
PARTNER B: Not at all. I'd be glad to.

1. You've finished dinner. You're about to wash the dinner dishes. You want the other person to dry them.
2. You're feeling tired. A friend has arrived to pick you up for a party, but you've decided not to go.
3. One of you says that you're going to a particular store. The other one also wants something from that store but doesn't have time to go there.
4. One of you wants to ask the other a personal question.
5. You've bought a new cell phone. You don't know how to send a text message, but your friend does. You want to learn how to do it.

❑ **Exercise 9. Looking at grammar.** (Charts 9-2 → 9-4)
Complete the polite requests with your own words. Try to imagine what the speaker might say in the given situation.

1.   JACK: What's the trouble, Officer?

    OFFICER: You made an illegal U-turn.

    JACK: I did?

    OFFICER: Yes. May _____*I see your driver's license*_____?

    JACK: Certainly. It's in my wallet.

    OFFICER: Would _____*you please remove it from your wallet*_____?

2.   WAITER: Good evening. Are you ready to order?

    CUSTOMER: No, we're not. Could _____?

    WAITER: Certainly. I'll be back shortly.

3.   SALLY: Are you driving to the meeting tonight?

    SAM: Uh-huh, I am.

    SALLY: Could _____?

    SAM: Sure. I'll pick you up at 7:00.

4. MR. PENN: Something's come up, and I can't meet with you Tuesday. Would you mind

    _____?

    MS. GRAY: Let me check my calendar.

5. MECHANIC: What seems to be the trouble with your car?

   CUSTOMER: Something's wrong with the brakes, I think. Could _____?

   MECHANIC: Sure. Just pull the car into the garage.

6. SHELLEY: Are you enjoying the movie?

   MIKE: Yeah, you?

   SHELLEY: Yes, but I can't see over the man in front of me. Would you mind _____?

   MIKE: Not at all. I see two empty seats across the aisle.

❏ **Exercise 10. Let's talk: pairwork.** (Charts 9-2 → 9-4)
Work with a partner. Make up a short dialogue for each situation. The dialogue should contain a polite request and a response to that request.

Example: Janet and Sara are roommates and good friends. Janet doesn't have enough money to go to a movie tonight. She wants to borrow some from Sara.
JANET: There's a movie I really want to see tonight, but I'm running a little low on money right now. Could I borrow a few dollars? I'll pay you back Friday.
SARA: Sure. No problem. How much do you need?

1. Rashid is walking down the hall of his office building. He needs to know what time it is. He asks Elena, a co-worker he's seen before but has never met.
2. Larry is trying to study. His roommate, Matt, is playing a CD very loudly. This is bothering Larry, who is trying to be polite even though he feels frustrated and a little angry.
3. Ms. Jackson is in the middle of the city. She's lost. She's trying to find the bus station. She stops a friendly-looking stranger on the street to ask for directions.
4. Paul just arrived at work and remembered that he left his stove on in his apartment. His neighbor Mrs. Wu has a key to the front door, and Paul knows that Mrs. Wu hasn't left for work yet. Anxiously, he telephones Mrs. Wu for help.

❏ **Exercise 11. Let's talk.** (Charts 9-2 → 9-4)
What are some polite requests you have heard (or have said) in the given locations? Create typical dialogues.

1. in this classroom	3. at a restaurant	5. on the telephone
2. at an airport	4. at a grocery store	6. at a clothing store

❏ **Exercise 12. Warm-up.** (Chart 9-5)
Read the statements. Choose the more typical context (a. or b.) for the words in blue. Discuss their meanings.

1. Gosh! Look at the time. I've got to go. I have class in five minutes!
   a. everyday conversation   b. formal writing

2. All applicants must be 18 years of age and must have a valid driver's license.
   a. everyday conversation   b. formal writing

3. We have to prepare a research paper on global warming in Dr. Chen's seminar this term. I think it'll be interesting.
   a. everyday conversation   b. formal writing

9-5 Expressing Necessity: *Must, Have To, Have Got To*

Must, Have To

(a) All applicants *must take* an entrance exam. (b) All applicants *have to take* an entrance exam.	*Must* and *have to* both express necessity. The meaning is the same in (a) and (b): *It is necessary for every applicant to take an entrance exam. There is no other choice. The exam is required.*
(c) I'm looking for Sue. I *have to talk* to her about our lunch date tomorrow. I can't meet her for lunch because I have to go to a business meeting at 1:00. (d) Where's Sue? I *must talk* to her right away. I have an urgent message for her.	In everyday statements of necessity, *have to* is used more commonly than *must*. *Must* is usually stronger than *have to* and can indicate urgency or stress importance. The meaning in (c): *I need to do this, and I need to do that.* The meaning in (d) is stronger: *This is very important!* Because it is a strong word, *must* (meaning necessity) is relatively rare in conversation. It is usually found in legal or academic writing.
(e) I *have to* ("hafta") be home by eight. (f) He *has to* ("hasta") go to a meeting tonight.	NOTE: Native speakers often say "hafta" and "hasta," as in (e) and (f).

Have Got To

(g) I *have got to go* now. I have a class in ten minutes. (h) I *have to go* now. I have a class in ten minutes.	*Have got to* also expresses the idea of necessity: (g) and (h) have the same meaning. *Have got to* is informal and is used primarily in spoken English. *Have to* is used in both formal and informal English.
(i) I *have got to go* ("I've gotta go / I gotta go") now.	The usual pronunciation of *got to* is "gotta." Sometimes *have* is dropped in speech: "I gotta do it."

Past Necessity

(j) PRESENT or FUTURE I *have to* / *have got to* / *must study* tonight. (k) PAST I *had to study* last night.	*Had to* expresses past necessity. In (j): *had to* = *needed to: I needed to study last night.* There is no other past form for *must* (when it means necessity) or *have got to*.

❑ **Exercise 13. Let's talk.** (Chart 9-5)
Answer the questions in complete sentences using *must, have to, had to,* or *have got to.*
Work in pairs, in small groups, or as a class.

1. What are some things you have to do after class today?
2. What have you got to do before you go to bed tonight? Is there any place you have got to go later today?
3. Think about everyday life. What are some things you must have in order to survive?
4. Think about your plans for the next week. What are some things you have to do?
5. Think about your activities last week. What were some things you had to do?
6. Think of the job of a doctor. What kinds of things must a doctor know about? What are some things a doctor has to do every day?

❏ **Exercise 14. Warm-up.** (Chart 9-6)
Choose the sentences that Speaker B might say in response to Speaker A.

SPEAKER A: The meeting starts in an hour. We have plenty of time.
SPEAKER B: 1. We must not hurry.
2. We don't have to hurry.
3. We don't need to hurry.

9-6 Lack of Necessity and Prohibition: *Have To* and *Must* in the Negative

Lack of Necessity	
(a) Tomorrow is a holiday. We ***don't have to go*** to class. (b) I can hear you. You ***don't have to shout.***	When used in the negative, ***must*** and ***have to*** have different meanings.
	Negative form: ***do not have to*** = lack of necessity. The meaning in (a): *We don't need to go to class tomorrow because it is a holiday.*
Prohibition	
(c) You ***must not tell*** anyone my secret. Do you promise?	***must not*** = prohibition (DO NOT DO THIS!) The meaning in (c): *Do not tell anyone my secret. I forbid it. Telling anyone my secret is prohibited.* Negative contraction: ***mustn't**. (The first "t" is silent: "muss-ənt.")
(d) ***Don't tell*** anyone my secret. (e) You ***can't tell*** anyone my secret. (f) You ***'d better not tell*** anyone my secret.	Because ***must not*** is so strong, speakers also express prohibition with imperatives, as in (d), or with other modals, as in (e) and (f).

*Lack of necessity may also be expressed by ***need not*** + *the simple form of a verb:* You ***needn't shout.*** The use of ***needn't*** as an auxiliary is chiefly British except in certain common expressions such as *You needn't worry.*

❏ **Exercise 15. Looking at grammar.** (Chart 9-6)
Complete the sentences with ***must not*** or ***do/does not have to***.

1. I've already finished all my work, so I ____*don't have to*____ study tonight. I think I'll read for a while.

2. In order to be a good salesclerk, you _____ be rude to customers.

3. You _____ introduce me to Dr. Gray. We've already met.

4. A person _____ become rich and famous in order to live a successful life.

5. If you encounter a growling dog, you _____ show any signs of fear. If a dog senses fear, it is more likely to attack a person.

6. I _____ go to the doctor. I'm feeling much better.

7. We _____ go to the concert if you don't want to, but it might be good.

8. A person _____ get married in order to lead a happy and fulfilling life.

❏ **Exercise 16. Let's talk.** (Chart 9-6)
What do you look for in a leader? What qualities do you think a leader needs in order to be effective? Complete the sentences with *must, must not, has to,* or *doesn't have to.* Discuss your answers.

An effective leader of a country . . .

1. _____ be well educated.

2. _____ be flexible and open to new ideas.

3. _____ be wealthy.

4. _____ have a family (spouse and children).

5. _____ have a military background.

6. _____ use his or her power for personal financial gain.

7. _____ ignore the wishes of the majority of the people.

8. _____ be a good public speaker.

❏ **Exercise 17. Listening.** (Chart 9-6)

CD 1
Track 46

Complete the sentences with *must, must not,* or *don't have to* using the information you hear. Finish the first situation before moving on to the second.

SITUATION 1: Class registration

1. New students _____ register in person.

2. Returning students _____ register in person.

3. New students _____ forget their ID.

SITUATION 2: Class changes and tuition

4. All students _____ make class changes in person.

5. Students _____ pay their tuition at the time of registration.

6. Students _____ pay their tuition late.

❏ **Exercise 18. Warm-up.** (Chart 9-7)
Read the situation. What advice would you give Amir?

SITUATION: Amir has a bad toothache.

1. He should see a dentist immediately.
2. He should wait and see if the pain goes away.
3. He should call an ambulance.
4. He should put an ice-pack on his cheek.
5. He should take some pain medicine.
6. He should get his cousin to pull the tooth right away.

9-7 Advisability: *Should, Ought To, Had Better*

(a) You *should study* harder. You *ought to study* harder. (b) Drivers *should obey* the speed limit. Drivers *ought to obey* the speed limit.	*Should* and *ought to* both express advisability. Their meaning ranges in strength from a suggestion (*This is a good idea*) to a statement about responsibility or duty (*This is a very important thing to do*). The meaning in (a): *This is a good idea. This is my advice.* In (b): *This is an important responsibility.*
(c) You *shouldn't leave* your keys in the car.	Negative contraction: *shouldn't*.* NOTE: the /t/ is often hard to hear in relaxed, spoken English.
(d) I *ought to* ("otta") *study* tonight, but I think I'll watch TV instead.	Native speakers often pronounce *ought to* as "otta" in informal speech.
(e) The gas tank is almost empty. We *had better stop* at the next gas station. (f) You *had better take* care of that cut on your hand soon, or it will get infected.	In meaning, *had better* is close to *should* and *ought to*, but *had better* is usually stronger. Often *had better* implies a warning or a threat of possible bad consequences. The meaning in (e): *If we don't stop at a service station, there will be a bad result. We will run out of gas.* Notes on the use of *had better*: • It has a present or future meaning. • It is followed by the simple form of a verb. • It is more common in speaking than writing.
(g) You *'d better* take care of it. (h) You *better* take care of it.	Contraction: *'d better,* as in (g). Sometimes in speaking, *had* is dropped, as in (h).
(i) You *'d better not* be late.	Negative form: *had better* + *not*

*****Ought to** is not commonly used in the negative. If it is, the **to** is sometimes dropped: *You **oughtn't (to) leave** your keys in the car.*

❏ **Exercise 19. Looking at grammar.** (Chart 9-7)
Complete the dialogues with your own words. Use *should, ought to,* or *had better* to give advice.

1. A: The shoes I bought last week don't fit.

   B: You _____

2. A: Have you gotten your airplane ticket?

   B: No, not yet.

   A: Flights fill up fast near the holidays. You _____

3. A: Yikes! My class starts in five minutes. I wasn't watching the time.

   B: You _____

4. A: I have the hiccups.

   B: You _____

5. A: I bought these organic apples, and all of them are rotten inside.

   B: You _____

Exercise 20. Let's talk: pairwork. (Chart 9-7)
Work with a partner. Partner A presents the problem. Partner B gives advice using *should,*
ought to, or *had better*.

Example:
PARTNER A (*book open*):   I have a test tomorrow.
PARTNER B (*book closed*): You should / ought to / had better study tonight.

  1. I can't see the board when I sit in the back row.
  2. My roommate snores, and I can't get to sleep.
  3. Pam's younger brother, who is 18, is using illegal drugs. How can she help him?

Change roles.
  4. My apartment is a mess, and my mother is coming to visit tomorrow!
  5. I have six months to improve my English.
  6. The Taylors' daughter is very excited about going to Denmark for a vacation.

Exercise 21. Let's talk: pairwork. (Chart 9-7)
Work with a partner. Complete the dialogues with your own words.

  1. A: Oops! I spilled _____ *coffee on my shirt.* _____

      B: You'd better _____ *run it under hot water before the stain sets.* _____

  2. A: My doctor said I should _____ , but I _____ .

      B: Well, I think you'd better _____

  3. A: I've been studying for three days straight.

      B: I know. You should _____

  4. A: Do you think I ought to _____ or _____

      B: I think you'd better _____

      If you don't, _____

  5. A: Lately I can't seem to concentrate on anything. I feel _____

      B: Maybe you should _____

      Or have you thought about _____

Exercise 22. Let's talk. (Charts 9-5 → 9-7)
Which sentence in each pair is stronger? Discuss situations in which a speaker might say these
sentences.

  1. a. You *should go* to a doctor.
      b. You*'d better go* to a doctor.

  2. a. Mary *should go* to work today.
      b. Mary *must go* to work today.

  3. a. We*'ve got to go* to class.
      b. We *ought to go* to class.

  4. a. I *have to go* to the post office.
      b. I *should go* to the post office.

  5. a. We *shouldn't go* into that room.
      b. We *must not go* into that room.

  6. a. You*'d better not go* there alone.
      b. You *shouldn't go* there alone.

Exercise 23. Looking at grammar. (Charts 9-5 → 9-7)
Complete the sentences with **should** or **must/have to**. In some sentences either one is possible, but the meaning is different. Discuss the difference in meanings.

1. A person _____ *must / has to* _____ eat in order to live.

2. A person _____ *should* _____ eat a balanced diet.

3. If you want to become a doctor, you _____ go to medical school for many years.

4. I don't have enough money to take the bus, so I _____ walk home.

5. Walking is good exercise. You say you want to get more exercise. You _____ walk to and from work instead of taking the bus.

6. We _____ go to Colorado for our vacation.

7. According to my advisor, I _____ take another English course.

8. Rice _____ have water in order to grow.

9. This pie is very good. You _____ try a piece.

10. This pie is excellent! You _____ try a piece.★

❏ **Exercise 24. Listening.** (Charts 9-5 → 9-7)
Listen to each sentence and choose the answer (a. or b.) that has the same meaning. In some cases <u>both</u> answers are correct.

CD 1
Track 47

Example: You will hear: During the test, do not look at your neighbor's paper.
You will choose: a. You don't have to look at you neighbor's paper.
ⓑ You must not look at your neighbor's paper.

1. a. You don't have to lock the door.
   b. You must not lock the door.

2. a. You must show proof of citizenship.
   b. You have to show proof of citizenship.

3. a. You ought to arrive early.
   b. You should arrive early.

4. a. To enter the boarding area, passengers should have boarding passes.
   b. To enter the boarding area, passengers must have boarding passes.

★Sometimes in speaking, **must** has the meaning of a very enthusiastic **should**.

❑ **Exercise 25. Warm-up.** (Chart 9-8)
Choose the student (Jason or Jim) who said this sentence: "I should have studied."

Jason   Jim

9-8 The Past Form of *Should*

(a) I had a test this morning. I didn't do well on the test because I didn't study for it last night. I *should have studied* last night.	Past form: ***should have*** + *past participle.** The meaning in (a): ***I should have studied*** = *Studying was a good idea, but I didn't do it. I made a mistake.*
(b) You were supposed to be here at 10:00 P.M., but you didn't come until midnight. We were worried about you. You *should have called* us. (You did not call.)	Usual pronunciation of ***should have***: "should-əv" or "should-ə."
(c) My back hurts. I *should not have carried* that heavy box up two flights of stairs. (I carried the box, and now I'm sorry.)	The meaning in (c): ***I should not have carried*** = *I carried something, but it turned out to be a bad idea. I made a mistake.* Usual pronunciation of ***should not have***:
(d) We went to a movie, but it was a waste of time and money. We *should not have gone* to the movie.	"shouldn't-əv" or "shouldn't-ə."

*The past form of ***ought to*** is ***ought to have*** + *past participle* (*I ought to have studied.*). It has the same meaning as the past form of ***should***. In the past, ***should*** is used more commonly than ***ought to***. ***Had better*** is used only rarely in a past form (e.g., *He **had better have taken care** of it.*) and usually only in speaking, not writing.

❑ **Exercise 26. Listening.** (Chart 9-8)
Listen to each situation and choose the best advice (a. or b.). In some cases, <u>both</u> answers are correct.

CD 1
Track 48

Example: You will hear: Your report had spelling errors because you didn't run a spellcheck.
You will choose: (a.) I should have run a spellcheck.
b. I shouldn't have run a spellcheck.

1. a. She should have spent more money.
    b. She shouldn't have spent so much money.

2. a. I should have gone with them.
    b. I shouldn't have stayed home.

3. a. He shouldn't have had so much coffee.
   b. He should have had more coffee.

4. a. She shouldn't have been dishonest.
   b. She should have been more honest.

❑ **Exercise 27. Let's talk.** (Chart 9-8)
Speaker A presents the given situation. Speaker B comments on it using ***should/shouldn't have*** + *past participle*. Work in pairs, in groups, or as a class.

Example:
SPEAKER A (*book open*):   I didn't invite Sonya to my party. That made her feel bad. I'm sorry I didn't invite her.
SPEAKER B (*book closed*):   You should have invited Sonya to your party.

1. Tim made a mistake yesterday. He left the door to his house open, and a bird flew in. He had a terrible time catching the bird.

2. There was an important meeting yesterday afternoon, but you decided not to go. That was a mistake. Now your boss is angry.

3. Emily didn't feel good a couple of days ago. I told her to see a doctor, but she didn't. That was a mistake. Now she is very sick.

4. Nick signed a contract to buy some furniture without reading it thoroughly. Now he has discovered that he is paying a higher interest rate than he expected. He made a mistake.

❑ **Exercise 28. Let's talk: pairwork.** (Chart 9-8)
Work with a partner. Partner A presents the situation. Partner B comments on it using ***should/shouldn't have*** + *past participle*.

Example:
PARTNER A (*book open*):   You failed the test because you didn't study.
PARTNER B (*book closed*):   I should have studied.

1. You are cold because you didn't wear a coat.
2. Your friend is upset because you didn't return his call.
3. The room is full of flies because you opened the window.
4. You don't have any food for dinner because you didn't go to the grocery store.
5. You bought a friend a box of candy for her birthday, but she doesn't like candy.

Change roles.
6. John loved Marta, but he didn't marry her. Now he is unhappy.
7. John loved Marta, and he married her. But now he is unhappy.
8. The weather was beautiful yesterday, but you stayed inside all day.
9. You lent your car to your friend, but she had an accident because she was driving on the wrong side of the road.
10. You overslept this morning because you didn't set your alarm clock.

Exercise 29. Let's talk or write. (Chart 9-8)
Discuss or write what you think the people in the given situations **should have done** or **shouldn't have done**.

Example: Tom didn't study for the test. During the exam, he panicked and started looking at other students' test papers. He didn't think the teacher saw him, but she did. She warned him once to stop cheating, but he continued. As a result, the teacher took Tom's test paper, told him to leave the room, and failed him on the exam.

→ *Tom should have studied for the test.*
→ *He shouldn't have looked at other students' papers during the test.*
→ *He shouldn't have started cheating.*
→ *He should have known the teacher would see him cheating.*
→ *He should have stopped cheating after the first warning.*
→ *The teacher should have ripped up Tom's paper and sent him out of the room the first time she saw him cheating.*

1. Kazu and his wife, Julie, had good jobs as professionals in New York City. Kazu was offered a high-paying job in Chicago, which he immediately accepted. Julie was shocked when he came home that evening and told her the news. She liked her job and the people she worked with. She didn't want to move away and look for another job.

2. For three years, Donna had been saving her money for a trip to Europe. Her brother, Hugo, had a good job, but he spent all of his money on expensive cars, clothes, and entertainment. Suddenly, Hugo was fired from work and had no money to support himself while he looked for another job. Donna lent him nearly all of her savings, and within three weeks he spent it all on his car, more clothes, and expensive restaurants.

❑ **Exercise 30. Warm-up.** (Chart 9-9)
Correct the errors in the form of **be supposed to**.

1. The building custodian ∧ supposed to* unlock the doors every morning.
   (is)

2. We're not suppose to open that door.

3. I have a meeting at seven tonight. I suppose to be there a little early to discuss the agenda.

4. I'm suppose to be at the meeting. I suppose* I'd better go.

5. Where have you been? You suppose be here an hour ago!

---

*COMPARE: ***He is supposed to*** = *He is expected to.*
               I suppose = *I guess, I think, I believe.*

9-9 Obligation: *Be Supposed To*

(a) The game *is supposed to begin* at 10:00. (b) The committee *is supposed to vote* by secret ballot.	**Be supposed to** expresses the idea that someone (*I, we, they, the teacher, lots of people, my father, etc.*) expects something to happen. **Be supposed to** often expresses expectations about scheduled events, as in (a), or correct procedures, as in (b).
(c) I *am supposed to go* to the meeting. My boss told me that he wants me to attend. (d) The children *are supposed to put away* their toys before they go to bed.	**Be supposed to** also expresses expectations about behavior. The meaning is the same in (c) and (d): *Someone else expects (requests or requires) certain behavior.*
(e) Jack *was supposed to call* me last night. I wonder why he didn't.	**Be supposed to** in the past (*was/were supposed to*) expresses unfulfilled expectations. The meaning in (e): *I expected Jack to call, but he didn't.*

❏ **Exercise 31. Let's talk.** (Chart 9-9)
Answer the questions in complete sentences. Use *be supposed to*. Work in pairs, in small groups, or as a class.

Example:
SPEAKER A (*book open*):   If you're driving and a traffic light turns red, what are you supposed to do?
SPEAKER B (*book closed*): You're supposed to come to a complete stop.★

1. What are you supposed to do if you're involved in a traffic accident?

2. What are you supposed to do prior to takeoff in an airplane?

3. What are some things athletes in training are supposed to do, and some things they're not supposed to do?

4. If you're driving and an ambulance with flashing lights and blaring sirens comes up behind you, what are you supposed to do?

(Change roles if working in pairs).

5. Can you think of something you were supposed to do yesterday (or sometime in the past) but didn't do?

6. What are we supposed to be doing right now?

7. Tell me about any job you've had. What were you supposed to do on a typical day?

8. In the place you live or work, who is supposed to do what? In other words, what are the duties or responsibilities of the people who live or work with you?

★Note the use of impersonal *you*. See Chart 8-5, p. 147.

❑ **Exercise 40. Warm-up.** (Chart 9-12)
Read the conversation. Whose suggestion seems stronger, Alice's or Roberto's?

Carl   Alice   Roberto

Carl: Something's wrong with my bike. How will I get to school tomorrow?

Alice: You could take the bus.

Roberto: You should walk.

9-12 Making Suggestions: *Could* vs. *Should*

— *What should we do tomorrow?* (a) Why don't we go on a picnic? (b) We *could go* on a picnic.	***Could*** can be used to make suggestions. The meanings in (a) and (b) are similar: The speaker is suggesting a picnic.
— *I'm having trouble in math class.* (c) You *should talk* to your teacher. (d) *Maybe* you *should talk* to your teacher. — *I'm having trouble in math class.* (e) You *could talk* to your teacher. Or you *could ask* Ann to help you with your math lessons. Or I *could try* to help you.	***Should*** gives definite advice and is stronger than ***could***. The meaning in (c): *I believe it is important for you to do this. This is what I recommend.* In (d), the use of ***maybe*** softens the strength of the advice. ***Could*** offers suggestions or possibilities. The meaning in (e): *I have some possible suggestions for you. It is possible to do this. Or it is possible to do that.**
— *I failed my math class.* (f) You *should have talked* to your teacher and gotten some help from her during the term. — *I failed my math class.* (g) You *could have talked* to your teacher. Or you *could have asked* Ann to help you with your math. Or I *could have tried* to help you.	***Should have*** (past form) gives "hindsight" advice.** The meaning in (f): *It was important for you to talk to the teacher, but you didn't do it. You made a mistake.* ***Could have*** (past form) offers "hindsight" possibilities. The meaning in (g): *You had the chance to do this or that. It was possible for this or that to happen. You missed some good opportunities.*

***Might** (but not **may**) can also be used to make suggestions (*You **might** talk to your teacher.*), but **could** is more common.
**Hindsight refers to looking back at something after it happens.

□ **Exercise 41. Looking at grammar.** (Chart 9-12)
Discuss Speaker B's and C's use of *should* and *could*. What are the differences in meaning?

1. A: Ted doesn't feel good. He has a bad stomachache. What do you think he should do?
   B: He *should see* a doctor.
   C: Well, I don't know. He *could call* a doctor. He *could call* Dr. Sung. Or he *could call* Dr. Jones. Or he *could* simply *stay* in bed for a day and hope he feels better tomorrow.

2. A: I need to get to the airport.
   B: You *should take* the airport bus. It's cheaper than a taxi.
   C: Well, you *could take* the airport bus. Or you *could take* a taxi. Maybe Matt *could take* you. He has a car.

3. A: I took a taxi to the airport, and it cost me a fortune.
   B: You *should have taken* the airport bus.
   C: You *could have taken* the airport bus. Or maybe Matt *could have taken* you.

□ **Exercise 42. Let's write: pairwork.** (Chapter 9)
Work with a partner. Write a letter to an advice columnist in a newspaper. Make up a personal problem for the columnist to solve. Then give your letter to another pair, who will write an answer.

Example letter:

Dear Annie,

   My husband and my sister had an argument over a year ago, and they haven't spoken to each other since. My husband accused my sister of insulting him about his baldness. Then he told my sister that her hair looked like straw. He said he'd rather be bald than have that kind of hair. My sister insists on an apology. My husband refuses until she apologizes to him first.

   The problem is that I'm planning a graduation party for my daughter. My husband insists that I not invite my sister. I tell him I have to invite her. He says he'll leave the party if my sister walks in the door. My daughter is very close to my sister and very much wants her to come to the celebration.

   What should I do? I feel I must include my sister in the graduation party, but I don't want to anger my husband.

Yours truly,
Confused and Torn

Example response:

Dear Confused and Torn,

   Tell your husband that this party is your daughter's time to have her whole family around her and that you're going to invite your sister to the family celebration. This is certainly a time he has to put his daughter's needs first.

   And you should tell both your husband and your sister that it's time to get past their silly argument and act like grownups instead of ten-year-olds. You could offer to serve as an intermediary to get them together to apologize to each other. If you present a reasonable, adult way of handling the problem, they may start behaving like adults. Good luck.

Annie

Chapter 10
Modals, Part 2

❑ **Exercise 1. Warm-up.** (Chart 10-1)
A man walked into Ramon's apartment and stole his guitar. The thief accidentally left his hat in the apartment. A policewoman at the scene asks Ramon, "Whose hat is this?" How would he answer her question? Match Ramon's thoughts in Column A to his statements in Column B.

Column A

1. Ramon thinks the hat looks familiar, but he's not certain whose it is.
2. Ramon thinks he recognizes the hat. He's almost sure he knows the owner.
3. Ramon has no doubts. He knows whose hat it is.

Column B

a. "It is Joe Green's hat."
b. "It could belong to Joe Green. It might be Al Goldberg's. Or it may belong to Mr. Perez across the hall."
c. "It must be Joe Green's hat."

10-1 Degrees of Certainty: Present Time

— *Why isn't John in class?* **100% sure**: He *is* sick. **95% sure**: He *must be* sick. **50% sure or less**: ⎧ He *may be* sick. ⎨ He *might be* sick. ⎩ He *could be* sick. NOTE: These percentages are approximate.	*Degree of certainty* refers to how sure we are — what we think the chances are — that something is true. If we are sure something is true in the present, we don't need to use a modal. For example, if I say, "John is sick," I am sure; I am stating a fact that I am sure is true. My degree of certainty is 100%.
— *Why isn't John in class?* (a) He *must be* sick. (Usually he is in class every day, but when I saw him last night, he wasn't feeling good. So my best guess is that he is sick today. I can't think of another possibility.)	***Must*** expresses a strong degree of certainty about a present situation, but the degree of certainty is still less than 100%. In (a): The speaker is saying, "Probably John is sick. I have evidence to make me believe that he is sick. That is my logical conclusion, but I do not know for certain."
— *Why isn't John in class?* (b) He *may be* sick. (c) He *might be* sick. (d) He *could be* sick. (I don't really know. He may be at home watching TV. He might be at the library. He could be out of town.)	***May***, ***might***, and ***could*** express a weak degree of certainty. In (b), (c), and (d): The meanings are all the same. The speaker is saying, "Perhaps, maybe,* possibly John is sick. I am only making a guess. I can think of other possibilities."

***Maybe** (one word) is an adverb: ***Maybe** he is sick*. **May be** (two words) is a verb form: *He **may be** sick*.

180

Exercise 2. Looking at grammar. (Chart 10-1)
Complete the sentences by using **must** or **may/might/could** with the expressions in the list or your own words.

> ✓be very proud   fit Jimmy   miss them very much
> be at a meeting   have the wrong number

1. A: I've heard that your daughter recently graduated from law school and that your son has

   gotten a scholarship to the state university. You _____*must be very proud*_____ of them.

   B: We are.

2. A: Hello?

   B: Hello. May I speak to Ron?

   A: I'm sorry. You _____

   There's no one here by that name.

3. A: Where's Ms. Adams? She's not in her office.

   B: I don't know. She _____, or maybe she's in the

   employee lounge.

4. A: This winter jacket is still in good shape, but Brian has outgrown it. Do you think it

   would fit one of your sons?

   B: Well, it's probably too small for Danny too, but it _____

5. A: How long has it been since you last saw your family?

   B: More than a year.

   A: You _____

3. A: I'm trying to be a good host. I've offered Rosa a glass of water, a cup of coffee or tea, and a soft drink. She doesn't want anything.

   B: She must not . . .

4. A: I offered Mr. Chang some nuts, but he refused them. Then I offered him some candy, and he accepted.

   B: He must not . . .

5. A: Mrs. Garcia seems very lonely to me.

   B: I agree. She must not . . .

❏ **Exercise 8. Let's talk: pairwork.** (Chart 10-2)
Work with a partner. Give possible reasons for Speaker B's conclusions.

Example: A: Someone is knocking at the door. It might be Mary.

   B: It couldn't be Mary.

   (*Reason? Mary is in Moscow. / Mary went to a movie tonight. / Etc.*)

1. A: Someone left this wool hat here. I think it belongs to Alex.

   B: It couldn't belong to him. (*Reason?*)

2. A: Someone told me that Karen is in Norway.

   B: That can't be right. She couldn't be in Norway. (*Reason?*)

3. A: Look at that big animal. Is it a wolf?

   B: It couldn't be a wolf. (*Reason?*)

4. A: Someone told me that Marie quit her job.

   B: You're kidding! That can't be true. (*Reason?*)

❏ **Exercise 9. Listening.** (Charts 10-1 and 10-2)
Listen to the conversation and write the verbs you hear.

CD 1
Track 49 SITUATION: Tom and his young son Billy hear a noise on the roof.

TOM: I wonder what that noise is.

BILLY: It _____ a bird.
                    1

TOM: It _____ a bird. It's running across the roof. Birds _____
                 2   3

across roofs.

BILLY: Well, some birds do. It _____ a big bird that's running fast.
                                              4

TOM: No, I think it _____ some kind of animal. It _____ a
                              5   6

mouse.

BILLY: It sounds much bigger than a mouse. It _____ a dragon!
                                                               7

TOM: Son, it _____ a dragon. We don't have any dragons around here.
                        8

They exist only in storybooks.

BILLY: It _____ a little dragon that you don't
              9
know about.

TOM: Well, I suppose it _____ some kind
                                10
of lizard.

BILLY: _____ look.
              11

TOM: That's a good idea.

BILLY: Guess what, Dad. It _____ a rat!
                                          12

❑ **Exercise 10. Let's talk: pairwork.** (Charts 10-1 and 10-2)
Work with a partner. Create a dialogue based on the given situation. Role-play your dialogue for the class or a group of classmates.

SITUATION: You and your friend are at home. You hear a noise. You discuss the noise: What *may / might / could / must / may not / couldn't / must not* be the cause. Then you finally find out what is going on.

❑ **Exercise 11. Warm-up.** (Chart 10-3)
Decide which past modal in the list best completes each sentence. One of the modals is <u>not</u> appropriate for any of the sentences.

| must have left | couldn't have left | should have left | might have left |

SITUATION: Jackie can't find her sunglasses.

1. Laura thinks it's possible that Jackie left them on the table at the restaurant. She says, "You _____ them on the table at the restaurant, but I'm just guessing."

2. Sergio disagrees. He looked at everything on the table before they left and doesn't remember seeing her sunglasses there. He thinks it is impossible that Jackie left them there, so he says, "You _____ them there. I'm sure they are somewhere else. Did you check your purse?"

3. Maya disagrees with Sergio. She remembers seeing the sunglasses on the table, so she says, "You _____ them there. That's the only logical explanation I can think of."

10-3 Degrees of Certainty: Past Time

Past Time: Affirmative

	— Why wasn't Mary in class?		In (a): The speaker is sure.
(a)	**100%:**	She *was* sick.	In (b): The speaker is making a logical conclusion, e.g., "I saw Mary yesterday and found out that she was sick. I assume that is the reason why she was absent. I can't think of any other good reason."
(b)	**95%:**	She *must have been* sick.	
(c)	**50% sure or less:**	She *may have been* sick. She *might have been* sick. She *could have been* sick.	In (c): The speaker is mentioning one possibility.

Past Time: Negative

	— Why didn't Sam eat?		In (d): The speaker is sure.
(d)	**100%:**	Sam *wasn't* hungry.	In (e): The speaker believes that it is impossible for Sam to have been hungry.
(e)	**99%:**	Sam *couldn't have been* hungry. Sam *can't have been* hungry.	
(f)	**95%:**	Sam *must not have been* hungry.	In (f): The speaker is making a logical conclusion.
(g)	**50% sure or less:**	Sam *may not have been* hungry. Sam *might not have been* hungry.	In (g): The speaker is mentioning one possibility.

❑ **Exercise 12. Looking at grammar.** (Chart 10-3)
Use past modals to restate each sentence in parentheses. In some cases, more than one modal may be possible.

SITUATION 1: The doorbell rang, but I was in bed trying to take a nap. So I didn't get up. I wonder who it was.

1. *(Maybe it was a friend.)* It ____*may / might / could have been*____ a friend.

2. *(It's not possible that it was my next-door neighbor. He was at work.)*

    It _____ my next-door neighbor.

3. *(I'm 95% sure it was a delivery person. There was a package outside my door when I got up.)*

    It _____ a delivery person.

SITUATION 2: I sent my best friend a birthday present, but she never responded or thanked me. That's not like her. I wonder why I never heard from her.

4. *(She probably never got it. That's the only reason I can think of for her not responding to me.)*

    I believe she _____ it.

5. *(My mother thinks it's possible that it got lost in the mail, but she's just guessing.)*

    My mother thinks it _____ lost in the mail. I guess that's possible.

Exercise 13. Let's talk. (Chart 10-3)

Make guesses using past modals.

SITUATION: Dan, David, Dylan, Dick, and Doug are all friends. One of them got engaged last night. Who do you think it is?

1. Dan had a huge argument with his girlfriend last night.
   → *It couldn't/must not have been Dan because he fought with his girlfriend last night.*
2. David met with his girlfriend's parents two nights ago.
3. Dylan invited his girlfriend to dinner and took a diamond ring with him.
4. Dick is going to wait to get married until he has a better job.
5. Doug isn't sure if he's ready for marriage. He thinks he's a little young to be a husband.

Exercise 14. Let's talk or write. (Chart 10-3)

Give several answers for each question, orally or in writing.

1. In 1957 the first animal (Laika, a Russian dog) went into space. How do you think she felt? In 1961 the Russian cosmonaut Yuri Gagarin went into space. How do you think he felt?
2. A fire started in the city park around midnight. A large crowd of people had been there earlier watching a fireworks display. What do you think caused the fire?
3. While the Browns were away on vacation, the security alarm went off at their home. The police arrived and checked the house. No doors had been opened. No windows were broken. Everything looked normal. What do you think set it off? What don't you think set it off?

Exercise 15. Let's talk. (Chart 10-3)

Speaker A asks a question, and Speaker B responds with **may have/might have/could have**. Speaker A provides more information. This time, Speaker B responds with **must have**. Work in pairs, in small groups, or as a class.

Example:
SPEAKER A: Larry was absent yesterday afternoon. Where was he?
SPEAKER B: I don't know. He *may have* been at home. He *might have* gone to a movie. He *could have* decided to go to the zoo because the weather was so nice.
SPEAKER A: Then you overhear him say, "My sister's plane was late yesterday afternoon. I had to wait almost three hours." Now what do you think?
SPEAKER B: He *must have* gone to the airport to meet his sister's plane.

1. A TO B: Beth didn't stay home last night. Where did she go?
   A TO B: Now, what if you overhear her say . . . ?

2. A TO B: How did Claudio get to school today?
   A TO B: Now, what if you hear him say . . . ?

3. A TO B: Sami walked into class yesterday . . . .
   A TO B: Then you overhear him say . . . . Now what do you think?

4. A TO B: (*name of a classmate*) took a vacation in a warm . . . .
   A TO B: Now, what if you overhear him/her say . . . . Now what do you think?

Exercise 16. Looking at grammar. (Charts 10-1 → 10-3)
Complete the dialogues with **must** and the verbs in parentheses. Use **not** if necessary.

1. A: Paula fell asleep in class this morning.

   B: She (*stay up*) _____*must have stayed up*_____ too late last night.

2. A: Jim is eating everything in the salad but the onions. He's pushed all of the onions to the side of his plate.

   B: He (*like*) _____ onions.

3. A: Marco had to give a speech in front of 500 people.

   B: Whew! That's a big audience. He (*be*) _____ nervous.

   A: He was, but no one could tell.

4. A: What time is it?

   B: Well, we came at seven, and I'm sure we've been here for at least an hour. So it (*be*) _____ around eight o'clock.

5. A: I met Ayako's husband at the reception. We said hello to each other, but when I asked him a question in English, he just smiled and nodded.

   B: He (*speak*) _____ much English.

6. A: Listen. Do you hear a buzzing sound in the kitchen?

   B: No, I don't hear a thing.

   A: You don't? Then something (*be*) _____ wrong with your hearing.

7. A: You have a black eye! What happened?

   B: I walked into a door.

   A: Ouch! That (*hurt*) _____.

8. A: Who is your teacher?

   B: I think his name is Mr. Rock, or something like that.

   A: Mr. Rock? Oh, you (*mean*) _____ Mr. Stone.

9. A: I grew up in a small town.

   B: That (*be*) _____ dull.

   A: It wasn't at all. You can't imagine the fun we had.

❏ **Exercise 17. Warm-up.** (Chart 10-4)
Match each sentence to the percentage it best describes.

1. We might get some snow tomorrow.
2. We will get some snow tomorrow.
3. We may get some snow tomorrow.
4. We should get some snow tomorrow.
5. We could get some snow tomorrow.

100%   50%   90%

10-4 Degrees of Certainty: Future Time

100% sure:	Kay *will do* well on the test.	→ The speaker feels sure.
90% sure:	{ Kay *should do* well on the test. Kay *ought to do* well on the test. }	→ The speaker is almost sure.
50% sure or less:	{ She *may do* well on the test. She *might do* well on the test. She *could do* well on the test. }	→ The speaker is guessing.

(a) Kay has been studying hard. She *should do / ought to do* well on the test tomorrow.	***Should/ought to*** can be used to express expectations about future events. In (a): The speaker is saying, "Kay will probably do well on the test. I expect her to do well. That is what I think will happen."
(b) I wonder why Sue hasn't written us. We *should have heard / ought to have heard* from her last week.	The past form of ***should/ought to*** is used to mean that the speaker expected something that did not occur.

❑ **Exercise 18. Looking at grammar.** (Chart 10-4)
Complete the sentences with the speakers' names based on how certain they are.

SITUATION: Jan asked her roommates, "What time are you going to be home tonight?"
CERTAINTY: **Marco** feels 100% sure.
  Linda is almost sure.
  Ned doesn't know. He's guessing.

1. _____ said, "I might be back by ten."

2. _____ said, "I'll be home by eight."

3. _____ said, "I should be here around nine."

❑ **Exercise 19. Looking at grammar.** (Charts 4-2, 10-1, and 10-4)
Complete the sentences with *will*, *should/ought to*, or *must*. In some cases, more than one modal is possible. Discuss the meanings that the modals convey.★

1. Lots of people are standing in line to get into that movie. It ____*must*____ be good.

2. Let's go to the lecture tonight. It ___*should / ought to* OR *will*___ be interesting.

3. Look. Jack's car is in front of his house. He _____ be at home. Let's stop and visit him.

4. A: Hello. May I speak to Elena?
   B: She isn't here right now, but she _____ be home around nine or so.

★COMPARE: *Must* expresses a strong degree of certainty about a present situation. (See Chart 10-1.) *Should* and *ought to* express a fairly strong degree of certainty about a future situation. (See Chart 10-4.) *Will* indicates that there is no doubt in the speaker's mind about a future event. (See Chart 4-2, p. 63.)

5. A: Who do you think is going to win the game tomorrow?

B: Well, our team has better players, so we _____ win, but you never know. Anything can happen in sports.

6. A: It's very important for you to be there on time.

B: I _____ be there at seven o'clock. I promise!

7. A: Susie is yawning and rubbing her eyes.

B: She _____ be sleepy. Let's put her to bed early tonight.

8. A: Martha has been working all day. She left for work early this morning.

B: She _____ be really tired tonight.

9. A: When's dinner?

B: We're almost ready to eat. The rice _____ be done in five minutes.

10. Ed has been acting strangely lately. He _____ be in love.

11. Hmmm. I wonder what's causing the delay. Ellen's plane _____ been here an hour ago.

12. I thought I had some money in my wallet, but I don't. I _____ spent it.

❏ **Exercise 20. Looking at grammar.** (Charts 10-1 → 10-4)
Complete the sentences based on the facts of each situation.

SITUATION 1: Someone's knocking at the door. I wonder who it is.
FACTS: **Ross** is out of town.
Fred called half an hour ago and said he would stop by this afternoon.
Alice is a neighbor who sometimes drops by in the middle of the day.

1. It must be _____Fred_____.

2. It couldn't be _____Ross_____.

3. I suppose it might be _____Alice_____.

Situation 2: Someone ran into the tree in front of our house. I wonder who did it.
  Facts: **Stacy** has a car, and she was out driving last night.
    Beth doesn't have a car and doesn't know how to drive.
    Ron has a car, but I'm pretty sure he was at home last night.
    Barb was out driving last night, and today her car has a big dent in the front.

4. It couldn't have been _____.

5. It must not have been _____.

6. It could have been _____.

7. It must have been _____.

Situation 3: There is a hole in the bread. It looks like something ate some of the bread. The bread was in a closed drawer until I opened it.
  Facts: **A mouse** likes to eat bread and often gets into drawers. In fact, we found one last week.
    A cat can't open a drawer. And most cats don't like bread.
    A rat can sometimes get into a drawer, but I've never seen one in our house.

8. It could have been _____.

9. It couldn't have been _____.

10. It must have been _____.

Situation 4: My friends Mark and Carol were in the next room with my neighbor. I heard someone playing a very difficult piece on the piano.
  Facts: **Mark** has no musical ability at all and doesn't play any instrument.
    Carol is an excellent piano player.
    I don't think **my neighbor** plays the piano, but I'm not sure.

11. It couldn't have been _____.

12. I suppose it could have been _____.

13. It must have been _____.

Situation 5: The meeting starts in fifteen minutes. I wonder who is coming.
  Facts: I just talked to **Bob** on the phone. He's on his way.
    Stephanie rarely misses a meeting.
    Andre comes to the meetings sometimes, and sometimes he doesn't.
    Janet is out of town.

14. _____ won't be at the meeting.

15. _____ should be at the meeting.

16. _____ will be here.

17. _____ might come.

☐ **Exercise 21. Listening.** (Chapter 9 and Charts 10-1 → 10-4)

The spoken forms of some modals are often reduced. For example, ***may have gone*** may sound like "may-uv gone" or "may-uh gone." Listen for the spoken forms of modals and write the non-reduced forms of the words you hear.

Example: You will hear: You shouldn't have done that.
            You will write: You _____*shouldn't have done*_____ that.

What's wrong? Your parents look upset.

1. We _____ them.

2. We _____ them.

3. You _____ them.

4. You _____ to find out.

5. Maybe you _____ out so late.

6. You _____ a good excuse for being late.

7. You _____ them what you planned to do.

8. You _____ your behavior would cause problems.

☐ **Exercise 22. Let's talk: pairwork.** (Charts 10-1 → 10-4)

Work with a partner. Choose one of the given situations and complete the dialogue. Then present your dialogue to the rest of the class. Try to include modals in your conversation.

SITUATION 1: Your teacher is always on time, but today it is fifteen minutes past the time class begins, and he/she still isn't here. You try to figure out why he/she isn't here yet and what you should do.

A: Mr./Mrs./Ms.*/Miss/Dr./Professor (_____) should have been here fifteen minutes ago. I wonder where he/she is. Why do you suppose he/she hasn't arrived yet?
B: I don't know . . . .
Etc.

SITUATION 2: The two of you are supposed to meet Anita and Pablo at the park for a picnic. You are almost ready to leave when the sky gets dark and the wind starts blowing very hard.

A: Is the picnic basket all packed?
B: Yes. Everything's ready.
A: Wow! Do you feel that wind?
B: Yeah, and look at the sky!
Etc.

---

*In American English, a period is used with the abbreviations *Mr./Mrs./Ms.;* British English does not use a period with these abbreviations.
  American: *Mr. Black/Mrs. Green/Ms. Brown*
  British: *Mr Black/Mrs Green/Ms Brown*

SITUATION 3: It is late at night. The roads are icy. Your eighteen-year-old son, who had gone to a party with some friends, was supposed to be home an hour ago. (The two of you are either a married couple or a parent and his/her friend.) You are getting worried. You are trying to figure out where he might be, what might or must have happened, and what you should do, if anything.

A: It's already _____ o'clock and _____ isn't home yet. I'm getting worried.
B: So am I. Where do you suppose he is?
Etc.

❑ **Exercise 23. Warm-up.** (Chart 10-5)
Do the verbs in blue express the idea that something is (or may be) in progress right now, at the time of speaking? Circle *yes* or *no*.

		IN PROGRESS?	
1.	Grandpa takes a nap every afternoon.	yes	no
2.	Grandpa may take a nap this afternoon.	yes	no
3.	Shhh. Grandpa is taking a nap.	yes	no
4.	Shhh. Grandpa may be taking a nap.	yes	no

10-5 Progressive Forms of Modals

(a) Let's just knock on the door lightly. Tom *may be sleeping.* (*right now*)	Progressive form, present time: *modal* + ***be*** + ***-ing***
(b) All of the lights in Ann's room are turned off. She *must be sleeping.* (*right now*)	Meaning: *in progress right now*
(c) Sue wasn't at home last night when we went to visit her. She *might have been studying* at the library.	Progressive form, past time: *modal* + ***have been*** + ***-ing***
(d) Joe wasn't at home last night. He has a lot of exams coming up soon, and he is also working on a term paper. He *must have been studying* at the library.	Meaning: *in progress at a time in the past*

❑ **Exercise 24. Looking at grammar.** (Chart 10-5)
Complete the sentences. Use the appropriate progressive forms of ***must, should,*** or ***may/might/could*** and the verbs in parentheses.

1. A: Look. Those people who are coming in the door are carrying wet umbrellas.

   B: It (*rain*) _____*must be raining*_____.

2. A: Why is Margaret in her room?

   B: I don't know. She (*do*) _____*may / might / could be doing*_____ her homework.

3. A: Do you smell smoke?

   B: I sure do. Something (*burn*) _____ in the kitchen.

4. A: The line's been busy for over an hour. Who do you suppose Julio is talking to?

   B: I don't know. He (*talk*) _____ to his parents. Or he

   (*talk*) _____ to his sister in Chicago.

5. A: What's all that noise upstairs? It sounds like a herd of elephants.

   B: The children (*play*) _____ some kind of game.

   A: That's what it sounds like to me too. I'll go see.

6. A: I need to call Howard. Do you know which hotel he's staying at in Boston?

   B: Well, he (*stay*) _____ at the Hilton, but I'm not sure.

   He (*stay*) _____ at the Holiday Inn.

7. A: What are you doing?

   B: I'm writing a letter to a friend, but I (*study*) _____. I have a

   test tomorrow.

8. A: Did you know that Majid just quit school and is hitchhiking to Alaska?

   B: What? You (*joke*) _____?

9. A: Did Joe mean what he said about Majid yesterday?

   B: I don't know. He (*joke*) _____ when he said that, but

   who knows?

10. A: Did Joe really mean what he said yesterday?

    B: No, I don't think so. I think he (*joke*) _____.

❏ **Exercise 25. Let's talk.** (Chart 10-5)
Discuss what the students on the bus **should** and **should not be doing**.

*Example: The student in the middle of the bus **shouldn't be climbing** out of the window to the top of the bus.*

❑ **Exercise 26. Looking at grammar.** (Charts 9-8 and 10-1 → 10-5)
Complete each sentence with the appropriate form of the words in parentheses. Add *not* if necessary.

1. Alex has a test tomorrow that he needs to study for. He (*should + watch*)

   _____*shouldn't be watching*_____ TV right now.

2. There's Mr. Chang. He's standing at the bus stop. He (*must + wait*)

   _____ for the two o'clock bus.

3. Kathy lost her way while driving to River City. She (*should + leave*)

   _____ her road map at home.

4. My leather jacket isn't in my closet. I think my roommate (*might + borrow*)

   _____ it. He often borrows my clothes without asking me.

5. When I walked into the room, the TV was on, but the room was empty. Dad

   (*must + watch*) _____ TV a short while before I came

   into the room. He (*must + forget*) _____ to turn it off

   before he left the room.

6. A: Why wasn't Mai at the meeting last night?

   B: She (*may + attend*) _____ the lecture at Shaw Hall. I know she

   really wanted to hear the speaker.

7. A: Where's that cold air coming from?

   B: Someone (*must + leave*) _____ the door open.

8. A: Where's Jessica? I haven't seen her for weeks.

   B: I'm not sure. She (*might + travel*) _____ in Europe.

   I think I heard her mention something about spending a few weeks in Europe this

   spring.

9. A: When I arrived, Tarek looked surprised.

   B: He (*must + expect*) _____ you.

10. A: Why didn't Roberto answer the teacher when she asked him a question?

    B: He was too busy staring out the window. He (*must + daydream*) _____

    _____. He (*should + pay*) _____

    attention. He (*should + stare*) _____ out the

    window during class.

❑ **Exercise 27. Let's talk or write.** (Charts 10-1 → 10-5)
Discuss and/or write about the people and activities in the picture. Include any factual information you can get from the picture and make guesses about the people: their ages, occupations, activities, etc.

❑ **Exercise 28. Let's talk.** (Charts 10-1 → 10-5)
A man and woman are sitting at a table having a conversation. In pairs or small groups, make guesses about the two people and what's happening. What possibilities can you think of? Answer the questions and add your own to the discussion.

MAN: I don't think you should do this alone.
WOMAN: But you don't understand. I have to.
MAN: Let me go with you. (*taking out his wallet*) Just give me a minute to pay the bill.
WOMAN: No, I'll be fine.
MAN: You must let me help.
WOMAN: There's nothing you can do. (*standing*) This is something I need to do for myself.
MAN: Okay. If that's the way you want it.
WOMAN: (*leaving*) I'll call you.

1. Where are the man and woman?
2. Who are they? What is their relationship?
3. Where's the woman going?
4. Why does she want to go alone?
5. Why does the man want to go with her?

Exercise 29. Looking at grammar. (Charts 10-1 → 10-5)
Choose the best completion for each sentence.

1. — Is Jeff a good student?
   — He _____ . I don't know him well, but I heard he got a scholarship for next year.
   a. must be   b. could be   c. is

2. — Do you know where Eva is?
   — She _____ at Barbara's house. She said something about wanting to visit after work today, but I'm really not sure.
   a. must be   b. could be   c. is

3. — I stayed up all night finishing this report for the boss.
   —You _____ really tired.
   — I do.
   a. must feel   b. might feel   c. feel

4. —Where's the leftover chicken from dinner last night?
   — I just saw it when I got some ice cubes. It _____ in the freezer.
   a. must be   b. might be   c. is

5. — It's supposed to rain tomorrow.
   — I know, but the forecast _____ wrong. Weather forecasts are far from 100 percent accurate.
   a. must be   b. could be   c. is

6. — I heard that Junko has received a scholarship and will be able to attend the university in the fall.
   —Wonderful! That's good news. She _____ very happy to have the matter finally settled.
   a. must be   b. may be   c. is

7. — Excuse me. Could you tell me which bus I should take to get to City Hall?
   — Hmmm. Bus number 63 _____ there. But you'd better ask the driver.
   a. must go   b. might go   c. goes

8. —Which bus should I take to get to the main post office?
   — Bus number 39. It _____ right to the post office.
   a. must go   b. could go   c. goes

9. — Do you suppose Mrs. Chu is sick?
   — She _____ . I can't think of anything else that would have kept her from coming to this meeting.
   a. must be   b. may be   c. is

10. — Is that Adam's brother standing with him in the cafeteria line?
    — It _____ , I suppose. He does look a little like Adam.
    a. must be   b. could be   c. is

11. — Let's be really quiet when we go into the baby's room. The baby _____ , and we don't want to wake her up.

— Okay.

a. might sleep   b. might be sleeping   c. might have been sleeping

12. — I wonder why the radio is on in the den. No one's in there.

— Grandma _____ to turn it off. She was in the den earlier and was probably listening to it.

a. must forget   b. must have forgotten   c. must be forgetting

❑ **Exercise 30. Warm-up.** (Chart 10-6)
Which sentence expresses

a. a physical ability?
b. an acquired skill?
c. possibility?
d. permission?

1. _____ Isabel can play chess very well.

2. _____ Yes, Ben, you can go outside to play, but be back before dinner.

3. _____ Dogs can hear higher-pitched sounds than humans can.

4. _____ I'm free for lunch tomorrow. I can meet you at the café around noon if you'd like.

10-6 Ability: *Can* and *Could*

(a) Tom is strong. He *can lift* that heavy box.	***Can*** is used to express physical ability, as in (a).
(b) I *can see* Central Park from my apartment.	***Can*** is frequently used with verbs of the five senses: *see, hear, feel, smell, taste*, as in (b).
(c) Maria *can play* the piano. She's been taking lessons for many years.	***Can*** is used to express an acquired skill. In (c): *can play = knows how to play.*
(d) You *can buy* a hammer at the hardware store.	***Can*** is used to express possibility. In (d): *you can buy = it is possible for one to buy.*
COMPARE: (e) I'm not quite ready to go, but you *can leave* if you're in a hurry. I'll meet you later. (f) When you finish the test, you *may leave.*	***Can*** is used to give permission in informal situations, as in (e). In formal situations, ***may*** rather than ***can*** is usually used to give permission, as in (f).
(g) Dogs *can bark*, but they *cannot/can't talk*.	Negative form: ***cannot*** or ***can't***
(h) Tom *could lift* the box, but I *couldn't*.	The past form of ***can*** meaning "ability" is ***could***, as in (h). Negative form: ***could not*** or ***couldn't***

Exercise 31. Listening. (Chart 10-6)

In spoken English, **can** is typically unstressed and pronounced /kən/. **Can't** is unstressed and is usually pronounced /kænt/ although the "t" is often not heard. Listen to the sentences and write the words you hear.★

CD 1
Track 51

1. The secretary _____ help you.

2. My mother _____ speak English.

3. My friend _____ meet you at the airport.

4. Mr. Smith _____ answer your question.

5. We _____ come to the meeting.

6. _____ you come?★★

7. You _____ take that course.

8. I _____ cook.

9. I _____ drive a stick-shift car.

10. Our son _____ count to ten.

❏ **Exercise 32. Let's talk.** (Charts 10-4 and 10-6)

Make sentences, answer questions, and/or discuss meanings as suggested in each item. Work in pairs, in small groups, or as a class.

1. Name a physical ability that you have and a physical ability you don't have. Name an acquired skill that you have and an acquired skill you don't have.

2. There's no class tomorrow. What can you do tomorrow? What may/might you do tomorrow? What are you going to do tomorrow?

3. What are the possible ways you can get to school? What are the possible ways you may get to school tomorrow?

4. What is the difference in the use of **can** and **may** in the following?
   a. Sure! You can borrow five dollars from me. You can pay me back later.
   b. You may pay the bill either in person or by mail.

5. Compare the following using **can** and **can't**: people and animals; adults and children; women and men.

6. Plan your next vacation and describe what you may do on your vacation; what you can do on your vacation; and what you will do on your vacation.

7. What is something you could do as a child that you can't do now?

★Sometimes even native speakers have difficulty in distinguishing between **can** and **can't**. Also, British and American pronunciations of **can't** are different. British: **can't** = /kant/ (cawhnt). American: **can't** = /kænt/ (rhymes with *rant*).
★★NOTE: "t" + "you" = "chu" (*can't you* = /kænču/).

Exercise 33. Let's listen and talk. (Charts 10-1 → 10-6)

CD 1
Track 52

Listen to the short talk on human behavior with your book closed. Then open your book and answer the questions.

1. Who did the researcher talk to first?
2. Who did the researcher talk to later?
3. What three questions did the researcher ask each group?
4. How many people in the first group answered "yes" to the questions about their ability to dance, sing, and draw?
5. What differences were there in the answers of the first group and the second group?
6. What do you think explains these differences?

❏ **Exercise 34. Warm-up.** (Chart 10-7)

Are the meanings of the two sentences the same or different?

1. When I was a child, I used to play in the street with the other children.
2. When I was a child, I would play in the street with the other children.

10-7 **Using *Would* to Express a Repeated Action in the Past**	
(a) When I was a child, my father *would read* me a story at night before bedtime. (b) When I was a child, my father *used to read* me a story at night before bedtime.	***Would*** can be used to express *an action that was repeated regularly in the past.* When ***would*** is used to express this idea, it has the same meaning as ***used to*** (*habitual past*). Sentences (a) and (b) have the same meaning.
(c) I *used to live* in California. He *used to be* a Boy Scout. They *used to have* a Ford.	***Used to*** expresses *a situation that existed in the past,* as in (c). In this case, ***would*** may not be used as an alternative. ***Would*** is used only for regularly repeated *actions* in the past.

❏ **Exercise 35. Looking at grammar.** (Chart 10-7)

Use ***would*** and the words in parentheses to express a repeated action in the past. Use ***used to*** to express a past situation.

1. I (*be*) _____used to be_____ very shy. Whenever a stranger came to our house, I (*hide*)
   _____would hide_____ in a closet.

2. I remember my Aunt Susan very well. Every time she came to our house, she (*give*)
   _____ me a big kiss and pinch my cheek.

3. Illiteracy is still a problem in my country, but it (*be*) _____
   much worse.

4. I (*be*) _____ afraid of flying. My heart (*start*) _____
   pounding every time I stepped on a plane. But now I'm used to flying and enjoy it.

5. When I was a child, I (*take*) _____ a flashlight to bed with me so that I could read comic books without my parents knowing about it.

6. My sister (*live*) _____ in Montana, and when I visited her, we (*go*) _____ on weeklong backpacking trips in the mountains. Every morning, we (*wake*) _____ up to the sound of singing birds. During the day, we (*hike*) _____ through woods and along mountain streams. Often we (*see*) _____ deer. Once we saw a bear, but it went off in the opposite direction.

7. I (*be*) _____ an anthropology major. Once, I was a member of an archeological expedition. Every morning, we (*get*) _____ up before dawn. After breakfast, we (*spend*) _____ our entire day in the field. Sometimes one of us (*find*) _____ a particularly interesting item, perhaps an arrowhead or a piece of pottery. When that happened, other members of the group (*gather*) _____ around to see what had been unearthed.

❏ **Exercise 36. Warm-up.** (Chart 10-8)
Answer the questions. Use **would rather** and complete sentences.

1. You are at school right now. Where would you rather be?
2. What would you rather do than go to class?
3. What did you do last night? What would you rather have done?
4. What are you doing right now? What would you rather be doing?

10-8 Expressing Preference: *Would Rather*

(a) I *would rather go* to a movie tonight *than study* grammar. (b) I'*d rather study* history *than* (*study*) biology.	***Would rather*** expresses preference. In (a): Notice that the simple form of a verb follows both ***would rather*** and ***than***. In (b): If the verb is the same, it usually is not repeated after ***than***.
— *How much do you weigh?* (c) I'*d rather not tell* you.	Contraction: **I would = I'd** Negative form: **would rather + not**
(d) The movie was okay, but I *would rather have gone* to the concert last night.	The past form: **would rather have** + *past participle*. Usual pronunciation: "I'd rather-əv"
(e) I'*d rather be lying* on a beach in India than (*be*) *sitting* in class right now.	Progressive form: **would rather + be + -ing**

❑ **Exercise 37. Looking at grammar.** (Chart 10-8)
Complete the sentences with ***would rather*** and your own words.

1. A: Do you want to go to the concert tonight?

   B: Not really. I _____

2. A: Did you go to the concert last night?

   B: Yes, but I _____

3. A: What are you doing right now?

   B: I'm studying grammar, but I _____

4. A: I _____ than _____

   B: Not me. I _____ than _____

❑ **Exercise 38. Let's talk: interview.** (Chart 10-8)
Interview your classmates. Begin each question with ***Would you rather***.

Would you rather . . .
1. go to Paris, Cairo, or Bogota? Why?
2. see a movie, a play, or an opera? Why?
3. use a bike, a motorcycle, or a car for transportation? Why?
4. prepare your own meals, have someone at home prepare them, or eat out? Why?
5. be playing soccer, shopping for clothes, or feeding birds in the park today? Why?
6. have been born in an earlier century? Why?
7. be swimming at a beach or pool right now or doing this interview? Why?

❑ **Exercise 39. Warm-up.** (Chart 10-9)
Check (✓) each correct sentence.

1. ____ I will can stay late at the office today.
2. ____ I will be able stay late today.
3. ____ I may have to stay late today.
4. ____ I may be able to stay late today.
5. ____ I will have to stay late today.
6. ____ I'm going to have to stay late today.

10-9 Combining Modals with Phrasal Modals

(a) INCORRECT: Janet will ~~can~~ help you tomorrow.	A modal cannot be immediately followed by another modal. In (a): The modal ***will*** cannot be followed by ***can***, which is another modal.
(b) Janet ***will be able to*** help you tomorrow. (c) You ***will have to*** pick her up at her home.	A modal can, however, be followed by the phrasal modals ***be able to*** and ***have to***. In (b): The modal ***will*** is correctly followed by the phrasal modal ***be able to***.
(d) Tom ***isn't going to be able to*** help you tomorrow.	It is also sometimes possible for one phrasal modal to follow another phrasal modal. In (d): ***be going to*** is followed by ***be able to***. This form is more common in negatives and questions.

□ **Exercise 40. Looking at grammar.** (Chart 10-9)
Complete the sentences with the words in *italics*.

1. *be able to \ you \ get \ will*

    What time _____ here?

2. *have to \ take \ be going to*

    You _____ algebra again next year if you

    don't pass the course this year.

3. *be able to \ attend \ be going to \ not*

    I _____ my friend

    Jess's wedding next month due to a previously scheduled business trip.

□ **Exercise 41. Looking at grammar.** (Chart 10-9)
Complete the sentences with the verb phrases in the list. In some cases, more than one
completion may be possible. Discuss the differences in meaning.

have to be able to	must not have been able to
should not have to	would rather not have to
✓not be going to be able to	

1. My schedule is completely full for the next few weeks. I *'m not going to be able to* _____

    meet with you until the end of the month.

2. You need to see a doctor you feel comfortable talking to. It's important that she knows

    how you feel. You _____ tell her exactly

    how you're feeling.

3. Jill just called from work. She sounded upset, but she won't tell me what's wrong. She

    was planning to ask her supervisor for a raise today. I bet that's the problem. She

    _____ get the raise.

4. Let's get to the movie a little late. I don't mind if we miss the previews. It's freezing

    outside, and I _____ stand in a long line

    outdoors until the movie begins.

5. Children, this room is a mess! I am not going to tell you again to clean it up. Really, I

    _____ tell you this more than once!

10-10 Summary Chart of Modals and Similar Expressions

Auxiliary	Uses	Present/Future	Past
may	(1) polite request (only with "I" or "we")	*May* I *borrow* your pen?	
	(2) formal permission	You *may leave* the room.	
	(3) 50% or less certainty	— *Where's John?* He *may be* at the library.	He *may have been* at the library.
might	(1) 50% or less certainty	— *Where's John?* He *might be* at the library.	He *might have been* at the library.
	(2) polite request (*rare*)	*Might* I *borrow* your pen?	
should	(1) advisability	I *should study* tonight.	I *should have studied* last night, but I didn't.
	(2) 90% certainty (*expectation*)	She *should do* well on the test tomorrow.	She *should have done* well on the test.
ought to	(1) advisability	I *ought to study* tonight.	I *ought to have studied* last night, but I didn't.
	(2) 90% certainty (*expectation*)	She *ought to do* well on the test tomorrow.	She *ought to have done* well on the test.
had better	(1) advisability with threat of bad result	You *had better be* on time, or we will leave without you.	(*past form uncommon*)
be supposed to	(1) expectation	Class *is supposed to begin* at 10:00.	
	(2) unfulfilled expectation		Class *was supposed to begin* at 10:00, but it began at 10:15.
must	(1) strong necessity	I *must go* to class today.	(I *had to go* to class yesterday.)
	(2) prohibition (*negative*)	You *must not* open that door.	
	(3) 95% certainty	Mary isn't in class. She *must be* sick.	Mary *must have been* sick yesterday.
have to	(1) necessity	I *have to go* to class today.	I *had to go* to class yesterday.
	(2) lack of necessity (*negative*)	I *don't have to go* to class today.	I *didn't have to go* to class yesterday.
have got to	(1) necessity	I *have got to go* to class today.	(I *had to go* to class yesterday.)
will	(1) 100% certainty	He *will be* here at 6:00.	
	(2) willingness	— *The phone's ringing.* I*'ll get* it.	
	(3) polite request	*Will* you please help me?	
be going to	(1) 100% certainty (*prediction*)	He *is going to be* here at 6:00.	
	(2) definite plan (*intention*)	I*'m going to paint* my bedroom.	
	(3) unfulfilled intention		I *was going to paint* my room, but I didn't have time.

Auxiliary	Uses	Present/Future	Past
can	(1) ability/possibility	I *can run* fast.	I *could run* fast when I was a child, but now I can't.
	(2) informal permission	You *can use* my car tomorrow.	
	(3) informal polite request	*Can* I *borrow* your pen?	
	(4) impossibility (*negative only*)	That *can't be* true!	That *can't have been* true!
could	(1) past ability		I *could run* fast when I was a child.
	(2) polite request	*Could* I *borrow* your pen? *Could* you *help* me?	
	(3) suggestion (*affirmative only*)	— *I need help in math.* You *could talk* to your teacher.	You *could have talked* to your teacher.
	(4) 50% or less certainty	— *Where's John?* He *could be* at home.	He *could have been* at home.
	(5) impossibility (*negative only*)	That *couldn't be* true!	That *couldn't have been* true!
be able to	(1) ability	I *am able to help* you. I *will be able to help* you.	I *was able to help* him.
would	(1) polite request	*Would* you please *help* me? *Would* you *mind* if I left early?	
	(2) preference	I *would rather go* to the park than *stay* home.	I *would rather have gone* to the park.
	(3) repeated action in the past		When I was a child, I *would visit* my grandparents every weekend.
	(4) polite for "want" (with "like")	I *would like* an apple, please.	
	(5) unfulfilled wish		I *would have liked* a cookie, but there were none in the house.
used to	(1) repeated action in the past.		I *used to visit* my grandparents every weekend.
	(2) past situation that no longer exists		I *used to live* in Spain. Now I live in Korea.
shall	(1) polite question to make a suggestion	*Shall* I *open* the window?	
	(2) future with *I* or *we* as subject	I *shall arrive* at nine. ("will" = more common)	

NOTE: The use of modals in reported speech is discussed in Chart 12-7, p. 261. The use of modals in conditional sentences is discussed in Chapter 20.

□ **Exercise 42. Let's talk.** (Chapters 9 and 10)
Discuss the differences in meaning, if any, in each group of sentences. Describe situations in which these sentences might be used. Work in pairs, in small groups, or as a class.

1. a. May I use your phone?
   b. Could I use your phone?
   c. Can I use your phone?

2. a. You should take an English course.
   b. You ought to take an English course.
   c. You're supposed to take an English course.
   d. You must take an English course.

3. a. You should see a doctor about that cut on your arm.
   b. You had better see a doctor about that cut on your arm.
   c. You have to see a doctor about that cut on your arm.

4. a. You must not use that door.
   b. You don't have to use that door.

5. a. I will be at your house by six o'clock.
   b. I should be at your house by six o'clock.

6. — *There is a knock at the door. Who do you suppose it is?*
   a. It might be Wendy.
   b. It may be Wendy.
   c. It could be Wendy.
   d. It must be Wendy.

7. — *There's a knock at the door. I think it's Ibrahim.*
   a. It may not be Ibrahim.
   b. It couldn't be Ibrahim.
   c. It can't be Ibrahim.

8. a. The family in the picture must be at a restaurant.
   b. The family in the picture are at a restaurant.

9. — *Where's Jeff?*
   a. He might have gone home.
   b. He must have gone home.
   c. He had to go home.

10. a. Each student should have health insurance.
    b. Each student must have health insurance.

11. a. If you're having a problem, you could talk to Mrs. Ang.
    b. If you're having a problem, you should talk to Mrs. Ang.
    c. If you're having a problem, you should have told Mrs. Ang.
    d. If you're having a problem, you could have told Mrs. Ang.

❏ **Exercise 43. Looking at grammar.** (Chapters 9 and 10)
Use a modal or phrasal modal with each verb in parentheses. More than one auxiliary may be possible. Use the one that seems most appropriate to you and explain why.

1. It looks like rain. We (*shut*) _____*should / had better / ought to shut*_____ the windows.

2. Anya, (*you, hand*) _____ me that dish? Thanks.

3. Spring break starts on the thirteenth. We (*go, not*) _____ to classes again until the twenty-second.

4. The baby is only a year old, but she (*say, already*) _____ a few words.

5. In the United States, elementary education is compulsory. All children (*attend*) _____ six years of elementary school.

6. There was a long line in front of the theater. We (*wait*) _____ almost an hour to buy our tickets.

7. A: I'd like to go to a warm, sunny place next winter. Any suggestions?
   B: You (*go*) _____ to Hawaii or Mexico. Or how about Indonesia?

8. A: Mrs. Wilson got a traffic ticket. She didn't stop at a stop sign.
   B: That's surprising. Usually she's a very cautious driver and obeys all the traffic laws. She (*see, not*) _____ the sign.

9. A: This is Steve's laptop, isn't it?
   B: It (*be, not*) _____ his. He doesn't have a laptop computer, at least not that I know of. It (*belong*) _____ to Jana or to Mindy. They sometimes bring their laptops to class.

10. In my country, a girl and boy (*go, not*) _____ out on a date unless they are accompanied by a chaperone.

11. Jimmy was serious when he said he wanted to be a cowboy when he grew up. We (*laugh, not*) _____ at him. We hurt his feelings.

12. A: This is a great open-air market. Look at all this wonderful fresh fish! What kind of fish is this?
    B: I'm not sure. It (*be*) _____ salmon. Let's ask.

Exercise 44. Listening. (Chapters 9 and 10)

Listen to each situation and choose the statement (a. or b.) you would most likely say. In some cases, <u>both</u> answers may be possible.

CD 1
Track 53

Example: You will hear: It's almost 5:00. Peter's mom will be home soon. She told him to clean his room today, but it's still a mess. She's going to be really mad.

You will choose: a. He might clean it up right away.
                 (b.) He'd better clean it up right away.

1. a. He should have come.
    b. He must have come.

2. a. I am supposed to go to the mall and shop.
    b. I would rather lie in the sun and read a novel.

3. a. He may have gotten caught in traffic.
    b. He ought to have called by now.

4. a. He's not going to be able to go to work for a few days.
    b. He might not have to go to work today.

5. a. She could have been daydreaming.
    b. She must have been daydreaming.

❑ **Exercise 45. Check your knowledge.** (Chapters 9 and 10)
Correct the errors.

1. If you have a car, you can traveled around the United States.

2. During class the students must to sit quietly.

3. When you send for the brochure, you should included a self-addressed, stamped envelope.

4. A film director must has control over every aspect of a movie.

5. When I was a child, I can climb to the roof of my house and saw all the other houses and

    streets.

6. We need to reschedule. I won't can see you at the time we scheduled for tomorrow.

7. I used to break my leg in a soccer game three months ago.

8. May you please help me with this?

9. Many students would rather to study on their own than going to classes.

10. We supposed to bring our books to class every day.

11. You can having a very good time as a tourist in my country. My country has many

    different climates, so you have better plan ahead before you came.

12. When you visit a big city in my country, you must to be paying attention to your wallet when you are in a crowded place because a thief maybe try to steal it.

❑ **Exercise 46. Let's talk: pairwork.** (Chapters 9 and 10)
Work with a partner. Complete the dialogues with your own words.

Example:
SPEAKER A: Why don't we . . . *go to Luigi's Restaurant for lunch?*
SPEAKER B: Thanks, but I can't. I have to . . . *stay and finish this report during lunchtime.*
SPEAKER A: That's too bad.
SPEAKER B: I should have . . . *come early this morning to finish it,* but I couldn't. I had to . . . *drop my daughter off at school and meet with her teacher.*

1. A: I . . . .
   B: You shouldn't have done that!
   A: I know, but . . . .
   B: Well, why don't . . . ?

2. A: Did you hear the news? We don't have to . . . .
   B: Why not?
   A: . . . .

3. A: Whose . . . ?
   B: I don't know. It . . . , or it . . . .
   A: Can . . . ?
   B: I'll try.

4. A: Did . . . ?
   B: I would have liked to, but I . . . .

5. A: I heard that . . . .
   B: That can't be true! She couldn't . . . .
   A: Oh? Why not? Why do you say that?
   B: Because . . . .

6. A: Did you have to . . . ?
   B: Yes.
   A: Are you going to have to do the same tonight?
   B: I think so. So I'm probably not going to be able to . . . .
      But I might be able to . . . .

7. A: I don't want . . . .
   B: Well, you'd better . . . , or . . . .
   A: I know, but . . . .

❑ **Exercise 47. Let's talk.** (Chapters 9 and 10)
In small groups, debate one, some, or all of the given statements. At the end of the discussion time, choose one member of your group to summarize for the rest of the class the main ideas expressed during your discussion.

Do you agree with these statements? Why or why not?
1. Violence on television influences people to act violently.
2. Cigarette smoking should be banned from all public places.
3. Books, films, and news should be censored by government agencies.
4. People of different religions should not marry.
5. People shouldn't marry until they are at least 25 years old.
6. All nuclear weapons in the possession of any nation should be destroyed.
7. All people of the world should speak the same language.

Exercise 48. Let's write or talk. (Chapters 9 and 10)

Write a short paragraph on one or more of the given topics or discuss some of them in small groups or as a class.

Topics:

1. Write about when, where, and why you should (or should not) have done something in your life.

2. Write about a time in your life when you did something you did not want to do. Why did you do it? What could you have done differently? What should you have done? What would you rather have done?

3. Look at your future. What will, might, or should it be like? Write about what you should, must, or can do now in order to make your life what you want it to be.

4. Write about one embarrassing incident in your life. What could, should, or might you have done to avoid it?

5. Look at the world situation and the relationships between nations. What could, should (or should not), must (or must not) be done to promote peace?

6. Choose one of the environmental problems we are facing today. What could, should, may, must, or might be done to solve this problem?

Chapter 11
The Passive

❑ **Exercise 1. Warm-up.** (Chart 11-1)
Match the sentences to the pictures. Which sentence is grammatically incorrect?

1. The girl hit the ball.
2. The ball was hit by the girl.
3. The girl was hit by the ball.
4. The ball hit the girl.
5. The girl was hitting the ball.
6. The girl was hit the ball.

Picture A   Picture B

11-1	Active vs. Passive	
Active:	(a) <u>Mary</u> (subject) <u>helped</u> (verb) <u>the boy</u>. (object)	In the passive, *the object* of an active verb becomes *the subject* of the passive verb: **the boy** in (a) becomes the subject of the passive verb in (b).
Passive:	(b) <u>The boy</u> (subject) <u>was helped</u> (verb) by Mary.	Notice that the subject of an active verb follows **by** in a passive sentence. The noun that follows **by** is called the "agent." In (b): **Mary** is the agent. Sentences (a) and (b) have the same meaning.
Passive:	(c) He *is* *helped* by her. / He *was* *helped* by her. / He *will be* *helped* by her. (**be** + *past participle*)	Form of the passive: **be** + *past participle*
Active: Passive:	(d) An accident *happened*. (e) (none)	Only transitive verbs (verbs that can be followed by an object) are used in the passive. It is not possible to use intransitive verbs (such as *happen, sleep, come, seem, die*) in the passive. (See Appendix Chart A-1.)

❑ **Exercise 2. Looking at grammar.** (Chart 11-1)
Decide if the sentences are active (A) or passive (P).

1. __A__ Kate prepared the salad.

2. __P__ The rice was prepared by Jamal.

3. _____ Shirley was preparing the dessert.

4. _____ Andy has prepared the tea.

5. _____ New species of insects are discovered by scientists every year.

6. _____ Our papers will be collected by the teacher next week.

7. _____ Dinosaurs existed millions of years ago.

8. _____ Anna's car was stopped by the police.

9. _____ Mr. Brown painted our house.

10. _____ Hiroki came to our apartment for dinner last night.

❑ **Exercise 3. Warm-up.** (Chart 11-2)
Complete the sentences. Change the verbs in *italics* from active to passive.

1. Tom *opens* the door.   → The door ___is opened___ by Tom.

2. Tom *is opening* the door.   The door _____ by Tom.

3. Tom *has opened* the door.   The door _____ by Tom.

4. Tom *opened* the door.   The door _____ by Tom.

5. Tom *was opening* the door.   The door _____ by Tom.

6. Tom *had opened* the door.   The door _____ by Tom.

7. Tom *will open* the door.   The door _____ by Tom.

8. Tom *is going to open* the door.   The door _____ by Tom.

9. Tom *will have opened* the door.   The door _____ by Tom.

10. *Did* Tom *open* the door?   _____ the door _____ by Tom?

11. *Will* Tom *open* the door?   _____ the door _____ by Tom?

12. *Has* Tom *opened* the door?   _____ the door _____ by Tom?

11-2 Tense Forms of the Passive

		Active			Passive		
(a) simple present	Mary	*helps*	the boy.	The boy	*is*	*helped*	by Mary.
(b) present progressive	Mary	*is helping*	the boy.	The boy	*is being*	*helped*	by Mary.
(c) present perfect*	Mary	*has helped*	the boy.	The boy	*has been*	*helped*	by Mary.
(d) simple past	Mary	*helped*	the boy.	The boy	*was*	*helped*	by Mary.
(e) past progressive	Mary	*was helping*	the boy.	The boy	*was being*	*helped*	by Mary.
(f) past perfect*	Mary	*had helped*	the boy.	The boy	*had been*	*helped*	by Mary.
(g) simple future	Mary	*will help*	the boy.	The boy	*will be*	*helped*	by Mary.
(h) *be going to*	Mary	*is going to help*	the boy.	The boy	*is going to be*	*helped*	by Mary.
(i) future perfect*	Mary	*will have helped*	the boy.	The boy	*will have been*	*helped*	by Mary.

(j) **Was** the boy *helped* by Mary? (k) **Has** the boy *been helped* by Mary?	In the question form of passive verbs, an auxiliary verb precedes the subject.

*The progressive forms of the *present perfect, past perfect,* and *future perfect* are rarely used in the passive.

❏ **Exercise 4. Looking at grammar.** (Charts 11-1 and 11-2)

Part I. Change the active to passive.
1. Shakespeare *wrote* that play. → *That play was written by Shakespeare.*
2. Waitresses and waiters *serve* customers.
3. The teacher *is going to explain* the lesson.
4. Two horses *were pulling* the farmer's wagon.
5. Toshi *will invite* Yoko to the party.
6. Alex *is preparing* that report.
7. Kathy *had returned* the book to the library.
8. Miriam *has designed* several public buildings.
9. His tricks *won't fool* me.
10. I *didn't write* that note. *Did* Jim *write* it?
11. *Does* Prof. Shapiro *teach* that course? No, he *doesn't teach* it.
12. Mrs. Andrews *hasn't signed* those papers yet. *Has* Mr. Andrews *signed* them yet?

Part II. Change the passive to active.
13. The speech *was given* by Anwar. → *Anwar gave the speech.*
14. Our assignments *are going to be corrected* by the teaching assistant.
15. *Was* the electric light bulb *invented* by Thomas Edison?
16. The speed limit on Highway 5 *isn't obeyed* by most drivers.
17. *Have* you *been informed* of the rent increase by the building manager?

❏ **Exercise 5. Looking at grammar.** (Charts 11-1 and 11-2)
Change the active verbs to passive if possible. Some verbs are intransitive and cannot be changed.

1. A strange thing happened yesterday. (*no change*)
2. Jackie scored the winning goal. → *The winning goal was scored by Jackie.*
3. I agree with Dr. Ikeda's theory.
4. Dr. Ikeda developed that theory.
5. A hurricane destroyed the small fishing village.

6. A large vase stands in the corner of our front hallway.

7. The children seemed happy when they went to the zoo.

8. After class, one of the students always erases the board.

9. The solution to my problem appeared to me in a dream.

10. Our plan succeeded at last.

11. Barbara traveled to Uganda last year.

12. A special committee is going to settle the dispute.

13. Did the police catch the thief?

14. This room is a mess. What happened?

❑ **Exercise 6. Warm-up.** (Chart 11-3)
Tell the class where something that you're wearing or own was made (e.g., your shoes, shirt, cell phone, etc.). Do you know who made these items? Is it important to know?

11-3 Using the Passive

(a) Rice *is grown* in India. (b) Our house *was built* in 1980. (c) This olive oil *was imported* from Crete.	Usually the passive is used without a *by*-phrase. The passive is most frequently used when it is not known or not important to know exactly who performs an action. In (a): Rice is grown in India by people, by farmers, by someone. It is not known or important to know exactly who grows rice in India. Examples (a), (b), and (c) illustrate the most common use of the passive, i.e., without the *by*-phrase.
(d) My aunt *made* this rug. (*active*)	If the speaker knows who performs an action, usually the active is used, as in (d).
(e) This rug *was made* by my aunt. That rug *was made* by my mother. (f) *Life on the Mississippi was written* by Mark Twain.	Sometimes, even when the speaker knows who performs an action, he/she chooses to use the passive with the *by*-phrase in order to focus attention on the subject of a sentence. In (e): The focus of attention is on two rugs. In (f): The focus is on the book, but the *by*-phrase is included because it contains important information.

❑ **Exercise 7. Looking at grammar.** (Charts 11-1 → 11-3)
Discuss why passive was chosen for these sentences instead of active.

1. My sweater *was made* in England.
   → *The speaker or writer probably uses the passive here because he or she doesn't know who made the sweater. Using an active sentence (Someone made my sweater in England) wouldn't add any important information.*

2. The new highway *will be completed* sometime next month.

3. The World Cup soccer games *are being televised* all over the world this year.

4. This composition *was written* by Ali. That one *was written* by Mariko.

5. The Washington Monument *is visited* by hundreds of people every day.

6. Bananas originated in Asia but now *are grown* in the tropics of both hemispheres of the world. They *were introduced* to the Americas in 1516.

❑ **Exercise 8. Reading and grammar.** (Charts 11-1 → 11-3)
Read the paragraph. <u>Underline</u> the passive verbs. Discuss why the writer chose to use passive rather than active. Answer the questions in complete sentences.

Early Writing Materials

The chief writing material of ancient times was papyrus. It <u>was used</u> in Egypt, Greece, and other Mediterranean lands. Parchment, another writing material that was widely used in ancient times, was made from the skins of animals, such as sheep and goats. After the hair had been removed, the skins were stretched and rubbed smooth to make a writing surface. Paper, the main writing material today, was invented by the Chinese.

Ink has been used for writing and drawing throughout history. No one knows when the first ink was developed. The ancient Egyptians and Chinese made ink from various natural substances such as berries, soot, and tree bark. Through the centuries, thousands of different formulas have been developed for ink. Most ink today is made from synthetic chemicals.

1. Before paper was invented, what materials were used for writing?
2. What was parchment made from?
3. What three things were done to animal skins to make writing material?
4. Who first used paper?
5. When was ink first used?
6. In ancient times, what ingredients did the Egyptians and Chinese use for ink?
7. What substances are in ink today?

❑ **Exercise 9. Looking at grammar.** (Charts 11-1 → 11-3)
Make complete sentences with the given words. Use the simple past. Some are active, and some are passive.

1. We \ allow, not \ to go to the park alone when we were young
    → *We weren't allowed to go to the park alone when we were young.*
2. A package \ deliver \ to our apartment yesterday
3. Maria \ teach \ her son to read when he was three
4. When I was in elementary school, we \ require \ to wear uniforms
5. As we watched, the airplane \ disappear \ into the clouds
6. I \ agree \ with your decision yesterday
7. Timmy \ drop \ a plate after dinner last night
8. The plate \ fall \ to the floor with a crash
9. What \ happen \ yesterday
10. Something very sad \ happen \ yesterday
11. My cat \ hit \ by a speeding truck
12. She \ kill \ instantly
13. She \ die \ instantly

□ **Exercise 10. Listening.** (Charts 11-1 → 11-3)

Choose the sentence (a. or b.) that has the same meaning as the one you hear.

CD 1
Track 54

Example: You will hear: The assistant manager interviewed Mr. Evans for the sales job.

You will choose: ⓐ Mr. Evans was interviewed.

b. The assistant manager was interviewed.

1. a. Someone would like the architect to design the new library.
   b. A famous architect would like to design the new library.

2. a. The kids told others to leave.
   b. Someone told the kids to leave.

3. a. I ignored the salesclerk.
   b. The salesclerk ignored me.

4. a. The speaker will be asked questions.
   b. The audience will be asked questions.

5. a. A party is being planned by Dr. Wilson.
   b. A party is being planned by the staff.

6. a. Natural habitats have altered human development.
   b. Natural habitats have been altered by human development.

□ **Exercise 11. Looking at grammar.** (Charts 11-1 → 11-3)

Change each news headline into a complete sentence. Work in pairs, in small groups, or as a class.

1. 5 PEOPLE KILLED BY TORNADOES

   Five people _____ yesterday.

2. DECISION ON TAX INCREASE TO BE ANNOUNCED SOON

   A decision on a tax increase _____ soon.

3. MORE THAN 2 BILLION CUPS OF COFFEE CONSUMED WORLDWIDE

   More than two billion cups of coffee _____ worldwide each day.

4. 200,000 CARS RECALLED FOR BRAKE DEFECTS SINCE LAST YEAR

   Two hundred thousand cars _____ for brake defects since last year.

5. NEW HIGH-SPEED COMPUTER CHIPS DELAYED

   New high-speed computer chips _____ until next year.

□ **Exercise 12. Game.** (Charts 11-1 → 11-3)

Work in teams with your books closed. Your teacher will say a sentence. Change it to passive if possible. Use the *by*-phrase only if necessary. Your team wins one point for each correct sentence.

1. Someone invited you to a party.
2. People grow rice in many countries.
3. Someone is televising the tennis match.

4. Someone told you to be here at ten.
5. Someone is going to serve dinner at six.
6. Someone has made a mistake.
7. An accident happened at the corner of Fifth and Main.
8. Ivan's daughter drew that picture. My son drew this picture.
9. The judges will judge the applicants on their creativity.
10. My sister's plane will arrive at 10:35.
11. Is Professor Rivers teaching that course this semester?
12. The mail carrier had already delivered the mail by the time I left for school this morning.
13. When is someone going to announce the results of the contest?
14. After the concert was over, hundreds of fans surrounded the rock star outside the theater.

❏ **Exercise 13. Let's talk.** (Charts 11-1 → 11-3)
Your teacher will read each sentence and the question that follows. Student A will change the sentence to the passive. Student B will answer the question with the information provided by Student A. Close your book for this activity.

Example: *To* A: People speak Arabic in many countries. *To* B: Is Arabic a common language?
TEACHER (*book open*):   People speak Arabic in many countries.
STUDENT A (*book closed*): Arabic is spoken in many countries.
TEACHER (*book open*):   Is Arabic a common language?
STUDENT B (*book closed*): Yes. It is spoken in many countries.

1. *To* A: Someone stole your pen. *To* B: What happened to (_____)'s pen?

2. *To* A: People play soccer in many countries. *To* B: Is soccer a popular sport?

3. *To* A: Someone returned your letter. *To* B: (_____) sent a letter last week, but he/she put the wrong address on it. What happened to the letter?

4. *To* A: Someone robbed the bank. *To* B: What happened to the bank?

5. *To* A: The police caught the bank robber. *To* B: Did the bank robber get away?

6. *To* A: A judge sent the thief to jail. *To* B: What happened to the thief?

7. *To* A: The government requires international students to have visas.
   To B: Is it necessary for international students to have visas?

8. *To* A: Someone had already made the coffee by the time you got up this morning.
   To B: Did (_____) have to make the coffee when he/she got up?

9. *To* A: Someone discovered gold in California in 1848.
   To B: What happened in California in 1848?

10. *To* A: People used candles for light in the 17th century.
    To B: Was electricity used for light in the 17th century?

11. *To* A: There is a party tomorrow night. Someone invited you to go.
    To B: Is (_____) invited to the party?

12. *To* A: You wanted to buy a chair, but you needed time to make up your mind. Finally you decided to buy it, but someone had already sold it by the time you returned to the store.
    To B: Did (_____) buy the chair?

Complete the sentences with the passive form of the verbs in the list. Use any appropriate tense.

build	divide	✓invent	order	surprise
cause	expect	kill	report	surround
confuse	frighten	offer	spell	wear

1. The electric light bulb _____was invented_____ by Thomas Edison in 1879.

2. An island _____ by water.

3. The -ing form of sit _____ with a double "t."

4. Even though construction costs are high, a new dormitory _____ next year.

5. The class was too large last semester, so it _____ into two sections.

6. A bracelet _____ around the wrist.

7. The Johnsons' house burned down. According to the inspector, the fire _____ _____ by lightning.

8. Al got a ticket for reckless driving. When he went to traffic court, he _____ _____ to pay a large fine.

9. I read about a hunter who _____ accidentally _____ by another hunter.

10. The hunter's fatal accident _____ in the newspaper yesterday.

11. I didn't expect Lisa to come to the meeting last night, but she was there. I _____ _____ to see her.

12. Last week I _____ a job at a local bank, but I didn't accept it.

13. The children _____ in the middle of the night when they heard strange noises in the house.

14. Could you explain this math problem to me? Yesterday in class I _____ by the teacher's explanation.

15. A: Is the plane going to be late?
    B: No. It _____ to be on time.

Exercise 15. Listening. (Charts 11-1 → 11-3)

Listen to the report about chocolate with your book closed. Then open your book and listen again. Complete the sentences with the verbs you hear.

CD 1
Track 55

How Chocolate Is Made

Chocolate _____ from the seeds of roasted cocoa beans. After the seeds
              1

_____, the inside of the seed _____ into a liquid. This
          2   3

liquid _____ chocolate liquor. The liquor _____ fat,
            4   5

which _____ from the liquor. After this _____, a solid
          6   7

_____. This solid, which _____ as cocoa cake,
        8   9

_____ up and becomes unsweetened cocoa. This is a very bitter
      10

chocolate. To make it taste better, other substances such as cocoa butter and sugar

_____ later.
      11

❑ **Exercise 16. Looking at grammar.** (Charts 11-1 and 11-3)

Complete the sentences with the active or passive form of the verbs in parentheses. Use any appropriate tense.

1. Gold (*discover*) _____*was discovered*_____ in California in 1848.

2. The Amazon valley is extremely important to the ecology of the earth. Forty percent of the world's oxygen (*produce*) _____ there.

3. Right now Roberto is in the hospital.* He (*treat*) _____ for a bad burn on his arm.

4. In my country, certain prices, such as the price of medical supplies, (*control*) _____ _____ by the government. Other prices (*determine*) _____ _____ by how much consumers are willing to pay for a product.

5. Richard Anderson is a former astronaut. Several years ago, when he was 52, Anderson (*inform*) _____ by his superior at an aircraft corporation that he could no longer be a test pilot. He (*tell*) _____ that he was being relieved of his duties because of his age. Anderson took the corporation to court for age discrimination.

6. Frostbite may occur when a person's skin (*expose*) _____ to extreme cold. It most frequently (*affect*)** _____ the skin of the cheeks, chin, ears, fingers, nose, and toes.

---

*in the hospital = American English; in hospital = British English.

NOTE: ***affect* = a verb (e.g., *The weather **affects** my moods.*).
    effect = a noun (e.g., *The weather has an **effect** on my moods.*).

7. Since the beginning of the modern industrial age, many of the natural habitats of plants and animals (*destroy*) _____ by industrial development and pollution.

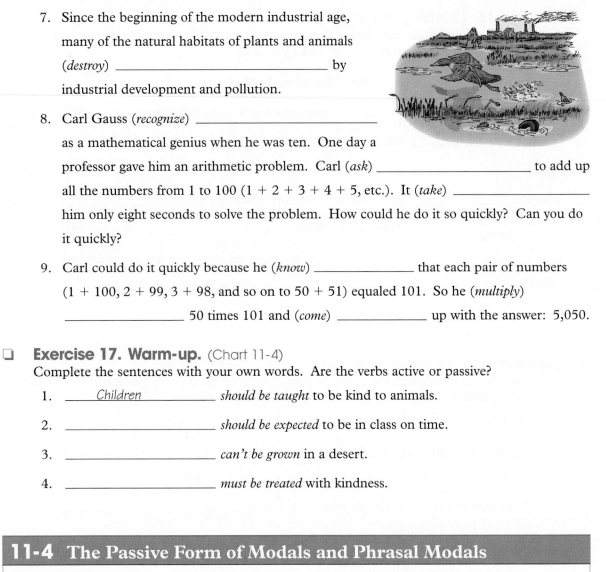

8. Carl Gauss (*recognize*) _____ as a mathematical genius when he was ten. One day a professor gave him an arithmetic problem. Carl (*ask*) _____ to add up all the numbers from 1 to 100 (1 + 2 + 3 + 4 + 5, etc.). It (*take*) _____ him only eight seconds to solve the problem. How could he do it so quickly? Can you do it quickly?

9. Carl could do it quickly because he (*know*) _____ that each pair of numbers (1 + 100, 2 + 99, 3 + 98, and so on to 50 + 51) equaled 101. So he (*multiply*) _____ 50 times 101 and (*come*) _____ up with the answer: 5,050.

❏ **Exercise 17. Warm-up.** (Chart 11-4)
Complete the sentences with your own words. Are the verbs active or passive?

1. ___*Children*___ *should be taught* to be kind to animals.

2. _____ *should be expected* to be in class on time.

3. _____ *can't be grown* in a desert.

4. _____ *must be treated* with kindness.

11-4 The Passive Form of Modals and Phrasal Modals

Passive form:	**modal*** +	***be*** +	**past participle**	
(a) Tom	*will*	*be*	*invited*	to the picnic.
(b) The window	*can't*	*be*	*opened.*	
(c) Children	*should*	*be*	*taught*	to respect their elders.
(d)	*May I*	*be*	*excused*	from class?
(e) This book	*had better*	*be*	*returned*	to the library before Friday.
(f) This letter	*ought to*	*be*	*sent*	before June 1st.
(g) Mary	*has to*	*be*	*told*	about our change in plans.
(h) Fred	*is supposed to*	*be*	*told*	about the meeting.

Past-passive form:	**modal** +	***have been*** +	**past participle**	
(i) The letter	*should*	*have been*	*sent*	last week.
(j) This house	*must*	*have been*	*built*	over 200 years ago.
(k) Eric	*couldn't*	*have been*	*offered*	the job.
(l) Jill	*ought to*	*have been*	*invited*	to the party.

*See Chapters 9 and 10 for a discussion of the form and use of modals and phrasal modals.

Exercise 18. Looking at grammar. (Chart 11-4)

Complete the sentences with the words in parentheses. Use the appropriate form, active or passive.

1. James (*should + tell*) _____*should be told*_____ the news as soon as possible.

2. Someone (*should + tell*) _____*should tell*_____ James the news immediately.

3. James (*should + tell*) _____*should have been told*_____ the news a long time ago.

4. Meat (*must + keep*) _____ in a refrigerator or it will spoil.

5. You (*must + keep*) _____ meat in a refrigerator or it will spoil.

6. We tried, but the window (*couldn't + open*) _____.
   It was painted shut.

7. I tried, but I (*couldn't + open*) _____ the window.

8. Good news! I (*may + offer*) _____ a job soon. I had an interview at an engineering firm yesterday.

9. Chris has good news. The engineering firm where she had an interview yesterday (*may + offer*) _____ her a job soon.

10. I hope Chris accepts our job offer, but I know she's been interviewing with several companies. She (*may + already + offer*)★ _____ a job by a competing firm before we made our offer.

11. A competing firm (*may + already + offer*) _____ Chris a job before we made our offer.

12. The class for next semester is too large. It (*ought to + divide*) _____ _____ in half, but there's not enough money in the budget to hire another teacher.

13. Last semester's class was too large. It (*ought to + divide*) _____ _____ in half.

14. These books (*have to + return*) _____ to the library by tomorrow.

15. Polly (*have to + return*) _____ these books by next Friday. If she doesn't return them, she (*will + have to + pay*) _____ a fine to the library.

★A midsentence adverb such as **already** may be placed after the first auxiliary (e.g., *might* **already** *have come*) or after the second auxiliary (e.g., *might have* **already** *come*).

16. A: Andy, your chores (*had better + finish*) _____
    by the time I get home, including taking out the garbage.
    B: Don't worry, Mom. I'll do everything you told me to do.

17. A: Andy, you (*had better + finish*) _____ your chores before
    Mom gets home.
    B: I know. I'll do them in a minute. I'm busy right now.

18. This application (*be supposed to + send*) _____
    to the personnel department soon.

19. Ann's birthday was on the 5th, and today is the 8th. Her birthday card (*should + send*)
    _____ a week ago. Maybe we'd better give her a call to
    wish her a belated happy birthday.

20. A: Yoko didn't expect to see her boss at the labor union meeting.
    B: She (*must + surprise*) _____ when she saw him.
    A: She was.

☐ **Exercise 19. Looking at grammar.** (Chart 11-4)
   Make complete sentences with the given words.

   Example: must   a. Seat belts \ wear \ during takeoff and landing
                       → *Seat belts must be worn during takeoff and landing.*
                    b. All passengers \ wear \ their seat belts during takeoff and landing
                       → *All passengers must wear their seat belts during takeoff and landing.*

   1. will   a. Many lives \ save \ with the new medical procedure
                  b. The procedure \ save \ many lives

   2. can   a. Shoppers \ look for \ product information on the internet every day
                  b. Product information \ find \ on the internet

   3. should   a. People \ check \ smoke alarm batteries once a month
                  b. Smoke alarm batteries \ test \ once a month

   4. may   a. The typhoon \ kill \ hundreds of villagers yesterday
                  b. Hundreds of villagers \ kill \ in the typhoon yesterday
                  c. Hundreds of villagers \ die \ in the typhoon yesterday

   5. had better a. Medical supplies \ deliver \ soon
                  b. Villagers \ receive \ medical supplies soon

❏ **Exercise 20. Let's talk.** (Chart 11-4)
Use passive modals to restate the computer lab rules. Make at least two sentences for each rule. Work in pairs or small groups.

Example: Do not bring food into the lab.
→ *Food **must** not be brought into the lab.*
→ *Food **cannot** be brought into the lab.*
→ *Food **must** be left outside.*

Computer lab rules:
1. Turn off cell phones.
2. Computers are for school use only.
3. Do not play computer games.
4. Do not download music from the internet.
5. Use the printer for schoolwork only.

❏ **Exercise 21. Looking at grammar.** (Chart 11-4)
Complete the sentences with the verbs in parentheses. Use the modal or phrasal modal that sounds best to you. All of the sentences are passive.

1. The entire valley (*see*) _____ can be seen _____ from the mountain top.

2. He is wearing a gold band on his fourth finger. He (*marry*) _____.

3. According to our teacher, all of our compositions (*write*) _____
   in ink. He won't accept papers written in pencil.

4. I found this book on my desk when I came to class. It (*leave*) _____
   by one of the students in the earlier class.

5. Your daughter has a good voice. Her interest in singing (*encourage*) _____
   _____.

6. Some UFO sightings (*explain, not*) _____ easily. They are
   inexplicable.

7. Try to speak slowly when you give your speech. If you don't, some of your words
   (*misunderstand*) _____.

The Passive **223**

8. What? You tripped over a chair at the party and dropped your plate of food into a woman's lap? You (*embarrass*) _____.

9. The hospital in that small town is very old and can no longer serve the needs of the community. A new hospital (*build*) _____ years ago.

10. Blue whales and other endangered species (*save*) _____ from extinction. Do you agree?

❑ **Exercise 22. Listening and grammar.** (Charts 11-1 → 11-4)

Part I. Listen to the lecture on the 2004 Indian Ocean tsunami with your book closed. Then open your book and choose all the grammatically correct sentences in each group.

CD 1
Track 56

1. a. An earthquake hit the Indian Ocean.
   b. The Indian Ocean was hit by an earthquake.
   c. An earthquake was hit the Indian Ocean.

2. a. Millions of lives were changed forever by the earthquake.
   b. Millions of lives changed forever by the earthquake.

3. a. The quake followed by giant tsunami waves.
   b. The quake was followed by giant tsunami waves.
   c. Giant tsunami waves were followed the earthquake.
   d. Giant tsunami waves followed the earthquake.

4. a. Thousands of people swept out to sea.
   b. Thousands of people were swept out to sea.
   c. The tsunami wave swept thousands of people out to sea.

5. a. Nearly 300,000 people died.
   b. Nearly 300,000 people were died.
   c. Nearly 300,000 people were killed.
   d. Nearly 300,000 people killed.

6. a. The damage could have been lessened by a tsunami early-warning system.
   b. A tsunami early-warning system could have lessened the damage.
   c. A tsunami early-warning system could have been lessened the damage.

7. a. An early-warning system already exists for the Pacific Ocean.
   b. An early-warning system already is existed for the Pacific Ocean.

Part II. Listen again. Complete the sentences with the verbs you hear.

The 2004 Indian Ocean Tsunami

In 2004, several countries that border the Indian Ocean, including Indonesia, Thailand, India,

Malaysia, and Somalia, _____ by an earthquake and subsequent tsunami.
1

(As you may already know, a tsunami is a giant ocean wave.) In just a few short hours, millions

of lives _____ forever. The earthquake _____
2 3

at 9.3 on the Richter scale. It was the fourth largest earthquake since 1900 and the second

largest that _____ on the Richter scale.
4

The quake _____ by four giant waves as high as 100 feet
5

(or 30 meters). Whole villages _____. Thousands of people
6

_____ out to sea, and many others _____ due to lack of
7 8

medical care. In total, almost 300,000 people _____, and 1.3 million
9

people _____ homeless. Aftershocks from the earthquake
10

_____ for several days.
11

Tragically, the damage _____ if there had been a
12

tsunami early-warning system. Such a system already _____ for the Pacific
13

Ocean, but it _____ to the Indian Ocean. Since the tsunami disaster,
14

governments _____ together to develop an early-warning system
15

so that Southeast Asia _____ such destruction again from a tsunami.
16

❑ **Exercise 23. Looking at grammar.** (Charts 11-1 → 11-4)
Change the verbs to the passive as appropriate. Discuss why you decided that certain verbs
should be in the passive but that others should remain active.

It is used

(1) Paper is a common material. ~~People use it~~ everywhere in the world. Throughout

history, people have made it from various plants such as rice and papyrus, but today wood is the

chief source of paper. In the past, people made paper by hand, but now machines do most of

the work.* Today people make paper from wood pulp by using either a mechanical or a

chemical process.

---

*Whether or not to use the passive in the second half of this sentence is a stylistic choice. Either the active or the passive can
appropriately be used. Some writers might prefer the passive so that both halves of the sentence are parallel in structure.

(2) In the mechanical process, someone grinds the wood into small chips. During the grinding, someone sprays it with water to keep it from burning from the friction of the grinder. Then someone soaks the chips in water.

(3) In the chemical process, first someone washes the wood, and then someone cuts it into small pieces in a chipping machine. Then someone cooks the chips in certain chemicals. After someone cooks the wood, someone washes it to get rid of the chemicals.

(4) The next steps in making paper are the same for both the mechanical and the chemical processes. Someone drains the pulp to form a thick mass, bleaches it with chlorine, and then thoroughly washes it again. Next someone puts the pulp through a large machine that squeezes the water out and forms the pulp into long sheets. After the pulp sheets go through a drier and a press, someone winds them onto rolls. These rolls of paper are then ready for use.

(5) The next time you use paper, you should think about its origin and how people make it. And you should ask yourself this question: What would the world be like without paper? If you can imagine how different today's world would be without paper, you will immediately understand how essential paper has been in the development of civilization.

❏ **Exercise 24. Let's write.** (Charts 11-1 → 11-4)
Write about how something is made. Choose one of these topics.

Topics:
1. Write about something you know how to make. *Possible subjects:* a kite, a ceramic pot, a bookcase, a sweater, a bead necklace, a special kind of food, etc.

2. Use a reference tool such as the internet to find out how something is made, and then summarize this information. It's not necessary to go into technical detail. Read about the process and then describe it in your own words. *Possible subjects:* a candle, a pencil, glass, steel, silk thread, bronze, leather, etc.

❏ **Exercise 25. Warm-up.** (Chart 11-5)
Look around the room and answer these questions.

1. Are the windows closed?
2. Is the door shut?
3. Are the lights turned on?
4. Is anything broken? If so, what?

11-5 Non-Progressive Passive

(a) The door is *old*. (b) The door is *green*. (c) The door is *locked*.	In (a) and (b): **old** and **green** are adjectives. They describe the door. In (c): **locked** is a past participle. It is used as an adjective. It describes the door.
(d) I locked the door five minutes ago. (e) The door was locked by me five minutes ago. (f) Now the door *is locked*.	When the passive form is used to describe an existing situation or state, as in (c), (f), and (i), it is called the "non-progressive passive." In the non-progressive: • no action is taking place; the action happened earlier. • there is no *by*-phrase. • the past participle functions as an adjective.
(g) Ann broke the window yesterday. (h) The window was broken by Ann. (i) Now the window *is broken*.	
(j) I *am interested in* Chinese art. (k) He *is satisfied with* his job. (l) Ann *is married to* Alex.	Prepositions other than **by** can follow non-progressive passive verbs. (See Chart 11-6.)
(m) I don't know where I am. I *am lost*. (n) I can't find my purse. It *is gone*. (o) I *am finished with* my work. (p) I *am done with* my work.	Sentences (m) through (p) are examples of idiomatic usage of the passive form in common, everyday English. These sentences have no equivalent active sentences.

❑ **Exercise 26. Looking at grammar.** (Chart 11-5)
Complete the sentences with the non-progressive passive of the verbs in parentheses. Use the simple present or the simple past.

1. Olga is wearing a blouse. It (*make*) _____ is made _____ of cotton.

2. The door to this room (*shut*) _____.

3. The lights in this room (*turn*) _____ on.

4. This room (*crowd, not*) _____.

5. We can leave now because class (*finish*) _____.

6. It is hot in this room because the window (*close*) _____.

7. Yesterday it was hot in this room because the window (*close*) _____

   _____.

8. We are ready to sit down and eat dinner. The table (*set*) _____,

   the meat and rice (*do*) _____, and the candles (*light*)

   _____.

9. Where's my wallet? It (*go*) _____! Did you take it?

10. Hmmm. My dress (*tear*) _____. I wonder how that happened.

□ **Exercise 27. Looking at grammar.** (Chart 11-5)
Complete each sentence with an appropriate form of the words in the list.

bear (born)*	crowd	locate	plug in	spoil
block	divorce	✓lose	qualify	stick
confuse	exhaust	marry	schedule	turn off

1. Excuse me, sir. Could you give me some directions? I _____ *am lost* _____.

2. Let's find another restaurant. This one _____ too _____. We would have to wait at least an hour for a table.

3. The meeting _____ for tomorrow at nine.

4. That's hard work! I _____. I need to rest for a while.

5. You told me one thing, and John told me another. I don't know what to think. I
_____.

6. Annie can't close the window. It _____.

7. Louise is probably sleeping. The lights in her room

_____.

8. Carolyn and Joe were married to each other for five years,
but now they _____.

9. I'm sorry. You _____ not
_____ for the job. We need someone
with a degree in electrical engineering.

10. I love my wife. I _____ to a wonderful woman.

11. We can't eat this fruit. It _____. We'll have to throw it out.

12. We'd better call a plumber. The water won't go down the drain. The drain
_____ with food.

13. Vietnam _____ in Southeast Asia.

14. A: How old is Juan?
B: He _____ in 1980.

15. A: The TV set isn't working.
B: Are you sure? _____ it _____?

---

*In the passive, **born** is used as the past participle of **bear** to mean "given birth to."

228 CHAPTER 11

□ **Exercise 28. Warm-up.** (Chart 11-6)
Answer the questions.

What is something that you are . . .

1. interested in?
2. annoyed by?
3. concerned about?
4. scared of?
5. excited about?
6. accustomed to?

11-6 Common Non-Progressive Passive Verbs + Prepositions

(a) I'm interested *in* Greek culture. (b) He's worried *about* losing his job.	Many non-progressive verbs are followed by prepositions other than *by*.

be concerned be excited } *about* be worried	be composed be made } *of* be tired	be acquainted be associated be cluttered
be discriminated *against*	be frightened be scared } *of/by* be terrified	be crowded be done be equipped } *with* be filled
be known be prepared be qualified } *for* be remembered be well known	be accustomed be addicted be committed be connected be dedicated be devoted } *to* be engaged be exposed be limited be married be opposed be related	be finished be pleased be provided be satisfied
be divorced be exhausted be gone } *from* be protected		be annoyed be bored } *with/by* be covered
be dressed be interested } *in* be located		
be disappointed be involved } *in/with*		

□ **Exercise 29. Looking at grammar.** (Chart 11-6)
Complete the sentences with the correct prepositions.

SITUATION: Maya is a toymaker. She makes simple toys from wood.

1. She is excited ___*about*___ creating toys children enjoy.

2. She is known _____ creating high-quality toys.

3. She is interested _____ how children play with one another.

4. She is pleased _____ the response to her toys.

5. Her toys are made _____ wood.

6. The materials in her toys are limited _____ wood.

7. She is disappointed _____ many of the popular toys in stores today.

8. She worries _____ toys that don't encourage children to use their imagination.

❏ **Exercise 30. Listening.** (Chart 11-6)

Listen to the sentences. They contain non-progressive passive verbs plus prepositions. Write the prepositions you hear.

Example: You will hear: Carol is interested in ancient history.
            You will write: _____*in*_____

1. _____   5. _____

2. _____   6. _____

3. _____   7. _____

4. _____   8. _____

❏ **Exercise 31. Looking at grammar.** (Chart 11-6)

Complete the sentences with the correct prepositions.

1. Jack is married _____ Joan.

2. Could I please have the dictionary when you are finished _____ it?

3. My car is equipped _____ air-conditioning and a sun roof.

4. Gandhi was committed _____ nonviolence. He believed in it all of his life.

5. Barbara turned off the TV because she was tired _____ listening to the news.

6. The choices in that restaurant are limited _____ pizza and sandwiches.

7. Their apartment is always messy. It's cluttered _____ newspapers, books, clothes, and dirty dishes.

8. A: Are you in favor of a worldwide ban on nuclear weapons, or are you opposed

      _____ it?

   B: I'm in favor of it. I'm terrified _____ the possibility of a nuclear war starting by

      accident. But my wife is against disarmament.

9. A: Are you still associated _____ the International Red Cross and Red Crescent?

   B: I was, until this year. Are you interested _____ working with them?

   A: I think I'd like to. They are dedicated _____ helping people in times of crisis,

      and I admire the work they've done. Can you get me some information?

Exercise 32. Looking at grammar. (Chart 11-6)
Complete each sentence with the non-progressive passive form of the given verb and an appropriate preposition. Use the simple present.

1. cover   It's winter, and the ground _____ *is covered with* _____ snow.

2. finish   Pat _____ her composition.

3. addict   Ann laughingly calls herself a "chocoholic." She says she
              _____ chocolate.

4. satisfy   I _____ the progress I have made.

5. engage   Hashim _____ Fatima.

6. divorce   Elaine _____ Pierre.

7. relate   Your name is Mary Smith. _____ you
              _____ John Smith?

8. dedicate   Mrs. Robinson works in an orphanage. She _____
              her work.

9. dress   Miguel _____ a tuxedo for his wedding today.

10. commit   The administration _____ improving the quality of
              education at our school.

11. prepare   We finished packing our sleeping bags, tent, first-aid kit, food, and warm
              clothes. We are finally _____ our camping trip.

12. do   We are _____ this exercise.

❑ **Exercise 33. Let's talk.** (Chart 11-6)
Think about changes that modern life has brought in communications, travel, work, school, daily life, etc. Complete the phrases with the correct prepositions and answer the questions. Work in pairs or small groups.

What changes or innovations are you (or people you know) . . .

1. excited _____?

2. concerned _____?

3. opposed _____?

4. annoyed _____?

5. addicted _____?

6. not accustomed _____?

❏ **Exercise 34. Looking at grammar.** (Chart 11-6)
Add the missing preposition to each sentence.

1. I'm not acquainted $\wedge$ that man. Do you know him?
   with

2. The department store was filled toys for the holiday sale.

3. Bert's bald head is protected the hot sun when he's wearing his hat.

4. Your leg bone is connected your hip bone.

5. A person who is addicted drugs needs professional medical help.

6. What? You're still dressed your pajamas? You'll never make it to work on time.

7. The school children were exposed the flu by a student who had it.

8. The electronic items were priced so low for the sale that they were gone the store shelves in minutes.

9. Roberta didn't get the job even though she was qualified it.

10. My office is located a building next to the park on Fifth Avenue.

❏ **Exercise 35. Warm-up.** (Chart 11-7)
Complete the sentences with the words in the list. Notice the word forms that follow the verb **get**.

dirty	dressed	hungry	hurt	lost	wet

1. When the children played in the mud, their clothes *got* _____.

2. We didn't have a map, so we *got* _____.

3. Don't go out in the rain without a coat. You*'ll get* _____.

4. I'll be ready to leave as soon as I *get* _____. It'll just take a few minutes.

5. If I skip breakfast, I always *get* _____ during my late morning class.

6. It was a bad accident, but luckily no one *got* _____.

11-7 The Passive with *Get*

Get + Adjective

(a) I'm *getting hungry*. Let's eat soon. (b) I stopped working because I *got sleepy*.	**Get** may be followed by certain adjectives. **Get** gives the idea of change — the idea of becoming, beginning to be, growing to be. In (a): **I'm getting hungry** = I wasn't hungry before, but now I'm beginning to be hungry.

Common adjectives that follow *get*

angry	cold	fat	hungry	quiet	tall
anxious	comfortable	full	late	ready	thirsty
bald	dark	good	light	rich	warm
better	dizzy	hard	mad	ripe	well
big	easy	healthy	nervous	serious	wet
busy	empty	heavy	noisy	sick	worse
chilly	famous	hot	old	sleepy	

Get + Past Participle

(c) I stopped working because I *got tired*. (d) They *are getting married* next month.	**Get** may also be followed by a past participle. The past participle functions as an adjective; it describes the subject. The passive with **get** is common in spoken English, but not in formal writing.

Common past participles with *get*

get accepted (for, into)	get dressed (in)	get invited (to)
get accustomed to	get drunk (on)	get involved (in, with)
get acquainted (with)	get elected (to)	get killed (by, with)
get arrested (for)	get engaged (to)	get lost (in)
get bored (with)	get excited (about)	get married (to)
get confused (about)	get finished (with)	get prepared (for)
get crowded (with)	get fixed (by)	get scared (of)
get divorced (from)	get hurt (by)	get sunburned
get done (with)	get interested (in)	get worried (about)

❏ **Exercise 36. Looking at grammar.** (Chart 11-7)
Complete the sentences with words that make sense. More than one answer may be correct for each sentence.

1. The meeting starts in an hour. I need to get _____ for it.
   a. prepare   b. prepared   c. ready   d. readying

2. I think I'll stop working for the day. I'm getting _____.
   a. tire   b. tired   c. dark   d. late

3. Sonia stopped working because it was getting _____.
   a. late   b. dark   c. tired   d. sleepy

4. We can leave as soon as you get _____.
   a. pack   b. finish   c. packed   d. finished

5. Sam was supposed to be home an hour ago, but he still isn't here. I'm getting _____.
    a. nervous   b. anxious   c. worry   d. worried

6. I didn't stay for the end of the movie because I got _____.
    a. bore   b. bored   c. interested   d. am bored

7. When are you going to get _____?
    a. marriage   b. marry   c. married   d. engage

❑ **Exercise 37. Looking at grammar.** (Chart 11-7)
Complete the sentences with any appropriate tense of **get** and the given adjectives.

accustom	do	✓hungry	pay
better	engage	invite	remarry
dark	fire	marry	well
depress	hire	nervous	wet
divorce			

1. What time are we going to eat? I _____*am getting hungry*_____.

2. I didn't have an umbrella, so I _____ while I was waiting for the bus yesterday.

3. Every time I have to give a speech, I _____.

4. Would you mind turning on the light? It _____ in here.

5. Maria's English is improving. It _____.

6. My friend was sick, so I sent him a card. It said, "_____ soon."

7. How long did it take you to _____ to living here?

8. We can leave as soon as I _____ with this work.

9. Chris _____ when she lost her job, so I tried to cheer her up.

10. I got an invitation. _____ you _____ to the party too?

11. I _____ on Fridays. I'll give you the money I owe you next Friday. Okay?

12. After Ed graduated, he _____ by an engineering firm.

13. But later he _____ because he didn't do his work.

14. Ben and Sara have had an interesting relationship. First, they _____.
Then, they _____. Later, they _____.
Finally, they _____. Today they are a happily married couple.

❑ **Exercise 38. Let's talk: interview.** (Chart 11-7)
Interview your classmates. Share some of their answers with the class.

Example: Have you ever gotten dizzy? Tell me about it.
→ *Yes. I got dizzy when I went on a ride at the carnival last summer. But it was a lot of fun!*

1. Tell me about a time you got lost. Where were you and what happened?

2. Do you ever get sleepy during the day? If so, tell me about it. If not, when do you get sleepy?

3. Have you ever gotten really scared? What scared you?

4. Think of the world situation today. What things are getting better, and what things are getting worse?

5. Have you ever gotten hurt in a traffic accident or any kind of accident? What happened?

6. Tell me about a time you got confused about something.

7. Have you or has someone you know ever gotten cheated when you bought something? Tell me about it.

8. Is there an election coming up in this country or another country that interests you? If so, who do you think is going to get elected? Who got elected in the last election in this country?

❑ **Exercise 39. Warm-up.** (Chart 11-8)
The teacher in the picture is lecturing her class about healthy food.

1. How would you describe the teacher: boring or bored?
2. How would you describe the students: boring or bored?

11-8 Participial Adjectives

(a) — The problem confuses the students. It is *a confusing problem*.	The *present participle* serves as an adjective with an active meaning. The noun it modifies performs an action. In (a): The noun **problem** does something; it *confuses*. Thus, it is described as a "confusing problem."
(b) — The students are confused by the problem. They are *confused students*.	The *past participle* serves as an adjective with a passive meaning. In (b): The students are confused by something. Thus, they are described as "confused students."
(c) — The story amuses the children. It is *an amusing story*.	In (c): The noun **story** performs the action.
(d) — The children are amused by the story. They are *amused children*.	In (d): The noun **children** receives the action.

❑ **Exercise 40. Looking at grammar.** (Chart 11-8)
Match the sentences to the pictures. Some sentences describe <u>neither</u> picture.

Picture A   Picture B

1. The monster is frightened.
2. The monster is frightening.
3. The child is frightened.
4. The child is frightening.
5. The tiger is frightened.
6. The tiger is frightening.

❑ **Exercise 41. Looking at grammar.** (Chart 11-8)
Complete each sentence with the present or past participle of the verb in *italics*.

1. The class *bores* the students. It is a _____*boring*_____ class.

2. The students *are bored* by the class. They are _____*bored*_____ students.

3. The game *excites* the people. It is an _____ game.

4. The people *are excited* by the game. They are _____ people.

5. The news *surprised* the man. It was _____ news.

6. The man *was surprised* by the news. He was a _____ man.

7. The child *was frightened* by the strange noise. The _____ child sought comfort from her father.

8. The strange noise *frightened* the child. It was a _____ sound.

9. The work *exhausted* the men. It was _____ work.

10. The men *were exhausted*. The _____ men sat down to rest under the shade of a tree.

❑ **Exercise 42. Let's talk.** (Chart 11-8)
Your teacher will read the questions. Answer them as a class (or individually) with a present or past participle. Close your book for this activity.

Example: If a book confuses you, how would you describe the book? How would you describe yourself?
TEACHER (*book open*):   If a book confuses you, how would you describe the book?
SPEAKER A (*book closed*): confusing
TEACHER (*book open*):   How would you describe yourself?
SPEAKER B (*book closed*): confused

1. If a story amazes you, how would you describe the story? How would you describe yourself?
2. If a story depresses you, how would you describe the story? How would you describe yourself?
3. If some work tires you, . . . ?
4. If a movie bores you, . . . ?
5. If a painting interests you, . . . ?
6. If a situation embarrasses you, . . . ?
7. If a book disappoints you, . . . ?
8. If a person fascinates you, . . . ?
9. If an assignment frustrates you, . . . ?
10. If a noise annoys you, . . . ?
11. If an event shocks you, . . . ?
12. If an experience thrills you, . . . ?

❑ **Exercise 43. Listening.** (Chart 11-8)
Listen to the sentences. Choose the words you hear.

CD 1
Track 58

Example: You will hear: Something's wrong with the refrigerator. It's been making an annoying buzz all day.
         You will choose: annoy   (annoying)   annoyed

1. miss   missing   missed
2. satisfy   satisfying   satisfied
3. frighten   frightening   frightened
4. marry   marrying   married
5. scare   scary   scared
6. finish   finishing   finished

❑ **Exercise 44. Listening.** (Chart 11-8)

Listen to the sentences. Choose the correct completions.

Example: You will hear: I attended a great lecture last night. It was _____ .

You will choose: (fascinating)   fascinated

You will hear: The audience listened carefully to the lecture. They were _____ .

You will choose: fascinating   (fascinated)

1. thrilling	thrilled		5. delightful	delighted
2. thrilling	thrilled		6. delightful	delighted
3. shocking	shocked		7. confusing	confused
4. shocking	shocked		8. confusing	confused

❑ **Exercise 45. Looking at grammar.** (Chart 11-8)

Complete the sentences with the present or past participle of the verbs in parentheses.

1. The thief tried to pry open the (*lock*) _____locked_____ cabinet.

2. I found myself in an (*embarrass*) _____ situation last night.

3. The (*injure*) _____ woman was put into an ambulance.

4. The teacher gave us a (*challenge*) _____ assignment, but we all enjoyed doing it.

5. The (*expect*) _____ event did not occur.

6. The invention of the (*print*) _____ press was one of the most important events in the history of the world.

7. (*Experience*) _____ travelers pack lightly. They carry little more than necessities.

8. A (*grow*) _____ child needs a (*balance*) _____ diet.

9. No one appreciates a (*spoil*) _____ child.

10. There is an old saying: "Let (*sleep*) _____ dogs lie." It means "Don't bring up past problems."

11. We had a (*thrill*) _____ but hair-raising experience on our backpacking trip into the wilderness.

12. The (*abandon*) _____ car was towed away by a tow truck.

13. (*Pollute*) _____ water is not safe for drinking.

14. I don't have any furniture of my own. Do you know where I can rent a (*furnish*) _____ apartment?

15. The equator is the (*divide*) _____ line between the Northern and Southern hemispheres.

16. We all expect our (*elect*) _____ officials to be honest.

17. The psychologist spoke to us about some of the (*amaze*) _____ coincidences in the lives of twins living apart from each other from birth.

❏ **Exercise 46. Let's talk: interview.** (Charts 11-5 → 11-7)
Make questions with the given words. Interview two students for each question. Share some of their answers with the class.

1. What \ be \ you \ worried about in today's world?
   → *What are you worried about in today's world?*
2. What \ be \ you \ tired of?
3. What (or who) \ be \ you \ pleased with?
4. What \ you \ get \ really nervous about?
5. What \ you \ want \ to be \ remembered for?
6. What \ be \ excite \ to you?
7. What \ you \ get excited about?
8. What \ be \ confuse \ to students?
9. What \ be \ you \ confused by?
10. What \ confuse \ to children?

❏ **Exercise 47. Listening.** (Chapter 11)
Part I. Listen to the lecture about the early Olympic Games with your book closed. Then open your book and read the statements. Circle "T" for true and "F" for false.

CD 1
Track 60

1. The Olympic Games were established so that men and women could compete against one another.   T   F

2. Greece invited other nations to the games to encourage good relationships among countries.   T   F

3. The winning athletes were considered heroes.   T   F

Part II. Listen again. Complete the sentences with the verbs you hear.

The Olympic Games

The Olympic Games _____ more than 2,000 years ago in Olympia, a
₁

small town in Greece. The games _____ for two purposes. One was
₂

to showcase the physical qualities and athletic performances of its young men. At that time,

only Greek males _____ to compete. In fact, women
₃

_____ to watch the games, and the only spectators were
₄

men. The other goal _____ to encourage good relationships among Greek cities.
₅

People of other nationalities _____ to participate.
₆

The winner of each event _____ with a wreath made of olive leaves.
₇

Additionally, his statue _____ in Olympia for all to see.
₈

_____ athletes _____ as heroes when they
₉   ₁₀

returned to their cities because with their victory, they _____ fame and
₁₁

honor to their hometowns.

❏ **Exercise 48. Let's talk.** (Chapter 11)
Discuss these questions. Work in small groups or as a class.

1. What is one of the most satisfying experiences in your life?
2. Do you ever get stressed? What stresses you?
3. Are you concerned about global warming? Why or why not?
4. What things in your daily life do you sometimes get tired of doing?
5. We all want to accomplish good things in our life and be good people. After you're gone,
   how do you want to be remembered?

❏ **Exercise 49. Let's talk or write.** (Chapter 11)
Discuss and/or write about one or more of the topics.

Topics:
1. *Athletes as Heroes*
   What are the most popular sports in your country and who are today's sports heroes? Who
   were your sports heroes (if any) when you were a child? How are athletes viewed by the
   general public in your country? Do you feel athletes are important role models for
   children?

2. *Men's vs. Women's Sports*
   When you were growing up, were girls' sports and boys' sports considered to be of equal
   importance in your school? Traditionally, women's sports have been viewed as less
   significant than men's sports, but today men's and women's sports are treated equally in
   the Olympics. Do you feel that women's sports are as valuable and entertaining as men's
   sports? If you are a fan of one but not the other, why?

3. *International Competition*
   Sports are competitive activities with winners and losers, yet the modern Olympics can be seen as valuable in creating international understanding and cooperation. What do you feel is the value (if any) of international sports competitions such as the Olympics?

❏ **Exercise 50. Check your knowledge.** (Chapter 11)
Correct the errors.

         interested
1. I am ~~interesting~~ in his ideas.

2. Two people got hurted in the accident and were took to the hospital by an ambulance.

3. The movie was so bored that we fell asleep after an hour.

4. The students helped by the clear explanation that the teacher gave.

5. The winner of the race hasn't been announcing yet.

6. When and where has the automobile invented?

7. My brother and I have always been interesting in learning more about our family tree.★

8. I am not agree with you, and I don't think you'll ever convince me.

9. It was late, and I was getting very worry about my mother.

10. Many strange things were happened last night.

11. I didn't go to dinner with them because I had already been eaten.

12. In class yesterday, I was confusing. I didn't understand the lesson.

13. When we were children, we are very afraid of caterpillars. Whenever we saw one of these monsters, we were run to our house before the caterpillars could attack us. I still get scare when I saw a caterpillar close to me.

14. One day, while the old man was cutting down a big tree near the stream, his axe was fallen into the river. He sat down and begin to cry because he does not have enough money to buy another axe.

★*family tree* = a genealogical diagram that shows how family members are related; each generation is represented by a new "branch" of the tree.

Chapter 12
Noun Clauses

❑ **Exercise 1. Warm-up.** (Chart 12-1)
Check (✓) the complete sentences.

1. __✓__ Jin studies business.
2. ____ What does Jin study?
3. ____ What Jin studies?
4. ____ What Jin studies is business.
5. ____ His books.
6. ____ I don't know how much his books cost.
7. ____ How much his books cost?
8. ____ How much do his books cost?

12-1	Introduction	
independent clause (a) ⌈Sue lives in Tokyo.⌉	A clause is a group of words containing a subject and a verb.* An INDEPENDENT CLAUSE (or *main clause*) is a complete sentence. It contains the main subject and verb of a sentence. Examples (a) and (b) are complete sentences. Example (a) is a statement; (b) is a question.	
independent clause (b) ⌈Where does Sue live?⌉		
dependent clause (c) ⌈where Sue lives⌉	A DEPENDENT CLAUSE (or *subordinate clause*) is not a complete sentence. Example (c) is a dependent clause.	
noun clause (d) I know ⌈*where Sue lives.*⌉	Example (d) is a complete sentence, with a main subject (*I*) and verb (*know*) followed by a dependent clause. *Where Sue lives* is called a *noun clause*.	
S V O (e) I **know** ⌈*what he said.*⌉ S V (f) ⌈*What he said*⌉ **is** true.	A NOUN CLAUSE has the same uses in a sentence as a noun: it is used as an object or a subject. In (e): The noun clause is the object of the verb **know**. In (f): The noun clause is the subject of the verb **is**.	

*A *phrase* is a group of words that does NOT contain a subject and a verb.

❏ **Exercise 2. Looking at grammar.** (Chart 12-1)

Underline the noun clause in each sentence. Some sentences do not have one.

1. I couldn't hear <u>what the teacher said</u>.

2. What did the teacher say? (*no noun clause*)

3. No one knows where Tom went.

4. Where Tom went is a secret.

5. What does Nancy want?

6. We need to know what Nancy wants.

❏ **Exercise 3. Looking at grammar.** (Chart 12-1)

Add punctuation and capitalization. Underline the noun clauses.

1. Where did Sara go did she go home → *Where did Sara go?* ***D****id she go home?*

2. I don't know <u>where Sara went</u> → *I don't know where Sara went.*

3. What does Alex need do you know

4. Do you know what Alex needs

5. What Alex needs is a new job

6. We talked about what Alex needs

7. What do you need did you talk to your parents about what you need

8. My parents know what I need

❏ **Exercise 4. Looking at grammar.** (Chart 12-1)

Are these sentences true for you? Circle *yes* or *no*. Discuss your answers.

1. What my family thinks of me is very important to me.	yes	no
2. I always pay attention to what other people think of me.	yes	no
3. Where we live is exciting.	yes	no
4. Where we live is expensive.	yes	no
5. I think how most celebrities behave is admirable.	yes	no
6. I usually don't believe what I read in advertisements.	yes	no

❏ **Exercise 5. Warm-up.** (Chart 12-2)
Choose the correct sentences.

1. Where does Brad live?
   a. I'm not sure where he lives.
   b. I'm not sure where does he live.

2. I'm looking for Brad.
   a. Could you tell me where is Brad?
   b. Could you tell me where Brad is?

12-2 Noun Clauses Beginning with a Question Word

Question	Noun Clause	
Where does she live? What did he say? When do they arrive?	(a) I don't know *where she lives*. (b) I couldn't hear *what he said*. (c) Do you know *when they arrive*?	In (a): *where she lives* is the object of the verb *know*. In a noun clause, the subject precedes the verb. Do not use question word order in a noun clause. Notice: *does*, *did*, and *do* are used in questions but not in noun clauses. See Appendix Chart B-2 for more information about question words and question forms.
S **V** Who lives there? Who is at the door?	**S** **V** (d) I don't know *who lives there*. (e) I wonder *who is at the door*.	In (d) and (e): The word order is the same in both the question and the noun clause because *who* is the subject in both.
V **S** Who are those men? Whose house is that?	**S** **V** (f) I don't know *who those men are*. (g) I wonder *whose house that is*.	In (f): *those men* is the subject of the question, so it is placed in front of the verb *be* in the noun clause.*
What did she say? What should they do?	(h) *What she said* surprised me. **S** **V** (i) ⌐*What they should do*¬ is obvious.	In (h): *What she said* is the subject of the sentence. Notice in (i): A noun clause subject takes a singular verb (e.g., *is*).

*COMPARE: *Who **is** at the door?* = *who* is the subject of the question.
            *Who **are** those men?* = *those men* is the subject of the question, so *be* is plural.

❏ **Exercise 6. Looking at grammar.** (Chart 12-2)
Change each question in parentheses to a noun clause.

1. (*How old is he?*) I don't know _____*how old he is*_____.

2. (*What was he talking about?*) _____ was interesting.

3. (*Where do you live?*) Please tell me _____.

4. (*Where did she go?*) _____ is none of your business.

5. (*When are they coming?*) Do you know _____?

6. (*Which one does he want?*) Let's ask him _____.

7. (*What happened?*) I don't know _____.

8. (*Who opened the door?*) I don't know _____.

9. (*Why did they leave the country?*) _____ is a secret.

10. (*What are we doing in class?*) _____ is easy.

11. (*Who are those people?*) I don't know _____.

12. (*Whose pen is this?*) Do you know _____?

❏ **Exercise 7. Looking at grammar.** (Chart 12-2)
Change the questions to noun clauses. Begin with **Can you tell me**.

Example: What time does the computer lab close?
→ *Can you tell me what time the computer lab closes?*

1. How is this word pronounced?
2. What does this mean?
3. What was my grade?
4. Who am I supposed to talk to?
5. When is our next assignment due?
6. How much time do we have for the test?
7. When do classes end for the year?
8. Where is our class going to meet?

❏ **Exercise 8. Let's talk.** (Chart 12-2)
Speaker A asks a question. Speaker B responds beginning with **I don't know** OR **I wonder**.
Use the names of your classmates. Work in pairs, in groups, or as a class.

Example: Where is (_____)?
SPEAKER A (*book open*): Where is Marco?
SPEAKER B (*book closed*): I don't know where Marco is. OR I wonder where Marco is.

(Change roles if working in pairs.)

1. Where does (_____) live?
2. What country is (_____) from?
3. How long has (_____) been living here?
4. What is (_____) telephone number?
5. Where is the post office?
6. How far is it to the South Pole?
7. What kind of watch does (_____) have?
8. Why was (_____) absent yesterday?
9. What is (_____) favorite color?
10. How long has (_____) been married?
11. Why are we doing this exercise?
12. Who turned off the lights?
13. Where are you going to eat lunch/dinner?
14. Where did (_____) go after class yesterday?
15. Why is (_____) smiling?
16. How often does (_____) go to the library?
17. Whose book is that?
18. How much did that book cost?

Exercise 9. Looking at grammar. (Chart 12-2)
Make questions from the given sentences. The words in parentheses should be the answer to
the question you make. Begin with a question word (**who, what, how, when, where, why**).
Then change the question to a noun clause.

1. Tom will be here (*next week*).

   QUESTION: _____When will Tom be here?_____

   NOUN CLAUSE: Please tell me _____when Tom will be here._____

2. He is coming (*because he wants to visit his friends*).

   QUESTION: _____

   NOUN CLAUSE: Please tell me _____

3. He'll be on flight (*645, not flight 742*).

   QUESTION: _____

   NOUN CLAUSE: Please tell me _____

4. (*Jim Hunter*) is going to meet him at the airport.

   QUESTION: _____

   NOUN CLAUSE: Please tell me _____

5. Jim Hunter is (*his roommate*).

   QUESTION: _____

   NOUN CLAUSE: Please tell me _____

6. He lives (*on Riverside Road in Columbus, Ohio, USA*).

   QUESTION: _____

   NOUN CLAUSE: Please tell me _____

7. He was (*in Chicago*) last week.

   QUESTION: _____

   NOUN CLAUSE: Please tell me _____

8. He has been working for Sony Corporation (*since 2000*).

   QUESTION: _____

   NOUN CLAUSE: Do you know _____

9. He has (*a Sony*) computer at home.

   QUESTION: _____

   NOUN CLAUSE: Do you know _____

❑ **Exercise 10. Looking at grammar.** (Chart 12-2)
Complete each sentence with the words in parentheses. Use any appropriate verb tense. Some of the completions contain noun clauses, and some contain questions.

1. A: Where (*Ruth, go*) _____did Ruth go_____? She's not in her room.

   B: I don't know. Ask her friend Tina. She might know where (*Ruth, go*)

   _____Ruth went_____.

2. A: Oops! I made a mistake. Where (*my eraser, be*) _____?
   Didn't I lend it to you?

   B: I don't have it. Ask Sally where (*it, be*) _____. I think I saw her using it.

3. A: The door isn't locked! Why (*Franco, lock, not*) _____ it
   before he left?*

   B: Why ask me? How am I supposed to know why (*he, lock, not*) _____
   _____ it? Maybe he just forgot.

4. A: Mr. Lee is a recent immigrant, isn't he? How long (*he, be*) _____ in
   this country?

   B: I have no idea, but I'll be seeing Mr. Lee this afternoon. Would you like me to ask him
   how long (*he, be*) _____ here?

5. A: Help! Quick! Look at that road sign! Which road (*we, be supposed*) _____
   _____ to take?

   B: Don't look at me! You're the driver. I don't know which road (*we, be supposed*)
   _____ to take. I've never been here before.

---

*Word order in negative questions:
  Usual: *Why didn't you call me?* (with *did* + *not* contracted)
  Very formal: *Why did you not call me?*

❏ **Exercise 11. Listening.** (Chart 12-2)
Listen to the dialogues. Choose the completions you hear.

1. a. how far it is.
   b. How far is it?

2. a. how far it is.
   b. How far is it?

3. a. why we watched the whole thing.
   b. Why did we watch the whole thing?

4. a. why you watched it.
   b. why did you watch it?

5. a. how old she is.
   b. How old is she?

6. a. how this word is pronounced.
   b. How is this word pronounced?

7. a. what the problem is.
   b. what is the problem?

❏ **Exercise 12. Let's talk: interview.** (Chart 12-2)
Ask your classmates if they can answer questions based on the given information. Begin with
Do you know followed by a question word (***who, what, when, where, how many, how
long, how far***). If no one in the class knows the answer to a question, research the answer.
Share any information you get with the rest of the class.

Example: the shortest month of the year
SPEAKER A: Do you know *what* the shortest month of the year is?
SPEAKER B: Yes. It's February. OR No, I don't know what the shortest month is.

1. the number of minutes in 24 hours
2. the year the first man walked on the moon
3. the winner of the Nobel Peace Prize last year
4. the place Buddha was born
5. the distance from the earth to the sun
6. the time it takes for the moon to rotate around the earth

❏ **Exercise 13. Warm-up.** (Chart 12-3)
Underline the noun clauses. What words are added when a yes/no question is changed to a
noun clause?

QUESTION: Has the mail arrived?
NOUN CLAUSE: I wonder <u>if the mail has arrived</u>.
              I wonder whether the mail has arrived.
              I wonder whether or not the mail has arrived.
              I wonder whether the mail has arrived or not.
              I wonder if the mail has arrived or not.

12-3 Noun Clauses Beginning with *Whether* or *If*

Yes/No Question	Noun Clause	

Will she come?
 	
Does he need help?
	(a) I don't know *whether she will come.*
	    I don't know *if she will come.*
	
	(b) I wonder *whether he needs help.*
	    I wonder *if he needs help.*
		When a yes/no question is changed to a noun clause, ***whether*** or ***if*** is used to introduce the clause.
		
		NOTE: ***Whether*** is more common than ***if*** in formal English. Both ***whether*** and ***if*** are commonly used in speaking.

	(c) I wonder *whether or not* she will come. (d) I wonder *whether* she will come *or not.* (e) I wonder *if* she will come **or not.**	In (c), (d), and (e): Notice the patterns when ***or not*** is used.
	(f) ***Whether she comes or not*** is unimportant to me.	In (f): Notice that the noun clause is in the subject position.

□ **Exercise 14. Looking at grammar.** (Chart 12-3)
Complete the sentences by changing the questions to noun clauses.

SITUATION: You're at the office.

Example: Let me know if . . .
    Did you finish the sales report? → *Let me know if you finished the sales report.*

Let me know if . . .
1. Is the financial report ready?
2. Will it be ready tomorrow?
3. Does the copy machine need paper?
4. Is someone waiting for me?
5. Do we need anything for the meeting?
6. Are you going to be there?

Please check whether . . .
7. Did they get my message?
8. Is the copy machine working?
9. Is there any paper left?
10. Is this information correct?
11. Did the fax come in?
12. Are we going to have Monday off?

□ **Exercise 15. Let's talk.** (Chart 12-3)
Speaker A asks a question. Speaker B responds beginning with ***I wonder***. Work in pairs, in small groups, or as a class.

Example:
SPEAKER A (*book open*):   Does Anna need any help?
SPEAKER B (*book closed*): I wonder whether/if Anna needs any help.

1. Where is Tom?
2. Should we wait for him?
3. Is he having trouble?
4. When was the first book written?
5. What causes earthquakes?
6. How long does a butterfly live?

(Change roles if working in pairs.)
7. Whose dictionary is this?
8. Does it belong to William?
9. Why did dinosaurs become extinct?
10. Is there life on other planets?
11. How did life begin?
12. Will people live on the moon someday?

❏ **Exercise 16. Let's talk: interview.** (Chart 12-3)
Interview students in your class. Ask each one a different question. Begin with **Can/Could you tell me.** Share a few of your answers with the class.

1. Have you ever won a prize? What?
2. Have you ever played a joke on someone? Describe it.
3. Have you ever stayed up all night? Why?
4. Have you ever felt embarrassed? Why?
5. Have you ever been in an earthquake? Where? When?
6. Do you have a talent like singing or dancing (*or something else*)? What?
7. Are you enjoying this interview? Why or why not?

❏ **Exercise 17. Let's talk: pairwork.** (Charts 12-1 → 12-3)
Work with a partner to create short dialogues. Partner A asks a question. Partner B answers the question beginning with the words in *italics*.

SITUATION: You're late for school. You need help finding your things.

Example: I don't know . . . .
         Where are my glasses?
PARTNER A (*book open*):   Where are my glasses?
PARTNER B (*book closed*): I don't know where your glasses are.

SITUATION 1: You're late for work.

I don't know . . . .

1. Where did I leave my keys?
2. Where did I put my shoes?
3. Where's my other sock?
4. What did I do with my briefcase?

SITUATION 2: You have a new neighbor.

I'll find out . . . .

5. Where's he from?
6. What does he do?
7. Where does he work?
8. Would he like to come to dinner?

Change roles.
SITUATION 3: You're at a tourist center.

Let's ask . . . .

9. Where is the bus station?
10. How much does the city bus cost?
11. Do the city buses carry bikes?
12. Is this bus schedule correct?

We need to figure out . . . .

13. How far is it from here to town?
14. How much does it cost to take a taxi from here to downtown?
15. How can we get our money changed here?

❏ **Exercise 18. Looking at grammar.** (Charts 12-1 → 12-3)
Correct the errors.

1. Please tell me what ~~is your name~~ . *your name is*

2. No one seems to know when will Maria arrive.

3. I don't know what does that word mean.

4. I wonder does the teacher know the answer?

5. I'll ask her would she like some coffee or not.

6. Be sure to tell the doctor where does it hurt.

7. Why am I unhappy is something I can't explain.

8. Nobody cares do we stay or leave.

9. I need to know who is your teacher.

10. I don't understand why is the car not running properly.

11. My young son wants to know where do the stars go in the daytime?

❏ **Exercise 19. Let's talk.** (Charts 12-1 → 12-3)
Work in small groups. What would you say in each situation? Use noun clauses.

Example: Someone asks you about the time the mail comes. You're not sure.
Possible answers: I'm not sure what time the mail comes.
I don't know when the mail is supposed to be here.
Etc.

1. You see a restaurant. You can't tell if it's open yet. You ask a man standing outside.
2. You were absent yesterday. You want to know the homework. You ask another student.
3. Someone asks you the date. You don't know, but you tell them you'll find out.
4. Someone asks you about the weather tomorrow. Is it supposed to be sunny? You haven't heard.
5. You're at a clothing store. You're buying a coat and want to know about the return policy. How many days do you have to return it? You ask a salesperson.
6. Your friend asks you if you want to go to a movie or get a DVD to watch at home. Both sound good to you. You tell your friend you don't care which you do.
7. You have a late fee on your bill. You want to know why. You call the company and ask.
8. You are planning a hiking trip with a friend. This friend wants to bring his dog and asks you if it is okay. It doesn't matter to you.

❏ **Exercise 20. Warm-up.** (Chart 12-4)
Complete the second sentence of each pair with an infinitive. Use *to get* or *to do*. Is the meaning in each pair the same or different?

1. a. Susan doesn't know what she should do.

   b. Susan doesn't know what _____.

2. a. She needs to figure out how she will get home.

   b. She needs to figure out how _____ home.

> What should I do?
> I don't have any money
> for the bus. How am
> I going to get home?

12-4 Question Words Followed by Infinitives

(a) I don't know *what I should do*. (b) I don't know *what to do*. (c) Pam can't decide *whether she should go or stay home*. (d) Pam can't decide *whether to go or (to) stay home*. (e) Please tell me *how I can get to the bus station*. (f) Please tell me *how to get to the bus station*. (g) Jim told us *where we could find it*. (h) Jim told us *where to find it*.	Question words (*when, where, how, who, whom, whose, what, which,* and *whether*) may be followed by an infinitive. Each pair of sentences in the examples has the same meaning. Notice that the meaning expressed by the infinitive is either *should* or *can/could*.

❑ **Exercise 21. Looking at grammar.** (Chart 12-4)
Make sentences with the same meaning by using infinitives.

1. Sally told me when I should come. → *Sally told me when to come.*

2. The plumber told me how I could fix the leak in the sink.

3. Please tell me where I should meet you.

4. Robert had a long excuse for being late for their date, but Sandy didn't know whether she should believe him or not.

5. Jim found two shirts he liked, but he had trouble deciding which one he should buy.

6. I've done everything I can think of to help Andy get his life straightened out. I don't know what else I can do.

❑ **Exercise 22. In your own words.** (Chart 12-4)
Complete the sentences with your own words. Use infinitives in your completions.

1. A: I can't decide _____ *what to wear* _____ to the reception.

   B: How about your green suit?

2. A: Where are you going to live when you go to the university?

   B: I'm not sure. I can't decide whether _____ or

   _____ .

3. A: Do you know how _____ ?

   B: No, but I'd like to learn.

4. A: I don't know what _____ for her birthday. Got any ideas?

   B: How about a book?

5. My cousin has a dilemma. He can't decide whether _____ or

   _____ . What do you think he should do?

6. Before you leave on your trip, read this tour book. It tells you where

   _____ and how _____ .

❑ **Exercise 23. Warm-up.** (Chart 12-5)
Check (✓) the grammatically correct sentences.

1. ___✓___ We know *that the planets revolve around the sun.*

2. _____ Centuries ago, people weren't aware *that the planets revolved around the sun.*

3. _____ *That the planets revolve around the sun* is now a well-known fact.

4. _____ Is clear *that the planets revolve around the sun.*

12-5 Noun Clauses Beginning with *That*

Verb + *That*-Clause

(a) I **think** *that Bob will come.* (b) I **think** *Bob will come.*	In (a): *that Bob will come* is a noun clause. It is used as the object of the verb **think**. The word *that* is usually omitted in speaking, as in (b). It is usually included in formal writing. See the list below for verbs commonly followed by a *that*-clause.

agree that	*feel* that	*know* that	*remember* that
believe that	*find out* that	*learn* that	*say* that
decide that	*forget* that	*notice* that	*tell* someone that
discover that	*hear* that	*promise* that	*think* that
explain that	*hope* that	*read* that	*understand* that

Person + *Be* + Adjective + *That*-Clause

(c) **Jan is happy** (*that*) *Bob called.*	*That*-clauses commonly follow certain adjectives, such as *happy* in (c), when the subject refers to a person (or persons). See the list below.

I'm *afraid* that*	Al is *certain* that	We're *happy* that	Jan is *sorry* that
I'm *amazed* that	Al is *confident* that	We're *pleased* that	Jan is *sure* that
I'm *angry* that	Al is *disappointed* that	We're *proud* that	Jan is *surprised* that
I'm *aware* that	Al is *glad* that	We're *relieved* that	Jan is *worried* that

It + *Be* + Adjective + *That*-Clause

(d) **It is clear** (*that*) *Ann likes her new job.*	*That*-clauses commonly follow adjectives in sentences that begin with *it* + *be*, as in (d). See the list below.

It's *amazing* that	It's *interesting* that	It's *obvious* that	It's *true* that
It's *clear* that	It's *likely* that	It's *possible* that	It's *undeniable* that
It's *good* that	It's *lucky* that	It's *strange* that	It's *well-known* that
It's *important* that	It's *nice* that	It's *surprising* that	It's *wonderful* that

That-Clause Used as a Subject

(e) *That Ann likes her new job* is clear.	It is possible but uncommon for *that*-clauses to be used as the subject of a sentence, as in (e). The word *that* is not omitted when the *that*-clause is used as a subject.
(f) **The fact** (*that*) *Ann likes her new job* is clear. (g) **It is a fact** (*that*) *Ann likes her new job.*	More often, a *that*-clause in the subject position begins with **the fact that**, as in (f), or is introduced by **it is a fact**, as in (g).

To be afraid has two possible meanings:
    (1) It can express fear: *I'm afraid of dogs. I'm afraid that his dog will bite me.*
    (2) It often expresses a meaning similar to "to be sorry": *I'm afraid that I can't accept your invitation. I'm afraid you have the wrong number.*

□ **Exercise 24. In your own words.** (Chart 12-5)
Complete the sentences with your own words.

1. I recently heard on the news that . . . .
2. When I was young, I found out that . . . .
3. I sometimes forget that . . . .
4. All parents hope that . . . .
5. Most people in my country believe that . . . .
6. Do you feel that . . . ?
7. I recently read that . . . .
8. Scientists have discovered that . . . .
9. Students understand that . . . .
10. Have you noticed that . . . ?

□ **Exercise 25. Let's talk: interview.** (Chart 12-5)
Interview your classmates. Ask each one a different question. Their answers should follow this pattern: *I'm* + *adjective* + *that*-clause.

Example: What is something in your life that you're glad about?
→ *I'm glad that my family is supportive of me.*

1. What is something that disappointed you in the past?
2. What is something that annoys you?
3. What is something about your friends that pleases you?
4. What is something about nature that amazes you?
5. What is something about another culture's traditions that surprises you?
6. What is something that you are afraid will happen in the future?
7. What is something about your future that you are sure of?

□ **Exercise 26. Looking at grammar.** (Chart 12-5)
Make noun clauses using *it* and any appropriate word(s) from the list. Make an equivalent sentence by using a *that*-clause as the subject.

apparent	a pity	surprising	unfair
clear	a shame	too bad	unfortunate
a fact	strange	true	a well-known fact
obvious			

1. The world is round.
   → *It is a fact that the world is round.*
   → *That the world is round is a fact.*
2. Tim hasn't been able to make any friends.
3. The earth revolves around the sun.
4. Exercise can reduce heart disease.
5. Drug abuse can ruin one's health.
6. Some women do not earn equal pay for equal work.
7. Irene, who is an excellent student, failed her entrance examination.
8. English is the principal language of business throughout much of the world.

❑ **Exercise 27. Game.** (Chart 12-5)
Work in teams. Agree or disagree with the given statements. If you think the statement is true, begin with *It's a fact that*. If you think the statement is false, begin with *It isn't true that*. If you're not sure, guess. Choose one person to write your team's statements. The team with the most correct statements wins.★

1. ___*It's a fact that*___ most spiders have eight eyes.

2. ___*It isn't true that*___ some spiders have twelve legs.

3. _____ more males than females are colorblind.

4. _____ people's main source of vitamin D is fruit.

5. _____ the Great Wall of China took more than 1,000 years to build.

6. _____ twenty-five percent of the human body is water.

7. _____ a substance called chlorophyll makes plant leaves green.

8. _____ the World Wide Web went online in 2000.

9. _____ elephants have the longest pregnancy of any land animal.

10. _____ the first wheels were made out of stone.

11. _____ a diamond is the hardest substance found in nature.

❑ **Exercise 28. Looking at grammar.** (Chart 12-5)
A *that*-clause is frequently used with *the fact*. Combine the sentences. Introduce each noun clause with *The fact that*.

1. Ann was late. *That* didn't surprise me.
   → *The fact that Ann was late didn't surprise me.*
2. Rosa didn't come. *That* made me angry.
3. Many people in the world live in intolerable poverty. *That* must concern all of us.
4. I was supposed to bring my passport to the exam for identification. I was not aware of *that*.
5. The people of the town were given no warning of the approaching tornado. Due to *that*, there were many casualties.

❑ **Exercise 29. Looking at grammar.** (Chart 12-5)
Restate the sentences. Begin with *The fact that*.

1. It's understandable that you feel frustrated.
   → *The fact that you feel frustrated is understandable.*
2. It's undeniable that traffic is getting worse every year.
3. It's unfortunate that the city has no funds for the project.
4. It's obvious that the two leaders don't respect each other.
5. It's a miracle that there were no injuries from the car accident.

---

*Only the teacher should look at the answers, which can be found in the Answer Key for Chapter 12.

□ **Exercise 30. Let's talk.** (Chart 12-5)
Work in small groups. Do you agree or disagree with the statements? Circle *yes* or *no*.

1.	It's undeniable that smoking causes cancer.	yes	no
2.	It's a well-known fact that young boys are more aggressive than young girls.	yes	no
3.	It's unfortunate that people eat meat.	yes	no
4.	It's true that women are more nurturing than men.	yes	no
5.	That someday all countries in the world will live in peace is unlikely.	yes	no
6.	That governments need to pay more attention to global warming is a fact.	yes	no
7.	It's clear that life is easier now than it was 100 years ago.	yes	no
8.	That technology has given us more free time is clearly true.	yes	no

□ **Exercise 31. Reading comprehension.** (Chart 12-5)
Part I. Read the article.

canned   fresh

Canned vs. Fresh: Which Is Better?

Do you avoid eating canned fruits and vegetables because you think they may be less nutritious than fresh fruits and vegetables? Do you think they might be less healthy? For many people, the idea of eating canned fruits or vegetables is really not very appealing, and they would rather buy fresh produce. But what are the differences between canned and fresh produce? Let's take a look at the two.

Many people are surprised to hear that canned food can have as many nutrients as fresh. This is true because the fruits and vegetables are put into the cans shortly after being picked. Because the food is canned so quickly, the nutritional content is locked in. Food in a can will stay stable for two years.

256 CHAPTER 12

Fresh produce, on the other hand, may need to be transported. This can take up to two weeks. Fresh produce will continue to lose important nutrients until it is eaten. The sooner you can eat fresh produce, the more nutritious it will be.

There are also advantages to some fruits when they are first cooked and then canned. Tomatoes, for instance, have a substance called lycopene. This is a cancer-fighting ingredient that is found in cooked tomatoes. Fresh tomatoes do not have a significant amount of lycopene. It is better to eat tomato sauce from a can rather than fresh tomato sauce if you want to have lycopene in your diet.

Of course, there are disadvantages to canned foods. They tend to have a higher salt and sugar content. People who need to watch their salt or sugar intake should try to find cans low in salt or sugar. Also, because the canning process requires heat, some loss of vitamin C may occur, but most essential nutrients remain stable.

Finally, there is the issue of taste. For many, there is no comparison between the taste of fresh fruits and vegetables versus canned. No matter what the benefits of canning, some people refuse to eat anything that isn't fresh. How about you? Which do you prefer?

Part II. Read the statements. Circle "T" for true and "F" for false.

1. According to the article, it's surprising to many people that canned produce
   can be as nutritious as fresh produce.   T   F

2. It's a fact that food in a can will last for two years.   T   F

3. It's a well-known fact that canned tomatoes contain a cancer-fighting ingredient.   T   F

4. That fresh produce and canned produce taste the same is undeniable.   T   F

5. It's obvious that the writer believes canned food is better than fresh.   T   F

❑ **Exercise 32. Warm-up.** (Chart 12-6)
Read the words in the picture. Then look at the quoted speech below it. Circle the quotation marks. Is the punctuation inside or outside the quotation marks? In item 3, what do you notice about the punctuation?

1. "Watch out!" Mrs. Brooks said.

2. "Are you okay?" she asked.

3. "You look like you're going to fall off that ladder," she said.

12-6 Quoted Speech

Quoted speech refers to reproducing words exactly as they were originally spoken.* Quotation marks ("...") are used.**

Quoting One Sentence

(a) She said, " *My* brother is a student."	In (a): Use a comma after **she said**. Capitalize the first word of the quoted sentence. Put the final quotation marks outside the period at the end of the sentence.
(b) "My brother is a student," she said.	In (b): Use a comma, not a period, at the end of the quoted sentence when it precedes **she said**.
(c) "My brother," she said, " *is* a student."	In (c): If the quoted sentence is divided by **she said**, use a comma after the first part of the quote. Do not capitalize the first word after **she said**.

Quoting More Than One Sentence

(d) "My brother is a student. He is attending a university," she said.	In (d): Quotation marks are placed at the beginning and end of the complete quote. Notice: There are no quotation marks after **student**.
(e) "My brother is a student," she said. " *He* is attending a university."	In (e): Since **she said** comes between two quoted sentences, the second sentence begins with quotation marks and a capital letter.

Quoting a Question or an Exclamation

(f) She asked, "When will you be here?"	In (f): The question mark is inside the closing quotation marks.
(g) "When will you be here?" she asked.	In (g): Since a question mark is used, no comma is used before *she asked*.
(h) She said, "Watch out!"	In (h): The exclamation point is inside the closing quotation marks.
(i) "My brother is a student," *said Anna*. "My brother," *said Anna*, "is a student."	In (i): The noun subject (**Anna**) follows **said**. A noun subject often follows the verb when the subject and verb come in the middle or at the end of a quoted sentence. NOTE: A pronoun subject almost always precedes the verb. *"My brother is a student,"* **she said**. VERY RARE: *"My brother is a student,"* **said she**.
(j) "Let's leave," *whispered* Dave. (k) "Please help me," *begged* the unfortunate man. (l) "Well," Jack *began*, "it's a long story."	*Say* and *ask* are the most commonly used quote verbs. Some others: *add, agree, announce, answer, beg, begin, comment, complain, confess, continue, explain, inquire, promise, remark, reply, respond, shout, suggest, whisper.*

Quoted speech is also called "direct speech." *Reported speech* (discussed in Chart 12-7) is also called "indirect speech."

**In British English, quotation marks are called "inverted commas" and can consist of either double marks (") or a single mark ('): *She said, 'My brother is a student'.*

❏ **Exercise 33. Looking at grammar.** (Chart 12-6)
Add punctuation and capitalization.

1. Henry said   there is a phone call for you

2. There is a phone call for you   he said

3. There is   said Henry a phone call for you

4. There is a phone call for you   it's your sister   said Henry

5. There is a phone call for you   he said   it's your sister

6. I asked him   where is the phone

7. Where is the phone   she asked

8. Stop the clock   shouted the referee   we have an injured player

9. Who won the game   asked the spectator

10. I'm going to rest for the next three hours   she said   I don't want to be disturbed

    That's fine   I replied   you get some rest   I'll make sure no one disturbs you

❏ **Exercise 34. Looking at grammar.** (Chart 12-6)
Add punctuation and capitalization. Notice that a new paragraph begins each time the speaker changes.

When the police officer came over to my car, he said   let me see your driver's license, please

What's wrong, Officer   I asked   was I speeding

No, you weren't speeding   he replied you went through a red light at the corner of Fifth Avenue and Main Street   you almost caused an accident

Did I really do that   I said   I didn't see a red light

Exercise 35. Let's write. (Chart 12-6)
Write fables using quoted speech.

Summer

Winter

1. In fables, animals have the power of speech. Discuss what is happening in the illustrations of the grasshopper and the ants. Then write a fable based on the illustrations. Use quoted speech in your fable. Read your fable to a partner or small group.

2. Write a fable that is well known in your country. Use quoted speech.

❏ **Exercise 36. Warm-up.** (Chart 12-7)
Read the conversation between Mr. and Mrs. Cook. Then read the description. What do you notice about the verbs in blue?

DESCRIPTION:
Mr. Cook *said* he knew why Mrs. Cook couldn't find her glasses. He *told* her that they were on her head.

Quoted Speech	Reported Speech	
(a) "I *watch* TV every day."	→ She said she *watched* TV every day.	*Reported speech* refers to using a noun clause to report what someone has said. No quotation marks are used.
(b) "I *am watching* TV."	→ She said she *was watching* TV.	
(c) "I *have watched* TV."	→ She said she *had watched* TV.	
(d) "I *watched* TV."	→ She said she *had watched* TV.	
(e) "I *had watched* TV."	→ She said she *had watched* TV.	If the reporting verb (the main verb of the sentence, e.g., *said*) is simple past, the verb in the noun clause will usually also be in a past form, as in these examples.
(f) "I *will watch* TV."	→ She said she *would watch* TV.	
(g) "I *am going to watch* TV."	→ She said she *was going to watch* TV.	
(h) "I *can watch* TV."	→ She said she *could watch* TV.	
(i) "I *may watch* TV."	→ She said she *might watch* TV.	
(j) "I *must watch* TV."	→ She said she *had to watch* TV.	
(k) "I *have to watch* TV."	→ She said she *had to watch* TV.	
(l) "I *should watch* TV."	→ She said she *should watch* TV.	In (l): *should*, *ought to*, and *might* do not change.
"I *ought to watch* TV."	→ She said she *ought to watch* TV.	
"I *might watch* TV."	→ She said she *might watch* TV.	
(m) Immediate reporting: — What did the teacher just say? I didn't hear him. — He said he *wants* us to read Chapter 6.		Changing verbs to past forms in reported speech is common in both speaking and writing.
(n) Later reporting: — I didn't go to class yesterday. Did Mr. Jones give any assignments? — Yes. He said he *wanted* us to read Chapter 6.		However, sometimes in spoken English, no change is made in the noun clause verb, especially if the speaker is reporting something immediately or soon after it was said.
(o) "The world *is* round."	→ She said the world *is* round.	Also, sometimes the present tense is retained even in formal English when the reported sentence deals with a general truth, as in (o).
(p) "I *watch* TV every day."	→ She *says* she *watches* TV every day.	When the reporting verb is simple present, present perfect or future, the noun clause verb is not changed.
(q) "I *watch* TV every day."	→ She *has said* that she *watches* TV every day.	
(r) "I *watch* TV every day."	→ She *will say* that she *watches* TV every day.	
(s) "*Watch* TV."	→ She *told* me *to watch* TV.*	In reported speech, an imperative sentence is changed to an infinitive. *Tell* is used instead of *say* as the reporting verb. See Chart 14-6, p. 313, for other verbs followed by an infinitive that are used to report speech.

*NOTE: **Tell** is immediately followed by a (pro)noun object, but **say** is not: *He told **me** he would be late. He said he would be late.*
Also possible: *He said **to me** he would be late.*

❑ **Exercise 37. Looking at grammar.** (Chart 12-7)
Complete the sentences by reporting the speaker's words. Use noun clauses. Use past verb forms in noun clauses if appropriate.

1. Pedro said, "I will help you." Pedro said . . . .
   → *Pedro said (that) he would help me.*
2. "Do you need a pen?" Elena asked. Elena asked me . . . .
3. Jennifer asked, "What do you want?" Jennifer asked me . . . .
4. Talal asked, "Are you hungry?" Talal wanted to know . . . .
5. "I want a sandwich," Elena said. Elena said . . . .
6. "I'm going to move to Ohio," said Bruce. Bruce informed me . . . .
7. "Did you enjoy your trip?" asked Kim. Kim asked me . . . .
8. Oscar asked, "What are you talking about?" Oscar asked me . . . .
9. Maria asked, "Have you seen my grammar book?" Maria wanted to know . . . .
10. Amy said, "I don't want to go." Amy said . . . .
11. "Can you help me with my report?" asked David. David asked me . . . .
12. "I may be late," said Mitch. Mitch told me . . . .
13. Felix said, "You should work harder." Felix told me . . . .
14. Nadia said, "I have to go downtown." Nadia said . . . .
15. "Why is the sky blue?" my young daughter often asks. My young daughter often asks me . . . .
16. My mother asked, "Where is everyone?" My mother wondered . . . .
17. "I will come to the meeting," said Pavel. Pavel told me . . . .
18. Ms. Adams just asked Ms. Chang, "Will you be in class tomorrow?" Ms. Adams wanted to know . . . .
19. "I think I'll go to the library to study." Joe said . . . .
20. "Does Omar know what he's doing?" I wondered . . . .
21. "Is what I've heard true?" I wondered . . . .
22. "The sun rises in the east," said Mr. Clark. Mr. Clark, an elementary school teacher, explained to his students that . . . .
23. "Someday we'll be in contact with beings from outer space." The scientist predicted that . . . .

❑ **Exercise 38. Let's talk.** (Chart 12-7)
Students A and B have their books open. They read the dialogue aloud. Student C's book is closed. Your teacher asks Student C about the dialogue.

Example:
STUDENT A (*book open*):   What time is it?
STUDENT B (*book open*):   Two-thirty.
TEACHER: What did Manuel (*Student A*) want to know?
STUDENT C (*book closed*): He wanted to know what time it was (OR is).
TEACHER: What did Helen (*Student B*) say?
STUDENT C (*book closed*): She told him that it was (OR is) two-thirty.

1. STUDENT A: Can you speak Arabic?
   STUDENT B: A little.
   TEACHER: What did (*Student A*) ask?
              What did (*Student B*) say?

2. STUDENT A: Where is your grammar book?
   STUDENT B: In my backpack.
   TEACHER: What did (*Student A*) want to know?
   What did (*Student B*) tell (*Student A*)?

3. STUDENT A: What courses are you taking?
   STUDENT B: I'm taking three science courses this term.
   TEACHER: What did (*Student A*) want to know?
   What did (*Student B*) say?

4. STUDENT A: Did you finish your assignment?
   STUDENT B: Oh, no, my assignment! I totally forgot about it.
   TEACHER: What did (*Student A*) ask?
   What did (*Student B*) tell (*Student A*)?

5. STUDENT A: Have you had lunch already?
   STUDENT B: Yes, I just finished.
   TEACHER: What did . . . ?

6. STUDENT A: Where will you be tomorrow around three o'clock?
   STUDENT B: I have a doctor's appointment at 2:45.

7. STUDENT A: How do you like living here?
   STUDENT B: It's okay.

8. STUDENT A: Is what you said really true?
   STUDENT B: Yes, it's the truth. I'm not making it up.

9. STUDENT A: How many people have you met since you came here?
   STUDENT B: Lots. People here have been very friendly.

10. STUDENT A: Is what you want to talk to me about really important?
    STUDENT B: Yes, it's very important. We need to sit down and have a serious conversation.

❑ **Exercise 39. Let's talk.** (Charts 12-1 → 12-7)
Speaker A asks a question — whatever comes to mind — using each item and a question word (***when, how, where, what, why,*** *etc.*). Speaker B answers the question in a complete sentence. Speaker C reports what Speaker A and Speaker B said. Work in small groups or as a class.

Example: tonight
SPEAKER A (*Rosa*): What are you going to do tonight?
SPEAKER B (*Ali*): I'm going to study.
SPEAKER C (*Yung*): Rosa asked Ali what he was going to do tonight. Ali replied that he was going to study.

1. this evening	5. book	9. television
2. music	6. this city	10. dinner
3. courses	7. population	11. next year
4. tomorrow	8. last year	12. vacation

☐ **Exercise 40. Looking at grammar.** (Chart 12-7)
Complete the sentences with a past form of the verbs in parentheses.

1. A: The test is scheduled for Monday.

   B: Really? I heard it (*schedule*) _____ for Tuesday.

2. A: It's raining outside.

   B: Really? I thought it (*snow*) _____ .

3. A: Tony needs to borrow your bike for Saturday.

   B: Are you sure? I heard he (*need*) _____ to borrow it for Sunday.

4. A: Marita hasn't applied for a job yet.

   B: That's not what I heard. I heard she (*apply*) _____ for work
   at her uncle's company.

5. A: Mikhail can't come tonight.

   B: Are you sure? I heard he (*come*) _____ tonight.

6. A: Ms. Alvarez is going to retire.

   B: Really? I thought she (*continue*) _____ in her sales
   position for another year.

☐ **Exercise 41. Listening.** (Chart 12-7)
Listen to the sentences. Complete them using past verb forms to report speech.

CD 2
Track 2

1. The speaker said that she _____*wasn't going*_____ to the personnel meeting
   because she _____*had to*_____ finish a report.

2. The speaker said that he _____ Marta any money because his
   wallet _____ in his coat pocket back at home.

3. The speaker said that someone in the room _____ very strong
   perfume and it _____ her a headache.

4. The speaker said that he _____ Emma at the coffee shop at 9:00.
   He said he _____ not to be late.

5. The speaker said she _____ looking for a new job and asked
   her friend what he _____ she _____ .

6. The speaker said that they _____ late for the concert
   because his wife _____ attend a business function after work.

❏ **Exercise 42. Looking at grammar.** (Chart 12-7)
Change quoted speech to reported speech. Study the example carefully and use the same
pattern: ***said that . . . and that***.

1. "My father is a businessman. My mother is an engineer."

   He said that _____*his father was a businessman and that his mother was an engineer.*_____

2. "I'm excited about my new job. I've found a nice apartment."

   I got an email from my sister yesterday. She said _____

   _____

3. "I expect you to be in class every day. Unexcused absences may affect your grades."

   Our sociology professor said _____

   _____

4. "Highway 66 will be closed for two months. Commuters should seek alternate routes."

   The newspaper said _____

   _____

5. "Every obstacle is a steppingstone to success. You should view problems in your life as

   opportunities to prove yourself."

   My father often told me _____

   _____

❏ **Exercise 43. Let's write.** (Charts 12-1 → 12-7)
Read each dialogue and write a report about it. Your report should include an accurate idea of
the speaker's words, but it doesn't have to use the exact words.

Example: Jack said, "I can't go to the game."
  Tom said, "Oh? Why not?"
  "I don't have enough money for a ticket," replied Jack.

Possible written reports:
→ Jack told Tom that he couldn't go to the game because he didn't have enough money for
  a ticket.
→ When Tom asked Jack why he couldn't go to the game, Jack said he didn't have enough
  money for a ticket.
→ Jack said he couldn't go to the game. When Tom asked him why not, Jack replied that he
  didn't have enough money for a ticket.

Write reports for these dialogues.
1.   "What are you doing?" Alex asked.
    "I'm drawing a picture," I said.

2.   Asako said, "Do you want to go to a movie
    Sunday night?"

Cho said, "I'd like to, but I have to study."

3.   "How old are you, Mrs. Robinson?" the little boy asked.

Mrs. Robinson said, "It's not polite to ask people their age."

"How much money do you make?" the little boy asked.

"That's impolite too," Mrs. Robinson said.

4.   "Is there anything you especially want to watch on TV tonight?" my sister asked.

"Yes," I replied. "There's a show at eight that I've been waiting to see for a long time."

"What is it?" she asked.

"It's a documentary on green sea turtles," I said.

"Why do you want to see that?"

"I'm doing a research paper on sea turtles. I think I might be able to get some good information from the documentary. Why don't you watch it with me?"

"No, thanks," she said. "I'm not especially interested in green sea turtles."

❑ **Exercise 44. Check your knowledge.** (Charts 12-1 → 12-7)
Correct the errors.

1. Tell the taxi driver where do you want to go.

2. My roommate came into the room and asked me why aren't you in class? I said I am waiting for a telephone call from my family.

3. It was my first day at the university, and I am on my way to my first class. I wondered who else will be in the class. What the teacher would be like?

4. He asked me that what did I intend to do after I graduate?

5. What does a patient tell a doctor it is confidential.

6. What my friend and I did it was our secret. We didn't even tell our parents what did we do.

7. The doctor asked that I felt okay. I told him that I don't feel well.

8. I asked him what kind of movies does he like, he said me, I like romantic movies.

9. Is true you almost drowned? my friend asked me. Yes, I said. I'm really glad to be alive. It was really frightening.

10. It is a fact that I almost drowned makes me very careful about water safety whenever I go swimming.

11. I didn't know where am I supposed to get off the bus, so I asked the driver where is the science museum. She tell me the name of the street. She said she will tell me when should I get off the bus.

12. My mother did not live with us. When other children asked me where was my mother, I told them she is going to come to visit me very soon.

13. When I asked the taxi driver to drive faster, he said I will drive faster if you pay me more. At that time I didn't care how much would it cost, so I told him to go as fast as he can.

14. My parents told me is essential to know English if I want to study at an American university.

❏ **Exercise 45. Let's talk.** (Charts 12-1 → 12-7)
Give a one-minute impromptu speech on any topic that interests you (insects, soccer, dogs, etc.). Your classmates will take notes as you speak. Later, in a short paragraph or orally, they will report what you said.

❏ **Exercise 46. Let's talk and write.** (Charts 12-1 → 12-7)
You and your classmates are newspaper reporters at a press conference. You will all interview your teacher or a person whom your teacher invites to class. Your assignment is to write a newspaper article about the person whom you interviewed.

Take notes during the interview. Write down some of the important sentences so that you can use them for quotations in your article. Ask for clarification if you do not understand something the interviewee has said. It is important to report information accurately.

In your article, try to organize your information into related topics. For example, if you interview your teacher, you might use this outline:

    I. General introductory information
   II. Professional life
      A. Present teaching duties
      B. Academic duties and activities outside of teaching
      C. Past teaching experience
      D. Educational background
  III. Personal life
      A. Basic biographical information (e.g., place of birth, family background, places of residence)
      B. Free-time activities and interests
      C. Travel experiences

This outline only suggests a possible method of organization. You must organize your own article, depending upon the information you have gained from your interview.

When you write your report, most of your information will be presented in reported speech; use quoted speech only for the most important or memorable sentences.

NOTE: When you use quoted speech, be sure you are presenting the interviewee's *exact words*. If you are simply paraphrasing what the interviewee said, do not use quotation marks.

❑ **Exercise 47. Let's talk and write.** (Charts 12-1 → 12-7)
Work in small groups. Discuss one (or more) of the given statements. Write a report of the main points made by each speaker in your group. (Do not attempt to report every word that was spoken.)

In your report, use words such as *think*, *believe*, *say*, *remark*, and *state* to introduce noun clauses. When you use *think* or *believe*, you will probably use present tenses (e.g., *Omar **thinks** that money **is** the most important thing in life.*). When you use *say*, *remark*, or *state*, you will probably use past tenses (e.g., *Olga **said** that many other things **were** more important than money.*).

Do you agree with these statements? Why or why not?

1. Money is the most important thing in life.
2. A woman can do any job a man can do.
3. When a person decides to get married, his or her love for the other person is the only important consideration.
4. A world government is both desirable and necessary. Countries should simply become the states of one nation, the Earth. In this way, wars could be eliminated and wealth could be equally distributed.

❑ **Exercise 48. Warm-up.** (Chart 12-8)
Read the sentences. Then substitute the phrases in the list for the words in blue.

SITUATION: Mr. and Mrs. Smith plan to retire soon and travel around the world.

in any way that	anything that	any place that	at any time that

1. They'll go wherever they want.
2. They'll leave whenever they want.
3. They'll do whatever they want.
4. They'll help people however they can.

12-8 Using *-ever* Words

The following *-ever* words give the idea of "any." Each pair of sentences in the examples has the same meaning.

whoever	(a)	***Whoever*** wants to come is welcome. *Anyone who* wants to come is welcome.
	(b)	He makes friends easily with ***whoever*** he meets.* He makes friends easily with *anyone who* he meets.
whatever	(c)	He always says ***whatever*** comes into his mind. He always says *anything that* comes into his mind.
whenever	(d)	You may leave ***whenever*** you wish. You may leave *at any time that* you wish.
wherever	(e)	She can go ***wherever*** she wants to go. She can go *anyplace that* she wants to go.
however	(f)	The students may dress ***however*** they please. The students may dress *in any way that* they please.

*In (b): ***whomever*** is also possible; it is the object of the verb ***meets***. In American English, ***whomever*** is rare and very formal. In British English, ***whoever*** (not ***whomever***) is used as the object form: *He makes friends easily with whoever he meets.*

268 CHAPTER 12

❑ **Exercise 49. Looking at grammar.** (Chart 12-8)
Complete the sentences with *-ever* words.

1. Mustafa is free to go anyplace he wishes. He can go _____*wherever*_____ he wants.

2. Mustafa is free to go anytime he wishes. He can go _____ he wants.

3. I don't know what you should do about that problem. Do _____ seems best to you.

4. I want you to be honest. I hope you feel free to say _____ is on your mind.

5. _____ leads a life full of love and happiness is rich.

6. If you want to rearrange the furniture, go ahead. You can rearrange it _____ you want. I don't care one way or the other.

7. Those children are wild! I feel sorry for _____ has to be their babysitter.

8. I have a car. I can take you _____ you want to go.

9. Irene does _____ she wants to do, goes _____ she wants to go, gets up _____ she wants to get up, makes friends with _____ she meets, and dresses _____ she pleases.

Chapter **13**
Adjective Clauses

❏ **Exercise 1. Warm-up.** (Chart 13-1)
The sentences are all correct. The words in blue are all pronouns. What nouns do they refer to? How does the noun affect the choice of the pronoun?

    1. a. We helped the man. He was lost in the woods.
        b. We helped the man who was lost in the woods.
        c. We helped the man that was lost in the woods.

    2. a. The new computer is fast. It is in my office.
        b. The new computer which is in my office is fast.
        c. The new computer that is in my office is fast.

13-1	**Adjective Clause Pronouns Used as the Subject**	
	I thanked the woman. **She** helped me. ↓	In (a): ***I thanked the woman*** = a main clause; ***who helped me*** = an adjective clause.*
(a) I thanked the woman	*who* helped me.	An adjective clause modifies a noun.
(b) I thanked the woman	*that* helped me.	In (a): the adjective clause modifies ***woman***.
	The book is mine. **It** is on the table. ↓	In (a): ***who*** is the subject of the adjective clause. In (b): ***that*** is the subject of the adjective clause.
(c) The book *which*	*is on the table* is mine.	NOTE: (a) and (b) have the same meaning; (c) and (d)
(d) The book *that*	*is on the table* is mine.	have the same meaning.
		who = used for people ***which*** = used for things ***that*** = used for both people and things
(e) CORRECT: The book ***that is on the table*** is mine. (f) INCORRECT: The book is mine ~~that is on the table.~~		An adjective clause closely follows the noun it modifies.

*A *clause* is a structure that has a subject and a verb. There are two kinds of clauses: **independent** and **dependent**.
   In example (a):
   • The main clause (*I thanked the woman*) is also called an **independent** clause. An independent clause is a complete sentence and can stand alone.
   • The adjective clause (*who helped me*) is a **dependent** clause. A dependent clause is NOT a complete sentence and cannot stand alone. A dependent clause must be connected to an independent clause.

Exercise 2. Looking at grammar. (Chart 13-1)

Choose all the possible completions for each sentence. Do not add any commas or capital letters.

1. I met the doctor _____ helped my father after the accident.
   (a.) who   (b.) that   c. which   d. she

2. Where is the magazine _____ has the story about online theft?
   a. who   b. that   c. which   d. it

3. Did I tell you about the car salesman _____ tried to sell me a defective truck?
   a. who   b. that   c. which   d. he

4. The house _____ is across the street from us is going to be rented soon.
   a. who   b. that   c. which   d. it

Exercise 3. Looking at grammar. (Chart 13-1)

Combine the two sentences. Use the second sentence as an adjective clause.

1. I saw the man. He closed the door. → *I saw the man* $\begin{Bmatrix} who \\ that \end{Bmatrix}$ *closed the door.*
2. The girl is happy. She won the race.
3. The student is from China. He sits next to me.
4. The students are from China. They sit in the front row.
5. We are studying sentences. They contain adjective clauses.
6. I am using a sentence. It contains an adjective clause.

Exercise 4. Let's talk. (Chart 13-1)

Make true statements. Use *who* as the subject of an adjective clause. Work in pairs, in small groups, or as a class.

Example: I like teachers who . . . .
I like teachers who have a good sense of humor.
I like teachers who don't give tests. Etc.

1. People who . . . amaze me.
2. I don't like people who . . . .
3. Friends who . . . frustrate me.
4. Famous athletes who . . . are not good role models for children.

Exercise 5. Listening. (Chart 13-1)

Part I. When *who* is contracted with an auxiliary verb, the contraction is often hard to hear. Listen to the following sentences. What is the full, uncontracted form of the *italicized* verb?

CD 2
Track 3

1. He has a friend *who'll* help him. (*full form = who will*)
2. He has a friend *who's* helping him.
3. He has a friend *who's* helped him.
4. He has friends *who're* helping him.
5. He has friends *who've* helped him.
6. He has a friend *who'd* helped him.
7. He has a friend *who'd* like to help him.

Part II. Complete the sentences with the verbs you hear, but write the full, uncontracted form of each verb.

Example: You will hear: I know a man who's lived in 20 different countries.

You will write: I know a man who _____*has lived*_____ in 20 different countries.

8. We know a person who _____ great for the job.

9. We know a person who _____ to apply for the job.

10. That's the man who _____ the speech at our graduation.

11. I know a nurse who _____ around the world helping people.

12. Let's talk to the people who _____ the protest march.

13. There are people at the factory who _____ there all their adult lives.

14. The doctor who _____ care of my mother retired.

❑ **Exercise 6. Warm-up.** (Chart 13-2)
Read the passage and complete the sentences.

When William and Eva started their family, they decided that Eva would continue to work and William would quit his job to stay home with the children.

William has been a stay-at-home dad for the last seven years, but now both children are in school, and he's going back to work. He's looking for a job that will still allow him to spend time with his children. What kind of job do you think he is looking for?

He is looking for a job that/which . . . OR *He is not looking for a job that/which . . .*

1. leave him free on weekends
2. require him to work on weekends
3. include a lot of long-distance travel
4. have minimal travel requirements
5. have a long commute
6. be close to home
7. demand sixteen-hour work days
8. have flexible hours

13-2 Adjective Clause Pronouns Used as the Object of a Verb

The man was Mr. Jones. I saw **him**. ↓ (a) The man *who(m)* *I saw* was Mr. Jones. (b) The man *that* *I saw* was Mr. Jones. (c) The man Ø *I saw* was Mr. Jones.	Notice in the examples: The adjective clause pronouns are placed at the beginning of the clause.
The movie wasn't very good. We saw **it** last night. ↓ (d) The movie *which* *we saw last night* wasn't very good. (e) The movie *that* *we saw last night* wasn't very good. (f) The movie Ø *we saw last night* wasn't very good.	In (a): **who** is usually used instead of **whom**, especially in speaking. **Whom** is generally used only in very formal English. In (c) and (f): An object pronoun is often omitted (Ø) from an adjective clause. (A subject pronoun, however, may not be omitted.) **who(m)** = used for people **which** = used for things **that** = used for both people and things

(g) *INCORRECT:* The man who(m) I saw ~~him~~ was Mr. Jones.
               The man that I saw ~~him~~ was Mr. Jones.
               The man I saw ~~him~~ was Mr. Jones.
	In (g): The pronoun **him** must be removed. It is unnecessary because *who(m)*, *that*, or Ø functions as the object of the verb **saw**.

❏ **Exercise 7. Looking at grammar.** (Chart 13-2)
Choose all the possible completions for each sentence. Do not add any commas or capital letters.

1. Tell me about the people _____ you visited when you were in Oxford.
   (a.) who   (b.) that   c. which   d. she   (e.) whom   (f.) Ø

2. Do you want to see the pictures _____ the photographer took?
   a. who   b. that   c. which   d. they   e. whom   f. Ø

3. The people _____ I call most often on my cell phone are my mother and my sister.
   a. who   b. that   c. which   d. she   e. whom   f. Ø

4. The apartment _____ we wanted to rent is no longer available.
   a. who   b. that   c. which   d. it   e. whom   f. Ø

5. The children _____ the Smiths adopted are from three different countries.
   a. who   b. that   c. which   d. they   e. whom   f. Ø

❏ **Exercise 8. Looking at grammar.** (Chart 13-2)
Combine the two sentences. Use the second sentence as an adjective clause. Give all the possible patterns, orally or in writing.

1. The book was good. I read it.
   → *The book that/which/Ø I read was good.*
2. I liked the woman. I met her at the party last night.
3. I liked the composition. You wrote it.
4. The people were very nice. We visited them yesterday.
5. The man is standing over there. Ann brought him to the party.

❏ **Exercise 9. Warm-up.** (Chart 13-3)
Compare the <u>underlined</u> adjective clause in sentence a. with the one in sentence b. What differences do you notice? NOTE: Both sentences are correct.

1. a. I think Lee is a person <u>who you can have fun with</u>.
   b. Do you think Lee is a person <u>with whom you can have fun</u>?

2. a. The art school <u>which Lori applied to</u> is very demanding.
   b. Do you know the name of the art school <u>to which Lori applied</u>?

13-3 Adjective Clause Pronouns Used as the Object of a Preposition

					In very formal English, the preposition comes at the beginning of the adjective clause, as in (a) and (e). Usually, however, in everyday usage, the preposition comes after the subject and verb of the adjective clause, as in the other examples.
	She is the woman.				
	I told you *about her*.				
		↓			
(a)	She is the woman	*about whom*	*I told you.*		
(b)	She is the woman	*who(m)*	*I told you about.*		
(c)	She is the woman	*that*	*I told you about.*		
(d)	She is the woman	Ø	*I told you about.*		

						NOTE: If the preposition comes at the beginning of the adjective clause, only ***whom*** or ***which*** may be used. A preposition is never immediately followed by ***that*** or ***who***.
	The music was good.					
	We listened *to it* last night.					
			↓			
(e)	The music	*to which*	*we listened*	*last night*	was good.	INCORRECT: She is the woman ~~about who~~ I told you.
(f)	The music	*which*	*we listened to*	*last night*	was good.	
(g)	The music	*that*	*we listened to*	*last night*	was good.	INCORRECT: The music ~~to that~~ we listened last night was good.
(h)	The music	Ø	*we listened to*	*last night*	was good.	

❏ **Exercise 10. Looking at grammar.** (Chart 13-3)
Choose all the possible completions for each sentence. Which one seems the most formal?

1. The sunglasses _____ were under the sofa.

   a. which I was looking for
   b. that I was looking for
   c. I was looking for
   d. I was looking
   e. I was looking for them

2. The health-care workers _____ were helpful.

   a. who I spoke to
   b. that I spoke to
   c. who I spoke to them
   d. to whom I spoke
   e. to who I spoke
   f. I spoke to

❏ **Exercise 11. Looking at grammar.** (Chart 13-3)
Combine the two sentences. Use the second sentence as an adjective clause. Give all the possible patterns, orally or in writing.

1. The man is standing over there. I was telling you about him.
2. I must thank the people. I got a present from them.
3. The meeting was interesting. Omar went to it.

❑ **Exercise 12. Looking at grammar.** (Charts 13-1 → 13-3)
Give all the possible completions for each sentence.

1. The dress ____*that / which / Ø*____ she is wearing is new.

2. Did I tell you about the woman _____ I met last night?

3. The report _____ Joe is writing must be finished by Friday.

4. The doctor _____ examined the sick child was gentle.

5. Did you hear about the earthquake _____ occurred in California?

6. The woman _____ I was dancing with stepped on my toes.

❑ **Exercise 13. Looking at grammar.** (Charts 13-1 → 13-3)
<u>Underline</u> the adjective clause in each sentence. Give all other possible patterns.

1. The woman <u>that I spoke to</u> gave me good advice.
   → *who(m) I spoke to*
   → *I spoke to*
   → *to whom I spoke*

2. I returned the money which I had borrowed from my roommate.

3. Yesterday I ran into an old friend I hadn't seen for years.

4. Marie lectured on a topic she knew very little about.

5. I read about a man who keeps chickens in his apartment.

❑ **Exercise 14. Check your knowledge.** (Charts 13-1 → 13-3)
Correct the errors in the adjective clauses.

1. In our village, there were many people didn't have much money.

2. I enjoyed the book that you told me to read it.

Adjective Clauses **275**

3. I still remember the man who he taught me to play the guitar when I was a boy.

4. I showed my father a picture of the car I am going to buy it as soon as I save enough money.

5. The woman about who I was talking about suddenly walked into the room. I hope she didn't hear me.

6. The people appear in the play are amateur actors.

7. I don't like to spend time with people which loses their temper easily.

8. While the boy was at the airport, he took pictures of people which was waiting for their planes.

9. People who works in the hunger program they estimate that 45,000 people worldwide die from starvation and malnutrition-related diseases every single day of the year.

10. In one corner of the marketplace, an old man who was playing a violin.

❑ **Exercise 15. Looking at grammar: pairwork.** (Charts 13-1 → 13-3)
Work with a partner. Speaker A looks at the cue briefly. Then, without looking at the text, Speaker A says the cue to Speaker B. Speaker B begins the answer with *Yes*.

Examples:
SPEAKER A (*book open*): You drank *some* tea. Did it taste good?
SPEAKER B (*book closed*): Yes, *the* tea I drank tasted good.

SPEAKER A (*book open*): A police officer helped you. Did you thank her?
SPEAKER B (*book closed*): Yes, I thanked *the* police officer who helped me.

1. You are sitting in a chair. Is it comfortable?
2. You saw a man. Was he wearing a brown suit?
3. A woman stepped on your toes. Did she apologize?
4. Some students took a test. Did most of them pass?
5. You were reading a book. Did you finish it?
6. A taxi driver took you to the bus station. Did you have a conversation with her?

Change roles.
7. You stayed at a hotel. Was it in the center of town?
8. A waiter served you at a restaurant. Was he polite?
9. A woman came into the room. Did you recognize her?
10. Some students are sitting in this room. Can all of them speak English?
11. You were looking for a dictionary. Did you find it?
12. A clerk cashed your check. Did he ask for identification?

□ **Exercise 16. Warm-up.** (Chart 13-4)
Check (✓) the sentences that are grammatically correct .

1. ___ I have a friend. His purpose in life is to help others.
2. ___ I have a friend whose purpose in life is to help others.
3. ___ I have a friend who his purpose in life is to help others.
4. ___ I have a friend that his purpose in life is to help others.

13-4 Using *Whose*

I know the man. **His bicycle** was stolen.
↓
(a) I know the man *whose bicycle* was stolen.
	Whose is used to show possession. It carries the same meaning as other possessive pronouns used as adjectives: *his, her, its,* and *their*.
	Like *his, her, its,* and *their,* **whose** is connected to a noun:
	  his bicycle → whose bicycle
	  her composition → whose composition

The student writes well. I read **her composition**. ↓ (b) The student *whose composition* I read writes well.	Both **whose** and the noun it is connected to are placed at the beginning of the adjective clause. **Whose** cannot be omitted.
(c) I worked at a **company** *whose employees* wanted to form a union.	**Whose** usually modifies people, but it may also be used to modify things, as in (c).
(d) That's the boy *whose parents* you met. (e) That's the boy *who's* in my math class. (f) That's the boy *who's been living* at our house since his mother was arrested.*	**Whose** and **who's** have the same pronunciation. **Who's** can mean **who is**, as in (e), or **who has**, as in (f).

*When **has** is a helping verb in the present perfect, it is usually contracted with **who** in speaking and sometimes in informal writing, as in (f).
When **has** is a main verb, it is NOT contracted with **who**: *I know a man **who has** a cook.*

□ **Exercise 17. Looking at grammar.** (Chart 13-4)
Complete the sentences with **who** or **whose**.

1. I know a doctor ___whose___ last name is Doctor.
2. I know a doctor ___who___ lives on a sailboat.
3. The woman _____ wallet was stolen called the police.
4. The woman _____ found my wallet called me immediately.
5. The professor _____ teaches art history is excellent.
6. The professor _____ course I am taking is excellent.
7. I apologized to the man _____ coffee I spilled.
8. I made friends with a man _____ is in my class.

Adjective Clauses **277**

❑ **Exercise 18. Looking at grammar.** (Chart 13-4)
Combine the two sentences. Use the second sentence as an adjective clause.

1. I met the woman. Her husband is the president of the corporation.
   → *I met the woman whose husband is the president of the corporation.*
2. Mrs. North teaches a class for students. Their native language is not English.
3. The people were nice. We visited their house.
4. I live in a dormitory. Its residents come from many countries.
5. I have to call the man. I accidentally picked up his umbrella after the meeting.
6. The man poured a glass of water on his face. His beard caught on fire when he lit a cigarette.

❑ **Exercise 19. Listening.** (Chart 13-4)
Circle the words you hear: ***who's*** or ***whose***.

CD 2
Track 4

Example: You will hear: The man who's standing over there is Mr. Smith.
            You will choose: (who's)   whose

1. who's whose	5. who's whose
2. who's whose	6. who's whose
3. who's whose	7. who's whose
4. who's whose	8. who's whose

❑ **Exercise 20. Let's talk: pairwork.** (Chart 13-4)
Work with a partner. Pretend you are in a room full of people. You and your partner are speaking. Together, you are identifying various people in the room. Begin each sentence with **There is**. Alternate items, with Partner A doing item 1, Partner B doing item 2, Partner A doing item 3, etc.

1. That man's wife is your teacher.
   → PARTNER A: *There is the man whose wife is my teacher.*
2. That woman's husband is a football player.
   → PARTNER B: *There is the woman whose husband is a football player.*
3. That girl's mother is a dentist.
4. That person's picture was in the newspaper.
5. That woman's car was stolen.
6. That man's daughter won a gold medal at the Olympic Games.
7. You found that woman's keys.
8. You are in that teacher's class.
9. You read that author's book.
10. You borrowed that student's lecture notes.

Exercise 21. Listening. (Chart 13-4)

Listen to the sentences in normal, contracted speech. You will hear: *whose*, *who's* (meaning *who is*), or *who's* (meaning *who has*). Circle the correct meaning.

Example: You will hear: I know a woman who's a taxi driver.
        You will choose: whose   (who is)   who has

1. whose   who is   who has   5. whose   who is   who has

2. whose   who is   who has   6. whose   who is   who has

3. whose   who is   who has   7. whose   who is   who has

4. whose   who is   who has   8. whose   who is   who has

❏ **Exercise 22. Let's talk: small groups.** (Chart 13-1 → 13-4)

Complete the sentences orally in small groups. Discuss each other's choices and opinions.

1. A famous person _____ life I admire is _____.
2. _____ is a famous person _____ has made the world a better place.
3. A person _____ is having a good influence on world affairs today is _____.
4. _____ is a country _____ is having a bad influence on world affairs today.
5. _____ is a country _____ leadership on issues of global warming is much admired throughout the world.

❏ **Exercise 23. Warm-up.** (Chart 13-5)

All of these sentences have the same meaning, and all of them are grammatically correct. The adjective clauses are in blue. What differences do you notice?

1. The **town** where I grew up is very small.
2. The **town** in which I grew up is very small.
3. The **town** which I grew up in is very small.
4. The **town** that I grew up in is very small.
5. The **town** I grew up in is very small.

13-5 Using *Where* in Adjective Clauses

	The building is very old. He lives **there** (*in that building*).			*Where* is used in an adjective clause to modify a place (*city, country, room, house, etc.*).
(a)	The building	*where*	*he lives*	is very old.	If *where* is used, a preposition is NOT included in the adjective clause, as in (a).
(b)	The building	*in which*	*he lives*	is very old.	
	The building	*which*	*he lives in*	is very old.	If *where* is not used, the preposition must be included, as in (b).
	The building	*that*	*he lives in*	is very old.	
	The building	Ø	*he lives in*	is very old.	

❏ **Exercise 24. Looking at grammar.** (Chart 13-5)
Combine the two sentences. Use the second sentence as an adjective clause.

1. The city was beautiful. We spent our vacation there (in that city).
2. That is the restaurant. I will meet you there (at that restaurant).
3. The office is busy. I work there (in that office).
4. That is the drawer. I keep my jewelry there (in that drawer).

❏ **Exercise 25. Warm-up.** (Chart 13-6)
All of these sentences have the same meaning, and all of them are grammatically correct. The adjective clauses are in blue. What differences do you notice?

1. I clearly remember the **day** when I rode a bike for the first time.
2. I clearly remember the **day** on which I rode a bike for the first time.
3. I clearly remember the **day** that I rode a bike for the first time.
4. I clearly remember the **day** I rode a bike for the first time.

13-6 Using *When* in Adjective Clauses

		I'll never forget the day. I met you **then** (**on that day**).	*When* is used in an adjective clause to modify a noun of time (*year, day, time, century,* etc.).
(a)	I'll never forget the day	*when* I met you.	The use of a preposition in an adjective clause that modifies a noun of time is somewhat different from that in other adjective clauses: a preposition is used preceding *which*, as in (b); otherwise, the preposition is omitted.
(b)	I'll never forget the day	*on which* I met you.	
(c)	I'll never forget the day	*that* I met you.	
(d)	I'll never forget the day	Ø I met you.	

❏ **Exercise 26. Looking at grammar.** (Chart 13-6)
Combine the two sentences. Use the second sentence as an adjective clause.

1. Monday is the day. They will come then (on that day).

2. 7:05 is the time. My plane arrives then (at that time).

3. 1960 is the year. The revolution took place then (in that year).

4. July is the month. The weather is usually the hottest then (in that month).

Exercise 27. Looking at grammar. (Charts 13-5 and 13-6)
Combine the two sentences. Use **where** or **when** to introduce an adjective clause.

1. That is the place. The accident occurred there.
   → *That is the place* **where** *the accident occurred.*
2. There was a time. Movies cost a dime then.
   → *There was a time* **when** *movies cost a dime.*
3. A café is a small restaurant. People can get a light meal there.
4. Every neighborhood in Brussels has small cafés. Customers drink coffee and eat pastries there.
5. There was a time. Dinosaurs dominated the earth then.
6. The house was destroyed in an earthquake ten years ago. I was born and grew up there.
7. The miser hid his money in a place. It was safe from robbers there.
8. There came a time. The miser had to spend his money then.

❑ **Exercise 28. Let's talk: interview.** (Charts 13-1 → 13-6)
Interview two classmates for each item. Encourage them to use adjective clauses that modify the nouns in **bold**. Share a few of their answers with the class.

Example: What kind of **food** don't you like?
   → *I don't like* **food** *that is too sugary.*

1. What kind of **people** do you like to spend time with?
2. What kind of **people** do you prefer to avoid?
3. What kind of **cities** do you like to visit?
4. What kind of **teachers** do you learn best from?
5. What kind of **place** would you like to live in?
6. What **time of day** do you feel most energetic?

❑ **Exercise 29. Listening.** (Charts 13-1 → 13-6)
Listen to the sentences. Choose the correct meanings for each sentence.

CD 2
Track 6 *Example:* You will hear: The nurse who gave the medicine to the patients seemed confused.
   You will choose: a. The patients were confused.
                  (b.) The patients received medicine from the nurse.
                  (c.) The nurse was confused.

1. a. A man organized the dinner.
   b. The man is the speaker's friend.
   c. The speaker organized the dinner.

2. a. Two people were killed in an accident.
   b. Two people blocked all lanes of the highway for two hours.
   c. An accident blocked all lanes of the highway for two hours.

3. a. The speaker lives in a large city.
   b. The speaker was born in a small town.
   c. The speaker was born in a large city.

4. a. The music teacher and the students play in a rock band.
   b. The music teacher directs a rock band.
   c. The music teacher plays in a rock band.

5. a. The speaker gave Jack a camera for his birthday.
   b. The camera takes excellent pictures.
   c. Jack takes excellent pictures.

6. a. The speaker often invites the neighbor to dinner.
   b. The neighbor often visits at dinnertime.
   c. The speaker visits the neighbor at dinnertime.

❑ **Exercise 30. Let's talk.** (Charts 13-1 → 13-6)
Work in small groups or as a class. The leader will ask Speaker A a question. The leader will then ask Speaker B to summarize the information in Speaker A's response in one sentence beginning with ***The***. Speaker B will use an adjective clause. Only the leader's book is open.

Example:
LEADER: Who got an email yesterday?
SPEAKER A (*Ali*):   I did.
LEADER to A: Who was it from?
SPEAKER A: My brother.
LEADER to B: Summarize this information. Begin with ***The***.
SPEAKER B: The email (*Ali*) got yesterday was from his brother.

(Change leaders if working in groups.)

1. Who lives in an apartment?
   Is it close to school?

2. Who is wearing earrings?
   What are they made of?

3. Pick up something that doesn't belong to you.
   What is it? Whose is it?

7. What did you have for dinner last night?
   Was it good?

8. Who watched a TV program last night?
   What was it about?

9. Who has borrowed something recently?
   What did you borrow?
   Who does it belong to?

(Change leaders if working in groups.)

4. Who grew up in a small town?
   In what part of the country is it located?

5. Who has bought something recently?
   Was it expensive?

6. Who went to a restaurant yesterday?
   Was it crowded?

(Change leaders if working in groups.)

10. Who shops for groceries?
    What is the name of the store?

11. Who eats lunch away from home?
    Where do you usually eat?
    Does it have good food?

12. Who took the bus to class today?
    Was it late or on time?

❑ **Exercise 31. Warm-up.** (Chart 13-7)
Underline each adjective clause. Draw an arrow to the word it modifies.

1. A: Is it okay if I come along on the picnic?
   B: Absolutely! Anyone who wants to come is more than welcome.

2. A: Should I apply for the opening in the sales department?
   B: I don't think so. They're looking for somebody who speaks Spanish.

3. A: Everything the Smiths do costs a lot of money.
   B: It's amazing, isn't it?

4. A: You're the only one who really understands me.
   B: Oh, that can't be true.

1. Did you hear about the man who rowed a boat across the Atlantic Ocean?

2. My uncle who loves boating rows his boat across the lake near his house nearly every day.

3. Tea which is a common drink throughout the world is made by pouring boiling water onto the dried leaves of certain plants.

4. Tea which is made from herbs is called herbal tea.

5. Toys which contain lead paint are unsafe for children.

6. Lead which can be found in paint and plastics is known to cause brain damage in children.

❑ **Exercise 37. Looking at grammar.** (Chart 13-8)
Add commas where necessary. Change the adjective clause pronoun to *that* if possible. Read the sentences aloud, pausing where necessary.

1. Mariko and Jackie, who didn't come to class yesterday, explained their absence to the teacher. (***Who*** *cannot be changed to* ***that***. *Pauses are used in speaking; add commas.*)

2. The students who did not come to class yesterday explained their absence to the teacher. (***Who*** *can be changed to* ***that***; *no commas.*)

3. The Mississippi River which flows south from Minnesota to the Gulf of Mexico is the major commercial river in the United States.

4. A river which is polluted is not safe for swimming.

5. Mr. Trang whose son won the spelling contest is very proud of his son's achievement. The man whose daughter won the science contest is also very pleased and proud.

6. Goats which were first tamed more than 9,000 years ago in Asia have provided people with milk, meat, and wool since prehistoric times.

7. Mrs. Clark has two goats. She's furious at the goat which got on the wrong side of the fence and is eating her flowers.

Exercise 38. Pronunciation and grammar. (Chart 13-8)
Read the sentences aloud. Choose the correct meaning (a. or b.) for each sentence.

1. The teacher thanked the students, who had given her some flowers.
   a. The flowers were from *only some* of the students.
   b. The flowers were from *all* of the students. (circled)

2. The teacher thanked the students who had given her some flowers.
   a. The flowers were from *only some* of the students. (circled)
   b. The flowers were from *all* of the students.

3. There was a terrible flood. The villagers who had received a warning of the impending flood escaped to safety.
   a. *Only some* of the villagers had been warned; only some escaped.
   b. *All* of the villagers had been warned; all escaped.

4. There was a terrible flood. The villagers, who had received a warning of the impending flood, escaped to safety.
   a. *Only some* of the villagers had been warned; only some escaped.
   b. *All* of the villagers had been warned; all escaped.

5. Natasha reached down and picked up the grammar book, which was lying upside down on the floor.
   a. There was *only one* grammar book near Natasha.
   b. There was *more than one* grammar book near Natasha.

6. Natasha reached down and picked up the grammar book which was lying upside down on the floor.
   a. There was *only one* grammar book near Natasha.
   b. There was *more than one* grammar book near Natasha.

□ **Exercise 39. Listening.** (Chart 13-8)
Listen to the sentences. Choose the correct meaning (a. or b.) for each sentence.

CD 2
Track 9

1. a. She threw away all of the apples.
   b. She threw away only the rotten apples.

2. a. She threw away all of the apples.
   b. She threw away only the rotten apples.

3. a. Some of the students were excused from class early.
   b. All of the students were excused from class early.

4. a. Some of the students were excused from class early.
   b. All of the students were excused from class early.

□ **Exercise 40. Looking at grammar.** (Chart 13-8)
Add commas where necessary. Read the sentences aloud, paying attention to pauses.

1. We enjoyed the city where we spent our vacation.

2. We enjoyed Mexico City where we spent our vacation.

3. One of the elephants which we saw at the zoo had only one tusk.

4. One of the most useful materials in the world is glass which is made chiefly from sand, soda, and lime.

5. You don't need to take heavy clothes when you go to Bangkok which has one of the highest average temperatures of any city in the world.

6. Child labor was a social problem in late eighteenth-century England where employment in factories became virtual slavery for children.

7. We had to use a telephone, so we went to the nearest house. The woman who answered our knock listened cautiously to our request.

8. I watched a scientist conduct an experiment on bees. The research scientist who was wearing protective clothing before she stepped into the special chamber holding the bees was not stung. A person who was unprotected by the special clothing could have gotten 300 to 400 bee stings within a minute.

❏ **Exercise 41. Reading and grammar.** (Charts 13-1 → 13-8)
Part I. Answer these questions. Then read the article. Notice the adjective clauses in blue.

1. Do you have a computer?
2. Do you know the name of its operating system?

The History of DOS

As you know, a computer needs to have an operating system in order to run programs. When most people think about the first operating systems that were developed for the personal computer, Microsoft or Bill Gates may come to mind. Actually, the truth is somewhat different.

In the late 1970s, there was a man in Seattle named Tim Paterson who worked for a company that was called Seattle Computer. He was a computer programmer and needed an operating system for his computer. Paterson got tired of waiting for another company to create one and decided to develop his own program. He called it QDOS, which meant "quick and dirty operating system." It took him about four months to develop it.

At the same time, Microsoft was quietly looking for an operating system to run a personal computer that I.B.M. was developing. Microsoft saw the program that Tim had written and in 1980, paid him $25,000 for a license for DOS. A year later they paid another $50,000 to acquire the rights. It became known as the Microsoft disk operating system (MS-DOS), and the rest is history. Microsoft and Bill Gates became very successful using Paterson's operating system.

Part II. Complete the sentences with information from the article. Use adjective clauses in your completions.

1. Tim Paterson was the person who _____

2. Seattle Computer was the company that _____

3. The abbreviation for the program was QDOS, which _____

4. I.B.M. was a company that _____

5. Microsoft, which _____

6. Microsoft acquired rights to a program that _____

❑ **Exercise 42. Warm-up.** (Chart 13-9)
Choose the correct meaning (a. or b.) for each sentence.

1. The couple has thirteen children, only a few of whom live at home.
   a. Ten children live at home.
   b. A few of the couple's children live at home.

2. Victoria bought a dozen dresses, most of which she later returned to the store.
   a. Victoria returned a dozen dresses.
   b. Victoria kept a few of the dresses.

13-9 Using Expressions of Quantity in Adjective Clauses

In my class there are 20 students. *Most of **them*** are from Asia.	An adjective clause may contain an expression of quantity with ***of***: *some of, many of, most of, none of, two of, half of, both of,* etc.
(a) In my class there are 20 students, *most of **whom*** are from Asia.	
(b) He gave several reasons, *only a few of **which*** were valid.	The expression of quantity precedes the pronoun. Only ***whom**, **which***, and ***whose*** are used in this pattern. This pattern is more common in writing than speaking. Commas are used.
(c) The teachers discussed Jim, *one of **whose** problems* was poor study habits.	

❑ **Exercise 43. Looking at grammar.** (Chart 13-9)
Combine the two sentences in each item. Use the second sentence as an adjective clause.

1. The city has sixteen schools. Two of them are junior colleges.
   → *The city has sixteen schools, two of which are junior colleges.*
2. Last night the orchestra played three symphonies. One of them was Beethoven's Seventh.
3. I tried on six pairs of shoes. I liked none of them.
4. The village has around 200 people. The majority of them are farmers.
5. That company currently has five employees. All of them are computer experts.
6. After the riot, over 100 people were taken to the hospital. Many of them had been innocent bystanders.

❑ **Exercise 44. In your own words.** (Chart 13-9)
Complete the sentences with your own words. Use adjective clauses.

1. Al introduced me to his roommates, both of _____whom are from California._____

2. The Paulsons own four automobiles, one of _____

3. I have three brothers, all of _____

4. I am taking four courses, one of _____

5. I have two roommates, neither of _____

6. This semester I had to buy fifteen books, most of _____

7. The company hired ten new employees, some of _____

8. In my apartment building, there are twenty apartments, several of _____

_____

❑ **Exercise 45. Warm-up.** (Chart 13-10)
What does **which** refer to in each sentence?

1. The soccer team worked very hard to win**,** **which** made their coach very proud.
2. Some of the athletes in the class cheated on the final exam**,** **which** disappointed their coach.
3. Sam took the final exam**,** **which** he passed without cheating.

13-10 Using *Which* to Modify a Whole Sentence

(a) Tom was late. **That** surprised me.	The pronouns **that** and **this** can refer to the idea of a whole sentence which comes before.
(b) Tom was late**,** *which surprised me.*	In (a): The word **that** refers to the whole sentence **Tom was late**.
(c) The elevator is out of order. **This** is too bad.	Similarly, an adjective clause with **which** may modify the idea of a whole sentence.
(d) The elevator is out of order**,** *which is too bad.*	In (b): The word **which** refers to the whole sentence **Tom was late**.
	Using **which** to modify a whole sentence is informal and occurs most frequently in spoken English. This structure is generally not appropriate in formal writing. Whenever it is written, however, it is preceded by a comma to reflect a pause in speech.

❏ **Exercise 46. Looking at grammar.** (Chart 13-10)
Combine the two sentences. Use the second sentence as an adjective clause.

1. Sonya lost her job. That wasn't surprising.
   → *Sonya lost her job, which wasn't surprising.*

2. She usually came to work late. That upset her boss.

3. So her boss fired her. That made her angry.

4. She hadn't saved any money. That was unfortunate.

5. So she had to borrow some money from me. I didn't like that.

6. She has found a new job. That is lucky.

7. So she has repaid the money she borrowed from me. I appreciate that.

8. She has promised herself to be on time to work every day. That is a good idea.

❏ **Exercise 47. Looking at grammar.** (Charts 13-1 → 13-10)
Combine sentences a. and b. Use b. as an adjective clause. Use formal written English.
Punctuate carefully.

1. a. An antecedent is a word.
   b. A pronoun refers to this word.
      → *An antecedent is a word to which a pronoun refers.*

2. a. The blue whale is considered the largest animal that has ever lived.
   b. It can grow to 100 feet and 150 tons.

3. a. The plane was met by a crowd of 300 people.
   b. Some of them had been waiting for more than four hours.

4. a. In this paper, I will describe the basic process.
   b. Raw cotton becomes cotton thread by this process.

5. a. The researchers are doing case studies of people to determine the importance of
      heredity in health and longevity.
   b. These people's families have a history of high blood pressure and heart disease.

6. a. At the end of this month, scientists at the institute will conclude their AIDS research.
   b. The results of this research will be published within six months.

7. a. According to many education officials, "math phobia" (that is, a fear of mathematics) is
      a widespread problem.
   b. A solution to this problem can and must be found.

8. a. The art museum hopes to hire a new administrator.
   b. Under this person's direction, it will be able to
      purchase significant pieces of art.

9. a. The giant anteater licks up ants for its dinner.
   b. Its tongue is longer than 30 centimeters
      (12 inches).

10. a. The anteater's tongue is sticky.
    b. It can go in and out of its mouth 160 times a minute.

❑ **Exercise 48. Reading and grammar.** (Charts 13-1 → 13-10)
Read about Ellen and her commute to work. Underline what the words in blue refer to.

(1) Ellen lives on an island and commutes to work by passenger ferry, which means she takes a boat with other foot passengers to the city where they work.

(2) She leaves her house at 6:00, which is earlier than she'd like but necessary because the ferry ride takes 30 minutes. Ellen needs 20 minutes to drive to the parking lot where she leaves her car and boards the ferry. Once she's on the other side, she catches a bus which takes her to her office.

(3) Traffic is usually heavy at that hour, so she's on the bus for another 30 minutes. On the bus, she usually reads reports that she was too tired to finish the night before.

(4) The bus drops her off a few blocks from her office. Sometimes she stops at an espresso stand and picks up coffee for her co-workers, for which they reimburse her later.

(5) By the time she gets to her office, she has been commuting for an hour and a half, which she wishes she didn't have to do but isn't going to change because she enjoys her life on the island so much.

❑ **Exercise 49. Let's talk or write.** (Charts 13-1 → 13-10)
Discuss and/or write definitions for one or more of the given topics. Include an adjective clause in each definition. If you are writing, choose only one item and expand your definition to a paragraph.

The ideal . . .

1. friend	5. school	9. job
2. mother	6. vacation	10. doctor
3. father	7. teacher	11. lifestyle
4. spouse	8. student	12. (*your choice*)

Look at the words in blue. What differences do you notice between each pair of sentences?
NOTE: Sentences a. and b. have the same meaning.

1. a. I talked to the people who were sitting beside me at the ball game.
   b. I talked to the people sitting beside me at the ball game.

2. a. The notebooks that are on my desk are mine.
   b. The notebooks on my desk are mine.

3. a. I read an article about Marie Curie, who was a famous French scientist.
   b. I read an article about Marie Curie, a famous French scientist.

13-11 Reducing Adjective Clauses to Adjective Phrases

CLAUSE: *A clause* is a group of related words that contains a subject and a verb.
PHRASE: *A phrase* is a group of related words that does not contain a subject and a verb.

(a) CLAUSE: The girl *who is sitting next to me* is Mai. (b) PHRASE: The girl *sitting next to me* is Mai. (c) CLAUSE: The girl (*whom*) *I saw* was Mai. (d) PHRASE: (*none*)	An adjective phrase is a reduction of an adjective clause. It modifies a noun. It does not contain a subject and verb. Examples (a) and (b) have the same meaning. Only adjective clauses that have a subject pronoun — **who, which**, or **that** — are reduced to modifying adjective phrases. The adjective clause in (c) cannot be reduced to an adjective phrase.	
(e) CLAUSE: The man *who is talking* to John is from Korea. PHRASE: The man Ø Ø *talking* to John is from Korea. (f) CLAUSE: The ideas *which are presented* in that book are good. PHRASE: The ideas Ø Ø *presented* in that book are good. (g) CLAUSE: Ann is the woman *that is responsible* for the error. PHRASE: Ann is the woman Ø Ø *responsible* for the error.	There are two ways in which an adjective clause is changed to an adjective phrase. **1.** If the adjective clause contains the **be** form of a verb, omit the subject pronoun and the **be** form, as in (e), (f), and (g).*	
(h) CLAUSE: English has an alphabet *that consists* of 26 letters. PHRASE: English has an alphabet Ø *consisting* of 26 letters. (i) CLAUSE: Anyone *who wants* to come with us is welcome. PHRASE: Anyone Ø *wanting* to come with us is welcome.	**2.** If there is no **be** form of a verb in the adjective clause, it is sometimes possible to omit the subject pronoun and change the verb to its **-ing** form, as in (h) and (i).	
(j) *Paris,* which is the capital of France, is an exciting city. (k) *Paris,* the capital of France, is an exciting city.	If the adjective clause requires commas, as in (j), the adjective phrase also requires commas, as in (k). An adjective phrase in which a noun follows another noun, as in (k), is called an *appositive*.	

*If an adjective clause that contains **be** + *a single adjective* is changed, the adjective is moved to its normal position in front of the noun it modifies.

    CLAUSE: **Fruit that is fresh** *tastes better than old, soft, mushy fruit.*
    CORRECT PHRASE: **Fresh fruit** *tastes better than old, soft, mushy fruit.*
    INCORRECT PHRASE: *Fruit fresh tastes better than old, soft, mushy fruit.*

❑ **Exercise 51. Looking at grammar.** (Charts 13-10 and 13-11)
Change the adjective clauses to adjective phrases.

1. Do you know the woman who is coming toward us?
   → *Do you know the woman coming toward us?*
2. The scientists who are researching the causes of cancer are making progress.
3. We have an apartment which overlooks the park.
4. The photographs which were published in the newspaper were extraordinary.
5. The rules that allow public access to wilderness areas need to be reconsidered.
6. The psychologists who study the nature of sleep have made important discoveries.
7. Antarctica is covered by a huge ice cap that contains 70 percent of the earth's fresh water.
8. When I went to Alex's house to drop off some paperwork, I met Jacob, who is his partner.
9. Many of the students who hope to enter this university will be disappointed because only one-tenth of those who apply for admission will be accepted.
10. Kuala Lumpur, which is the capital of Malaysia, is a major trade center in Southeast Asia.

❑ **Exercise 52. Listening.** (Charts 13-10 and 13-11)
Listen to the sentences. Choose the correct meaning (a. or b.) for each sentence. In some cases, both a. and b. are correct.

CD 2
Track 10

Example: You will hear: The experiment conducted by the students was successful.
You will choose: ⓐ The students conducted an experiment.
ⓑ The experiment was successful.

1. a. There is a fence around our house.
   b. Our house is made of wood.

2. a. All schoolchildren receive a good education.
   b. That school provides a good education.

3. a. The university president will give a speech.
   b. Dr. Stanton will give a speech.

4. a. There is a galaxy called the Milky Way.
   b. Our solar system is called the Milky Way.

❑ **Exercise 53. Looking at grammar.** (Charts 13-10 and 13-11)
Change the adjective phrases to adjective clauses.

1. We visited Barcelona, a city in northern Spain.
   → *We visited Barcelona, which is a city in northern Spain.*

2. Corn was one of the agricultural products introduced to the European settlers by the Indians. Some of the other products introduced by the Indians were potatoes, peanuts, and tobacco.

3. Mercury, the nearest planet to the sun, is also the smallest of the planets orbiting our sun.

4. The pyramids, the monumental tombs of ancient Egyptian pharaohs, were constructed more than 4,000 years ago.

5. Any student not wanting to go on the trip should inform the office.

6. Be sure to follow the instructions given at the top of the page.

Exercise 54. Looking at grammar. (Charts 13-10 and 13-11)
Change the adjective clauses to adjective phrases.

Early Failures of Famous People

(1) Many famous people did not enjoy immediate success in their early lives. Abraham Lincoln, ~~who was~~ one of the truly great presidents of the United States, ran for public office 26 times and lost 23 of the elections.

(2) Walt Disney, who was the creator of Mickey Mouse and the founder of his own movie production company, once was fired by a newspaper editor because he had no good ideas.

(3) Thomas Edison, who was the inventor of the light bulb and the phonograph, was believed by his teachers to be too stupid to learn.

(4) Albert Einstein, who was one of the greatest scientists of all time, performed badly in almost all of his high school courses and failed his first college entrance exam.

❏ **Exercise 55. Looking at grammar.** (Charts 13-10 and 13-11)
Complete the sentences in Part II by turning the information in Part I into adjective phrases. Use commas as necessary.

Part I.
  a. It is the lowest place on the earth's surface.
✓b. It is the highest mountain in the world.
  c. It is the capital of Iraq.
  d. It is the capital of Argentina.
  e. It is the largest city in the Western Hemisphere.
  f. It is the largest city in the United States.
  g. It is the most populous country in Africa.
  h. It is the northernmost country in Latin America.
  i. They are sensitive instruments that measure the shaking of the ground.
  j. They are devices that produce a powerful beam of light.

Part II.
  1. Mount Everest ⎯, *the highest mountain in the world,* ⎯⎯⎯ is in the Himalayas.

  2. One of the largest cities in the Middle East is Baghdad ⎯⎯⎯⎯⎯⎯

  3. Earthquakes are recorded on seismographs ⎯⎯⎯⎯⎯⎯

  4. The Dead Sea ⎯⎯⎯⎯⎯⎯
     is located in the Middle East between Jordan and Israel.

  5. The newspaper reported an earthquake in Buenos Aires ⎯⎯⎯⎯⎯⎯

  6. Industry and medicine are continually finding new uses for lasers ⎯⎯⎯⎯⎯⎯

     ⎯⎯⎯⎯⎯⎯⎯⎯⎯⎯⎯⎯⎯⎯⎯⎯⎯⎯

7. Mexico _____

   lies just south of the United States.

8. The nation Nigeria _____ consists

   of over 250 different cultural groups even though English is the official language.

9. Both Mexico City _____ and New York City

   _____ face challenging futures.

☐ **Exercise 56. Listening.** (Chapters 12 and 13)

Part I. Listen to the lecture about animals and earthquake predictions with your book closed. Then open your book and read the statements. Circle "T" for true and "F" for false.

1. That animals can predict earthquakes is an indisputable fact.   T   F

2. Some animals exhibit unusual behavior before an earthquake.   T   F

3. According to the lecture, scientists are certain that the energy in the air changes before an earthquake.   T   F

4. Some scientists believe that animal behavior can be helpful in earthquake prediction.   T   F

Part II. Listen again. Complete the sentences with the words you hear.

Animals and Earthquakes

_____ animals can predict earthquakes has been widely debated for
                   1

hundreds of years. In fact, as far back as 373 B.C., villagers _____
                                                      2

hundreds of animals deserted the Greek town of Helice a few days before an earthquake

destroyed it. There are other interesting phenomena _____.
                                                 3

For example, before an earthquake, dogs may begin barking or howling for no reason; chickens

might stop laying eggs; and some pets will go into hiding.

   In Asia in 2004, many animals _____ accustomed to being
                                                4

on the beach in the early morning refused to go there the morning of the big tsunami. In

Thailand, a herd of buffalo on a beach noticed or heard _____
                                               5

made them run to the top of a hill before the tsunami was anywhere in sight. The villagers

_____ them were saved.
                   6

What causes this strange behavior in animals? One theory _____
_____ 7
can sense the earth move before people can. There are vibrations deep in the earth

_____ before an earthquake can be detected. Another idea
_____ 8
_____ the energy in the air changes _____ animals are disturbed
_____ 9 _____ 10
by these changes.

Some scientists dismiss these ideas, while others _____ they are worth
_____ 11
researching further. Those scientists _____ witnessed this strange animal
_____ 12
behavior _____ animals are far more sensitive to subtle changes in the
_____ 13
earth than people are _____ studying their behavior can be useful in
_____ 14
the prediction of earthquakes.

❏ **Exercise 57. Looking at grammar.** (Chapter 13)
Combine each group of short, choppy sentences into one sentence. Use the <u>underlined</u>
sentence as the independent clause and build your sentence around it. Use adjective clauses
and adjective phrases wherever possible.

1. <u>Chihuahua is divided into two regions</u>. It is the largest Mexican state. One region is a
mountainous area in the west. The other region is a desert basin in the north and east.

Chihuahua, the largest Mexican state, is divided into two regions, a mountainous

area in the west and a desert basin in the north and east.

2. <u>Disney World covers a large area of land</u>. It is an amusement park. It is located in
Orlando, Florida. The land includes lakes, golf courses, campsites, hotels, and a wildlife
preserve.

_____

_____

3. <u>Jamaica is one of the world's leading producers of bauxite</u>. It is the third largest island in
the Caribbean Sea. Bauxite is an ore. Aluminum is made from this ore.

_____

_____

4. <u>Robert Ballard made headlines in 1985</u>. He is an oceanographer. In 1985 he discovered the remains of the *Titanic*. The *Titanic* was the "unsinkable" passenger ship. It has rested on the floor of the Atlantic Ocean since 1912. It struck an iceberg in 1912.

_____

_____

_____

5. <u>The Republic of Yemen is an ancient land</u>. It is located at the southwestern tip of the Arabian Peninsula. This land has been host to many prosperous civilizations. These civilizations include the Kingdom of Sheba and various Islamic empires.

_____

_____

_____

❑ **Exercise 58. Check your knowledge.** (Chapter 13)
Correct the errors. All of the sentences are adapted from student writing.

1. Baseball is the only sport in which I am interested in it.

2. My favorite teacher, Mr. Chu, he was always willing to help me after class.

3. It is important to be polite to people who lives in the same building.

4. My sister has two children, who their names are Ali and Talal.

5. He comes from Venezuela that is a Spanish-speaking country.

6. There are some people in the government who is trying to improve the lives of the poor.

7. My classroom is located on the second floor of Carver Hall that is a large brick building in the center of the campus.

8. A myth is a story expresses traditional beliefs.

9. There is an old legend telling among people in my country about a man lived in the seventeenth century and saved a village from destruction.

10. An old man was fishing next to me on the pier was muttering to himself.

11. The road that we took it through the forest it was narrow and steep.

12. There are ten universities in Thailand, seven of them are located in Bangkok is the capital city.

13. At the national park, there is a path leads to a spectacular waterfall.

14. At the airport, I was waiting for some relatives which I had never met them before.

15. It is almost impossible to find two persons who their opinions are the same.

16. On the wall, there is a colorful poster which it consists of a group of young people who dancing.

17. The sixth member of our household is Pietro that is my sister's son.

18. Before I came here, I didn't have the opportunity to speak with people who English is their native tongue.

❏ **Exercise 59. Let's write.** (Chapter 13)
Write a paragraph on one or more of the given topics. Try to use adjective clauses and phrases.

Topics:
1. Write about three historical figures from your country. Give your reader information about their lives and accomplishments.
2. Write about your favorite TV shows. What are they? What are they about? Why do you enjoy them?
3. Who are some people in your country who are popular with young people (e.g., singers, movie stars, political figures, etc.)? Tell your readers about these people. Assume your readers are completely unfamiliar with them.
4. You are a tourist agent for your hometown/country. Write a descriptive brochure that would make your readers want to visit your hometown/country.

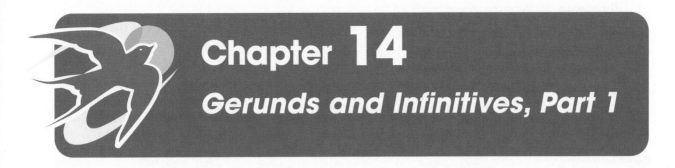

Chapter 14
Gerunds and Infinitives, Part 1

❑ **Exercise 1. Warm-up.** (Chart 14-1)
Complete the sentences with the words in the list. Give your own opinion. Then answer the questions.

baseball	golf	badminton
basketball	soccer	tennis

1. **Playing** _____ is fun.

2. My friends and I enjoy **playing** _____.

3. I don't know much about **playing** _____.

In which sentence is **playing**

a. the object of the verb?

b. the subject?

c. the object of a preposition?

14-1 Gerunds: Introduction

(a) $\overset{S}{Playing}$ tennis $\overset{V}{is}$ fun.	A *gerund* is the **-ing** form of a verb used as a noun.* A gerund is used in the same ways as a noun, i.e., as a subject or as an object.
(b) $\overset{S}{We}$ $\overset{V}{enjoy}$ $\overset{O}{playing}$ tennis.	In (a): **playing** is a gerund. It is used as the subject of the sentence. **Playing tennis** is a *gerund phrase*.
(c) He's excited $\overset{PREP}{about}$ $\overset{O}{playing}$ tennis.	In (b): **playing** is a gerund used as the object of the verb **enjoy**.
	In (c): **playing** is a gerund used as the object of the preposition **about**.

*Compare the uses of the **-ing** form of verbs:
  (1) **Walking** *is good exercise.* → **walking** = a gerund used as the subject of the sentence.
  (2) *Bob and Ann are* **playing** *tennis.* → **playing** = a present participle used as part of the present progressive tense.
  (3) *I heard some* **surprising** *news.* → **surprising** = a present participle used as an adjective.

Exercise 2. Warm-up. (Chart 14-2)
Each phrase in blue contains a preposition. What do you notice about the form of the verb that follows each preposition?

1. Sonya is excited about **moving** to a new city.
2. You'd better have a good excuse for **being** late.
3. I'm looking forward to **going** on vacation soon.

14-2 Using Gerunds as the Objects of Prepositions

(a) We talked *about going* to Canada for our vacation. (b) Sue is in charge *of organizing* the meeting. (c) I'm interested *in learning* more about your work.	A gerund is frequently used as the object of a preposition.
(d) I*'m used to sleeping* with the window open. (e) I*'m accustomed to sleeping** with the window open. (f) I *look forward to going* home next month.	In (d) through (f): *to* is a preposition, not part of an infinitive form, so a gerund follows.
(g) We *talked about not going* to the meeting, but finally decided we should go.	NEGATIVE FORM: *not* precedes a gerund.

Common preposition combinations followed by gerunds

be excited
be worried } *about doing* it

complain
dream
talk
think } *about/of doing* it

apologize
blame someone
forgive someone
have an excuse
have a reason
be responsible
thank someone } *for doing* it

keep someone
prevent someone
prohibit someone
stop someone } *from doing* it

be interested
believe
participate
succeed } *in doing* it

be accused
be capable
be guilty
instead
take advantage
take care } *of doing* it

be tired
insist *on doing* it } *of/from doing* it

be accustomed
in addition
be committed
be devoted
look forward
object
be opposed
be used } *to doing* it

*Possible in British English: *I'm accustomed to sleep with the window open.*

❏ **Exercise 3. Looking at grammar.** (Chart 14-2)
Complete each sentence with a preposition and a form of *go*.

1. We thought _____*about going*_____ to the beach.

2. We talked _____ there.

3. We're interested _____ there.

4. My family is excited _____ there.

5. The children insisted _____ there.

6. They're looking forward _____ there.

7. The rain prevented us _____ there.

8. A storm kept us _____ there.

❏ **Exercise 4. Looking at grammar.** (Chart 14-2)
Complete each sentence with a preposition and a form of the verb in parentheses.

Sɪᴛᴜᴀᴛɪᴏɴ 1: An airplane flight.

1. Two children are excited (*take*) _____*about taking*_____ their first flight.

2. They have been looking forward (*be*) _____ above the clouds.

3. A first-time flyer is worried (*fly*) _____ in stormy weather.

4. One passenger is blaming another passenger (*spill*) _____
his coffee.

5. A man is complaining (*have*) _____ an aisle seat rather than a
window seat.

6. The pilot was late, but he had an excuse (*be*) _____ late.

7. The co-pilot will be responsible (*fly*) _____ the plane.

8. Security personnel are prohibiting a woman (*get*) _____ on
the flight.

SITUATION 2: At a police station.

9. The teenager has been accused (*steal*) _____ a purse.

10. An elderly woman said he was responsible (*take*) _____ it.

11. The police are blaming him (*do*) _____ it.

12. The teenager said he was trying to prevent someone else (*take*) _____ it.

13. He is upset. The police are listening to the woman instead (*listen*) _____ to his version of the story.

14. He has not yet succeeded (*convince*) _____ the police of his innocence.

❑ **Exercise 5. Looking at grammar.** (Chart 14-2)
Complete each sentence with an appropriate preposition and the **-ing** form of the given verb.

1. look   Alice isn't interested _____*in looking*_____ for a new job.

2. do   You are capable _____ better work.

3. have   I'm accustomed _____ a big breakfast.

4. help   Thank you _____ me carry my suitcases.

5. know   Mrs. Grant insisted _____ the whole truth.

6. be   I believe _____ honest at all times.

7. live   You should take advantage _____ here.

8. go, not   Fatima had a good reason _____ to class yesterday.

9. search   Everyone in the neighborhood participated _____ for the lost child.

10. make   I apologized to Yoko _____ her wait for me.

11. go   In addition _____ to school full-time, Spiro has a part-time job.

12. run   I stopped the child _____ into the street.

13. go   Where should we go for dinner tonight? Would you object _____ to an Italian restaurant?

14. clarify   The mayor made another public statement for the purpose _____ the new tax proposal.

15. wear   Larry isn't used _____ a suit and tie every day.

❑ **Exercise 6. Listening.** (Chart 14-2)

Listen to each dialogue. Summarize it by completing each sentence with a preposition and a gerund phrase.

CD 2
Track 12

1. The man apologized _____ *for being late.* _____

2. The woman succeeded _____

3. Both speakers are complaining _____

4. The man thanked his friend _____

5. The man didn't have an excuse _____

6. The woman isn't used _____

7. The flu kept the man _____

❑ **Exercise 7. Let's talk: interview.** (Chart 14-2)

Interview two classmates for each question. Share some of their answers with the class.

1. Where \ you \ think \ go \ today?
   → *Where are you thinking about going today?*

2. What \ you \ not accustomed \ do?

3. What \ you \ interested \ find out about?

4. Where \ you \ look forward \ go \ on your next trip?

5. What \ be \ a good reason \ not \ do \ your homework?

❑ **Exercise 8. Let's talk.** (Chart 14-2)

Answer the questions in complete sentences. Use prepositions followed by gerunds in your answers. Work in pairs or small groups.

Example:

SPEAKER A (*book open*):   Your friend was rude. Did she apologize?
SPEAKER B (*book closed*): Yes, she apologized *for being* rude. OR No, she didn't apologize *for being* rude.

1. Your neighbor helped you carry heavy boxes. Did you thank him/her?
2. You're going to visit your friends in another town this weekend. Are you looking forward to that?
3. You didn't come to class on time yesterday. Did you have a good excuse?
4. You're living in a cold/warm climate. Are you accustomed to that?
5. You're going to a tropical island for vacation. Are you excited?
6. A customer interrupted you while you were talking to the store manager. Did she apologize?
7. The students in the class did role-plays. Did all of them participate?

Gerunds and Infinitives, Part 1   **305**

(Change roles if working in pairs.)

8. Someone broke the window. Do you know who was responsible?
9. People in some countries have their biggest meal at lunch. Are you used to doing that?
10. The weather is hot/cold. What does that prevent you from doing?
11. The advanced students have to do a lot of homework. Do they complain?
12. Your wallet was missing after your friend visited. Do you blame him?
13. You didn't study grammar last night. What did you do instead?
14. You studied last weekend. What did you do in addition?

❏ **Exercise 9. Let's talk.** (Chart 14-2)
Answer the questions with **by** + *a gerund or gerund phrase* to express how something is done. Work in pairs, in small groups, or as a class.

1. How do you turn off a cell phone? → *By pushing a button.*
2. How can students improve their listening comprehension?
3. How do people satisfy their hunger?
4. How do people quench their thirst?
5. How did you find out what *quench* means?
6. What are some ways employees get in trouble with their manager?
7. How do dogs show they are happy?
8. In a restaurant, how do you catch the server's attention?

❏ **Exercise 10. Let's talk: interview.** (Chart 14-2)
Part I. Interview your classmates about the different ways people express emotions. Answers can include descriptions of facial expressions, actions, what people say, etc. Try to use **by** + *gerund* in your answers. Share some of the answers with the class.

Example: excitement
SPEAKER A: How do people show excitement at a sports event?
SPEAKER B: People show excitement at a sports event by clapping their hands, jumping up and down, and yelling.

1. happiness	3. anger	5. confusion	7. agreement
2. sadness	4. frustration	6. disagreement	8. surprise

Part II. Draw a face that shows an emotion. Ask a classmate to guess which emotion you've tried to show.

❏ **Exercise 11. Warm-up.** (Chart 14-3)
Complete the sentences with phrases in the list that are true for you. What do you notice about the form of the verbs in these phrases?

buying things online	surfing the internet
going online to get news	talking about politics
reading newspapers	watching commercials on TV
spending hours at a computer	watching the news on TV

1. I enjoy _____.

2. I don't enjoy _____.

3. I avoid _____.

14-3 Common Verbs Followed by Gerunds

verb + gerund (a) I *enjoy* *playing* tennis.	Gerunds are used as the objects of certain verbs. In (a): *enjoy* is followed by a gerund (*playing*). *Enjoy* is not followed by an infinitive. INCORRECT: I enjoy ~~to play~~ tennis. Common verbs that are followed by gerunds are listed below.
(b) Joe *quit smoking*. (c) Joe *gave up smoking*.	Examples (b) and (c) have the same meaning. Some phrasal verbs,* e.g., *give up*, are followed by gerunds. See these phrasal verbs in parentheses below.

Verb + gerund

enjoy	quit (give up)	avoid	consider
appreciate	finish (get through)	postpone (put off)	discuss
mind	stop**	delay	mention
		keep (keep on)	suggest

*A *phrasal verb* consists of a verb and a particle (a small word such as a preposition) that together have a special meaning. For example, *put off* means "postpone."

Stop can also be followed by an infinitive of purpose. *He **stopped** at the station (**in order**) **to get** some gas.* See *infinitives of purpose*, Charts 14-7, p. 317, and 15-1, p. 331.

❏ **Exercise 12. Looking at grammar.** (Chart 14-3)
Make sentences with the given words. Use any tense and subject. Work in pairs, in small groups, or as a class.

Example: enjoy \ drink tea
SPEAKER A: enjoy [*pause*] drink tea
SPEAKER B: I enjoy drinking tea with breakfast.

(*Change roles if working in pairs.*)

1. mind \ open the window	7. postpone \ do my work
2. finish \ eat dinner	8. put off \ do my work
3. get through \ eat dinner	9. delay \ leave on vacation
4. stop \ rain	10. consider \ get a job
5. keep \ work	11. talk about \ go to a movie
6. keep on \ work	12. mention \ go out of town

□ **Exercise 13. Listening.** (Chart 14-3)

Listen to the conversations. Complete the sentences with appropriate verbs.

CD 2
Track 13

1. The speakers enjoy _____*watching*_____ movies on weekends.

2. The speakers have given up _____ for better weather.

3. The speakers are going to keep on _____.

4. The speakers are discussing _____ to a concert in the city.

5. The speakers have put off _____ their homework.

6. The speakers are going to delay _____ the office.

□ **Exercise 14. Looking at grammar.** (Chart 14-3)

Complete the sentences with appropriate gerunds.

1. When Beth got tired, she stopped _____*working / studying*_____.

2. Would you mind _____ the door? Thanks.

3. I have a lot of homework tonight, but I'd still like to go with you later on. I'll call you when I get through _____.

4. Where are you considering _____ for your break?

5. Sometimes I put off _____ my apartment.

6. You have to decide where you want to go to school next year. You can't postpone _____ that decision much longer.

7. I wanted to go to Mexico. Sally suggested _____ to Hawaii.

8. Tony mentioned _____ the bus to school instead of walking.

9. I appreciate _____ able to study in peace and quiet.

□ **Exercise 15. Warm-up.** (Chart 14-4)

Complete the sentences by circling all the activities that are true for you. All the choices end in **-ing**. What do you notice about the verbs in blue?

1. Last week I went *shopping running biking dancing.*

2. I like to go *hiking swimming camping sightseeing.*

3. I've never gone *fishing bowling skiing diving.*

308 CHAPTER 14

14-4 *Go* + Gerund

(a) Did you *go shopping*? (b) We *went fishing* yesterday.	*Go* is followed by a gerund in certain idiomatic expressions to express, for the most part, recreational activities.

Go + gerund

go biking	go dancing	go running	go skiing
go birdwatching	go fishing*	go sailing	go skinnydipping
go boating	go hiking	go shopping	go sledding
go bowling	go hunting	go sightseeing	go snorkeling
go camping	go jogging	go skating	go swimming
go canoeing/kayaking	go mountain climbing	go skateboarding	go window shopping

*Also, in British English: *go angling*.

❏ **Exercise 16. Let's talk.** (Chart 14-4)
Discuss the activities listed in Chart 14-4. Work in pairs, in small groups, or as a class.

1. Which ones have you done? When? Briefly describe your experiences.
2. Which ones do you like to do?
3. Which ones do you never want to do?
4. Which ones have you not done but would like to do?

❏ **Exercise 17. Listening.** (Chart 14-4)
CD 2
Track 14
Listen to the story with your book closed. Then open your book and listen again. Complete the sentences with a form of *go* and any verb that makes sense.

1. The first thing Saturday morning, Ron _____*went canoeing*_____.

2. He brought a fishing rod so he could _____.

3. He saw some friends on a sailboat but didn't _____ with them.

4. He _____ instead.

5. After lunch, he _____.

6. He finished the day by _____ with some of his friends.

❑ **Exercise 18. Let's talk.** (Chart 14-4)
Make a sentence that is true for you using the words in parentheses. Then ask a classmate, "How about you?"

Example: I (*enjoy, don't enjoy*) \ go \ shop \ for clothes
SPEAKER A: I don't enjoy going shopping for clothes. How about you?
SPEAKER B: No, I don't enjoy it either. OR Actually, I enjoy it.

1. I (*go, never go*) \ dance \ on weekends
2. I (*like to go, don't like to go*) \ bowl
3. I (*sometimes postpone, never postpone*) \ do \ my homework
4. I (*really appreciate, don't appreciate*) \ get \ emails from advertisers
5. I (*am considering, am not considering*) \ look \ for a new place to live
6. I (*enjoy, don't enjoy*) \ play \ card games
7. I (*used to go, never went*) \ fish \ as a child
8. I (*go, never go*) \ jog \ for exercise

❑ **Exercise 19. Warm-up.** (Chart 14-5)
Read the story. Look at the phrases in blue. <u>Underline</u> the verb that follows each phrase. What form do these verbs take?

Ms. Jones, the teacher, is new and inexperienced. She speaks very quickly, so students have a hard time <u>following</u> her. Because they have difficulty understanding her, they spend a lot of class time asking questions. In response, Ms. Jones gives long, wordy explanations and wastes a lot of class time trying to make herself understood. The students sit at their desks looking confused, and Ms. Jones stands in front of the class feeling frustrated.

14-5 Special Expressions Followed by *-ing*

(a) We *had fun* We *had a good time* } *playing* volleyball.	*-ing* forms follow certain special expressions: ***have fun/a good time* + *-ing*** ***have trouble/difficulty* + *-ing*** ***have a hard time/difficult time* + *-ing***
(b) I *had trouble* I *had difficulty* I *had a hard time* I *had a difficult time* } *finding* his house.	
(c) Sam *spends most of his time studying*.	***spend* + expression of time or money + *-ing***
(d) I *waste a lot of time watching* TV.	***waste* + expression of time or money + *-ing***
(e) She *sat at her desk writing* a letter.	***sit* + expression of place + *-ing***
(f) I *stood there wondering* what to do next.	***stand* + expression of place + *-ing***
(g) He *is lying in bed reading* a novel.	***lie* + expression of place + *-ing***
(h) When I walked into my office, I *found George using* my telephone.	***find* + (pro)noun + *-ing*** ***catch* + (pro)noun + *-ing*** In (h) and (i): Both ***find*** and ***catch*** mean "discover." ***Catch*** often expresses anger or displeasure.
(i) When I walked into my office, I *caught* a thief *looking* through my desk drawers.	

❏ **Exercise 20. Looking at grammar.** (Chart 14-5)
Complete the sentences with appropriate *-ing* verbs.

1. We had a lot of fun _____*playing*_____ games at the picnic.

2. I have trouble _____ Mrs. Maxwell when she speaks. She talks too fast.

3. I spent five hours _____ my homework last night.

4. Olga is standing at the corner _____ for the bus.

5. Ricardo is sitting in class _____ notes.

6. It was a beautiful spring day. Dorothy was lying under a tree _____ to the birds sing.

7. We wasted our money _____ to that movie. It was very boring.

8. Ted is an indecisive person. He has a hard time _____ up his mind about anything.

9. I wondered what the children were doing while I was gone. When I got home, I found them _____ TV.

10. When Mr. Chan walked into the kitchen, he caught the children _____ some candy even though he'd told them not to spoil their dinners.

❏ **Exercise 21. Let's talk: pairwork.** (Chart 14-5)
Work with a partner. Complete a sentence about yourself using an *-ing* verb. Ask your partner, "How about you?"

Example: Sometimes I have trouble . . . .
SPEAKER A: Sometimes I have trouble understanding spoken English. How about you?
SPEAKER B: Yeah. Me too. I have a lot of trouble understanding people in TV shows especially.

1. Every week I spend at least an hour . . . .
2. In my free time, I have fun . . . .
3. Sometimes I sit in class . . . .
4. Sometimes I waste money . . . .
5. If you come to my home at midnight, you will find me . . . .

Change roles.
6. I think it's fun to spend all day . . . .
7. Sometimes I have trouble . . . .
8. You will never catch me . . . .
9. I *am/am not* a decisive person. I have a *hard/easy* time . . . .
10. When I'm on a picnic, I always have a good time . . . .

Exercise 22. Listening. (Chart 14-5)

Listen to the sentences. Complete the sentences, orally or in writing, using *-ing* verbs.

CD 2
Track 15

Example: You will hear:　　　　　I play soccer every day. I love it!

You will write (or say): The speaker has fun ____*playing soccer*____.

1. The speaker has trouble _____.

2. The speaker caught his son _____.

3. The speaker stands at the kitchen counter in the mornings _____.

4. The speaker has a hard time _____.

5. The speaker wasted two hours _____.

6. The speaker had a good time _____.

7. The speaker found Tom _____.

8. The speaker spent an hour _____.

❏ **Exercise 23. Let's talk: interview.** (Chart 14-5)

Make questions with the given words. Interview two people for each item. Share some of the answers with the class.

1. What \ you \ have difficulty \ remember?
2. What \ you \ have a hard time \ learn?
3. What \ you \ have a good time \ play?
4. What English sounds \ you \ have a hard time \ pronounce?
5. What \ people \ waste money \ do?
6. What \ people \ waste time \ do?

❏ **Exercise 24. Warm-up.** (Chart 14-6)

Check (✓) all the correct sentences.

1. a. ____ We hope visiting them soon.

　　b. ____ We hope to visit them soon.

　　c. ____ We hope you to visit them soon.

2. a. ____ We told you to call us.

　　b. ____ We told to call us.

　　c. ____ We told calling us.

3. a. ____ I invited to go to the party.

　　b. ____ I invited Ella to go to the party.

　　c. ____ Ella was invited to go to the party.

14-6 Common Verbs Followed by Infinitives

Verb + Infinitive

(a) I *hope to see* you again soon. (b) He *promised to be* here by ten.	An *infinitive* = *to* + *the simple form of a verb* (*to see, to be, to go,* etc.).
	Some verbs are followed immediately by an infinitive, as in (a) and (b).
(c) He *promised not to be* late.	Negative form: *not* precedes the infinitive, as in (c).

Common verbs followed by infinitives

hope to (do something)	promise to	seem to	expect to
plan to	agree to	appear to	would like to
intend to*	offer to	pretend to	want to
decide to	refuse to	ask to	need to

Verb + Object + Infinitive

(d) Mr. Lee *told me to be* here at ten o'clock. (e) The police *ordered the driver to stop*.	Some verbs are followed by a (pro)noun object and then an infinitive, as in (d) and (e).
(f) I *was told to be* here at ten o'clock. (g) The driver *was ordered* to stop.	These verbs are followed immediately by an infinitive when they are used in the passive, as in (f) and (g).

Common verbs followed by (pro)nouns and infinitives

tell someone to	invite someone to	require someone to	expect someone to
advise someone to**	permit someone to	order someone to	would like someone to
encourage someone to	allow someone to	force someone to	want someone to
remind someone to	warn someone to	ask someone to	need someone to

Verb + Infinitive/Verb + Object + Infinitive

(h) I *expect to pass* the test. (i) I *expect Mary to pass* the test.	Some verbs have two patterns: • *verb + infinitive*, as in (h) • *verb + object* + infinitive, as in (i) COMPARE: In (h): I think I will pass the test. In (i): I think Mary will pass the test.

Common verbs followed by infinitives or by objects and then infinitives

ask to / ask someone to	want to / want someone to
expect to / expect someone to	would like to / would like someone to
need to / need someone to	

*__Intend__ is usually followed by an infinitive (*I **intend to go** to the meeting.*) but sometimes may be followed by a gerund (*I **intend** going to the meeting.*) with no change in meaning.

A gerund is used after **advise (active) if there is no noun or pronoun object.
  COMPARE:
    (1) *He advised buying a Fiat.*
    (2) *He advised me to buy a Fiat. I was advised to buy a Fiat.*

❏ **Exercise 25. Looking at grammar.** (Chart 14-6)
Complete the sentences with *to leave* or *me to leave*. In some cases, both completions are possible.

1. He told _____ *me to leave* _____.

2. He decided _____ *to leave* _____.

3. He asked _____ *to leave / me to leave* _____.

4. He offered _____.

5. She wanted _____.

6. He agreed _____.

7. She would like _____.

8. He warned _____.

9. She refused _____.

10. He promised _____.

11. She hoped _____.

12. He permitted _____.

13. She expected _____.

14. He forced _____.

15. She allowed _____.

16. He reminded _____.

17. She planned _____.

18. He pretended _____.

❏ **Exercise 26. Looking at grammar.** (Chart 14-6)
Report what was said by using the verbs in the list to introduce an infinitive phrase.

advise	encourage	order	require
allow	expect	permit	tell
ask	force	remind	warn

1. The professor said to Alan, "You may leave early."

   → *The professor allowed Alan to leave early.* OR

   → *Alan was allowed to leave early.*

2. Roberto said to me, "Don't forget to take your book back to the library."

3. Mr. Chang thinks I have a good voice, so he said to me, "You should take singing lessons."

4. Mrs. Alvarez was very stern and a little angry. She shook her finger at the children and said to them, "Don't play with matches!"

5. I am very relieved because the Dean of Admissions said to me, "You may register for school late."

6. The law says, "Every driver must have a valid driver's license."

7. My friend said to me, "You should get some automobile insurance."

8. The robber had a gun. He said to me, "Give me all of your money."

9. My boss said to me, "Come to the meeting ten minutes early."

❑ **Exercise 27. Let's talk.** (Chart 14-6)
Work in small groups. Speaker A forms the question, and Speaker B gives the answer.
Speaker C changes the sentence to passive (the *by*-phrase can be omitted).

Example: What \ someone \ remind \ you \ do \ recently?
SPEAKER A: What did someone remind you to do recently, Mario?
SPEAKER B: My roommate reminded me to recharge my cell phone.
SPEAKER C: Mario was reminded to recharge his cell phone.

1. What \ a family member \ remind \ you \ do \ recently?

2. Where \ a friend \ ask \ you \ go \ recently?

3. What \ the government \ require \ people \ do?

4. What \ doctors \ advise \ patients \ do?

5. What \ teachers \ expect \ students \ do?

6. What \ our teacher \ tell \ you \ do \ recently?

7. What \ the laws \ not permit \ you \ do?

8. Where \ parents \ warn \ their kids \ not \ go?

9. What \ our teacher \ encourage \ us \ do to practice our English?

❑ **Exercise 28. Looking at grammar.** (Charts 14-3 and 14-6)
Complete each sentence with a gerund or an infinitive.

1. We're going out for dinner. Would you like _____*to join*_____ us?

2. Jack avoided _____*looking at*_____ me.

3. I was broke, so Jenny offered _____ me a little money.

4. Would you mind _____ the door for me?

5. Even though I asked the people in front of me at the movie _____ quiet,
   they kept _____.

6. Lucy pretended _____ the answer to my question.

7. The teacher seems _____ in a good mood today, don't you think?

8. I don't mind _____ alone.

9. Mrs. Jackson warned her young son not
   _____ the hot stove.

10. Residents are not allowed _____
    pets in my apartment building.

11. All applicants are required _____
    an entrance examination.

12.   My boss expects me _____ the work ASAP.*

13.   Joan and David were considering _____ married in June, but they finally
      decided _____ until August.

14.   Jack advised me _____ a new apartment.

15.   I was advised _____ a new apartment.

16.   Jack advised _____ a new apartment.

17.   Jack suggested _____ a new apartment.

18.   When we were in New York, we had a really good time _____ in Central
      Park on sunny days.

19.   This is my first term at this school. I haven't really had any problems, but sometimes I
      have trouble _____ the lectures. Some professors speak too fast.

20.   Ms. Gray is a commuter. Every workday, she spends almost two hours
      _____ to and from work.

❏   **Exercise 29. Warm-up.** (Chart 14-7)
Which pairs (a. and b.) have basically the same meaning? Which pairs have different
meanings?

1. a. It began to snow.
    b. It began snowing.

2. a. I remembered to call my parents.
    b. I remembered calling my parents.

3. a. We love to listen to music.
    b. We love listening to music.

4. a. He forgot to buy a gift.
    b. He forgot buying a gift.

5. a. I stopped to talk to my friend.
    b. I stopped talking to my friend.

---

*ASAP = *as soon as possible.*

14-7 Common Verbs Followed by Either Infinitives or Gerunds

Some verbs can be followed by either an infinitive or a gerund, sometimes with no difference in meaning, as in Group A below, and sometimes with a difference in meaning, as in Group B below.

Group A: Verb + Infinitive or Gerund, with No Difference in Meaning

begin start continue	like love prefer*	hate can't stand can't bear	The verbs in Group A may be followed by either an infinitive or a gerund with little or no difference in meaning.

(a) It *began to rain*. / It *began raining*. (b) I *started to work*. / I *started working*.	In (a): There is no difference between **began to rain** and **began raining**.
(c) It *was beginning to rain*.	If the main verb is progressive, an infinitive (not a gerund) is usually used, as in (c).

Group B: Verb + Infinitive or Gerund, with a Difference in Meaning

remember forget	regret try	stop	The verbs in Group B may be followed by either an infinitive or a gerund, but the meaning is different.

(d) Judy always *remembers to lock* the door.	**Remember** + *infinitive* = remember to perform responsibility, duty, or task, as in (d).
(e) Sam often *forgets to lock* the door.	**Forget** + *infinitive* = forget to perform a responsibility, duty, or task, as in (e).
(f) I *remember seeing* the Alps for the first time. The sight was impressive.	**Remember** + *gerund* = remember (recall) something that happened in the past, as in (f).
(g) I*'ll never forget seeing* the Alps for the first time.	**Forget** + *gerund* = forget something that happened in the past, as in (g).**
(h) I *regret to tell* you that you failed the test.	**Regret** + *infinitive* = regret to say, to tell someone, to inform someone of some bad news, as in (h).
(i) I *regret lending* him some money. He never paid me back.	**Regret** + *gerund* = regret something that happened in the past, as in (i).
(j) I*'m trying to learn* English.	**Try** + *infinitive* = make an effort, as in (j).
(k) The room was hot. I *tried opening* the window, but that didn't help. So I *tried turning* on the fan, but I was still hot. Finally, I turned on the air conditioner.	**Try** + *gerund* = experiment with a new or different approach to see if it works, as in (k).
(l) The students *stopped talking* when the professor entered the room. The room became quiet.	**Stop** + *gerund* = stop an activity.
(m) When Ann saw her professor in the hallway, she *stopped* (*in order*) *to talk* to him.	**Stop** can also be followed immediately by an infinitive of purpose, as in (m): Ann stopped walking in order to talk to her professor. (See Chart 15-1, p. 331.)

*Notice the patterns with **prefer**:
   prefer + *gerund*: I **prefer staying** home **to going** to the concert.
   prefer + *infinitive*: I'd **prefer to stay** home (rather) **than** (**to**) **go** to the concert.

Forget followed by a gerund usually occurs in a negative sentence or in a question: e.g., *I'll never forget, I can't forget, Have you ever forgotten*, and *Can you ever forget* are often followed by a gerund phrase.

Complete each sentence with the correct form of the verb in parentheses.

1. I always remember (*turn*) _____to turn_____ off all the lights before I leave my house.

2. I remember (*play*) _____ with dolls when I was a child.

3. What do you remember (*do*) _____ when you were a child?

4. What do you remember (*do*) _____ before you leave for class every day?

5. What did you forget (*do*) _____ before you left for class this morning?

6. I won't ever forget (*watch*) _____ our team score the winning goal in the last seconds of the championship game.

7. Don't forget (*do*) _____ your homework tonight.

8. Please stop (*bite*) _____ your fingernails.

9. I stopped (*get*) _____ gas yesterday and was shocked at the high price.

10. I stopped (*drive*) _____ so much because of the high price of gas.

❑ **Exercise 31. Listening.** (Chart 14-7)

CD 2
Track 16

Listen to each sentence and choose the sentence (a. or b.) with the same meaning.

1. a. Joan thought about her phone call with her husband.
   b. Joan didn't forget to call her husband.

2. a. Rita was thinking about the times she went to the farmers' market with her grandmother.
   b. Rita didn't forget to go to the farmers' market with her grandmother.

3. a. Roger got a cigarette and began to smoke.
   b. Roger quit smoking.

4. a. Mr. and Mrs. Olson finished eating.
   b. Mr. and Mrs. Olson got something to eat before the movie.

5. a. The speaker is sorry about something he did.
   b. The speaker is delivering some bad news.

❑ **Exercise 32. Looking at grammar.** (Charts 14-3 → 14-7)
Complete each sentence with the correct form of the verb in parentheses.

1. Maria loves (*swim*) _____swimming / to swim_____ in the ocean.

2. After a brief interruption, the professor continued (*lecture*) _____.

3. I hate (*see*) _____ any living being suffer. I can't bear (*watch*) _____ news reports of children who are starving. I can't stand (*read*) _____ about animals that have been cruelly abused by people.

4. I'm afraid of flying. When a plane begins (*move*) _____ down the runway, my heart starts (*race*) _____. Uh-oh! The plane is beginning (*move★*) _____, and my heart is starting (*race*) _____.

5. When I travel, I prefer (*drive*) _____ to (*take*) _____ a plane.

6. I prefer (*drive*) _____ rather than (*take*) _____ a plane.

7. I regret (*inform*) _____ you that your loan application has not been approved.

8. I regret (*listen, not*) _____ to my father's advice. He was right.

9. When a student asks a question, the teacher always tries (*explain*) _____ the problem as clearly as possible.

10. I tried everything, but the baby still wouldn't stop (*cry*) _____.

I tried (*hold*) _____ him, but that didn't help.

I tried (*feed*) _____ him, but he refused the food and continued (*cry*) _____.

I tried (*burp*) _____ him.

I tried (*change*) _____ his diaper.

Nothing worked. The baby wouldn't stop crying.

★If possible, native speakers usually prefer to use an infinitive following a progressive verb instead of using two **-ing** verbs in a row.

    Usual: *The baby is starting **to walk**.* (instead of *walking*)

If the main verb is not progressive, either form is used:

    *Babies **start to walk** around one.* OR *Babies **start walking** around one.*

Speaker A gives the cues. Speaker B makes sentences from the verb combinations. Any name, verb tense, or modal can be used. Work in pairs or small groups.

Examples:
SPEAKER A (*book open*):   like \ go
SPEAKER B (*book closed*):   I like to go (OR going) to the park.

SPEAKER A (*book open*):   ask \ open
SPEAKER B (*book closed*):   Kostas asked me to open the window.

1. advise \ go
2. offer \ lend
3. start \ laugh
4. remind \ take
5. be allowed \ have

Change roles.
6. postpone \ go
7. look forward to \ see
8. forget \ bring
9. remember \ go
10. suggest \ go

Change roles.
11. continue \ walk
12. finish \ do
13. encourage \ go
14. can't stand \ have to wait
15. regret \ take

Change roles.
16. decide \ ask \ come
17. stop \ walk
18. consider \ not go
19. keep \ put off \ do
20. intend \ finish

❑ **Exercise 34. Let's talk: interview.** (Charts 14-3 → 14-7)
Make true sentences about yourself using the words in parentheses. Ask other students about themselves using the given question word. Share some of the answers with the class.

Example: (like \ go \ on weekends) Where?
→ *I like to go to Central Park on weekends. How about you? Where do you like to go on weekends?*

1. (enjoy \ listen to) What?
2. (be interested in \ learn) What?
3. (be used to \ have \ for breakfast) What?
4. (prefer \ go to bed) What time?
5. (can't stand \ watch) What?
6. (decide \ study English) Why?

❑ **Exercise 35. Looking at grammar.** (Charts 14-3 → 14-7)
Complete each sentence with an appropriate form of the verb in parentheses.

1. Mary reminded me (*be, not*) _____ not to be _____ late for the meeting.

2. I've volunteered (*help*) _____ at the local school during my time off and (*paint*) _____ the lunchroom.

3. We discussed (*quit*) _____ our jobs and (*open*) _____ our own business.

4. I'm getting tired. I need (*take*) _____ a break.

5. Sometimes students avoid (*look*) _____ at the teacher if they don't want (*answer*) _____ a question.

6. Most children prefer (*watch*) _____ television to (*listen*) _____ to the radio.

7. The taxi driver refused (*take*) _____ a check. He wanted the passenger (*pay*) _____ cash.

8. The travel agent advised us (*wait, not*) _____ until August (*make*) _____ a reservation.

9. Keep (*talk*) _____. I'm listening to you.

10. Linda offered (*water*) _____ my plants while I was out of town.

11. Igor suggested (*go*) _____ (*ski*) _____ in the mountains this weekend. How does that sound to you?

12. The doctor ordered Mr. Gray (*smoke, not*) _____.

13. Don't tell me his secret. I prefer (*know, not*) _____.

14. Toshi was allowed (*renew*) _____ his student visa.

15. Don't forget (*tell*) _____ Jane (*call*) _____ me about (*go*) _____ (*swim*) _____ tomorrow.

16. Sally reminded me (*ask*) _____ you (*tell*) _____ Bob (*remember*) _____ (*bring*) _____ his soccer ball to the picnic.

17. Recently, Jo has been spending most of her time (*do*) _____ research for a book on pioneer women.

18. The little boy had a lot of trouble (*convince*) _____ anyone he had seen a mermaid.

□ **Exercise 36. Warm-up.** (Chart 14-8)
All of the sentences are correct. What differences do you notice in their grammatical structure?
Do you agree or disagree with the statements? Why or why not?

1. Speaking a second language without an accent is nearly impossible for adult language learners.
2. To speak a second language without an accent is nearly impossible for adult language learners.
3. It is nearly impossible for adult language learners to speak a second language without an accent.

14-8 *It* + Infinitive; Gerunds and Infinitives as Subjects

(a) *It* is difficult *to learn* a second language.	Often an infinitive phrase is used with *it* as the subject of a sentence. The word *it* refers to and has the same meaning as the infinitive phrase at the end of the sentence. In (a): *It* means "to learn a second language."
(b) *Learning* a second language is difficult.	A gerund phrase is frequently used as the subject of a sentence, as in (b).
(c) *To learn* a second language is difficult.	An infinitive can also be used as the subject of a sentence, as in (c), but far more commonly an infinitive phrase is used with *it*, as in (a).
(d) It is easy *for young children* to learn a second language. *Learning* a second language is easy *for young children*. *To learn* a second language is easy *for young children*.	The phrase *for (someone)* may be used to specify exactly who the speaker is talking about, as in (d).

□ **Exercise 37. Looking at grammar.** (Chart 14-8)
Make sentences beginning with *it*. Use a form of the given word followed by an infinitive phrase for each sentence.

1. be dangerous → *It's dangerous to ride a motorcycle without wearing a helmet.*
2. be important
3. not be easy
4. be silly
5. must be interesting
6. be always a pleasure
7. be smart
8. not cost much money
9. be necessary
10. take time

❏ **Exercise 38. Looking at grammar.** (Chart 14-8)

Add *for* (*someone*) and any other words to give a more specific and accurate meaning to each sentence.

1. It isn't possible to be on time.
   → *It isn't possible for me to be on time for class if the bus drivers are on strike and I have to walk to class in a rainstorm.*
2. It's easy to speak Spanish.
3. It's important to learn English.
4. It is essential to get a visa.
5. It's important to take advanced math courses.
6. It's difficult to communicate.
7. It was impossible to come to class.
8. It is a good idea to study gerunds and infinitives.

❏ **Exercise 39. Let's talk: pairwork.** (Chart 14-8)

Work with a partner. Speaker A gives the cue. Speaker B completes the sentence with an infinitive phrase. Speaker A restates the sentence using a gerund phrase as the subject.

Example:
SPEAKER A (*book open*):   It's fun . . .
SPEAKER B (*book closed*):   . . . to ride a horse.
SPEAKER A (*book open*):   Riding a horse is fun.

	Change roles.
1. It's dangerous . . .	5. It is wrong . . .
2. It's easy . . .	6. It takes a lot of time . . .
3. It's impolite . . .	7. It's a good idea . . .
4. It is important . . .	8. Is it difficult . . . ?

❏ **Exercise 40. Let's talk: interview.** (Chart 14-8)

Interview two different students for each item. Ask the students to answer each question using a gerund phrase as the subject.

1. What is easy for you?
2. What is hard for you?
3. What is or isn't interesting for you?
4. What has been a good experience for you?
5. What sounds like fun to you?
6. What is considered impolite in your country?
7. What is a complicated process?
8. What demands patience and a sense of humor?

Verbs with a bullet (•) can also be followed by infinitives. See Chart 14-10.

1.	admit	He *admitted stealing* the money.
2.	advise•	She *advised waiting* until tomorrow.
3.	anticipate	I *anticipate having* a good time on vacation.
4.	appreciate	I *appreciated hearing* from them.
5.	avoid	He *avoided answering* my question.
6.	can't bear•	I *can't bear waiting* in long lines.
7.	begin•	It *began raining*.
8.	complete	I finally *completed writing* my term paper.
9.	consider	I *will consider going* with you.
10.	continue•	He *continued speaking*.
11.	delay	He *delayed leaving* for school.
12.	deny	She *denied committing* the crime.
13.	discuss	They *discussed opening* a new business.
14.	dislike	I *dislike driving* long distances.
15.	enjoy	We *enjoyed visiting* them.
16.	finish	She *finished studying* about ten.
17.	forget•	I*'ll never forget visiting* Napoleon's tomb.
18.	hate•	I *hate making* silly mistakes.
19.	can't help	I *can't help worrying* about it.
20.	keep	I *keep hoping* he will come.
21.	like•	I *like going* to movies.
22.	love•	I *love going* to operas.
23.	mention	She *mentioned going* to a movie.
24.	mind	Would *you mind helping* me with this?
25.	miss	I *miss being* with my family.
26.	postpone	Let's *postpone leaving* until tomorrow.
27.	practice	The athlete *practiced throwing* the ball.
28.	prefer•	Ann *prefers walking* to driving to work.
29.	quit	He *quit trying* to solve the problem.
30.	recall	I *don't recall meeting* him before.
31.	recollect	I *don't recollect meeting* him before.
32.	recommend	She *recommended seeing* the show.
33.	regret•	I *regret telling* him my secret.
34.	remember•	I *can remember meeting* him when I was a child.
35.	resent	I *resent her interfering* in my business.
36.	resist	I *couldn't resist eating* the dessert.
37.	risk	She *risks losing* all of her money.
38.	can't stand•	I *can't stand waiting* in long lines.
39.	start•	It *started raining*.
40.	stop	She *stopped going* to classes when she got sick.
41.	suggest	She *suggested going* to a movie.
42.	tolerate	She *won't tolerate cheating* during an examination.
43.	try•	I *tried changing* the light bulb, but the lamp still didn't work.
44.	understand	I *don't understand his leaving* school.

Verbs with a bullet (•) can also be followed by gerunds. See Chart 14-9.

Verbs Followed Immediately by an Infinitive

1.	afford	I *can't afford to buy* it.
2.	agree	They *agreed to help* us.
3.	appear	She *appears to be* tired.
4.	arrange	I*'ll arrange to meet* you at the airport.
5.	ask	He *asked to come* with us.
6.	can't bear•	I *can't bear to wait* in long lines.
7.	beg	He *begged to come* with us.
8.	begin•	It *began to rain.*
9.	care	I *don't care to see* that show.
10.	claim	She *claims to know* a famous movie star.
11.	consent	She finally *consented to marry* him.
12.	continue•	He *continued to speak.*
13.	decide	I *have decided to leave* on Monday.
14.	demand	I *demand to know* who is responsible.
15.	deserve	She *deserves to win* the prize.
16.	expect	I *expect to enter* graduate school in the fall.
17.	fail	She *failed to return* the book to the library on time.
18.	forget•	I *forgot to mail* the letter.
19.	hate•	I *hate to make* silly mistakes.
20.	hesitate	*Don't hesitate to ask* for my help.
21.	hope	Jack *hopes to arrive* next week.
22.	intend	He *intends to be* a firefighter.
23.	learn	He *learned to play* the piano.
24.	like•	I *like to go* to the movies.
25.	love•	I *love to go* to operas.
26.	manage	She *managed to finish* her work early.
27.	mean	I *didn't mean to hurt* your feelings.
28.	need	I *need to have* your opinion.
29.	offer	They *offered to help* us.
30.	plan	I*'m planning to have* a party.
31.	prefer•	Ann *prefers to walk* to work.
32.	prepare	We *prepared to welcome* them.
33.	pretend	He *pretends not to understand.*
34.	promise	I *promise not to be* late.
35.	refuse	I *refuse to believe* his story.
36.	regret•	I *regret to tell* you that you failed.
37.	remember•	I *remembered to lock* the door.
38.	seem	That cat *seems to be* friendly.
39.	can't stand•	I *can't stand to wait* in long lines.
40.	start•	It *started to rain.*
41.	struggle	I *struggled to stay* awake.
42.	swear	She *swore to tell* the truth.
43.	talk	He *tends to talk* too much.
44.	threaten	She *threatened to tell* my parents.
45.	try•	I*'m trying to learn* English.
46.	volunteer	He *volunteered to help* us.
47.	wait	I*'ll wait to hear* from you.
48.	want	I *want to tell* you something.
49.	wish	She *wishes to come* with us.

Verbs Followed by a (Pro)noun + an Infinitive

50.	advise•	She *advised me to wait* until tomorrow.
51.	allow	She *allowed me to use* her car.
52.	ask	I *asked John to help* us.
53.	beg	They *begged us to come.*
54.	cause	Her laziness *caused her to fail.*
55.	challenge	She *challenged me to race* her to the corner.
56.	convince	I couldn't *convince him to accept* our help.
57.	dare	He *dared me to do* better than he had done.
58.	encourage	He *encouraged me to try* again.
59.	expect	I *expect you to be* on time.
60.	forbid	I *forbid you to tell* him.
61.	force	They *forced him to tell* the truth.
62.	hire	She *hired a boy to mow* the lawn.
63.	instruct	He *instructed them to be* careful.
64.	invite	Harry *invited the Johnsons to come* to his party.
65.	need	We *needed Chris to help* us figure out the solution.
66.	order	The judge *ordered me to pay* a fine.
67.	permit	He *permitted the children to stay* up late.
68.	persuade	I *persuaded him to come* for a visit.
69.	remind	She *reminded me to lock* the door.
70.	require	Our teacher *requires us to be* on time.
71.	teach	My brother *taught me to swim.*
72.	tell	The doctor *told me to take* these pills.
73.	urge	I *urged her to apply* for the job.
74.	want	I *want you to be* happy.
75.	warn	I *warned you not to drive* too fast.

❑ **Exercise 41. Let's talk: pairwork.** (Charts 14-9 and 14-10)
Work with a partner. Partner A gives the cue. Partner B completes the sentence with *doing it* or *to do it*. Check Charts 14-9 and 14-10 for the correct verb form if necessary.

Example: I promise
PARTNER A (*book open*): I promise . . .
PARTNER B (*book closed*): . . . to do it.

1. We plan . . .
2. I can't afford . . .
3. She didn't allow me . . .
4. I don't care . . .
5. Please remind me . . .
6. I am considering . . .
7. Our director postponed . . .
8. He persuaded me . . .
9. I don't mind . . .
10. Everyone avoided . . .

Change roles.
11. I refused . . .
12. I hope . . .
13. She convinced me . . .
14. He mentioned . . .
15. I expect . . .
16. I encouraged him . . .
17. I warned him not . . .
18. We prepared . . .
19. I don't recall . . .
20. We decided . . .

Change roles.
21. He resented . . .
22. When will you finish . . . ?
23. Did you practice . . .
24. She agreed . . .
25. They consented . . .

26. Stop . . .
27. I didn't force him . . .
28. I couldn't resist . . .
29. Somehow, the cat managed . . .
30. Did the little boy admit . . . ?

Change roles.
31. He denied . . .
32. I didn't mean . . .
33. She swore . . .
34. I volunteered . . .
35. He suggested . . .
36. He advised me . . .
37. He struggled . . .
38. I don't want to risk . . .
39. Do you recommend . . . ?
40. I miss . . .

Change roles.
41. I can't imagine . . .
42. She threatened . . .
43. He seems to dislike . . .
44. The children begged . . .
45. She challenged me . . .
46. Did he deny . . . ?
47. She taught me . . .
48. Do you anticipate . . . ?
49. I don't recollect . . .
50. I'll arrange . . .

❑ **Exercise 42. Game.** (Charts 14-9 and 14-10)
Divide into teams. Your teacher will begin a sentence by using any of the verbs in Charts 14-9 and 14-10. Complete the sentence with *to do it* or *doing it,* or with your own words. Each correct completion scores one point.

Example:
TEACHER: I reminded Mario . . .
STUDENT A: . . . to do it. OR . . . to be on time.
TEACHER: Yes. One point!

❑ **Exercise 43. Looking at grammar.** (Charts 14-9 and 14-10)
Choose the correct form of the verbs in *italics*. In some sentences, both verbs are correct.

1. Hassan volunteered *bringing / to bring* some food to the reception.

2. The students practiced *pronouncing / to pronounce* the "th" sound in the phrase "these thirty-three dirty trees."

3. In the fairy tale, the wolf threatened *eating / to eat* a girl named Little Red Riding Hood.

4. The movers struggled *lifting / to lift* the piano up the stairs.

5. Anita demanded *knowing / to know* why she had been fired.

6. My skin can't tolerate *being / to be* in the sun all day. I get sunburned easily.

7. Mr. Kwan broke the antique vase. I'm sure he didn't mean *doing / to do* it.

8. Fred Washington claims *being / to be* a descendant of George Washington.

9. Linda failed *passing / to pass* the entrance exam.

10. I hate *getting / to get* to work late.

11. I can't bear *seeing / to see* animals suffer.

12. Ming Wan just started a new business. He risks *losing / to lose* everything if it doesn't succeed.

❑ **Exercise 44. Looking at grammar.** (Charts 14-9 and 14-10)
Complete each sentence with an appropriate form of the verb in parentheses.

1. How did you manage (*find*) _____to find_____ out about the surprise party?

2. I think Sam deserves (*have*) _____ another chance.

3. Olga finally admitted (*be*) _____ responsible for the problem.

4. Mrs. Freeman can't help (*worry*) _____ about her children.

5. Children, I forbid you (*play*) _____ in the street. There's too much traffic.

6. Lori suggested (*leave*) _____ around six. Is that too early for you?

7. I urged Omar (*return*) _____ to school and (*finish*) _____ his education.

8. Oscar keeps (*hope*) _____ and (*pray*) _____ that things will get better.

9. Nadia keeps (*promise*) _____ (*visit*) _____ us, but she never does.

10. My little cousin is a blabbermouth! He can't resist (*tell*) _____ everyone my secrets!

11. I finally managed (*persuade*) _____ Yoko (*stay*) _____ in school and (*finish*) _____ her degree.

12. Margaret challenged me (*race*) _____ her across the pool.

❏ **Exercise 45. Let's talk.** (Chapter 14)
Work in groups of three to five. Choose one of the story beginnings or make up your own. Each group member continues the story by adding a sentence or two. At least one of the sentences should contain words from the list on page 329, plus a gerund or infinitive phrase (but it is okay to continue the story without using a gerund or infinitive if it works out that way). As a group, use as many of the words in the list as you can.

Example: Yoko had a bad night last night. First, when she got home, she discovered that . . .
SPEAKER A: . . . her door was unlocked. She didn't ***recall leaving*** her door unlocked. She always ***remembers to lock*** her door and in fact specifically ***remembered locking*** it that morning. So she became afraid that someone had broken into her apartment.
SPEAKER B: She ***thought about going*** inside, but then decided ***it*** would be better ***not to go*** into her apartment alone. What if there was a burglar inside?
SPEAKER C: ***Instead of going*** into her apartment alone, Yoko walked to her next-door neighbor's door and knocked.
SPEAKER D: Her neighbor answered the door. He could see that something was the matter. "Are you all right?" he asked her.
Etc.

Story beginnings:
1. (_____) is having trouble with (her/his) roommate, whose name is (_____). (Her/His) roommate keeps many pets even though the lease they signed forbids residents to keep animals in their apartments. Yesterday, one of these pets, a/an . . . .

2. It was a dark and stormy night. (_____) was all alone at home. Suddenly . . . .

3. Not long ago, (_____) and (_____) were walking home together after dark. They heard a strange whooshing sound. When they looked up in the night sky, they saw a huge hovering aircraft. It glowed! It was round and green! (_____) was frightened and curious at the same time. (She/He) wanted to . . . , but . . . .

4. Once upon a time, (_____) lived in a faraway village in a remote mountainous region. All of the villagers were terrified because of the dragon that lived nearby. At least once a week, the dragon would descend on the village and . . . .

5. (_____) had a bad day yesterday. First of all, when (she/he) got up in the morning, (she/he) discovered that . . . .

List of words and phrases to use in your story:

Prepositional expressions followed by gerunds	Verbs followed by gerunds or infinitives		*It* + an infinitive or a gerund subject
be accused of	admit	mind	be a bad experience
be accustomed to	advise	need	be a bad idea
in addition to	afford	offer	be better
be afraid of	agree	permit	be clever
apologize (to someone) for	ask	persuade	be dangerous
believe in	avoid	plan	be difficult
blame (someone) for	beg	postpone	be easy
be capable of	begin	prefer	be essential
be committed to	consider	prepare	be foolish
complain about	continue	pretend	be a good experience
dream of	convince	promise	be a good idea
be excited about	decide	quit	be fun
forgive (someone) for	demand	recall	be hard
be guilty of	deny	refuse	be important
instead of	discuss	regret	be impossible
be interested in	dislike	remember	be interesting
look forward to	encourage	remind	be necessary
be opposed to	enjoy	risk	be a pleasure
prevent (someone) from	expect	seem	be possible
be scared of	fail	start	be relaxing
stop (someone) from	force	stop	take effort
succeed in	forget	struggle	take energy
take advantage of	hesitate	suggest	take money
be terrified of	hope	threaten	take patience
thank (someone) for	invite	wait	take time
think of	learn	want	
be tired of	like	warn	
be worried about	manage		

Exercise 46. Check your knowledge. (Chapter 14)
Correct the errors.

1. I don't mind to have a roommate.

2. Most students want return home as soon as possible.

3. Learning about another country it is very interesting.

4. I tried very hard to don't make any mistakes.

5. The task of find a person who could tutor me in English wasn't difficult.

6. All of us needed to went to the ticket office before the game yesterday.

7. I'm looking forward to go to swimming in the ocean.

8. Ski in the Alps it was a big thrill for me.

9. Don't keep to be asking me the same questions over and over.

10. During a fire drill, everyone is required leaving the building.

11. I don't enjoy to play card games. I prefer to spend my time for read or watch movies.

12. Is hard for me understand people who speak very fast.

13. When I entered the room, I found my young son stand on the kitchen table.

14. When I got home, Irene was lying in bed think about what a wonderful time she'd had.

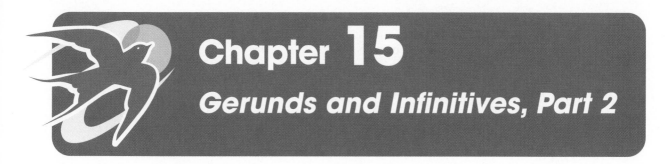

Chapter 15
Gerunds and Infinitives, Part 2

❑ **Exercise 1. Warm-up.** (Chart 15-1)
Which sentences answer the question "Why"?

1. Joe went to the library to study last night.
   → *Why did Joe go to the library last night? To study.*
2. Lucy wants to leave now.
   → *(The sentence doesn't answer the question "Why?")*
3. Eva opened the window to let in some fresh air.
4. Oscar came to this school in order to learn English.
5. Rick needs to call his mother.
6. Rick needs to call his mother to tell her the good news.

15-1 Infinitive of Purpose: *In Order To*

(a) He came here *in order to study* English. (b) He came here *to study* English.	*In order to* is used to express *purpose*. It answers the question "Why?" *In order* is often omitted, as in (b).
(c) INCORRECT: He came here ~~for studying~~ English. (d) INCORRECT: He came here ~~for to study~~ English. (e) INCORRECT: He came here ~~for study~~ English.	To express purpose, use (*in order*) *to*, not *for*, with a verb.*
(f) I went to the store *for* some bread. (g) I went to the store *to buy* some bread.	*For* can be used to express purpose, but it is a preposition and is followed by a noun object, as in (f).

*Exception: The phrase *be used for* expresses the typical or general purpose of a thing. In this case, the preposition *for* is followed by a gerund: *A saw is used for cutting* wood. Also possible: *A saw is used to cut* wood.

However, to talk about a particular thing and a particular situation, *be used* + *an infinitive* is used: *A chain saw was used to cut* (NOT *for cutting*) down the old oak tree.

❑ **Exercise 2. Looking at grammar.** (Chart 15-1)
Complete the sentences with *to* or *for*.

Isabella spent a month in Miami. She went there . . .

1. ____to____ see her cousins.

2. ____for____ a vacation.

3. _____ business.

4. _____ meet with company executives.

5. _____ discuss long-term plans for the company.

6. _____ spend time with her parents.

7. _____ a visit with childhood friends.

❏ **Exercise 3. In your own words.** (Chart 15-1)
Complete the sentences with your own words. Express the purpose of the action.

1. I went to Chicago to ____*visit my grandparents.*_____

2. Ron went to Chicago for ____*a medical conference.*_____

3. I went to the grocery store for _____

4. Reisa went to the grocery store to _____

5. I went to the doctor to _____

6. My son went to the doctor for _____

7. I swim every day to _____

8. Kevin swims every day for _____

❏ **Exercise 4. Looking at grammar.** (Chart 15-1)
Add *in order* wherever possible. If nothing should be added, write Ø.

1. I went to the garden center _____*in order*_____ to get some fertilizer for my flowers.

2. When the teacher asked him a question, Scott pretended _____*Ø*_____ to understand what she was saying.

3. My roommate asked me _____ to clean up the dishes after dinner.

4. Mustafa climbed onto a chair _____ to change a light bulb in the ceiling.

5. Rita has to work at two jobs _____ to support herself and her three children.

6. I really want _____ to learn Italian before I visit Venice next year.

7. I jog three times a week _____ to stay healthy.

8. Karen finally went to the dentist _____ to get some relief from her toothache.

9. It's easier for me _____ to understand written English than it is to understand spoken English.

10. Is it important _____ to speak English without an accent as long as people understand what you're saying?

□ **Exercise 5. Check your knowledge.** (Chart 15-1)
Correct the errors.

1. I went to the library ~~for~~ *to* study last night.

2. Helen borrowed my dictionary for to look up the spelling of *occurred*.

3. The teacher opened the window for letting some fresh air into the room.

4. I came to this school for learn English.

5. I traveled to Osaka for to visit my sister.

□ **Exercise 6. Let's talk: interview.** (Chart 15-1)
Ask two classmates each question. Share some of their responses with the class.

What are two reasons why some people . . .

1. go to Hawaii for vacation?
2. exercise?
3. cheat on exams?
4. meditate?
5. tell white lies?*
6. become actors?

□ **Exercise 7. Warm-up.** (Chart 15-2)
Look at the adjectives in blue. What do you notice about the words that come after them? about the words that come before them?

1. Anya *was* sorry *to hear* that her favorite restaurant closed.
2. Nate *is* certain *to pass* his test.
3. Timmy *was* sad *to learn* his pet goldfish had died.
4. I would *be* happy *to help* you.

15-2 Adjectives Followed by Infinitives

(a) We *were* **sorry to** *hear* the bad news. (b) I *was* **surprised to** *see* Ted at the meeting.	Certain adjectives can be immediately followed by infinitives, as in (a) and (b). In general, these adjectives describe a person (or persons), not a thing. Many of these adjectives describe a person's feelings or attitudes.

Common adjectives followed by infinitives

glad to (do it)	sorry to*	ready to	careful to	surprised to*
happy to	sad to*	prepared to	hesitant to	amazed to*
pleased to	upset to*	anxious to	reluctant to	astonished to*
delighted to	disappointed to*	eager to	afraid to	shocked to*
content to		willing to		stunned to*
relieved to	embarrassed to	motivated to	certain to	
lucky to	proud to	determined to	likely to	
fortunate to	ashamed to		unlikely to	

*The expressions with asterisks are usually followed by infinitive phrases with verbs such as *see, learn, discover, find out, hear.*

---

white lies = lies that aren't considered serious, e.g., telling a friend her dress looks nice when you don't think it does.

❏ Exercise 8. In your own words. (Chart 15-2)

Complete the sentences using the expressions listed in Chart 15-2 and your own words. Use infinitive phrases in your completions.

1. Nicole always speeds on the expressway. She's . . . .
   → *She's certain to get stopped by the police.*
   → *She's likely to get a ticket.*
2. I've worked hard all day long. Enough's enough! I'm . . . .
3. Next month, I'm going to a family reunion — the first one in 25 years. I'm very much looking forward to it. I'm . . . .
4. Some children grow up in unhappy homes. My family, however, has always been loving and supportive. I'm . . . .
5. Ivan's run out of money again, but he doesn't want anyone to know his situation. He needs money desperately, but he's . . . .
6. Rosalyn wants to become an astronaut. That has been her dream since she was a little girl. She has been working hard toward her goal and is . . . .
7. Our neighbors had extra tickets to the ballet, so they invited us to go with them. Since both of us love the ballet, we were . . . .
8. Andrea recently told me what my wayward brother is up to these days. I couldn't believe my ears! I was . . . .

❏ Exercise 9. Let's talk. (Chart 15-2)

Work in small groups. Complete the sentences with adjectives from Chart 15-2 that make sense. Discuss your answers.

SITUATION 1: Mr. Wah was offered an excellent job in another country. He sees advantages and disadvantages to moving.

He is . . .

1. _____sad to / prepared to / reluctant to_____ leave his country.

2. _____ move away from his parents.

3. _____ take his wife and children away from family and friends.

4. _____ try a new job.

5. _____ learn a new language.

SITUATION 2: There have been a lot of nighttime burglaries in the town of Viewmont.

The residents have been . . .

6. _____ leave their homes overnight.

7. _____ lock their doors and windows at night.

8. _____ watch for strangers on the streets.

9. _____ have weekly meetings with the police for updates on their progress.

10. _____ hear that the police suspect neighborhood teenagers.

❑ **Exercise 10. Let's talk: interview.** (Chart 15-2)
Make questions using the words in parentheses. Ask two classmates each question. Share some of their answers with the class.

1. What are children sometimes (afraid \ do)?
2. When you're tired in the evening, what are you (content \ do)?
3. What should drivers be (careful \ do) in traffic?
4. If one of your friends has a problem, what are you (willing \ do)?
5. What are people who don't speak English well (reluctant \ do)?
6. What are you (determined \ do) before you are too old?
7. What are some things people are (ashamed \ do)?
8. Can you tell me something you were (shocked \ find out)?
9. Can you tell me something you were (sad \ hear)?
10. What are you (eager \ do) in the near future?

❑ **Exercise 11. Warm-up.** (Chart 15-3)
In which sentences are the speakers expressing a negative idea (in other words, expressing the idea that there's something wrong or that there's a bad result)?

1. The soup is too spicy. I can't eat it.
2. The soup is very spicy, but I like it.
3. It's very late, but the restaurant is still open.
4. We're too late. The restaurant has closed.

15-3 Using Infinitives with *Too* and *Enough*

COMPARE: (a) That box is *too heavy* for Bob to lift. (b) That box is *very heavy*, but Bob can lift it.	In the speaker's mind, the use of *too* implies a negative result. In (a): *too heavy* = It is *impossible* for Bob to lift that box. In (b): *very heavy* = It is *possible but difficult* for Bob to lift that box.
(c) I am *strong enough to lift* that box. I can lift it. (d) I have *enough strength to lift* that box. (e) I have *strength enough to lift* that box.	*Enough* follows an adjective, as in (c). Usually *enough* precedes a noun, as in (d). In formal English, it may follow a noun, as in (e).

❑ **Exercise 12. Let's talk.** (Chart 15-3)
Work in pairs, in small groups, or as a class.

Part I. Think of a negative result for each sentence. Make negative statements using infinitive phrases.

1. That ring is too expensive.
   → Negative result: *I can't buy it. That ring is too expensive for me to buy.*
2. I'm too tired.
   → Negative result: *I don't want to go to the meeting. I'm too tired to go to the meeting.*
3. It's too late.
4. It's too cold.
5. Physics is too difficult.
6. I'm too busy.
7. My son is too young.
8. The mountain cliff is too steep.

Part II. Now think of a positive result for each sentence. Make positive statements using infinitive phrases.

9. That ring is very expensive, but it isn't too expensive.
   → Positive result: *I can buy it. That ring isn't too expensive for me to buy.*
10. I'm very tired, but I'm not too tired.
11. My suitcase is very heavy, but it's not too heavy.
12. I'm very busy, but I'm not too busy.

❑ **Exercise 13. Let's talk.** (Chart 15-3)
Discuss possible answers to the given questions. Work in pairs, in small groups, or as a class.

1. What is a child too young to do but an adult old enough to do?
2. What is your pocket big enough to hold? What is it too small to hold?
3. What do you have enough time to do after class today? Are you too busy to do something you'd like to do or should do?
4. Is there enough space in this classroom for 100 people? Or is it too small to hold that many people? How many people is this room big enough to hold comfortably?
5. Here's an English saying: "Too many cooks spoil the soup." What do you think it means?
6. Do you think it is very important to practice your English? Do you get enough practice? In your opinion, how much practice is enough?
7. Is it very difficult or too difficult to learn English?

❑ **Exercise 14. Listening.** (Chart 15-3)
Listen to Speaker A. Choose the response that you expect Speaker B to give.

CD 2
Track 17

Example: You will hear: Oh, no. I spilled the coffee!

You will choose: a. I'm sorry. I didn't fill your cup full enough.

ⓑ I'm sorry. I filled your cup too full.

336 CHAPTER 15

SPEAKER B:

1. a. Yes. It was too good to eat.
   b. Yes. It was very good.

2. a. No. She's old enough to stay home alone.
   b. Never. She's too young to stay home alone.

3. a. I agree. It can be very difficult at times.
   b. I agree. It's too difficult.

4. a. Really well. They're too clean. Thanks.
   b. Really well. They're very clean. Thanks.

5. a. I know. He shouldn't be driving.
   b. I know he's very old, but it's okay for him to keep driving.

6. a. I guess we don't have enough big envelopes.
   b. I guess we don't have big enough envelopes.

❏ **Exercise 15. Grammar and speaking.** (Charts 14-7, 14-8, 14-11, and 15-1 → 15-3)
Complete the sentences with your own words. Try to use a gerund or infinitive in each
statement. Then work with a partner. Ask him/her to agree or disagree with your statements
(and to explain why). Share some of their answers with the class.

		PARTNER AGREES?	
1.	It's important for _____	yes	no
2.	A person should never forget to _____	yes	no
3.	Teachers often advise their students to _____	yes	no
4.	I'm not willing to _____	yes	no
5.	It's too difficult for most people to _____	yes	no
6.	In order to _____, employees should _____	yes	no
	_____		
7.	It's easy to _____	yes	no
8.	It's hard to get accustomed to _____	yes	no

❏ **Exercise 16. Warm-up.** (Chart 15-4)
Choose the correct form of the passive verbs. Reminder: A passive verb is *a form of* **be** + *the
past participle.*★ For example, *the patient* **was seen** *by a specialist.*

1. The patient appreciated (*to be seen / being seen*) by a specialist.
2. It was important for him (*to be seen / being seen*) by a specialist.

★See Chart 11-2, p. 213.

15-4 Passive Infinitives and Gerunds

(a) I didn't *expect to be asked* to his party.	PASSIVE INFINITIVE: ***to be*** + *past participle* In (a): ***to be asked*** is a passive infinitive. The understood *by*-phrase is *by him: I didn't expect to be asked to his party (by him).*
(b) I *enjoyed being asked* to his party.	PASSIVE GERUND: ***being*** + *past participle* In (b): ***being asked*** is a passive gerund. The understood *by*-phrase is *by him: I enjoyed being asked to his party (by him).*

❏ **Exercise 17. Looking at grammar.** (Chart 15-4)
Complete the sentences with the passive form of ***invite***.

1. Sam would like _____<u>to be invited</u>_____ to Ann's birthday party.

2. Mark also hopes _____.

3. Maria has no doubts. She expects _____ to it.

4. Omar is looking forward to _____ too.

5. I would enjoy _____ to it, but I probably won't be.

6. Everyone I know wants _____ to Ann's birthday party.

❏ **Exercise 18. Looking at grammar.** (Chart 15-4)
Complete each sentence with the correct form of the verb in parentheses.

1. I don't enjoy (*laugh*) _____<u>being laughed</u>_____ at by other people.

2. Ryan is a convincing liar. It's easy (*fool*) _____<u>to be fooled</u>_____ by his lies.

3. Sometimes adolescents complain about not (*understand*) _____
   by their parents.

4. Your compositions are supposed (*write*) _____ in ink.

5. Ms. Thompson is always willing to help if there is a problem in the office, but she doesn't
   want (*call*) _____ at home unless there is an emergency.

6. Despite his name, Freddie Frankenstein has a good chance of (*elect*) _____
   _____ to the local school board.

7. You must tell me the truth. I insist on your (*tell*) _____ the truth.

8. Don't all of us want (*love*) _____ and (*need*) _____
   by other people?

Exercise 19. Let's talk. (Chart 15-4)
Agree or disagree with the following statements and explain your reasons why. Work in pairs, in small groups, or as a class.

1. I appreciate *being given* advice by my family and friends.
2. I didn't like *being given* advice by my family when I was young.
3. I always expect *to be told* the absolute and complete truth by everyone at all times.
4. I would like *to be invited* to an event where there are a lot of famous people.

Exercise 20. Warm-up. (Chart 15-5)
Make statements that are true for you. Use the same noun to complete each sentence. Do the sentences have the same or different meanings?

1. I need to clean my _____ .

2. My _____ needs cleaning.

3. My _____ needs to be cleaned.

15-5 Using Gerunds or Passive Infinitives Following *Need*

(a) I *need to paint* my house. (b) John *needs to be told* the truth.	Usually an infinitive follows ***need***, as in (a) and (b).
(c) My house *needs painting*. (d) My house *needs to be painted*.	In certain circumstances, a gerund may follow ***need***, as in (c). In this case, the gerund carries a passive meaning. Usually the situations involve fixing or improving something. Examples (c) and (d) have the same meaning.

Exercise 21. Looking at grammar. (Chart 15-5)
Complete each sentence with an appropriate form of the verb in parentheses.

1. The chair is broken. I need (*fix*) ____to fix____ it. The chair needs (*fix*)
   ____fixing / to be fixed____ .

2. The baby's diaper is wet. It needs (*change*) _____ .

3. What a mess! This room needs (*clean*) _____ up. We need
   (*clean*) _____ it up before the company arrives.

4. My shirt is wrinkled. It needs (*iron*) _____ .

5. There is a hole in our roof. The roof needs (*repair*) _____ .

6. I have books and papers all over my desk. I need (*take*) _____ some time to
   straighten up my desk. It needs (*straighten*) _____ up.

7. The apples on the tree are ripe. They need (*pick*) _____ .

8. The dog's been digging in the mud. He needs (*wash*) _____ .

❏ **Exercise 22. Let's talk.** (Chart 15-5)
Look at the picture. What needs doing/to be done?

❏ **Exercise 23. Let's talk or write.** (Chart 15-5)
Choose a situation. Think about what needs to be done and make a list of all the tasks. Then talk or write about your list.

Situations:

1. a student applying to a university
2. a parent trying to get young children off to school in the morning
3. a group of students planning for an end-of-the-year party
4. a person going on vacation to another country for a month
5. an engaged couple making plans for a wedding
6. a farmer on a large farm in the early morning
7. a restaurant owner preparing to open for dinner

❏ **Exercise 24. Warm-up.** (Chart 15-6)
See and *hear* are called "verbs of perception." In other words, they express things that we can perceive (become aware of) through our physical senses. What do you notice about the verb forms following *see* and *hear?*

1. a. CORRECT: I **saw** Mr. Reed give something to the boss.
   b. CORRECT: I **saw** Mr. Reed giving something to the boss.
   c. INCORRECT: I **saw** Mr. Reed ~~to~~ give something to the boss.

2. a. CORRECT: I **heard** Mr. Reed say something to the boss.
   b. CORRECT: I **heard** Mr. Reed saying something to the boss.
   c. INCORRECT: I **heard** Mr. Reed ~~to~~ say something to the boss.

15-6 Using Verbs of Perception

(a) I *saw* my friend *run* down the street.	Certain verbs of perception are followed by either *the simple form** or *the -ing form*** of a verb.
(b) I *saw* my friend *running* down the street.	Examples (a) and (b) have essentially the same meaning, except that the *-ing* form emphasizes the idea of "while." In (b): I saw my friend while she was running down the street.
(c) I *heard* the rain *fall* on the roof.	
(d) I *heard* the rain *falling* on the roof.	
(e) When I walked into the apartment, I *heard* my roommate *singing* in the shower.	Sometimes (not always) there is a clear difference between using the simple form or the *-ing* form.
(f) I *heard* a famous opera star *sing* at the concert last night.	The use of the *-ing* form gives the idea that an activity is already in progress when it is perceived, as in (e): The singing was in progress when I first heard it.
	In (f): I heard the singing from beginning to end. It was not in progress when I first heard it.

Verbs of perception followed by the simple form or the *-ing* form

see	look at	hear	feel	smell
notice	observe	listen to		
watch				

**The simple form of a verb* = the infinitive form without *to*. INCORRECT: I saw my friend ~~to~~ run down the street.

**The -ing form refers to the present participle.

❑ **Exercise 25. Let's talk.** (Chart 15-6)
Describe what you see and hear.

1. Ask a classmate to stand up and sit back down. What did you just see him/her do?
2. Close your eyes. What do you hear happening right now?
3. Ask a classmate to do something. As he/she continues to do this, describe what you see and hear him/her doing.

❑ **Exercise 26. Looking at grammar.** (Chart 15-6)
Part I. Complete the sentences with any appropriate verbs. Both the simple form and the *-ing* form are possible with little or no difference in meaning.

1. Polly was working in her garden, so she didn't hear the phone _____*ring / ringing*_____.

2. I like to listen to the birds _____ when I get up early in the morning.

3. The guard observed a suspicious-looking person _____ into the bank.

4. There was an earthquake in my hometown last year. It was just a small one, but I could feel the ground _____.

5. I was almost asleep last night when I suddenly heard someone _____ on the door.

6. While I was waiting for my plane, I watched other planes _____ and _____.

Part II. Read each situation. Complete the sentence below it with the verb form that seems better to you. Remember that the **-ing** form gives the idea that an activity is in progress when it is perceived.

Both the simple form and the **-ing** form of a verb are grammatically correct, so you can't make a grammar mistake. But a speaker might choose one instead of the other.

SITUATION 1: *I smell smoke. Something must be burning.*

Do you smell something _____*burning*_____? I do.

SITUATION 2: *The front door slammed. I got up to see if someone had come in.*

When I heard the front door _____, I got up to see if someone had come in.

SITUATION 3: *Uncle Ben is in the bedroom. He is snoring.*

I know Uncle Ben is in the bedroom because

I can hear him _____.

SITUATION 4: *When I walked past the park, some children were playing softball.*

When I walked past the park, I saw some children _____ softball.

SITUATION 5: *It was graduation day in the auditorium. When the school principal called my name, I walked to the front of the room.*

When I heard the school principal _____ my name, I walked to the front of the auditorium to receive my diploma.

SITUATION 6: *I glanced out the window. Adam was walking toward the house. I was surprised.*

I was surprised when I saw Adam _____ toward the house.

SITUATION 7: *A fly landed on the table. I swatted it with a rolled-up newspaper.*

As soon as I saw the fly _____ on the table, I swatted it with a rolled-up newspaper.

SITUATION 8: *Someone is calling for help in the distance. I suddenly hear that.*

Listen! Do you hear someone _____ for help? I do.

❑ **Exercise 27. Warm-up.** (Chart 15-7)
Check (✓) the sentences that are correct.

1. ____ My parents let me sleep late on weekends.

2. ____ My parents let me to sleep late on weekends.

3. ____ After I wake up, I help them do the chores.

4. ____ After I wake up, I help them to do the chores.

15-7 Using the Simple Form after *Let* and *Help*

(a) My father *lets* me *drive* his car. (b) I *let* my friend *borrow* my bicycle. (c) *Let's go* to a movie.	*Let* is followed by the simple form of a verb, not an infinitive. INCORRECT: My father lets me ~~to~~ drive his car.
(d) My brother *helped* me *wash* my car. (e) My brother *helped* me *to wash* my car.	*Help* is often followed by the simple form of a verb, as in (d). Although less common, an infinitive is also possible, as in (e). Both (d) and (e) are correct.

❏ **Exercise 28. In your own words.** (Chart 15-7)
Complete the sentences with your own words. Use verb phrases.

1. Don't let me ___*forget to take my house keys with me.*___

2. The teacher usually lets us _____

3. Why did you let your roommate _____

4. You shouldn't let other people _____

5. A stranger helped the lost child _____

6. It was very kind of my friend to help me _____

7. Keep working. Don't let me _____

8. Could you help me _____

❏ **Exercise 29. Warm-up.** (Chart 15-8)
Match the conversations with the descriptions that follow them.

1. ADAM: Mom, can I go out and play?
   MRS. LEE: No, Adam, you cannot go out and play until you clean up your room. I don't know
             how many times I have to say this. Go clean up your room, and I mean now!
   ADAM: Okay, okay!

2. ADAM: Mom, can I go out and play?
   MRS. LEE: Well, let's make a deal. First you clean up your room. Then you can go out
             and play. How does that sound? It needs to be clean before Grandma comes
             for a visit this evening. And if you do it now, you can stay out and play until
             dark. You won't have to come home early to clean your room. Okay?
   ADAM: Okay.

3. ADAM: Mom, can I go out and play?
   MRS. LEE: Sure, but first you need to clean up your room. Okay?
   ADAM: Okay.

Descriptions of conversations:
  a. Mrs. Lee got Adam to clean up his room.   _____
  b. Mrs. Lee made Adam clean up his room.   _____
  c. Mrs. Lee had Adam clean up his room.   _____

15-8 Using Causative Verbs: *Make, Have, Get*

(a) I *made* my brother *carry* my suitcase. (b) I *had* my brother *carry* my suitcase. (c) I *got* my brother *to carry* my suitcase.	**Make**, **have**, and **get** can be used to express the idea that "X" causes "Y" to do something. When they are used as causative verbs, their meanings are similar but not identical. In (a): My brother had no choice. I insisted that he carry my suitcase. In (b): My brother carried my suitcase because I asked him to. In (c): I managed to persuade my brother to carry my suitcase.

Forms				
X	*makes*	Y	*do* something.	(*simple form*)
X	*has*	Y	*do* something.	(*simple form*)
X	*gets*	Y	*to do* something.	(*infinitive*)

Causative *Make*

(d) Mrs. Lee *made* her son *clean* his room. (e) Sad movies *make* me *cry*.	Causative **make** is followed by the simple form of a verb, not an infinitive. *INCORRECT:* She made him ~~to~~ clean his room. **Make** gives the idea that "X" **gives** "Y" **no choice**. In (d): Mrs. Lee's son had no choice.

Causative *Have*

(f) I *had* the plumber *repair* the leak. (g) Jane *had* the waiter *bring* her some tea.	Causative **have** is followed by the simple form of a verb, not an infinitive. *INCORRECT:* I had him ~~to~~ repair the leak. **Have** gives the idea that "X" **requests** "Y" to do something. In (f): The plumber repaired the leak because I asked him to.

Causative *Get*

(h) The students *got* the teacher *to dismiss* class early. (i) Jack *got* his friends *to play* soccer with him after school.	Causative **get** is followed by an infinitive. **Get** gives the idea that "X" **persuades** "Y" to do something. In (h): The students managed to persuade the teacher to let them leave early.

Passive Causatives

(j) I *had* my watch *repaired* (by someone). (k) I *got* my watch *repaired* (by someone).	The past participle is used after **have** and **get** to give a passive meaning. In this case, there is usually little or no difference in meaning between **have** and **get**. In (j) and (k): I caused my watch to be repaired by someone.

❏ **Exercise 30. Looking at grammar.** (Chart 15-8)
Choose the meaning that is closest to the meaning of the verb in **boldface**.

1. The teacher **had** her class write a composition.
   a. gave them no choice   b. persuaded them   c. requested them to do this

2. Mrs. Wilson **made** the children wash their hands before dinner.
   a. gave them no choice   b. persuaded them   c. requested them to do this

3. Kostas **got** some neighborhood kids to help him clean out his garage.
   a. gave them no choice   b. persuaded them   c. requested them to do this

4. My boss **made** me redo my report because he wasn't satisfied with it.
   a. gave me no choice   b. persuaded me   c. requested me to do this

5. I **got** Rosa to lend me some lunch money.
   a. gave her no choice   b. persuaded her   c. requested her to do this

6. The police officer **had** the driver get out of his car.
   a. gave him no choice   b. persuaded him   c. requested him to do this

❑ **Exercise 31. Looking at grammar.** (Chart 15-8)
Complete the sentences with the correct form of the verbs in parentheses.

1. I made my son (*wash*) _____*wash*_____ the windows before he could go outside to play.

2. Mrs. Crane had her house (*paint*) _____*painted*_____.

3. I went to the bank to have a check (*cash*) _____.

4. Tom had a bad headache yesterday, so he got his twin brother, Tim, (*go*)

   _____ to class for him. The teacher didn't know the difference.

5. When Scott went shopping, he found a jacket that he

   really liked. After he had the sleeves (*shorten*)

   _____, it fit him perfectly.

6. When my laptop stopped working, I took it to the

   computer store to have it (*fix*) _____.

7. Peeling onions always makes me (*cry*) _____.

8. Tom Sawyer was supposed to paint the fence, but he

   didn't want to do it. He was a very clever boy. Somehow he got his friends (*do*)

   _____ it for him.

9. We had a professional photographer (*take*) _____ pictures of everyone at

   the wedding. We had over 500 pictures (*take*) _____.

❑ **Exercise 32. Let's talk or write.** (Chart 15-8)
Think about the shopping area nearest your home. What can people do there? Make
sentences with *can* and *can't*.

At the shopping area nearest my home, people can/can't get . . .

1. car \ fix
2. hair \ cut
3. checks \ cash
4. laundry \ do
5. picture \ take
6. blood pressure \ check
7. shoes \ repair
8. clothes \ dry-clean
9. money \ exchange

❏ **Exercise 33. Let's talk or write.** (Chart 15-8)
Ask and answer the questions. Work in pairs, in small groups, or as a class.

1. What do children sometimes try to **get** their parents **to do** (perhaps at a toy store or grocery store)?
2. What do bosses sometimes **make** their employees **do**?
3. What does our teacher sometimes **have** us **do**?
4. Do teachers usually **let** their students **leave** the classroom whenever they want to? What kinds of things do teacher usually not **let** their students **do** inside a classroom?
5. What do your classmates (or friends) sometimes **help** you **do**?

(Change roles if working in pairs.)
6. What didn't your parents **let** you **do** when you were a child?
7. Will you **let** your children **do** those things? (Or, if you're a parent, do you **let** your children **do** those things?)
8. Did your parents **make** you **do** certain things when you were a child?
9. What do you sometimes **have** the server at a restaurant **do**?
10. What do you sometimes **get** your friends **to do**?

❏ **Exercise 34. Check your knowledge.** (Chapter 15)
Correct the errors.

1. My parents made me ~~to~~ promise to write them once a week.

2. I asked my roommate to let me to use his shoe polish.

3. I heard a car door to open and closing.

4. I had my friend to lend me his car.

5. You should visit my country. It is too beautiful.

6. I went to the college bookstore for getting my books for the new term.

7. One of our fights ended up with me having to sent to the hospital for getting stitches.

8. Lilly deserves to be tell the truth about what happened last night.

9. Barbara always makes me laughing. She has a great sense of humor.

10. Stop telling me what to do! Let me to make up my own mind.

11. I went to the pharmacy for having my prescription to be filled.

12. You shouldn't let children playing with matches.

13. When Shelley needed a passport photo, she had her picture taking by a professional photographer.

14. I've finally assembled enough information for beginning writing my research paper.

15. Omar is at the park right now. He is sit on a park bench watch the ducks swimming in the pond. The sad expression on his face makes me to feel sorry for him.

16. The music director tapped his baton for beginning the rehearsal.

❏ **Exercise 35. Looking at grammar.** (Chapters 14 and 15)
Choose the correct completions.

1. My cousins helped me _____ into my new apartment.
   (a.) move   (b.) to move   c. moving   d. being moved

2. It was a hot day, and the work was hard. I could feel sweat _____ down my back.
   a. trickle   b. to trickle   c. trickling   d. trickled

3. You can lead a horse to water, but you can't make him _____.
   a. drink   b. to drink   c. drinking   d. to be drunk

4. As he contemplated the meaning of life, Edward stood on the beach _____ out over the ocean.
   a. look   b. to look   c. looking   d. looked

5. He's a terrific soccer player! Did you see him _____ that goal?
   a. make   b. to make   c. making   d. made

6. We spent the entire class period _____ about the revolution.
   a. talk   b. to talk   c. talking   d. being talked

7. Only seven people applied for the sales job, so Maleek has a good chance of _____ for an interview.
   a. chosen   b. being chosen   c. to be chosen   d. to choose

8. If you hear any news, I want _____ immediately.
   a. told   b. being told   c. to be told   d. telling

9. I was getting sleepy, so I had my friend _____ the car.
   a. drive   b. being driven   c. to be driven   d. to drive

10. The witness to the murder wanted her name kept secret. She asked not _____ in the newspaper.
    a. identify   b. being identified   c. to be identified   d. to identify

☐ **Exercise 36. Reading and listening.** (Chapters 14 and 15)

CD 2
Track 18

First, read the paragraph and try to complete the sentences using the words in the list. Second, listen to the paragraph and check your answers.

to be understood	to solve	to read
able to read	using	being

An Issue in Health Care: Illiteracy

According to some estimates, well over half of the people in the world are functionally illiterate. This means they are unable to perform everyday tasks because they can't read, understand, and respond appropriately to information. One of the problems this creates in health care is that millions of people are not _____ directions on

1

medicine bottles or packages. Imagine _____ a parent with a sick

2

child and being unable _____ the directions on a medicine bottle. We

3

all know that it is important for medical directions _____ clearly.

4

One solution is pictures. Many medical professionals are working today

_____ this problem by _____ pictures to

5   6

convey health-care information.

☐ **Exercise 37. Looking at grammar.** (Chapters 14 and 15)

Complete each sentence with an appropriate form of the verb in parentheses.

1. My children enjoy (allow) ___*being allowed*___ to stay up late when there's something special on TV.

2. I couldn't get to sleep last night, so for a long time I just lay in bed (think) _____ about my career and my future.

3. Jacob's at an awkward age. He's old enough (*have*) _____ adult problems but too young (*know*) _____ how (*handle*) _____ them.

4. I don't anticipate (*have*) _____ any difficulties (*adjust*) _____ to a different culture when I go abroad.

5. We sat in his kitchen (*sip*) _____ very hot, strong tea and (*eat*) _____ pastries from the bakery.

6. I don't like (*force*) _____ (*leave*) _____ the room (*study*) _____ whenever my roommate feels like (*have*) _____ a party.

7. Let's (*have*) _____ Ron and Maureen (*join*) _____ us for dinner tonight, okay?

8. Do you know that your co-workers complain about your* (*come*) _____ late to work and (*leave*) _____ early?

9. Fish don't use their teeth for (*chew*) _____. They use them for (*grab*) _____, (*hold*) _____, or (*tear*) _____. Most fish (*swallow*) _____ their prey whole.

10. It is the ancient task of the best artists among us (*force*) _____ us (*use*) _____ our ability (*feel*) _____ and (*share*) _____ emotions.

11. Traffic has become too heavy for the Steinbergs (*commute*) _____ easily to their jobs in the city from their suburban apartment. They're considering (*move*) _____ to an apartment in the city (*be*) _____ closer to their work. Both of them hate the long commute. They want (*spend*) _____ more time (*do*) _____ things they really enjoy (*do*) _____ in their free time rather than being tied up on the highway during rush hour.

---

*In formal English, a possessive adjective (e.g., *your coming*) is used to modify a gerund. In informal English, the object form of a pronoun is frequently used (*you coming*).

❑ **Exercise 38. Looking at grammar.** (Chapters 14 and 15)
Complete each sentence with the correct form of the verb in parentheses.

1. I was tired, so I just watched them (*play*) _____ volleyball instead of
   (*join*) _____ them.

2. Emily stopped her car (*let*) _____ a black cat (*run*) _____ across the
   street.

3. I'm tired. I wouldn't mind just (*stay*) _____ home tonight and (*get*)
   _____ to bed early.

4. I can't seem (*get*) _____ rid of the cockroaches in my apartment. Every night I
   see them (*run*) _____ all over my kitchen counters. It drives me crazy. I'm
   considering (*have*) _____ the whole apartment (*spray*)
   _____ by a professional pest control expert.

5. Last week I was sick with the flu. It made me (*feel*) _____ awful. I didn't have
   enough energy (*get*) _____ out of bed. I just lay there (*feel*) _____
   sorry for myself. When my father heard me (*sneeze*) _____ and
   (*cough*) _____, he opened my bedroom door (*ask*) _____ me if
   I needed anything. I was really happy to see his kind and caring face, but there wasn't
   anything he could do to make the flu (*go*) _____ away.

❑ **Exercise 39. Let's talk and listen.** (Chapters 14 and 15)

Part I. Answer these questions. Then listen to the lecture on lightning storms with your
book closed.

CD 2
Track 19

1. Have you ever been in a lightning storm?
2. How did you protect yourself?

Part II. Open your book and read the statements. Circle "T" for true and "F" for false.

1. It's important to hide under a tree during a lightning storm.   T   F

2. It's advisable to make yourself as small as possible when a storm is nearby.   T   F

3. If you are lucky enough to be near a car during a storm, get inside it.   T   F

4. Few lightning deaths occur after a storm has passed.   T   F

Part III. Listen to the lecture again. Complete the sentences with the words you hear.

Protecting Yourself in a Lightning Storm

Lightning storms can occur suddenly and without warning. It's important

_____ safe if you're outside when a storm begins. Some people
                1

stand under trees or in open shelters like picnic areas _____ themselves.
                                                                  2

They are _____ that this can be a fatal mistake. Tall objects are
              3

_____ lightning, so when you are out in the open, you should try
              4

_____ yourself as small as possible. _____
              5   6

into a ball lessens the chance that a lightning bolt will strike you. _____
                                                                                    7

a depression in the ground to hide in, like a hole or a ditch, is even better.

_____ a building is safer than _____, but it's not
              8   9

without dangers. _____ away from doors and windows. If
                              10

you're talking on a phone with a cord, hang up. Lightning has been known to travel along a

phone cord and strike the person holding the phone. Even TVs can conduct lightning through

the cable or antenna, so it's a good idea _____ away from the television. It's also
                                                        11

inadvisable _____ a shower or bath since plumbing can conduct electricity
                    12

from lightning. How safe are cars? Surprisingly, the inside of a car is safe as long as it has a

metal roof, but _____ any part of the car that leads to the outside.
                        13

There's a 30/30 rule regarding lightning. As soon as you see lightning, _____
                                                                                          14

the seconds until you hear thunder. If you hear thunder before you reach 30, this means you

_____ shelter immediately. Additionally, even if the storm
              15

_____, you want _____ in a protected place for 30 minutes
              16   17

after you hear the last sounds of thunder or have seen the last flashes of lightning. Many

lightning deaths, in fact more than half in the United States, occur after a storm has passed.

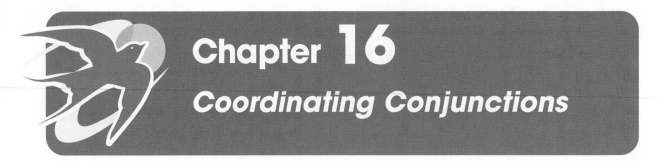

Chapter 16
Coordinating Conjunctions

❑ **Exercise 1. Warm-up.** (Chart 16-1)
Identify the parts of speech of the words in blue and the word that connects them. What do you notice about the words in blue?

	Part of speech	Connective
1. The old man is extremely kind and generous.	*adjective*	*and*
2. He received a book and a sweater for his birthday.		
3. She spoke angrily and bitterly about the war.		
4. In my spare time, I enjoy reading novels or watching television.		
5. He will leave early but arrive late.		

16-1 Parallel Structure

One use of a conjunction is to connect words or phrases that have the same grammatical function in a sentence. This use of conjunctions is called "parallel structure." The conjunctions used in this pattern are **and**, **but**, **or**, and **nor**. These words are called "coordinating conjunctions."

(a) *Steve* **and** his *friend* are coming to dinner.	In (a): *noun* + **and** + *noun*
(b) Susan *raised* her hand **and** *snapped* her fingers.	In (b): *verb* + **and** + *verb*
(c) He *is waving* his arms **and** (*is*) *shouting* at us.	In (c): *verb* + **and** + *verb* (The second auxiliary may be omitted if it is the same as the first auxiliary.)
(d) These shoes are *old* **but** *comfortable*.	In (d): *adjective* + **but** + *adjective*
(e) He wants *to watch* TV **or** (*to*) *listen* to some music.	In (e): *infinitive* + **or** + *infinitive* (The second *to* is usually omitted.)

❑ **Exercise 2. Looking at grammar.** (Chart 16-1)
Choose the correct completions.

1. My roommate is friendly and _____.
   (a.) helpful   (b.) kind   c. kindness

2. Jack opened the window and _____.
   a. turn on the fan   b. turning on the fan   c. turned on the fan

3. Honesty and _____ are admirable qualities in a person.
   a. generous   b. generosity   c. intelligence

4. Kate was listening to the radio and _____ at the same time.
   a. study   b. studying   c. studies

5. I was tired and _____ after our long hike.
   a. hungry   b. hunger   c. thirsty

6. Everyone had a good time at the party and _____ home happy.
   a. go   b. went   c. going

7. No one wanted to stay after the party and _____ up.
   a. clean   b. cleaning   c. cleaned

8. No one enjoys staying and _____ up at the end of a party.
   a. clean   b. cleaning   c. cleaned

❑ **Exercise 3. Looking at grammar.** (Chart 16-1)
Complete each sentence with <u>one</u> word that gives the same idea as the words in parentheses.

1. Lisa was saddened and _____<u>upset</u>_____ by the news.
   (*her feelings were upset*)

2. We enjoy fish and _____ for dinner.
   (*we eat vegetables*)

3. The clerk spoke impatiently and _____ when I asked for help.
   (*her words were rude*)

4. Mr. Evans is very old but _____.
   (*has a lot of strength*)

5. The driver ran a stop sign and _____ down the street.
   (*he was driving at a high speed*)

❑ **Exercise 4. Warm-up.** (Chart 16-2)
Check (✓) the sentences that are correctly punctuated. Notice the use of commas.

1. ___ Oranges, and strawberries are high in vitamin C. (*not correct*)

2. ✓ Oranges and strawberries are high in vitamin C.

3. ___ Oranges, strawberries, and broccoli are high in vitamin C.

4. ___ Oranges, strawberries and broccoli are high in vitamin C.

5. ___ Oranges strawberries and broccoli are high in vitamin C.

6. ___ Oranges, strawberries, and broccoli, are high in vitamin C.

16-2 Parallel Structure: Using Commas

(a) **Steve** and **Joe** are in class.	No commas are used when *and* connects **two** parts of a parallel structure, as in (a).
(b) *INCORRECT PUNCTUATION:* Steve, and Joe are in class.	
(c) **Steve, Joe** *and* **Rita** are in class. (d) **Steve, Joe,** *and* **Rita** are in class.	When *and* connects **three or more** parts of a parallel structure, a comma is used between the first items in the series.
(e) **Steve, Joe, Rita, Jan** *and* **Kim** are in class. (f) **Steve, Joe, Rita, Jan,** *and* **Kim** are in class.	A comma may also be used before *and,* as in (d) and (f). The use of this comma is optional (i.e., the writer can choose).* NOTE: A comma often represents a pause in speech.

*The purpose of punctuation is to make writing clear for readers. This chart and others in this chapter describe the usual use of commas in parallel structures. Sometimes commas are required according to convention (i.e., the expected use by educated language users). Sometimes use of commas is a stylistic choice made by the experienced writer.

❏ **Exercise 5. Listening and punctuation.** (Chart 16-2)

CD 2
Track 20

Listen to the sentences and add commas as necessary. Practice pronouncing the sentences.

1. My bedroom has a bed, a desk (*optional comma*), and a lamp.
2. The price of the meal includes a salad a main dish and dessert.
3. The price of the meal includes a salad and a main dish.
4. Elias waited for his son wife and daughter.
5. Elias waited for his son's wife and daughter.
6. Susan raised her hand snapped her fingers and asked a question.
7. Red yellow gold and olive green are the main colors in the fabric.
8. I love films full of action adventure and suspense.
9. I love action and adventure films.
10. "Travel is fatal to prejudice bigotry and narrow-mindedness." —*Mark Twain**

❏ **Exercise 6. Looking at grammar.** (Charts 16-1 and 16-2)

Parallel structure makes repeating the same words unnecessary. Cross out the words that are unnecessary, and then combine the two given sentences into one concise sentence that contains parallel structure.

1. Molly opened the door. ~~Molly~~ greeted her guests.
   → *Molly opened the door* **and** *greeted her guests.*
2. Molly is opening the door. Molly is greeting her guests.
3. Molly will open the door. Molly will greet her guests.
4. Linda is kind. Linda is generous. Linda is trustworthy.
5. Please try to speak more loudly. Please try to speak more clearly.

---

*Mark Twain (1835–1910) is a well-known American writer and humorist. His most famous novel is *The Adventures of Huckleberry Finn.* He is also famous for his witty quotations.

6. He gave her flowers on Sunday. He gave her candy on Monday. He gave her a ring on Tuesday.

7. He decided to quit school. He decided to go to California. He decided to find a job.

8. I am looking forward to going to Italy. I am looking forward to eating wonderful pasta every day.

9. The boy was old enough to work. The boy was old enough to earn some money.

10. I should have finished my homework. Or I should have cleaned up my room.

11. I like coffee. I do not like tea.

   → *I like coffee **but** not tea.*

12. I have met his mother. I have not met his father.

13. Jake would like to live in Puerto Rico. He would not like to live in Iceland.

❑ **Exercise 7. Looking at grammar.** (Charts 16-1 and 16-2)
First, complete the unfinished sentence in each group. Second, combine the sentences into one concise sentence that contains parallel structure.

1. The country lane was narrow.
   The country lane was steep.

   The country lane was _____<u>muddy</u>_____.

   The country lane was narrow, _____<u>steep, and muddy</u>_____.

2. I dislike living in a city because of the air pollution.
   I dislike living in a city because of the crime.

   I dislike living in a city because of _____.

   I dislike living in a city because of the air pollution, _____

   _____.

3. Hawaii has a warm climate.
   Hawaii has beautiful beaches.
   Hawaii has many interesting tropical trees.

   Hawaii has many interesting tropical _____.

   Hawaii has a warm climate, beautiful beaches, _____

   _____.

4. Mary Hart would make a good president because she works effectively with others.
   Mary Hart would make a good president because she has a reputation for integrity.
   Mary Hart would make a good president because she has a reputation for independent thinking.

   Mary Hart would make a good president because she _____.

   Mary Hart would make a good president because she works effectively with others,

   _____.

❏ **Exercise 8. Looking at grammar.** (Charts 16-1 and 16-2)
Complete the sentences with your own words. Use parallel structure.

1. Judge Holmes served the people of this country with fairness, ability, and _____*honesty*_____ .

2. Ms. Garcia has proven herself to be a hard-working, responsible, and _____

   manager.

3. The professor walked through the door and _____ .

4. I was listening to music and _____

   when I heard a knock at the door.

5. I get up at seven every morning, eat a light breakfast, and _____ .

6. _____ and attending concerts in the park

   are two of the things my wife and I like to do on summer weekends.

7. Our whole family enjoys camping. We especially enjoy fishing in mountain streams and

   _____ .

❏ **Exercise 9. Let's talk.** (Charts 16-1 and 16-2)
Complete the sentences in pairs or small groups. Share some of your completions with the class.

1. A good friend needs to be _____ and _____ .

2. English teachers should have these qualities: _____ ,

   _____ , and _____ .

3. Parents need to _____ and _____ .

4. Doctors should _____ or _____ .

5. _____ , _____ , and _____

   are three easy ways for me to relax at the end of the day.

6. In my free time, I like to _____ , _____ , and

   _____ .

7. Three activities I don't enjoy are _____ , _____ , and

   _____ .

8. _____ , _____ , and _____ are difficult

   subjects for me.

❑ **Exercise 10. Check your knowledge.** (Charts 16-1 and 16-2)
Correct the errors. All of the sentences are adapted from student writing.

1. By obeying the speed limit, we can save energy, lives, and it costs us less.

2. My home offers me a feeling of security, warm, and love.

3. The pioneers hoped to clear away the forest and planting crops.

4. When I refused to help Alice, she became very angry and shout at me.

5. When Nadia moved, she had to rent an apartment, make new friends, and to find a job.

6. All plants need light, to have a suitable climate, and an ample supply of water and minerals from the soil.

7. Slowly and being cautious, the firefighter climbed the burned staircase.

8. On my vacation, I lost a suitcase, broke my glasses, and I missed my flight home.

9. With their keen sight, fine hearing, and they have a refined sense of smell, wolves hunt elk, deer, moose, and caribou.

10. When Anna moved, she had to rent an apartment, make new friends, and to find a job.

11. The Indian cobra snake and the king cobra use poison from their fangs in two ways: by injecting it directly into their prey or they spit it into the eyes of the victim.

❑ **Exercise 11. Warm-up.** (Chart 16-3)
What do you notice about the subject-verb agreement in each pair of sentences?

1. a. Either my brother or my sister is going to tutor me in science.
   b. Either my brother or my sisters are going to tutor me in science.

2. a. Neither my brother nor my sister is a teacher.
   b. Neither my brother nor my sisters are teachers.

3. a. Not only my brother but also my sister has a doctorate in science.
   b. Not only my brother but also my sisters have doctorates in science.

16-3 Paired Conjunctions: *Both . . . And; Not Only . . . But Also; Either . . . Or; Neither . . . Nor*

(a) **Both** my mother **and** my sister **are** here.	Two subjects connected by **both . . . and** take a plural verb, as in (a).
(b) **Not only** my mother **but also** my sister **is** here. (c) **Not only** my sister **but also** my parents **are** here. (d) **Neither** my mother **nor** my sister **is** here. (e) **Neither** my sister **nor** my parents **are** here.	When two subjects are connected by **not only . . . but also**, **either . . . or**, or **neither . . . nor**, the subject that is closer to the verb determines whether the verb is singular or plural.
(f) The research project will take **both** time **and** money. (g) Sue *saw* **not only** a fox in the woods **but** *(also)* a bear. (h) I'll take **either** chemistry **or** physics next quarter. (i) That book is **neither** interesting **nor** accurate.	Notice the parallel structure in the examples. The same grammatical form should follow each part of the paired conjunctions.*
	In (f): **both** + *noun* + **and** + *noun* In (g): **not only** + *noun* + **but also** + *noun* In (h): **either** + *noun* + **or** + *noun* In (i): **neither** + *adjective* + **nor** + *adjective* NOTE: Paired conjuctions are usually used for emphasis; they draw attention to both parts of the parallel structure.

*Paired conjunctions are also called "correlative conjunctions."

❑ **Exercise 12. Looking at grammar.** (Chart 16-3)
Complete the sentences with *is/are*.

1. Both the teacher and the student _____*are*_____ here.

2. Neither the teacher nor the student _____ here.

3. Not only the teacher but also the student _____ here.

4. Not only the teacher but also the students _____ here.

5. Either the students or the teacher _____ planning to come.

6. Either the teacher or the students _____ planning to come.

7. Both the students and the teachers _____ planning to come.

8. Both the students and the teacher _____ planning to come.

❑ **Exercise 13. Looking at grammar.** (Chart 16-3)
Answer the questions. Use paired conjunctions. Work in pairs, in small groups, or as a class.

Part I. Use *both . . . and*.

1. You've met his father. Have you met his mother?
   → *Yes. I've met both his father and his mother.*
2. The driver was injured in the accident. Was the passenger injured in the accident?
3. Wheat is grown in Kansas. Is corn grown in Kansas?
4. The city suffers from air pollution. Does it suffer from water pollution?

Part II. Use ***not only . . . but also***.

5. I know you are studying math. Are you studying chemistry too?

   → *Yes. I'm studying not only math but also chemistry.*

6. I know his cousin is living with him. Is his mother-in-law living with him too?

7. I know you lost your wallet. Did you lose your keys too?

8. I know she goes to school. Does she have a full-time job too?

Part III. Use ***either . . . or***.

9. Omar has your book, or Rosa has your book. Is that right?

   → *Yes. Either Omar or Rosa has my book.*

10. You're going to give your friend a book for her birthday, or you're going to give her some jewelry. Is that right?

11. Your sister will meet you at the airport, or your brother will meet you there. Right?

12. They can go swimming, or they can play tennis. Is that right?

Part IV. Use ***neither . . . nor***.

13. He doesn't like coffee. Does he like tea?

    → *No. He likes neither coffee nor tea.*

14. Her husband doesn't speak English. Do her children speak English?

15. They don't have a refrigerator for their new apartment. Do they have a stove?

16. The result wasn't good. Was the result bad?

❏ **Exercise 14. Listening.** (Chart 16-3)

CD 2
Track 21

Choose the sentence (a. or b.) that has the same meaning as the sentence you hear.

Example: You will hear: Sarah is working on both a degree in biology and a degree in chemistry.

You will choose: a. Sarah is working on only one degree.

   (b.) Sarah is working on two degrees.

1. a. Ben will call Mary and Bob.
   b. Ben will call one of them but not both.

2. a. My mother and my father talked to my teacher.
   b. Either my mother or my father talked to my teacher.

3. a. Simon saw both a whale and a dolphin.
   b. Simon didn't see a whale, but he did see a dolphin.

4. a. Our neighborhood had electricity but not water.
   b. Our neighborhood didn't have electricity or water.

5. a. We will have two teachers today.
   b. We will have one teacher today.

Exercise 15. Looking at grammar. (Chart 16-3)
Combine each pair of sentences into one new sentence with parallel structure. Use *both . . . and; not only . . . but also; either . . . or; neither . . . nor*.

1. He does not have a pen. He does not have paper.
   → *He has neither a pen nor paper.*
2. You can have tea, or you can have coffee.
   → *You can have tea or coffee.*
3. Tanya enjoys horseback riding. Beth enjoys horseback riding.
4. Arthur is not in class today. Ricardo is not in class today.
5. Arthur is absent. Ricardo is absent.
6. We can fix dinner for them here, or we can take them to a restaurant.
7. The leopard faces extinction. The tiger faces extinction.
8. The library doesn't have the book I need. The bookstore doesn't have the book I need.
9. We could fly, or we could take the train.
10. The hospital will not confirm the story. The hospital will not deny the story.
11. Coal is an irreplaceable natural resource. Oil is an irreplaceable natural resource.
12. Her roommates don't know where she is. Her brother doesn't know where she is.

Exercise 16. Listening. (Charts 16-1 → 16-3)

CD 2
Track 22

Part I. Answer these questions. Then listen to the short lecture on bats with your book closed.

1. Do you ever see bats?
2. Are you afraid of them?

Part II. Open your book. Choose the correct completions. Then listen again and check your answers.

Bats

(1) What do people in your country think of bats? Are they mean and scary creatures, or are they symbols of both happiness and ((luck), *lucky*)?

(2) In Western countries, many people have an unreasoned fear of bats. According to scientist Dr. Sharon Horowitz, bats are not only (*harm, harmless*) but also (*benefit, beneficial*) mammals. "When I was a child, I believed that a bat would attack me and (*tangle, tangled*) itself in my hair. Now I know better," said Dr. Horowitz.

(3) Contrary to popular Western myths, bats do not (*attack, attacking*) humans. Although a few bats may have diseases, they are not major carriers of rabies or other frightening diseases. Bats help natural plant life by pollinating plants, spreading seeds, and (*to eat, eating*) insects. If you get rid of bats that eat overripe fruit, then fruit flies can flourish and (*destroy, destruction*) the fruit industry.

(4) According to Dr. Horowitz, bats are both gentle and (*train, trainable*) pets. Not many people, however, own or train bats, and bats themselves prefer to avoid people.

❏ **Exercise 17. Warm-up.** (Chart 16-4)
Check (✓) the items with correct punctuation. NOTE: Only one of the items has incorrect punctuation.

1. ___ Thunder clouds rolled by. Flashes of lightning lit the sky.

2. ___ Thunder clouds rolled by, flashes of lightning lit the sky.

3. ___ Thunder clouds rolled by, and flashes of lightning lit the sky.

4. ___ Thunder clouds rolled by. And flashes of lightning lit the sky.

16-4 Separating Independent Clauses with Periods; Connecting Them with *And* and *But*

(a) It was raining hard. There was a strong wind.	Example (a) contains two *independent clauses* (i.e., two complete sentences).
(b) *INCORRECT PUNCTUATION:* It was raining hard, there was a strong wind.	PUNCTUATION: A period,* NOT A COMMA, is used to separate two independent clauses. The punctuation error in (b) is called a "run-on sentence." In spoken English, a pause, slightly longer than a pause for a comma, separates the two sentences.
(c) It was raining hard, *and* there was a strong wind. (d) It was raining hard. *And* there was a strong wind. (e) It was raining hard *and* there was a strong wind. (f) It was late, *but* he didn't care. (g) It was late. *But* he didn't care.	*And* and *but* (coordinating conjunctions) are often used to connect two independent clauses. PUNCTUATION: Usually a comma immediately precedes the conjunction, as in (c) and (f). In informal writing, a writer might choose to begin a sentence with a conjunction, as in (d) and (g). In a very short sentence, a writer might choose to omit the comma in front of *and,* as in (e). (Omitting the comma in front of *but* is rare.)

*In British English, a period is called a "full stop."

❏ **Exercise 18. Looking at grammar.** (Chart 16-4)
Punctuate the sentences by adding commas and periods. Do not add any words. Add capitalization as necessary.

1. The boys walked the girls ran.
   → *The boys walked. The girls ran.*

2. The boys walked and the girls ran.

3. The teacher lectured the students took notes.

4. The teacher lectured and the students took notes.

5. Elena came to the meeting but Pedro stayed home.

6. Elena came to the meeting her brother stayed home.

□ **Exercise 19. Listening and grammar.** (Chart 16-4)

Listen to the sentences, paying special attention to pauses. Add periods and commas where you hear pauses. Add capitalization as necessary.

CD 2
Track 23

1. Both Jamal and I had many errands to do yesterday. Jamal had to go to the post office and the bookstore I had to go to the post office the travel agency and the bank.

2. Roberto slapped his hand on his desk in frustration he had failed another examination and had ruined his chances for a passing grade in the course.

3. When Alex got home he took off his coat and tie threw his briefcase on the kitchen table and opened the refrigerator looking for something to eat Ann found him sitting at the kitchen table when she got home.*

4. When Tara went downtown yesterday she bought birthday presents for her children shopped for clothes and saw a movie at the theater it was a busy day but she felt fine because it ended on a relaxing note.

5. It was a wonderful picnic the children waded in the stream collected rocks and insects and flew kites the teenagers played an enthusiastic game of baseball the adults busied themselves preparing the food supervising the children and playing some volleyball.

□ **Exercise 20. Looking at grammar.** (Charts 16-2 and 16-4)

Punctuate the sentences by adding commas and periods. Do not add any words. Add capitalization as necessary.

1. Janice entered the room and looked around she knew no one.

2. A thermometer is used to measure temperature a barometer measures air pressure.

3. Derek made many promises but he had no intention of keeping them.

4. The earthquake was devastating tall buildings crumbled and fell to the ground.

5. Birds have certain characteristics in common they have feathers wings and a beak with no teeth birds lay hard-shelled eggs and their offspring are dependent on parental care for an extended period after birth.

6. The ancient Egyptians had good dentists archeologists have found mummies that had gold fillings in their teeth.

---

* See Chart 17-1, p. 365, for the punctuation of adverb clauses. Commas are used when the adverb clause comes before the main clause but not when it comes after the main clause.

    Examples: ***When the phone rang,*** *I answered it.* (comma used)

                 I answered the phone ***when it rang.*** (no comma used)

❏ **Exercise 21. Listening and grammar.** (Chart 16-4)

Part I. Read the passage on butterflies quickly. How does the lack of punctuation and capitalization make a difference in how easily you can read the passage?

CD 2
Track 24

Butterflies

A butterfly is a marvel it begins as an ugly caterpillar and turns into a work of art the sight of a butterfly floating from flower to flower on a warm, sunny day brightens anyone's heart a butterfly is a charming and gentle creature caterpillars eat plants and cause damage to some crops but adult butterflies feed principally on nectar from flowers and do not cause any harm when cold weather comes some butterflies travel great distances to reach tropical climates they can be found on every continent except Antarctica because they are so colorful and beautiful butterflies are admired throughout the world.

Part II. Listen to the passage with your book open. Listen for pauses and add periods, commas, and capital letters as necessary. Then read the passage again and make sure it is punctuated the way you think is best.

Part III. Listen to the passage one more time to see if your punctuation reflects the spoken pauses.

❏ **Exercise 22. Let's read and talk.** (Chapter 16)

Part I. Read the paragraph about Dr. Martin Luther King, Jr.

Martin Luther King, Jr., was the leader of the 1960s civil rights movement in the United States that sought to end segregation and racial discrimination against African-Americans. In 1964, Dr. King became the youngest person to receive the Nobel Peace Prize. He was assassinated in 1968, but his powerful and inspiring words still live.

Part II. Underline the parallel structures that you find in these quotes from the speeches and writings of Dr. Martin Luther King, Jr. Discuss the ideas. Work in pairs, in small groups, or as a class.

1. "The hope of a <u>secure and livable</u> world lies with disciplined nonconformists who are dedicated to justice, peace and brotherhood."

2. "The ultimate measure of a man is not where he stands in moments of comfort and convenience, but where he stands at times of challenge and controversy."

3. "In the end, we will remember not the words of our enemies, but the silence of our friends."

4. "Nonviolence is the answer to the crucial political and moral question of our time: the need for mankind to overcome oppression and violence without resorting to oppression and violence. Mankind must evolve for all human conflict a method which rejects revenge, aggression, and retaliation. The foundation of such a method is love."

Choose one of the given topics. Write two versions of the same paragraph. The first version should be a draft in which you get your ideas on paper. Then the second version should be a "tightened" revision of the first. Look for places where two or three sentences can be combined into one by using parallel structure. In the second version, use as few words as possible and still communicate your meaning.

Topics:

1. Give a physical description of your place of residence (apartment, dorm room, etc.)
2. Describe the characteristics and activities of a successful student.
3. Give your reader directions for making a particular food dish.

Example:

First Draft: You'll need several ingredients to make spaghetti sauce. You'll need some ground beef. Probably about one pound of ground beef is enough. You should also have an onion. If the onions are small, you should use two. Also, find a green pepper and put it in the sauce. Of course, you will also need some tomato sauce or tomatoes.

Revision: To make spaghetti sauce, you will need one pound of ground beef, one large or two small onions, a green pepper, and some tomato sauce or tomatoes.

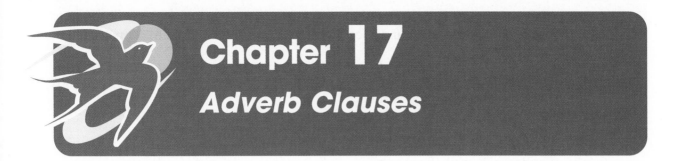

Chapter **17**
Adverb Clauses

❏ **Exercise 1. Warm-up.** (Chart 17-1)
The words in blue are adverb clauses. What do you notice about their sentence placement and punctuation?

1. He closed the window when it got windy.
2. Because it got windy, he closed the window.
3. Even though it was windy, he opened the window.
4. Would you please close the window if it gets windy?

17-1 Introduction

Adverb clauses are used to show relationships between ideas. They show relationships of *time, cause and effect, contrast,* and *condition.*

adverb clause main clause (a) ***When the phone rang,*** the baby woke up. (b) The baby woke up ***when the phone rang.***	In (a) and (b): ***when the phone rang*** is an adverb clause of time. Examples (a) and (b) have the same meaning. PUNCTUATION: When an adverb clause precedes a main clause, as in (a), a comma is used to separate the clauses. When the adverb clause follows, as in (b), usually no comma is used.
(c) ***Because he was sleepy,*** he went to bed. (d) He went to bed ***because he was sleepy.***	In (c) and (d), ***because*** introduces an adverb clause that shows a cause-and-effect relationship.

(e) INCORRECT PUNCTUATION:
     When we were in New York. We saw several plays.
 (f) INCORRECT PUNCTUATION:
     He went to bed. Because he was sleepy.
	Adverb clauses are dependent clauses. They cannot stand alone as a sentence in written English. They must be connected to a main (or independent) clause.*

Summary list of words used to introduce adverb clauses**

TIME		CAUSE AND EFFECT	CONTRAST	CONDITION
after	by the time (that)	because	even though	if
before	once	now that	although	unless
when	as/so long as	since	though	only if
while	whenever			whether or not
as	every time (that)		DIRECT CONTRAST	even if
as soon as	the first time (that)		while	in case
since	the last time (that)			
until	the next time (that)			

*See Chart 13-1, p. 270, for the definition of dependent and independent clauses.

**Words that introduce adverb clauses are called "subordinating conjunctions."

□ **Exercise 2. Looking at grammar.** (Chart 17-1)
Check (✓) the sentences that are grammatically complete and contain the correct punctuation.

1. ✓ I woke up.
2. ___ When the door slammed.
3. ___ I woke up. When the door slammed.
4. ___ I woke up when the door slammed.
5. ___ When the door slammed, I woke up.
6. ___ The door slammed. I woke up.
7. ___ As soon as you finish dinner, you will need to pick up Andy at work.
8. ___ The first time I saw you at the school dance last February.
9. ___ Every time the phone rings and I answer it.
10. ___ We won't know the results until the doctor calls.
11. ___ We got something to eat. After we went to the movie.

□ **Exercise 3. Looking at grammar.** (Chart 17-1)
<u>Underline the adverb clauses</u>. Add punctuation and capitalization as necessary. Do not add or delete any words.

       W
1. <u>when Abder was in New York</u>, he stayed with his cousins.

2. we went inside when it began to rain

3. it began to rain we went inside

4. when it began to rain we went inside

5. when the mail comes my assistant opens it

6. my assistant opens the mail when it comes

7. the mail comes around ten o'clock every morning my assistant opens it

□ **Exercise 4. Looking at grammar.** (Charts 16-2, 16-4, and 17-1)
Add punctuation and capitalization as necessary. Do not add or delete any words.

1. As soon as the rain began the children wanted to go outdoors they love to play outside in the warm summer rain I used to do the same thing when I was a child.

2. I had a cup of tea before I left for work this morning but I didn't have anything to eat I rarely eat breakfast.

3. When Jack and his wife go on vacation they have to drive or take the train because his wife is afraid of flying.

4. After Ellen gets home from work she likes to read the newspaper she follows the same routine every day after work as soon as she gets home she changes her clothes gets a snack and a drink and sits down in her favorite chair to read the newspaper in peace and quiet she usually has about half an hour to read the paper before her husband arrives home.

5. When you speak to someone who is hard of hearing you do not have to shout it is important to face the person directly and speak clearly my elderly father is hard of hearing but he can understand me when I look directly at him and say each word clearly.

6. Jane wears contact lenses because she is near-sighted without them, she can't see from one end of a basketball court to the other when one of her contacts popped out during a recent game both teams stopped playing and searched the floor for the lens.

❑ **Exercise 5. Warm-up.** (Chart 17-2)
Add the word(s) in parentheses to the correct place in each sentence. Add commas and capitalization as necessary.

1. Anya listened to some music _{while} she was working at her computer. (*while*)

2. I go to bed I always brush my teeth. (*before*)

3. I was a child I've been interested in butterflies. (*ever since*)

4. I'm going to meet some friends I leave class today. (*after*)

5. People speak English too fast Oscar can't catch the meaning. (*when*)

6. The teacher speaks too fast Oscar is going to ask her to slow down. (*the next time*)

17-2 Using Adverb Clauses to Show Time Relationships

after*	(a) **After** she graduates, she will get a job.	A present tense, NOT a future tense, is used
	(b) **After** she (had) graduated, she got a job.	in an adverb clause of time, as in (a) and (c)
before*	(c) I will leave **before** he comes.	(See Chart 4-3, p. 67, for tense usage in
	(d) I (had) left **before** he came.	future time clauses.)
when	(e) **When** I arrived, he *was talking* on the phone.	**when** = at that time
	(f) **When** I got there, he *had* already *left.*	Notice the different time relationships
	(g) **When** it began to rain, I *stood* under a tree.	expressed by the tenses.
	(h) **When** I was in Chicago, I *visited* the museums.	
	(i) **When** I see him tomorrow, I *will ask* him.	
while	(j) **While** I was walking home, it began to rain.	**while, as** = during that time
as	(k) **As** I was walking home, it began to rain.	
by the time	(l) **By the time** he arrived, we *had* already *left.*	**by the time** = one event is completed before *another event*
	(m) **By the time** he comes, we *will have* already *left.*	Notice the use of the past perfect and future perfect in the main clause.
since	(n) I *haven't seen* him **since** he left this morning.	**since** = from that time to the present
	(o) I*'ve known* her **ever since** I was a child.	In (o): **ever** adds emphasis.
		NOTE: The present perfect is used in the main clause.
until	(p) We stayed there **until** we finished our work.	**until, till** = to that time and then no longer
till	(q) We stayed there **till** we finished our work.	(**Till** is used more in speaking than in writing; it is generally not used in formal English.)
as soon as	(r) **As soon as** it stops raining, we will leave.	**as soon as, once** = when one event happens, another event happens soon afterward
once	(s) **Once** it stops raining, we will leave.	
as long as	(t) I will never speak to him again **as long as** I live.	**as long as, so long as** = during all that time, from beginning to end
so long as	(u) I will never speak to him again **so long as** I live.	
whenever	(v) **Whenever** I see her, I say hello.	**whenever** = every time
every time	(w) **Every time** I see her, I say hello.	
the first time	(x) **The first time** (that) I went to New York, I went to an opera.	Adverb clauses can be introduced by:
the last time	(y) I saw two plays **the last time** (that) I went to New York.	the { first / second / third, etc. / last / next / etc. } time (that)
the next time	(z) **The next time** (that) I go to New York, I'm going to see a ballet.	

After and *before* are commonly used in the following expressions:

shortly after	**shortly** before
a short time after	**a short time** before
a little while after	**a little while** before
not long after	**not long** before
soon after	

Exercise 6. Looking at grammar. (Charts 17-1 and 17-2)
Complete the sentences with your own words. Add brackets around the adverb clause in each sentence.

1. I will call you [before I _____ *come over* _____.]

2. Last night I went to bed after I _____ my homework.

3. Tonight I will go to bed after I _____ my homework.

4. Ever since I was a child, I _____ afraid of dogs.

5. Be sure to reread your composition for errors before you _____ it to the teacher tomorrow.

6. By the time I left my apartment this morning, the mail carrier _____ the mail.

7. I have known Jim Bates since he _____ ten years old.

8. A black cat ran across the road as I _____ my car to work this morning.

9. By the time I leave this city, I _____ here for four months.

10. Whenever Mark _____ angry, his nose gets red.

11. I _____ to the beach whenever the weather was nice, but now I don't have time to do that because I have to study.

12. We will have a big party when _____.

13. The next time I _____ to Hawaii, I'm going to visit Mauna Loa, the world's largest active volcano.

14. I had fried chicken the last time I _____ at that restaurant.

□ **Exercise 7. Looking at grammar.** (Charts 17-1 and 17-2)
Combine each pair of sentences with the words in parentheses. Add commas as necessary.

1. The other passengers will get on the bus soon. We'll leave. (*as soon as*)
   → *As soon as the other passengers get on the bus, we'll leave.*
2. I left the room. I turned off the lights. (*after*)
3. I left the room. I turned off the lights. (*before*)
4. Suki feels nervous. She bites her nails. (*whenever*)
5. The frying pan caught on fire. I was making dinner. (*while*)
6. We were sitting down to eat. Someone knocked on the door. (*just as**)

Just adds the idea of "immediately":
  just as = at that immediate or same moment.
  just before = immediately before.
  just after = immediately after.

7. The audience burst into applause. The singer finished her song. (*as soon as*)

8. We have to wait here. Nancy will come. (*until*)

9. Julia will come. We can leave for the theater. (*as soon as*)

10. My roommate walked into the room. I knew something was wrong. (*just as soon as*)

11. I stood up to give my speech. I got butterflies in my stomach. (*just before*)

12. I saw the great pyramids of Egypt in the moonlight. I was speechless. (*the first time*)

13. Lori started working at this company six months ago. Lori has gotten three promotions in the last six months. (*since*)

14. The weather will get warmer soon. We can start spending more time outside. (*once*)

15. Shakespeare died in 1616. He had written more than 37 plays. (*by the time*)

16. Sam will go to get his driver's license. He'll remember to take his glasses. (*the next time*)

❏ **Exercise 8. Looking at grammar.** (Chart 17-2)
Choose the best completions.

1. As soon as Martina saw the fire, she _____ the fire department.
   a. was telephoning   c. had telephoned
   (b.) telephoned   d. has telephoned

2. Before Jennifer won the lottery, she _____ any kind of contest.
   a. hasn't entered   c. wasn't entering
   b. doesn't enter   d. hadn't entered

3. Every time Prakash sees a movie made in India, he _____ homesick.
   a. will have felt   c. feels
   b. felt   d. is feeling

4. Since I left Venezuela six years ago, I _____ to visit friends and family several times.
   a. return   c. am returning
   b. will have returned   d. have returned

5. While he was washing his new car, Mr. De Rosa _____ a small dent in the rear fender.
   a. has discovered   c. is discovering
   b. was discovering   d. discovered

6. Yesterday while I was attending a sales meeting, Matthew _____ on the company's annual report.
   a. was working   c. has worked
   b. had been working   d. works

7. Tony _____ to have children until his little daughter was born. After she won his heart, he decided he wanted a big family.
   a. doesn't want   c. wasn't wanting
   b. hadn't wanted   d. hasn't wanted

8. After the horse threw her to the ground for the third time, Jennifer picked herself up and said, "I _____ on another horse as long as I live."
    a. never ride
    b. have never ridden
    c. will never ride
    d. do not ride

9. The next time Paul _____ to New York, he will visit the Metropolitan Museum of Art's famous collection of international musical instruments.
    a. will fly
    b. flies
    c. has flown
    d. will have flown

10. Ever since Maurice arrived, he _____ quietly in the corner. Is something wrong?
    a. sat
    b. has been sitting
    c. had been sitting
    d. will have sat

11. After Nela _____ for twenty minutes, she began to feel tired.
    a. jogging
    b. had been jogging
    c. has been jogging
    d. has jogged

12. Peter, _____ since you got home from football practice?
    a. have you eaten
    b. will you eat
    c. are you eating
    d. do you eat

13. By the time the young birds _____ the nest for good, they will have learned how to fly.
    a. will leave
    b. will have left
    c. are leaving
    d. leave

14. The last time I _____ in Athens, the weather was hot and humid.
    a. had been
    b. was
    c. am
    d. will have been

❏ **Exercise 9. Looking at grammar.** (Charts 17-1 and 17-2)
Read the description of events. Make sentences using the words below the example.

Events:
    4:00   Judy parked her car at the mall and went to buy some jeans.
    4:03   A thief broke into her car and stole her radio.
    4:30   Judy returned to her car.
    4:31   Judy called the police.
    4:35   The police arrived.
    4:35   Judy began crying in frustration.

Example: just after
    → Just after Judy parked her car, a thief broke into it.

1. just after
2. just as
3. when
4. while
5. by the time
6. as soon as

Exercise 10. Let's talk. (Charts 17-1 and 17-2)
Work in small groups. Complete the sentences with your own words. Each member of the group should finish each sentence.

Example: After I left class yesterday, ...
→ *After I left class yesterday, I met my cousin for tea.*

1. After I leave class today, ...
2. Before I go to bed tonight, ...
3. As soon as I get up tomorrow, ...
4. Whenever I feel nervous, ...
5. The first time I came to this class, ...
6. Ever since I was a child, ...
7. As long as I live, ...
8. Just as I was falling asleep last night, ...

❑ **Exercise 11. Listening and grammar.** (Charts 17-1 and 17-2)

CD 2
Track 25
Listen to the story about Marco's and Anya's cultural misunderstandings with your book closed. Then open your book and complete the sentences.

1. The first time Marco was asked "How's it going?", _____

_____

2. At first, every time someone asked Anya how she was, _____

_____

3. The next time Marco wants to get the server's attention at a restaurant, _____

_____

4. Since Marco and Anya have come to this country, _____

_____

5. Whenever they have a cultural misunderstanding, _____

_____

❑ **Exercise 12. Warm-up.** (Chart 17-3)
Which adverb clauses give the idea of "because"?

1. Now that I've finished art school, I can focus on finding work as an illustrator.
2. Since I was young, I have been artistic.
3. Since you're artistic, you can illustrate the story.

17-3 Using Adverb Clauses to Show Cause and Effect

because	(a) **Because** he was sleepy, he went to bed. (b) He went to bed **because** he was sleepy.	An adverb clause may precede or follow the independent clause. Notice the punctuation in (a) and (b).
now that	(c) **Now that** I've finished the semester, I'm going to rest a few days and then take a trip. (d) Jack lost his job. **Now that** he's unemployed, he can't pay his bills.	**Now that** means "because now." In (c): **Now that I've finished the semester** means "because the semester is now over." **Now that** is used for present causes of present or future situations.
since	(e) **Since** Monday is a holiday, we don't have to go to work. (f) **Since** you're a good cook and I'm not, you should cook the dinner.	When **since** is used to mean "because," it expresses a known cause; it means "because it is a fact that" or "given that it is true that." Cause-and-effect sentences with **since** say, "Given the fact that X is true, Y is the result." In (e): "Given the fact that Monday is a holiday, we don't have to go to work."
	(g) **Since** I came here, I have met many people.	NOTE: **Since** has two meanings. One is "because." It is also used in time clauses, as in (g). See Chart 17-2.

❏ **Exercise 13. Looking at grammar.** (Chart 17-3)
Combine each pair of sentences with the words in parentheses. Add commas as necessary.

1. We can go swimming every day. The weather is warm. (*now that*)
   → *We can go swimming every day now that the weather is warm.*
2. The students had done poorly on the test. The teacher decided to give it again. (*since*)
   → *Since the students had done poorly on the test, the teacher decided to give it again.*
3. Cold air hovers near the earth. It is heavier than hot air. (*because*)
4. You paid for the theater tickets. Please let me pay for our dinner. (*since*)
5. Do you want to go for a walk? The rain has stopped. (*now that*)
6. Our TV set was broken. We listened to the news on the radio. (*because*)
7. Many young people move to the cities in search of employment. There are few jobs available in the rural areas. (*since*)
8. The civil war has ended. A new government is being formed. (*now that*)
9. Ninety-two thousand people already have reservations with an airline company for a trip to the moon. I doubt that I'll get the chance to go on one of the first tourist flights. (*since*)

❑ **Exercise 14. Looking at grammar.** (Chart 17-3)
Complete the sentences with your own words. Punctuate carefully.

1. Now that I've finally finished _____

2. The teacher didn't _____

   because _____

3. Since it's too expensive to _____

4. Gary can't stay out all night with his friends now that _____

   _____

5. Since we don't have class tomorrow _____

   _____

❑ **Exercise 15. Warm-up.** (Chart 17-4)
Which sentence expresses an unexpected result?

1. Because I was very tired, I went to bed early.
2. Even though I was very tired, I stayed up late.

17-4	Expressing Contrast (Unexpected Result): Using *Even Though*	
(a)	*Because* the weather was cold, I *didn't go* swimming.	*Because* is used to express expected results.
(b)	*Even though* the weather was cold, I *went* swimming.	*Even though* is used to express unexpected results.*
(c)	*Because* I wasn't tired, I *didn't go* to bed.	NOTE: Like *because, even though* introduces an adverb clause.
(d)	*Even though* I wasn't tired, I *went* to bed.	

*Although and *though* have basically the same meaning and use as *even though*. See Chart 19-6, p. 406, for information on the use of *although* and *though*.

❑ **Exercise 16. Looking at grammar.** (Chart 17-4)
Choose the correct completions.

1. Because it was a dark, cloudy day, _____.
   (a.) I didn't put on my sunglasses   b. I put on my sunglasses

2. Even though it was a dark, cloudy day, _____.
   a. I put on my sunglasses   b. I didn't put on my sunglasses

3. Even though Mira has a cold, _____.
   a. she feels okay   b. she feels tired

4. Because gas is so expensive, _____.
   a. I drive my car a lot   b. I avoid driving my car a lot

❑ **Exercise 17. Looking at grammar.** (Chart 17-4)
Complete the sentences with **even though** or **because**.

1. Tim's in good shape physically _____*even though*_____ he doesn't get much exercise.

2. Barry's in good shape physically _____*because*_____ he gets a lot of exercise.

3. _____ Melissa has a job, she doesn't make enough money to support her four children.

4. _____ Yoko has a job, she is able to pay her rent and feed her family.

5. Sherry didn't learn Spanish _____ she lived in Mexico for a year.

6. Joe speaks Spanish well _____ he lived in Mexico for a year.

7. Jing-Won jumped into the river to rescue a little girl who was drowning

   _____ he wasn't a good swimmer.

8. A newborn kangaroo can find its mother's pouch _____ its eyes are not yet open.

9. Some people protest certain commercial fishing operations _____ dolphins, considered to be highly intelligent and social mammals, are killed unnecessarily.

10. _____ the earthquake damaged the bridge across Skunk River, the

   Smiths were able to cross the river _____ they had a boat.

❑ **Exercise 18. Let's talk.** (Chart 17-4)
Work in pairs, in small groups, or as a class. Speaker A asks the question. Speaker B answers the question beginning with **Yes/No** and followed by **Even though**.

Examples:
SPEAKER A (*book open*):   It was raining. Did you go to the zoo anyway?
SPEAKER B (*book closed*): Yes. Even though it was raining, I went to the zoo.

SPEAKER A (*book open*):   You studied hard. Did you pass the test?
SPEAKER B (*book closed*): No. Even though I studied hard, I didn't pass the test.

1. You weren't tired. Did you go to bed anyway?
2. The phone rang many times, but did you wake up?
3. The food was terrible. Did you eat it anyway?
4. You didn't study. Did you pass the test anyway?
5. The weather is terrible today. Did you stay home?
6. You fell down the stairs. Did you get hurt?

(*Change roles if working in pairs.*)
7. You told the truth, but did anyone believe you?
8. You turned on the air conditioner. Is it still hot in here?
9. You mailed the letter a week ago. Has it arrived yet?
10. You have a lot of money. Can you afford to buy an airplane?
11. Your grandmother is ninety years old. Is she still young at heart?
12. (. . .) told a joke. You didn't understand it. Did you laugh anyway?

Exercise 19. Warm-up. (Chart 17-5)
Check (✓) the sentences that show contrast (i.e., show that "this" is the opposite of "that").

1. ____ I am a vegetarian, while my husband is a meat-eater.

2. ____ While I was shopping, I ran into some friends from high school.

3. ____ While some people prefer hot weather, I prefer cooler climates.

17-5 Showing Direct Contrast: *While*

(a) Mary is rich, *while John is poor.*	***While*** is used to show direct contrast: "this" is exactly the opposite of "that."*
(b) John is poor, *while Mary is rich.*	Examples (a), (b), (c), and (d) all have the same meaning.
(c) *While John is poor,* Mary is rich.	Note the use of the comma in (a) and (b): In using ***while*** for direct contrast, a comma is often used even if the *while*-clause comes second (unlike the punctuation of most other adverb clauses).
(d) *While Mary is rich,* John is poor.	
COMPARE: (e) The phone rang *while I was studying.*	REMINDER: ***While*** is also used in time clauses and means "during that time," as in (e). See Chart 17-2.

*****Whereas*** can have the same meaning and use as ***while***, but it occurs mostly in formal written English and occurs with considerably less frequency than ***while***: *Mary is rich, **whereas** John is poor.*

❑ **Exercise 20. Looking at grammar.** (Chart 17-5)
Choose the best completion for each sentence.

1. Some people are tall, while others are ____.
    a. intelligent
    b. thin
    (c.) short
    d. large

2. A box is square, while ____.
    a. a rectangle has four sides
    b. my village has a town square in the center
    c. we use envelopes for letters
    d. a circle is round

3. While some parts of the world get an abundance of rain, others ____.
    a. are warm and humid
    b. are cold and wet
    c. get little or none
    d. get a lot

4. In some nations the favorite beverage is coffee, while ____.
    a. I like tea
    b. it has caffeine
    c. in others it is tea
    d. they drink tea

5. Some people like cream and sugar in their coffee, while ____.
    a. others like it black
    b. others drink hot coffee
    c. milk is good in coffee too
    d. sugar can cause cavities

6. Steve is an interesting storyteller and conversationalist, while his brother ____.
    a. is a newspaper reporter
    b. bores other people by talking about himself all the time
    c. has four children
    d. knows a lot of stories too

Exercise 21. Let's talk. (Chart 17-5)
Ask two classmates to complete each sentence. Share some of their completions with the class.

Example: Some people are talkative, while . . . .
→ *Some people are talkative, while others are quiet.*
→ *While some people are talkative, others are quiet.*

1. Some people have curly hair, while . . . .
2. Some people prefer to live in the country, while . . . .
3. While some people know only their native language, ...
4. The climate at sea level at the equator is always hot, while the climate at the North and South poles . . . .
5. Some people . . . , while . . . .
6. Some countries . . . , while . . . .

□ **Exercise 22. Warm-up.** (Chart 17-6)
Check (✓) the sentence with *if* that is grammatically correct.

1. _____ If I will need help, I will ask you.
2. _____ If I need help, I will ask you.
3. _____ If I will need help, I ask you.

17-6 Expressing Conditions in Adverb Clauses: *If*-Clauses

(a) **If** it **rains** tomorrow, I **will take** my umbrella.	*If*-clauses (also called "adverb clauses of condition") present possible conditions. The main clause expresses RESULTS. In (a): POSSIBLE CONDITION = *it may rain tomorrow* RESULT = *I will take my umbrella* A present tense, not a future tense, is used in an *if*-clause even though the verb in the *if*-clause may refer to a future event or situation, as in (a).*

Words that introduce adverb clauses of condition (*if*-clauses)		
if	even if	unless
whether or not	in case	only if

*See Chapter 20 for uses of other verb forms in sentences with *if*-clauses.

□ **Exercise 23. Looking at grammar.** (Chart 17-6)
Make sentences with *if* using the given conditions.

Example: It may be cold tomorrow.
→ *If it's cold tomorrow, I'm going to stay home.*
→ *We can't go on a picnic if it's cold tomorrow.*

1. The teacher may not be in class tomorrow.
2. You will stay up until two in the morning.
3. Maybe the sun will be shining when you get up tomorrow morning.
4. Predictions about global warming may be correct.
5. Think of something that may happen this year in world politics.

❏ **Exercise 24. Warm-up.** (Chart 17-7)
Check (✓) the sentences that logically follow the question and are grammatically correct.

Do you have your cell phone with you?

1. ____ If you do, could I use it?

2. ____ If so, could I use it?

3. ____ If not, I can use the pay phone.

4. ____ If you don't, I can use the pay phone.

5. ____ If you are, could I use it?

17-7 Shortened *If*-Clauses

(a) Are you a student? *If so / If you are*, the ticket is half-price. *If not / If you aren't*, the ticket is full price.	When an *if*-clause refers to the idea in the sentence immediately before it, it is sometimes shortened. In (a): **If so / If you are** = *If you are a student* **If not / If you aren't** = *If you aren't a student*
(b) It's a popular concert. Do you have a ticket? *If so / If you do*, you're lucky. *If not / If you don't*, you're out of luck.	In (b): **If so / If you do** = *If you have a ticket* **If not / If you don't** = *If you don't have a ticket*

❏ **Exercise 25. Looking at grammar.** (Chart 17-7)
First, complete the sentences in two ways:

    a. Use *so* or *not*.
    b. Use a helping verb or main verb *be*.

Second, give the full meaning of the shortened *if*-clause.

1. Does Lisa want to go out to dinner with us?

    a. If _____*so*_____, tell her to meet us at 8:00.

    b. If she _____*does*___, tell her to meet us at 8:00.

        → *Meaning: if Lisa wants to go out to dinner with us*

2. Are you free this weekend?

    a. If _____, do you want to go to a movie?

    b. If you _____, do you want to go to a movie?

3. Do you have a ride to the theater?

    a. If _____, would you like to ride with us?

    b. If you _____, would you like to ride with us?

4. Are you coming to the meeting?

    a. If _____, I'll see you there.

    b. If you _____, I'll see you there.

5. Did you use a spellcheck on your email to me?

    a. If _____, it didn't catch all the spelling errors.

    b. If you _____, it didn't catch all the spelling errors.

6. We need some rice. Can you stop at the store on your way home today?

    a. If _____, I'll do it.

    b. If you _____, I'll do it.

❑ **Exercise 26. Warm-up.** (Chart 17-8)
Check (✓) all the sentences that are true for David.

SITUATION: If David gets married, he will be happy. If he doesn't get married, he will be happy.

1. ____ David will be happy if he doesn't get married.

2. ____ If he gets married, David won't be happy.

3. ____ Even if David gets married, he won't be happy.

4. ____ Even if David doesn't get married, he will be happy.

5. ____ David will be happy whether or not he gets married.

6. ____ Whether or not David gets married, he will be happy.

17-8 Adverb Clauses of Condition: Using *Whether Or Not* and *Even If*

Whether or not

(a) I'm going to go swimming tomorrow *whether or not it is cold.* OR *whether it is cold or not.*	*Whether or not* expresses the idea that neither this condition nor that condition matters; the result will be the same.
	In (a): "If it is cold, I'm going swimming. If it is not cold, I'm going swimming. I don't care about the temperature. It doesn't matter."

Even if

(b) I have decided to go swimming tomorrow. *Even if the weather is cold*, I'm going to go swimming.	Sentences with *even if* are close in meaning to those with *whether or not*.
	Even if gives the idea that a particular condition does not matter. The result will not change.

Choose the sentence (a. or b.) that has the same meaning as the given sentence.

1. Even if I get an invitation to the reception, I'm not going to go.
   a. I won't go to the reception without an invitation.
   b. I don't care if I get an invitation. I'm not going.

2. Even if the weather improves, I won't go to the beach.
   a. I'm going to the beach if the weather improves.
   b. I don't care if the weather improves. I'm not going to the beach.

3. Whether or not you want help, I plan to be at your house at 9:00.
   a. I'm going to help you because I think you need help.
   b. I'm going to help you because you want me to.

4. I won't tell even if someone pays me.
   a. I won't tell whether or not someone gives me money.
   b. If someone pays me enough money, I will tell.

5. Even if John apologizes, I won't forgive him!
   a. John needs to apologize for me to forgive him.
   b. I don't care if John apologizes. It doesn't matter.

6. I have to go to work tomorrow whether I feel better or not.
   a. Whether I go to work or not depends on how I feel.
   b. I'm going to work tomorrow no matter how I feel.

❏ **Exercise 28. Looking at grammar.** (Chart 17-8)
Use the given information to complete sentences a. and b.

SITUATION 1: *Usually people need to graduate from school to get a good job. But it's different for Ed. Maybe Ed will graduate from school, and maybe he won't. It doesn't matter because he has a good job waiting for him in his father's business.*

    a. Ed will get a good job whether or not . . . .
       → *Ed will get a good job whether or not he graduates.*
    b. Ed will get a good job even if . . . .
       → *Ed will get a good job even if he doesn't graduate.*

SITUATION 2: *Cindy's uncle tells a lot of jokes. Sometimes they're funny, and sometimes they're not. It doesn't matter.*

    a. Cindy laughs at the jokes whether . . . or not.
    b. Cindy laughs at the jokes even if . . . .

SITUATION 3: *Maybe you are finished with the exam, and maybe you're not. It doesn't matter. The time is up.*

    a. You have to hand in your examination paper whether . . . or not.
    b. You have to hand in your examination paper even if . . . .

SITUATION 4: *It might snow, or it might not. We don't want to go camping in the snow, but it doesn't matter.*

    a. We're going to go camping in the mountains whether . . . or not.
    b. We're going to go camping in the mountains even if . . . .

SITUATION 5: *Max's family doesn't have enough money to send him to college. He would like to get a scholarship, but it doesn't matter because he's saved some money to go to school and has a part-time job.*

     a. Max can go to school whether or not . . . .
     b. Max can go to school even if . . . .

SITUATION 6: *Sometimes the weather is hot, and sometimes the weather is cold. It doesn't matter. My grandfather always wears his gray sweater.*

     a. My grandfather wears his gray sweater whether or not . . . .
     b. My grandfather always wears his gray sweater even if . . . .

SITUATION 7: *Your approval doesn't matter to me.*

     a. I'm going to marry Harry whether . . . or not.
     b. I'm going to marry Harry even if . . . .

❑ **Exercise 29. Warm-up.** (Chart 17-9)
Choose the sentence (1. or 2.) that has the same meaning as the given sentence.

If by chance you have trouble, you can reach me at this number.

    1. In case you have trouble, you can reach me at this number.
    2. When you have trouble, you can reach me at this number.

17-9 Adverb Clauses of Condition: Using *In Case*

(a) I'll be at my uncle's house *in case* you *(should)* need to reach me.	***In case*** expresses the idea that something probably won't happen, but it might. ***In case*** means "if by chance this should happen."
	NOTE: Using ***should*** in an adverb clause emphasizes the speaker's uncertainty that something will happen.

❑ **Exercise 30. Looking at grammar.** (Chart 17-9)
Combine each pair of sentences. Begin your new sentence with ***In case***.

   1. You probably won't need to get in touch with me, but maybe you will. If so, I'll give you my phone number.
     → *In case you (should) need to get in touch with me, I'll give you my phone number.*

   2. You probably won't need to see me, but maybe you will. If so, I'll be in my office tomorrow morning around ten.

   3. I don't think you need any more information, but maybe you do. If so, you can call me.

   4. You probably don't have any more questions, but maybe you do. If so, ask Dr. Smith.

   5. Russ probably won't call, but maybe he will. If so, please tell him that I'm at the library.

   6. You will probably be satisfied with your purchase, but maybe not. If not, you can return it to the store.

❏ **Exercise 31. Looking at grammar.** (Charts 17-8 and 17-9)
Complete the sentences with your own words. Work in pairs, in small groups, or as a class.

1. I have my umbrella with me just in case . . . .

2. It's a good idea for you to keep a written record of your credit card numbers in case . . . .

3. Our boss doesn't accept illness as an excuse for missing work. We have to go to work even if . . . .

4. I think I'd better clean up the apartment in case . . . .

5. Are you planning to apply for a scholarship? If so, ...

6. Do you have to work this Saturday? If not, ...

❏ **Exercise 32. Warm-up.** (Chart 17-10)
Choose the logical completions.

1. I'll be at work on time tomorrow if there (*is, isn't*) a lot of heavy traffic.

2. I'll be at work on time tomorrow unless there (*is, isn't*) a lot of heavy traffic.

3. We'll have the party outside unless it is (*rainy, sunny*).

4. We'll have the party inside unless it is (*rainy, sunny*).

17-10 Adverb Clauses of Condition: Using *Unless*

(a) I'll go swimming tomorrow *unless* it's cold.	*unless* = *if . . . not*
(b) I'll go swimming tomorrow *if* it isn't cold.	In (a): *unless it's cold* means "if it isn't cold."
	Examples (a) and (b) have the same meaning.

❏ **Exercise 33. Looking at grammar.** (Chart 17-10)
Make sentences with the same meaning as the given sentences. Use ***unless***.

1. I will go to the zoo if it isn't cold.
   → *I will go to the zoo unless it's cold.*

2. You can't travel abroad if you don't have a passport.

3. You can't get a driver's license if you're not at least sixteen years old.

4. If I don't get some new batteries for my camera, I won't be able to take pictures when Laura and Rob get here.

5. You'll get hungry during class if you don't eat breakfast.

❏ **Exercise 34. Looking at grammar.** (Chart 17-10)
Complete the sentences with your own words. Work in pairs, in small groups, or as a class.

1. Your letter won't be delivered unless . . . .
   → *Your letter won't be delivered unless it has the correct postage.*

2. I'm sorry, but you can't see the doctor unless . . . .

3. I can't graduate from school unless . . . .

4. . . . unless you put it in the refrigerator.

5. Unless it rains, ...

6. Certain species of animals will soon become extinct unless . . . .

7. . . . unless I get a raise in salary.

8. Tomorrow I'm going to . . . unless . . . .

9. The political situation in . . . will continue to worsen unless . . . .

10. Unless you . . . .

□ **Exercise 35. Warm-up.** (Chart 17-11)
Answer the questions about Scott.

SITUATION: Scott closes his bedroom window at night only if it's raining hard.

1. Does Scott close his bedroom window if the temperature is below freezing?

2. Does Scott close his bedroom window if it's windy outside?

3. Does Scott close his bedroom window if there's a light rain?

4. Does Scott close his bedroom window if there is a heavy rain?

17-11 Adverb Clauses of Condition: Using *Only If*

(a) The picnic will be canceled *only if* it rains. If it's windy, we'll go on the picnic. If it's cold, we'll go on the picnic. If it's damp and foggy, we'll go on the picnic. If it's unbearably hot, we'll go on the picnic.	*Only if* expresses the idea that there is only one condition that will cause a particular result.
(b) *Only if* it rains *will* the picnic *be canceled.*	When *only if* begins a sentence, the subject and verb of the main clause are inverted, as in (b).* No commas are used.

*Other subordinating conjunctions and prepositional phrases preceded by *only* at the beginning of a sentence require subject-verb inversion in the main clause:
> *Only when* the teacher dismisses us *can we stand* and *leave* the room.
> *Only after* the phone rang *did I realize* that I had fallen asleep in my chair.
> *Only in* my hometown *do I feel* at ease.

□ **Exercise 36. Looking at grammar.** (Chart 17-11)
Check (✓) the sentences that are true for this situation.

SITUATION: You can take Saturday off only if you work Thursday.

1. ____ You must work Thursday if you want Saturday off.

2. ____ You can take Saturday off if you work another day of your choice.

3. ____ If you work Thursday, you don't have to work Saturday.

4. ____ You can work Thursday, but it's not a requirement if you want Saturday off.

❏ **Exercise 37. Looking at grammar.** (Chart 17-11)

Part I. Read the situations and complete the sentences. Work in pairs, in small groups, or as a class.

SITUATION 1: *John must take an additional science class in order to graduate. That is the only condition under which he can graduate. If he doesn't take an additional science class, he can't graduate.*

> He can graduate only if . . . .
> → *He can graduate only if he takes an additional science class.*

SITUATION 2: *You have to have an invitation in order to go to the party. That is the only condition under which you will be admitted. If you don't have an invitation, you can't go.*

> You can go to the party only if . . . .

SITUATION 3: *You have to have a student visa in order to study here. Unless you have a student visa, you can't go to school here.*

> You can attend this school only if . . . .

SITUATION 4: *Jimmy's mother doesn't want him to chew gum, but sometimes he chews it anyway.*

> Jimmy . . . only if he's sure his mother won't find out.

SITUATION 5: *If you want to go to the movie, we'll go. If you don't want to go, we won't go.*

> We . . . only if you want to.

SITUATION 6: *The temperature has to reach 32°F / 0°C before water will freeze.*

> Water will freeze only if . . . .

SITUATION 7: *You must study hard. Then you will pass the exam.*

> Only if you study hard . . . .

SITUATION 8: *You have to have a ticket. Then you can get into the soccer stadium.*

> Only if you have a ticket . . . .

SITUATION 9: *His parents make Steve finish his homework before he can watch TV in the evening.*

> Only if Steve's homework is finished . . . .

SITUATION 10: *I have to get a job. Then I will have enough money to go to school.*

> Only if I get a job . . . .

Part II. Complete the sentences with your own words.

1. Yes, Paul, I will marry you — but only if . . . .
2. I . . . only if . . . .
3. Only if . . . .

❑ **Exercise 38. Looking at grammar.** (Charts 17-10 and 17-11)
Make sentences with the same meaning as the given sentences. Use *only if* and *unless*.

1. If you don't study hard, you won't pass the test.
   → *You will pass the test only if you study hard.*
   → *You won't pass the test unless you study hard.*
2. If I don't get a job, I can't pay my bills.
3. Your clothes won't get clean if you don't use soap.
4. I can't take any pictures if the flash doesn't work.
5. I don't wake up if the alarm clock doesn't ring.
6. If eggs aren't kept at the proper temperature, they won't hatch.
7. Don't borrow money from friends if you don't absolutely have to.
8. Anita doesn't talk in class if the teacher doesn't ask her specific questions.

❑ **Exercise 39. Looking at grammar.** (Charts 17-6 → 17-11)
Combine these two sentences using the words below the example.

It may or may not rain. The party will be held inside/outside.

Example: if
   → *If it rains, the party will be held inside.*
   → *If it doesn't rain, the party will be held outside.*

1. even if   3. in case   5. only if
2. whether or not   4. unless

❑ **Exercise 40. Reading and grammar.** (Chapter 17)
Part I. Read the passage about the ways people learn.

How Do People Learn Best?

How do people learn best? There is not one answer because much depends on individual learning styles and needs. Over 300 years ago, however, the noted inventor Benjamin Franklin made some observations regarding learning that still hold true for a great many learners today: "Tell me and I forget. Teach me and I remember. Involve me and I learn."

Benjamin Franklin

Imagine that you are learning how to fold a paper airplane. The person teaching you presents the information verbally. She begins by saying:

Take a piece of paper.
Fold it in half.
Open the paper.
Look at the crease in the middle.
Now take one corner and fold it down along the crease.

The instructions continue this way. How well are you going to learn how to fold a paper airplane?

Now imagine that your instructor is standing before you with paper and gives the directions while folding the paper herself. Will this help you more?

Finally, imagine that both you and your instructor have paper. Each time she gives you instructions, both you and she fold your own papers.

Of the three methods, which one will be the most effective in helping you learn how to fold a paper airplane?

It's interesting to think about Benjamin Franklin's quote in relation to learning English. How do you learn English best? Is "being told" effective for you? What about "being taught"? How about "being involved"?

Part II. Think about your experiences learning English vocabulary and complete the sentences with your own words. Punctuate carefully.

1. I remember new words best when _____

2. I often forget the meanings of new words unless _____

3. Even if I _____

4. I _____ only if _____

5. If you want to increase your vocabulary, _____
    _____

6. If teachers want to help their class learn new vocabulary, they _____
    _____

7. Although _____
    _____

8. When I am involved in my learning, I feel _____
    _____

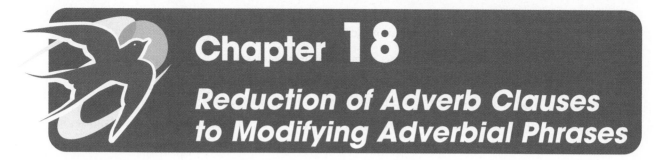

Chapter 18
Reduction of Adverb Clauses to Modifying Adverbial Phrases

❏ **Exercise 1. Warm-up.** (Charts 18-1 and 18-2)
Check (✓) the sentences that are grammatically correct.

1. ____ While sitting at my desk, I fell asleep.
2. ____ While I was sitting at my desk, I fell asleep.
3. ____ While was sitting at my desk, I fell asleep.
4. ____ Before I went into the theater, I turned off my cell phone.
5. ____ Before go into the theater, I turned off my cell phone.
6. ____ Before going into the theater, I turned off my cell phone.

18-1 Introduction

(a) Adverb clause:	*While I was walking* to class, I ran into an old friend.	In Chapter 13, we discussed changing adjective clauses to modifying phrases. (See Chart 13-11, p. 294.) Some adverb clauses may also be changed to modifying phrases, and the ways in which the changes are made are the same:
(b) Modifying phrase:	*While walking* to class, I ran into an old friend.	
(c) Adverb clause:	*Before I left for work,* I ate breakfast.	• If there is a *be* form of the verb, omit the subject of the dependent clause and *be* verb, as in (b). OR
(d) Modifying phrase:	*Before leaving for work,* I ate breakfast.	• If there is no *be* form of a verb, omit the subject and change the verb to *-ing,* as in (d).
(e) Change possible:	*While I was sitting in class, I* fell asleep. *While sitting in class, I* fell asleep.	An adverb clause can be changed to a modifying phrase **only when the subject of the adverb clause and the subject of the main clause are the same.**
(f) Change possible:	*While Ann was sitting in class, she* fell asleep. (clause) *While sitting in class, Ann* fell asleep.	A *modifying adverbial phrase* that is the reduction of an adverb clause *modifies the subject* of the main clause.
(g) No change possible:	*While the teacher was lecturing to the class, I* fell asleep.*	No reduction (i.e., change) is possible if the subjects of the adverb clause and the main clause are different, as in (g).
(h) *INCORRECT:*	~~While watching TV last night,~~ the phone rang.	In (h): *While watching* is called a "dangling modifier" or a "dangling participle," i.e., a modifier that is incorrectly "hanging alone" without an appropriate noun or pronoun subject to modify.

While lecturing to the class, **I fell asleep means "While **I** was lecturing to the class, **I** fell asleep."*

❏ **Exercise 2. Looking at grammar.** (Chart 18-1)
Check (✓) the sentences that are grammatically correct.

1. ____ While sitting at my computer, the fire alarm went off.
2. _✓_ While sitting at my computer, I heard the fire alarm go off.
3. ____ While standing on the top floor of the building, the crowd below looked like ants.
4. ____ While standing on the top floor of the building and looking down, Patrick suddenly felt dizzy.
5. ____ Before getting up, Mary likes to lie in her warm bed and plan her day.
6. ____ Before getting up, Mary's alarm clock went off three times by accident.
7. ____ While working on his new novel, William found himself telling the story of his childhood.
8. ____ After standing in line for hours to buy concert tickets, the theater manager told us the concert was sold out.

18-2 Changing Time Clauses to Modifying Adverbial Phrases

(a) Clause:	*Since Maria came* to this country, she has made many friends.	Adverb clauses beginning with *after*, *before*, *while*, and *since* can be changed to modifying adverbial phrases.
(b) Phrase:	*Since coming* to this country, Maria has made many friends.	
(c) Clause:	*After he (had) finished* his homework, Peter went to bed.	In (c): There is no difference in meaning between *After he finished* and *After he had finished*. (See Chart 3-5, p. 50.)
(d) Phrase:	*After finishing* his homework, Peter went to bed.	In (d) and (e): There is no difference in meaning between *After finishing* and *After having finished*.
(e) Phrase:	*After having finished* his homework, Peter went to bed.	
(f) Phrase:	Peter went to bed *after finishing* his homework.	The modifying adverbial phrase may follow the main clause, as in (f).

❏ **Exercise 3. Looking at grammar.** (Charts 18-1 and 18-2)
Underline the subject of the adverb clause and the subject of the main clause in each sentence. Change the adverb clauses to modifying adverbial phrases if possible.

1. While Joe was driving to school yesterday, he had an accident.
   → *While driving to school yesterday, Joe had an accident.*
2. While Joe was watching TV last night, the telephone rang. (*no change*)
3. Before I came to class, I had a cup of coffee.
4. Before the student came to class, the teacher had already given a quiz.
5. Since I came here, I have learned a lot of English.
6. Since Alberto opened his new business, he has been working 16 hours a day.
7. Omar left the house and went to his office after he (had) finished breakfast.

8. Before the waiter came to our table, I had already made up my mind to order shrimp.

9. You should always read a contract before you sign your name.

10. While Jack was trying to sleep last night, a mosquito kept buzzing in his ear.

11. While Susan was climbing the mountain, she lost her footing and fell onto a ledge several feet below.

12. After I heard Marika describe how cold it gets in Minnesota in the winter, I decided not to go there for my vacation in January.

❏ **Exercise 4. Let's talk: interview.** (Chart 18-2)
Ask two classmates each question. Ask them to answer in complete sentences. Share some of their answers with the class.

What do you do . . .
1. before going to bed?
2. after waking up?
3. after arriving at school?
4. while sitting in class?
5. before leaving school for the day?
6. while preparing for a difficult exam?

❏ **Exercise 5. Warm-up.** (Charts 18-3 and 18-4)
Read the sentences and answer the questions.

1. Hiking through the woods yesterday, Alan saw a bear.
   QUESTION: Who was hiking through the woods?

2. Walking through the woods, the bear spotted Alan.
   QUESTION: Who was walking through the woods?

18-3 Expressing the Idea of "During the Same Time" in Modifying Adverbial Phrases

(a) *While I was walking* down the street, *I* ran into an old friend. (b) *While walking* down the street, *I* ran into an old friend. (c) *Walking* down the street, *I* ran into an old friend.	Sometimes *while* is omitted, but the *-ing* phrase at the beginning of the sentence gives the same meaning (i.e., "during the same time"). Examples (a), (b), and (c) have the same meaning.

18-4 Expressing Cause and Effect in Modifying Adverbial Phrases

(a) *Because she needed* some money to buy a book, *Sue* cashed a check.	Often an *-ing* phrase at the beginning of a sentence gives the meaning of "because."
(b) *Needing* some money to buy a book, *Sue* cashed a check.	Examples (a) and (b) have the same meaning.
(c) *Because he lacked* the necessary qualifications, *he* was not considered for the job.	*Because* is not included in a modifying phrase. It is omitted, but the resulting phrase expresses a cause-and-effect relationship, as in (b) and (d).
(d) *Lacking* the necessary qualifications, *he* was not considered for the job.	
(e) *Having seen* that movie before, *I don't want* to go again.	*Having* + *past participle* gives the meaning not only of "because" but also of "before."
(f) *Having seen* that movie before, *I didn't want* to go again.	
(g) *Because she was unable* to afford a car, *she* bought a bicycle.	A form of *be* in the adverb clause may be changed to *being*. The use of *being* makes the cause-and-effect relationship clear.
(h) *Being unable* to afford a car, *she* bought a bicycle.	Examples (g), (h), and (i) have the same meaning.
(i) *Unable* to afford a car, *she* bought a bicycle.	

❏ **Exercise 6. Looking at grammar.** (Charts 18-3 and 18-4)
Underline the modifying adverbial phrases and discuss their meanings. Which ones give the meaning of "because"? Which ones give the meaning of "while"? Do some of the sentences give the idea of both?

1. Driving to my grandparents' house last night, I saw a young woman who was selling flowers. I stopped so that I could buy some for my grandmother. (*Meaning* = "while")

2. Being a widow with three children, Mrs. Romero has no choice but to work.

3. Sitting on the airplane and watching the clouds pass beneath me, I let my thoughts wander to the new experiences that were in store for me during the next two years of living abroad.

4. Having guessed at the answers for most of the test, I did not expect to get a high score.

5. Realizing that I had made a dreadful mistake when I introduced him as George Johnson, I walked over to him and apologized. I know his name is John George.

6. Tapping his fingers loudly on the airline counter, Todd made his impatience known.

7. Having broken her arm in a fall, Elena had to learn to write with her left hand.

8. Lying on her bed in peace and quiet, Lisa soon forgot her troubles.

❏ **Exercise 7. Looking at grammar.** (Chart 18-4)
Change the adverb clauses to modifying adverbial phrases.

1. Because Sam didn't want to hurt her feelings, he didn't tell her the bad news.
   → *Not wanting to hurt her feelings, Sam didn't tell her the bad news.*

2. Because the little boy believed no one loved him, he ran away from home.

3. Because I had forgotten to bring a pencil to the examination, I had to borrow one.

4. Because Chelsea is a vegetarian, she does not eat meat.

☐ **Exercise 8. Looking at grammar.** (Charts 18-2 → 18-4)
Choose all the possible answers for each sentence.

1. Before _____ to you, I had never understood that formula.
   a. talked   (b.) talking   (c.) I talked

2. After _____ the chapter four times, I finally understood the author's theory.
   a. I read   b. read   c. reading

3. Since _____ his bachelor's degree, he has had three jobs, each one better than the last.
   a. he completed   b. completing   c. completed

4. _____ across Canada, I could not help being impressed by the great differences in terrain.
   a. Traveling   b. While I was traveling   c. While traveling

5. _____ national fame, the union leader had been an electrician in a small town.
   a. Before gaining   b. Gaining   c. Before he gained

6. _____ in an airplane before, the little girl was surprised and a little frightened when her ears popped.
   a. Had never flown   b. Having never flown   c. Because she had never flown

7. Before _____ vice-president of marketing and sales, Peter McKay worked as a sales representative.
   a. became   b. becoming   c. he became

8. _____ the cool evening breeze and listening to the sounds of nature, we lost track of time.
   a. Because enjoying   b. Enjoying   c. We were enjoying

9. _____ to spend any more money this month, Jim decided against going to a restaurant for lunch. He made himself a sandwich instead.
   a. Not wanting   b. Because he didn't want   c. Because not wanting

☐ **Exercise 9. Looking at grammar.** (Charts 18-3 and 18-4)
If possible, combine each pair of sentences by making a modifying phrase out of the first sentence.

1. The children had nothing to do. They were bored.
   → *Having nothing to do, the children were bored.*
2. The children were bored. I offered to play a game with them. (*no change*)
3. Anna kept one hand on the steering wheel. She paid the bridge toll with her free hand.
4. Anna kept one hand on the steering wheel. Bob put the money for the bridge toll in her free hand.
5. I heard that Nadia was in the hospital. I called her family to find out what was wrong.
6. We slowly approached the door to the hospital. The nurse stepped out to help us.
7. I live a long distance from my work. I have to commute daily by train.
8. Abdul lives a long distance from his work. His car is essential.
9. I am a married man. I have many responsibilities.
10. Martha was picking strawberries in the garden. A bumblebee stung her.
11. I recognized his face, but I had forgotten his name. I just smiled and said, "Hi."
12. Ann was convinced that she could never learn to play the piano. She stopped taking lessons.

❏ **Exercise 10. Game.** (Charts 18-3 and 18-4)
Work in teams. Make sentences by combining the ideas in Column A and Column B. Use the idea in Column A as a modifying adverbial phrase. Show logical relationships. The first group to combine all the ideas correctly is the winner.

Example: Having sticky pads on their feet, flies can easily walk on the ceiling.

Column A

1. They have sticky pads on their feet.
2. She has done very well in her studies.
3. She was born two months prematurely.
4. He had done everything he could for the patient.
5. She had never eaten Thai food before.
6. He had no one to turn to for help.
7. They are extremely hard and nearly indestructible.
8. They are able to crawl into very small places.

Column B

a. Marta didn't know what to expect when she went to the Thai restaurant for dinner.
b. Mice can hide in almost any part of a house.
c. Sayid was forced to work out the problem by himself.
d. The doctor left to attend other people.
e. Nancy expects to be hired by a top company after graduation.
f. Diamonds are used extensively in industry to cut other hard minerals.
✓ g. Flies can easily walk on the ceiling.
h. Monique needed special care for the first few days of her life.

❏ **Exercise 11. Looking at grammar.** (Charts 18-1 → 18-4)
Check (✓) the sentences that are grammatically correct. Rewrite the incorrect sentences.

1. __✓__ After leaving the theater, we stopped at a coffee shop for a late-night snack.

2. _____ After leaving the theater, Tom's car wouldn't start, so we had to take a taxi home.
    → *After we left the theater, Tom's car wouldn't start, so we had to take a taxi home.*
    → *After leaving the theater, we discovered that Tom's car wouldn't start, so we took a taxi home.*

3. _____ Not wanting to interrupt the conversation, I stood quietly and listened until I could have a chance to talk.

4. _____ Being too young to understand death, my mother gave me a simple explanation of where my grandfather had gone.

5. _____ When asked to explain his mistake, the new employee cleared his throat nervously.

6. _____ While working in my office late last night, someone suddenly knocked loudly at my door and nearly scared me to death!

7. _____ After hurrying to get ready for the picnic, it began to rain just as we were leaving.

8. _____ While walking across the street at a busy intersection, a truck nearly hit me.

□   **Exercise 12. Warm-up.** (Chart 18-5)
Which sentences have the same meaning?

    1. When Sharon heard the news of her friend's death, she began to cry.
    2. Upon hearing the news of her friend's death, Sharon began to cry.
    3. On hearing the news of her friend's death, Sharon began to cry.

18-5 Using *Upon* + *-ing* in Modifying Adverbial Phrases

(a) ***Upon reaching*** the age of 21, I received my inheritance.	Modifying adverbial phrases beginning with ***upon*** + ***-ing*** usually have the same meaning as adverb clauses introduced by ***when***.
(b) ***When I reached*** the age of 21, I received my inheritance.	Examples (a) and (b) have the same meaning.
(c) ***On reaching*** the age of 21, I received my inheritance.	***Upon*** can be shortened to ***on***. Examples (a), (b), and (c) all have the same meaning.

□   **Exercise 13. Looking at grammar.** (Chart 18-5)
Make sentences using ***upon*** + ***-ing***.

    1. When Carl saw his wife and child get off the airplane, he broke into a big smile.
       → *Upon seeing his wife and child get off the airplane, Carl broke into a big smile.*
    2. When Tina crossed the marathon finish line, she fell in exhaustion.
    3. When I looked in my wallet, I saw I didn't have enough money to pay my restaurant bill.

    4. Sam found that he had made a math error when he re-read the data.
    5. When you finish the examination, bring your paper to the front of the room.
    6. There must have been 300 students in the room on the first day of class. The professor slowly read through the list of names. When I heard my name, I raised my hand to identify myself.
    7. Captain Cook had been sailing for many weeks with no land in sight. Finally, one of the sailors shouted, "Land ho!" When he heard this, Cook grabbed his telescope and searched the horizon.

❑ **Exercise 14. Looking at grammar.** (Charts 18-1 → 18-5)
Change the adverb clause in each sentence to a modifying adverbial phrase if possible. Change punctuation, capitalization, and word order as necessary.

1. After it spends some time in a cocoon, a caterpillar will emerge as a butterfly.
    → *After spending some time in a cocoon, a caterpillar will emerge as a butterfly.*

2. When the movie started, it suddenly got very quiet inside the theater. (*no change*)

3. When we entered the theater, we handed the usher our tickets.
    → *Upon entering the theater, we handed the usher our tickets.*

4. Because I was unprepared for the test, I didn't do well.
    → *Being unprepared for the test, I didn't do well.* OR *Unprepared for the test, I didn't do well.*

5. Before I left on my trip, I checked to see what shots I would need.

6. Jane's family hasn't received any news from her since she arrived in Kenya two weeks ago.

7. Because I hadn't understood the directions, I got lost.

8. My father reluctantly agreed to let me attend the game after he had talked it over with my mother.

9. When I discovered I had lost my key to the apartment, I called the building superintendent.

10. Because the forest area is so dry this summer, it is prohibited to light campfires.

11. After we had to wait for more than half an hour, we were finally seated at the restaurant.

❑ **Exercise 15. Let's talk.** (Chapter 18)
Work in small groups. Imagine your friend is traveling to a foreign country and has never been abroad before. Give advice by making several suggestions for each item.

1. Before leaving on your trip, . . .
    → *you'll need to get a visa.*
    → *you should find out if you need immunizations.*
    → *give a friend or family member your itinerary.*
    → *don't forget to have someone pick up your mail.*
2. Upon arriving at the airport, . . .
3. After getting to your destination, . . .
4. When talking with the local people, . . .
5. While visiting tourist sites, . . .
6. Before leaving for home, . . .
7. In general, when traveling to a foreign country, . . .

❑ **Exercise 16. Listening.** (Chapter 18)

CD 2
Track 26

Listen to each conversation. Choose the sentence (a. or b.) that has the same meaning.

Example: You will hear: A: William, don't forget to pick up some groceries after work.
                       B: Oh yeah, thanks. That's the first thing I'll do when I leave the office.

         You will choose: (a.) After leaving work, William will stop at the grocery store.
                        b. Before leaving work, William will pick up some groceries.

1. a. Fearing people will laugh at her if she plays the piano, Rose doesn't want to play at the family gathering.
   b. Knowing she plays beautifully, Rose is happy to play the piano at the family gathering.

2. a. Not wanting to upset him, Jan isn't going to talk to Thomas this afternoon.
   b. Hoping to change Thomas' work behavior, Jan is going to talk to him this afternoon.

3. a. Upon finding her wedding ring, Susan hid it in a box.
   b. On finding her wedding ring, Susan felt relieved.

4. a. Never having voted in an election, Sam is taking it very seriously.
   b. Having done a lot of research before choosing a candidate, Sam voted in the presidential election.

❑ **Exercise 17. Reading and grammar.** (Chapter 18)
Part I. Read the passage and <u>underline</u> the modifying adverbial phrases.

The First Telephone

Alexander Graham Bell, a teacher of the deaf in Boston, invented the first telephone. One day in 1875, <u>while running a test on his latest attempt to create a machine that could carry voices</u>, he accidentally spilled acid on his coat. Naturally, he called for his assistant, Thomas A. Watson, who was in another room. Bell said, "Mr. Watson, come here. I want you." Upon hearing words coming from the machine, Watson immediately realized that their experiments had at last been successful. He rushed excitedly into the other room to tell Bell that he had heard his words over the machine.

After successfully testing the new machine again and again, Bell confidently announced his invention to the world. For the most part, scientists appreciated his accomplishment, but the general public did not understand the revolutionary nature of Bell's invention. Believing the telephone was a toy with little practical application, most people paid little attention to Bell's announcement.

Part II. Read the statements. Circle "T" for true and "F" for false.

1. Bell was testing a machine when Watson made a discovery.   T   F

2. Watson heard words coming from the machine.   T   F

3. Watson tested the new device again and again.   T   F

4. Bell announced his phone was a toy.   T   F

❏ **Exercise 18. Listening.** (Chapter 18)

Part I. Look at the picture of the keyboard while listening to the lecture.

CD 2
Track 27

QWERTY keyboard

Part II. Read the statements. Circle "T" for true and "F" for false.

1. While working on a typewriter design, Sholes came up up with more than one pattern for the keyboard.   T   F

2. Upon discovering that the keys hit one another if the letters were in alphabetical order, Sholes developed a keyboard called "QWERTY."   T   F

3. Needing a keyboard that allowed typists to type letters as rapidly as possible, Sholes decided his design would be the best choice.   T   F

4. Having a long history of successful use, QWERTY is not likely to be replaced any time soon.   T   F

Chapter 19

Connectives That Express Cause and Effect, Contrast, and Condition

❏ **Exercise 1. Warm-up.** (Chart 19-1)
Which sentences express the same meaning as the given situation?

SITUATION: Monday was a holiday.
RESULT: All schools were closed.

1. All schools were closed on Monday because it was a holiday.
2. Because of the holiday, all schools were closed on Monday.
3. Due to the holiday, all schools were closed on Monday.
4. Due to the fact that it was a holiday, all schools were closed on Monday.
5. Because all schools were closed on Monday, it was a holiday.

19-1 Using *Because Of* and *Due To*

(a) *Because* the weather was cold, we stayed home.	*Because* introduces an adverb clause; it is followed by a subject and a verb, as in (a).
(b) *Because of* the cold weather, we stayed home. (c) *Due to* the cold weather, we stayed home.	*Because of* and *due to* are phrasal prepositions; they are followed by a noun object, as in (b) and (c).
(d) *Due to the fact that* the weather was cold, we stayed home.	Sometimes (usually in more formal writing) *due to* is followed by a noun clause introduced by *the fact that*.
(e) We stayed home *because of the cold weather*. We stayed home *due to the cold weather*. We stayed home *due to the fact that the weather was cold*.	Like adverb clauses, these phrases can also follow the main clause, as in (e).

❏ **Exercise 2. Looking at grammar.** (Charts 17-3 and 19-1)
Identify the cause and effect in each pair of sentences. Then combine the sentences with *because*.

1. Jon is a heavy smoker. Jon has breathing problems.
2. Martina feels homesick. Martina moved to a new town.
3. Mr. Jordan's house has no heat. Mr. Jordan lost his job.
4. Victor has gained weight. Victor is going to eat less.

□ **Exercise 3. Looking at grammar.** (Charts 17-3 and 19-1)
Complete the sentences with *because* or *because of*.

1. We postponed our trip _____ the bad driving conditions.

2. Sue's eyes were red _____ she had been swimming in a chlorinated pool.

3. We can't visit the museum tomorrow _____ it isn't open.

4. Jim had to give up jogging _____ his sprained ankle.

5. _____ heavy fog at the airport, our plane was delayed for several hours.

6. _____ the elevator was broken, we had to walk up six flights of stairs.

7. Thousands of Irish people emigrated to the United States _____ the potato famine in Ireland in the mid-19th century.

□ **Exercise 4. Looking at grammar.** (Chart 19-1)
Complete the sentences with the ideas in parentheses.

1. (*The traffic was heavy.*) We were late to the meeting due to _____<u>the heavy traffic</u>_____.

2. (*Bill's wife is ill.*) Bill has to do all of the cooking and cleaning because of _____
_____.

3. (*It was noisy in the next apartment.*) I couldn't get to sleep last night because of
_____.

4. (*Our parents are generous.*) Because of _____,
all of the children in our family have received the best of everything.

5. (*Circumstances are beyond our control.*) Due to _____
_____, our office is closed today.

□ **Exercise 5. Warm-up.** (Chart 19-2)
Check (✓) the sentences that logically complete the idea of the given sentence.

Nadia likes fresh vegetables.

1. ____ Therefore, she has a vegetable garden in her yard.
2. ____ As a result, she doesn't grow her own vegetables.
3. ____ Therefore, she buys canned vegetables at the store.
4. ____ As a result, she buys produce from local farmers.
5. ____ She eats a lot of frozen vegetables, therefore.
6. ____ Consequently, she eats produce from her garden.

19-2 Cause and Effect: Using *Therefore, Consequently,* and *So*

(a) Al failed the test because he didn't study. (b) Al didn't study. *Therefore,* he failed the test. (c) Al didn't study. *Consequently,* he failed the test.	Examples (a), (b), and (c) have the same meaning. ***Therefore*** and ***consequently*** mean "as a result." In grammar, they are called *transitions* (or *conjunctive adverbs*). Transitions connect the ideas between two sentences. They are used most commonly in formal written English and rarely in spoken English.

(d) Al didn't study. *Therefore,* he failed the test.
(e) Al didn't study. He, *therefore,* failed the test.
(f) Al didn't study. He failed the test, *therefore*.
 	
POSITIONS OF A TRANSITION:
transition + S + V (+ rest of sentence)
     S + ***transition*** + V (+ rest of sentence)
     S + V (+ rest of sentence) + ***transition***
	A transition occurs in the second of two related sentences.
	
	Notice the patterns and punctuation in the examples. A period (NOT a comma) is used at the end of the first sentence.* The transition has several positions in the second sentence. The transition is separated from the rest of the sentence by commas.

(g) Al didn't study, *so* he failed the test.	In (g): ***So*** is used as a *conjunction* between two independent clauses. It has the same meaning as ***therefore***. ***So*** is common in both formal written and spoken English. A comma usually precedes ***so*** when it connects two sentences, as in (g).

*A semicolon is also possible in this situation. See the footnote to Chart 19-3.

❑ **Exercise 6. Looking at grammar.** (Chart 19-2)
Rewrite the sentence with the given words. Punctuate carefully.

The children stayed home because a storm was approaching.

1. therefore   _____

2. consequently _____

3. so   _____

❑ **Exercise 7. Looking at grammar.** (Charts 17-3, 19-1, and 19-2)
Punctuate the sentences. Add capital letters as necessary. NOTE: Two sentences need no changes.

1. *adverb clause:*   Because it was cold she wore a coat.

2. *adverb clause:*   She wore a coat because it was cold.

3. *prepositional phrase:* Because of the cold weather she wore a coat.

4. *prepositional phrase:* She wore a coat because of the cold weather.

5. *transition:*   The weather was cold therefore she wore a coat.

6. *transition:*   The weather was cold she wore a coat therefore.

7. *conjunction:*   The weather was cold so she wore a coat.

❑ **Exercise 8. Looking at grammar.** (Charts 17-3, 19-1, and 19-2)
Punctuate the sentences. Add capital letters as necessary.

1. Pat always enjoyed studying sciences in high school therefore she decided to major in biology in college.

2. Due to recent improvements in the economy fewer people are unemployed.

3. Last night's storm damaged the power lines consequently the town was without electricity.

4. Due to the snowstorm only five students came to class the teacher therefore canceled the class.

❑ **Exercise 9. Warm-up.** (Chart 19-3)
Check (✓) the sentences that have the correct punctuation.

1. ____ Doctors sometimes recommend yoga for their patients. Because it can lower stress.

2. ____ Because yoga can lower stress doctors sometimes recommend it for their patients.

3. ____ Yoga can lower stress. Doctors, therefore, sometimes recommend it for their patients.

4. ____ Yoga can lower stress, so doctors sometimes recommend it for their patients.

19-3 Summary of Patterns and Punctuation

Adverb Clauses	(a) *Because* it was hot**,** we went swimming. (b) We went swimming *because* it was hot.	An *adverb clause* may precede or follow an independent clause. PUNCTUATION: A comma is used if the adverb clause comes first.
Prepositions	(c) *Because of* the hot weather**,** we went swimming. (d) We went swimming *because of* the hot weather.	A *preposition* is followed by a noun object, not by a subject and verb. PUNCTUATION: A comma is usually used if the prepositional phrase precedes the subject and verb of the independent clause.
Transitions	(e) It was hot. *Therefore,* we went swimming. (f) It was hot. We**,** *therefore,* went swimming. (g) It was hot. We went swimming**,** *therefore.*	A *transition* is used with the second sentence of a pair. It shows the relationship of the second idea to the first idea. A transition is movable within the second sentence. PUNCTUATION: A period is used between the two independent clauses.* A comma may NOT be used to separate the clauses. Commas are usually used to set the transition off from the rest of the sentence.
Conjunctions	(h) It was hot**,** *so* we went swimming.	A conjunction comes between two independent clauses. PUNCTUATION: Usually a comma is used immediately in front of a conjunction.

*A semicolon (;) may be used instead of a period between the two independent clauses.
  It was hot; therefore, we went swimming.
  It was hot; we, therefore, went swimming.
  It was hot; we went swimming, therefore.
In general, a semicolon can be used instead of a period between any two sentences that are closely related in meaning: *Peanuts are not nuts; they are beans.* Notice that a small letter, NOT a capital letter, immediately follows a semicolon.

❏ **Exercise 10. Looking at grammar.** (Charts 17-3 and 19-3)
Combine the sentences using the given words. Discuss correct punctuation.

We postponed our trip. The weather was bad.

Example: because → *We postponed our trip* **because** *the weather was bad.*
→ **Because** *the weather was bad, we postponed our trip.*

1. therefore   3. so   5. consequently
2. since   4. because of   6. due to the fact that

❏ **Exercise 11. Looking at grammar.** (Charts 17-3, 19-2, and 19-3)
Combine each pair of ideas with the words in parentheses.

1. My cell phone doesn't work. The battery is dead. (*because*)
   → *My cell phone doesn't work because the battery is dead.* OR
   → *Because the battery is dead, my cell phone doesn't work.*
2. Pat doesn't want to return to the Yukon to live. The winters are too severe. (*because*)
3. It is important to wear a hat on cold days. We lose sixty percent of our body heat through our head. (*since*)
4. Bill couldn't pick us up after the concert. His car wouldn't start. (*therefore*)
5. When I was in my teens and twenties, it was easy for me to get into an argument with my father. Both of us can be stubborn and opinionated. (*because*)
6. A camel can go completely without water for eight to ten days. It is an ideal animal for desert areas. (*due to the fact that*)
7. Robert emailed the software company for technical support. He got some new business software that didn't work. (*so*)
8. A tomato is classified as a fruit, but most people consider it a vegetable. It is often eaten in salads along with lettuce, onions, cucumbers, and other vegetables. (*since*)
9. There is consumer demand for ivory. Many African elephants are being slaughtered ruthlessly. Many people who care about saving these animals from extinction refuse to buy any item made from ivory. (*due to, consequently*)
10. Most 15th-century Europeans believed the world was flat and that a ship could conceivably sail off the end of the earth. Many sailors of the time refused to venture forth with explorers into unknown waters. (*because*)

❏ **Exercise 12. Warm-up.** (Chart 19-4)
Read about Alan and Lisa. Imagine their reactions as parents and complete the sentences with phrases in the list or your own ideas. What do you notice about **so/such** and the words in blue?

SITUATION: Alan and Lisa are the proud parents of triplets. Before their triplets were born, however, they were told they were going to have twins. Imagine their surprise when they found out they were the parents of three babies. Alan was incredibly happy. Lisa was utterly exhausted.

began to cry	couldn't laugh or cry	fell asleep
called friends	danced around the room	went into shock

1. Ed was *so* happy that he . . . .   3. Ed was *such* a happy dad that he . . . .
2. Lisa was *so* tired that she . . . .   4. Lisa was *such* a tired mom that she . . . .

19-4 Other Ways of Expressing Cause and Effect: *Such . . . That* and *So . . . That*

(a) Because the weather was nice, we went to the zoo. (b) It was *such nice weather that* we went to the zoo. (c) The weather was *so nice that* we went to the zoo.	Examples (a), (b), and (c) have the same meaning.
(d) It was *such good coffee that* I had another cup. (e) It was *such a foggy day that* we couldn't see the road.	*Such . . . that* encloses a modified noun: *such* + *adjective* + *noun* + *that*
(f) The coffee is *so hot that* I can't drink it. (g) I'm *so hungry that* I could eat a horse. (h) She speaks *so fast that* I can't understand her. (i) He walked *so quickly that* I couldn't keep up with him.	*So . . . that* encloses an adjective or adverb: *so* + { *adjective* or *adverb* } + *that*
(j) She made *so many mistakes that* she failed the exam. (k) He has *so few friends that* he is always lonely. (l) She has *so much money that* she can buy whatever she wants. (m) He had *so little trouble* with the test *that* he left twenty minutes early.	*So . . . that* is used with *many*, *few*, *much*, and *little*.
(n) It was *such a good book* (*that*) I couldn't put it down. (o) I was *so hungry* (*that*) I didn't wait for dinner to eat something.	Sometimes, primarily in speaking, *that* is omitted.

❑ **Exercise 13. Looking at grammar.** (Chart 19-4)
Complete the sentences with *so* or *such*.

1. It was ___such___ an enjoyable party that no one wanted to leave.

2. The party was ___so___ enjoyable that no one wanted to leave.

3. We had ___so___ much fun that no one wanted to leave.

4. Maya is _____ afraid of flying that she travels by train or bus.

5. You've been _____ kind that I don't know how to thank you.

6. The article had _____ little current information that it wasn't useful.

7. The teacher has repeated herself _____ many times that it's becoming a joke.

8. It was _____ a long trip abroad that I got very homesick.

9. My elderly aunt has _____ few friends that I am beginning to worry about her.

❑ **Exercise 14. Let's talk.** (Chart 19-4)
Work in small groups. Take turns making sentences using *so/such . . . that* with the given ideas. Try to exaggerate your answers. Share your favorite sentences with the class.

Example: I'm hungry. In fact, I'm . . . .
→ *I'm **so** hungry. In fact, I'm **so** hungry (**that**) I could eat a horse.*

1. I'm really tired. In fact, I'm . . . .
2. I didn't expect it! I was really surprised. In fact, I was . . . .

3. I took a very slow bus to town. In fact, it was . . . .
4. I saw a shark while I was swimming in the ocean. I was frightened. In fact, I was . . . .
5. We rented a video. It was a very exciting movie. In fact, it was . . . .
6. The weather was really, really hot. In fact, it was . . . .
7. My wallet fell out of my pocket and I lost a lot of money. In fact, I lost . . . .
8. I ordered an expensive meal at a restaurant. The server brought a small plate with a tiny amount of food to your table. In fact, it was . . . .

❏ **Exercise 15. Looking at grammar.** (Chart 19-4)
Make sentences using *so* or *such* by combining the ideas in Column A and Column B.

Example: The wind was strong. → *The wind was **so** strong that it blew my hat off my head.*

Column A	**Column B**
1. The wind was strong.	a. It burned my tongue.
2. The radio was too loud.	b. She was fired from her job.
3. Olga did poor work.	✓c. It blew my hat off my head.
4. The food was too hot.	d. The teacher postponed the test.
5. There are many leaves on a single tree.	e. It is impossible to count them.
6. The tornado struck with great force.	f. It lifted cars off the ground.
7. Few students showed up for class.	g. I couldn't hear what Michael was saying.
8. Charles used too much paper when he was writing his report.	h. The wastepaper basket overflowed.

❏ **Exercise 16. Warm-up.** (Chart 19-5)
Check (✓) the sentences that correctly complete the given sentence.

Kay got a new job so that . . .
1. _____ she could be closer to home.
2. _____ she is very excited.
3. _____ her husband is taking her out to dinner to celebrate.
4. _____ she could earn more money.

19-5 Expressing Purpose: Using *So That*

(a) I turned off the TV **in order to** enable my roommate to study in peace and quiet.	**In order to** expresses *purpose.* (See Chart 15-1, p. 331.)
(b) I turned off the TV **so (that)** my roommate could study in peace and quiet.	In (a): I turned off the TV for a purpose. The purpose was to make it possible for my roommate to study in peace and quiet.

So That + *Can* or *Could*

(c) I'm going to cash a check **so that I can** buy my textbooks. (d) I cashed a check **so that I could** buy my textbooks.	**So that** also expresses *purpose.** It expresses the same meaning as **in order to**. The word "that" is often omitted, especially in speaking. **So that** is often used instead of **in order to** when the idea of ability is being expressed. **Can** is used in the adverb clause for a present/future meaning. In (c): **so that I can buy** = in order to be able to buy **Could** is used after **so that** in past sentences, as in (d).**

So That + *Will / Would* or Simple Present

(e) I'll take my umbrella **so that I won't** get wet. (f) Yesterday I took my umbrella **so that I wouldn't** get wet. (g) I'll take my umbrella **so that I don't** get wet.	In (e): **so that I won't get wet** = in order to make sure that I won't get wet **Would** is used in past sentences, as in (f). In (g): It is sometimes possible to use the simple present after **so that** in place of **will**; the simple present expresses a future meaning.

*NOTE: *In order that* has the same meaning as *so that* but is less commonly used.
     Example: *I turned off the TV **in order that** my roommate could study in peace and quiet.*
Both *so that* and *in order that* introduce adverb clauses. It is unusual but possible to put these adverb clauses at the beginning of a sentence: ***So that** my roommate could study in peace and quiet, I turned off the TV.*

Also possible but less common: the use of ***may* or ***might*** in place of ***can*** or ***could*** (e.g., *I cashed a check **so that I might** buy my textbooks.*).

❏ **Exercise 17. Looking at grammar.** (Chart 19-5)
Combine each set of ideas by using *so* (*that*).

1. Please turn down the radio. I want to be able to get to sleep.
   → *Please turn down the radio so (that) I can get to sleep.*
2. My wife turned down the radio. I wanted to be able to get to sleep.
   → *My wife turned down the radio so (that) I could get to sleep.*
3. Put the milk in the refrigerator. We want to make sure it won't (OR doesn't) spoil.
   → *Put the milk in the refrigerator so (that) it won't (OR doesn't) spoil.*
4. I put the milk in the refrigerator. I wanted to make sure it didn't spoil.
   → *I put the milk in the refrigerator so (that) it wouldn't spoil.*
5. Please be quiet. I want to be able to hear what Sharon is saying.
6. I asked the children to be quiet. I wanted to be able to hear what Sharon was saying.
7. I'm going to cash a check. I want to make sure that I have enough money to go to the store.
8. I cashed a check yesterday. I wanted to make sure that I had enough money to go to the store.

9. Ann and Larry have a six-year-old child. Tonight they're going to hire a babysitter. They want to be able to go out with some friends.

10. Last week Ann and Larry hired a babysitter. They wanted to be able to go to a dinner party at the home of Larry's boss.

11. Be sure to put the meat in the oven at 5:00. You want to be sure that it will be (OR is) ready to eat by 6:30.

12. Yesterday I put the meat in the oven at 5:00. I wanted it to be ready to eat by 6:30.

13. I'm going to leave the party early. I want to be able to get a good night's sleep tonight.

14. When it started to rain, Harry opened his umbrella. He wanted to be sure he didn't get wet.

15. The little boy pretended to be sick. He wanted to stay home from school.

❑ **Exercise 18. Looking at grammar.** (Charts 19-2 and 19-5)
Add *that* to the sentence if *so* means *in order that*. If *so* means *therefore*, add a comma.

1. I borrowed some money so ∧ I could pay my rent. *(that)*

2. I didn't have enough money for a movie**,** so I went home and watched TV.

3. I need a visa so I can travel overseas.

4. I needed a visa so I went to the embassy to apply for one.

5. Marta is trying to improve her English so she can become a tour guide.

6. Olga wants to improve her English so she has hired a tutor.

7. Tarek borrowed money from his parents so he could start his own business.

8. I turned off the TV so I could concentrate on my paperwork.

❑ **Exercise 19. Warm-up.** (Chart 19-6)
Usually when someone breaks an arm, he/she goes to a doctor. That is expected behavior. Answer the same question about expected behavior for each statement. Circle *yes* or *no*.

	EXPECTED BEHAVIOR?	
1. Ron broke his arm, but he didn't go to the doctor.	yes	no
2. Joe went to the doctor because he broke his arm.	yes	no
3. Sue broke her arm, so she went to the doctor.	yes	no
4. Amy broke her arm; nevertheless, she didn't go to the doctor.	yes	no
5. Despite having a broken arm, Rick didn't go to the doctor.	yes	no
6. Eva was in so much pain from her broken arm that she went to the doctor.	yes	no
7. Jeff broke his arm; therefore, he went to the doctor.	yes	no

19-6 Showing Contrast (Unexpected Result)

All of these sentences have the same meaning. The idea of cold weather is contrasted with the idea of going swimming. Usually if the weather is cold, one does not go swimming, so going swimming in cold weather is an "unexpected result." It is surprising that the speaker went swimming in cold weather.

Adverb Clauses	*even though*	(a) *Even though* it was cold, I went swimming.
	although	(b) *Although* it was cold, I went swimming.
	though	(c) *Though* it was cold, I went swimming.
Conjunctions	*but . . . anyway*	(d) It was cold, *but* I went swimming *anyway*.
	but . . . still	(e) It was cold, *but* I *still* went swimming.
	yet . . . still	(f) It was cold, *yet* I *still* went swimming.
Transitions	*nevertheless*	(g) It was cold. *Nevertheless*, I went swimming.
	nonetheless	(h) It was cold; *nonetheless*, I went swimming.
	however . . . still	(i) It was cold. *However*, I *still* went swimming.
Prepositions	*despite*	(j) I went swimming *despite* the cold weather.
	in spite of	(k) I went swimming *in spite of* the cold weather.
	despite the fact that	(l) I went swimming *despite the fact that* the weather was cold.
	in spite of the fact that	(m) I went swimming *in spite of the fact that* the weather was cold.

❏ **Exercise 20. Looking at grammar.** (Charts 19-2 and 19-6)
Complete the sentences with *inside* or *outside* to make logical statements.

1. It rained, but we still had our wedding _____.

2. It rained, so we had our wedding _____.

3. It rained; nevertheless, we had our wedding _____.

4. Though it rained, we had our wedding _____.

5. Even though it rained, we had our wedding _____.

6. Although it rained, we had our wedding _____.

7. Despite the fact that it rained, we had our wedding _____.

8. It rained; therefore, we had our wedding _____.

❏ **Exercise 21. Looking at grammar.** (Chart 19-6)
Complete the sentences with *am* or *am not* to make logical statements.

1. The roads are icy; nevertheless, I _____ going shopping.

2. Though the roads are icy, I _____ staying home.

3. Even though the roads are icy, I _____ going shopping.

4. I _____ going shopping although the roads are icy.

5. The roads are icy, yet I _____ going shopping anyway.

6. Despite the fact that the roads are icy, I _____ staying home.

7. In spite of the icy roads, I _____ going shopping.

❏ **Exercise 22. Looking at grammar.** (Chart 19-6)
Complete the sentences with the given words. Notice the use of punctuation and capitalization.

Part I. Complete the sentences with **but, even though**, or **nevertheless**.

1. Bob ate a large dinner. _____, he is still hungry.

2. Bob ate a large dinner, _____ he is still hungry.

3. Bob is still hungry _____ he ate a large dinner.

4. I had a lot of studying to do, _____ I went to a movie anyway.

5. I had a lot of studying to do. _____, I went to a movie.

6. _____ I had a lot of studying to do, I went to a movie.

7. I finished all of my work _____ I was very sleepy.

8. I was very sleepy, _____ I finished all of my work anyway.

9. I was very sleepy. _____, I finished all of my work.

Part II. Complete the sentences with **yet, although**, or **however**.

10. I washed my hands. _____, they still looked dirty.

11. I washed my hands, _____ they still looked dirty.

12. _____ I washed my hands, they still looked dirty.

13. Diana didn't know how to swim, _____ she jumped into the pool.

14. _____ Diana didn't know how to swim, she jumped into the pool.

15. Diana didn't know how to swim. _____, she jumped into the pool.

❏ **Exercise 23. Looking at grammar.** (Chart 19-6)
Add commas, periods, and capital letters as necessary. Do not add, omit, or change any words.

1. Anna's father gave her some good advice nevertheless she did not follow it.
   → *Anna's father gave her some good advice.* **N**evertheless, *she did not follow it.*

2. Anna's father gave her some good advice but she didn't follow it.

3. Even though Anna's father gave her some good advice she didn't follow it.

4. Anna's father gave her some good advice she did not follow it however.

5. Thomas was thirsty I offered him some water he refused it.

6. Thomas refused the water although he was thirsty.

7. Thomas was thirsty nevertheless he refused the glass of water I brought him.

8. Thomas was thirsty yet he refused to drink the water that I offered him.

❏ **Exercise 24. Looking at grammar.** (Chart 19-6)
Combine the sentences using the given words. Discuss correct punctuation. Use the negative if necessary to make a logical statement.

His grades were low. He was admitted to the university.

1. even though
2. but . . . anyway
3. yet . . . still

4. nonetheless
5. despite
6. because of

❏ **Exercise 25. Warm-up.** (Chart 19-7)
Read the question and the answers that follow. Which answers express "direct contrast," i.e., the idea that "this" is the opposite of "that"?

hurricane

tornado

What is the difference between hurricanes and tornadoes?

1. Hurricanes develop over warm oceans while tornadoes form over land.
2. Hurricanes develop while they are traveling over warm ocean water.
3. Hurricanes develop over warm oceans, but tornadoes form over land.
4. Hurricanes develop over warm oceans; however, tornadoes form over land.
5. Hurricanes develop over warm oceans; on the other hand, tornadoes form over land.

19-7 Showing Direct Contrast

All of the sentences have the same meaning: "This" is the opposite of "that."

Adverb Clauses	*while*	(a) Mary is rich, *while* John is poor.* (b) John is poor, *while* Mary is rich.
Conjunctions	*but*	(c) Mary is rich, *but* John is poor. (d) John is poor, *but* Mary is rich.
Transitions	*however*	(e) Mary is rich; *however*, John is poor. (f) John is poor; Mary is rich, *however*.
	on the other hand	(g) Mary is rich. John, *on the other hand*, is poor. (h) John is poor. Mary, *on the other hand*, is rich.

*Sometimes a comma precedes a *while*-clause that shows direct contrast. A comma helps clarify that *while* is being used to express contrast rather than time. The use of a comma in this instance is a stylistic choice by the writer.

❏ **Exercise 26. Looking at grammar.** (Chart 19-7)
Make two sentences with the same meaning as the given sentence. Use **however** or **on the other hand**. Punctuate carefully.

1. Florida has a warm climate, while Alaska has a cold climate.
2. While Fred is a good student, his brother is lazy.
3. Elderly people in my country usually live with their children, but the elderly in the United States often live by themselves.

❏ **Exercise 27. Looking at grammar.** (Chart 19-7)
Complete the sentences with your own words.

1. Some people really enjoy swimming, while others . . . *are afraid of water.*
2. In the United States, people drive on the right-hand side of the road. However, people in . . . .
3. While my desk always seems to be a mess, my . . . .
4. My oldest son is shy, while my youngest son . . . .

❏ **Exercise 28. Let's talk or write.** (Chart 19-7)
Part I. Read the information below about extroverts and introverts. Make several sentences with the words in the list, either orally or in writing using the words **but, however, on the other hand,** or **while**.

General Characteristics of Extroverts and Introverts

Extroverts . . .
like to be the center of attention.
like to talk more than listen.
enjoy meeting people.
prefer being active.
like to work in groups.
don't always think before speaking.
don't mind noise.
like crowds.
are energized by being with others.

Introverts . . .
are uncomfortable being the center of attention.
like to listen more than talk.
are reserved when meeting people.
like to spend time alone.
don't like to work in groups.
think carefully before speaking.
prefer the quiet.
avoid crowds.
can find it tiring to spend time with others.

Examples:
→ *Extroverts like to talk more than listen, **while** introverts like to listen more than talk.*
→ *Introverts like to listen more than talk. Extroverts, **however**, like to talk more than listen.*

Part II. Are you an extrovert or introvert? Compare yourself to someone you know who is different from you. Make several sentences.

❏ **Exercise 29. Let's talk.** (Chart 19-7)
Think of two different countries you are familiar with. How are they different? Use **while, however, on the other hand,** and **but**. Work in pairs, in small groups, or as a class.

1. size
2. population
3. food
4. time of meals
5. economic system
6. educational system
7. role of women
8. language
9. educational costs
10. medical care
11. public transportation
12. dating customs

❑ **Exercise 30. Warm-up.** (Chart 19-8)
Choose the logical verb for each sentence: **can** or **can't**.

SITUATION: Sarah drinks coffee every morning. It wakes her up.

1. If Sarah drinks coffee in the morning, she *can / can't* wake up quickly.

2. Unless Sarah drinks coffee in the morning, she *can / can't* wake up quickly.

3. Sarah drinks coffee every morning; otherwise, she *can / can't* wake up quickly.

4. Sarah drinks coffee in the morning, or else she *can / can't* wake up quickly.

19-8 Expressing Conditions: Using *Otherwise* and *Or (Else)*

Adverb Clauses	(a) *If I don't eat breakfast,* I get hungry. (b) You'll be late *if you don't hurry.* (c) You'll get wet *unless you take your umbrella.*	*If* and *unless* state conditions that produce certain results. (See Charts 17-6 and 17-10, pp. 377 and 382.)
Transitions	(d) I always eat breakfast. *Otherwise,* I get hungry during class. (e) You'd better hurry. *Otherwise,* you'll be late. (f) Take your umbrella. *Otherwise,* you'll get wet.	*Otherwise* expresses the idea "if the opposite is true, then there will be a certain result." In (d): *otherwise* = if I don't eat breakfast
Conjunctions	(g) I always eat breakfast, *or (else)* I get hungry during class. (h) You'd better hurry, *or (else)* you'll be late. (i) Take your umbrella, *or (else)* you'll get wet.	*Or else* and *otherwise* have the same meaning.

❑ **Exercise 31. Looking at grammar.** (Chart 19-8)
Make sentences with the same meaning as the given sentence. Use *otherwise*.

1. If I don't call my mother, she'll start worrying about me.
   → *I am going to / should / had better / have to / must call my mother. Otherwise, she'll start worrying about me.*

2. If you don't leave now, you'll be late for class.

3. Unless you have a ticket, you can't get into the theater.

4. You can't enter that country unless you have a passport.

5. If Tom doesn't get a job soon, his family won't have enough money for food.

6. Only if you speak both Japanese and Chinese fluently will you be considered for that job.*

7. Mary can go to school only if she gets a scholarship.

8. If I don't wash my clothes tonight, I won't have any clean clothes to wear tomorrow.

---

*Notice that the subject and verb in the main clause are inverted because the sentence begins with *only if.* See Chart 17-11, p. 383.

19-9 Summary of Connectives: Cause and Effect, Contrast, and Condition

	Adverb Clause Words	Transitions	Conjunctions	Prepositions
Cause and Effect	because so (that) since now that	therefore consequently	so	because of due to
Contrast	even though while although though	however nevertheless nonetheless on the other hand	but (. . . anyway) yet (. . . still)	despite in spite of
Condition	if in case unless only if even if whether or not	otherwise	or (else)	

❏ **Exercise 32. Looking at grammar.** (Chart 19-9)
Using the two ideas of "to study" and "to pass or fail the exam," complete the sentences. Punctuate and capitalize as necessary.

1. Because I did not study __, I failed the exam._____

2. I failed the exam because _____

3. Although I studied _____

4. I did not study therefore _____

5. I did not study however _____

6. I studied nevertheless _____

7. Even though I did not study _____

8. I did not study so _____

9. Since I did not study _____

10. If I study for the exam _____

11. Unless I study for the exam _____

12. I must study otherwise _____

13. Even if I study _____

14. I did not study consequently _____

15. I did not study nonetheless _____

16. I will probably fail the exam whether _____

17. Only if I study _____

18. I studied hard yet _____

19. You'd better study or else _____

❏ **Exercise 33. Listening.** (Chart 19-9)

Listen to each sentence and choose the logical completion (a. or b.).

CD 2
Track 28

Example: You will hear: I was exhausted when I got home, but . . .

You will choose: (a.) I didn't take a nap.   b. I took a nap.

1. a. my back gets sore.   b. my back doesn't get sore.

2. a. my old one works fine.   b. my old one doesn't work.

3. a. I hurry.   b. I don't hurry.

4. a. I hurried.   b. I didn't hurry.

5. a. our offices are hot.   b. our offices aren't hot.

6. a. the noise bothers me.   b. the noise doesn't bother me.

7. a. I fell asleep during dinner.   b. I didn't fall asleep during dinner.

❏ **Exercise 34. Game.** (Charts 17-2, 19-4, and 19-9)

Work in teams. Combine these two ideas using the words below the example. The time is now, so use present and future tenses. The team that correctly combines the most sentences wins.

to go (or not to go) to the beach \ hot, cold, nice weather

Example: because
→ ***Because** the weather is cold, we aren't going to go to the beach.*
→ *We're going to go to the beach **because** the weather is hot.*

1. so . . . that	8. because of	15. therefore
2. so	9. consequently	16. only if
3. nevertheless	10. as soon as	17. nonetheless
4. despite	11. such . . . that	18. in spite of
5. now that	12. since	19. even if
6. once	13. but . . . anyway	20. yet . . . still
7. although	14. unless	21. whether . . . or not

412 CHAPTER 19

❑ **Exercise 35. Reading.** (Chart 19-9)

Part I. Read the passage comparing optimists and pessimists.

Optimists vs. Pessimists

Have you ever heard the expression that a glass is half full or half empty? If not, imagine that you are looking at a glass that is filled exactly halfway with liquid. Now, is the glass half full or half empty to you? People who say it is half full are called optimists, while people who say it is half empty are called pessimists. In simple terms, optimists see the best in the world, while pessimists see the worst.

One of the clearest ways to see the differences between the two is to look at the way optimists and pessimists explain events. When something bad happens, optimists tend to see the event as a single event which does not affect other areas of their lives. For example, Sarah is an optimistic person. When she gets a low grade on a test, she will say something like this to herself: "Oh well, that was one test I didn't do well on. I wasn't feeling well that day. I have another test in a few weeks. I'll do better on that one."

Pessimists, on the other hand, will feel that an event is just one of a string of bad events affecting their lives, and that they're somehow the cause of it. Let's take a look at Susan. She is a pessimist. When she gets a low grade on a test, she might say: "I failed again. I never do well on tests. I'm stupid. I should just quit trying." And when something does go well for Susan, she often attributes her success to luck. She may say, "I was just lucky that time," and she doesn't expect to do well again. While optimists don't see themselves as failures, pessimists do.

Research has shown that optimism can be a learned trait and that, despite their upbringing, people can train themselves to respond to events in more positive terms. For example, Paul has a tendency to react negatively to events. The first thing he has to do is become conscious of that behavior. Once he identifies how he is reacting, he can reframe his thoughts in more positive terms, as Sarah did when she failed the test. As Paul begins to do more of this, he forms new patterns of response, and over time these responses become more automatic. Gradually he can develop a more positive outlook on life.

What about you? How do you see life? Is the glass half full or half empty?

Part II. Complete the sentences with information from the reading.

1. Optimists think positively about life, while . . . .
2. An optimist may do poorly on a test; nevertheless, ...
3. Things sometimes go well for a pessimist; however, ...
4. Pessimists see themselves as failures; on the other hand, ...
5. Optimists don't see a single event affecting other areas of their lives; consequently, ...
6. Optimists see the best in the world; therefore, ...
7. Optimists see the best in the world; however, ...
8. Although people may have been raised as pessimists, ...
9. If a pessimist wants to change how he reacts, ...

Exercise 36. Listening. (Chapters 17 → 19)

Part I. Answer these questions. Then listen to the lecture with your book closed.

CD 2
Track 29

1. What makes you yawn?
2. Do you yawn when others around you yawn?

Part II. Open your book and read the statements. Circle "T" for true and "F" for false.

1. Yawning is so contagious that when one person
   yawns, others nearby may yawn as well.   T   F

2. According to the speaker, people are not necessarily
   tired even though they may yawn.   T   F

3. According to the speaker, people yawn
   only if others around them yawn.   T   F

4. It's been proven that unless people yawn,
   they can't stay awake.   T   F

5. It's possible that at some point in history, people
   yawned so that they could stay awake and keep others
   awake in times of danger.   T   F

6. According to the speaker, if you are talking to people
   and they begin yawning, you can be certain that they
   have become bored by you.   T   F

Exercise 37. Check your knowledge. (Chapters 1 → 19)

These sentences are taken from student writing. You are the editor for these students. Rewrite the sentences, correcting errors, combining ideas, and making whatever revisions in phrasing or vocabulary you feel will help the writers say what they intended to say.

Example: My idea of the most important thing in life. It is to be healthy. Because a person can't enjoy life without health.
> → *In my opinion, the most important thing in life is good health because a person cannot enjoy life fully without it.*

1. We went shopping after ate dinner. But the stores were closed. We had to go back home

   even we hadn't found what were we looking for.

2. I want explain that I know a lot of grammars but is my problem I haven't enough

   vocabularies.

3. When I got lost in the bus station a kind man helped me, he explained how to read the

   huge bus schedule on the wall. Took me to the window to buy a ticket and showed me

   where was my bus, I will always appreciate his kindness.

4. I had never understand the important of know English language. Until I worked at a large international company.

5. Since I was young my father found an American woman to teach me and my brothers English, but when we move to other town my father wasn't able to find other teacher for other five years.

6. I was surprised to see the room that I was given at the dormitory. Because there aren't any furniture, and dirty.

7. When I meet Mr. Lee for the first time, we played video games at the student center even though we can't communicate very well, but we had a good time.

8. Because the United States is a large and also big country. It means that they're various kinds of people live there and it has a diverse population.

9. My grammar class was start at 10:35. When the teacher was coming to class, she returned the last quiz to my classmates and I. After we have had another quiz.

10. If a wife has a work, her husband should share the houseworks with her. If both of them help, the houseworks can be finish much faster.

11. The first time I went skiing. I was afraid to go down the hill. But then I think to myself, "Why not? Give it a try. You'll make it!" After stand around for ten minutes without moving. Finally, I decided go down that hill.

❑ **Exercise 38. Listening and writing.** (Chapter 19)

CD 2
Track 30

Listen to each passage twice. Then work together in pairs or small groups to write out the passage. Summarize what you heard. Then listen again and revise your writing as necessary.

PASSAGE 1: Turtles
PASSAGE 2: Boy or Girl?

Chapter 20
Conditional Sentences and Wishes

❏ **Exercise 1. Warm-up.** (Chart 20-1)
Each sentence talks about a "condition" and the "result" of this condition. <u>Underline</u> the result clause in each sentence. Notice the verbs in blue. In which sentence does a past verb refer to present or future time?

1. If I have extra money, <u>I usually buy computer equipment with it</u>.
2. I will buy a new laptop computer next month if I have some extra money.
3. If I had some extra money, I would buy a new laptop today or tomorrow.
4. I would have bought a new laptop last month if I had had some extra money.

20-1	Overview of Basic Verb Forms Used in Conditional Sentences		
Situation	***If*-clause**	**Result clause**	**Examples**
True in the Present/Future	simple present	*will* + *simple form*	If I *have* enough time, I *watch* TV every evening. If I *have* enough time, I *will watch* TV later on tonight.
Untrue in the Present/Future	simple past	*would* + *simple form*	If I *had* enough time, I *would watch* TV now or later on.
Untrue in the Past	past perfect	*would have* + *past participle*	If I *had had* enough time, I *would have watched* TV yesterday.

❏ **Exercise 2. Looking at grammar.** (Chart 20-1)
Complete the sentences with the verbs in parentheses.

1. I usually send my parents an email every week. That is a true fact. In other words:

   If I (*have*) _____*have*_____ enough time, I (*send*) _____*send*_____ my parents an email **every week**.

2. I may have enough time to send my parents an email later tonight. I want to send them an email tonight. Both of those things are true. In other words:

   If I (*have*) _____ enough time, I (*send*) _____ my parents an email **later tonight**.

3. I don't have enough time right now, so I won't send my parents an email. I'll try to do it later. I want to email them, but the truth is that I just don't have enough time right now. In other words:

If I (*have*) _____ enough time **right now**, I (*send*) _____ my parents an email.

4. I won't have enough time tonight, so I won't send my parents an email. I'll try to do it tomorrow. I want to email them, but the truth is that I just won't have enough time. In other words:

If I (*have*) _____ enough time **later tonight**, I (*send*) _____ my parents an email.

5. I wanted to send my parents an email last night, but I didn't have enough time. In other words:

If I (*have*) _____ enough time, I (*send*) _____ my parents an email **last night**.

❑ **Exercise 3. Warm-up.** (Chart 20-2)
Discuss the differences in meaning, if any, in each pair of sentences.

1. a. If it rains, the streets get wet.
   b. If it rains tomorrow, the streets will get wet.

2. a. If you heat water, it boils.
   b. If you heat water, it will boil.

3. a. If it should rain tomorrow, we'll cancel the picnic.
   b. If it rains tomorrow, we'll cancel the picnic.

20-2 True in the Present or Future

(a) If I *don't eat* breakfast, I always *get* hungry during class.	In conditional sentences that express true, factual ideas in the present/future, the *simple present* (not the simple future) is used in the *if*-clause.
(b) Water *freezes* OR *will freeze* if the temperature *reaches* 32°F/0°C.	The result clause has various possible verb forms. A result clause verb can be:
(c) If I *don't eat* breakfast tomorrow morning, I *will get* hungry during class.	• the *simple present,* to express a habitual activity or situation, as in (a).
(d) If it *rains*, we *should stay* home. If it *rains*, I *might decide* to stay home. If it *rains*, we *can't go*. If it *rains*, we*'re going to stay* home.	• either the *simple present* or the *simple future,* to express an established, predictable fact or general truth, as in (b). • the *simple future,* to express a particular activity or situation in the future, as in (c). • *modals* and *phrasal modals* such as **should, might, can, be going to,** as in (d).* • an *imperative* verb, as in (e).
(e) If anyone *calls,* please *take* a message.	
(f) If anyone *should* call, please take a message.	Sometimes **should** is used in an *if*-clause. It indicates a little more uncertainty than the use of the simple present, but basically the meaning of examples (e) and (f) is the same.

*See Chart 9-1, p. 157, for a list of modals and phrasal modals.

❏ **Exercise 4. Let's talk.** (Chart 20-2)
Answer the questions. Work in pairs, in small groups, or as a class.

1. If it's cold tomorrow, what are you going to wear to class?
2. If it's cold, what do you usually wear?
3. Fish can't live out of water. If you take a fish out of water, what will happen/what happens?
4. If I want to learn English faster, what should I do?
5. Tell me what to do, where to go, and what to expect if I visit your hometown as a tourist.

❏ **Exercise 5. Looking at grammar.** (Chart 20-2)
Choose the correct verb for the result clauses. In some cases, both answers are correct.

1. If I find out the answer, I *will let / let* you know.

2. If I have extra time, I *tutor / am going to tutor* students in math.

3. If it snows, the roads *are / will be* closed.

4. If you run up a hill, your heart *beats / will beat* fast.

5. If it should rain tomorrow, we *might change / will change* our plans.

6. If my cell phone battery goes dead, I *will recharge / would recharge* it.

❏ **Exercise 6. Listening.** (Chart 20-2)

CD 2
Track 31

If + *pronoun* can be difficult to hear at the beginning of sentences because these words are generally unstressed. Additionally, *if* at the beginning of a sentence is often reduced to /f/. Listen to the sentences spoken in casual, relaxed English. Complete the sentences with the non-reduced forms of the words you hear.

Example: You will hear: If I hear anything, I'll tell you.

You will write: _____ *If I hear* _____ anything, I'll tell you.

1. _____ too fast, please tell me.

2. _____ married, everyone will be shocked.

3. _____ okay, I'll ask for some advice.

4. _____ to quit, I hope he lets us know soon.

5. _____ , we'll need to try something else.

6. _____ harder, I'm sure she'll succeed.

7. _____ the job, I'll call you right away.

❏ **Exercise 7. Warm-up.** (Chart 20-3)
Choose the correct completions.

1. If Tom were a teacher, he would teach law.
   a. Tom *is / isn't* a teacher.
   b. Tom *teaches / doesn't teach* law.

2. If it were 5:00, we could leave.
   a. It *is / isn't* 5:00.
   b. We *can / can't* leave now.

20-3 Untrue (Contrary to Fact) in the Present or Future

(a) If I *taught* this class, I *wouldn't give* tests.	In (a): In truth, I don't teach this class.
(b) If he *were* here right now, he *would help* us.	In (b): In truth, he is not here right now.
(c) If I *were* you, I *would accept* their invitation.	In (c): In truth, I am not you.
	NOTE: *Were* is used for both singular and plural subjects. *Was* (with *I, he, she, it*) is sometimes used in informal speech: *If I was you, I'd accept their invitation.*
COMPARE: (d) If I had enough money, I *would* buy a car. (e) If I had enough money, I *could* buy a car.	In (d): The speaker wants a car but doesn't have enough money. *Would* expresses desired or predictable results. In (e): The speaker is expressing one possible result. *could* = *would be able to*; *could* expresses possible options.

❏ **Exercise 8. Looking at grammar.** (Charts 20-2 and 20-3)
Complete the sentences with the verbs in parentheses.

1. If I have enough apples, I (*bake*) _____will bake_____ an apple pie this afternoon.

2. If I had enough apples, I (*bake*) ___would bake / could bake___ an apple pie.

3. I will fix your bicycle if I (*have*) _____ a screwdriver of the proper size.

4. I would fix your bicycle if I (*have*) _____ a screwdriver of the proper size.

5. I (*go*) _____ to a movie tonight if I don't have any homework to do.

6. I (*go*) _____ to a movie tonight if I didn't have any homework to do.

7. Sally always answers the phone if she (*be*) _____ in her office.

8. Sally would answer the phone if she (*be*) _____ in her office right now.

❏ **Exercise 9. Let's talk.** (Chart 20-3)
Discuss the questions. Work in small groups or as a class.

Under what conditions, if any, would you . . .
1. exceed the speed limit while driving?
2. lie to your best friend?
3. disobey an order from your boss?
4. steal food?
5. carry a friend on your back?
6. not pay your rent?

❏ **Exercise 10. Looking at grammar.** (Charts 20-2 and 20-3)
Complete the sentences with the verbs in parentheses. Work in pairs or small groups.

1. I (*be, not*) _____ a student in this class if English (*be*) _____ my
   native language.

2. Most people know that oil floats on water. If you pour oil on water, it (*float*)

   _____ .

3. If there (be) _____ no oxygen on earth, life as we know it (exist, not) _____ .

4. My evening newspaper has been late every day this week. If the paper (arrive, not) _____ on time today, I'm going to cancel my subscription.

5. If I (be) _____ a bird, I (want, not) _____ to live my whole life in a cage.

6. How long (human beings, live) _____ _____ if all diseases in the world were completely eradicated?

7. If you boil water, it (disappear) _____ into the atmosphere as vapor.

8. If people (have) _____ paws instead of hands with fingers and opposable thumbs, the machines we use in everyday life (have to) _____ be constructed very differently. We (be, not) _____ able to turn knobs, push small buttons, or hold tools and utensils securely.

❏ **Exercise 11. Let's talk: interview.** (Chart 20-3)
Find a partner to interview. Give him/her a fact. Ask your partner to make an unreal "if" statement. Change roles after item 3. Share some of the statements with the class.

Example: Ocean water is salty.
→ *If ocean water weren't salty, people could drink it and there would be enough water for everyone in the world.*

Facts:
1. There is gravity on the earth.
2. People don't have wings.
3. Cars can't fly.
4. Children don't get everything they want.
5. Guns exist.
6. There isn't enough food on the earth for everyone.

❏ **Exercise 12. Warm-up.** (Chart 20-4)
Check (✓) the sentences that have a past meaning.

1. _____ If Ann were available, she would help us.
2. _____ If Ann had been available, she would have helped us.
3. _____ If Ann is available, she will help us.
4. _____ If Ann had been available, she could have helped us.

20-4 Untrue (Contrary to Fact) in the Past

(a) If you *had told* me about the problem, I *would have helped* you.	In (a): In truth, you did not tell me about it.
(b) If they *had studied*, they *would have passed* the exam.	In (b): In truth, they did not study. Therefore, they failed the exam.
(c) If I *hadn't slipped* on the stairs, I *wouldn't have broken* my arm.	In (c): In truth, I slipped on the stairs. I broke my arm.
	NOTE: The auxiliary verbs are often reduced in speech. "If you'd told me, I would've helped you (OR *I-duv* helped you)."*
COMPARE:	In (d): *would* expresses a desired or predictable result.
(d) If I had had enough money, I *would* have bought a car.	In (e): *could* expresses a possible option.
(e) If I had had enough money, I *could* have bought a car.	*could have bought* = *would have been able to buy*

*In casual, informal speech, some native speakers sometimes use *would have* in an *if*-clause: *If you **would've told** me about the problem, I would've helped you.* This verb form usage is generally considered to be grammatically incorrect in standard English, but it occurs fairly commonly.

❑ **Exercise 13. Looking at grammar.** (Chart 20-4)
Complete the sentences with a factual or truthful statement.

1. If I had worn a jacket, I wouldn't have been so cold at the park, but the truth is . . . .
   → *I didn't wear a jacket.*

2. If Martin hadn't become a soccer player, he would have been a soccer coach, but the truth is . . . .

3. If I hadn't answered my cell phone while I was driving, I wouldn't have caused the accident, but the truth is . . . .

4. If Professor Stevens had given a fair test, more students would have passed, but the truth is . . . .

❑ **Exercise 14. Looking at grammar.** (Charts 20-1 → 20-4)
<u>Underline</u> the clause that expresses a condition. Write "T" if the condition is a true condition (i.e., a condition that exists in fact). Write "U" if the condition is untrue (i.e., a condition that does not exist in fact). Then decide if the sentence refers to present/future or past time.

1. __T__ <u>If the weather is warm</u>, we'll eat outdoors.   (present/future)   past

2. __U__ <u>If the weather were warm</u>, we would eat outdoors.   (present/future)   past

3. _____ If the weather had been warm, we would have
          eaten outdoors.   present/future   past

4. _____ If I had more money, I would work less.   present/future   past

5. _____ If I had had more money, I would have worked less.   present/future   past

6. _____ If I take time off from work, I feel more relaxed.   present/future   past

7. _____ If I hadn't had to work, I could have seen you.   present/future   past

8. _____ If I didn't have to work, I could see you.   present/future   past

❏ **Exercise 15. Looking at grammar.** (Charts 20-1 → 20-4)
Complete each sentence with **would do, will do,** or **would have done.**

1. Rita believes in hard work and wants her children to work hard. She always tells them,

    "If you work hard every day, you _____ well."

2. Scott is smart, but he doesn't work very hard. As a result, he is not very successful at

    his job. His co-workers often tell him, "If you worked hard every day, you

    _____ well."

3. Mark planned to study hard for a test yesterday, but some friends called, and he decided to

    go out with them. He didn't do well on his test the next day. His teacher told him, "If you

    had worked hard yesterday, you _____ well on the test."

❏ **Exercise 16. Looking at grammar.** (Charts 20-1 → 20-4)
Complete the sentences with the verbs in parentheses.

1. If I (*have*) _____ enough money, I will go with you.

2. If I (*have*) _____ enough money, I would go with you.

3. If I (*have*) _____ enough money, I would have gone with you.

4. If the weather is nice tomorrow, we (*go*) _____ to the zoo.

5. If the weather were nice today, we (*go*) _____ to the zoo.

6. If the weather had been nice yesterday, we (*go*) _____ to the zoo.

7. If Sally (*be*) _____ at home tomorrow, I am going to visit her.

8. Jim isn't home right now. If he (*be*) _____ at home

    right now, I (*visit*) _____ him.

9. Linda wasn't at home yesterday. If she (*be*)

    _____ at home yesterday, I (*visit*)

    _____ her.

10. Last night Alex ruined his sweater when he washed it.

    If he (*read*) _____ the label, he (*wash, not*)

    _____ it in hot water.

Exercise 17. Looking at grammar. (Charts 20-1 → 20-4)
Answer the questions with *yes* or *no*.

1. If the weather had been good yesterday, we would not have canceled the picnic.

    a. Was the picnic canceled? ____yes____

    b. Was the weather good? ____no____

2. If I had an envelope and a stamp, I would mail this letter today.

    a. Do I have an envelope and a stamp right now? _____

    b. Do I want to mail this letter today? _____

    c. Am I going to mail this letter today? _____

3. Ann would have made it to class on time this morning if the bus hadn't been late.

    a. Did Ann try to make it to class on time? _____

    b. Did Ann make it to class on time? _____

    c. Was the bus late? _____

4. If I didn't have any friends, I would be lonely.

    a. Am I lonely? _____

    b. Do I have friends? _____

❑ **Exercise 18. Let's talk.** (Chart 20-4)
Work with a partner. Speaker A gives the cue. Speaker B begins the response with ***But if I had known***.

Example:
SPEAKER A (*book open*):   There was a test yesterday. You didn't know that, so you didn't study.
SPEAKER B (*book closed*):   But if I had known (that there was a test yesterday), I would have studied.

1. Your friend was in the hospital. You didn't know that, so you didn't visit her.
2. I've never met your friend. You didn't know that, so you didn't introduce me.
3. There was a meeting last night. You didn't know that, so you didn't go.
4. Your friend's parents are in town. You didn't know that, so you didn't invite them to dinner.

Change roles.
5. I wanted to go to the soccer game. You didn't know that, so you didn't buy a ticket for me.
6. I was at home last night. You didn't know that, so you didn't visit me.
7. Your sister wanted a gold necklace for her birthday. You didn't know that, so you didn't buy her one.
8. I had a problem. You didn't know that, so you didn't offer to help.

❑ **Exercise 19. Let's listen and talk.** (Chart 20-4)

Part I. Answer this question: Why do you think dinosaurs became extinct? Then close your book and listen to the short talk on dinosaurs.

CD 2
Track 32

Part II. Open your book and read the statements. Circle "T" for true and "F" for false.

1. According to one theory, if an asteroid had collided with the earth, several disastrous changes in the earth's climate would have taken place.　　　T　　F

2. This theory suggests that if an asteroid had not collided with the earth, dinosaurs would still exist.　　　T　　F

Part III. Discuss these questions.

1. If dinosaurs still existed, what do you think the world would be like?
2. Would it be possible for dinosaurs and human beings to coexist on the same planet?

❑ **Exercise 20. Listening.** (Charts 20-1 → 20-4)

In conditional sentences, /h/ is often dropped in the auxiliary verbs *have* and *had*. Listen to the sentences spoken in casual, relaxed English. Complete the sentences with the non-reduced forms of the words you hear.

CD 2
Track 33

SITUATION: Jon told several good friends a lie, and they recently found out. Here are their reactions:

Example: You will hear: If he had been truthful, he wouldn't have lost my trust.
　　　　　　You will write: _____*If he had been*_____ truthful, _____*he wouldn't have lost*_____ my trust.

1. _____ the truth sooner, _____ differently.

2. _____ him, _____ so foolish.

3. _____ me what a great guy Jon was, _____

_____ him so easily.

4. _____ another person, _____ so shocked.

5. _____ , _____ more respect for him.

❑ **Exercise 21. Looking at grammar.** (Charts 20-1 → 20-4)
Complete the sentences with the verbs in parentheses.

1. You should tell your father exactly what happened. If I (*be*) _____ you, I (*tell*) _____ him the truth as soon as possible.

2. If I (*have*) _____ my camera with me yesterday, I (*take*) _____ _____ a picture of Alex standing on his head.

3. I'm almost ready to plant my garden. I have a lot of seeds. Maybe I have more than I need. If I (*have*) _____ more seeds than I need, I (*give*) _____ some to my neighbor.

4. George has only two pairs of socks. If he (*have*) _____ more than two pairs of socks, he (*have to, not*) _____ wash his socks so often.

5. The cowboy pulled his gun to shoot at the rattlesnake, but he was too late. If he (*be*) _____ quicker to pull the trigger, the snake (*bite, not*) _____ _____ him on the foot. It's a good thing he was wearing heavy leather boots.

6. What (*we, use*) _____ to look at ourselves when we comb our hair if we (*have, not*) _____ mirrors?

7. It's been a long drought. It hasn't rained for over a month. If it (*rain, not*) _____ soon, a lot of crops (*die*) _____. If the crops (*die*) _____, many people (*go*) _____ hungry this coming winter.

8. A: Shhh! Your father is taking a nap. Uh-oh. You woke him up.

   B: Gee, I'm sorry, Mom. If I (*realize*) _____ he was sleeping, I (*make, not*) _____ so much noise when I came in.

9. A: Since I broke my foot, I haven't been able to get to the basement to wash my clothes.

   B: Why didn't you say something? I (*come*) _____ over and (*wash*) _____ them for you if you (*tell*) _____ me.

   A: I know you (*come*) _____ right away if I (*call*) _____ you. I guess I didn't want to bother you.

   B: Nonsense! What are good neighbors for?

Exercise 22. Listening. (Charts 20-1 → 20-4)

Listen to the statements and answer the questions.

Example: You will hear: If Bob had asked me to keep the news about his marriage a secret, I wouldn't have told anybody. I know how to keep a secret.

You will answer: a. Did I tell anybody the news?   ___*yes*___

b. Did Bob ask me to keep it a secret?   ___*no*___

1. a. Am I going to go to the art museum?   _____

b. Do I have enough time?   _____

2. a. Did Mrs. Jones receive immediate medical attention?   _____

b. Did she die?   _____

3. a. Am I a carpenter?   _____

b. Do I want to build my own house?   _____

c. Am I going to build my own house?   _____

4. a. Was the hotel built to withstand an earthquake?   _____

b. Did the hotel collapse?   _____

❏ **Exercise 23. Looking at grammar.** (Charts 20-1 → 20-4)

Complete each sentence with an appropriate auxiliary verb.

1. I don't have a pen, but if I _____*did*_____, I would lend it to you.

2. He is busy right now, but if he _____*weren't*_____, he would help us.

3. I didn't vote in the election, but if I _____*had*_____, I would have voted for Senator Todd.

4. I don't have enough money, but if I _____, I would buy that book.

5. The weather is cold today, but if it _____, I'd go swimming.

6. She didn't come, but if she _____, she would have met my brother.

7. I'm not a good cook, but if I _____, I would make all of my own meals.

8. He didn't go to a doctor, but if he _____, the cut on his hand wouldn't have gotten infected.

9. I always pay my bills. If I _____, I'd get in a lot of trouble.

10. Helium is lighter than air. If it _____, a helium-filled balloon wouldn't float upward.

11. I called my husband to tell him I would be late. If I _____, he would have gotten worried about me.

❑ **Exercise 24. Let's talk: pairwork.** (Charts 20-1 → 20-4)
Work with a partner. Speaker A asks the questions. Speaker B begins the answers with
No, but.

Example:
SPEAKER A (*book open*):   Do you have a dollar?
SPEAKER B (*book closed*):   No, but if I did (No, but if I had a dollar), I would lend it to you.

Change roles.

1. Are you rich?
2. Do you have a car?
3. Are you a bird?
4. Did you forget to bring a pen to class today?
5. Do you have your own airplane?
6. Are you the teacher of this class?

7. Are you at home right now?
8. Do you speak (*another language*)?
9. Did you forget to bring your grammar book to class today?
10. Is the weather hot/cold today?
11. Do you live in (*a different city*)?
12. Are you hungry?

❑ **Exercise 25. Warm-up.** (Chart 20-5)
Match the true or factual sentences in Column A to the conditional sentences in Column B.

Column A

1. I was painting my apartment when you asked me to go to a movie.
2. I am painting my apartment right now.

Column B

a. If I weren't painting my apartment, I would go to a movie with you.
b. If I hadn't been painting my apartment, I would have gone to a movie with you.

20-5 Using Progressive Verb Forms in Conditional Sentences

Notice the use of progressive verb forms in these examples. Even in conditional sentences, progressive verb forms are used in progressive situations. (See Chart 1-2, p. 3, for a discussion of progressive verbs.)

(a)	True:	It *is raining* right now, so I *will not go* for a walk.
(b)	Conditional:	If it ***were not raining*** right now, I *would go* for a walk.
(c)	True:	It *was raining* yesterday afternoon, so I *did not go* for a walk.
(d)	Conditional:	If it ***had not been raining,*** I *would have gone* for a walk.

❑ **Exercise 26. Looking at grammar.** (Chart 20-5)
Change the statements to conditional sentences.

1. You weren't listening, so you didn't understand the directions. But . . . .
   → *if you had been listening, you would have understood the directions.*
2. You aren't wearing a coat, so you're cold. But . . . .
3. Joe got a ticket because he was driving too fast. But . . . .
4. I'm enjoying myself, so I won't leave. But . . . .
5. You were sleeping, so I didn't tell you the news as soon as I heard it. But . . . .

□ **Exercise 27. Looking at grammar.** (Chart 20-5)
Complete each sentence with the correct form of the verb in parentheses. Make untrue or contrary-to-fact statements.

1. It's snowing. We can't go to the park.

    If it (*snow*) _____*weren't snowing*_____, we could go to the park.

2. It wasn't snowing. We went to the park.

    If it (*snow*) _____*had been snowing*_____,
    we wouldn't have gone to the park.

3. Elena just got out of the shower. She's
    drying her hair with a hair dryer, so she can't
    hear the phone ring.

    If Elena (*dry*) _____
    her hair, she could hear the phone ring.

4. Elena was waiting for a phone call from Tom, but as it happened, she was drying her hair when he called and couldn't hear the phone ring.

    If Elena (*dry*) _____ her hair when Tom called, she could have heard the phone ring.

5. Max is at a party at his friend's apartment, but he's not having any fun. He wants to leave.

    Max wouldn't want to leave early if he (*have*) _____ fun.

6. Mrs. Chang was talking on her cell phone while she was driving and wasn't paying enough attention to traffic. When the car in front of her stopped, she crashed into it.

    If Mrs. Chang (*talk*) _____ on her cell phone, she probably wouldn't have gotten into an accident.

□ **Exercise 28. Warm-up.** (Chart 20-6)
Choose the correct time words.

1. If I had done my homework (*now / earlier*), I would know the answers (*now / earlier*).

2. Anita wouldn't be sick (*now / earlier*) if she had followed the doctor's orders (*now / earlier*).

20-6 Using "Mixed Time" in Conditional Sentences

Frequently the time in the *if*-clause and the time in the result clause are different: one clause may be in the present and the other in the past. Notice that past and present times are mixed in these sentences.

(a) True:	I *did not eat* breakfast several hours ago, so I *am* hungry now.	
(b) Conditional:	If I *had eaten* breakfast several hours ago, I *would not be* hungry now.	
	(past)	(present)
(c) True:	He *is not* a good student. He *did not study* for the test yesterday.	
(d) Conditional:	If he *were* a good student, he *would have studied* for the test yesterday.	
	(present)	(past)

□ **Exercise 29. Looking at grammar.** (Chart 20-6)
Change the statements to conditional sentences. Begin each one with ***But***.

1. I'm hungry now because I didn't eat dinner.
   → *But if I'd eaten dinner, I wouldn't be hungry now.*
2. The room is full of flies because you left the door open.
3. You are tired this morning because you didn't go to bed at a reasonable hour last night.
4. I didn't finish my report yesterday, so I can't begin a new project today.
5. I'm not you, so I didn't tell him the truth.
6. I don't know anything about plumbing, so I didn't fix the leak in the sink myself.
7. Anita got sick because she didn't follow the doctor's orders.

□ **Exercise 30. Warm-up.** (Chart 20-7)
The following sentences are correct. Make sentences with the same meaning using ***if***. Notice the order of the words in blue.

1. Were I the teacher, I would give fewer tests.
2. Had I known about your problem, I would have helped you.
3. Should anyone come, please tell them I'm asleep.

20-7 Omitting *If*	
(a) *Were I* you, I wouldn't do that. (b) *Had I known,* I would have told you. (c) *Should anyone call,* please take a message.	With ***were***, ***had*** (past perfect), and ***should***, sometimes ***if*** is omitted and the subject and verb are inverted. In (a): ***Were I you*** = *if I were you* In (b): ***Had I known*** = *if I had known* In (c): ***Should anyone call*** = *if anyone should call*

□ **Exercise 31. Looking at grammar.** (Chart 20-7)
Make sentences with the same meaning by omitting ***if***.

1. If you should need more money, go to the bank before six o'clock.
   → *Should you need more money, go to the bank before six o'clock.*
2. If I were you, I wouldn't do that.
3. If they had realized the danger, they would have done it differently.
4. If I were your teacher, I would insist you do better work.
5. If you should change your mind, please let me know immediately.
6. She would have gotten the job if she had been better prepared.
7. Your boss sounds like a real tyrant. If I were you, I would look for another job.
8. I'll be out of the office until June 12th. If you should need to reach me, I'll be at our company headquarters in Seoul.
9. The artists and creative thinkers throughout the history of the world have changed all of our lives. If they had not dared to be different, the history of civilization would have to be rewritten.
10. If there should be a global nuclear war, life on earth as we know it would end forever.

❏ **Exercise 32. Listening.** (Chart 20-7)

Choose the sentence that best expresses the meaning of the sentence you hear.

CD 2
Track 35

Example: You will hear: Should you need help, I'll be in the room next door.

You will choose: a. I'll be helping others in the room.
(b.) I'm available to help you.
c. You shouldn't ask me for help.
d. Do you need help from me?

1. a. I get a lot of speeding tickets.
   b. I was driving too fast.
   c. I like to drive fast.
   d. I didn't get a ticket.

2. a. You shouldn't call me on my cell.
   b. Did you have questions?
   c. Call me soon.
   d. Call me if you have questions.

3. a. We're glad you told us.
   b. We were happy to help you.
   c. We needed to know earlier.
   d. Why did you tell us so soon?

4. a. I took the fastest way to the theater.
   b. I didn't take the fastest way.
   c. The theater was too far away.
   d. I took several different routes.

5. a. We stayed home.
   b. We didn't stay home.
   c. Someone warned us.
   d. Several people warned us.

6. a. Are we rich?
   b. Rich people live in houses overlooking the ocean.
   c. We aren't rich.
   d. We live in a house overlooking the ocean.

❏ **Exercise 33. Warm-up.** (Chart 20-8)

Read the paragraph. Check (✓) the sentences that are true.

One night a fire started in Janet's apartment. A blanket on the sofa got too close to an electric heater. Janet was in a deep sleep and wasn't aware of the fire. Fortunately, her neighbors saw smoke coming out of the window and threw rocks at her bedroom window to wake her up. Janet was very grateful that she wasn't killed or injured in the fire.

1. _____ Janet would have kept sleeping, but the neighbors woke her up.

2. _____ Janet would have awakened without her neighbors' help.

3. _____ Janet was awakened by her neighbors; otherwise, she wouldn't have woken up.

20-8 Implied Conditions

(a) I *would have gone* with you, *but I had to study.* (b) I never *would have succeeded* without your help.	Often the *if*-clause is implied, not stated. Conditional verbs are still used in the result clause. In (a): the implied condition = *if I hadn't had to study* In (b): the implied condition = *if you hadn't helped me*
(c) She ran; *otherwise,* she *would have missed* her bus.	Conditional verbs are frequently used following ***otherwise.*** In (c), the implied *if*-clause = *if she had not run*

❑ **Exercise 34. Looking at grammar.** (Chart 20-8)
Identify the implied conditions by making sentences using *if*-clauses.

1. I would have visited you, but I didn't know that you were at home.
   → *I would have visited you if I had known you were at home.*
2. It wouldn't have been a good meeting without Rosa.
   → *It wouldn't have been a good meeting if Rosa hadn't been there.*
3. I would have answered the phone, but I didn't hear it ring.
4. I couldn't have finished the work without your help.
5. I like to travel. I would have gone to Nepal last summer, but I didn't have enough money.
6. I stepped on the brakes. Otherwise, I would have hit the child on the bicycle.
7. Olga turned down the volume on the CD player. Otherwise, the neighbors probably would have called to complain about the noise.
8. Tarek would have finished his education, but he had to quit school and find a job in order to support his family.

❑ **Exercise 35. Listening.** (Chart 20-8)
Choose the statement (a. or b.) that is true for each sentence you hear. In some cases both answers are correct.

CD 2
Track 36

Example: You will hear: I canceled your dentist appointment for Tuesday. Otherwise, you would have had two appointments in one day.
      You will choose: a. I thought you needed two appointments.
                    (b.) I didn't think you wanted two appointments.

1. a. If I had had your number, I would have called.
   b. I didn't have your number; otherwise, I would have called.

2. a. If my parents hadn't helped me, I wouldn't have gone to college.
   b. If I hadn't gone to college, my parents wouldn't have helped me.

3. a. I picked up your clothes.
   b. I wasn't able to pick up your clothes.

4. a. If someone had told us about the party, we would have come.
   b. We came to the party even though you didn't tell us about it.

5. a. If I'd had your advice, I would have known what to do.
   b. Because of your advice, I knew what to do.

❑ **Exercise 36. Looking at grammar.** (Charts 20-1 → 20-8)
Complete each sentence with the verb in parentheses. Some of the verbs are passive.

1. If I could speak Japanese, I (*spend*) _____ next year studying in Japan.

2. Had I known Mr. Jung was in the hospital, I (*send*) _____ him a note and some flowers.

3. We will move into our new house next month if it (*complete*) _____
   _____ by then.

4. It's too bad that it's snowing. If it (*snow, not*) _____, we could go for a drive.

5. I was very tired. Otherwise, I (*go*) _____ to the party with you last night.

6. I'm glad I have so many friends and such a wonderful family. Life without friends or family (*be*) _____ lonely for me.

7. If you (*sleep, not*) _____ last night when we arrived, I would have asked you to go with us, but I didn't want to wake you up.

8. Bill has such a bad memory that he (*forget*) _____ his head if it (*be, not*) _____ attached to his body.

9. A: What would you be doing right now if you (*be, not*) _____ in class?

   B: I (*sleep*) _____ .

10. A: Boy, is it ever hot today!

    B: You said it! If there (*be*) _____ only a breeze, it (*be, not*) _____ _____ quite so unbearable.

11. A: Hi. Sorry I'm late.

    B: That's okay.

    A: I (*be*) _____ here sooner, but I had car trouble.

12. A: Want to ride on the roller coaster?

    B: No way! I (*ride, not*) _____ on the roller coaster even if you paid me a million dollars!

13. A: Are you coming to the party?

    B: I don't think so, but if I change my mind, I (*tell*) _____ you.

❏ **Exercise 37. In your own words.** (Charts 20-1 → 20-8)
Complete the sentences with your own words, either orally or in writing. If written, add commas as necessary.

1. If it hadn't rained . . . .
2. If it weren't raining . . . .
3. You would have passed the test had . . . .
4. It's a good thing we took a map with us. Otherwise . . . .

5. Without electricity modern life . . . .

6. If you hadn't reminded me about the meeting tonight . . . .

7. Should you need any help . . . .

8. If I could choose any profession I wanted . . . .

9. If I were at home right now . . . .

10. Without your help yesterday . . . .

11. Were I you . . . .

12. What would you do if . . . .

13. If I had the chance to live my childhood over again . . . .

14. Had I known . . . .

15. Can you imagine what life would be like if . . . .

❏ **Exercise 38. Let's talk.** (Charts 20-1 → 20-8)
Explain what you would do in these circumstances. Work in pairs or small groups.

Example:
SPEAKER A (*book open*):   Suppose the student sitting next to you drops her pen.
                                    What would you do?
SPEAKER B (*book closed*):   I would pick it up for her.

1. Suppose/pretend there is a fire in this building right now. What would you do?

2. Suppose there is a fire in your room or apartment or house. You have time to save only one thing. What would you save?

3. Suppose you go to the bank to cash a check for (twenty dollars). The bank teller cashes your check and you leave, but when you count the money, you find she gave you (thirty dollars) instead of (twenty). What would you do?

4. Same situation, but she gave you only (fifteen dollars) instead of (twenty).

5. John was cheating during an examination. Suppose you were the teacher and you saw him. What would you have done?

6. You are at a party. A man starts talking to you, but he is speaking so fast that you can't catch what he is saying. What would you do?

7. Late at night you're driving your car down a deserted street. You're all alone. In an attempt to avoid a dog in the road, you swerve and hit a parked car. You know that no one saw you. What would you do?

8. Ricardo goes to a friend's house for dinner. His friend serves a dish that he can't stand/doesn't like at all. What if you were Ricardo?

9. Suppose you go to another city to visit a friend. You have never been there before. Your friend said he would meet you at the airport, but he's not there. You wait a long time, but he never shows up. You try to call him, but nobody answers the phone. Now what?

❏ **Exercise 39. Warm-up.** (Chart 20-9)
Which sentences are true for you? Circle *yes* or *no*. What do you notice about the words in blue?

1. I wish I were someplace else right now.	yes	no
2. I wish I could travel all around the world next year.	yes	no
3. I wish I had learned English when I was a child.	yes	no

20-9 Verb Forms Following *Wish*

Wish is used when the speaker wants reality to be different, to be exactly the opposite.

	"True" Statement	Verb Form Following *Wish*	*Wish* is followed by a noun clause. (See Chart 12-5, p. 253.) Past verb forms, similar to those in conditional sentences, are used in the noun clause.
A Wish about the Future	(a) She *will not tell* me. (b) He *isn't going to be* here. (c) She *can't come* tomorrow.	I *wish* (that) she *would tell* me. I *wish* he *were going to be* here. I *wish* she *could come* tomorrow.	For example, in (a): *would*, the past form of *will*, is used to make a wish about the future.
A Wish about the Present	(d) I *don't know* French. (e) It *is raining* right now. (f) I *can't speak* Japanese.	I *wish* I *knew* French. I *wish* it *weren't raining* right now. I *wish* I *could speak* Japanese.	In (d): the simple past (*knew*) is used to make a wish about the present.
A Wish about the Past	(g) John *didn't come.* (h) Mary *couldn't come.*	I *wish* John *had come.** I *wish* Mary *could have come.*	In (g): the past perfect (*had come*) is used to make a wish about the past.

*Sometimes in very informal speaking: *I wish John **would have** come.*

❑ **Exercise 40. Looking at grammar.** (Chart 20-9)
Complete the sentences with an appropriate verb form.

1. Our classroom doesn't have any windows. I wish our classroom _____*had*_____ windows.

2. The sun isn't shining. I wish the sun _____ right now.

3. I didn't go shopping. I wish I _____ shopping.

4. I don't know how to dance. I wish I _____ how to dance.

5. It's cold today. I'm not wearing a coat. I wish I _____ a coat.

6. I don't have enough money to buy that book. I wish I _____ enough money.

7. I can't go with you tomorrow, but I wish I _____.

8. My friend won't ever lend me his car. I wish he _____ me his car for my date tomorrow night.

9. Mrs. Takasawa isn't coming to dinner with us tonight. I wish she _____ _____ to dinner with us.

10. The teacher is going to give an exam tomorrow. I wish he _____ _____ us an exam tomorrow.

11. You can't meet my parents. I wish you _____ them, but they're out of town.

12. Khalid didn't come to the meeting. I wish he _____ to the meeting.

13. I'm not lying on a sunny beach. I wish I _____ on a sunny beach.

❑ **Exercise 41. Let's talk: interview.** (Chart 20-9)
Ask two classmates each question. Share some of their answers with the class.

1. What is something you can't do but you wish you could do?
2. What do you wish you were doing right now?
3. What is something you don't have but wish you had?
4. What is something that didn't happen yesterday but that you wish had happened?
5. What is something you don't know but wish you knew?
6. What is something that has never happened in your life but that you wish would happen?
7. What is something that happened in your life but that you wish had not happened?
8. What is something you have to do but wish you didn't have to do?
9. What is something that will not happen tomorrow but that you wish would happen?
10. What is something you were unable to do yesterday but you wish you could have done?

❑ **Exercise 42. Looking at grammar.** (Chart 20-9)
Complete the sentences with an appropriate auxiliary verb.

1. I'm not at home, but I wish I _____*were*_____ .

2. I don't know her, but I wish I _____*did*_____ .

3. I can't sing well, but I wish I _____*could*_____ .

4. I didn't go, but I wish I _____*had*_____ .

5. He won't talk about it, but I wish he _____*would*_____ .

6. I didn't read that book, but I wish I _____ .

7. I want to go, but I can't. I wish I _____ .

8. I don't have a bicycle, but I wish I _____ .

9. He didn't buy a ticket to the game, but he wishes he _____ .

10. It probably won't happen, but I wish it _____ .

11. He isn't old enough to drive a car, but he wishes he _____ .

12. They didn't go to the movie, but they wish they _____ .

13. I don't have a driver's license, but I wish I _____ .

14. I'm not living in an apartment, but I wish I _____ .

❑ **Exercise 43. Warm-up.** (Chart 20-10)
Choose the correct time word for each sentence. What do you notice about the verbs in blue and the tenses?

1. Jim's neighbors play loud music. He wishes they were quieter (*now* / *soon*).
2. Jim's neighbors are going to move. He wishes they would move (*soon* / *last week*).

20-10 Using *Would* to Make Wishes about the Future

(a) It is raining. I *wish* it *would stop*. (*I want it to stop raining.*) (b) I'm expecting a call. I *wish* the phone *would ring*. (*I want the phone to ring.*)	***Would*** is usually used to indicate that the speaker wants something to happen or someone other than the speaker to do something in the future. The wish may or may not come true (be realized).
(c) It's going to be a good party. I *wish* you *would come*. (d) We're going to be late. I *wish* you *would hurry*.	In (c) and (d): ***I wish you would*** . . . is often used to make a request.

❏ **Exercise 44. Looking at grammar.** (Charts 20-9 and 20-10)
Use the given information to answer each pair of questions. Use ***wish*** + ***would***.

Example:
TOM: Why are you watching the telephone?
SUE: I'm waiting to hear from Sam. I want him to call me. I need to talk to him right now. We had an argument. I need to make sure everything's okay.

    (a) What does Sue want to happen in the near future?
      → *She **wishes** the phone **would** ring.*
    (b) What else does Sue wish?
      → *She **wishes** Sam **would** call her. She wishes she could talk to Sam right now. She probably wishes she and Sam hadn't had an argument.*

1. ANNA: Can't you come to the concert? Please change your mind. I'd really like you to come.

   YOKO: No, I can't. I have to work.

    (a) What does Anna want Yoko to do?
    (b) What else does Anna wish?

2. Helen is a neat and orderly person. Judy, her roommate, is messy. Judy never picks up after herself. She leaves dirty dishes in the sink. She drops her clothes all over the apartment. She never makes her bed. Helen nags Judy to pick up after herself.

    (a) What does Helen want Judy to do?
    (b) What does Judy probably wish?

❏ **Exercise 45. Listening.** (Charts 20-9 and 20-10)
Listen to the sentences spoken in casual, relaxed English. Complete the sentences with the non-reduced forms of the words you hear.

CD 2
Track 37

Example: You will hear: I wish I didn't need so much sleep. I could get so much more done in a day!
          You will write: I wish I _____*didn't need*_____ so much sleep.

1. Alice doesn't like her job as a nurse. She wishes _____

   to nursing school.

2. A: I wish _____ go to work today.

   B: So do I. I wish _____ a holiday.

3. We had a good time in the mountains over vacation. I wish _____ with us. If _____ with us, _____ a good time.

4. I know that something's bothering you. I wish _____ me what it is. Maybe I can help.

5. A: My feet are killing me! I wish _____ more comfortable shoes.

   B: Yeah, me too. I wish _____ that we were going to have to walk this much.

❑ **Exercise 46. Let's talk.** (Charts 20-9 and 20-10)
Answer the questions. Use *wish*. Work in pairs, in small groups, or as a class.

1. Where do you wish you were right now? What do you wish you were doing?
2. Are you pleased with the weather today, or do you wish it were different?
3. Look around this room. What do you wish were different?
4. Is there anything you wish were different about the place you are living?
5. What do you wish were different about this city/town?
6. What do you wish were different about this country?
7. What do you wish were different about a student's life? about a worker's life?
8. Your friend gave you his phone number, but you didn't write it down because you thought you would remember it. Now you have forgotten the number. What do you wish?
9. You didn't eat breakfast/lunch/dinner before you came to class. Now you are hungry. What do you wish?
10. (_____) stayed up very late last night. Today she is tired and sleepy. What does she probably wish?

❑ **Exercise 47. Let's talk or write.** (Chapter 20)
Answer the questions, either orally or in writing. If orally, work in pairs, in small groups, or as a class.

1. If you could have free service for the rest of your life from a chauffeur, cook, housekeeper, or gardener, which would you choose? Why?
2. If you had to leave your country and build a new life, where would you go? Why?
3. If you had control of all medical research in the world and, by concentrating funds and efforts, could find the cure for only one disease in the next 25 years, which disease would you select? Why?
4. You have promised to spend an evening with your best friend. Then you discover you have the chance to spend the evening with (*name of a famous person*). Your friend is not invited. What would you do? Why?
5. Assume that you have a good job. If your boss told you to do something that you think is wrong, would you do it? Why or why not? (You understand that if you don't do it, you will lose your job.)
6. If you had to choose among perfect health, a loving family, and wealth (and you could have only one of the three during the rest of your life), which would you choose? Why?

Appendix
Supplementary Grammar Charts

UNIT A: Basic Grammar Terminology

A-1 Subjects, Verbs, and Objects

(a)   **S**   **V**
     Birds *fly.*
    (noun) (verb)
	Almost all English sentences contain a subject (**S**) and a verb (**V**). The verb may or may not be followed by an object (**O**).

(b)   The *baby* *cried.*
       S   **V**
       (noun)   (verb)
	VERBS: Verbs that are not followed by an object, as in (a) and (b), are called "intransitive verbs."
	
	 Common intransitive verbs: *agree, arrive, come, cry, exist, go, happen, live, occur, rain, rise, sleep, stay, walk.*

(c)   The *student* *needs* a *pen.*
       S   **V**   **O**
       (noun)   (verb)   (noun)
	Verbs that are followed by an object, as in (c) and (d), are called "transitive verbs."
	
	 Common transitive verbs: *build, cut, find, like, make, need, send, use, want.*

(d)   My *friend* *enjoyed* the *party.*
       S   **V**   **O**
       (noun)   (verb)   (noun)
	Some verbs can be either intransitive or transitive.
	    Intransitive: *A student studies.*
	    Transitive: *A student studies books.*

	SUBJECTS AND OBJECTS: The subjects and objects of verbs are nouns (or pronouns). Examples of nouns: *person, place, thing, John, Asia, pen, information, appearance, amusement.*

A-2 Adjectives

(a)   Ann is an ***intelligent*** *student.*
             (adjective)   (noun)
 	
 (b)   The ***hungry*** *child* ate fruit.
        (adjective) (noun)
	Adjectives describe nouns. In grammar, we say that adjectives modify nouns. The word *modify* means "change a little." Adjectives give a little different meaning to a noun: *intelligent student, lazy student, good student.*
	
	 Examples of adjectives: *young, old, rich, beautiful, brown, French, modern.*

(c) I saw some ***beautiful*** *pictures.* *INCORRECT:* beautiful~~s~~ pictures	An adjective is neither singular nor plural. A final **-s** is never added to an adjective.

A-3 Adverbs

(a) He walks *quickly*. 　　　　　(adverb) (b) She opened the door *quietly*. 　　　　　　　　　　　　(adverb)	Adverbs modify verbs. Often they answer the question "How?" In (a): *How does he walk?* Answer: *Quickly.* Adverbs are often formed by adding **-ly** to an adjective. 　　Adjective: *quick* 　　Adverb:　 *quickly*
(c) I am *extremely happy*. 　　　(adverb)　(adjective)	Adverbs are also used to modify adjectives, i.e., to give information about adjectives, as in (c).
(d) Ann will come *tomorrow*. 　　　　　　　　　(adverb)	Adverbs are also used to express time or frequency. Examples: *tomorrow, today, yesterday, soon, never, usually, always, yet.*
MIDSENTENCE ADVERBS: (e) Ann *always comes* on time. (f) Ann *is always* on time. (g) Ann *has always come* on time. (h) *Does she always come* on time?	Some adverbs may occur in the middle of a sentence. Midsentence adverbs have usual positions; they • come in front of simple present and simple past verbs (except **be**), as in (e); • follow **be** (simple present and simple past), as in (f); • come between a helping verb and a main verb, as in (g). In a question, a midsentence adverb comes directly after the subject, as in (h).

Common midsentence adverbs

ever	usually	generally	seldom	never	already
always	often	sometimes	rarely	not ever	finally
	frequently	occasionally	hardly ever		just
					probably

A-4 Prepositions and Prepositional Phrases

Common prepositions

about	at	beyond	into	since	up
above	before	by	like	through	upon
across	behind	despite	near	throughout	with
after	below	down	of	till	within
against	beneath	during	off	to	without
along	beside	for	on	toward(s)	
among	besides	from	out	under	
around	between	in	over	until	

S　　　**V**　　**PREP**　**O of PREP** (a) The 'student' 'studies' 'in' the 'library.' 　　　　　　　　　　　　　　　　(noun) 　　　　**S**　　**V**　　　　**O**　**PREP**　**O of PREP** (b) 'We' 'enjoyed' the 'party' 'at' your 'house.' 　　　　　　　　　　　　　　　　　　　(noun)	An important element of English sentences is the prepositional phrase. It consists of a preposition (**PREP**) and its object (**O**). The object of a preposition is a noun or pronoun. In (a): ***in the library*** is a prepositional phrase.
(c) We went　　*to the zoo*　　*in the afternoon*. 　　　　　　　　(Place)　　　　　　(Time) (d) *In the afternoon,* we went to the zoo.	In (c): In most English sentences, "place" comes before "time." In (d): Sometimes a prepositional phrase comes at the beginning of a sentence.

A-5 The Verb *Be*

(a) John *is* **a student**.
     (be)   (noun)
 	
(b) John *is* **intelligent**.
     (be) (adjective)
 	
(c) John *was* **at the library**.
     (be)   (prep. phrase)
	A sentence with **be** as the main verb has three basic patterns:
	   In (a): **be** + a noun
	   In (b): **be** + an adjective
	   In (c): **be** + a prepositional phrase

(d) Mary *is* writing a letter. (e) They *were* listening to some music. (f) That letter *was* written by Alice.	**Be** is also used as an auxiliary verb in progressive verb tenses and in the passive. In (d): **is** = auxiliary; **writing** = main verb

Tense Forms of *Be*

	SIMPLE PRESENT	SIMPLE PAST	PRESENT PERFECT
Singular	*I am* *you are* *he, she, it is*	*I was* *you were* *he, she, it was*	*I have been* *you have been* *he, she, it has been*
Plural	*we, you, they are*	*we, you, they were*	*we, you, they have been*

A-6 Linking Verbs

(a) The soup *smells* *good*. (linking verb) (adjective) (b) This food *tastes delicious*. (c) The children *feel happy*. (d) The weather *became cold*.	Other verbs like **be** that may be followed immediately by an adjective are called "linking verbs." An adjective following a linking verb describes the subject of a sentence.* Common verbs that may be followed by an adjective: • *feel, look, smell, sound, taste* • *appear, seem* • *become* (and *get, turn, grow* when they mean "become")

*COMPARE:
(1) *The man looks angry.* → An adjective (**angry**) follows **look**. The adjective describes the subject (**the man**). **Look** has the meaning of "appear."
(2) *The man looked at me angrily.* → An adverb (**angrily**) follows **look at**. The adverb describes the action of the verb. **Look at** has the meaning of "regard, watch."

Ann *is* **at the laudromat**.
She *looks* very *busy*.

UNIT B: Questions

B-1 Forms of Yes/No and Information Questions

A yes/no question = a question that may be answered by *yes* or *no*

A: Does he live in Chicago?
B: Yes, he does. OR No, he doesn't.

An information question = a question that asks for information by using a question word

A: Where does he live?
B: In Chicago.

Question word order = (*Question word*) + *helping verb* + *subject* + *main verb*

Notice that the same subject-verb order is used in both yes/no and information questions.

(Question Word)	Helping Verb	Subject	Main Verb	(Rest of Sentence)	
(a) (b) Where	Does does	she she	live live?	there?	If the verb is in the simple present, use **does** (with *he, she, it*) or **do** (with *I, you, we, they*) in the question. If the verb is simple past, use **did**. Notice: The main verb in the question is in its simple form; there is no final **-s** or **-ed**.
(c) (d) Where	Do do	they they	live live?	there?	
(e) (f) Where	Did did	he he	live live?	there?	
(g) (h) Where	Is is	he he	living living?	there?	If the verb has an auxiliary (a helping verb), the same auxiliary is used in the question. There is no change in the form of the main verb. If the verb has more than one auxiliary, only the first auxiliary precedes the subject, as in (m) and (n).
(i) (j) Where	Have have	they they	lived lived?	there?	
(k) (l) Where	Can can	Mary Mary	live live?	there?	
(m) (n) Where	Will will	he he	be living be living?	there?	
(o) Who (p) Who	Ø can	Ø Ø	lives come?	there?	If the question word is the subject, usual question-word order is not used; **does, do,** and **did** are not used. The verb is in the same form in a question as it is in a statement. Statement: *Tom came.* Question: *Who came?*
(q) (r) Where	Are are	they they?	Ø Ø	there?	Main verb **be** in the simple present (*am, is, are*) and simple past (*was, were*) precedes the subject. It has the same position as a helping verb.
(s) (t) Where	Was was	Jim Jim?	Ø Ø	there?	

B-2 Question Words

	Question	Answer	
When	(a) *When* did they arrive? *When* will you come?	Yesterday. Next Monday.	*When* is used to ask questions about *time*.
Where	(b) *Where* is she? *Where* can I find a pen?	At home. In that drawer.	*Where* is used to ask questions about *place*.
Why	(c) *Why* did he leave early? *Why* aren't you coming with us?	Because he's ill. I'm tired.	*Why* is used to ask questions about *reason*.
How	(d) *How* did you come to school? *How* does he drive?	By bus. Carefully.	*How* generally asks about *manner*.
	(e) *How much* money does it cost? *How many* people came?	Ten dollars. Fifteen.	*How* is used with **much** and **many**.
	(f) *How old* are you? *How cold* is it? *How soon* can you get here? *How fast* were you driving?	Twelve. Ten below zero. In ten minutes. 50 miles an hour.	*How* is also used with adjectives and adverbs.
	(g) *How long* has he been here? *How often* do you write home? *How far* is it to Miami from here?	Two years. Every week. 500 miles.	*How long* asks about *length of time*. *How often* asks about *frequency*. *How far* asks about *distance*.
Who	(h) *Who* can answer that question? *Who* came to visit you?	I can. Jane and Eric.	*Who* is used as the subject of a question. It refers to people.
	(i) *Who* is coming to dinner tonight? *Who* wants to come with me?	Ann, Bob, and Al. We do.	*Who* is usually followed by a singular verb even if the speaker is asking about more than one person.
Whom	(j) *Who(m)* did you see? *Who(m)* are you visiting? (k) *Who(m)* should I talk *to*? *To whom* should I talk? (formal)	I saw George. My relatives. The secretary.	*Whom* is used as the object of a verb or preposition. In everyday spoken English, **whom** is rarely used; **who** is used instead. *Whom* is used only in formal questions. NOTE: **Whom**, not **who**, is used if preceded by a preposition.
Whose	(l) *Whose* book did you borrow? *Whose* key is this? (*Whose* is this?)	David's. It's mine.	*Whose* asks questions about *possession*.

(continued)

	Question	Answer	
What	(m) *What* made you angry? *What* went wrong?	His rudeness. Everything.	*What* is used as the subject of a question. It refers to things.
	(n) *What* do you need? *What* did Alice buy?	I need a pencil. A book.	*What* is also used as an object.
	(o) *What* did he talk *about*? *About what* did he talk? (formal)	His vacation.	
	(p) *What kind of* soup is that? *What kind of* shoes did he buy?	It's bean soup. Sandals.	*What kind of* asks about the particular variety or type of something.
	(q) *What did* you *do* last night? *What is* Mary *doing*?	I studied. Reading a book.	*What* + *a form of* *do* is used to ask questions about activities.
	(r) *What countries* did you visit? *What time* did she come? *What color* is his hair?	Italy and Spain. Seven o'clock. Dark brown.	*What* may accompany a noun.
	(s) *What is* Ed *like*?	He's kind and friendly.	*What* + *be like* asks for a general description of qualities.
	(t) *What is* the weather *like*?	Hot and humid.	
	(u) *What does* Ed *look like*?	He's tall and has dark hair.	*What* + *look like* asks for a physical description.
	(v) *What does* her house *look like*?	It's a two-story,* red brick house.	
Which	(w) I have two pens. *Which pen* do you want? ⎫ *Which one* do you want? ⎬ *Which do* you want? ⎭	The blue one.	*Which* is used instead of *what* when a question concerns choosing from a definite, known quantity or group.
	(x) *Which book* should I buy?	That one.	
	(y) *Which countries* did he visit? *What countries* did he visit?	Peru and Chile.	In some cases, there is little difference in meaning between *which* and *what* when they accompany a noun, as in (y) and (z).
	(z) *Which class* are you in? *What class* are you in?	This class.	

*American English: *a two-**story** house.*
British English: *a two-**storey** house.*

B-3 Shortened Yes/No Questions

(a) *Going to bed now?* = *Are you going to bed now?* (b) *Finish your work?* = *Did you finish your work?* (c) *Want to go to the movie with us?* = *Do you want to go to the movie with us?*	Sometimes in spoken English, the auxiliary and the subject *you* are dropped from a yes/no question, as in (a), (b), and (c).

B-4 Negative Questions

(a) *Doesn't she live* in the dormitory? (b) *Does she not live* in the dormitory? (very formal)	In a yes/no question in which the verb is negative, usually a contraction (e.g., *does* + *not* = *doesn't*) is used, as in (a). Example (b) is very formal and is usually not used in everyday speech. Negative questions are used to indicate the speaker's idea (i.e., what she/he believes is or is not true) or attitude (e.g., surprise, shock, annoyance, anger).
(c) Bob returns to his dorm room after his nine o'clock class. Matt, his roommate, is there. Bob is surprised. Bob says, "*What are you doing here? Aren't you supposed to be in class now?*"	In (c): Bob believes that Matt is supposed to be in class now. *Expected answer:* **Yes**.
(d) Alice and Mary are at home. Mary is about to leave on a trip, and Alice is going to take her to the airport. Alice says, "*It's already two o'clock. We'd better leave for the airport. Doesn't your plane leave at three?*"	In (d): Alice believes that Mary's plane leaves at three. She is asking the negative question to make sure that her information is correct. *Expected answer:* **Yes**.
(e) The teacher is talking to Jim about a test he failed. The teacher is surprised that Jim failed the test because he usually does very well. The teacher says: "*What happened? Didn't you study?*"	In (e): The teacher believes that Jim did not study. *Expected answer:* **No**.
(f) Barb and Ron are riding in a car. Ron is driving. He comes to a corner where there is a stop sign, but he does not stop the car. Barb is shocked. Barb says, "*What's the matter with you? Didn't you see that stop sign?*"	In (f): Barb believes that Ron did not see the stop sign. *Expected answer:* **No**.

B-5 Tag Questions

(a) Jack *can* come, *can't* he? (b) Fred *can't* come, *can* he?	A tag question is a question added at the end of a sentence. Speakers use tag questions mainly to make sure their information is correct or to seek agreement.*

AFFIRMATIVE SENTENCE + NEGATIVE TAG → AFFIRMATIVE ANSWER EXPECTED

Mary *is* here,	*isn't* she?	Yes, she is.
You *like* tea,	*don't* you?	Yes, I do.
They *have left,*	*haven't* they?	Yes, they have.

NEGATIVE SENTENCE + AFFIRMATIVE TAG → NEGATIVE ANSWER EXPECTED

Mary *isn't* here,	*is* she?	No, she isn't.
You *don't like* tea,	*do* you?	No, I don't.
They *haven't left,*	*have* they?	No, they haven't.

(c) *This/That* is your book, isn't *it*? *These/Those* are yours, aren't *they*?	The tag pronoun for ***this/that*** = ***it***. The tag pronoun for ***these/those*** = ***they***.
(d) *There is* a meeting tonight, *isn't there*?	In sentences with ***there*** + ***be***, ***there*** is used in the tag.
(e) *Everything* is okay, isn't *it*? (f) *Everyone* took the test, didn't *they*?	Personal pronouns are used to refer to indefinite pronouns. ***They*** is usually used in a tag to refer to ***everyone***, ***everybody***, ***someone***, ***somebody***, ***no one***, ***nobody***.
(g) *Nothing is* wrong, *is* it? (h) *Nobody called* on the phone, *did* they? (i) You *'ve never been* there, *have* you?	Sentences with negative words take affirmative tags.
(j) *I am* supposed to be here, *am I not*? (k) *I am* supposed to be here, *aren't I*?	In (j): ***am I not?*** is formal English. In (k): ***aren't I?*** is common in spoken English.

*A tag question may be spoken:

   (1) with a rising intonation if the speaker is truly seeking to ascertain that his/her information, idea, belief is correct (e.g., *Ann lives in an apartment, doesn't she?*); OR

   (2) with a falling intonation if the speaker is expressing an idea with which she/he is almost certain the listener will agree (e.g., *It's a nice day today, isn't it?*).

Jim *could* use some help, *couldn't* he?

UNIT C: Contractions

C Contractions

IN SPEAKING: In everyday spoken English, certain forms of *be* and auxiliary verbs are usually contracted with pronouns, nouns, and question words.

IN WRITING: (1) In written English, contractions with pronouns are common in informal writing, but they're not generally acceptable in formal writing.

(2) Contractions with nouns and question words are, for the most part, rarely used in writing. A few of these contractions may be found in quoted dialogue in stories or in very informal writing, such as a chatty letter to a good friend, but most of them are rarely if ever written.

In the following, quotation marks indicate that the contraction is frequently spoken but rarely, if ever, written.

	With Pronouns	**With Nouns**	**With Question Words**
am	*I'm* reading a book.	Ø	*"What'm"* I supposed to do?
is	*She's* studying. *It's* going to rain.	My *"book's"* on the table. *Mary's* at home.	*Where's* Sally? *Who's* that man?
are	*You're* working hard. *They're* waiting for us.	My *"books're"* on the table. The *"teachers're"* at a meeting.	*"What're"* you doing? *"Where're"* they going?
has	*She's* been here for a year. *It's* been cold lately.	My *"book's"* been stolen! *Sally's* never met him.	*Where's* Sally been living? *What's* been going on?
have	*I've* finished my work. *They've* never met you.	The *"books've"* been sold. The *"students've"* finished the test.	*"Where've"* they been? *"How've"* you been?
had	*He'd* been waiting for us. *We'd* forgotten about it.	The *"books'd"* been sold. *"Mary'd"* never met him before.	*"Where'd"* you been before that? *"Who'd"* been there before you?
did	Ø	Ø	*"What'd"* you do last night? *"How'd"* you do on the test?
will	*I'll* come later. *She'll* help us.	The *"weather'll"* be nice tomorrow. *"John'll"* be coming soon.	*"Who'll"* be at the meeting? *"Where'll"* you be at ten?
would	*He'd* like to go there. *They'd* come if they could.	My *"friends'd"* come if they could. *"Mary'd"* like to go there too.	*"Where'd"* you like to go?

UNIT D: Negatives

D-1 Using *Not* and Other Negative Words

(a) AFFIRMATIVE: The earth is round. (b) NEGATIVE: The earth is *not* flat.	***Not*** expresses a *negative* idea.

AUX + *NOT* + MAIN VERB
(c) I *will*   *not*   *go*   there.
    I *have* *not* *gone* there.
    I *am*   *not* *going* there.
    I *was*   *not*   there.
    I *do*   *not*   *go*   there.
   He *does* *not*   *go*   there.
    I *did*   *not*   *go*   there.
	Not immediately follows an auxiliary verb or ***be***.
	
	NOTE: If there is more than one auxiliary, ***not*** comes immediately after the first auxiliary: *I **will not be** going there.*
	
	Do or ***does*** is used with ***not*** to make a simple present verb (except ***be***) negative.
	
	Did is used with ***not*** to make a simple past verb (except ***be***) negative.

Contractions of auxiliary verbs with *not*

are not = aren't*	has not = hasn't	was not = wasn't
cannot = can't	have not = haven't	were not = weren't
could not = couldn't	had not = hadn't	will not = won't
did not = didn't	is not = isn't	would not = wouldn't
does not = doesn't	must not = mustn't	
do not = don't	should not = shouldn't	

(d) I almost *never* go there.
    I have *hardly ever* gone there.
	In addition to *not*, the following are negative adverbs:
	   never, rarely, seldom
	   hardly (ever), scarcely (ever), barely (ever)

(e) There's *no* chalk in the drawer.	***No*** also expresses a negative idea.

COMPARE: *NOT* VS. *NO* (f) I *do not have* any money. (g) I have *no money*.	***Not*** is used to make a verb negative, as in (f). ***No*** is used as an adjective in front of a noun (e.g., *money*), as in (g). NOTE: Examples (f) and (g) have the same meaning.

*Sometimes in spoken English you will hear "ain't." It means "am not," "isn't," or "aren't." *Ain't* is not considered proper English, but many people use *ain't* regularly, and it is also frequently used for humor.

D-2 Avoiding Double Negatives

(a) INCORRECT: I ~~don't~~ have ~~no~~ money. (b) CORRECT: I *don't* have *any money*. CORRECT: I have *no money*.	Sentence (a) is an example of a "double negative," i.e., a confusing and grammatically incorrect sentence that contains two negatives in the same clause. One clause should contain only one negative.*

*Negatives in two different clauses in the same sentence cause no problems; for example:
   *A person who **doesn't** have love **can't** be truly happy.*
   *I **don't** know why he **isn't** here.*

D-3 Beginning a Sentence with a Negative Word

(a) *Never will I do* that again! (b) *Rarely have I eaten* better food. (c) *Hardly ever does he come* to class on time.	When a negative word begins a sentence, the subject and verb are inverted (i.e., question word order is used).*

*Beginning a sentence with a negative word is relatively uncommon in everyday usage; it is used when the speaker/writer wishes to emphasize the negative element of the sentence and be expressive.

UNIT E: Preposition Combinations

E Preposition Combinations with Adjectives and Verbs

A
be absent from
be accused of
be accustomed to
be acquainted with
be addicted to
be afraid of
agree with
be angry at, with
be annoyed with, by
apologize for
apply to, for
approve of
argue with, about
arrive in, at
be associated with
be aware of

B
believe in
blame for
be blessed with
be bored with, by

C
be capable of
care about, for
be cluttered with
be committed to
compare to, with
complain about, of
be composed of
be concerned about
be connected to
consist of
be content with
contribute to
be convinced of
be coordinated with
count (up)on
be covered with
be crowded with

D
decide (up)on
be dedicated to
depend (up)on
be devoted to
be disappointed in, with
be discriminated against
distinguish from
be divorced from
be done with

dream of, about
be dressed in

E
be engaged in, to
be envious of
be equipped with
escape from
excel in, at
be excited about
excuse for
be exhausted from
be exposed to

F
be faithful to
be familiar with
feel like
fight for
be filled with
be finished with
be fond of
forget about
forgive for
be friendly to, with
be frightened of, by
be furnished with

G
be gone from
be grateful to, for
be guilty of

H
hide from
hope for

I
be innocent of
insist (up)on
be interested in
introduce to
be involved in

J
be jealous of

K
keep from
be known for

L
be limited to
be located in
look forward to

M
be made of, from
be married to

O
object to
be opposed to

P
participate in
be patient with
be pleased with
be polite to
pray for
be prepared for
prevent from
prohibit from
be protected from
be proud of
provide with

Q
be qualified for

R
recover from
be related to
be relevant to
rely (up)on
be remembered for
rescue from
respond to
be responsible for

S
be satisfied with
be scared of, by
stare at
stop from
subscribe to
substitute for
succeed in

T
take advantage of
take care of
talk about, of
be terrified of, by
thank for
think about, of
be tired of, from

U
be upset with
be used to

V
vote for

W
be worried about

UNIT F: The Subjunctive in Noun Clauses

F Using the Subjunctive in Noun Clauses

(a) The teacher *demands* that we *be* on time.	A subjunctive verb uses the simple form of a verb. It does not have present, past, or future forms; it is neither singular nor plural.
(b) I *insisted* that he *pay* me the money.	
(c) I *recommended* that she *not go* to the concert.	Sentences with subjunctive verbs generally *stress importance or urgency.* A subjunctive verb is used in *that*-clauses that follow the verbs and expressions listed below.
(d) *It is important* that they *be told* the truth.	In (a): *be* is a subjunctive verb; its subject is *we*.
	In (b): *pay* (not *pays*, not *paid*) is a subjunctive verb; it is in its simple form, even though its subject (*he*) is singular.
	Negative: *not* + *simple form*, as in (c).
	Passive: *simple form of be* + *past participle*, as in (d).
(e) I *suggested* that she *see* a doctor.	*Should* is also possible after *suggest* and *recommend*.*
(f) I *suggested* that she *should see* a doctor.	

Common verbs and expressions followed by the subjunctive in a noun clause

advise (that)	propose (that)	it is critical (that)	it is important (that)
ask (that)	recommend (that)	it is essential (that)	it is necessary (that)
demand (that)	request (that)	it is imperative (that)	it is vital (that)
insist (that)	suggest (that)		

*The subjunctive is more common in American English than British English. In British English, ***should*** + *simple form* is more usual than the subjunctive: *The teacher **insists** that we **should be** on time.*

UNIT G: Troublesome Verbs

G Raise / Rise, Set / Sit, Lay / Lie

Transitive	Intransitive	
(a) *raise, raised, raised* Tom **raised** his hand.	(b) *rise, rose, risen* The sun **rises** in the east.	**Raise**, **set**, and **lay** are *transitive* verbs; they are followed by an object. **Rise**, **sit**, and **lie** are intransitive; they are NOT followed by an object.*
(c) *set, set, set* I **will set** the book on the desk.	(d) *sit, sat, sat* I **sit** in the front row.	In (a): **raised** is followed by the object **hand**. In (b): **rises** is not followed by an object.

(e) *lay, laid, laid*
I **am laying** the book on the desk.
	(f) *lie,** lay, lain*
	He **is lying** on his bed.
		NOTE: **Lay** and **lie** are troublesome for native speakers too and are frequently misused.
		    lay = put
		    lie = recline

*See Appendix Chart A-1 for information about transitive and intransitive verbs.

****Lie** is a regular verb (*lie, lied*) when it means "not tell the truth": *He **lied** to me about his age.*

Listening Script

Please note: You may want to pause the audio after each item or in longer passages so that there is enough time to complete each task.

Chapter 1: Overview of Verb Tenses

Exercise 4, p. 2.
1. I cooked my own dinner last night.
2. I bought a textbook yesterday.
3. I get on the internet every day.
4. I will be home tonight.
5. I am going to watch a movie this weekend.

Exercise 6, p. 3.
1. At midnight last night, I was sleeping.
2. Right now I am thinking about grammar.
3. Tomorrow I will be sitting in class at this time.
4. Tonight at 9:00, I will be watching TV.
5. Last night at 9:00, I was watching TV.

Exercise 8, p. 4.
1. I have done my homework already.
2. Before I went to bed last night, I had done all my homework.
3. By the time I finish this chapter, I will have done several verb exercises.
4. I have studied all the English verb tenses.
5. Before I began this class, I had studied all the English verb tenses.

Exercise 15, p. 9.
1. Hoped. We hoped to see you last week. Hoped.
2. Stopped. The rain finally stopped. Stopped.
3. Waiting. The taxi is waiting. Waiting.
4. Sitting. He's sitting in a taxi. Sitting.
5. Started. The movie started late. Started.
6. Happened. What happened yesterday? Happened.
7. Planning. We're planning a birthday party. Planning.
8. Enjoyed. We enjoyed our vacation. Enjoyed.
9. Worried. We worried about you. Worried.
10. Studying. I'm studying English. Studying.

Exercise 18, p. 12.
1. We are renting an apartment in the city.
2. We preferred to rent and see how we liked city life.
3. The earthquake destroyed the town.
4. Our children visited their grandparents.
5. We gained a little weight on our vacation.
6. I'm planning a short trip this summer.
7. I'm taking a few weeks off from work.
8. Right now I am replying to several emails.
9. I'm done. I replied to all of them.

Chapter 2: Present and Past; Simple and Progressive

Exercise 5, p. 15.
1. Hey, look out the window! It's raining . . .
2. We get a lot of rain here . . .
3. Besides the rain, it also snows here a little . . .
4. Did you hear? We can go skiing this weekend. It's snowing in the mountains . . .
5. We go hiking a lot. We especially like to hike in the mountains . . .
6. Our son is spending some time in the mountains . . .

Exercise 12, p. 22.
1. Did she lose her notebook?
2. Did she forget her homework?
3. Did she make a lot of mistakes on the writing test?
4. Did she write several words incorrectly?
5. Did she take another student's homework to copy?
6. Did he do his homework?
7. Did he understand the homework?
8. Did he bring his homework to class?
9. Did he get a good grade on the test?
10. Did he know all the answers on the test?
11. Did she begin class on time?
12. Did she speak clearly?
13. Did she give a fair test?
14. Did she spend extra time helping her students?
15. Did she tell her students jokes?
16. Did she teach her students a song?
17. Did she sing with her students?

Exercise 14, p. 23.
1. Did they swim in the water?
2. Did they stand in the waves?
3. Did they fall down in the waves?
4. Did they run barefoot on the sand?
5. Did they lie in the sun?
6. Did they wear sunscreen?
7. Did they dig in the sand?
8. Did they build giant sandcastles?
9. Did they write their names in the sand?
10. Did they draw pictures in the sand?
11. Did they hide their feet in the sand?
12. Did they sing songs?
13. Did some bees sting them?
14. Did they see the sunset?

Exercise 16, p. 24.
1. Did she wake up sick?
2. Did she catch a cold?
3. Did her head hurt?
4. Did she take her temperature?
5. Did she have a fever?
6. Did she feel bad?
7. Did she keep her pajamas on?
8. Did she lie on the couch?
9. Did she sleep for several hours?
10. Did she dream about scary things?
11. Did she eat some chicken soup?
12. Did she speak to the doctor?
13. Did she take some medicine?
14. Did she read the instructions on the label?

Exercise 18, p. 25.
1. Yesterday I felt . . .
2. Yesterday Mr. Jones taught . . .
3. Did you fill . . .
4. The children drew . . .
5. The man hid . . .
6. One student withdrew . . .
7. When I was cooking dinner, I burnt . . .
8. Did you shrink . . .
9. The audience wept . . .
10. The plants grew . . .

Exercise 19, p. 25.
Part I.

A Scary Night

I had a terrible experience last night. You won't believe what happened! A thief burst into my apartment while I was asleep. There I was, just sleeping peacefully when someone broke the glass in the sliding door!

The sound woke me up. I heard the sliding door open, so I reached for the phone by the bed and called the police. My voice shook as I told the operator there was an intruder in my home.

I hid in my bedroom closet while the thief was creeping around my office. Soon I heard sirens as the police sped to my building. From the crack in the closet door, I saw the thief as he ran outside with my computer.

The police jumped out of their cars and followed the thief, but he managed to get away in a car that was waiting for him. The police got back in their cars and drove after him. Later I learned that they caught the thief a few miles from my building.

I felt really frightened by all this. It really upset me, as you can imagine. I think I'll stay at my sister's house tonight.

Part II.
1. The thief entered quietly.
2. He opened a window.
3. The woman spoke with the intruder.
4. The woman went into her closet.
5. The police caught the thief in the woman's apartment.
6. The woman felt relaxed at the end of the story.

Exercise 20, p. 26.
1. lasted, tried
2. helped, stopped
3. described, wanted
4. invited, wanted
5. believed, kissed
6. missed, reached
7. saved, smelled
8. watched, asked
9. finished, robbed

Exercise 21, p. 27.
1. typed
2. closed
3. rented
4. replied
5. succeeded
6. looked
7. canceled
8. finished
9. counted

Exercise 22, p. 27.
1. Olga blinked (blink/t/), yawned (yawn/d/), and stretched (stretch/t/).
2. Mrs. Olsen mopped (mop/t/) the kitchen floor, vacuumed (vacuum/d/) the carpet, and dusted (dust/əd/) the furniture.
3. The meeting started (start/əd/) late and ended (end/əd/) early.
4. My friend jumped (jump/t/) up and down and yelled (yell/d/) when she got the news.
5. The airplane departed (depart/əd/) at six and landed (land/əd/) at eight.
6. When I asked (ask/t/) the doctor about some medication, he suggested (suggest/əd/) a new one.

Exercise 29, p. 32.

First Day of Class

It was my first day of class. I finally found the right room. The room was already full of students.

On one side of the room, students were talking to each other in Japanese or Arabic. On the other side, students were speaking in Spanish or Portuguese. It sounded like the United Nations. Some of the students, however, were sitting quietly by themselves, not talking to anyone.

I looked for an empty seat in the last row and sat down. In a few minutes, the teacher walked into the room, and all the multilingual conversation suddenly stopped.

Chapter 3: Perfect and Perfect Progressive Tenses

Exercise 2, p. 37.
1. I wrote a book. Have you ever . . .
2. I lost my wallet. Have you ever . . .
3. I climbed a mountain last year. Have you ever . . .
4. I gave a speech to a large audience. Have you ever . . .
5. I told a lie. Have you ever . . .
6. I once sang in public. Have you ever . . .
7. I rode on a motorcycle once. Have you ever . . .
8. I drank Turkish coffee. Have you ever . . .
9. I took a cooking class. Have you ever . . .
10. I shook hands with a famous person. Have you ever . . .
11. I helped another person with English. Have you ever . . .
12. I slept in a tent. Have you ever . . .
13. I drove a truck. Have you ever . . .
14. I had a car accident. Have you ever . . .
15. I studied biology. Have you ever . . .
16. I once played a violin. Have you ever . . .

Exercise 10, p. 41.
1. The Browns have decided to grow their own vegetables.
2. It's past midnight. Where have you been?
3. Laura has offered to help us move into our new apartment.
4. Is Nick in trouble again? What's he done this time?
5. Janet has traveled all over the world.
6. Her parents have traveled a lot too.

Exercise 11, p. 42.
1. My teacher's in the classroom.
2. Your teacher has already left.
3. All of the other teachers have already left too.
4. You're late! Where have you been?
5. Susan has a guilty look on her face. What's she done?
6. Finally! The mail's come.
7. My neighbors have lived in the same apartment for over thirty years.
8. Vicky's planning a trip to Brazil.
9. It's great to see you. How have you been?
10. India's been an independent country since 1947.
11. The weather's very nice.
12. The weather's been warm lately.
13. The children have finished their drawings.
14. Ruth has read four novels so far this month.

Exercise 18, p. 48.
A: Good to see you! So, what have you been up to lately?
B: Not too much. I've been taking it easy.
A: How nice! Glad to hear you haven't been working too hard. By the way, how are your parents? I haven't seen them for a while.
B: They're doing great. They're traveling now that they're retired.
A: How long have they been retired?
B: Gosh, I don't know. It's been a couple of years now.
A: So, they've been traveling a lot?
B: Yeah. They've been staying in warm, sunny places in the winter and spending summers here.
A: What a great way to spend retirement! I'm glad to hear they're enjoying themselves.

Exercise 20, p. 49.
1. Susan got to the doctor's office at 9:00 A.M. It is now 9:30, and she's still in the waiting room.
2. Alexi arrived in this country last month. He bought a motorcycle right away and uses it to get around town.
3. Joe will soon make his decision about which job to take.
4. Mika is stuck in rush-hour traffic. She's going to be late for her first day of work at a new job. She left home at 7:00 and now it's 8:30.
5. Andrew and Donna are in the middle of a chess match. They're getting tired and would like some lunch. Their chess match started three hours ago.

Exercise 25, p. 52.
1. I'm sorry we missed the meeting. We had forgotten about it.
2. The movie had already begun by the time we got there.
3. I couldn't change my schedule. I had already planned my day.
4. I got home late. My roommate had already gone to bed.

Exercise 26, p. 53.
1. We had never seen it. He had never seen it. They had never seen it.
2. We got home late. The children had already fallen asleep.
3. My roommates had finished dinner by the time I got home.
4. My roommates had dinner early.
5. We couldn't drive across the river. The flood had washed away the bridge.
6. You were at Jim's at 8:00. Where had you been before that?
7. I had never visited there before. I'd like to go again. I had a good time.

Exercise 27, p. 53.

1. You're a new student, aren't you? How long've you been in this country?
2. You must miss your old neighbor. How long had you known Mr. Kim before he moved away?
3. You're looking for Jack? Jack has left. He isn't here.
4. We were late, and Natasha had left by the time we got there.
5. Unfortunately, I didn't have my cell phone with me when we got lost. I'd left it at home.
6. Since we're teachers, we have the summers off and do a lot of traveling. We'd like to travel to Africa next.
7. Talk about long marriages! Can you believe that Mr. and Mrs. Cho have been married for 65 years?
8. Serena's an amazing chef. She's created so many new and popular dishes that it's almost impossible to get a reservation at her restaurant.

Exercise 28, p. 54.

A Pleasant Surprise

Last night Amy got home from work two hours late. Usually she's home by 7:30, but last night she didn't get there until almost 9:30.

When she got home, her husband, Jamal, had already eaten dinner and was washing the dishes. With a worried tone in his voice, he asked her where she'd been. She told him she'd had to work late, and then, on her way home, there'd been a big accident that had slowed traffic to a crawl. He asked her why she hadn't called. She said she'd forgotten to recharge her cell phone, so she couldn't call him.

Jamal smiled warmly and said that he was just glad that she was safely home. Then he offered to make her dinner — which she gratefully accepted. A home-cooked meal sounded wonderful. It'd been a long day!

Exercise 33, p. 58.

1. Yoko has recently learned to ski.
2. Yoko has been learning how to ski.
3. Mia has worked as an auto mechanic, but she prefers other types of work.
4. Jon has been traveling since he received his job promotion a month ago.
5. Jon had been working in sales when he became vice-president for human resources.

Chapter 4: Future Time

Exercise 3, p. 61.

1. Let's go to the beach. The children enjoy going there.
2. Yes, I'm sure they'll enjoy it.
3. The children'll enjoy going to the beach.
4. We meet at the library every Wednesday night for our book club.
5. We'll meet you in the reference section of the library.

6. Where'll I find information on organic gardening?
7. You'll find the information you're looking for in the gardening section of our bookstore.
8. These books have the information you're looking for.

Exercise 5, p. 62.

1. You'll need to turn in all your assignments by tomorrow.
2. We'll review for the final exam on Monday.
3. The test'll have 50 questions.
4. There'll be 50 questions on the exam.
5. You'll have the whole hour to complete the test.
6. It's a long exam. Sorry, but nobody'll finish early.
7. It'll be a lot of work. Study hard!
8. The results'll be available in my office the next day.

Exercise 6, p. 62.

1. Next in the news: The United Nations is going to vote on the new trade resolution tomorrow afternoon.
2. The election's almost here. I think I'm going to (gonna) vote for Carol Johnson. I like her.
3. Good evening, ladies and gentleman. It is clear that our town has a number of problems. What are we going to do to make our town a better place to live? I'd like to offer a few suggestions this evening.
4. Oh, no! We're out of gas. We're in the middle of nowhere. It's past midnight. Yikes! What're we going to (gonna) do?

Exercise 12, p. 66.

1. So, you were talking about your plans for the summer. What are you going to do?
2. Can you help me out? I've got to get this letter in the mail by noon.
3. Tell me again. Why are you leaving work early?
4. Darn, this flashlight doesn't work.
5. Here's the broom. What did you want it for?

Chapter 5: Review of Verb Tenses

Exercise 4, p. 78.

A Silly Mistake

When I got home to my apartment last night, I took out my key to open the door as usual. As always, I put it in the lock, but the door didn't open. I tried my key again and again with no luck. So I knocked on the door for my wife to let me in. Finally the door opened, but I didn't see my wife on the other side. I saw a stranger. I had been trying to get into the wrong apartment! I quickly apologized and went to my own. I felt very stupid about what I had done.

Exercise 8, p. 80.

1. Flight 907 landed at 8:06 P.M.
2. It was evening, and Greg was home alone. He was lying on his couch in the living room. He had been listening to classical music for almost an hour.

3. This wet weather is getting very tiresome. It's been raining for days.
4. On the way to the theater, we got stuck in traffic, so we were late. The concert was just starting as we walked in.
5. Janice is interested in learning to fly a small plane. She's had two lessons so far.
6. There was a robbery at the bank ten minutes ago, and the police still haven't come. By the time they get here, the thief'll be far away.

Chapter 6: Subject-Verb Agreement

Exercise 3, p. 85.
1. ride/z/
2. write/s/
3. rob/z/
4. rug/z/
5. sleep/s/
6. lock/s/
7. wish/əz/
8. page/əz/
9. month/s/

Exercise 5, p. 86.
1. Cats sleep eighteen hours a day.
2. People come in many shapes and sizes.
3. Maria practices pronunciation by reading sentences aloud.
4. The cafeteria serves good sandwiches.
5. Our teacher encourages us to speak English outside of class.
6. When Jack has a cold, he coughs and sneezes.

Exercise 9, p. 88.
1. The students . . .
2. The students in this classroom . . .
3. Each student . . .
4. Every student . . .
5. Every student in Mrs. Walker's classes . . .
6. The students and teachers . . .
7. Every student and teacher . . .
8. Each student and teacher . . .

Exercise 15, p. 91.
1. Still hungry? There're some leftovers in the fridge.
2. If you want more to eat, there's an apple left over from lunch.
3. Don't leave yet. There're email messages waiting for your response.
4. Excuse me. There's someone on the phone for you.
5. I need your help. Is there a place we could go to talk?
6. It's very crowded. Are there chairs for us to sit down?
7. I think there're extra chairs in the hallway.
8. Moving is a lot of work. Is there anything I can do to help?

Chapter 7: Nouns

Exercise 14, p. 108.
1. Joseph and Rob are taxi drivers.
2. They're drivers. They drive taxis for a living.
3. Maria and her sister have good jobs. They're office managers.
4. Managers of big offices have a lot of responsibilities.
5. I don't enjoy traveling in airplanes anymore. The seats are getting smaller and smaller.
6. Airplane seats are getting more and more uncomfortable, don't you think?
7. Schools often offer a lot of after-school activities for students.
8. Anna enjoys school activities such as playing on the soccer team and being in the debate club.

Exercise 23, p. 117.
1. My boss has unreasonable expectations.
2. This is not an easy situation to deal with.
3. I feel uneasy about this situation.
4. This is a difficult situation.
5. My boss has made an unreasonable request.
6. The speaker presented a complicated problem.
7. The speaker presented complicated problems.
8. The presentation was uncomplicated.

Exercise 30, p. 121.
Computer Bugs

When there is a problem with a computer, we often say we have a "computer bug." Of course, it's not a real insect. It refers to a technical difficulty we are having. The expression actually goes back to Thomas Edison, who was a famous inventor. When he was working on his first phonograph, he had a lot of problems. He attributed the problems to an imaginary insect that had hidden inside the machine. He is quoted in a newspaper as saying there was "a bug" in his phonograph. This was in 1889, and it is the first recorded use of the word *bug* in such a context.

Exercise 39, p. 128.
1. I don't really like much salt on my food.
2. I have a long plane ride ahead of me.
3. Mr. Hong arrived in Canada only a few days ago. He's never studied English. I think he knows how to say "hello," but I haven't heard him say any other English words.
4. Talk to Mr. Hong's daughter. She studied English in school before they emigrated. If you speak slowly, she'll understand you, and you can have a conversation with her.
5. Linda is in Mexico, but she can't speak Spanish. She can't find a job. She's almost out of money.

6. Billy has loving parents and grandparents. He's healthy and happy. He has cousins and friends to play with. He's a lucky little boy.
7. Mr. Perez doesn't know how to be a good boss. He has a bad temper and yells at people all the time about nothing.

Chapter 8: Pronouns

Exercise 10, p. 139.
1. Where's Kim?
   A: I don't know. I haven't seen him this morning.
   B: I think he's in the restroom.
   C: I'm looking for him too.
   D: Ask his assistant. He'll know.
   E: Have you tried looking in his office? I know he's not there much, but maybe he'll surprise you.

2. The Nelsons are giving their daughter a motorcycle for graduation.
   A: Hmmm. Does she like motorcycles that much?
   B: Really? Is she a motorcycle rider?
   C: That's an odd gift. I wonder what they were thinking.
   D: That's what the Smiths gave their son. I think he's already had an accident.
   E: I'm not a fan of motorcycles. Cars just don't see them in traffic.
   F: I think it's a wonderful gift! I've had mine for years, and it's been great.

Exercise 20, p. 146.
1. Hey Jon, I see you finally cleaned your apartment. How did you find the time to do it . . .
2. Do you like my dress? I made it . . .
3. We were going to take a trip with our cousins, but the plans got so complicated that we finally decided to go by . . .
4. My brother has an antique car. He restored it . . .
5. Mr. and Mrs. Peterson are planning to sell their house. They are going to put an ad in the paper and sell it . . .
6. My sister-in-law is an architect. She designed her office . . .

Exercise 30, p. 151.
1. This coffee is delicious. Could I please have another cup?
2. The coffee isn't in this grocery bag, so I'll look in the other one.
3. There are supposed to be ten chairs in the room, but I count only five. Where are the others?
4. No, let's not use this printer. Let's use the other one.

5. Bob is a nickname for Robert. Others are Rob and Robbie.
6. The sky is clearing. It's going to be another beautiful day.

Exercise 34, p. 154.
1. The teacher asked the students the same question. One after another they gave the wrong answer.
2. Mr. and Mrs. Clark lead such busy lives that they see each other only on weekends.
3. Mr. Perez is doing fine. Susan spoke with him just the other day.
4. A: I have a secret about Danny and me.
   B: Let me guess. You're engaged!
   A: Yes! But it's a secret. We haven't told anyone other than you.
5. A: Have you sent party invitations yet?
   B: Everyone except Jan knows about the surprise party.

Chapter 9: Modals, Part 1

Exercise 7, p. 161.
1. This is a non-smoking restaurant. Would you mind putting out your cigarette?
2. The music's awfully loud. Would you mind if I turned it down?
3. It's getting cool in here. Would you mind closing the window?
4. I can't reach the salt and pepper. Would you mind passing it to me?
5. I can't talk now. Mind if I called you back?

Exercise 17, p. 166.
Situation 1: Class registration
   Here is some important information you need for class registration next Monday. If you are a new student, you will need to register in person. Bring some form of photo ID, such as a passport or driver's license, or you cannot register. If you are a returning student, you can register online or in person.

Situation 2: Class changes and tuition
   If you want to change classes next week, you need to do so in person. You cannot do this online. Also, it is very important that you pay your tuition in full by the second week of classes, which is the deadline for payment, or you will have to drop your classes.

Exercise 24, p. 169.
1. The key's in the desk drawer, but it's not necessary to lock the front door when you leave.
2. When you apply for a visa, it's very important that you show proof of citizenship.
3. It's a good idea to arrive at the airport early tomorrow. The security lines will be long.
4. Only airline passengers with boarding passes will be allowed into the boarding area.

Exercise 26, p. 170.

1. Your sister is broke now because she spent all her money carelessly.
2. Your friends went to Hawaii over vacation. They had a good time. You didn't go with them, and now you are sorry.
3. Jack had too much coffee, and now he can't sleep.
4. The little girl told a lie. She got into a lot of trouble.

Chapter 10: Modals, Part 2

Exercise 9, p. 184.

Situation: Tom and his young son, Billy, hear a noise on the roof.

Tom: I wonder what that noise is.

Billy: It may be a bird.

Tom: It can't be a bird. It's running across the roof. Birds don't run across roofs.

Billy: Well, some birds do. It could be a big bird that's running fast.

Tom: No, I think it must be some kind of animal. It might be a mouse.

Billy: It sounds much bigger than a mouse. It may be a dragon!

Tom: Son, it couldn't be a dragon. We don't have any dragons around here. They exist only in storybooks.

Billy: It could be a little dragon that you don't know about.

Tom: Well, I suppose it might be some kind of lizard.

Billy: I'll go look.

Tom: That's a good idea.

Billy: Guess what, Dad. It's a rat!

Exercise 21, p. 192.

What's wrong? Your parents look upset.
1. We should ask them.
2. We shouldn't ask them.
3. You may have upset them.
4. You should try to find out.
5. Maybe you shouldn't have stayed out so late.
6. You'd better have a good excuse for being late.
7. You could have told them what you planned to do.
8. You must have known your behavior would cause problems.

Exercise 31, p. 199.

1. The secretary can help you.
2. My mother can't speak English.
3. My friend can meet you at the airport.
4. Mr. Smith can answer your question.
5. We can't come to the meeting.
6. Can't you come?
7. You can take that course.

8. I can't cook.
9. I can't drive a stick-shift car.
10. Our son can count to ten.

Exercise 33, p. 200.

An Experiment in Human Behavior

A researcher in human behavior conducted an experiment. First she talked to a group of four-year-olds.

"How many of you can dance?" All of the children raised their hands.

"How many of you can sing?" All of the hands shot up.

"And finally, how many of you can draw?" Every child's hand was raised.

Next the researcher went to a college class of twenty-five students in their late teens and early twenties.

"How many of you can dance?" she asked. About a third of the students raised their hands.

"How many of you can sing?" Some hands were raised, but fewer than were raised for the first question.

"How many of you can draw?" Only two hands went up.

Exercise 44, p. 208.

1. Carlos was planning to come to the party, but he didn't show up. It was a great party. There was delicious food, and we danced until midnight.
2. I have a whole lot of material I need to review before the exam, but I just don't feel like studying this afternoon.
3. Tony's over an hour late for our meeting. That's not like him. I hope nothing bad has happened.
4. Rick was supposed to be at work early today to train his new assistant, but he woke up with a high fever. He can't even get out of bed.
5. The teacher called on Sonya in class yesterday, but she kept looking out the window and didn't respond.

Chapter 11: The Passive

Exercise 10, p. 216.

1. A famous architect has been asked to design the new library.
2. There was a group of noisy kids at the movie theater. They had been told several times to leave.
3. I was ignored by the salesclerk while she spent five minutes talking on the phone.
4. After the speech, the audience will ask the speaker follow-up questions.
5. The staff is planning a retirement party for Dr. Wilson.
6. Since the beginning of the modern industrial age, many of the natural habitats of plants and animals have been altered or destroyed by human development.

Exercise 15, p. 219.

How Chocolate Is Made

Chocolate is made from the seeds of roasted cocoa beans. After the seeds have been roasted, the inside of the seed is pressed into a liquid. This liquid is called chocolate liquor. The liquor contains fat, which is separated from the liquor. After this has been done, a solid is left. This solid, which is known as cocoa cake, is ground up and becomes unsweetened cocoa. This is a very bitter chocolate. To make it taste better, other substances such as cocoa butter and sugar will be added later.

Exercise 22, p. 224.

The 2004 Indian Ocean Tsunami

In 2004, several countries that border the Indian Ocean, including Indonesia, Thailand, India, Malaysia, and Somalia, were hit by an earthquake and subsequent tsunami. (As you may already know, a tsunami is a giant ocean wave.) In just a few short hours, millions of lives were changed forever. The earthquake was measured at 9.3 on the Richter scale. It was the fourth largest earthquake since 1900 and the second largest that has ever been recorded on the Richter scale.

The quake was followed by four giant waves as high as 100 feet (or 30 meters). Whole villages were destroyed. Thousands of people were swept out to sea, and many others died due to lack of medical care. In total, almost 300,000 people were killed, and 1.3 million people were left homeless. Aftershocks from the earthquake continued for several days.

Tragically, the damage could have been lessened if there had been a tsunami early-warning system. Such a system already exists for the Pacific Ocean, but it doesn't reach to the Indian Ocean. Since the tsunami disaster, governments have been working together to develop an early-warning system so that Southeast Asia will not experience such destruction again from a tsunami.

Exercise 30, p. 230.
1. Water is composed of hydrogen and oxygen.
2. I am not acquainted with Dr. William's books.
3. I'm finally accustomed to living here.
4. You're so busy. I think you're involved in too many activities.
5. Are you prepared for the next test?
6. Mr. and Mrs. Miller are devoted to each other.
7. I'm concerned about my grandfather's health.
8. Are you satisfied with your progress?

Exercise 43, p. 237.
1. Excuse me. Your application form has some missing information.
2. As the owner of her own design business, Carol works hard to have satisfied customers.
3. After the earthquake, frightened residents were afraid to sleep indoors for several days.

4. I think James will be single forever. He's just not the marrying type.
5. The airplane pilot had a few scary moments when lightning hit his plane.
6. The finished product was exactly what the client had asked for.

Exercise 44, p. 238.
1. When I ride on a roller coaster, my heart pounds with excitement. The ride is . . .
2. During the ride, I feel . . .
3. The art museum has an exhibit that people are upset about. People who visit the museum are . . .
4. People say that the exhibit is . . .
5. My parents enjoy talking with my friend, Maria. They find her . . .
6. Maria gets along well with my parents. She thinks they are . . .
7. Not one of the students could understand Professor Steven's explanations. Whenever he explains a math problem, the students become more . . .
8. His explanations are terribly . . .

Exercise 47, p. 239.

The Olympic Games

The Olympic Games began more than 2,000 years ago in Olympia, a small town in Greece. The games were established for two purposes. One was to showcase the physical qualities and athletic performances of its young men. At that time, only Greek males were allowed to compete. In fact, women were not even permitted to watch the games, and the only spectators were men. The other goal was to encourage good relationships among Greek cities. People of other nationalities were not invited to participate.

The winner of each event was crowned with a wreath made of olive leaves. Additionally, his statue could be placed in Olympia for all to see. Winning athletes were treated as heroes when they returned to their cities because with their victory, they brought fame and honor to their hometowns.

Chapter 12: Noun Clauses

Exercise 11, p. 248.
1. A: It's a beautiful day. Let's walk over to Lakeside Park. It's not far from here, is it?
   B: Gosh, I don't know how far it is.
2. A: Do you want to walk to the farmers' market with me tomorrow morning? They have lots of fresh fruits and vegetables.
   B: Gee, I don't know. Maybe. How far is it?
3. A: That was a terrible movie!
   B: I agree. I don't know why we watched the whole thing.

4. A: I watched an awful movie on TV last night.
    B: Well, if it was awful, why did you watch it?

5. A: Is Jeannie going to be 49 or 50 this year?
    B: I don't know. I can never remember how old she is.

6. A: Excuse me. I'm still unsure about the pronunciation of that word.
    B: Which one?
    A: This one right here. How is this word pronounced?

7. A: You look upset.
    B: I am. I'm very upset.
    A: So, what is the problem?

Exercise 41, p. 264.

1. I'm not going to the personnel meeting because I have to finish a report.
2. I can't lend Marta any money because my wallet is in my coat pocket back at home.
3. Someone in this room is wearing very strong perfume. It's giving me a headache.
4. Hi, Emma. I'll meet you at the coffee shop at 9:00. I promise not to be late.
5. I'm considering looking for a new job. What do you think I should do?
6. We are going to be late for the concert. My wife has to attend a business function after work.

Chapter 13: Adjective Clauses

Exercise 5, p. 271.

Part I.
1. He has a friend who'll help him.
2. He has a friend who's helping him.
3. He has a friend who's helped him.
4. He has friends who're helping him.
5. He has friends who've helped him.
6. He has a friend who'd helped him.
7. He has a friend who'd like to help him.

Part II.
8. We know a person who'll be great for the job.
9. We know a person who'd like to apply for the job.
10. That's the man who's giving the speech at our graduation.
11. I know a nurse who's traveled around the world helping people.
12. Let's talk to the people who're planning the protest march.
13. There are people at the factory who've worked there all their adult lives.
14. The doctor who'd been taking care of my mother retired.

Exercise 19, p. 278.

1. I met the man who's going to become the new manager of our department.
2. I know someone who's never flown in an airplane.
3. I talked to the man whose wife was in the car accident on Fifth Street yesterday. She's in the hospital, but she's going to be okay.
4. I forget the name of the woman who's going to call you later — Mrs. Green or Mrs. White or something like that.
5. I need to hurry. The neighbor whose bike I borrowed is waiting for me to return it.
6. I got an email from a friend who's studying in Malaysia. It was really good to hear from her.
7. I recently heard from a friend who's been out of the country for over two months. He finally sent me an email.
8. I'm thinking about getting a pet. There's a woman at work whose dog just had puppies. I might adopt one.

Exercise 21, 279.

1. That's the person who's going to help us.
2. That's the person whose help we need.
3. I'd like to introduce you to a teacher who's spent time in Africa.
4. I'd like to introduce you to the teacher whose husband is from Africa.
5. The company is looking for a person who's bilingual.
6. The company is looking for a person whose native language is Arabic.
7. The company is looking for a person who's had a lot of experience in sales.
8. They want to hire a person who's familiar with their sales territory.

Exercise 29, p. 281.

1. The man who organized the community dinner is a friend of mine.
2. Two people died in the accident that blocked all lanes of the highway for two hours.
3. The small town where I was born is now a large city.
4. The music teacher who directs the school band plays in a rock band on weekends.
5. The camera that Jack gave me for my birthday takes excellent digital pictures.
6. My neighbor often drops in for a visit about the time when we would like to sit down to dinner.

Exercise 33, p. 284.

A: Do you see that guy who's wearing the baseball cap?
B: I see two guys that're wearing baseball caps. Do you mean the one whose T-shirt says "Be Happy"?
A: Yeah, him. Do you remember him from high school? He looks a little different now, doesn't he? Isn't he the one whose wife joined the circus?

B: Nah, I heard that story too. That was just a rumor. When the circus was in town last summer, his wife spent a lot of time there, so people started wondering why. Some people started saying she was working there as a performer. But the truth is that she was only visiting a cousin who's a manager for the circus. She just wanted to spend time with him while he was in town.

A: Well, you know, it was a story that sounded pretty fishy to me. But people sure enjoyed talking about it. The last thing that I heard was that she'd learned how to eat fire and swallow swords!

B: Rumors really take on a life of their own, don't they?!

Exercise 36, p. 286.

1. Did you hear about the man who rowed a boat across the Atlantic Ocean?
2. My uncle, who loves boating, rows his boat across the lake near his house nearly every day.
3. Tea, which is a common drink throughout the world, is made by pouring boiling water onto the dried leaves of certain plants.
4. Tea which is made from herbs is called herbal tea.
5. Toys which contain lead paint are unsafe for children.
6. Lead, which can be found in paint and plastics, is known to cause brain damage in children.

Exercise 39, p. 288.

1. My mother looked in the fruit basket and threw away the apples that were rotten.
2. My mother looked in the fruit basket and threw away the apples, which were rotten.
3. The students who had done well on the test were excused from class early.
4. The students, who had done well on the test, were excused from class early.

Exercise 52, p. 295.

1. The fence surrounding our house is made of wood.
2. The children attending that school receive a good education.
3. Dr. Stanton, the president of the university, will give a speech at the commencement ceremonies.
4. Our solar system is in a galaxy called the Milky Way.

Exercise 56, p. 297.

Animals and Earthquakes

Whether or not animals can predict earthquakes has been widely debated for hundreds of years. In fact, as far back as 373 B.C. villagers reported that hundreds of animals deserted the Greek town of Helice a few days before an earthquake destroyed it. There are other interesting phenomena that scientists have noted. For example, before an earthquake, dogs may begin barking or howling for no reason; chickens might stop laying eggs; and some pets will go into hiding.

In Asia in 2004, many animals that were accustomed to being on the beach in the early morning refused to go there the morning of the big tsunami. In Thailand, a herd of buffalo on a beach noticed or heard something which made them run to the top of a hill before the tsunami was anywhere in sight. The villagers who followed them were saved.

What causes this strange behavior in animals? One theory is that they can sense the earth move before people can. There are vibrations deep in the earth that begin before an earthquake can be detected. Another idea is that the energy in the air changes and that animals are disturbed by these changes.

Some scientists dismiss these ideas, while others believe that they are worth researching further. Those scientists who have witnessed this strange animal behavior are certain that animals are far more sensitive to subtle changes in the earth than people are and that studying their behavior can be useful in the prediction of earthquakes.

Chapter 14: Gerunds and Infinitives, Part 1

Exercise 6, p. 305.

1. A: I'm sorry I'm late.
   B: No problem. We have lots of time.
2. A: I finished the project early.
   B: That's great you got it done so quickly.
3. A: I hate to do housework.
   B: I know. I do too. It's a lot of work.
4. A: You were a big help. Thanks.
   B: Sure. I was happy to help out.
5. A: Your report isn't finished. What's your excuse?
   B: Uh, well, sorry. I don't really have one.
6. A: How do you like the food here?
   B: It's too spicy. I can't eat much of it.
7. A: How was your weekend? Did you go away for the holiday?
   B: No. I got the flu and spent the whole weekend in bed.

Exercise 13, p. 308.

1. A: What should we do tomorrow night?
   B: Let's just stay home and watch a movie. There's nothing I like to do better on a weekend.
   A: Sounds good to me.
2. A: I was really looking forward to the hike up to Skyline Ridge to see the mountains, but I guess we're not going to get there this month.
   B: It doesn't look like it. I don't think there's any hope. It's supposed to rain the rest of this week and into next week.
3. A: Do you want to take a break?
   B: No, we have to finish this report by 5:00. We don't have time for a break.
4. A: Let's go into the city this weekend. There's a great concert at the park. And it's free!
   B: Great idea! Who's playing?

5. A: Gosh, I'd really like to go out this evening, but I have all this work to do. I have three papers due, and I haven't begun to write any of them.
    B: I know how you feel. I'm way behind in my homework too.
6. A: I just heard that there's an accident on the freeway and nothing's moving. I don't want our drive home to take hours.
    B: Me neither. Let's not leave the office for another couple of hours. We can get caught up on our work.
    A: Good idea. I have so much to do.

Exercise 17, p. 309.

Ron's Busy Saturday

Ron is an active individual. On his days off, he likes to do several activities in one day. His friends can't keep up with him.

Last Saturday, for example, he began by going canoeing early in the morning. He finds early mornings on the lake very calm and relaxing. He brought a fishing rod with him so he could go fishing and perhaps catch something for dinner. He saw some friends getting their sailboat ready and thought about going sailing with them, but decided instead to go swimming. By that time, it was only noon!

After lunch, he went biking in the hills behind his town. He cooked a fish that he had caught for dinner, and it was delicious. Later, some friends called to invite him out, so he finished the day by going dancing with them.

Exercise 22, p. 312.

1. I have a terrible memory. I can't even remember my children's birthdays.
2. My teenage son tried to hide his report card, but I caught him.
3. I'm in a hurry in the mornings. I always stand at the kitchen counter and eat my breakfast.
4. Foreign languages are hard for me to learn.
5. I sat in traffic for two hours. It was a waste of time.
6. We sang songs on the bus trip. It was fun.
7. I looked all over for Tom. He was studying in the library.
8. There was a line to buy movie tickets. I had to wait for an hour.

Exercise 31, p. 318.

1. Joan remembered to call her husband before she left work yesterday.
2. Rita remembered going to the farmers' market with her grandmother.
3. Roger stopped smoking when the doctor told him he had heart disease.
4. Mr. and Mrs. Olson stopped to eat before the movie.
5. I regret leaving school before I graduated.

Chapter 15: Gerunds and Infinitives, Part 2

Exercise 14, p. 336.

1. That dinner was delicious, Nancy.
2. Do you leave your daughter home alone when you go out?
3. I think our English is getting a lot better, but learning a second language isn't easy.
4. I used a new laundry detergent on these shirts. How did it work?
5. Mr. Jones is 99 years old. He's too old to drive.
6. We need 20 big envelopes, but we only have 10.

Exercise 36, p. 348.

An Issue in Health Care: Illiteracy

According to some estimates, well over half of the people in the world are functionally illiterate. This means that they are unable to perform everyday tasks because they can't read, understand, and respond appropriately to information. One of the problems this creates in health care is that millions of people are not able to read directions on medicine bottles or packages. Imagine being a parent with a sick child and being unable to read the directions on a medicine bottle. We all know that it is important for medical directions to be understood clearly. One solution is pictures. Many medical professionals are working today to solve this problem by using pictures to convey health-care information.

Exercise 39, p. 350.

Protecting Yourself in a Lightning Storm

Lightning storms can occur suddenly and without warning. It's important to know how to stay safe if you're outside when a storm begins. Some people stand under trees or in open shelters like picnic areas in order to protect themselves. They are surprised to hear that this can be a fatal mistake. Tall objects are likely to attract lightning, so when you are out in the open, you should try to make yourself as small as possible. Crouching down or curling up into a ball lessens the chance that a lightning bolt will strike you. Finding a depression in the ground to hide in, like a hole or a ditch, is even better.

Being inside a building is safer than being outside, but it's not without dangers. Be careful to stay away from doors and windows. If you're talking on a phone with a cord, hang up. Lightning has been known to travel along a phone cord and strike the person holding the phone. Even TVs can conduct lightning through the cable or antenna, so it's a good idea to stay away from the television. It's also inadvisable to take a shower or bath since plumbing can conduct electricity from lightning. How safe are cars? Surprisingly, the inside of a car is safe as long as it has a metal roof, but avoid touching any part of the car that leads to the outside.

There's a 30/30 rule regarding lightning. As soon as you see lightning, begin counting the seconds until you hear thunder. If you hear thunder before you reach 30, this means you need to seek shelter immediately. Additionally, even if the storm has passed, you want to stay in a protected place for 30 minutes after you hear the last sounds of thunder or have seen the last flashes of lightning. Many lightning deaths, in fact more than half in the United States, occur after a storm has passed.

Chapter 16: Coordinating Conjunctions

Exercise 5, p. 354.
1. My bedroom has a bed, a desk, and a lamp.
2. The price of the meal includes a salad, a main dish, and dessert.
3. The price of the meal includes a salad and a main dish.
4. Elias waited for his son, wife, and daughter.
5. Elias waited for his son's wife and daughter.
6. Susan raised her hand, snapped her fingers, and asked a question.
7. Red, yellow, gold, and olive green are the main colors in the fabric.
8. I love films full of action, adventure, and suspense.
9. I love action and adventure films.
10. Travel is fatal to prejudice, bigotry, and narrow-mindedness.

Exercise 14, p. 359.
1. Ben will call either Mary or Bob.
2. Both my mother and father talked to my teacher.
3. Simon saw not only a whale but also a dolphin.
4. Our neighborhood had neither electricity nor water after the storm.
5. Either Mr. Anderson or Ms. Wiggins is going to teach our class today.

Exercise 16, p. 360.

Bats

(1) What do people in your country think of bats? Are they mean and scary creatures, or are they symbols of both happiness and luck?

(2) In Western countries, many people have an unreasoned fear of bats. According to scientist Dr. Sharon Horowitz, bats are not only harmless but also beneficial mammals. "When I was a child, I believed that a bat would attack me and tangle itself in my hair. Now I know better," said Dr. Horowitz.

(3) Contrary to popular Western myths, bats do not attack humans. Although a few bats may have diseases, they are not major carriers of rabies or other frightening diseases. Bats help natural plant life by pollinating plants, spreading seeds, and eating insects. If you get rid of bats that eat overripe fruit, then fruit flies can flourish and destroy the fruit industry.

(4) According to Dr. Horowitz, bats are both gentle and trainable pets. Not many people, however, own or train bats, and bats themselves prefer to avoid people.

Exercise 19, p. 362.
1. Both Jamal and I had many errands to do yesterday. Jamal had to go to the post office and the bookstore. I had to go to the post office, the travel agency, and the bank.
2. Roberto slapped his hand on his desk in frustration. He had failed another examination and had ruined his chances for a passing grade in the course.

3. When Alex got home, he took off his coat and tie, threw his briefcase on the kitchen table, and opened the refrigerator looking for something to eat. Ann found him sitting at the kitchen table when she got home.
4. When Tara went downtown yesterday, she bought birthday presents for her children, shopped for clothes, and saw a movie at the theater. It was a busy day, but she felt fine because it ended on a relaxing note.
5. It was a wonderful picnic. The children waded in the stream, collected rocks and insects, and flew kites. The teenagers played an enthusiastic game of baseball. The adults busied themselves preparing the food, supervising the children, and playing some volleyball.

Exercise 21, p. 363.

Butterflies

A butterfly is a marvel. It begins as an ugly caterpillar and turns into a work of art. The sight of a butterfly floating from flower to flower on a warm, sunny day brightens anyone's heart. A butterfly is a charming and gentle creature. Caterpillars eat plants and cause damage to some crops, but adult butterflies feed principally on nectar from flowers and do not cause any harm. When cold weather comes, some butterflies travel great distances to reach tropical climates. They can be found on every continent except Antarctica. Because they are so colorful and beautiful, butterflies are admired throughout the world.

Chapter 17: Adverb Clauses

Exercise 11, p. 372.

Cultural Misunderstandings

Since Marco and Anya came to this country, they've had some memorable misunderstandings due to language and culture. The first time Marco met someone at a party, he was asked "How's it going?" Marco thought that the person was asking him about leaving, and that seemed very strange.

Once, Anya walked into class, and a native speaker said, "Hi. How are you?" When Anya started to give a long answer, the native speaker looked at her rather oddly. This happened several times until Anya learned she was just supposed to say something like "Okay" or "Fine, thanks. And you?"

Another time, Marco was at a restaurant and wanted to get the server's attention. He snapped his fingers. The server was not pleased.

Since coming here, Marco and Anya have learned that cultural misunderstandings are a normal part of learning another language. They can be valuable and even entertaining learning experiences. Marco and Anya just smile at these misunderstandings now.

Chapter 18: Reduction of Adverb Clauses to Modifying Adverbial Phrases

Exercise 16, p. 395.

1. A: I don't want to play the piano at the family gathering. I don't play well enough. People will laugh at me.
   B: Oh, Rose, don't be silly. You play beautifully. Everyone will love hearing you.

2. A: Jan, are you going to tell Thomas that he needs to do more work on the project? He hasn't done his share. He's being really lazy.
   B: Well, he'll probably get upset, but I'm going to talk with him about it this afternoon.

3. A: I'm so relieved that I found my wedding ring. It'd been missing for a month. The next time I take it off, I'm going to put it in a box on top of my dresser drawer.
   B: That sounds like a wise thing to do, Susan. It'd be terrible to lose your wedding ring again.

4. A: This is the first year I'm eligible to vote in the presidential election. I'm going to research all the candidates extensively.
   B: They have very different positions, Sam. It's good to get as much information as you can.

Exercise 18, p. 396

The QWERTY Keyboard

Do you know why the letters on an English language keyboard are placed where they are? Take a minute and look at the second row on the keyboard in the picture. Notice that Q-W-E-R-T-Y are the first six letters beginning on the left. In fact, the keyboard is called "QWERTY." As you look at all the letters on the keyboard, does it seem to make any sense to you? Many people have wondered about this rather strange placement of keys, but as it turns out, there is a logical reason for the design.

A man named Christopher Sholes, the inventor of the typewriter, came up with this keyboard in the 1860s. Wanting to create a logical design, Sholes first placed the letters in alphabetical order on his typewriter. He put two rows from A to Z on the keyboard.

But Sholes found there was a problem. The letters were on typebars — typebars, by the way, are also called keys — and some of these keys crashed into one another. This happened when letters that often occur together in words, like "s" and "l," were near each other on the keyboard. The keys tended to hit each other and get stuck, and the typist would have to stop and pull them apart.

Trying to figure out a way to keep the keys from hitting one another, Sholes made a list of letters commonly used together in English, like the pair I already mentioned, "s" and "l," or, for example, "q" and "u." He then rearranged these letters so they would be on opposite sides of the keyboard. If you look at a keyboard, "q" is on the left side and "u" is on the right side. He put the keys that were most likely to be hit one after the other on opposite sides of the keyboard. This keyboard became known as QWERTY.

Nowadays, with computers, we don't have to worry about keys crashing into one another, so QWERTY is not necessarily the fastest and most efficient keyboard. Other people have come up with alternative keyboard patterns, but so far, none has gained much popularity. Having survived since the 1860s, QWERTY has demonstrated its longevity. It does not appear that it is going to be replaced any time soon by a faster, more efficient keyboard.

Chapter 19: Connectives That Express Cause and Effect, Contrast, and Condition

Exercise 33, p. 412.

1. Because I lift heavy boxes at work, . . .
2. I bought a new TV even though . . .
3. Even if I'm late for work, . . .
4. I was late for work this morning; nevertheless, . . .
5. The air-conditioning has been broken; therefore, . . .
6. Although I live in a noisy city, . . .
7. I was so tired last night that . . .

Exercise 36, p. 414.

Why We Yawn

Have you ever noticed that when a person near you yawns, you may start yawning too? This is called contagious yawning. *Contagious* in this sense means that the behavior spreads: when one person does something like yawn, it can cause others to do the same thing.

There are various theories about why people yawn. One popular idea is that yawning brings more oxygen into the brain to wake people up. Is that what you have thought? But in 2007, researchers at a university in New York came up with a new idea: yawning helps cool the brain.

Scientists found that people yawned more frequently in situations where their brains were warmer. The idea is that yawning cools the brain by increasing blood flow and bringing cooler air into the body. Cooler brains work better than warmer ones.

This may also help explain why yawning is contagious. People are more awake when their brains are cooler. As people evolved over time, contagious yawning helped people stay awake. This was important in times of danger. It's very possible that the person yawning could have been signaling to others to stay awake.

The next time you are talking to someone and that person yawns, you can tell yourself that he or she actually wants to stay awake, not go to sleep.

Exercise 38, p. 415.

Passage 1: Turtles

Turtles have survived on earth for more than 200 million years, but now many species face extinction. People in many parts of the world use them for food and for traditional medicine, so the demand for them is high. In spite of international trade laws that protect them, illegal traffic in turtles is increasing.

Passage 2: Boy or Girl?

Research shows that many parents prefer to have a boy rather than a girl because boys are expected to become better economic providers for their parents in their old age. In developed countries, however, more women than men go to a university. It's possible that in some places more women than men will be prepared for the high-paying jobs of the 21st century.

Chapter 20: Conditional Sentences and Wishes

Exercise 6, p. 418.

1. If I'm talking too fast, please tell me.
2. If we get married, everyone will be shocked.
3. If it's okay, I'll ask for some advice.
4. If he's planning to quit, I hope he lets us know soon.
5. If it's not working, we'll need to try something else.
6. If she works harder, I'm sure she'll succeed.
7. If I should get the job, I'll call you right away.

Exercise 19, p. 424.

The Extinction of Dinosaurs

There are several scientific theories as to why dinosaurs became extinct. One theory has to do with asteroids. Asteroids, as you may know, are rocky objects that orbit the sun. According to this theory, an asteroid collided with the earth millions of years ago, causing disastrous changes in the earth's climate, such as tsunamis, high winds, and dust in the atmosphere that blocked the sun. As a result, dinosaurs could no longer survive. Some scientists believe that if this asteroid had not collided with the earth, dinosaurs would not have become extinct.

Exercise 20, p. 424.

1. If I had known the truth sooner, I would have acted differently.
2. If we hadn't believed him, we wouldn't have felt so foolish.
3. If you hadn't told me what a great guy Jon was, I wouldn't have believed him so easily.

4. If it had been another person, I wouldn't have been so shocked.
5. If he hadn't lied, I would have had more respect for him.

Exercise 22, p. 426.

1. If I had enough time, I'd go to the art museum this afternoon. I love going to art museums.
2. Mrs. Jones is really lucky. If she hadn't received immediate medical attention, she would have died.
3. If I were a carpenter, I'd build my own house. I'd really enjoy that.
4. So many people died unnecessarily in the earthquake. If the hotel had been built to withstand an earthquake, it wouldn't have collapsed.

Exercise 32, p. 430.

1. If I hadn't been driving so fast, I wouldn't have gotten a speeding ticket.
2. Should you have questions, give me a call on my cell.
3. Had you told us sooner, we could have helped you.
4. If there had been a faster way to get to the theater, I would have taken it.
5. Had anyone warned us about the situation, we would have stayed home.
6. Were we rich, we would live in a house overlooking the ocean.

Exercise 35, p. 431.

1. I would have called, but I left your number at home.
2. I couldn't have gone to college without my parents' financial help.
3. I ran out of time. Otherwise, I would have picked up your clothes from the cleaners.
4. We would have come to the party, but no one told us about it.
5. Without your advice, I wouldn't have known what to do.

Exercise 45, p. 436.

1. Alice doesn't like her job as a nurse. She wishes she hadn't gone to nursing school.

2. A: I wish we didn't have to go to work today.
   B: So do I. I wish it were a holiday.

3. We had a good time in the mountains over vacation. I wish you had come with us. If you had come with us, you would have had a good time.

4. I know that something's bothering you. I wish you would tell me what it is. Maybe I can help.

5. A: My feet are killing me! I wish I had worn more comfortable shoes.
   B: Yeah, me too. I wish I had known that we were going to have to walk this much.

Index

Able to, 202, 205 *(Look on pages 202 and 205.)*	The numbers following the words listed in the index refer to page numbers in the text.
Continuous tenses, 3*fn.* *(Look at the footnote on page 3.)*	The letters *fn.* mean "footnote." Footnotes are at the bottom of a chart or the bottom of a page.

infos à connaître

LES VIKINGS

100

infos à connaître

LES VIKINGS

Fiona Macdonald

Consultant : Jeremy Smith

Piccolia

Remerciements :
aux artistes qui ont contribués
à l'élaboration de ce titre

Mark Davis - Peter Dennis - Mike Foster - Richard Hook - Kevin
Maddison - Janos Marffy - Alessandro Menchi - Peter Sarson - Mike
Saunders - Mike White - Rudi Vizi

Sommaire

Qui étaient les Vikings ?

GROENLAND

ISLANDE

N

W E

S

CANADA

TERRE NEUVE

**1 Les Vikings vivaient en Scandinavie
il y a plus de 1 000 ans.** Ils ont semé la
terreur dans toute l'Europe entre la fin du
VIIIe et la moitié du XIIe siècle ap. J-C. Les
guerriers vikings organisaient des
attaques meurtrières contre des villages
paisibles pour conquérir de nouvelles
terres, piller les trésors et revendre leurs
prisonniers comme esclaves. Les marchands
vikings parcouraient de longues distances
pour aller d'Europe au Moyen-Orient. Les Vikings ont
installé des fermes en Angleterre, en Irlande, en Écosse et en
France alors que leurs explorateurs partaient fonder de nouvelles
colonies en Islande, au Groenland et en Russie. Ce sont les
premiers à aller en Amérique vers 1000.

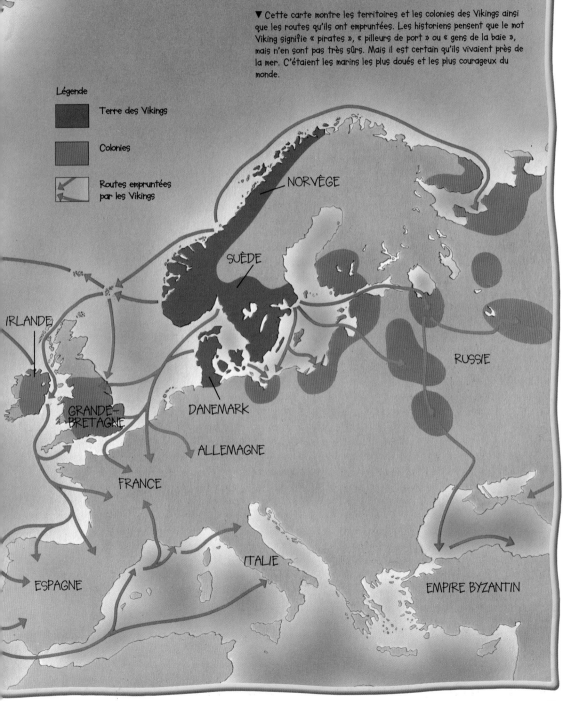

▼ Cette carte montre les territoires et les colonies des Vikings ainsi que les routes qu'ils ont empruntées. Les historiens pensent que le mot Viking signifie « pirates », « pilleurs de port » ou « gens de la baie », mais n'en sont pas très sûrs. Mais il est certain qu'ils vivaient près de la mer. C'étaient les marins les plus doués et les plus courageux du monde.

Légende

Terre des Vikings

Colonies

Routes empruntées par les Vikings

NORVÈGE

SUÈDE

IRLANDE

GRANDE-BRETAGNE

DANEMARK

RUSSIE

ALLEMAGNE

FRANCE

ITALIE

ESPAGNE

EMPIRE BYZANTIN

Les rois et le peuple

2 **La société viking était divisée en trois classes.** Au sommet, se trouvaient les nobles (les rois ou les chefs). Propriétaires des terres, ils étaient riches et avaient de nombreux serviteurs. Les hommes libres constituait la classe du milieu, qui comprenait les fermiers, les commerçants, les artisans et leurs épouses. Venaient ensuite les esclaves qui travaillaient dur au profit des nobles ou des hommes riches et n'avaient pas le droit de posséder des terres.

Guerrier viking

Fermier viking

Esclave viking

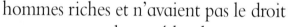

▲ Esclaves, fermiers et guerriers travaillaient dur, si bien que les Vikings étaient riches et puissants.

◀ Célèbre pour sa cruauté, Erik à la hache sanglante fut le dernier à régner sur le royaume de Northumbrie, au Nord-Est de l'Angleterre.

3 **Certains guerriers vikings devinrent rois.** Au début de l'histoire des Vikings, les chefs locaux contrôlaient de vastes territoires et possédaient des armées d'hommes libres. Au fil des siècles, les nobles s'enrichirent en pillant et en envahissant d'autres territoires. Vers 1050, un roi contrôlait un pays enfin unifié, l'actuelle Norvège.

4 **Erik à la hache sanglante tua ses frères.** Lorsqu'un roi viking mourait, chacun de ses fils avait le droit d'hériter du trône. D'ailleurs les membres de la famille se battaient souvent pour pouvoir régner. En 930, le roi Erik de Norvège tua ses frères pour régner seul.

5 **Le roi Harald à la dent Bleue laissa un magnifique mémorial.** Il régna sur le Danemark de 935 à 985. Ce fut le premier Viking à se convertir au christianisme. Il fit construire une église à Jelling, où ses parents furent inhumés. Juste à côté, il construisit un magnifique monument en forme de pyramide à leur mémoire. Cette « pierre de Jelling » est gravée de motifs vikings et chrétiens.

▶ La pierre de Jelling (tout à droite) représente un combat entre un serpent et un lion qui symbolisent les forces du bien et du mal.

6 **Le roi Knud Ier régnait sur un Empire européen, mais pas sur les vagues !** Le roi Knud fut l'un des plus puissants rois vikings. En 1028, il régnait sur l'Angleterre, le Danemark et la Norvège. Pourtant, il ne voulait pas paraître prétentieux. Un jour, il organisa une cérémonie sur la plage et demanda aux vagues de lui obéir. Comme elles n'en firent rien, il déclara : « Cela prouve que je suis faible, seul Dieu peut contrôler les vagues. »

INCROYABLE !

De nombreux chefs vikings avaient des noms qui traduisaient leur violence comme : Erik à la hache sanglante, Erik le Rouge, Magnus aux jambes nues, Thorfin le Pourfendeur.

9

Des marins et des pilleurs

7 **Les Vikings naviguaient dans des bateaux évoquant un dragon.** Ils possédaient différents types de bateaux. Les cargos étaient lents et lourds, avec de vastes soutes pour transporter les marchandises. Les bateaux de rivière étaient légers, solides et pouvaient contenir beaucoup de passagers. Les plus beaux bateaux étaient les drakkars (en forme de dragon), conçus pour la guerre. C'étaient de longues embarcations minces et rapides, à la proue et la poupe magnifiquement sculptées. Leur quille courte leur permettait d'accoster rapidement sur les plages.

Les rameurs s'asseyaient sur des bancs, un homme par rame.

Gouvernail

QUIZ

1. Qu'est-ce qu'un drakkar ?
2. Quand Sven Barbe fourchue régna-t-il sur le Danemark ?
3. Avec quel bois fabriquait-on la quille d'un navire ?

Réponses :
1. Un bateau viking.
2. Entre 987-1014. 3. Du chêne.

8 **Les marins se dirigeaient grâce aux étoiles.** Les vikings n'avaient ni radio ni satellites pour naviguer lorsqu'ils s'éloignaient des terres. Ils observaient attentivement le soleil et les étoiles pour déterminer leur position. Ils étudiaient également les vents, les vagues et les courants marins ainsi que les déplacements des bancs de poissons et des colonies d'oiseaux.

9 **Les constructeurs de bateaux avaient besoin de grands arbres.** Ils utilisaient du chêne pour fabriquer la quille (la colonne vertébrale) des bateaux. Les plus longues quilles venaient d'arbres mesurant au moins 40 mètres de haut. Les constructeurs utilisaient des planches de chêne ou de bouleau pour la coque. Pour le mât, ils avaient besoin de grands arbres, très droits, comme le pin.

Voile carrée de coton ou de laine

Proue gravée

▼ Drakkar viking. Sa coque longue et étroite est composée de planches superposées, fixées par des clous métalliques. Le mât est fabriqué dans un tronc de pin entier.

10 **Les pirates exigèrent de l'or pour s'en aller.** Les pirates vikings comme le roi Sven à la barbe fourchue du Danemark (985-1014) exigea de l'argent pour ne pas assaillir un peuple : il alla en Angleterre avec ses bateaux de guerre et promit d'attaquer le pays si on ne le payait pas. Sa tactique était efficace. Chaque fois qu'il retournait en Angleterre on lui donnait « l'or des Danois ».

Quille solide (permettait de fendre les vagues)

11 **Les pilleurs emportaient des trésors et des esclaves.** Les nobles vikings engageaient des hordes de guerriers qu'ils envoyaient en expédition. Ils attaquaient les villages ou les monastères pour s'emparer de leurs trésors et capturer des jeunes gens en bonne santé pour en faire des esclaves.

▼ Les familles qui vivaient en bord de mer étaient terrifiées par les Vikings.

Armes et guerriers

12 **Les Vikings préféraient la gloire à une longue vie paisible.** Ils pensaient que la gloire survivrait longtemps aux guerriers courageux et que leur nom ne serait jamais oublié. Selon les mythes et les légendes, les guerriers qui mourraient au combat allaient au Walhalla où ils festoyaient avec les dieux.

13 **Les Berserker étaient des fous de bataille.** Ils s'habillaient de peaux d'ours et se mettaient dans un état de transe avant de se lancer dans le combat. Ils chargeaient l'ennemi en hurlant comme des loups. Dans cet état, ils n'avaient peur de rien et se révélaient être des ennemis redoutables pour tous ceux qui se mettaient en travers de leur chemin.

▲ Les guerriers berserker se ruaient sur leurs ennemis, vêtus de peau de bêtes sur leur cotte de maille.

14

Les nobles conduisaient leurs hommes à la guerre. À l'époque des Vikings, il n'existait pas encore d'armée nationale. Tous les rois et les seigneurs conduisaient leurs hommes à la guerre contre un ennemi commun. Les guerriers se battaient pour gagner de l'argent et des récompenses, comme des bracelets d'argent, par exemple. Ils pouvaient même obtenir une part du butin.

15

Les guerriers donnaient un nom à leur épée. Une bonne épée était le trésor le plus précieux d'un Viking. Souvent, les guerriers donnaient un nom à leur arme comme Morsure de feu, par exemple, et se faisaient enterrer avec elle. Les épées vikings à double tranchant avaient de longues lames solides et flexibles de fer martelé. Les pommeaux étaient décorés d'or et d'argent.

16

Les soldats vikings vivaient dans des camps et des forts. Les guerres et les raids emmenaient souvent les guerriers loin de chez eux. En Angleterre, ils construisirent des camps de cabanes en bois, entourées d'un haut monticule de terre sur lequel ils avaient érigé un mur de bois.

Bouclier rond de bois, couvert de cuir. Le centre métallique protégeait la main du guerrier.

Longue épée

Couteau

Casque de fer décoré, avec masque protecteur autour des yeux.

Longue lance

▲ Les soldats vikings devaient posséder leurs armes et leur équipement. Les soldats pauvres portaient des casques de cuir et des tuniques et étaient armés de couteaux et de lances. Les Vikings plus fortunés pouvaient s'offrir des cottes de maille, des casques de métal et des épées tranchantes.

INCROYABLE !

Les femmes vikings allaient à la guerre, mais elles ne se battaient pas. Elles soignaient les guerriers blessés et préparaient les repas.

Marchands, explorateurs et colons

17 **Les marchands vikings voyageaient à dos de chameaux et portaient leurs bateaux.** Les Vikings étaient de grands aventuriers qui aimaient découvrir des nouveaux pays. Certains marchands traversaient la Russie pour se rendre à Constantinople en Turquie (aujourd'hui Istanbul) et à Jérusalem, en Israël. Ces voyages duraient plusieurs années. De plus, ils étaient obligés de porter leurs bateaux entre les rivières pour traverser les terres. Dans les déserts du Moyen-Orient, ils voyageaient à dos de chameau, comme les habitants de la région.

▼ Les Vikings faisaient de longs voyages en hiver. Il était plus facile de marcher sur un sol gelé que de naviguer.

◄ Les marchands vikings emportaient toujours des balances et des poids avec eux.

18 **Les marchands emportaient des balances et de l'argent.** Les Vikings faisaient du commerce avec toutes sortes de gens. Certains préféraient faire du troc, échanger des marchandises et d'autres utilisaient de la monnaie. Il n'y avait pas de banques à l'époque des Vikings, si bien qu'ils n'étaient jamais sûrs d'obtenir une somme équitable. Ils faisaient donc leur commerce en échangeant des pièces d'argent qu'ils pesaient sur des balances portables.

19 **Les marchands revenaient avec de nombreux achats.** Les Vikings achetaient des marchandises, tout autant qu'ils en vendaient. Ils allaient en Angleterre pour acheter du blé et des tissus de laine. En France, ils se procuraient du vin et des poteries. Ils achetaient du verre en Allemagne, des bijoux en Russie et des épices au Moyen-Orient.

20 Les Vikings installèrent des colonies de l'Écosse à la Sicile. Partout où ils allaient, les Vikings fondaient de nouveaux villages et de nouvelles villes. Soit ils se battaient avec les habitants de la région pour leur prendre leurs terres, soit ils vivaient avec eux pacifiquement.

21 Erik le Rouge utilisa une astuce pour faire venir ses compagnons au Groenland. Il fut le premier à découvrir cette terre vers 983. Certes le pays était glacé, il y avait peu de pâturages mais il voulait que des familles viennent s'installer dans ce pays. C'est pourquoi il l'appela « Groenland », pays vert. En 986, d'autres colons vinrent le rejoindre mais une fois qu'ils avaient découvert à quoi ressemblait le pays, il était trop tard pour faire demi-tour !

22 Les Vikings allèrent en Amérique par erreur !
En 986, Bjarni Herjólfsson, lors d'un voyage, aperçut une terre mais n'a pu y accoster à cause d'une violente tempête. Quelques années plus tard, un colon du Groenland, Leif Eriksson décida d'aller voir de plus près cette terre que Bjarni avait longée. Il accosta dans des lieux qu'il nomma Helluland, Markland et Vinland.

▶ Les Vikings s'installèrent sur les côtes du Groenland car l'intérieur des terres était couvert de glace. Ces colonies disparurent entre 1480 et 1500 car le climat était devenu encore plus froid.

Les maisons vikings

23 Dans les années 700 et 800, les Vikings comptaient parmi les meilleurs artisans du monde. Ils vivaient dans des environnements hostiles, aux hivers froids, avec des nuits très longues et devaient mettre leurs troupeaux à l'abri. Dans les villes, les cochons, les chèvres et les chevaux vivaient dans des granges, mais dans les campagnes, on construisait de longues maisons, avec un espace pour la famille d'un côté et un espace pour les animaux de l'autre.

24 Les Vikings couvraient les maisons avec de l'herbe. Dans de nombreuses régions où ils s'installèrent, comme les îles Orcades ou l'Islande, il y avait très peu d'arbres. Les familles vikings construisaient des maisons dont les fondations étaient de pierre et étaient recouvertes de tourbe et de terre où poussait encore de l'herbe. S'ils en avaient les moyens, ils tapissaient les murs de planches importées de Scandinavie Sinon, ils récupéraient des morceaux de bois apportés par les vagues.

Les animaux vivaient d'un côté de la maison

Métier à tisser

Murs de rondins

▶ Les longues maisons étaient généralement construites sur un terrain en pente pour que les déjections des animaux coulent le long de la colline, et non dans le quartier réservé aux hommes.

25

Les maisons vikings n'étaient pas très saines. Ces maisons étaient privées de fenêtres pour ne pas laisser entrer le froid. Elles étaient humides et enfumées à cause du feu qu'on y faisait. D'ailleurs, les vikings souffraient souvent de maladies des poumons et certains ont été tués par un gaz, le monoxyde de carbone, qui s'accumule au fur et à mesure que le feu consomme l'oxygène de la pièce.

INCROYABLE !

Les Vikings aimaient vivre dans leurs longues maisons car la chaleur des animaux fournissait une sorte de chauffage.

Tourbe et herbe sur le toit

Poutres de bois

Viande fumée pour la conservation

26

Les propriétaires de la maison s'asseyaient sur le haut siège. Les familles vikings possédaient très peu de meubles. Seuls les riches pouvaient s'offrir des lits ou des tables à pieds fixes. La plupart des maisons étaient meublées avec des tables à tréteaux et des bancs de bois. Le centre d'un des bancs était marqué par deux piliers de bois. C'était le haut siège, la place d'honneur du maître de la maison.

Sanitaires extérieurs

17

27 **Les Vikings pratiquaient l'élevage plutôt que la culture.** Dans les pays du Nord, le sol était trop mince et trop caillouteux pour des cultures telles que le blé ou l'orge. Les fermiers élevaient des moutons ou autres bétails pour avoir du lait et de la viande. Ces animaux avaient besoin d'herbe : c'est pourquoi les Vikings appréciaient les pâturages naturels.

28 **Le chanvre et le foin étaient les principales récoltes.** Les Vikings avaient besoin de fabriquer des vêtements et de nourrir leur bétail. Les vêtements chauds étaient en laine mais ils grattaient. Les femmes tissaient donc des tissus plus fins à porter sur la peau. Pour cela, elles utilisaient des tiges de chanvre que les fermiers plantaient sur des terrains humides. Quand venait l'hiver et que les pâturages des animaux étaient couverts de neige, le bétail avait besoin de foin (d'herbe sèche). Les Vikings faisaient pousser l'herbe dans des prairies bien entretenues, la fauchaient et la conservaient au sec.

Poissons mis à sécher au soleil

Herbe qui sèche pour en faire du foin

29 **Les chasseurs et les pêcheurs trouvaient leur nourriture près des côtes.**

Les Vikings vivaient près de côtes riches en poissons. À l'aide de filets et de pièges, les pêcheurs capturaient des morues, des harengs ou des poissons de rivière comme les truites et les anguilles. Ils ramassaient des moules et des huîtres et chassaient les baleines pour leur graisse.

Les jeunes gens escaladaient de dangereuses falaises pour dénicher les oiseaux et ramasser leurs œufs. Ils chassaient aussi les phoques et les morses.

Bateau ancré dans un port

Les paysans fauchent l'herbe

◀ Les Vikings ne passaient pas tout leur temps à piller et à voler. Ils se sont aperçus que les îles britanniques fournissaient de belles terres arables pour leurs colonies.

Labourage d'un champ avec les bœufs

30 **Les chasseurs traquaient les animaux sauvages.**

En Norvège et en Suède, il y avait de nombreux animaux sauvages, comme les ours, les loups et les renards. On les chassait pour leur fourrure, qui donnait des vêtements chauds ou qu'on pouvait vendre à de riches clients.

Ils chassaient aussi le cerf pour sa viande, sa peau et ses bois, avec lesquels on fabriquait des perles et des peignes.

La femme disperse des grains pour les poulets

Nourriture et fêtes

31 **Les Vikings mangeaient deux fois par jour.** Le matin, le repas du jour, était constitué de pain d'orge ou d'avoine, accompagné de beurre et de fromage. Le repas principal, ou repas du soir, était prévu en début de soirée. Au menu, on trouvait de la viande ou du poisson et des baies sauvages en été. Les repas étaient servis dans des assiettes de bois ou des bols de saponite (« pierre à savon »). On mangeait avec des couteaux en métal ou des cuillères en corne.

▼ Les objets fabriqués dans les cornes du bétail étaient très légers mais aussi très solides. C'étaient des instruments parfaits pour les voyages des marchands ou des guerriers.

Timbale argentée décorée utilisée par les riches

Poterie utilisée par les pauvres

Corne dans laquelle buvaient les guerriers

QUIZ

1. Dans quoi buvaient les guerriers vikings ?
2. Comment les Vikings faisaient-ils bouillir leur eau ?
3. Que signifie « abats » ?
4. Combien de temps duraient les fêtes ?

Réponses
1. Dans des cornes de bœuf
2. Sur des pierres chauffées au rouge
3. Le cœur, le foie et les poumons d'un animal
4. Une semaine ou plus

32 **Les guerriers buvaient dans des cornes de bœuf.** Les boissons préférées des Vikings étaient le lait, le petit lait (liquide qui reste après la fabrication du fromage), la bière (fabriquée avec de l'orge fermenté) et l'hydromel (du vin de miel). Les riches buvaient dans des verres ou des timbales d'argent ; les pauvres, eux, se contentaient de pots en terre. Lors des fêtes, les guerriers vikings buvaient dans des cornes creuses d'animaux.

 Les Vikings faisaient bouillir leur eau sur des pierres chauffées au rouge. Les Vikings possédaient rarement des fours. Les femmes et les servantes faisaient cuire les aliments dans des chaudrons de métal remplis d'eau qu'elles mettaient sur des pierres chauffées au rouge. C'était une méthode de cuisson très efficace.

34 **Les Vikings adoraient les saucisses au sang.** Les cuisinières préparaient les saucisses en versant le sang de l'animal tout juste tué et les abats (le cœur, le foie, les poumons) dans l'intestin nettoyé d'un mouton puis faisaient bouillir le tout. Parfois, elles ajoutaient de l'ail, du cumin ou des graines de genièvre. Les Vikings préféraient ce plat aux légumes comme les choux, les pois et les haricots.

▼ Les femmes et les esclaves préparaient les repas sur le feu et servaient les guerriers qui festoyaient.

Chou

Haricots

Ail

Petits pois

Oignon

▲ Les Vikings mangeaient déjà des petits pois, des haricots, des choux, des oignons et de l'ail.

35 **Les fêtes duraient souvent plus d'une semaine.** Après avoir remporté une victoire, les Vikings aimaient faire la fête. Les rois et les nobles offraient des festins pour récompenser les vaillants soldats. Les familles en organisaient aussi pour célébrer les mariages. Les invités revêtaient leurs plus beaux vêtements et les hôtes fournissaient une abondance de nourriture et de boissons. Tout le monde restait jusqu'à ce qu'il ne reste plus rien à manger.

Femmes et enfants

36 Les femmes vikings étaient très indépendantes. Elles prenaient les décisions importantes concernant la maison. Elles cuisinaient et fabriquaient les vêtements. Elles élevaient les enfants, dirigeaient les esclaves et s'occupaient de l'élevage du bétail ainsi que de l'artisanat.

FABRIQUE UN COLLIER VIKING

Tu auras besoin de :

Une ficelle de 40 centimètres

De la pâte à modeler

De la peinture blanche, jaune et brune

De peinture dorée ou argentée

1. Forme un croc d'animal de 4 cm de long dans la pâte à modeler.

2. Perce un trou près de la racine et attends que la dent sèche.

3. Peins le croc avec les peintures blanche, jaune et brune. Lorsque tout est sec, décore-le avec un peu de peinture argentée ou dorée.

4. Fais ainsi plusieurs crocs

5. Passe le fil à travers le trou des dents et attache-le autour de ton cou.

▲ Les femmes filaient la laine de mouton et la tissaient sur des métiers verticaux pour en faire des vêtements chauds.

37 Seules les veuves pouvaient épouser qui elles voulaient. Si un Viking voulait se marier, il devait demander l'autorisation au père de la jeune fille et verser une somme d'argent. Si le père acceptait, le mariage avait lieu, même si la fille ne le voulait pas. Les veuves disposaient de plus de liberté. Elles n'avaient pas besoin de la permission de quiconque pour se remarier. Les femmes avaient le droit de demander le divorce si leur mari les traitait mal.

38

Les vieilles femmes étaient respectées pour leur sagesse. De nombreuses femmes mouraient très jeunes en donnant naissance à leur enfant. Les personnes âgées de plus de 50 ans étaient rares dans la société viking. Tant qu'elles étaient en bonne santé, elles étaient utiles pour leurs connaissances et leur expérience ; mais faibles et malades, elles devenaient un fardeau pour la famille.

39

Les pères vikings choisissaient les enfants qui allaient survivre. Les parents comptaient sur leurs enfants pour assurer leurs vieux jours, il fallait donc qu'ils soient forts et solides. Le père examinait l'enfant à la naissance. S'il semblait en bonne santé, il l'aspergeait d'eau et lui donnait un nom pour montrer qu'il l'acceptait dans la famille. Si l'enfant était malade, il demandait aux esclaves de le laisser mourir dehors.

◀ Nourrir les poulets et ramasser les œufs était un travail de filles. Elles s'occupaient également de la culture des légumes et aidaient leur mère à faire la cuisine.

40

Les enfants vikings n'allaient pas à l'école. Les filles aidaient leur mère à faire la cuisine et à s'occuper des animaux. Elles allaient chercher de l'eau, des noix et des fruits. Elles apprenaient à filer, à tisser et à coudre. Les garçons aidaient leur père à l'atelier ou dans les champs. Ils apprenaient à monter à cheval et à se servir des armes. Ils devaient être prêts à se battre dès l'âge de quinze ou seize ans.

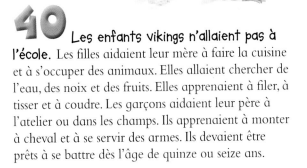

▲ Les garçons s'entraînaient au combat avec des épées de bois et de petits boucliers.

Vêtements et bijoux

41 Les Vikings portaient beaucoup de vêtements pour se protéger du froid.

Les femmes s'habillaient d'une longue robe de lin ou de laine recouverte d'une chasuble de laine. Les hommes étaient vêtus d'une tunique de laine sur une chemise de lin et portaient des pantalons de laine. Hommes et femmes portaient des gants, des manteaux, des chaussettes, des bottes et des chaussures de cuir. Les hommes couvraient leur tête de bonnets en peau de moutons ; les femmes, de foulards et de châles.

▶ Les femmes vikings aimaient les couleurs vives et les dessins. Elles ornaient souvent leurs vêtements de broderies.

42 Fourrure et plumes les aidaient à se tenir au chaud.

Les Vikings doublaient leurs vêtements en laine de fourrure ou les rembourraient avec des couches de duvet d'oie. Certains fabriquaient des manteaux dans des peaux de mouton, très résistantes et très chaudes.

43 Les Vikings attachaient leurs vêtements avec des broches.

Il y en avait de styles différents. Les hommes portaient de grosses broches rondes sur l'épaule gauche. Les femmes les portaient par paire, une sur chaque épaule pour attacher les bretelles de leur chasuble. Parfois, elles en avaient une autour du cou pour retenir leur manteau, et une autre munie d'un cordon, qui leur servait de porte-clés.

▶ Cette magnifique broche ornée de fil d'or appartenait à un riche noble viking.

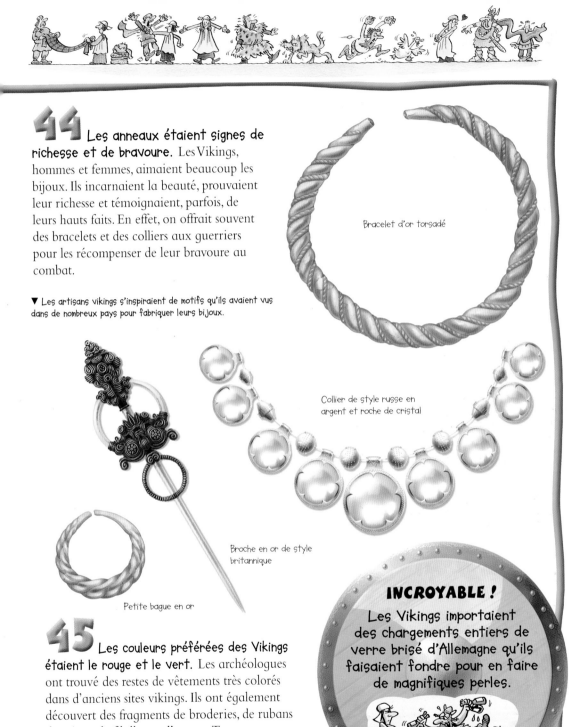

44 **Les anneaux étaient signes de richesse et de bravoure.** Les Vikings, hommes et femmes, aimaient beaucoup les bijoux. Ils incarnaient la beauté, prouvaient leur richesse et témoignaient, parfois, de leurs hauts faits. En effet, on offrait souvent des bracelets et des colliers aux guerriers pour les récompenser de leur bravoure au combat.

▼ Les artisans vikings s'inspiraient de motifs qu'ils avaient vus dans de nombreux pays pour fabriquer leurs bijoux.

Bracelet d'or torsadé

Collier de style russe en argent et roche de cristal

Broche en or de style britannique

Petite bague en or

45 **Les couleurs préférées des Vikings étaient le rouge et le vert.** Les archéologues ont trouvé des restes de vêtements très colorés dans d'anciens sites vikings. Ils ont également découvert des fragments de broderies, de rubans de soie et de fil d'or et d'argent. Tous ces éléments servaient à décorer les vêtements.

INCROYABLE !

Les Vikings importaient des chargements entiers de verre brisé d'Allemagne qu'ils faisaient fondre pour en faire de magnifiques perles.

Santé et beauté

46 **Les Anglais trouvaient les Vikings trop propres !** Ils disaient que les Vikings se coiffaient trop souvent, changeaient sans cesse de vêtements et prenaient un bain toutes les semaines. Ils se lavaient en versant de l'eau sur des pierres chauffées au rouge, créant ainsi des nuages de vapeur où ils restaient assis pour transpirer. Ensuite, ils se nettoyaient la peau avec des tiges de saule et plongeaient dans un bassin d'eau fraîche pour se rincer.

▲ Les Vikings se « baignaient » dans des bains de vapeur appelés sauna, toujours très en vogue en Scandinavie.

47 **Les Vikings emmenaient leur épée avec eux aux toilettes.** Les Vikings possédaient des toilettes extérieures qui consistaient en un seau ou un trou creusé dans le sol, surmonté d'un siège en bois. Les murs étaient souvent en osier. Mais en territoire ennemi, les Vikings procédaient autrement. Ils sortaient par groupe de quatre ou cinq hommes armés pour se protéger les uns les autres.

▲ Les toilettes vikings devaient ressembler un peu à cela. Ils utilisaient de la mousse ou des feuilles séchées comme papier toilette.

48

Les Vikings utilisaient les oignons pour diagnostiquer la gravité des blessures. Si un guerrier était blessé à l'estomac lors d'une bataille, ses camarades lui préparaient une bouillie de céréales avec beaucoup d'oignons et la lui faisait manger. Ils attendaient et respiraient la blessure. Si elle avait l'odeur d'oignon, ils laissaient l'homme mourir car ils savaient que la paroi de l'estomac avait été tranchée et qu'on ne pourrait plus le sauver.

▲ La foi dans les pouvoirs guérisseurs des runes a peut-être aidé les Vikings à moins souffrir.

50

Les Vikings soignaient beaucoup leurs cheveux. Les femmes portaient les cheveux longs et les laissaient lâchés jusqu'à leur mariage. En revanche, une fois mariées, elles les nouaient en une natte très sophistiquée sur le bas de la nuque. Les hommes prenaient également soin de leurs cheveux. Ils les coupaient courts sur la nuque mais les laissaient longs devant. Pour ne pas être gênés par les mèches devant les yeux, ils faisaient parfois des nattes.

INCROYABLE !

Les hommes vikings se maquillaient ! Ils utilisaient surtout de l'eye-liner, sans doute fait de suie ou de baies rouges écrasées. Ils trouvaient que cela les rendait plus beaux.

49

Les Vikings croyaient que les runes soulageaient la douleur. Ils fabriquaient des médicaments avec des herbes mais pensaient aussi que l'écriture de symboles avait des pouvoirs surnaturels. Ils écrivaient des formules magiques sur des morceaux d'os qu'ils laissaient près des malades. Ils en inscrivaient également sur les paumes des femmes pendant les accouchements pour leur éviter la douleur.

▲ Des styles de coiffure viking. Lors des fêtes, les femmes portaient des couronnes de fleurs dans les cheveux.

Des artisans talentueux

51 Les Vikings confectionnaient tous les objets dont ils avaient besoin. Les familles étaient obligées de fabriquer et de réparer tout ce qu'il leur fallait : maison, meubles, jouets pour les enfants, vêtements Ils ne disposaient d'aucune machine, si bien que ce travail leur prenait beaucoup de temps.

52 Les forgerons allaient de ferme en ferme. Les Vikings avaient souvent une petite forge chez eux et pouvaient ainsi fabriquer leurs outils. Mais, pour un travail plus complexe, ils comptaient sur les forgerons itinérants ou devaient entreprendre eux-mêmes un long voyage pour se rendre en ville.

▶ Les forgerons faisaient chauffer le fer jusqu'à ce qu'il devienne assez mou pour qu'on puisse le travailler et le transformer en arme.

53 Les os étaient joliment travaillés.

Les artisans doués fabriquaient des peignes dans les bois de cerf mais ils étaient trop chers pour les Vikings ordinaires. Ces derniers gravaient les os qui leur restaient après les repas pour en faire des peignes, des perles, des broches, des plaques d'identité et des tablettes de tissage pour les broderies.

54 Les vikings fabriquaient des tasses dans les carrières.

On trouvait des carrières de saponite dans de nombreuses régions vikings. Malgré sa beauté, cette pierre était très lourde. Alors, pour éviter de transporter de trop lourds fardeaux, les artisans fabriquaient grossièrement les objets sur place et les emmenaient chez eux pour les finitions.

Manche

Manche décoré

◄ Pour fabriquer les peignes, on fixait des rangées de dents dans un manche.

Dents d'os

55 Les bijoutiers avaient beaucoup de talent.

Pour faire une broche, ils martelaient un bloc de métal sur un motif déjà conçu, puis ajoutaient des détails en filigrane (avec des gouttelettes d'argent fondu) ou incrustaient les parties incisées d'une pâte noire appelée nielle. Pour fabriquer bracelets et colliers, ils torsadaient des fils d'argent.

◄ Ce collier est fait de plusieurs fils d'argents savamment torsadés.

Les villes vikings

56 **Les rois faisaient construire des villes pour favoriser le commerce.** Avant de devenir très puissants, les marchands allaient faire du commerce dans des foires qui n'avaient lieu qu'une ou deux fois par an. Les Vikings décidèrent donc de construire des villes pour pouvoir faire du commerce toute l'année. On prélevait des impôts sur les habitants et les marchands qui y passaient.

▶ Les marchés vikings se tenaient souvent sur les plages. Les familles de fermiers et les marchands s'y rencontraient pour vendre et acheter.

57 **Les villes constituaient des cibles faciles pour les attaquants.** Les pirates et les brigands venus de Russie et d'Allemagne traversaient la Baltique pour voler les marchandises précieuses. Les rois firent construir des enceintes de terre surmontées de murs en bois et envoyèrent des troupes de guerriers pour les protéger.

58 **Les maisons des villes étaient bien conçç pour les citadins.** En ville, les maisons étaient constru les unes contre les autres car l'espace était limité. Elles étaient plus petites que les maisons de la campagne co on n'avait pas besoin d'espace pour les animaux et les récoltes. La plupart étaient construites en bois avec de toits de chaume et possédaient souven atelier et une petite boutique.

INCROYABLE !

Les premiers Russes étaient des Vikings ! Le nom « Russie » vient du mot Rus, utilisé par les gens vivant à l'est de la Baltique pour désigner les colons qui s'installaient là-bas.

59 C'est en ville que furent fabriquées les premières pièces de monnaie. D'après ce que nous savons, il n'y avait pas de monnaie en Scandinavie avant les Vikings. Les marchands faisaient du troc en échangeant des marchandises ou payaient avec des petits morceaux d'argent qu'ils pesaient sur des balances portatives. Mais de nombreuses pièces étrangères sont arrivées chez les Vikings grâce à leurs voyages à l'étranger et aux pillages. Vers 825, les artisans de la ville de Hedeby (située aujourd'hui au nord de l'Allemagne) commencèrent à les copier. Plus tard, d'autres villes fabriquèrent leur monnaie.

60 Les Vikings se sont aussi installés en Russie. Les Vikings se rendirent sur les côtes est de la Baltique et s'y installèrent pour y pratiquer le commerce. Staraya Ladoga et Novgorod en Russie ainsi que Kiev en Ukraine comptaient parmi les villes les plus importantes en négoce.

◄ Cette pièce viking de la ville de Hedeby représente un navire marchand.

La loi et l'ordre

61 **Les Vikings observaient un strict code de l'honneur.** Les hommes et les femmes étaient très fiers, et l'honneur comptait beaucoup pour eux. Être traité de voleur, de tricheur ou de lâche était une disgrâce. Les Vikings appréciaient aussi la loyauté. Ils juraient fidélité à leur seigneur et à leurs camarades en se serrant la main pour sceller le contrat.

62 **Les querelles se réglaient souvent par un combat.** Les querelles entre familles créaient des inimitiés. Si quelqu'un était insulté ou tué, toute la famille avait pour devoir de le venger. Les conflits pouvaient durer des mois et de nombreuses personnes étaient tuées dans les deux camps. Quand les familles étaient enfin prêtes à accepter la paix, l'une devait payer à l'autre une certaine somme en compensation du préjudice causé.

▲ Les guerriers vikings défiaient ceux qui les avaient insultés en un combat mortel.

63 **Les lois vikings n'étaient pas écrites.** Un crieur de lois les apprenait par cœur et les récitait chaque année pour que tout le monde puisse les entendre et les comprendre. Grâce à leurs connaissances, les crieurs de lois devenaient souvent les conseillers des rois et des seigneurs.

64 **Les Vikings tenaient une assemblée générale annuelle.** C'était une assemblée à ciel ouvert qui réunissait tous les hommes libres d'un district. Elle punissait les criminels et établissait les nouvelles lois. En général, les punitions les plus sévères étaient de fortes amendes.

Ces assemblées permettaient aux gens des communautés éloignées de se rencontrer et d'échanger des nouvelles. De nombreux commerçants en profitaient et installaient leur étal tout autour.

▼ Tous les hommes libres, des seigneurs aux fermiers, pouvaient voter lors des assemblées.

65 **Les punitions étaient impitoyables.** La vie des Vikings n'était pas facile. Ils devaient travailler dur pour survivre et il n'y avait aucune place dans la communauté pour les faibles, les paresseux ou les gêneurs. Les voleurs étaient souvent pendus et les criminels qui refusaient de payer les amendes étaient bannis. C'était une punition très sévère. Sans maison ni famille, il était impossible de survivre.

QUIZ

1. Quels étaient les deux punitions les plus sévères ?

2. Comment les Vikings réglaient-ils les conflits familiaux ?

3. Pourquoi les Vikings se serraient-ils la main ?

4. Qui récitait les lois ?

Réponses :
1. La pendaison et le bannissement.
2. En se battant.
3. Pour sceller un contrat.
4. Le crieur de lois

33

Jeux, musiques et sports

▲ Les Vikings aimaient les histoires de dragons, d'elfes, de monstres, de créatures magiques tout autant que celles des héros locaux.

66 Les Vikings aimaient la musique, la danse et les clowns. Lors des fêtes, ils chantaient et dansaient. Selon ce qu'ils avaient bu, les danses étaient lentes ou agitées. Les rois payaient des danseurs, des clowns, des acrobates et des jongleurs pour animer leurs fêtes.

67 Les Vikings aimaient plaisanter et poser des énigmes. Ils avaient un sens de l'humour un peu grossier mais très vif et aimaient se faire des farces. Ils appréciaient les histoires où les héros et les dieux gagnaient en jouant des vilains tours. Ils s'amusaient aux dés et à d'autres jeux de société, comme les échecs (hnefatafl). Malheureusement, ils étaient très mauvais perdants et les jeux finissaient souvent en bagarres.

▶ Cette table de jeux servait à jouer au hnefatafl dont les règles étaient proches de celles des échecs.

68 La natation, la course et le saut étaient leurs jeux estivaux. En été, le temps était assez clément pour que les Vikings puissent se débarrasser de la plupart de leurs vêtements. Ils pouvaient donc bouger plus librement et courir rapidement. En hiver, dans leurs vêtements chauds, les Vikings pratiquaient les sports de neige comme le ski ou le patinage sur des lacs gelés.

▼ Les archers vikings utilisaient des arcs de bois d'if et des cordes de chanvre. Les flèches en bouleau étaient munies d'une pointe métallique.

INCROYABLE !

Un des récits favoris des Vikings raconte que le dieu Thor, célèbre pour sa barbe et sa force, s'était déguisé en fille pour épouser un géant. En fait, c'était une ruse pour récupérer le marteau magique que le géant lui avait dérobé.

69 Les sports vikings constituaient un entraînement parfait pour la guerre. Le lancer de javelot, l'escrime et le tir à l'arc étaient des sports très populaires. Les Vikings s'entraînaient également à la bataille et apprenaient à leurs fils à développer leur force et à manier les armes.

70 Les Vikings aimaient la lutte et les combats de chevaux. La lutte était également un bon entraînement pour la guerre. En effet, un guerrier pouvait perdre ses armes au combat et devait savoir se battre au corps à corps. Mais les Vikings aimaient regarder les combats pour s'amuser car ils adoraient la violence. Ils se distrayaient aussi en regardant les étalons se battre à coup de dents et de sabots.

Les dieux et les déesses

71 Les Vikings adoraient de nombreux dieux.

Les Ases ou dieux du ciel comprenaient Odin, Thor et Tyr (des dieux de la guerre) et Loki qui était un dieu farceur. Les Vanes, dieux de la terre et de l'eau, étaient Njord, le dieu de la mer, et Freyr, le dieu des fermiers. Avec sa sœur Freyja, il apportait la fertilité.

▼ Odin, le dieu de la guerre, chevauchait un cheval à huit pattes. Deux corbeaux, la Pensée et la Mémoire, l'accompagnaient toujours.

▼ La belle déesse Freyja se déplaçait dans un char tiré par des chats.

72 On pratiquait des sacrifices humains.

Les Vikings croyaient pouvoir obtenir les faveurs des dieux en leur faisant des cadeaux. Comme la vie était la chose la plus précieuse, on leur offrait des hommes vivants, généralement des prisonniers de guerre. Les Vikings cuisinaient également des repas qu'ils partageaient avec les dieux.

73 Le destin était le maître des Vikings.

Selon la légende, trois sœurs décidèrent du sort du monde. Elles s'assirent au pied d'Yggdrasil, le grand arbre qui soutient l'univers, et filèrent les « fils du destin ». Elles rendaient également visite à chaque bébé pour décider de son avenir. Une fois leur décision prise, rien ne pouvait la changer.

74 Après la mort, les Vikings allaient dans différents royaumes. Les guerriers qui mouraient au combat allaient soit au Walhalla, soit dans la demeure pacifique de Freyja. Les jeunes filles célibataires rejoignaient aussi Freyja et les hommes bons allaient vivre avec les dieux du ciel. Mais les Vikings qui menaient une vie ordinaire ou mouraient de maladie ne pouvaient que se réfugier dans le Niflheim. C'était un lieu sinistre, perpétuellement dans le brouillard, dirigé par une farouche déesse nommée Hel.

▶ Les Vikings demandaient au dieu farouche Tyr de les aider à remporter les batailles.

75 Vers la fin de l'ère viking, de nombreux hommes se convertirent au christianisme. Des missionnaires venus d'Angleterre, d'Allemagne et de France se rendirent dans les pays vikings. Les Vikings continuèrent à vénérer leurs dieux pendant quelques siècles. Vers l'an 1000, des rois vikings comme Harald à la dent Bleue et Olav Tryggvesson adoptèrent la foi chrétienne, leur permettant ainsi de renforcer leurs pouvoirs. Ils ont fait construire des églises et ont incité le peuple à se convertir.

▼ Njord, le dieu de la mer, épousa la géante Skadi qui veillait sur les montagnes enneigées.

QUIZ

1. Qui était Loki ?

2. Quel arbre soutenait l'univers ?

3. Où allaient les guerriers après leur mort ?

Réponses :
1. Un dieu farceur 2. Yggdrasil 3. Walhalla

Héros, légendes et sagas

◄ Les Vikings aimaient beaucoup les sagas, retraçant les vies des gens d'autrefois.

76 **Les Vikings honoraient les héros morts au combat.** Ils racontaient des histoires, nommées sagas, qui narraient leurs aventures à la guerre. Elles étaient contées de génération en génération afin qu'elles ne tombent jamais dans l'oubli. Après l'époque viking, on les écrivit.

77 **Les scaldes chantaient et racontaient des sagas.** Les rois vikings et les seigneurs engageaient des poètes appelés scaldes. Ils avaient pour fonction de réciter des poèmes à la gloire de leur patron et de distraire les invités lors des fêtes. La plupart jouaient de la harpe et accompagnaient leurs récits de chansons.

78 **Les Vikings avaient peur de la fin du monde.** De nombreux récits racontaient l'histoire de Ragnarok, la malédiction des dieux. Ce serait une époque terrible où les forces du mal et les forces du bien s'affronteraient. Les dieux vikings se battraient contre des monstres et des géants et perdraient la bataille. Ce serait la fin du monde.

▼ Les légendes Vikings prédisaient que la fin du monde aurait lieu au cours de la grande bataille de Ragnarok. Cependant, un nouveau monde devait renaître sur les ruines de l'ancien.

79 Les Vikings croyaient aux esprits et aux monstres. Pour eux, c'étaient des forces invisibles qui vivaient dans le monde des vivants. Certains, comme les elfes, étaient gentils et secourables. Ils apportaient de bonnes récoltes et donnaient de beaux enfants. D'autres, comme les géants, mangeaient les hommes et étaient cruels. Les Vikings imaginaient que les monstres ressemblaient à d'immenses animaux féroces. Ils gravaient leurs têtes sur les bateaux pour éloigner les esprits maléfiques.

▲ Les Vikings croyaient que les Walkyries, de farouches guerrières, conduisaient les hommes morts au combat au Walhalla où ils vivraient éternellement avec Odin.

◄ Une amulette viking (un porte-bonheur) en forme de marteau.

QUIZ

1. Comment les Vikings appelaient-ils la fin du monde ?

2. Que contaient les scaldes ?

3. Pourquoi les fermiers portaient-ils des marteaux autour du cou ?

4. Que mangeaient les géants ?

Réponses :
1. Ragnarok. 2. Les sagas de leur patron
3. Pour apporter fertilité aux troupeaux
et à la terre 4. Des hommes.

80 Les amulettes protégeaient les guerriers et les paysans. Ils portaient autour du cou des amulettes ayant la forme du marteau magique de Thor. Les guerriers pensaient que ces petits marteaux leur donneraient la force pour combattre. Les paysans espéraient que ces porte-bonheur apporteraient la fertilité.

Rites de mort

81 **Les Vikings enterraient déjà leurs morts.** Tout au début de l'âge viking, on brûlait les corps sur de grands feux de bois. Ensuite, on récupérait les cendres qu'on conservait dans des urnes de poterie. Entre 800 et 900, dans certaines régions, on commença à enterrer les corps directement dans la terre.

82 **Les morts emportaient des objets utiles dans l'autre monde.** Les Vikings croyaient que les âmes des morts survivaient dans l'autre monde. C'est pourquoi ils emportaient des objets qui leur seraient utiles après la mort. Les riches guerriers emportaient des vêtements, des armes, des chevaux et parfois, des femmes et des esclaves. Les femmes riches étaient enterrées avec des vêtements, des bijoux, des meubles et du matériel pour tisser et filer.

83
Les tombes vikings ont été préservées pendant des siècles.
Les archéologues ont découvert de nombreuses tombes dont le contenu était en très bon état. Certains objets, comme les bijoux, les poteries et les gravures sur pierre ne pourrissent jamais. D'autres comme les vêtements ont parfois eu la chance de résister. Même certains bateaux ont été préservés sous l'eau. Tous ces éléments nous ont donné des indications précieuses sur le mode de vie des Vikings.

▼ Ces pierres disposées en forme de coque de navire marque l'emplacement d'une ancienne sépulture.

84
Les Vikings espéraient que les bateaux emporteraient les âmes dans l'au-delà. Lorsqu'ils enterraient les urnes, ils les disposaient en forme de bateau. Certains emplacements très vastes pouvant mesurer jusqu'à 80 mètres de long servaient sans doute également de lieu de culte. Les personnalités très importantes étaient enterrées dans de véritables bateaux, avec de nombreux trésors.

◄ Protégé par une toile, le corps étaient installés dans un véritable bateau. Ensuite, on y mettait le feu pour que l'âme du mort puisse, à la fin de la crémation, s'envoler vers l'au-delà.

85
Les Vikings traitaient les corps avec beaucoup de respect. Ils les lavaient, les emballaient dans un tissu ou dans de l'écorce de bouleau avant de les enterrer ou de les brûler. Les Vikings craignaient que les morts reviennent les hanter s'ils n'étaient pas traités avec soin.

INCROYABLE !
Certains squelettes et bateaux vikings, enterrés dans des sols acides, ont totalement disparu. Néanmoins, ils ont laissé des traces dans la terre que les archéologues étudient attentivement.

Écriture et images

86 **La plupart des Vikings ne savaient ni lire ni écrire.** Ils se fiaient au langage parlé pour communiquer et à leur mémoire pour se souvenir de l'histoire du pays, de la famille et des événements importants. Au début de l'ère viking, tout le monde parlait la même langue, le *dönsk tunga*, mais après l'an 1000, de nouveaux dialectes sont apparus.

87 **L'écriture viking était composée de runes.** L'alphabet viking comprenait 16 lettres, appelées runes. Elles étaient utilisées pour marquer le nom du propriétaire sur les objets de valeur ou pour envoyer des messages. Les runes étaient constituées de lignes droites ; ainsi elles étaient faciles à graver sur le bois ou la pierre. Les Vikings ne connaissaient pas le papier.

▲Runes viking. De haut en bas, ces symboles pourraient se transcrire phonétiquement ainsi : F U Th É R K H N Aie É S T B M L R.

▼ Les Vikings utilisaient des pointes métalliques pour graver les objets précieux.

Bois de cerf décoré de runes

Calendrier viking

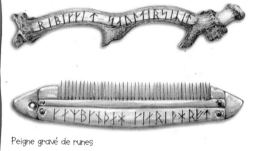

Peigne gravé de runes

88 **On utilisait aussi les runes pour écrire des formules magiques.** Parfois, les runes servaient à inscrire des messages codés, voire des formules magiques. Elles étaient censées donner un pouvoir particulier aux objets. Encore aujourd'hui, certains messages secrets ne sont pas encore décryptés.

89 Les pierres marquées de runes raconte histoires. Les riches familles payaient des artisans pour qu'ils gravent des inscriptions sur les pierres à la louange des parents ou des enfants défunts. Parfois, on y inscrivait les exploits du mort. Une fois le travail terminé, on dressait la pierre dans un lieu public afin que tout le monde puisse la voir.

▲ Les pierres gravées sont des traces des anciens citoyens vikings.

90 Les pierres gravées racontent de formidables aventures. Dans certaines régions, les vikings gravaient des dessins sur les pierres, et non des runes. Ils montraient des scènes de la vie du défunt et représentaient des dieux, des géants et des monstres.

▲ Certaines images racontaient les exploits des guerriers, d'autres honoraient l'être aimé.

ÉCRIS TON NOM EN RUNES

Avec la pierre gravée de la page 42, essaie d'écrire ton nom en runes. L'alphabet rune s'appelle aussi « futhark », rappelant ainsi la valeur phonétique des six premiers caractères. Il existe un caractère spécial pour le son « th » qu'on trouve encore en anglais, mais aucun pour les sons « i » et « o ». Même les vikings avaient du mal à écrire tous les mots !

La fin de l'époque viking

91 **Les rois écrasèrent la puissance viking.** Pendant des siècles, les rois d'Angleterre, d'Écosse et d'Irlande tentèrent vainement de chasser les Vikings de leurs terres. Mais après l'an 1000, ils commencèrent à avoir un peu plus de succès. Brian Boru, le roi d'Irlande vainquit les Vikings en 1014. La domination viking cessa également d'exister en Angleterre en 1042. Les rois de Norvège, descendants des Vikings, régnèrent encore sur une partie de l'Écosse jusqu'en 1266, et sur les îles Orcades et Shetland jusqu'en 1469.

▼ À la Saint-Brice, le 13 novembre 1002, le roi anglais Ethelred II donna l'ordre de tuer tous les Danois qui vivaient dans le pays.

92 **Les Vikings apprirent à vivre avec les autres.** Dans la plupart des endroits où ils s'installèrent, les Vikings ont épousé les femmes du pays et travaillaient avec les autres habitants. Certaines de leurs coutumes se sont mélangées aux locales, mais la plupart ont disparu. La tradition viking n'a survécu que dans les endroits où personne n'était là avant eux, comme l'Islande, les îles Orcades ou le nord de l'Écosse.

▲ En 1066, les Normands, descendants des Vikings qui s'étaient installés en Normandie, envahirent l'Angleterre. Cette scène de la tapisserie de Bayeux représente des bateaux de style viking.

93 **Le christianisme supplanta les dieux vikings.** Les Vikings croyaient que leurs dieux, tels que Thor ou Odin, puniraient ceux qui ne les vénéreraient pas et tueraient donc les missionnaires chrétiens. Mais les religieux survécurent si bien que les Vikings se convertirent au christianisme : ils se sont demandés si leurs dieux avaient réellement des pouvoirs.

◄ Les chrétiens qui vivaient en Scandinavie après la fin de la période viking fabriquèrent des statues de Jésus pour exprimer leur foi.

94 **Les Vikings installèrent de nouveaux royaumes en dehors de chez eux.** Dans des lieux très éloignés de leur pays, comme la Normandie ou Novgorod en Russie, les seigneurs vikings ont créé des royaumes qui se développèrent de manière indépendante. Au fil des ans, ils perdirent le contact avec leurs origines vikings et inventèrent leurs propres coutumes et leurs propres lois.

95 **Les colons vikings abandonnèrent l'Amérique.** Peu après l'an 1000, Thorfinn Karlsefni, un marchand viking originaire d'Islande, conduisit une centaine d'hommes et de femmes à Vinland, l'endroit où Leif Eriksson avait accosté en Amérique du Nord. Ils y passèrent deux ans avant de s'en aller, lassés des attaques incessantes des Amérindiens.

L'héritage viking

96 Plusieurs jours de la semaine portent toujours des noms vikings. Les noms de certains jours de la semaine ont été inspirés de noms vikings. En français, lundi est le jour de la Lune, en anglais, *sunday* est le jour du Soleil. Vendredi, *friday* en anglais, vient du nom de la déesse Freyja. Dans les langues scandinaves, le samedi est le « jour du bain », rappelant que les Vikings prenaient leur bain hebdomadaire ce jour-là.

97 Nous utilisons toujours de nombreux mots vikings aujourd'hui. Dans les régions où les Vikings se sont installés, ils ont donné des noms à leur environnement. C'est pourquoi de nombreux lieux ont des noms d'inspiration viking comme Turgis dont le nom vient du dieu Thor, ou encore Querqueville qui vient du mot kerke signifiant église.

98 Une histoire viking a inspiré une des pièces de Shakespeare. William Shakespeare, un auteur de théâtre anglais (1564-1616) a vécu 500 ans après les Vikings. Pourtant, il s'est inspiré d'un de leurs récits pour l'intrigue de sa pièce la plus célèbre *Hamlet*. Elle raconte l'histoire d'un prince du Danemark désemparé après la mort de son père.

▶ Dans la pièce de Shakespeare, le héros, Hamlet, réfléchit au sens de la vie et de la mort.

99
On célèbre toujours les fêtes vikings. Dans les îles Shetland, par exemple, où de nombreux Vikings s'étaient installés, on célèbre encore « Up-Helly-Aa », le dernier mardi du mois de janvier. C'est une fête qui marque la fin de Yule, la fête viking du milieu de l'hiver. Les gens se déguisent en Vikings, défilent dans les rues, puis brûlent une maquette géante de bateau viking.

100
Le Père Noël était autrefois un dieu viking.
Yule (le milieu de l'hiver) était l'une des fêtes vikings les plus importantes. Ils organisaient des banquets et échangeaient des cadeaux. Ils croyaient que les dieux traversaient le ciel pour apporter de très bonnes choses (comme le Père Noël !)

▶ Comme à l'époque des Vikings, les feux et la chaleur des fêtes de l'hiver apportent réconfort et espoir pendant une période difficile.

▲ Cette image moderne du Père Noël le montre traversant le ciel sur un traîneau tiré par des rennes.

Index

MERCIER AND CAMIER

Other Works by Samuel Beckett
Published by Grove Press

MERCIER AND CAMIER

Samuel Beckett

*Translated from the original French
by the author*

GROVE PRESS, INC., NEW YORK

Originally published in French as *Mercier et Camier*
by Les Editions de Minuit, Paris, 1970

First published in Great Britain in 1974 in the author's
translation by Calder & Boyars Ltd., London

ISBN: 0-394-17835-1
Grove Press ISBN: 0-8021-0109-7

Library of Congress Catalog Card Number: 74-21639

First Evergreen Edition, 1975

Printed and bound in the United States of America

Distributed by Random House, Inc., New York

GROVE PRESS, INC., 53 East 11th Street,
New York, New York 10003

MERCIER AND CAMIER

I

The journey of Mercier and Camier is one I can tell, if I
will, for I was with them all the time.

Physically it was fairly easy going, without seas or
frontiers to be crossed, through regions untormented on
the whole, if desolate in parts. Mercier and Camier did
not remove from home, they had that great good fortune.
They did not have to face, with greater or less success,
outlandish ways, tongues, laws, skies, foods, in sur-
roundings little resembling those to which first childhood, then boyhood, then manhood had inured them.
The weather, though often inclement (but they knew no
better), never exceeded the limits of the temperate,
that is to say of what could still be borne, without danger
if not without discomfort, by the average native fittingly
clad and shod. With regard to money, if it did not run
to first class transport or the palatial hotel, still there was
enough to keep them going, to and fro, without recourse
to alms. It may be said therefore that in this respect too
they were fortunate, up to a point. They had to struggle,
but less than many must, less perhaps than most of those
who venture forth, driven by a need now clear and now
obscure.

They had consulted together at length, before embarking

on this journey, weighing with all the calm at their command what benefits they might hope from it, what ills apprehend, maintaining turn about the dark side and the rosy. The only certitude they gained from these debates was that of not lightly launching out, into the unknown.

Camier was first to arrive at the appointed place. That is to say that on his arrival Mercier was not there. In reality Mercier had forestalled him by a good ten minutes. Not Camier then, but Mercier, was first to arrive. He possessed himself in patience for five minutes, with his eye on the various avenues of approach open to his friend, then set out for a saunter destined to last full fifteen minutes. Meantime Camier, five minutes having passed without sight or sign of Mercier, took himself off in his turn for a little stroll. On his return to the place, fifteen minutes later, it was in vain he cast about him, and understandably so. For Mercier, after cooling his heels for a further five minutes, had wandered off again for what he pleased to call a little stretch. Camier hung around for five more minutes, then again departed, saying to himself, Perhaps I'll run into him in the street. It was at this moment that Mercier, back from his breather, which as chance this time would have it had not exceeded ten minutes, glimpsed receding in the morning mist a shape suggestive of Camier's and which was indeed none other. Unhappily it vanished as though swallowed up by the cobbles, leaving Mercier to resume his vigil. But on expiry of what is beginning to look like the regulation five minutes he abandoned it again, feeling the need of a little motion. Their joy was thus for an instant unbounded, Mercier's joy and Camier's joy,

8

when after five and ten minutes respectively of uneasy prowl, debouching simultaneously on the square, they found themselves face to face for the first time since the evening before. The time was nine fifty in the morning.

In other words:

	Arr.	Dep.	Arr.	Dep.	Arr.	Dep.	Arr.
Mercier .	9.05	9.10	9.25	9.30	9.40	9.45	9.50
Camier .	9.15	9.20	9.35	9.40	9.50		

What stink of artifice.

They were still in each other's arms when the rain began to fall, with quite oriental abruptness. They made therefore with all speed to the shelter which, in the form of a pagoda, had been erected here as protection from the rain and other inclemencies, in a word from the weather. Shadowy and abounding in nooks and crannies it was a friend to lovers also and to the aged of either sex. Into this refuge, at the same instant as our heroes, bounded a dog, followed shortly by a second. Mercier and Camier, irresolute, exchanged a look. They had not finished in each other's arms and yet felt awkward about resuming. The dogs for their part were already copulating, with the utmost naturalness.

The place where they now found themselves, where they had agreed, not without pains, that they should meet, was not properly speaking a square, but rather a small public garden at the heart of a tangle of streets and lanes. It displayed the usual shrubberies, flower-beds, pools, fountains, statues, lawns and benches in strangulating profusion. It had something of the maze, irksome to perambulate, difficult of egress, for one not in its secrets. Entry was of course the simplest thing in the

9

world. In the centre, roughly, towered huge a shining copper beech, planted several centuries earlier, according to the sign rudely nailed to the bole, by a Field Marshal of France peacefully named Saint-Ruth. Hardly had he done so, in the words of the inscription, when he was struck dead by a cannon-ball, faithful to the last to the same hopeless cause, on a battlefield having little in common, from the point of view of landscape, with those on which he had won his spurs, first as brigadier, then as lieutenant, if that is the order in which spurs are won, on the battlefield. It was no doubt to this tree that the garden owed its existence, a consequence which can scarcely have occurred to the Field Marshal as on that distant day, well clear of the quincunxes, before an elegant and replete assistance, he held the frail sapling upright in the hole gorged with evening dew. But to have done with this tree and hear no more about it, from it the garden derived what little charm it still possessed, not to mention of course its name. The stifled giant's days were numbered, it would not cease henceforward to pine and rot till finally removed, bit by bit. Then for a while, in the garden mysteriously named, people would breathe more freely.

Mercier and Camier did not know the place. Hence no doubt their choice of it for their meeting. Certain things shall never be known for sure.

Through the orange panes the rain to them seemed golden and brought back memories, determined by the hazard of their excursions, to the one of Rome, of Naples to the other, mutually unavowed and with a feeling akin to shame. They should have felt the better for this glow of distant days when they were young, and warm, and loved art, and mocked marriage, and did not know each other, but they felt no whit the better.

Let us go home, said Camier.

Why? said Mercier.

It won't stop all day, said Camier.

Long or short, tis but a shower, said Mercier.

I can't stand there doing nothing, said Camier.

Then let us sit, said Mercier.

Worse still, said Camier.

Then let us walk up and down, said Mercier, yes, arm in arm let us pace to and fro. There is not much room, but there might be even less. Lay down our umbrella, there, help me off with our knapsack, so, thanks, and off we go.

Camier submitted.

Every now and then the sky lightened and the rain abated. Then they would halt before the door. This was the signal for the sky to darken again and the rain to redouble in fury.

Don't look, said Mercier.

The sound is enough, said Camier.

True, said Mercier.

After a moment of silence Mercier said:

The dogs don't trouble you?

Why does he not withdraw? said Camier.

He cannot, said Mercier.

Why? said Camier.

One of nature's little gadgets, said Mercier, no doubt to make insemination double sure.

They begin astraddle, said Camier, and finish arsy-versy.

What would you? said Mercier. The ecstasy is past,

they yearn to part, to go and piss against a post or eat a morsel of shit, but cannot. So they turn their backs on each other. You'd do as much, if you were they.

Delicacy would restrain me, said Camier.

And what would you do? said Mercier.

Feign regret, said Camier, that I could not renew such pleasure incontinent.

After a moment of silence Camier said:

Let us sit us down, I feel all sucked off.

You mean sit down, said Mercier.

I mean sit us down, said Camier.

Then let us sit us down, said Mercier.

On all hands already the workers were at it again, the air waxed loud with cries of pleasure and pain and with the urbaner notes of those for whom life had exhausted its surprises, as well on the minus side as on the plus. Things too were getting ponderously under way. It was in vain the rain poured down, the whole business was starting again with apparently no less ardour than if the sky had been a cloudless blue.

You kept me waiting, said Mercier.

On the contrary, said Camier.

I arrived at nine five, said Mercier.

And I at nine fifteen, said Camier.

You see, said Mercier.

Waiting, said Camier, and keeping waiting can only be with reference to a pre-arranged terminus.

And for what hour was our appointment, according to you? said Mercier.

Nine fifteen, said Camier.

Then you are grievously mistaken, said Mercier.

Meaning? said Camier.

12

Will you never have done astounding me? said Mercier.

Explain yourself, said Camier.

I close my eyes and live it over again, said Mercier, your hand in mine, tears rising to my eyes and the sound of my faltering voice, So be it, tomorrow at nine. A drunken woman passed by, singing a ribald song and hitching up her skirts.

She went to your head, said Camier. He took a note-book from his pocket, turned the leaves and read: Monday 15, St. Macarius, 9.15, St. Ruth, collect umbrella at Helen's.

And what does that prove? said Mercier.

My good faith, said Camier.

True, said Mercier.

We shall never know, said Camier, at what hour we arranged to meet today, so let us drop the subject.

In all this confusion one thing alone is sure, said Mercier, and that is that we met at ten to ten, at the same time as the hands, or rather a moment later.

There is that to be thankful for, said Camier.

The rain had not yet begun, said Mercier.

The morning fervour was intact, said Camier.

Don't lose our agenda, said Mercier.

At this moment suddenly appeared from nowhere the first of a long line of maleficent beings. His uniform, sickly green in colour, its place of honour rife with heroic emblems and badges, suited him down to the ground. Inspired by the example of the great Sarsfield he had risked his life without success in defence of a territory which in itself must have left him cold and considered as a symbol cannot have greatly heated him

13

either. He carried a stick at once elegant and massive and even leaned on it from time to time. He suffered torment with his hip, the pain shot down his buttock and up his rectum deep into the bowels and even as far north as the pyloric valve, culminating as a matter of course in uretro-scrotal spasms with quasi-incessant longing to micturate. Invalided out with a grudging pension, whence the sour looks of nearly all those, male and female, with whom his duties and remnants of bonhomie brought him daily in contact, he sometimes felt it would have been wiser on his part, during the great upheaval, to devote his energies to the domestic skirmish, the Gaelic dialect, the fortification of his faith and the treasures of a folklore beyond compare. The bodily danger would have been less and the benefits more certain. But this thought, when he had relished all its bitterness, he would banish from his mind, as unworthy of it. His moustache, once stiff as the lip it was grown to hide, was no longer so. From time to time, when he remembered, with a blast from below of fetid breath mingled with spittle, he straightened it momentarily. Motionless at the foot of the pagoda steps, his cape agape, streaming with rain, he darted his eyes to and fro, from Mercier and Camier to the dogs, from the dogs to Mercier and Camier.

Who owns that bicycle? he said.

Mercier and Camier exchanged a look.

We could have done without this, said Camier.

Shift her, said the ranger.

It may prove diverting, said Mercier.

Who owns them dogs? said the ranger.

I don't see how we can stay, said Camier.

Can it I wonder be the fillip we needed, to get us moving? said Mercier.

The ranger mounted the steps of the shelter and stood stock-still in the doorway. The air darkened immediately and turned a deeper yellow.

I think he is about to attack us, said Camier.

I leave the balls to you, as usual, said Mercier.

Dear sergeant, said Camier, what exactly can we do for you?

You see that bicycle? said the ranger.

I see nothing, said Camier. Mercier, do you see a bicycle?

Is she yours? said the ranger.

A thing we do not see, said Camier, for whose existence we have only your word, how are we to tell if it is ours, or another's?

Why would it be ours? said Mercier. Are these dogs ours? No. We see them today for the first time. And you would have it that the bicycle, assuming it exists, is ours? And yet the dogs are not ours.

Bugger the dogs, said the ranger.

But as if to give himself the lie he fell on them with stick and boot and drove them cursing from the pagoda. Tied together as they still were, by the post-coitus, their retreat was no easy matter. For the efforts they made to escape, acting equally in opposite directions, could not but annul each other. They must have greatly suffered.

He has now buggered the dogs, said Mercier.

He has driven them from the shelter, said Camier, there is no denying that, but by no means from the garden.

The rain will soon wash them loose, said Mercier.

Less rut-besotted they would have thought of it them-selves.

The fact is he has done them a service, said Camier.

Let us show him a little kindness, said Mercier, he's a hero of the great war. Here we were, high and dry, masturbating full pelt without fear of interruption, while he was crawling in the Flanders mud, shitting in his puttees.

Conclude nothing from those idle words, Mercier and Camier were old young.

It's an idea, said Camier.

Will you look at that clatter of decorations, said Mercier. Do you realize the gallons of diarrhoea that represents?

Darkly, said Camier, as only one so costive can.

Let us suppose this alleged bicycle is ours, said Mercier. Where lies the harm?

A truce to dissembling, said Camier, it is ours.

Shift her out of here, said the ranger.

The day has dawned at last, said Camier, after years of shilly-shally, when we must go, we know not whither, perhaps never to return . . . alive. We are simply waiting for the day to lift, then full speed ahead. Try and understand.

What is more, said Mercier, we have still thought to take, before it is too late.

Thought to take? said Camier.

Those were my words, said Mercier.

I thought all thought was taken, said Camier, and all in order.

All is not, said Mercier.

Will you shift her or won't you? said the ranger.

Are you venal, said Mercier, since you are deaf to reason?

Silence.

Can you be bought off? said Mercier.

Certainly, said the ranger.

Give him a bob, said Mercier. To think our first disbursement should be a sop to bribery and extortion.

The ranger vanished with a curse.

How of a piece they all are, said Mercier.

Now he'll prowl around, said Camier.

What can that matter to us? said Mercier.

I don't like being prowled around, said Camier.

Mercier took exception to this turn. Camier maintained it. This little game soon palled. It must have been near noon.

And now, said Mercier, the time is come for us.

For us? said Camier.

Precisely, said Mercier, for us, for serious matters.

What about a bite to eat? said Camier.

Thought first, said Mercier, then sustenance.

A long debate ensued, broken by long silences in which thought took place. At such times they would sink, now Mercier, now Camier, to such depths of meditation that the voice of one, resuming its drift, was powerless to bring the other back, or passed unheard. Or they would arrive simultaneously at often contrary conclusions and simultaneously begin to state them. Nor was it rare for one to lapse into a brood before the other had concluded his exposé. And there were times they would look long at each other, unable to utter a word, their minds two blanks. It was fresh from one such daze they decided to abandon their inquiry, for the time being. The afternoon was well advanced, the rain was falling still, the short winter day was drawing to a close.

It is you have the provisions, said Mercier.

On the contrary, said Camier.

True, said Mercier.

My hunger is gone, said Camier.

One must eat, said Mercier.

I see no point, said Camier.

We have a long hard road before us still, said Mercier.

The sooner we drop the better, said Camier.

True, said Mercier.

The ranger's head appeared in the doorway. Believe it or not, only his head was to be seen. It was to say, in his quaint way, they were free to spend the night for half-a-crown.

Is thought now taken, said Camier, and all in order?

No, said Mercier.

Will all ever be? said Camier.

I believe so, said Mercier, yes, I believe, not firmly, no, but I believe, yes, the day is coming when all will be in order, at last.

That will be delightful, said Camier.

Let us hope so, said Mercier.

A long look passed between them. Camier said to himself, Even him I cannot see. A like thought agitated his vis-à-vis.

Two points seemed nevertheless established as a result of this consultation.

1. Mercier would set off alone, awheel, with the raincoat. Wherever he should stop for the night, at the first stage, he would get all in readiness to receive

18

Camier. Camier would take the road as soon as the weather permitted. Camier would keep the umbrella. No mention of the sack.

2. It so chanced that Mercier, up to now, had shown himself the live wire, Camier the dead weight. The reverse was to be expected at any moment. On the less weak let the weaker always lean, for the course to follow. They might conceivably be valiant together. That would be the day. Or the great weakness might overtake them simultaneously. Let them in this case not give way to despair, but wait with confidence for the evil moment to pass. In spite of the vagueness of these expressions they understood each other, more or less.

Not knowing what to think, said Camier, I look away.

It would seem to be lifting, said Mercier.

The sun comes out at last, said Camier, that we may admire it sink, below the horizon.

That long moment of brightness, said Mercier, with its thousand colours, always stirs my heart.

The day of toil is ended, said Camier, a kind of ink rises in the east and floods the sky.

The bell rang, announcing closing time.

I sense vague shadowy shapes, said Camier, they come and go with muffled cries.

I too have the feeling, said Mercier, we have not gone unobserved since morning.

Are we by any chance alone now? said Camier.

I see no one, said Mercier.

Let us then go together, said Camier.

They left the shelter.

The sack, said Mercier.

The umbrella, said Camier.

The raincoat, said Mercier.

It I have, said Camier.

Is there nothing else? said Mercier.

I see nothing else, said Camier.

I'll get them, said Mercier, you mind the bicycle.

It was a woman's bicycle, without free wheel unfortunately. To brake one pedalled backwards.

The ranger, his bunch of keys in his hand, watched them recede. Mercier held the handlebar, Camier the saddle. The pedals rose and fell.

He cursed them on their way.

II

In the show windows the lights came on, went out, according to the show. Through the slippery streets the crowd pressed on as towards some unquestioned goal. A strange well-being, wroth and weary, filled the air. Close the eyes and not a voice is heard, only the on-ward panting of the feet. In this throng silence they advanced as best they could, at the edge of the sidewalk, Mercier in front, his hand on the handlebar, Camier behind, his hand on the saddle, and the bicycle slithered in the gutter by their side.

You hinder me more than you help me, said Mercier.

I'm not trying to help you, said Camier, I'm trying to help myself.

Then all is well, said Mercier.

I'm cold, said Camier.

It was indeed cold.

It is indeed cold, said Mercier.

Where do our feet think they're taking us? said Camier.

They would seem to be heading for the canal, said Mercier.

Already? said Camier.

Perhaps we shall be tempted, said Mercier, to strike

out along the towpath and follow it till boredom doth ensue. Before us, beckoning us on, without our having to lift our eyes, the dying tints we love so well.

Speak for yourself, said Camier.

The very water, said Mercier, will linger livid, which is not to be despised either. And then the whim, who knows, may take us to throw ourselves in.

The little bridges slip by, said Camier, ever fewer and farther between. We pore over the locks, trying to understand. From the barges made fast to the bank waft the watermen's voices, bidding us good-night. Their day is done, they smoke a last pipe before turning in.

Every man for himself, said Mercier, and God for one and all.

The town lies far behind, said Camier. Little by little night overtakes us, blueblack. We splash through puddles left by the rain. It is no longer possible to advance. Retreat is equally out of the question.

He added, some moments later:

What are you musing on, Mercier?

On the horror of existence, confusedly, said Mercier.

What about a drink? said Camier.

I thought we had agreed to abstain, said Mercier, except in the event of accident, or indisposition. Does not that figure among our many conventions?

I don't call drink, said Camier, a quick nip to put some life in us.

They stopped at the first pub.

No bikes here, said the publican.

Perhaps after all he was a mere hireling.

And now? said Camier.

We might chain it to a lamppost, said Mercier.

That would give us more freedom, said Camier. He added, Of movement.

In the end they fell back on a railing. It came to the same.

And now? said Mercier.

Back to no bikes? said Camier.

Never! said Mercier.

Never say that, said Camier.

So they adjourned across the way.

Sitting at the bar they discoursed of this and that, brokenly, as was their custom. They spoke, fell silent, listened to each other, stopped listening, each as he fancied or as bidden from within. There were moments, minutes on end, when Camier lacked the strength to raise his glass to his mouth. Mercier was subject to the same failing. Then the less weak of the two gave the weaker to drink, inserting between his lips the rim of his glass. A press of sombre shaggy bulks hemmed them about, thicker and thicker as the hour wore on. From their conversation there emerged in spite of all, among other points, the following.

1. It would be useless, nay, madness, to venture any further for the moment.

2. They need only ask Helen to put them up for the night.

3. Nothing would prevent them from setting out on the morrow, hail, rain or shine, at the crack of dawn.

4. They had nothing to reproach themselves with.

5. Did what they were looking for exist?

6. What were they looking for?

7. There was no hurry.

23

8. All their judgements relating to the expedition called for revision, in tranquillity.

9. Only one thing mattered: depart.

10. To hell with it all anyway.

Back in the street they linked arms. After a few hundred yards Mercier drew Camier's attention to the fact that they were not in step.

You have your gait, said Camier, I have mine.

I'm not accusing anyone, said Mercier, but it's wearing. We advance in jerks.

I'd prefer you to ask me straight out, said Camier, straight out plump and plain, either to let go your arm and move away or else to fall in with your titubations.

Camier, Camier, said Mercier, squeezing his arm.

They came to a crossroads and stopped.

Which way do we drag ourselves now? said Camier.

Our situation is no ordinary one, said Mercier, I mean in relation to Helen's home, if I know where we are. For these different ways all lead there with equal success.

Then let us turn back, said Camier.

And lose ground we can ill afford? said Mercier.

We can't stay stuck here all night, said Camier, like a couple of clots.

Let us toss our umbrella, said Mercier. It will fall in a certain way, according to laws of which we know nothing. Then all we have to do is press forward in the designated direction.

The umbrella answered, Left! It resembled a great wounded bird, a great bird of ill omen shot down by hunters and awaiting quivering the coup de grâce. The likeness was striking. Camier picked it up and hung it from his pocket.

24

It is not broken, I trust, said Mercier.

Here their attention was drawn to a strange figure, that of a gentleman wearing, despite the rawness of the air, a simple frock-coat and top-hat. He seemed, for the moment, to be going their way, for their view was of his rear. His hands, in a gesture coquettishly demential, held high and wide apart the skirts of his cutaway. He advanced warily, with stiff and open tread.

Do you feel like singing? said Camier.

Not to my knowledge, said Mercier.

The rain was beginning again. But had it ever ceased?

Let us make haste, said Camier.

Why do you ask me that? said Mercier.

Camier seemed in no hurry to reply. Finally he said: I hear singing.

They halted, the better to listen.

I hear nothing, said Mercier.

And yet you have good ears, said Camier, so far as I know.

Very fair, said Mercier.

Strange, said Camier.

Do you hear it still? said Mercier.

For all the world a mixed choir, said Camier.

Perhaps it's a delusion, said Mercier.

Possibly, said Camier.

Let's run, said Mercier.

They ran some little way in the dark and wet, without meeting a soul. When they had done running Mercier deplored the nice state, soaked to the buff, in which they would arrive at Helen's, to which in reply Camier described how they would immediately strip

25

and put their things to dry, before the fire or in the hot-cupboard with the boiler and hot water pipes.

Come to think of it, said Mercier, why didn't we use our umbrella?

Camier looked at the umbrella, now in his hand. He had placed it there that he might run more freely.

We might have indeed, he said.

Why burden oneself with an umbrella, said Mercier, and not put it up as required?

Quite, said Camier.

Put it up now, in the name of God, said Mercier.

But Camier could not put it up.

Give it here, said Mercier.

But Mercier could not put it up either.

This was the moment chosen by the rain, acting on behalf of the universal malignity, to come down in buckets.

It's stuck, said Camier, don't strain it whatever you do.

Mercier used a nasty expression.

Meaning me? said Camier.

With both hands Mercier raised the umbrella high above his head and dashed it to the ground. He used another nasty expression. And to crown all, lifting to the sky his convulsed and streaming face, he said, As for thee, fuck thee.

Decidedly Mercier's grief, heroically contained since morning, could be no longer so.

Is it our little omniomni you are trying to abuse? said Camier. You should know better. It's he on the contrary fucks thee. Omniomni, the all-unfuckable.

Kindly leave Mrs Mercier outside this discussion, said Mercier.

The mind has snapped, said Camier.

The first thing one noticed at Helen's was the carpet.

Will you look at that pile, said Camier.

Prime moquette, said Mercier.

Unbelievable, said Camier.

You'd think you never saw it till now, said Mercier, and you wallowing on it all these years.

I never did see it till now, said Camier, and now I can't forget it.

So one says, said Mercier.

If that evening the carpet in particular caught the eye, it was not alone in catching it, for a cockatoo caught it too. It clung shakily to its perch hung from a corner of the ceiling and dizzily rocked by conflicting swing and spin. It was wide awake, in spite of the late hour. Feebly and fitfully its breast rose and fell, faint quiverings ruffled up the down at every expiration. Every now and then the beak would gape and for what seemed whole seconds fishlike remain agape. Then the black spindle of the tongue was seen to stir. The eyes, averted from the light, filled with unspeakable bewilderment and distress, seemed all ears. Shivers of anguish rippled the plumage, blazing in ironic splendour. Beneath it, on the carpet, a great news-sheet was spread.

There's my bed and there's the couch, said Helen.

They're all yours, said Mercier. For my part I'll sleep with none.

A nice little suck-off, said Camier, not too prolonged, by all means, but nothing more.

Terminated, said Helen, the nice little suck-offs but nothing more.

I'll lie on the floor, said Mercier, and wait for dawn.

27

Scenes and faces will unfold before my gaze, the rain on the skylight sound like claws and night rehearse its colours. The longing will take me to throw myself out of the window, but I'll master it. He repeated, in a roar, I'll master it!

Back in the street they wondered what they had done with the bicycle. The sack too had disappeared.

Did you see the polly? said Mercier.

Pretty thing, said Camier.

It groaned in the night, said Mercier.

Camier questioned this.

It will haunt me till my dying day, said Mercier.

I didn't know she had one, said Camier, what haunts me is the Kidderminster.

Nor I, said Mercier. She says she's had it for years.

She's lying of course, said Camier.

It was still raining. They took shelter in an archway, not knowing where to go.

When exactly did you notice the sack was gone? said Mercier.

This morning, said Camier, when I went to get my sulfamides.

I see no sign of the umbrella, said Mercier.

Camier inspected himself, stooping and spreading out his arms as if concerned with a button.

We must have left it at Helen's, he said.

My feeling is, said Mercier, that if we don't leave this town today we never shall. So let us think twice before we start trying to———.

He almost said recoup.

What exactly was there in the sack? said Camier.

Toilet requisites and necessaries, said Mercier.

28

Superfluous luxury, said Camier.

A few pairs of socks, said Mercier, and one of drawers.

God, said Camier.

Some eatables, said Mercier.

Rotten ripe for the muckheap, said Camier.

On condition we retrieve them, said Mercier.

Let us board the first express southward bound! cried Camier. He added, more soberly, And so not be tempted to get out at the nearest stop.

And why south, said Mercier, rather than north, or east, or west?

I prefer south, said Camier.

Is that sufficient ground? said Mercier.

It's the nearest terminus, said Camier.

True, said Mercier.

He went out into the street and looked up at the sky, a grey pall, look where he would.

The sky is uniformly leaden, he said, resuming his place under the arch, we'll drown like rats without the umbrella.

Camier criticized this simile.

Like rats, said Mercier.

Even if we had the umbrella, said Camier, we could not use it, for it is broken.

What fresh extravagance is this? said Mercier.

We broke it yesterday, said Camier. Your idea.

Mercier took his head between his hands. Little by little the scene came back to him. Proudly he drew himself up, to his full height.

Come, he said, regrets are vain.

We'll wear the raincoat turn and turn about, said Camier.

We'll be in the train, said Mercier, speeding south.

Through the streaming panes, said Camier, we try to number the cows, shivering pitiably in the scant shelter of the hedges. Rooks take wing, all dripping and bedraggled. But gradually the day lifts and we arrive in the brilliant sunlight of a glorious winter's afternoon. It seems like Monaco.

I don't seem to have eaten for forty-eight hours, said Mercier. And yet I am not hungry.

One must eat, said Camier. He went on to compare the stomach with the bladder.

Apropos, said Mercier, how is your cyst?

Dormant, said Camier, but under the surface mischief is brewing.

What will you do then? said Mercier.

I dread to think, said Camier.

I could just manage a cream puff, said Mercier.

Wait here, said Camier.

No no! cried Mercier. Don't leave me! Don't let us leave each other!

Camier left the archway and began to cross the street. Mercier called him back and an altercation ensued, too foolish to be recorded, so foolish was it.

Another would take umbrage, said Camier. Not I, all things considered. For I say to myself, The hour is grave and Mercier . . . well . . . He advanced towards Mercier who promptly recoiled. I was only going to embrace you, said Camier. I'll do it some other time, when you're less yourself, if I think of it.

He went out into the rain and disappeared. Alone in the archway Mercier began pacing to and fro, deep in bitter thought. It was their first separation since the morning of the day before. Raising suddenly his eyes, as from a vision no longer to be borne, he saw two children, a little boy and a little girl, standing gazing at him. They wore little black oilskins with hoods, identical, and the boy had a little satchel on his back. They held each other by the hand.

Papa! they said, with one voice or nearly.

Good evening, my children, said Mercier, get along with you now.

But they did not get along with them, no, but stood their ground, their little clasped hands lightly swinging back and forth. Finally the little girl drew hers away and advanced towards him they had addressed as papa. She stretched out her little arms towards him, as if to invite a kiss, or at least a caress. The little boy followed suit, with visible misgiving. Mercier raised his foot and dashed it against the pavement. Be off with you! he cried. He bore down on them, wildly gesturing and his face contorted. The children backed away to the sidewalk and there stood still again. Fuck off out of here! screamed Mercier. He flew at them in a fury and they took to their heels. But soon they halted and looked back. What they saw then must have impressed them strongly, for they ran on and bolted down the first sidestreet. As for the unfortunate Mercier, satisfied after a few minutes of fuming tenterhooks that the danger was past, he returned dripping to the archway and resumed his reflections, if not at the point where they had been interrupted, at least at one near by.

Mercier's reflections were peculiar in this, that the same swell and surge swept through them all and cast the mind away, no matter where it embarked, on the same rocks invariably. They were perhaps not so much reflections as a dark torrent of brooding where past and future merged in a single flood and closed, over a present for ever absent. Ah well.

Here, said Camier, I hope you haven't been fretting.

Mercier extracted the cake from its paper wrapping and placed it on the palm of his hand. He bent forward and down till his nose was almost touching it and the eyes not far behind. He darted towards Camier, while still in this position, a sidelong look full of mistrust.

A cream horn, said Camier, the best I could find.

Mercier, still bent double, moved forward to the verge of the archway, where the light was better, and examined the cake again.

It's full of cream, said Camier.

Mercier slowly clenched his fist and the cake gushed between his fingers. The staring eyes filled with tears. Camier advanced to get a better view. The tears flowed, overflowed, all down the furrowed cheeks and vanished in the beard. The face remained unmoved. The eyes, still streaming and no doubt blinded, seemed intent on some object stirring on the ground.

If you didn't want it, said Camier, you had better given it to a dog, or to a child.

I'm in tears, said Mercier, don't intrude.

When the flow stopped Camier said:

Let me offer you our handkerchief.

There are days, said Mercier, one is born every minute. Then the world is full of shitty little Merciers. It's hell. Oh but to cease!

Enough, said Camier. You look like a capital S. Ninety if a day.

32

Would I were, said Mercier. He wiped his hand on the seat of his trousers. He said, I'll start crawling any minute.

I'm off, said Camier.

Leaving me to my fate, said Mercier. I knew it.

You know my little ways, said Camier.

No, said Mercier, but I was counting on your affection to help me serve my time.

I can help you, said Camier, I can't resurrect you.

Take me by the hand, said Mercier, and lead me far away from here. I'll trot along at your side like a little puppy dog, or a tiny tot. And the day will come——.

A terrible screech of brakes rent the air, followed by a scream and a resounding crash. Mercier and Camier made a rush (after a moment's hesitation) for the open street and were rewarded by the vision, soon hidden by a concourse of gapers, of a big fat woman writhing feebly on the ground. The disorder of her dress revealed an amazing mass of billowing underclothes, originally white in colour. Her lifeblood, streaming from one or more wounds, had already reached the gutter.

Ah, said Mercier, that's what I needed, I feel a new man already.

He was in fact transfigured.

Let this be a lesson to us, said Camier.

Meaning? said Mercier.

Never to despair, said Camier, or lose our faith in life.

Ah, said Mercier with relief, I was afraid you meant something else.

As they went their way an ambulance passed, speeding towards the scene of the mishap.

33

I beg your pardon? said Camier.

A crying shame, said Mercier.

I don't follow you, said Camier.

A six cylinder, said Mercier.

And what of it? said Camier.

And they talk about the petrol shortage, said Mercier.

There are perhaps more victims than one, said Camier.

It might be an infant child, said Mercier, for all they care.

The rain was falling gently, as from the fine rose of a watering pot. Mercier advanced with upturned face. Now and then he wiped it, with his free hand. He had not had a wash for some time.

Summary
of two preceding chapters

I

Outset.

Meeting of Mercier and Camier.

Saint Ruth Square.

The beech.

The rain.

The shelter.

The dogs.

Distress of Camier.

The ranger.

The bicycle.

Words with the ranger.

Mercier and Camier confer.

Results of this conference.

Bright too late.

The bell.

Mercier and Camier set out.

II

The town at twilight.

Mercier and Camier on the way to the canal.

Vision of the canal.

The bicycle.

First bar.
Mercier and Camier confer.
Results of this conference.
Mercier and Camier on the way to Helen's.
Doubts as to the way.
The umbrella.
The man in the frockcoat.
The rain.
Camier hears singing.
Mercier and Camier run.
The umbrella.
The downpour.
Distress of Mercier.
At Helen's.
The cockatoo.
The Kidderminster.
The second day.
The rain.
Disappearance of sack, bicycle and umbrella.
The archway.
Mercier and Camier confer.
Results of this conference.
Departure of Camier.
Distress of Mercier.
Mercier and the children.
Return of Camier.
The cream horn.
Distress of Mercier.
The fat woman.
Mercier and Camier depart.
Rain on Mercier's face.

III

I trust an only child, I was born at P——. My parents came from Q——. It was from them I received, together with the treponema pallidum, the huge nose whose remains you have before you. They were severe with me, but just. For the least peccadillo my father beat me till I bled, with his solid razor-strop. But he never failed to notify my mother that she might dress my wounds, with tincture of iodine or permanganate of potash. Here lies no doubt the explanation of my unconfiding character and general surliness. Unfitted for the pursuit of knowledge I was taken away from school at the age of thirteen and placed with farmers near by. Heaven, as they put it, having denied them offspring of their own, they fell back on me with very natural virulence. And when my parents perished, in a providential railway smash, they adopted me with all the forms and observances required by the law. But no less feeble of body than of mind I was for them a constant source of disappointment. To follow the plough, ply the scythe, flounder in the mangel-wurzels, and so on, were labours so far beyond my strength that I literally collapsed whenever forced to undertake them. Even as shepherd, cowherd, goatherd, pigherd, it was in vain

I strained every nerve, I could never give satisfaction. For the animals strayed, unnoticed by me, into the neighbouring properties and there ate their bellyful of vegetables, fruit and flowers. I pass over in silence the combats between rutting males, when I fled in terror to take shelter in the nearest outhouse. Add to this that the flock or herd, because of my inability to count beyond ten, seldom came home at full muster, and with this too I was deservedly reproached. The only branches in which I may boast of having, if not excelled, at least succeeded, were the slaughter of little lambs, calves, kids and porklings and the emasculation of little bullocks, rams, billy goats and piglets, on condition of course they were still unspoiled, all innocence and trustingness. It was therefore to these specialities I confined myself, from the age of fifteen. I have still at home some charming little—well, comparatively little— ram's testes dating from that happy time. In the fowl-yard too I was a terror of accuracy and elegance. I had a way of smothering geese that was the admiration and envy of all. Oh I know you are listening with only half an ear, and that half unwilling, but that is nothing to me. For my life is behind me and my only pleasure left to summon up, out loud, the good old days happily gone for ever. At the age of twenty, or possibly nine-teen, having been awkward enough to fecundate a milkmaid, I ran away, under cover of night, for I was closely watched. I improved this occasion by setting light to the barns, granaries and stables. But the flames were scarcely under way when they were doused by a downfall none could have foreseen, so starry was the sky at the moment of ignition. That was fifty years ago, feels like five hundred. He brandished his stick and brought it down with a thump on the seat which emitted instantaneously a cloud of fine ephemeral dust. Five hundred! he bellowed.

The train slowed down. Mercier and Camier exchanged a look. The train stopped.

Woe is us, said Mercier, we're in the slow and easy.

The train moved on.

We might have alit, said Mercier, now it's too late.

Next stop, said the old man, you alight with me.

This puts a fresh complexion on it, said Mercier.

Butcher's boy, said the old man, poulterer's boy, knacker's boy, undertaker's man, sexton, one corpse on top of another, there's my life for you. Gab was my salvation, every day a little more, a little better. The truth is I had that too in my bleeding blood, my father having sprung, with what alacrity you may imagine, from the loins of a parish priest, it was common knowledge. I infested the outlying whoreshops and saloons. Comrades, I said, having never learnt to write, comrades, Homer tells us, Iliad Book 3, lines 85 and following, in what consists happiness here below, that is to say happiness. Oh I gave it to them! *Potopompos scroton evohe!* Like that, hot and strong! Picked up at nightschool—he burst into a wild raucous laugh—free nightschool for glimmer-thirsty wrecks. Potopompos scroton evohe, the soft cock and buckets of the hard. Step out of here, I said, with a stout heart and your bollocks in your boots and come again tomorrow, tell the missus to go chase apes in hell. There were delicate moments. Then up I'd get, covered with blood and my

39

rags in ribbons, and at 'em again. Brats the offscourings of fornication and God Almighty a cheap scent in a jakes. I cleaned myself up and crashed their weddings, funerals, balls, wakes and christenings. They made me welcome, another ten years and I'd be popular. I let them have it on the lot, hymen, vaseline, the evil day from dawn to dark. Till I came in for the farm, or better still the farms, for there were two. The creatures bless their hearts, they loved me to the end. A good job for me they did, for my snout was starting to crumble. People love you less when your snout starts to crumble.

The train slowed down. Mercier and Camier drew in their legs to let him pass. The train stopped.

Not alighting? said the old man. You're right, only the damned alight here.

He wore gaiters, a yellow block-hat and a rusty frock-coat reaching down to his knees. He lowered himself stiffly to the platform, turned, slammed the door and raised towards them his hideous face.

The train moved on.

Adieu adieu, cried Mr Madden, they loved me to the end, they loved—.

Mercier, whose back was to the engine, saw him as he stood there, dead to the passengers hastening towards the exit, bow down his head till it lay on his hands at rest on the knob of his stick.

With what relief the eyes from this clutter to the empty sky, with what relief back again.

A fresh complexion, said Mercier, a totally fresh complexion.

Camier wiped the pane with the cuff of his sleeve caught between the palm and four crooked fingers.

It's the end, said Mercier, that just about—. He paused for thought. That just about finishes me, he said.

Visibility nil, said Camier.

You remain strangely calm, said Mercier. Am I right in thinking you took advantage of my condition to substitute this hearse for the express we agreed on?

Camier mumbled something about burnt bridges and indecent haste.

I knew it, said Mercier. I've been shamefully abused. I'd throw myself out of the window if I wasn't afraid I might sprain my ankle.

I'll explain everything, said Camier.

You'll explain nothing, said Mercier. You took advantage of my weakness to cod me I was getting on an express when in fact—. His face fell apart. More readily than Mercier's few faces fell apart. Words fail me, he said, to disguise what I feel.

But your weakness it was precisely, said Camier, that prompted this little subterfuge.

Explain yourself, said Mercier.

Seeing the state you were in, said Camier, it was imperative to go, and yet at the same time stay.

You are cheap, said Mercier.

We'll get down at the next stop, said Camier, and consider how to proceed. If we see fit to go on we'll go on. We'll have lost two hours. What are two hours?

I wouldn't like to say, said Mercier.

If on the other hand, said Camier, we see fitter to return to town—.

To town! cried Mercier.

To town, said Camier, to town we shall return.

But we have just come from town, said Mercier, and now you speak of returning there.

When we left town, said Camier, it was necessary to leave town. So we very properly left it. But we are not children and necessity has her whims. If having elected to drive us forth she now elects to drive us back shall we balk? I trust not.

The only necessity I know, said Mercier, is to get away from that hell as fast and as far as possible.

That remains to be seen, said Camier. Never trust the wind that swells your sails, it is always obsolete.

Mercier controlled himself.

A third and last possibility, said Camier, since none are to be neglected, is that we form the heroic resolution to stay where we are. In which case I have all we need.

A village just one long street, everything lined up in a row, dwellings, shops, bars, the two stations, railway and petrol, the two churches, graveyard and so on. A strait.

Take the raincoat, said Camier.

Pah I won't melt, said Mercier.

They entered an inn.

Wrong address, said the man. This is Messrs. Clappe and Sons, Wholesale Fruit and Vegetable Suppliers.

And what leads you to suppose, said Camier, that we have not business with father Clappe or one of his waste products?

They regained the street.

Is this an inn, said Camier, or is it the fish market?

This time the man made way, all of a flutter.

Come in, gentlemen, he said, step right in. It's not the Savoy, but it's . . . how shall I say? He took their

42

measure with a quick furtive look. How shall I say? he said.

Say it, said Camier, and put us out of our pain.

It's . . . snug, said the man, there is no other word. Patrick! he cried. But there was another word, for he added, in a tone of tentative complicity, whatever that sounds like, It's . . . *gemütlich*.

He takes us for globe-trotters, said Mercier.

Ah, said the man, rubbing his hands, physiognomies— pronouncing as was his right the *g*—have no secrets for me. It's not every day that I have the honour . . . He hesitated. That I have the honour, he said. Patrick!

Speaking for myself, said Mercier, I am happy to meet you at last, you have been haunting me this long time.

Ah, said the man.

Yes sir, said Mercier. You appear to me most often on a threshold, or at a window. Behind you torrents of light and joy which should normally annihilate your features, but do not. You smile. Presumably you do not see me, across the alley from where you stand and plunged in deepest shadow. I too smile—and pass on. Do you see me, in my dreams, Mr Gall?

Let me relieve you, said the man.

In any case it is a happiness to meet you again, said Mercier, in such happier circumstances.

Relieve us of what? said Camier.

Why, said the man, of your coats, your hats, how shall I say? Patrick!

But will you look at us, said Camier. Do we appear to be hatted? Are we wearing gloves, without our knowledge? Come sir!

43

A porter for our trunks, said Mercier, what are you waiting for?

Patrick! cried the man.

Vengeance! cried Mercier, taking a step forward.

It was fair day. The saloon was crowded with farmers, cattle-dealers and the like. The beasts proper were far on their way already, straggling along the miry backland roads, to the cries of the herds. Some would come at night to their familiar byres, others to others they knew not of. Bringing up the rear, behind the sodden ewes, a train of clattering carts. The herds held their pricks through the stuff of their pockets.

Mercier propped his elbows on the bar. Camier, on the contrary, leaned his back against it.

They guzzle with their hats on, he said.

Where is he now? said Mercier.

By the door, said Camier, observing us without appearing to do so.

Can one see his teeth? said Mercier.

His mouth is hidden behind his hand, said Camier.

I do not ask if his mouth is hidden, said Camier, I ask if one can see his teeth.

One cannot see his teeth from here, said Camier, owing to the hand that hides them.

What are we doing here? said Mercier.

First eat, said Camier. Barman, what are your titbits today?

The barman rattled off a list.

Mine will be a button-fish salad, said Camier, with Dutch dressing.

Not on today, said the barman.

Then make it a hopper sandwich, said Camier.

44

Just finished the last, said the barman. He had heard it was better to humour them.

You keep a civil tongue in your head, said Mercier. He turned to Camier. What kind of a kip is this? he said. What kind of a trip is this?

At this point the journey of Mercier and Camier seemed likely indeed to founder. That it did not was doubtless due to Camier, mirror of magnanimity and ingenuity.

Mercier, he said, leave it to me.

Do something for God's sake, said Mercier, do something? Why must I always be the one to lead the way?

Call your employer, said Camier.

The barman seemed reluctant.

Call him, my good fellow, said Mercier, call him when you're told. Make the little sound he can tell from every other and would not fail to hear even in a howling gale. Or the little beck that is lost on all but him and would bring him running though the heavens were to fall.

But he whom Mercier had called Mr Gall was already by their side.

Have I the honour of addressing the proprietor? said Camier.

I am the manager, said the manager, since he was the manager.

It appears there is no more hopper, said Mercier. You have a curious way of managing, for a manager. What have you done with your teeth? Is this what you call *gemütlich*?

The manager wore the air of one in thought. He had

no taste for trouble. The extremities of his drooping grey moustache seemed bent on meeting. The barman watched him closely. Mercier was struck by the scant grey strands, fine as a babe's, trained forward with pitiable coquetry from the back of the head across the crown. Mr Gall had never appeared to him thus, but always erect and smiling and radiant.

Ah well, said Mercier, no more about it, such shortage is understandable, after all.

Would you have a room by any chance, said Camier, where my friend might take a moment's rest? He is dropping with fatigue. He leaned towards the manager and whispered in his ear.

His mother? said the manager.

My mother is it? said Mercier. She died perpetrating me, the slut. Rather than meet my eye. What's all this? he said to Camier. Have you no respect for my family?

I could manage a room, said the manager, but of course—.

A moment's rest, said Camier, he is out on his feet.

Come on, nightmare pal, said Mercier, you can't refuse me that.

Of course at the full day rate, said the manager.

On an upper floor as far as possible, said Mercier, where I can throw myself out of the window without misgiving, should occasion arise.

You'll stick by him? said the manager.

To the last, said Camier.

Patrick! cried the manager. Where's Patrick? he said to the barman.

Out sick, said the barman.

46

What do you mean out sick? said the manager. I saw him last night. I even thought I saw him just now.

Out sick, said the barman. No hope they say. Sinking fast.

How aggravating, said the manager. What's the matter with him?

I do not know, said the barman.

And why was I not informed? said the manager.

We must have thought you knew, said the barman.

And who says it's serious? said the manager.

It's a rumour going the rounds, said the barman.

And where is he? said the manager. At home or—.

A pox on your Patrick! cried Mercier. Do you want to finish me?

Show the gentlemen up, said the manager. Take their order and hurry back.

Six? said the barman.

Or seven, said the manager. As the gentlemen prefer.

He watched them go. He poured himself a glass and tossed it off.

Ah Mr Graves, he said, good day, what are you taking?

Nice pair, said Mr Graves.

Oh that's nothing, said the manager, I'm used to it.

And where might I ask did you get used to it? said Mr Graves in his incipient pastoral patriarch's thick bass. Not among us, I vow.

Where I got used to it? said the manager. He closed his eyes the better to see what was still in spite of all a little dear to him. Among my masters, he said.

I'm happy to hear you say so, said Mr Graves. I wish you good day.

47

The manager capped this.

His weary gaze strayed over the saloon where the honourable yokels were making to depart. Mr Graves had given the signal, they would not be slow to follow an example of such moment.

The barman reported back.

Mr Gast did not at once reply, intent on the scene as it faded and gave way, before his open eyes, to a little grey medieval square where silent shapes, muffled up to the eyes, passed slowly with laboured tread in the deep snow.

They took both, said the barman.

Mr Gast turned towards him.

They ordered a bottle of malt, said the barman.

Have they settled? said Mr Gast.

Yes, said the barman.

Nothing else matters, said Mr Gast.

I don't like the look of them at all, said the barman. Particular the long hank with the beard. The little fat one I wouldn't mind so much.

You keep out of it, said Mr Gast.

He went and stood by the door to take civil leave of his customers whose departure, in a body, was now clearly imminent. Most of them climbed aboard old high-slung Fords, others dispersed through the village in search of bargains. Others gathered talking in the rain which did not seem to incommode them. They were perhaps so pleased, who knows, for professional reasons, to see it fall, that they were pleased to feel it fall, wetting them through. Soon they would be on their several ways, scattered along the muddy roads shadowy already in the last gleams of niggard day. Each hastens towards his little kingdom, his waiting wife, his beasts snugly stalled, his dogs listening for the coming of their lord.

Mr Gast returned to the saloon.

Have you served them? he said.

Yes, said the barman.

They made no remark? said Mr Gast.

Only not to be disturbed, said the barman.

Where's Patrick? said Mr Gast. At home or in hospital?

I think he's at home, said the barman, but I wouldn't vouch for it.

You don't know a great deal, said Mr Gast.

I keep my mind on my work, said the barman. He fixed Mr Gast in the eye. On my duties and prerogatives, he said.

You couldn't do better, said Mr Gast, that way greatness lies. He went to the door. If I'm wanted, he said, I've gone out and won't be long.

He went out sure enough and sure enough was not long.

Dead, he said.

The barman wiped his hands in haste and crossed himself.

His last words, said Mr Gast, before yielding up the ghost, were unintelligible. Not so his second last, a gem of their kind, namely, A pint, for the love of Christ, a pint.

What ailed him exactly? said the barman.

How many days had he coming to him? said the barman.

He drew on Saturday like the rest, said the barman.

Negligible so, said Mr Gast. I'll send a sheaf.

A good pal as ever was, said the barman.

Mr Gast shrugged his shoulders.

Where's Teresa? he said. Don't tell me she's been taken too. Teresa! he cried.

In the toilet, said the barman.

Nothing escapes you, said Mr Gast.

Coming! cried Teresa.

A buxom wench appeared, a big tray under her arm and a clout in her hand.

Look at this sty, said Mr Gast.

A man entered the saloon. He wore a cap, a trench-coat all tabs, flaps, pockets and leather buttons, riding-breeches and mountaineering boots. His still brawny back was bowed beneath a knapsack filled to bursting and he held a huge stick in his hand. He lurched across the saloon, dragging noisily his hobnailed soles.

Some are best limned at first sight, those liable to vanish and never reappear.

My parquet, said Mr Gast.

Water, said Mr Conaire (the name without delay).

Mr Gast did not budge, nor did the barman. Had Mr Gast budged, then doubtless the barman too had budged. But Mr Gast not budging the barman did not budge either.

Water first, said Mr Conaire, then floods of liquor. Thanks. Again. Thanks. Enough.

He shed his sack with convulsive contortions of shoulders and loins.

Gin, he said.

He took off his cap and shook it violently in all

directions. Then he put it back on his shining sugar-loaf.

You have before you, gentlemen, he said, a man. Make the most of it. I have footed it from the very core of the metropolitan gas-chamber without rest or pause except twice to—. He looked about him, saw Teresa (already seen, but now with ostentation), leaned across the bar and finished his phrase in a murmur. He looked from Mr Gast to George (as the barman now is called), from George to Mr Gast, as though to make sure his words had done their work. Then drawing himself up he declared in ringing tones, Little and often, little and often, and gently, gently, that's what I've come to. He leered at Teresa and broke into a strident laugh. Where's your convenience? he said, adding, Convenience! They call that a convenience!

Mr Gast described the way that led to it.

What complications, said Mr Conaire. Always the same abominable well-bred latency. In Frankfurt, when you get off the train, what is the first thing you see, in gigantic letters of fire? A single word: HIER. Gin.

Neat? said Mr Gast.

Mr Conaire stepped back and struck an attitude.

What age would you say I was? he said. He rotated slowly. Speak up, he said, don't spare me.

Mr Gast named a figure.

Damnation, said Mr Conaire, got it in one.

Tis the baldness is deceptive, said Mr Gast.

Not another word, said Mr Conaire. In the yard, did I hear you say?

At the back on the left, said Mr Gast.

And to win from here to there? said Mr Conaire.

Mr Gast renewed his directions.

Lest I be taken short, said Mr Conaire.

On his way out he paused for a brush with Teresa.

Hello sweety, he said.

Teresa eyed him.

Sir, she said.

What loveliness, said Mr Conaire. At the door he turned. And graciousness, he said, what graciousness. He went out.

Mr Gast and George exchanged a look. Get out your slate, said Mr Gast. His next words were for Teresa. You couldn't be a little more endearing? he said.

The old dirt, said Teresa.

No one is asking you to wallow on the floor, said Mr Gast. He began to pace up and down, then halted, his mind made up. Stop what you're doing, he said, and collect yourselves. I shall now treat of the guest, that wild lovable beast. A shame that Patrick is not here to hear me.

He threw back his head, clasped his hands behind him and treated of the guest. Even as he spoke he saw a little window opening on an empty place, a moor unbroken save for a single track, where no shade ever falls, winding out of sight its gentle alternate curves. Not a breath stirs the pale grey air. In the far distance here and there the seam of earth and sky exudes a sunflooded beyond. It seems an autumn afternoon, late November say. The little black mass slowly approaching gradually takes shape, a tilted wagon drawn by a black horse, without effort, saunteringly. The wagoner walks ahead, flourishing his whip. He wears a heavy greatcoat, light in colour, its skirts trailing on the ground. It may even be he is happy, for he sings as he goes, in snatches. Now and then he turns, no doubt to look inside. As he draws near he seems young, he lifts his head and smiles.

That will be all for today, said Mr Gast. Impregnate yourselves with these considerations. They are the fruit of an eternity of public fawning and private snarls. I make you a present of them. If I'm wanted I'm out. Call me at six as usual.

There's something in what he says, said George.

There's men all over for you, said Teresa, no more ideal than a monkey.

Mr Conaire reappeared, enchanted to have got it over so fast.

I had my work cut out, he said, but I did it, I did it. He shivered. Nice north pole you have here, he said, what will you take. Jump at the chance, I feel the other hell calling me back.

George jumped.

Your health, sir, he said.

Pledge it, pledge it, said Mr Conaire, none deserves it more. And rosebud here, he said, would she deign to clink with us?

She's married, said George, and mother of three.

Fie upon you! cried Mr Conaire. How can one say such things!

You're being stood a port, said George.

Teresa moved behind the bar.

When I think what it means, said Mr Conaire. The torn flesh! The pretty crutch in tatters! The screams! The blood! The glair! The afterbirth! He put his hand before his eyes. The afterbirth! he groaned.

All the best, said Teresa.

53

Drink, drink, said Mr Conaire, pay no heed to me. What an abomination! What an abomination!

He took away his hand and saw them smiling at him, as at a child.

Forgive me, he said, when I think of women I think of maidens, I can't help it. They have no hairs, they pee not neither do they cack.

Mention it not, said George.

I took you for a maiden, said Mr Conaire, I give you my oath, no flattery intended. On the buxom side I grant you, nice and plump, plenty of bounce, a bosom in a thousand, a bottom in a million, thighs—. He broke off. No good, he said, not a stir out of him.

Teresa went back to her work.

I now come to the object of my visit, said Mr Conaire. Would you happen to know of a man by the name of Camier?

No, said George.

Strange, said Mr Conaire, seeing I was to meet him here, this very place, this very afternoon. Here's his card.

George read:

F. X. Camier
Private Investigator
Soul of Discretion

New one on me, said George.

Small and fat, said Mr Conaire, red face, scant hair, four chins, protruding paunch, bandy legs, beady pig eyes.

There's a couple above, said George, showed up there a short time back.

54

What's the other like? said Mr Conaire.

A big bony hank with a beard, said George, hardly able to stand, wicked expression.

That's him, cried Mr Conaire, those are them! Slip up now and give him the word. Tell him Mr Conaire is waiting in the lounge. Co-naire.

They left word not to be disturbed, said George. They'd turn on you like a shot, I tell you.

Listen, said Mr Conaire.

George listened.

Well I don't mind trying, he said.

He went out and a moment later came back.

They're snoring, he said.

Rouse them, said Mr Conaire.

The bottle is empty, said George, and there they are—.

What bottle? said Mr Conaire.

They ordered a bottle of malt in the room, said George.

Oh the hogs, said Mr Conaire.

There they are stretched out side by side in their clothes on the floor, said George. Snoring hand in hand.

Oh the hogs, said Mr Conaire.

IV

The field lay spread before them. In it nothing grew, that is nothing of use to man. Nor was it clear at first sight what interest it could have for animals. Birds may have found the odd worm there. Its straggling expanse was bounded by a sickly hedge of old tree stumps and tangles of brambles perhaps good for a few bramble berries at bramble-berry time. Thistles and nettles, possible fodder at a pinch, contended for the soil with a sour blue grass. Beyond the hedge were other fields, similar in aspect, bounded by no less similar hedges. How did one get from one field to another? Through the hedges perhaps. Capriciously a goat, braced on its hind legs, its forefeet on a stump, was muzzling the brambles in search of the tenderer thorns. Now and then it turned with petulance away, took a few angry steps, stood still, then perhaps a little spring, straight up in the air, before returning to the hedge. Would it continue thus all round the field? Or weary first?

Some day someone would realize. Then the builders would come. Or a priest, with his sprinkler, and another acre would be God's. When prosperity returned.

Camier was reading in his notebook. He tore out the little leaves when read, crumpled them and threw them away. He watches me, he said, without a word. He drew a big envelope from his pocket, took from it and threw away the following: buttons, two specimens of head or body hair, an embroidered handkerchief, a number of laces (his speciality), one toothbrush, a strange piece of rubber, one garter, samples of material. The envelope too, when he had emptied it, he threw away. I might as well be picking my nose, he said, for all he cares. He rose, impelled by scruples that did him credit, and gathered up the crumpled leaves, those at least which the light morning breeze had not blown away, or hidden in a fold of the ground, or behind a clump of thistles. The leaves thus recovered he tore up and threw away. So, he said, I feel lighter now. He turned back towards Mercier. You're not sitting on the wet grass, I hope, he said.

I'm sitting on my half of our coat, said Mercier, clover is nothing to it.

Fine too early, said Camier, bad sign.

What is the weather doing, said Mercier, now you mention it.

Look and see, said Camier.

I'd rather you told me, said Mercier.

A pale raw blotch, said Camier, has appeared in the east, the sun presumably. Happily it is intermittent, thanks to a murk of tattered wrack driving from the west before its face. It is cold, but not yet raining.

Sit, said Mercier. I know you do not share my chilly nature, but profit by the bank just the same. Don't overdo it, Camier, a nice bloody fool I'd look if you caught pneumonia.

Camier sat.

Cuddle close, said Mercier, snug and warm. Now look, like me, wrap the slack round your legs. So. All we need now is the hard-boiled egg and bottle of pop.

I feel the damp creeping up my crack, said Camier.

So long as none creeps down, said Mercier.

I fear for my cyst, said Camier.

What you lack, said Mercier, is a sense of proportion.

I don't see the connexion, said Camier.

Just so, said Mercier, you never see the connexion. When you fear for your cyst think of your fistula. And when you tremble for your fistula consider your chancre. This method holds equally for what is called happiness. Take one for example entirely free from pain all over, both his body and the other yoke. Where can he turn for relief? Nothing simpler. To the thought of annihilation. Thus, whatever the conjuncture, nature bids us smile, if not laugh. And now, let us look things calmly in the face.

After a moment's silence Camier began to laugh. Mercier in due course was tickled too. Then they laughed long together, clutching each other by the shoulders so as not to collapse.

What innocent merriment, said Camier, finally.

Well you know what I mean, said Mercier.

Before going any further they asked and told each other how they felt. Then Mercier said:

What exactly did we decide? I remember we agreed, as indeed we always do, in the end, but I forgot as to what. But you must know, since it is your plan, is it not, we are putting into execution.

For me too, said Camier, certain details have faded, and certain refinements of reasoning. So if I have any light to throw it is rather on what we are going to do, or rather again on what we are going to try and do, than on why we are going to try and do it.

I'm ready to try anything, said Mercier, so long as I know what.

Well, said Camier, the idea is to return to town, at our leisure, and stay there for as long as necessary.

Necessary for what? said Mercier.

For retrieving our belongings, said Camier, or giving them up for lost.

It must indeed have been rich in refinements, said Mercier, the reasoning responsible for that.

It would seem to have seemed to us, said Camier, though I cannot swear to it, that the sack is the crux of the whole matter in that it contains, or did contain, certain objects we cannot dispense with.

But we have reviewed its entire contents, said Mercier, and deemed them superfluous without exception.

True, said Camier, and our conception of what is superfluous can scarcely have evolved since yesterday. Whence then our disquiet?

Well, whence? said Mercier.

From the intuition, said Camier, if I remember right, that the said sack contains something essential to our salvation.

But we know that is not so, said Mercier.

You know the faint imploring voice, said Camier, that drivels to us on and off of former lives?

I confuse it more and more, said Mercier, with the one that tries to cod me I'm not yet dead. But I take your meaning.

It would seem to be some such organ, said Camier,

that for the past twenty-four hours has not ceased to murmur, The sack! Your sack! Our latest heart to heart made this quite clear.

I recall nothing of the kind, said Mercier.

And so the need for us, said Camier, if not to find, at least to look for it, and for the bicycle, and for the umbrella.

I fail to see why, said Mercier. Why not the sack alone, since our concern is with the sack alone.

I too fail to see why, said Camier, exactly why. All I know is that yesterday we did see why, exactly why.

When the cause eludes me, said Mercier, I begin to feel uneasy.

Here Camier was alone in wetting his trousers.

Mercier does not join in Camier's laugh? said Camier.

Not just this once, said Mercier.

This thing we think we need, said Camier, once in our possession and now no longer so, we situate in the sack, as in that which contains. But on further thought nothing proves it is not in the umbrella, or fastened to some part of the bicycle. All we know is we had it once and now no more. And even that we do not know for sure.

There's premises for you if you like, said Mercier.

It boils down then to some unknown, said Camier, which not only is not necessarily in the sack, but which perhaps no sack of this type could possibly accommodate, the bicycle itself for example, or the umbrella, or both. By what token shall we know the truth? By a heightened sense of well-being? Unlikely.

60

I had a strange dream last night, said Mercier, I was in a wood with my grandmother, she was—.

Most unlikely, said Camier. No, but perhaps rather a gradual feeling of relief, spun out in time, reaching its paroxysm a fortnight or three weeks later, without our knowing exactly to what it was due. An example of bliss in ignorance, bliss at having recovered an essential good, ignorance of its nature.

She was carrying her breasts in her hands, said Mercier, by the nipples held between finger and thumb. But unfortunately—.

Camier flew into a rage, into a feigned rage that is, for into a true rage with Mercier Camier could not fly. The former sat agape. Drops seemingly from nowhere glistened in the grey tangles of his beard. The fingers fumbled at the great bony nose, its red skin stretched to bursting, delved furtively in the black holes, spread to feel their way down the channelled cheeks, began again. The ashen eyes stared into space aghast. The brow, scored deep with aliform furrows due less to meditation than to chronic amaze, this brow was perhaps, all things considered, of this grotesque head the least grotesque feature. It culminated in an unbelievably tousled mass of dirty hair comprising every tone from tow to snow. The ears—no.

Mercier had little to say for himself.

You ask me to explain, said Camier, I do so and you don't mind me.

It's my dream came over me again, said Mercier.

Yes, said Camier, instead of minding me you tell me your dreams. And yet you know our covenant: no communication of dreams on any account. The same holds for quotes. No dreams or quotes at any price. He got up. Do you feel strong enough to move? he said.

No, said Mercier.

Camier go get you food, said Camier.

Go, said Mercier.

The stout little bandy legs carried him in no time to the village, from the waist up all swagger and swing, an act. Mercier, alone in the lee of the bank, wavered between his two familiar leanings, not knowing which way to fall. Was not the outcome the same? In the end he said, I am Mercier, alone, ill, in the cold, the wet, old, half mad, no way on, no way back. He eyed briefly, with nostalgia, the ghastly sky, the hideous earth. At your age, he said. Another act. Immaterial.

I was about to go, said Mr Conaire, all hope abandoned.

George, said Camier, five sandwiches, four wrapped and one on the side. You see, he said, turning graciously to Mr Conaire, I think of everything. For the one I eat here will give me the strength to get back with the four others.

Sophistry, said Mr Conaire. You set off with your five, wrapped, feel faint, open up, take one out, eat, recuperate, push on with the others.

For all response Camier began to eat.

You'll spoil him, said Mr Conaire. Yesterday cakes, today sandwiches, tomorrow crusts and Thursday stones.

Mustard, said Camier.

Before leaving me yesterday, said Mr Conaire, for your matter of life and death, you appointed to meet me here, at this very place, that very afternoon. I arrive, ask George in what a state, with my invariable punctuality. I wait. Doubts gradually assail me. Can I have mistaken the place? The day? The hour? I unburden myself to the barman. I learn you are somewhere above-stairs, with your butty, for some time past what is more, the pair of you plunged in a crapulous stupor. I invoke the urgency of my business and request you be waked. No question. You are not to be disturbed, on any account. You entice me to this place and take measures to prevent my seeing you. I receive advice. Stay around, they'll soon be down. Weakly I stay. Are you soon down? Bah! I return to the charge. Wake him, tell him Mr Conaire is below. What a hope! The guest's desires are sacred. I offer threats. They laugh in my face. I press my point. By force. They bar the way. By stealth, sneaking up the stairs. They overtake me. I go down on my knees. General hilarity. They egg me on to drink, to stay for dinner, to stay the night. I'll see you in the morning. I'll be told the moment you're down. The saloon fills. Labourers, travellers. I get carried away. I come to on a couch. It is seven in the morning. You are gone. Why was I not told? No one knew. What time did you leave? No one knows. Are you expected back? No one knows.

Camier raised an imaginary tankard, with flexed fingers to clinch his meaning. The real he emptied slowly at a single draught, then caught up his packet and went to the door. There he turned.

Mr Conaire, he said, I present my apologies. There was a moment yesterday when you were much in my thoughts. Then suddenly pff! no longer, gone from them utterly. As if you had never been, Mr Conaire.

No, that's not right, as if you had ceased to be. No, that's not right either, as if you were without my knowledge. Don't take what I say in evil part, Mr Conaire, I have no wish to offend. The truth is I suddenly saw my work was over, I mean the work I am famous for, and that it was a mistake to have thought you might join me here, if only for a moment. I renew my apologies, Mr Conaire, and bid you farewell.

And my bitch! cried Mr Conaire.

Your old pet, said Camier. You miss her. You'd pay dear, what passes for dear, to get her back. You don't know when you're well off.

He went. Mr Conaire half made to follow him. But for some time past he had been fighting the need. On his return from the yard he went to the street door and looked out, then turned back into the saloon where such sadness overcame him that he ordered more gin.

My little bitch! he groaned.

Come, come, said George, we'll get you another.

Queenie! groaned Mr Conaire. Her smile was almost human!

One more out of the way, with any luck.

Mr Gast was nowhere to be seen, and with good reason, for he was looking for snowdrops in a little wood, snowdrops for Patrick's sheaf.

Blow, blow, thou ill wind.

Teresa was nowhere to be seen either, without regret be it said, Teresa was nowhere to be seen.

Mercier would not eat. But Camier made him.

You are green, said Camier.

I think I'm going to be sick, said Mercier.

He was not mistaken. Camier held him up.

You'll feel better without it, said Camier.

And sure enough, little by little, Mercier did feel better, better than before being sick that is.

It's all the dark thoughts I've been revolving, said Mercier, ever since you went. I even wondered if you had abandoned me.

Leaving you the raincoat? said Camier.

There is every reason to abandon me, I know, said Mercier. He reflected a moment. It takes Camier not to abandon Mercier, he said.

Can you walk? said Camier.

I'll walk, never fear, said Mercier. He got up and took a few steps. How's that? he said.

The raincoat, said Camier, why not dump it? What good is it?

It retards the action of the rain, said Mercier.

A cerecloth, said Camier.

You go too far, said Mercier.

Do you want my honest opinion? said Camier. The one who has it on is no less to be pitied, physically and morally, than the one who has it off.

There's something in what you say, said Mercier.

They contemplated the raincoat where it lay spread out at the foot of the bank. It looked flayed. Flitters of chequered lining, its ghostly tartan rending to behold, still clung to the shoulders. A paler yellow marked those patches where the wet had not yet soaked through.

Let us be gone from here, said Camier.

Shall we not throw it away? said Mercier.

Let it lie where it is, said Camier, no needless exertion.

I should have liked to launch it, said Mercier.

Let it lie there, said Camier. Soon no trace of our bodies will subsist. Under the action of the sun it will shrivel, like dead leaf.

We could bury it, said Mercier.

Don't be mawkish, said Camier.

Otherwise someone will come and take it, said Mercier, some verminous brute.

What do we care? said Camier.

True, said Mercier, but we do.

Camier moved off. After a little Mercier came up with him.

You may lean on me, said Camier.

Not now, not now, said Mercier irritably.

What has you looking back all the time? said Camier.

It moved, said Mercier.

To wave, said Camier.

We didn't leave anything in the pockets by any chance? said Mercier.

Punched tickets of all sorts, said Camier, spent matches, scraps of newspaper bearing in their margins the obliterated traces of irrevocable rendez-vous, the classic last tenth of pointless pencil, crumples of soiled bumf, a few porous condoms, dust. Life in short.

Nothing we'll be needing? said Mercier.

Did you not hear what I said? said Camier. Life.

They went a little way in silence, as every now and then it was their wont.

We'll take ten days if need be, said Camier.

No further transport? said Mercier.

What we seek is not necessarily behind the back of beyond, said Camier. So let our watchword be—.

Seek? said Mercier.

We are not faring for the love of faring, that I know of, said Camier. Cunts we may be, but not to that extent. He cast a cold eye on Mercier. Don't choke, he said. If you have anything to say, now speak.

I was thinking of saying something, said Mercier, but on second thoughts I'll keep it to myself.

Selfish pig, said Camier.

Go on you, said Mercier.

Where was I? said Camier.

Let our watchword be, said Mercier.

Ah yes, said Camier, lente, lente, and circum-spection, with deviations to right and left and sudden reversals of course. Nor let us hesitate to halt, for days and even weeks on end. We have all life before us, all the fag end that is.

What's the weather like now, said Mercier, if I look up I'll fall down.

Like what it's always like, said Camier, with this slight difference, that we're beginning to get used to it.

I thought I felt drops on my cheeks, said Mercier.

Cheer up, said Camier, we are coming to the station of the damned, I can see the steeple.

God be praised, said Mercier, now we can get some rest.

Summary
of two preceding chapters

III

The train.
Madden interlude I.
The slow train.
Madden interlude conclusion.
The village.
The inn.
Mr Gast.
The beasts on the roads.
The farmers.
Mercier's dream.
The journey in jeopardy.
Camier's presence of mind.
Patrick's illness.
Mercier and Camier mount.
Mr Graves.
Patrick's death.
His second-last words.
Conaire interlude I.
Mr Gast treats of the guest.
Mr Gast's vision.
Conaire interlude II.
Mercier and Camier sleep.

IV

Next day.
The field.
The goat.
The dawn.
Mercier and Camier laugh.
Mercier and Camier confer.
Camier laughs alone.
Mercier's face.
Camier departs.
Mercier alone.
The inn.
Conaire interlude conclusion.
The snowdrops.
Mercier eats and vomits.
The raincoat.
They press on.
The steeple of the damned.

V

The day came at last when lo the town again, first the outskirts, then the centre. They had lost the notion of time, but all pointed to the Lord's Day, or day of rest, the streets, the sounds, the passers-by. Night was falling. They prowled about the centre, at a loss where to go. Finally, at the suggestion of Mercier, whose turn it must have been to lead, they went to Helen's. She was in bed, a trifle unwell, but rose none the less and let them in, not without having first cried, from behind the door, Who goes there? They told her all the latest, their hopes both shattered and forlorn. They described how they had been chased by the bull. She left the room and came back with the umbrella. Camier manipulated it at length. But it's in perfect trim, he said, quite perfect. I mended it, said Helen. Perhaps even if possible more perfect than before, said Camier. If possible perhaps, said Helen. It opens like a dream, said Camier, and when I release—click!—the catch it collapses unaided. I open, I close, one, two, click, plop, click, pl—. Have done, said Mercier, before you break it on us again. I'm a trifle unwell, said Helen. No better omen, said Camier. But the sack was nowhere to be seen. I don't see the parrot, said Mercier. I put it out

70

in the country, said Helen. They passed a peaceful
night, for them, without debauch of any kind. All next
day they spent within doors. Time tending to drag,
they manstuprated mildly, without fatigue. Before the
blazing fire, in the twofold light of lamp and leaden day,
they squirmed gently on the carpet, their naked bodies
mingled, fingering and fondling with the languorous
tact of hands arranging flowers, while the rain beat on
the panes. How delicious that must have been! Towards evening Helen fetched up some vintage bottles
and they drifted off contentedly to sleep. Men less
tenacious might not have withstood the temptation to
leave it at that. But the following afternoon found them
in the street again, with no other thought than the goal
they had assigned themselves. Only a few more hours
and it would be night, nightfall, a few more leaden
hours, so no time was to be lost. Yet even total darkness, total but for the streetlamps, so far from hindering
their quest could only further it, all things considered.
For the district they now aimed to get to, one to which
they hardly knew the way, would be easier for them to
get to by night than by day, since the one time they had
got to it before, the one and only time, it had not been
day, no, but night, nightfall. So they entered a bar, for
it is in bars that the Merciers of this world, and the
Camiers, find it least tedious to await the dark. For this
they had another if less weighty reason, namely the
advantage to be derived, on the mental level too, from
immersion as complete as possible in that selfsame
atmosphere which had so unsteadied their first steps.
They set to therefore without delay. There is too much
at stake, said Camier, for us to neglect the elementary

precautions. Thus with a single stone they accounted for two birds, and even three. For they availed themselves of the respite to talk freely of this and that, with great profit, to themselves. For it is in bars that the Merciers of this heavenly planet, and the Camiers, talk with greatest freedom, greatest profit. Finally a great light bathed their understandings, flooding in particular the following concepts.

1. The lack of money is an evil. But it can turn to a good.

2. What is lost is lost.

3. The bicycle is a great good. But it can turn nasty, if ill employed.

4. There is food for thought in being down and out.

5. There are two needs: the need you have and the need to have it.

6. Intuition leads to many a folly.

7. That which the soul spews forth is never lost.

8. Pockets daily emptier of their last resources are enough to break the stoutest resolution.

9. The male trouser has got stuck in a rut, particularly the fly which should be transferred to the crotch and designed to open trapwise, permitting the testes, regardless of the whole sordid business of micturition, to take the air unobserved. The drawers should of course be transfigured in consequence.

10. Contrary to a prevalent opinion, there are places in nature from which God would appear to be absent.

11. What would one do without women? Explore other channels.

12. Soul: another four-letter word.

13. What can be said of life not already said? Many things. That its arse is a rotten shot, for example.

These illustrations did not blind them to the goal they had in view. This appeared to them, however, with ever increasing clarity as time wore on, one to be pursued with calm and collection. And being still just calm and collected enough to know they were no longer so they reached without difficulty the happy decision to postpone all action to the following day and even, if necessary, to the next but one. They returned then in excellent spirits to Helen's apartment and dropped asleep without further ceremony. And even the following day they refrained from the pretty frolics of wet forenoons, so keen were they to be on their toes for the trials to come.

It was chiming midday when they left the house. In the porch they paused.

Oh the pretty rainbow, said Camier.

The umbrella, said Mercier.

They exchanged a look. Camier vanished up the stairs. When he reappeared, with the umbrella, Mercier said:

You took your time.

Oh you know, said Camier, one does what one can. Are we to put it up?

Mercier scrutinized the sky.

What do you think? he said.

Camier left the shelter of the porch and submitted the sky to a thorough inspection, turning celtically to the north, the east, the south and finally the west, in that order.

Well? said Mercier.

Don't rush me, said Camier.

He advanced to the corner of the street, in order to reduce the risk of error. Finally he regained the porch and delivered his considered opinion.

In our shoes I wouldn't, he said.

And may one inquire why not? said Camier. It's coming down, if I am to believe my eyes. Can you not sense you're wet?

Your inclination would be to put it up? said Camier.

I don't say that, said Mercier, I simply ask myself when we'll put it up if we do not do so now.

To the unprejudiced eye it was less an umbrella than a parasol. From the tip of the spike to the ends of the stays or struts was a bare quarter of the total length. The stick was terminated by an amber knob with tassels. The material was red in colour, or had been, indeed still was in places. Shreds of fringe adorned the perimeter, at irregular intervals.

Look at it, said Camier. Take it in your hand. Come on, take it in your hand, it won't bite you.

Stand back! cried Mercier.

Where was it dug up at all? said Camier.

I bought it at Khan's, said Mercier, knowing we had only one raincoat to our name. He asked a shilling for it, I got it for eight pence. I thought he was going to embrace me.

It must have come out about 1900, said Camier. The year I believe of Ladysmith, on the Klip. Remember? Cloudless skies, garden parties daily. Life lay smiling before us. No hope was too high. We played at holding fort. We died like flies. Of hunger. Of cold. Of thirst. Of heat. Pom! Pom! The last rounds. Surrender!

Never! We eat our dead. Drink our pee. Pom! Pom! Two more we didn't know we had. But what is that we hear? A clamour from the watch-tower! Dust on the horizon! The column at last! Our tongues are black. Hurrah none the less. Rah! Rah! A craking as of crows. A quartermaster dies of joy. We are saved. The century was two months old.

Look at it now, said Mercier.

A silence ensued which Camier was the first to violate.

Well, he said, do we put it up now or wait for the weather to worsen?

Mercier scrutinized the inscrutable sky.

Go take a look, he said, and see what you think.

Camier again gained the corner of the street. On his return he said:

There is perhaps a little light below the verge. Would you have me go up on the roof?

Mercier concentrated. Finally he exclaimed, impulsively:

Let us put it up and pray for the best.

But Camier could not put it up.

Give it here to me, said Mercier.

But Mercier had no better success. He brandished it above his head, but controlled himself in time.

What have we done to God? he said.

Denied him, said Camier.

Don't tell me he is all that rancorous, said Mercier.

Camier took the umbrella and vanished up the stairs.

No sooner was he alone than Mercier went. His path crossed, at a given moment, that of an old man of weird and wretched aspect, carrying under his arm what looked like a board folded in two. It seemed to Mercier he had seen him somewhere before and he wondered as he went on his way where that somewhere could have been. The old man too, on whom for a wonder the transit of Mercier had not been lost, was left with the impression of a scarecrow encountered elsewhere and busied himself for a space with trying to recall in what circumstances. So, as with laboured steps they drew apart, each occupied the other's thoughts in vain. But the least little thing halts the Merciers of this world, a murmur coming to its crest and breaking, a voice saying how strange the autumn-tide of day no matter what the season. A new beginning, but with no life in it, how could there be? More manifest in town than in the country, but in the country too, where slowly over the vast empty space the peasant seems to stray, so aimless that night must surely overtake him far from the village nowhere, the homestead nowhere to be seen. There is no time left and yet how it drags. Even the flowers seem past their time to close and a kind of panic seizes on the tired wings. The hawk stoops always too soon, the rooks rise from the fallows while it is still light and flock to their places of assembly, there to croak and squabble till nightfall. Then, too late, they agitate to set out again. Day is over long before it ends, man ready to drop long before the hour of rest. But not a word, evening is all fever, a scurrying to and fro to no avail. So short it is not worth their while beginning, too long for them not to begin, that is the time they are pent up in, as cruelly as Balue in his cage. Ask the hour of a passer-by and he'll throw it at you over his shoulder at a venture and hurry on. But you may be easy in your mind, he is not far wrong who every few minutes consults his watch, sets it by official astronomic time, makes his reckonings, wonders how on earth to fit in all he has to do before the endless day comes to an end. Or with furious weary gesture he gives the hour that besets him, the hour it always was and will be, one that to the beauties of too late unites the charms of prematurity, that of the Never! without more of an even dreader raven. But all day that is how it is, from the first tick to the last tack, or rather from the third to the antepenultimate, allowing for the time it needs, the tamtam within, to drum you back into the dream and drum you back out again. And in between all are heard, every millet grain that falls, you look behind and there you are, every day a little closer, all life a little closer. Joy in saltspoonfuls, like water when it's thirst you're dying of, and a bonny little agony homeopathically distilled, what more can you ask? A heart in the room of the heart? Come come. But ask on the contrary your way of the passer-by and he'll take your hand and lead you, by the warren's beauty-spots, to the very place. It's a great grey barracks of a building, unfinished, unfinishable, with two doors, for those who enter and for those who leave, and at the windows faces peering out. The more fool you to have asked.

Mercier's hand released the railing to which this attack of wind had fastened it. But he had not gone far when he stopped again to observe, advancing towards him, a ragged shaggy old man plodding along beside a donkey. The latter, unbridled, set with small steps its dainty dogged course beside the curb, unswervingly except to circumvent a stationary vehicle or a group of urchins at marbles on their hunkers in the gutter. The man walked in the street, between the grey haunch and the hostile cars. They raised their eyes from the ground only when danger threatened, to take its measure. Mercier said to himself, disappointing again as usual, No outerness will ever disestablish that harmony. It was perhaps too great a call on his strength, this parting from Camier at so sombre an hour. Admittedly strength was needed for to stay with Camier, no less than for to stay with Mercier, but less than for the horrors of soliloquy. Yet there he is on his way again, the voice has ceased, he is over the worst of the old man and the donkey, his being fills again with that merciful fog which is the best he knows, he's good for the long road yet. His dim shape moves on, hugging the railing, in the shadow of God knows what evergreens so called, hollies perhaps, if shadow is the word for a light hardly less leaden than that of the bogland near by. The collar of his coat is turned up, his right hand is in his left sleeve and vice versa, they lie jogging on his belly in senile abandon, now and then he glimpses as through shifting seaweed a foot dragging on a flagstone. Heavy chains, hung between small stone pillars, festoon with their massy garlands the pavement on the street side. Once in motion they swing on and on, steadily or with serpentine writhings. Here Mercier would come to play when he was small. Running along the line of chains he set them going, one after another, with a stick, then turned back to look how the great jolts shook the pavement from end to end till it seemed they would never come to rest.

VI

Camier sat near the door at a small red table with a
thick glass top. On his left hand strangers were be-
littling equal strangers, while to his right the talk, in
undertones, was of the interest taken by Jesuits in
mundane matters. In this or some cognate connexion
an article was cited, recently appeared in some ecclesi-
astical rag, on the subject of artificial insemination, the
conclusion of which appeared to be that sin arose
whenever the sperm was of non-marital origin. On this
angelic sex issue was joined, several voices taking part.

Change the subject, said Camier, or I'll report you
to the archbishop. You're putting thoughts in my
head.

He could not distinguish clearly what lay before him,
all outline blurred in the smoke-laden air. Here and
then emerged, rifting the haze, the unanswerable
gesture complete with irrefutable pipe, the conical hat,
fragments of lower limbs and notably feet, shuffling and
fidgeting from one state of torment to the next, as
though the seat of the soul. But behind him he had the
stout old wall, plain and bare, he could feel it in his
rear, he laid the back of his head against it and rubbed.
He said to himself, When Mercier comes, for come he

will, I know my man, where will he sit? Here, at this
table? This problem absorbed him for a time. No, he
decided in the end, no, he must not, he Camier could
not bear it, why he knew not. What then? The better
to envisage this, that is to say what then, since Mercier
must not join him in his corner, Camier took his
hands from his pockets, disposed them before him on
the table in a snug little heap and rested his face thereon,
first gently, then with the full weight of the skull. And
the vision was not long in coming of Camier seeing
Mercier before Mercier Camier, rising and hastening
to the door. There you are at last, he cries, I thought
you had left me for ever, and he draws him to the bar-
counter, or deep into the saloon, or they go out together, though this is hardly likely. For Mercier is
weary, in want of rest and refreshment before going any
further, and has things to tell that can ill brook delay,
and Camier too has things to tell, yes, they have things
of moment to tell each other and they are weary, they
need to compose themselves, after this long separation,
and take their bearings, determine more or less how
they stand, whether the future is bright or dark or
merely dim as so often, and if there is one direction
rather than another in which preferably to bend their
steps, in a word collect themselves sufficiently to press
hotfoot on, all smiles and lucidity, towards one of the
innumerable goals indulgent judgement equivails, or
else all smiles (optional) do justice on this élan and
admire them from a distance, one after another, for
they are distant. It is then a glimpse is caught of what
might have been were one not as one had to be and it is
not every day such a hair is offered for splitting. For

once whelped all over bar the howling. Having thus cleaned up the immediate future Camier raised his head and saw before him a creature which he took some little time, so great was the resemblance, to recognize as Mercier, whence a tangle of reflections that left him no peace (but what peace then!) till the next day but one, with the comforting conclusion that what he had so dreaded as to deem it unbearable was not to feel his friend by his side, but to see him cross the sill and tread the last stage of the great space separating them since noon.

Mercier's entry had provoked some embarrassment in the saloon, a kind of uneasy chill. And yet the company was of dockers and sailors for the most part, with a sprinkling of excisemen, such as are not easily affected, as a rule, by singularity of exterior. A hush fell none the less as voices lulled, gestures froze, tankards trembled tilted on the brink and all eyes looked the same way. An acute observer, had one been present, but none was, might well have been put in mind of a flock of sheep, or a herd of oxen, startled by some dark threat. Their bodies rigid, drawn with fixed glare to face the common foe, they are stiller for a moment than the ground on which they graze. Then all to their heels, or full tilt at the intruder (if weak), or back to whatever they were about, cropping, chewing, coupling, gambolling. Or in mind of those walking sick who still all speech where they pass, dispel the body and fill the soul with dread, pity, anger, mirth, disgust. Yes, when you outrage nature you need be mighty careful if you don't want to hear the view-halloo or suffer the succour of some repugnant hand. For a moment it seemed to Camier that things were going to turn nasty and his hamstrings tensed under the table. But little by little a vast sigh arose, an exhalation higher and higher like a shoreward sweeping wave whose might in the end collapses in froth and clatter, for the glee of children.

What became of you? said Camier.

Mercier raised his eyes, but their stare was not at Camier, nor even at the wall. What on earth could it have been that they fixed with such intensity? One wonders.

Christ what a face, said Camier, you look straight from the infernal regions. What's that you say?

No doubt about it, Mercier's lips had moved.

I know of only one, said Mercier.

They didn't beat you? said Camier.

Across them the shadow fell of a huge man. His apron ended half way down his thighs. Camier looked at him, who looked at Mercier, who began to look at Camier. Thus were engendered, though no eyes met, images of extreme complexity enabling each to enjoy himself in three distinct simultaneous versions plus, on a more modest scale, the three versions of self enjoyed by each of the others, namely a total of nine images at first sight irreconcilable, not to mention the confusion of frustrated excitations jostling on the fringes of the field. In all a gruesome mess, but instructive, instructive. Add to this the many eyes fastened on the trio and a feeble idea may be obtained of what awaits him too smart not to know better, better than to leave his black cell and that harmless lunacy, faint flicker every other age or so, the consciousness of being, of having been.

What will it be? said the barman.

When we need you we'll tell you, said Camier.

What will it be? said the barman.

The same as before, said Mercier.

You haven't been served, said the barman.

The same as this gentleman, said Mercier.

The barman looked at Camier's empty glass.

I forget what it was, he said.

I too, said Camier.

I never knew, said Mercier.

Make an effort, said Camier.

You intimidate us, said Mercier, good for you.

We put a bold front on it, said Camier, though actually shitting with terror. Quick some sawdust, my good fellow.

And so on, each saying things he ought not to have said, till some kind of settlement was reached, sealed with sickly smiles and scurrilous civilities. The roar (of conversation) resumed.

Us, said Camier.

Mercier raised his glass.

I didn't mean that, said Camier.

Mercier set down his glass.

But why not, after all? said Camier.

So they raised their glasses and drank, both saying, at the same instant or almost, Here's to you. Camier added, And to the success of our—. But this was a toast he could not complete. Help me, he said.

I can think of no word, said Mercier, nor of any set of words, to express what we imagine we are trying to do.

Your hand, said Camier, your two hands.

83

What for? said Mercier.

To clasp in mine, said Camier.

The hands fumbled for one another beneath the table, found one another, clasped one another, one small between two big, one big between two small.

Yes, said Mercier.

What do you mean, yes? said Camier.

I beg your pardon, said Mercier.

You said yes, said Camier.

I said yes? said Mercier. I? Impossible. The last time I abused that term was at my wedding. To Toffana. The mother of my children. Mine own. Inalienable. Toffana. You never met her. She lives on. A tundish. Like fucking a quag. To think it was for this hectolitre of excrement I renegued my dearest dream. He paused coquettishly. But Camier was in no playful mood. So that Mercier resumed perforce, You are shy to ask me which. Then let me whisper it in your ear. That of leaving the species to get on as best it could without me.

I would have cherished a coloured baby, said Camier.

Ever since I favour the other form, said Mercier. One does what one can, but one can nothing. Only squirm and wriggle, to end up in the evening where you were in the morning. But! There's a vocable for you if you like! All is vox inanis save, certain days, certain conjunctions, such is Mercier's contribution to the squabble of the universals.

Where are our things? said Camier.

Where our umbrella? said Mercier.

As I was trying to help Helen, said Camier, my hand slipped.

Not another word, said Mercier.

I dumped it in the sluice, said Camier.

Let us go from here, said Mercier.

Where? said Camier.

Crooked ahead, said Mercier.

Our things? said Camier.

Less said the better, said Mercier.

You'll be my death, said Camier.

You want details? said Mercier.

Camier did not answer. Words fail him, said Mercier to himself.

You remember our bicycle? said Mercier.

Just, said Camier.

Speak up, said Mercier, I'm not deaf.

Yes, said Camier.

Of it there remains, said Mercier, securely chained to the railing, as much as may reasonably remain, after a week's incessant rain, of a bicycle relieved of both wheels, the saddle, the bell and the carrier. And the tail-light, he added, I nearly forgot. He struck his forehead a blow. What an addle-pate to be sure! he said.

And the pump of course, said Camier.

Believe it or not, said Mercier, it's all one to me, our pump has been spared.

And it such a fine pump, said Camier. Where is it?

Thinking it was a mere oversight, said Mercier, I left it where it was. It seemed the right thing to do. What is there for us to pump up now? That is to say I turned it upside down, I don't know why.

Does it fit as well so? said Camier.

Oh quite as well, said Mercier, quite, quite as well.

They went out. It was blowing.

Is it raining still? said Mercier.

85

Not for the moment, I fancy, said Camier.

And yet the air strikes damp, said Mercier.

If we have nothing to say, said Camier, let us say nothing.

We have things to say, said Mercier.

Then why don't we say them? said Camier.

We can't, said Mercier.

Then let us be silent, said Camier.

But we try, said Mercier.

We have got clear without mishap, said Camier, and unscathed.

What did I tell you? said Mercier. Continue.

We advance painfully—.

Painfully! cried Mercier.

Laboriously . . . laboriously through the dark streets, dark and comparatively deserted, because of the late hour no doubt, and the unsettled weather, not knowing who is leading, who following, whom.

By the ingle, said Mercier, snug and warm, they drowse away. Books fall from hands, heads on chests, flames die down, embers expire, dream steals from its lair towards its prey. But the watcher is on the watch, they wake and go to bed, thanking God for the position, dearly won, permitting of such joys, among so many others, such peace, while wind and rain lash against the panes and thought strays, spirit unalloyed, among those who have no refuge, the unable, the accursed, the weak, the unfortunate.

Do we as much as know, said Camier, what the other was up to all this time?

Again, said Mercier.

Camier repeated his remark.

Even side by side, said Mercier, as now, arm to arm, hand in hand, legs in unison, we are fraught with more events than could fit in a fat tome, two fat tomes, your fat tome and my fat tome. Whence no doubt our blessed sense of nothing, nothing to be done, nothing to be said. For man wearies in the end of trying to slake his drought at the fireman's hose and seeing his few remaining tapers, one after another, blasted by the oxyhydrogen blowpipe. So he gives himself over, once and for all, to thirsting in the dark. It's less nerve-rending. But forgive, there are days when fire and water invade my thoughts, and consequently my conversation, in so far as the two are connected.

I should like to ask some simple questions, said Camier.

Simple questions? said Mercier. Camier, you surprise me.

Their couching will be of the simplest, said Camier, all you have to do is reply without thinking.

If there's one thing I abominate, said Mercier, it's talking walking.

Our situation is desperate, said Camier.

Now now, said Mercier, none of your bombast. Would it be on account of the wind, do you suppose, that the rain has stopped, if it has?

Don't ask me, said Camier.

Let me tell you, said Mercier, before you go any further, I haven't an answer to my name. Oh there was a time I had, and none but the best, they were my only company, I even invented queries to go with them. But I sent them all packing long ago.

I don't mean that kind, said Camier.

And what kind so? said Mercier. This is looking up.

You'll see, said Camier. First, what news of the sack?

I hear nothing, said Mercier.

The sack, cried Camier, where is the sack?

Let's go down here, said Mercier, it's more sheltered.

They turned into a narrow street between high ancient houses.

Now, said Mercier.

Where is the sack? said Camier.

What possesses you to bring that up again? said Mercier.

You've told me nothing, said Camier.

Mercier stopped in his stride, which obliged Camier to stop in his too. Had not Mercier stopped in his stride, then Camier had not stopped in his either. But Mercier having stopped in his stride, Camier had to stop in his too.

Told you nothing? said Mercier.

Strictly nothing, said Camier.

What is there to tell, said Mercier, assuming I told you nothing?

Why, said Camier, if you found it, how things went, all that.

Mercier said, Let us resume our—. At a loss he gestured, with his free hand, towards his legs and those of his companion. There was a silence. Then they resumed that indescribable process not unconnected with their legs.

You were saying? said Mercier.

The sack, said Camier.

Would I appear to have it? said Mercier.

No, said Camier.

Well then? said Mercier.

So many things may have happened, said Camier. You may have looked for it, but in vain, found it and lost it again or even discarded it, said to yourself, It's not worth bothering about, or, Enough for today, tomorrow we'll see. How am I to know?

I looked for it in vain, said Mercier, longly, patiently, carefully, unsuccessfully.

He exaggerated.

Do I ask, said Mercier, how exactly you came to break the umbrella? Or what you went through before throwing it away? I combed innumerable sites, questioned innumerable parties, made allowance for the invisibility of things, the metamorphoses of time, the foible of folk in general, and of me in particular, for fabulation and fibbery, the wish to please and the urge to hurt, and had as well, just as well, stayed quietly where I was, no matter where, still trying to imagine against the endless approach, the shuffling slippers, the clinking keys, some better remedy than the yelp, the gasp, the whine, the skedaddle.

Camier said briefly what he thought of this.

Why do we insist, said Mercier, you and I for example, did you ever ask yourself that question, you who ask so many? Shall we fritter away what little is left of us in the tedium of flight and dreams of deliverance? Do you not inkle, like me, how you might adjust yourself to this preposterous penalty and placidly await the executioner, come to ratify you?

No, said Camier.

They held back on the brink of a great open space, a

square perhaps, all tumult, fluttering gleams, writhing shadows.

Let us turn back, said Mercier. This street is charming. That brothel perfume.

They set about the street the other way. It seemed changed, even in the dark. Not they, or scarcely.

I see distant lands——. said Mercier.

Where are we going? said Camier.

Shall I never shake you off? said Mercier.

Do you not know where we are going? said Camier.

What does it matter, said Mercier, where we are going? We are going, that's enough.

No need to shout, said Camier.

We go wherever the flesh creeps least, said Mercier. We dodge along, hugging the walls, wherever the shit lies least thick. We stumble on an alley in a thousand, all we need do is pace it to and fro till it's no better than the others, and you want to know where we are going. Where are your sensibilities this evening, Camier?

I recapitulate, said Camier.

He did, then asked his simple questions. This brought them to the end of the alley where, as one man, they turned back yet again.

We talk too much, said Mercier. I have heard and said more inanities, since you took me in tow, than in all the rest of my life.

Tis I am in tow, said Camier. He added, The days of our talking together may well soon be ended. So let us think twice before we hold our tongue. For then you will turn to me in vain, and I to you, to me and you not there, but elsewhere, no better off, or barely.

What's all this? said Mercier.

So much so that I often wonder, said Camier, quite often, if we had not better part now, here and now, without more ado.

If it's my feelings you're appealing to, said Mercier, you should know better.

No later than today, for example, said Camier, I was on the point of not keeping our appointment.

So they had an appointment.

How strange, said Mercier, I had to wrestle with just such an angel.

One of us will yield in the end, said Camier.

Quite so, said Mercier, no need for both to succumb.

It would not be a desertion, said Camier, not necessarily.

Far from it, said Mercier, far from it.

By that I mean a forsaking, said Camier.

I took you to, said Mercier.

But the chances are it would, said Camier.

Would what? said Mercier.

Be one, said Camier.

Well obviously, said Mercier. To go on alone, left or leaver . . . Allow me to leave the thought unfinished.

They paced on a little way in silence. Then Mercier said:

I smell kips.

All is in darkness, said Camier. No light of any colour. No number.

Let us ask this worthy constable, said Mercier.

They accosted the constable.

Pardon, Inspector, said Mercier, would you by any chance happen to know of a house . . . how shall I say, a bawdy or brothelhouse, in the vicinity.

The constable looked them up and down.

Guaranteed clean, said Mercier, as far as possible, we have a horror of the pox, my friend and I.

Are you not ashamed of yourselves, at your age? said the constable.

What is that to you? said Camier.

Ashamed? said Mercier. Are you ashamed of yourself, Camier, at your age?

Move on, said the constable.

I note your number, said Camier.

Have you our pencil? said Mercier.

Sixteen sixty-five, said Camier. The year of the plague. Easy to remember.

Look you, said Mercier, to renounce venery because of a simple falling off in erotogenesis would be puerile, in our opinion. You would not have us live without love, Inspector, were it but once a month, the night of the first Saturday for example.

And that's where the taxpayers' good-looking money goes, said Camier.

You're arrested, said the constable.

What is the charge? said Camier.

Venal love is the only kind left to us, said Mercier. Passion and dalliance are reserved for blades like you.

And solitary enjoyment, said Camier.

The constable seized Camier's arm and screwed it.

Help, Mercier, said Camier.

Unhand him please, said Mercier.

Camier gave a scream of pain. For the constable, holding fast his arm with one hand the size of two, with the other had dealt him a violent smack. His interest was awakening. It was not every night a diversion of

92

this quality broke the monotony of his beat. The profession had its silver lining, he had always said so. He unsheathed his truncheon. Come on with you now, he said, and no nonsense. With the hand that held the truncheon he drew a whistle from his pocket, for he was no less dexterous than powerful. But he had reckoned without Mercier (who can blame him?) and to his undoing, for Mercier raised his right foot (who could have foreseen it?) and launched it clumsily but with force among the testicles (to call a spade a spade) of the adversary (impossible to miss them). The constable dropped everything and fell howling with pain and nausea to the ground. Mercier himself lost his balance and came down cruelly on his hipbone. But Camier, beside himself with indignation, caught up the truncheon, sent the helmet flying with his boot and clubbed the defenceless skull with all his might, again and again, holding the truncheon with both hands. The howls ceased. Mercier rose to his feet. Help me! roared Camier. He tugged furiously at the cape, caught between the head and the cobbles. What do you want with that? said Mercier. Cover his gob, said Camier. They freed the cape and lowered it over the face. Then Camier resumed his blows. Enough, said Mercier, give me that blunt instrument. Camier dropped the truncheon and took to his heels. Wait, said Mercier. Camier halted. Mercier picked up the truncheon and dealt the muffled skull one moderate and attentive blow, just one. Like partly shelled hard-boiled egg, was his impression. Who knows, he mused, perhaps that was the finishing touch. He threw aside the truncheon and joined Camier, taking him by the arm. Look lively now, he said. On the edge of the square they were brought to a stand by the violence of the blast. Then slowly, head down, unsteadily, they pressed on through a tumult of shadow and clamour, stumbling on the cobbles strewn already with black boughs trailing grating before the wind or by little leaps and bounds as though on springs. On the far side debouched a narrow street the image of it they had just left.

He didn't hurt you badly, I hope, said Mercier.

The bastard, said Camier. Did you mark the mug?

This should greatly simplify matters, said Mercier.

And they talk of law and order, said Camier.

We would never have hit on it alone, said Mercier.

Best now go to Helen's, said Camier.

Indubitably, said Mercier.

Are you sure we were not seen? said Camier.

Chance knows how to handle it, said Mercier. Deep down I never counted but on her.

I don't see what difference it makes, said Camier.

You will, said Mercier. The flowers are in the vase and the flock back in the fold.

I don't understand, said Camier.

They went then mostly in silence the short way they had still to go, now exposed to the full fury of the wind, now through zones of calm, Mercier striving to grasp the full consequences for them of what had chanced, Camier to make sense of the phrase he had just heard. But they strove in vain, the one to conceive their good fortune, the other to arrive at a meaning, for they were weary, in need of sleep, buffeted by the wind, while in their skulls, to crown their discomfiture, a pelting of insatiable blows.

Summary
of two preceding chapters

V

Evening of the eighth (?) day.
At Helen's.
The umbrella.
Next day at Helen's.
Pastimes.
Next afternoon in the street.
The bar.
Mercier and Camier confer.
Result of this conference.
At Helen's.
Next day noon in front of Helen's.
The umbrella.
Looks at the sky.
The umbrella.
More looks at the sky.
Ladysmith.
The umbrella.
More looks at the sky.
The umbrella.
Mercier departs.
Mercier's encounters.
Mercier's mind.
The chains.

VI

Same evening.
Last bar but one.
Mother Church and artificial insemination.
The giant barman.
Mercier's contribution to the controversy of the universals.
The umbrella, end.
The bicycle, end.
In the street.
The ingle-nook.
The hose and the blowpipe.
The wind.
The fatal alley.
The sack.
The gulf.
The fatal alley.
Distant lands.
The fatal alley.
The constable.
The gulf.
"The flowers are in the vase."
The wind.
The endocranian blows.

VII

A road still carriageable climbs over the high moorland.
It cuts across vast turfbogs, a thousand feet above sea-
level, two thousand if you prefer. It leads to nothing
any more. A few ruined forts, a few ruined dwellings.
The sea is not far, just visible beyond the valleys dipping
eastward, pale plinth as pale as the pale wall of sky.
Tarns lie hidden in the folds of the moor, invisible from
the road, reached by faint paths, under high over-
hanging crags. All seems flat, or gently undulating, and
there at a stone's throw these high crags, all un-
suspected by the wayfarer. Of granite what is more. In
the west the chain is at its highest, its peaks exalt even
the most downcast eyes, peaks commanding the vast
champaign land, the celebrated pastures, the golden
vale. Before the travellers, as far as eye can reach, the
road winds on into the south, uphill, but imperceptibly.
None ever pass this way but beauty-spot hogs and
fanatical trampers. Under its heather mask the quag
allures, with an allurement not all mortals can resist.
Then it swallows them up or the mist comes down. The
city is not far either, from certain points its lights can
be seen by night, its light rather, and by day its haze.
Even the piers of the harbour can be distinguished, on

very clear days, of the two harbours, tiny arms in the glassy sea outflung, known flat, seen raised. And the islands and promontories, one has only to stop and turn at the right place, and of course by night the beacon lights, both flashing and revolving. It is here one would lie down, in a hollow bedded with dry heather, and fall asleep, for the last time, on an afternoon, in the sun, head down among the minute life of stems and bells, and fast fall asleep, fast farewell to charming things. It's a birdless sky, the odd raptor, no song. End of descriptive passage.

What is that cross? said Camier.

There they go again.

Planted in the bog, not far from the road, but too far for the inscription to be visible, a plain cross stood.

I once knew, said Mercier, but no longer.

I too once knew, said Camier, I'm almost sure.

But he was not quite sure.

It was the grave of a nationalist, brought here in the night by the enemy and executed, or perhaps only the corpse brought here, to be dumped. He was buried long after, with a minimum of formality. His name was Masse, perhaps Massey. No great store was set by him now, in patriotic circles. It was true he had done little for the cause. But he still had this monument. All that, and no doubt much more, Mercier and perhaps Camier had once known, and all forgotten.

How aggravating, said Camier.

Would you like to go and look? said Mercier.

And you? said Camier.

As you please, said Mercier.

They had cut themselves cudgels before leaving the

timber-line. They made good headway, for their age. They wondered which would drop first. They went a good half mile without a word, no longer arm in arm, but each keeping to his side of the road whose whole width therefore, or nearly, lay between them. They opened their mouths simultaneously, Mercier to say, Strange impression sometimes—, and Camier, Do you think there are worms—?

Pardon, said Camier, what was that you said?

No no, said Mercier, you.

No no, said Camier, nothing of interest.

No matter, said Mercier, let's have it.

I assure you, said Camier.

I beg of you, said Mercier.

After you, said Camier.

I interrupted you, said Mercier.

I interrupted *you*, said Camier.

Silence fell again. Mercier broke it, or rather Camier.

Have you caught a chill? said Mercier.

For Camier had coughed.

It's a little early to be sure, said Camier.

I do hope it's nothing, said Mercier.

What a beautiful day, said Camier.

Is it not? said Mercier.

How beautiful the bog, said Camier.

Most beautiful, said Mercier.

Will you look at that heather, said Camier.

Mercier looked with ostentation at the heather and whistled incredulously.

Underneath there is turf, said Camier.

One would never think so, said Mercier.

Camier coughed again.

Do you think there are worms, said Camier, the same as in the earth.

Turf has remarkable properties, said Mercier.

But are there worms? said Camier.

Shall we dig a little hole and see? said Mercier.

Certainly not, said Camier, what an idea.

He coughed a third time.

The day was indeed fine, at least what passes for fine, in those parts, but cool, and night at hand.

Where shall we pass the night, said Camier, have we thought of that?

Strange impression, said Mercier, strange impression sometimes that we are not alone. You not?

I am not sure I understand, said Camier.

Now quick, now slow, that is Camier all over.

Like the presence of a third party, said Mercier. Enveloping us. I have felt it from the start. And I am anything but psychic.

Does it bother you? said Camier.

At first no, said Mercier.

And now? said Camier.

It begins to bother me a little, said Mercier.

Night was indeed at hand, and a good thing for them, without perhaps their yet admitting it, that night was at hand.

Hell, said Mercier, who the devil are you, Camier?

Me? said Camier. I am Camier, Francis Xavier.

I might well ask myself the same question, said Mercier.

Where do we plan to pass the night? said Camier. Under the stars?

There are ruins, said Mercier, or we can walk till we drop.

A little further on they did indeed come to the ruins of a house. A good half-century old by the look of them. It was almost night.

Now we must choose, said Mercier.

Between what? said Camier.

Ruin and collapse, said Mercier.

Could we not somehow combine them? said Camier.

We shall never make the next, said Mercier.

They walked on, if it could be called walking. Finally Mercier said:

I don't think I can go much further.

So soon? said Camier. What is it? The legs? The feet?

The head rather, said Mercier.

It was now night. The road vanished in darkness a few yards ahead of them. It was too early for the stars to give light. The moon would not rise till later. It was the darkest hour. They stood still, all but hidden from each other by the width of the road. Camier approached Mercier.

We'll turn back, said Camier. Lean on me.

It's my head, I tell you, said Mercier.

You see shapes that do not exist, said Camier. Groves, where none are. Strange animals loom, giant horses and cows, out of the murk do you but raise your head. High barns too and enormous ricks. And all more and more blurred and fuzzy, as if you were going blind before your very eyes.

Take me by the hand if you wish, said Mercier.

So hand in hand they retraced their steps, the big

hand in the little, in silence. Finally Mercier said:

Your hand is clammy and you cough, perhaps you have senile tuberculosis.

Camier did not answer. They stumbled on. Finally Mercier said:

I hope we have not overstepped it.

Camier did not answer. There are times when the simplest words are slow to signify. Here "it" was the laggard. But do him justice, soon he called a sudden halt.

It's a little off the road, said Mercier, we may have passed it unawares, so black is the night.

One would have seen the track, said Camier.

So one would have thought, said Mercier.

Camier advanced, drawing Mercier in his wake.

Keep level with me for God's sake, said Camier.

Consider yourself fortunate, said Mercier, that you don't have to carry me. Lean on me, those were your words.

True, said Camier.

I decline, said Mercier, not wishing to be a burden. And when I lag a little you berate me.

Their progress was now no better than a totter. They overflowed on the bog, with risk of fatal consequences, to them, but nothing doing. Soon falls began to enter into play, now Camier accompanying Mercier (in his fall), now the reverse, and now the two collapsing simultaneously, as one man, without preconcertation and in perfect interindependency. They did not immediately rise, having practised in their youth the noble art, but rise in the end they did. And even at the worst moments their hands kept faith, although no knowing now which gave and which received the clasp, so confounded the confusion at this stage. Their anxiety (regarding the ruins) was no doubt in part to blame, and regrettably so, being ill-founded. For they came to them in the end, to those ruins they feared perhaps far behind them, they even had the strength to gain their inmost parts till these were all about them and they lay there as in a tomb. It was only then, sheltered from the cold they did not feel, from the unvexing damp, that they accepted rest, sleep rather, and that their hands were freed to go about their old business.

They sleep side by side, the deep doze of the old. They will speak together yet, but only at haphazard as the saying is. But did they ever speak together otherwise? In any case nothing is known for sure, henceforth. Here would be the place to make an end. After all it is the end. But there is still day, day after day, afterlife all life long, the dust of all that is dead and buried rising, eddying, settling, burying again. So let him wake, Mercier, Camier, no matter, Camier, Camier wakes, it's night, still night, he doesn't know the time, no matter, he gets up and moves away, in the dark, lies down again a little further on, still in the ruins, they are extensive. Why? No knowing. No knowing such things any more. Good reasons are never lacking for trying somewhere else, a little further on, a little further back. So good in the event that Mercier follows suit, at much the same moment no doubt. The whole question of priority, so luminous hitherto, is from now on obscure. There they are then lying, or perhaps merely crouching, at a reasonable remove from each other, compared to their customary cleavings. They drowse off again, or perhaps simply lose themselves in thought. Before dawn in any case, well before, one of them gets up, say Mercier, fair is fair, and goes to look if Camier is still there, that is in the place where he thinks he left him, that is in the place where in the first instance they had dropped as one. Is that clear? But Camier is no longer there, how could he be? Then Mercier to himself, Well I never, the little rascal, he has stolen a march on me, and picks his way through the rubble, his eyes agoggle (for the least ray of light), his arms like antennae probing the air, his feet fumbling, gains and climbs the track leading to the road. Almost at the same moment, not precisely, that wouldn't work, almost, a little sooner, a little later, no importance, hardly any, Camier executes the same manœuvre. The pig, he says, he has given me the slip, and gropes his way out with infinite precautions, life is so precious, pain so redoubtable, the old skin so slow to mend, out of this hospitable chaos, without a single word or other sign of gratitude, one does not return thanks to stone, one should. Such roughly must have been the course of events. There they are then back on the road, appreciably recruited in spite of all, and each knows the other is at hand, feels, believes, fears, hopes, denies he is at hand, and can do nothing about it. Now and then they halt, all ears for the footfalls, footfalls distinguishable from all the other footfalls, and they are legion, softly falling on the face of the earth, more or less softly, day and night. But in the dark a man sees what is not, hears what is not, gives way to imaginings, there is no sense in giving heed, and yet God wot he does. So it may well be that one or the other stops, sits down on the side of the road, almost in the bog, to rest, or the better to think, or the better to stop thinking, good reasons are never lacking for coming to a stop, and that the other catches up, the one left behind, and seeing this kind of shade does not believe his eyes, at least not enough to run to its arms, or to kick it arse over tip into the quags. The sitter sees too, unless his eyes are closed, in any case he hears, unless he has gone to sleep, and taxes himself with hallucination, but half-heartedly. Then gradually he rises and the other sits, and so on, you see the gag, it can last them all the way to town, each yeaing and naying the other to no avail. For needless to say it is townward they are bound, as always when they leave it, as after long vain reckonings the head falls back among the data. But beyond the eastering valleys the sky changes, it's the foul old sun yet again, punctual as a hangman. Take a firm hold on yourselves now, we're going to see the glories of the earth once more, and on top of that ourselves once more, the night won't have made a ha'porth of difference, it's only the lid on the latrine, lucky we it has one, our brethren are there to dispel our hopes if any, our multitudinous brethren, and the rising gorge, and all the hoary old pangs. So there they are in view again, of each other, what less can you expect, they had only to set out sooner. Whose turn now, Camier's, then turn worm and have a good look. You can't believe your eyes, no matter, you will, for it's himself and no error, your boon old weary hairy skeleton of a butty, bet to the world, within stone's throw, but don't throw it, think of the good old days when you wallowed in the swill together. Mercier himself bows to the irrecusable, a habit one contracts among the axioms, while Camier raises his hand in a gesture at once prudent, courtly, elegant and uncompromising. Mercier hesitates an instant before acknowledging this salute, unexpected to say the least, which opportunity to hurry on Camier is not slow to seize. But even to the dead a man may wave, they do not benefit but the hearse squad are gratified, and the friends and relatives, and the horses, it helps them to believe they are surviving, the waver himself is the livelier for it too. Finally Mercier not at all put out raises in his turn his hand, not any old hand but the heterologous, in the affably selfless flourish prelates use when consecrating some portion of favoured matter. But to have done with these inanities, at the first fork Camier stopped and his heart beat fast with the thought of what to pack into a last long salute gravid to bursting with unprecedented delicacy. It was true countryside at last, quickset hedgerows, mud, liquid manure, rocks, wallows, cow-shit, hovels, and here and there a form unmistakably human scratching at his plot since the first scabs of dawn, or shifting his dung, with a spade, having lost his shovel and his fork being broken. A giant tree, jumble of black boughs, stands between the branching roads. The left leads straight to the town, at least what passes for straight in those parts, the second after long meandering through a rash of pestilential hamlets. Camier then, having reached this juncture, stopped and turned, whereon Mercier also stopped and half turned, all set to fly. But his fears were unfounded, for Camier merely raised his hand, in a gesture of salute similar in all respects to that with which he had already so kindly obliged, while darting the other, rigid at full stretch and doubtless quivering, at the right branch. A moment thus and then, with a kind of heroic precipitancy, he sprang off in the direction indicated and vanished, as into a burning house where three generations of his nearest and dearest were awaiting rescue. Reassured, but not entirely, Mercier advanced with caution to the fork, looked in the direction Camier had taken, saw no sign of him and hastened away in the other. Unstuck at last! Such roughly must have been the course of events. The earth dragged on into the light, the brief interminable light.

VIII

That's it. It takes a little time to grasp more or less what happened. It's your sole excuse, the best in any case. Enough to tempt you joking apart to have another go, another go at getting up, dressing up (paramount), ingesting, excreting, undressing up, dossing down, and all the other things too tedious to enumerate, in the long run too tedious, requiring to be done and suffered. No danger of losing interest, under these conditions. You cultivate your memory till it's passable, a treasure-bin, stroll in your crypt, unlit, return to the scenes, call back the old sounds (paramount), till you have the lot off pat and you all at a loss, head, nose, ears and the rest, what remains to snuff up, they all smell equally sweet, what old jingles to play back. Pretty beyond! And all that can still happen to you! Such things! Such adventures! You think you have done with it all and then one fine day, bang! full in the eye. Or in the arse, or in the balls, or in the cunt, no lack of targets, above all below the waist. And they talk of stiffs being bored!

It's wearing naturally, all-absorbing, no time left for putting a shine on the soul, but you can't have every-thing, the body in bits, the mind flayed alive and the archeus (in the stomach) as in the days of innocency, before the flop, yes, it's a fact, no time left for eternity.

But one black beast is hard to keep at bay, the waiting for the night that makes it all plain at last, for it is not every night possesses this property. This can drag on for months, the betwixt and between, the long dull mawkish muddle of regrets, the dead and buried with the undying, you've been through it all a thousand times, the old joke that has ceased to amuse, the smile unsmilable smiled a thousand times. It's night, forenight, and there are no more sedatives. Fortunately it does not always last for ever, a few months do the trick as a rule, a few years, sudden ends have even been observed, in warm climates particularly. Nor is it of necessity unremitting, brief breaks for recreation are permitted, with the illusion of life they sometimes give, while they last, of time in motion, of a detail yet for the drain.

Then there are the pretty colours, expiring greens and yellows vaguely speaking, they pale to paler still but only the better to pierce you, will they ever die, yes, they will.

And to follow? That will be all, thank you. The bill.

Seen from outside it was a house like any other. Seen from inside too. And yet it emitted Camier. He still took the air in a small way, when the weather was fine. It was summer. Autumn would have suited better, late November, but there it is, it was summer. The sun was going down, the strings were tuning up, why God knows, before breaking into the old wail. Lightly attired Camier moved forward, his head resting on his breastbone. Every now and then he straightened up, with a sudden jerk instantaneously annulled, by way of looking to see where he was going. He had felt even worse, he was in one of his better days. He got many a knock from the other foot-passengers, but not deliberate, they would all have preferred not to touch him. He was off for a little turn, no more, a little turn, he would very soon feel tired, very tired. Then he would halt, open wide his little blue-red eyes and cast about him till he had his bearings. Comparison of his strength with that required to get him home often drove him to the nearest bar for more, and for a little courage, a little courage and confidence regarding the way back, of which often too he had only the haziest notion. He helped himself on by means of a stick with which he struck the ground at every step he took, not at every two, at every one.

A hand landed with a thump on his shoulder. Camier froze, shrunk, but did not raise his head. He had no objection, it was even better thus, simpler, but not to the point of his losing sight of the earth. He heard the words, It's a small world. Fingers raised his chin. He saw a figure of towering stature, squalidly clad. No point in detailing him. He seemed well on in years. He stunk with the double stink of the old and the unwashed, that strongish smell. Camier inhaled it connoisseurishly.

Have you met my friend Mercier? said the man.

Camier looked in vain.

Behind you, said the man.

Camier turned. Mercier, apparently intent on a hatter's show-window, presented his profile.

Allow me, said the man. Mercier, Camier, Camier, Mercier.

They stood in the attitude of two blind men whom not unwillingness, but want of vision alone, prevents from growing acquainted.

I see you have met before, said the man. I knew it. Don't salute each other whatever you do.

I don't think I recognize you, sir, said Camier.

I am Watt, said Watt. As you say, I'm unrecognizable.

Watt? said Camier. The name means nothing to me.

I am not widely known, said Watt, true, but I shall be, one day. Not universally perhaps, my notoriety is not likely ever to penetrate to the denizens of Dublin's fair city, or of Cuq-Toulza.

Where did you make my acquaintance? said Camier. You must forgive my want of memory. I have not yet had time to unravel all.

In your moses basket, said Watt. You haven't changed.

Then you knew my mother, said Camier.

A saint, said Watt. She changed your diapers every two hours till you were pushing five. He turned to Mercier. Whereas yours, he said, I only saw inanimate.

I knew a poor man named Murphy, said Mercier, who had a look of you, only less battered of course. But he died ten years ago, in rather mysterious circumstances. They never found the body, can you imagine.

My dream, said Watt.

So he doesn't know you either? said Camier.

Come now, my children, said Watt, be on speaking terms again. Don't mind me. I'm discretion itself. The wild horse's despair.

Gentlemen, said Camier, allow me to leave you.

Were I not without desires, said Mercier, I would buy me one of those hats, to wear on my head.

Come have one on me, said Watt. He added, Chaps, with a smile devoid of malice, almost tender.

Really—, said Camier.

That fawn billycock on the block, said Mercier.

Watt took hold of Mercier's right arm, then, after a brief scuffle, of Camier's left, and drew them along.

Jesus off again, said Camier.

Mercier espied, in the far distance, the chains of his childhood, the same that had served him as playmates. Watt admonished him:

If you picked up your feet you'd make better progress. We're not going to have your teeth out today.

They advanced into the sunset (you can't deny yourself everything), burning up the sky higher than the highest roofs.

A pity Dumas the Elder cannot see us, said Watt.

Or one of the Evangelists, said Camier.

A different class, Mercier and Camier, for all their faults.

My strength is limited, said Camier, if yours is not.

We're nearly home, said Watt.

A police constable barred their way.

This is a sidewalk, he said, not a circus ring.

What is that to you? said Camier.

Fuck along with you now, said Mercier, and no nonsense.

Easy! Easy! said Watt. He stooped towards the constable. Inspector, he said, have a heart, they are a little—he tapped his forehead—but they wouldn't hurt a fly. The long hank takes himself for John the Baptist, of whom you have certainly heard, and Runty on my right daren't sit on his glass arse. As for me I am resigned to the utilities I was stuck with at birth, one of which consists in promenading these gentlemen, weather permitting. Given all this we can hardly be expected to form up in Indian file, as propriety requires.

Go and promenade in the country, said the constable.

We have tried, said Watt, time and time again. But they see red at the mere sight of green. Is that not curious? Whereas the shop-windows, concrete, cement, asphalt, neon, pickpockets, dogberries and kips, all this calms them down and sows in them the seeds of a night's refreshing sleep.

You don't own the sidewalk, said the constable.

Look out! cried Watt. See how their agitation grows! God grant they don't prove too much for me! He let go their arms and encircled their waists, hugging them against him. Forward my hearties, he said. They reeled off in a tangle of legs. The constable cursed them on their way.

What do you take us for? said Camier. Let me go.

But we're doing fine, said Watt. We smell of putrefaction one and all. Did you see his snout? He was dying for a snite. That's why he let us go.

They collapsed pell-mell in a bar. Mercier and Camier strained towards the counter, but Watt sat them down at a table and called for three doubles at the top of his voice.

Don't say you never put foot in this joint before, said Watt, I can well believe you. Order grappa and you're ejected.

The whiskey came.

I too have sought, said Watt, all on my own, only I

thought I knew what. Can you beat that one? He raised his hands and passed them over his face, then slowly down his shoulders and front till they met again on his knees. Incredible but true, he said.

Disjointed members stirred in the grey air.

One shall be born, said Watt, one is born of us, who having nothing will wish for nothing, except to be left the nothing he hath.

Mercier and Camier paid scant heed to these sayings. They were beginning to look at each other again, with something of the old look.

I all but gave myself up, said Camier.

Did you return to the scene? said Mercier.

Watt rubbed his hands.

You do me good, he said, you really do me good. You almost comfort me.

Then I said to myself—, said Camier.

May you feel one day, said Watt, what now I feel. That won't prevent your having lived in vain, but it will, how shall I say—?

Then I said to myself, said Camier, that you might have had the same idea.

So you didn't, said Mercier.

A bit of warmth for the old cockles, said Watt, that's it, a touch of warmth for the poor old cockles.

I was afraid I might run into you, said Camier.

Watt banged the table, whereon an impressive silence fell. This was doubtless what he had in view, for into it he cast, in a voice crackling with vehemence:

Bugger life!

Indignant murmurs were heard. The manager approached, or perhaps even the proprietor. He was dressed with care. Some purists might have preferred, with his pearl-grey trousers, black shoes to the tan he wore. But after all he was on his own premises. By way of buttonhole he had chosen a tulip bud.

Out, he said.

Whence? said Camier. Hence?

Out to hell out of here, said the manager. It must have been the manager. But how different from Mr Gast!

He has just lost his unique child, said Camier, unique of its kind.

Bigeminal, said Mercier.

His grief boils over, said Camier, could anything he more natural?

His wife is at her last, said Mercier.

We dare not let him out of our sight, said Camier.

One more small double, said Mercier, if we can prevail on him to swallow it he's saved.

None more dearly than he, said Camier, loves life, the humble daily round, the innocent pleasures and very pains themselves that permit us to supply the deficiencies of the Redemption. Make this clear to these good gentlemen. A cry of revolt has escaped him. His loss is so recent. Tomorrow, before his porridge, he will redden at the recollection.

He will wipe his lips, said Mercier, slip his napkin back into its ring, clasp his hands and ejaculate, Blessed be the dead that die!

Had he broken a glass, said Camier, we would be the first to reprove him. But such is not the case.

Overlook this little incident, said Mercier, it will not occur again. Will it, daddy?

Pass the sponge, said Camier, according to Saint Matthew.

And give us the same, said Mercier, your whiskey likes us.

Buy what did you say? said the manager, his cupidity aroused.

Geminal, said Camier.

Yes, said Mercier, everything double but the arse. We bury him day after tomorrow. Don't we, daddy?

It's the organizer made a balls of it, said Camier.

The organizer? said the manager.

Each egg has its little life and soul of the party, said Camier. Did you not know that? Sometimes he nods. Could you blame him?

Calm him down, said the manager. Don't try me too far.

He withdrew. He had been firm without harshness, human and yet dignified. He had not lost face before his customers, butchers for the most part, whom the blood of the lamb had made rather intolerant.

The second round came. The change from the first still lay on the table. Help yourself, my good man, said Camier.

The manager moved from group to group. Gradually the saloon revived.

How can one say such things? said Camier.

To think them is a crime in itself, said Mercier.

Towards man, said Camier.

And beast, said Mercier.

God alone would agree with him, said Camier.

That lot, said Mercier.

Watt seemed asleep. He had not touched his second glass.

Perhaps a sip of water, said Camier.

Let him be, said Mercier.

Mercier rose and went to the window. He introduced his head between the curtain and the glass, which enabled him, as he had foreseen, to observe the heaven. Its colours were not quite spent. He remarked at the same time, as he had not suspected, that from it a fine and no doubt gentle rain was dropping. The glass was not wet. He returned to his seat.

You know what often comes back to me? said Camier.

It's raining, said Mercier.

The goat, said Camier.

Mercier was looking perplexedly at Watt.

Day was breaking, said Camier, drizzly day.

Where have I seen this johnny before? said Mercier. He drew back his chair, crouched down and peered up at the face dim under the lee of the hat.

Old Madden too—, said Camier.

Suddenly Watt seized Camier's stick, wrenched it clear, raised it aloft and slammed it down in a passion of rage on the next table where a man with side-whiskers was sitting quietly reading his newspaper and smoking his pipe, before a foaming pint. What had to happen did, the glass top flew into smithers, the stick broke in two, the pint overturned and the man with side-whiskers intact fell over backwards, still sitting on the chair, the pipe in his mouth and the latest news in his hand. The piece of stick remaining in his Watt now hurled at the counter where it brought down a number of bottles and glasses. Watt waited for all the clatter and clash to subside, then bawled:

Fuck life!

Mercier and Camier, as though activated by a single wire, drained their glasses in haste and made a dash for the exit. Once safely there they turned. A stifled roar rose briefly above the hubbub:

Up Quin!

It's raining, said Camier.

I told you so, said Mercier.

Then farewell, said Camier.

You wouldn't walk with me a bit of the way? said Mercier.

What way? said Camier.

I live now beyond the canal, said Mercier.

It's not my way, said Camier.

There's a prospect there would break your heart, said Mercier.

Too late, said Camier.

We'll have a last one, said Mercier.

I haven't a make, said Camier.

Mercier put his hand in his pocket.

No, said Camier.

I've enough, said Mercier.

No I tell you, said Camier.

Like arctic flowers, said Mercier. In half an hour they'll be gone.

Canals mean nothing to me now, said Camier.

They advanced in silence to the end of the street.

Here I go right, said Mercier. He halted.

What ails you now? said Camier.

I halt, said Mercier.

They turned right, Camier on the sidewalk, Mercier in the gutter.

Up who? said Camier.

I heard Quin, said Mercier.

That must be someone who does not exist, said Camier.

The whiskey had helped after all. They made good headway, for their age. Camier missed his stick sorely.

I miss my stick, said Camier, it was my father's.

I never heard you speak of it, said Mercier.

Looking back on it, said Camier, we heard ourselves speaking of everything but ourselves.

We didn't bring it off, said Mercier, I grant you that. He took thought a moment, then uttered this fragment, Perhaps we might—.

What a deathtrap, said Camier, wasn't it here we lost the sack?

Not far from here, said Mercier.

Between the high ancient houses the pale strip of sky seemed even narrower than the street. It should on the contrary have seemed wider. Night plays these little tricks.

All . . . more or less nowadays? said Mercier.

Pardon? said Camier.

I ask if all is, you know, more or less, with you, nowadays.

No, said Camier.

A few minutes later tears welled up into his eyes. Old men weep quite readily, contrary to what one might have expected.

And you? said Camier.

Nor, said Mercier.

The houses grew fewer, the street broader, the sky more ample, they could see each other again, they had only to turn their heads, one to the left, the other to the right, only to raise their heads and turn them. Then suddenly all fell open before them, as if space had gaped and earth vanished in the shadow it casts skywards. But these are diversions do not last and they were not slow to be struck by their situation, that of two old men, one tall, one short, on a bridge. It itself was charming, connoisseurs were heard to say, a charming, charming bridge. Why not? Its name in any case was Lock Bridge, and rightly so, one had only to lean over the parapet to be satisfied on that score.

Here we are, said Mercier.

Here? said Camier.

The end went like magic, said Mercier.

And your prospect? said Camier.

Are you eyeless? said Mercier.

Camier scanned the various horizons, destrorsum, as always.

Don't rush me, he said, I'll try again.

You see it better from the bank, said Mercier.

Then why arse around up here? said Camier. Have you some sighs on your chest?

They went down on the bank. A bench with backrest was there to receive them. They sat.

So that's it, said Camier.

The rain fell silently on the canal, to Mercier's no little chagrin. But high above the horizon the clouds were fraying out in long black strands, fine as weepers' tresses. Nature at her most thoughtful.

I see our sister-convict Venus, said Camier, foundering in the skywrack. I hope it's not for that you dragged me here.

Further, further, said Mercier.

Camier screened his eyes with his hand.

Further north, said Mercier. North, I said, not south.

Wait, said Camier.

A little more, a little less.

Is that your flowers? said Camier.

Did you see? said Mercier.

I saw a few pale gleams, said Camier.

You need to have the knack, said Mercier.

I'd do better with my knuckle in my eye, said Camier.

The ancients' Blessed Isles, said Mercier.

They weren't hard to please, said Camier.

You wait, said Mercier, you only barely saw, but you'll never forget, you'll be back.

What is that grim pile? said Camier.

A hospital, said Mercier. Diseases of the skin.

The very thing for me, said Camier.

And mucous membrane, said Mercier. He cocked an ear. Not all that howling this evening.

It must be too early, said Camier.

Camier rose and went to the water.

Careful! said Mercier.

Camier returned to the bench.

Do you remember the parrot? said Mercier.

I remember the goat, said Camier.

I have the feeling he's dead, said Mercier.

We did not meet many animals, said Camier.

I have the feeling he was already dead the day she told us she had put him out in the country.

Waste no grief on him, said Camier.

He went a second time to the water, pored over it a little, then returned to the bench.

Well, he said, I must go. Farewell, Mercier.

Sleep sound, said Mercier.

Alone he watched the sky go out, dark deepen to its full. He kept his eyes on the engulfed horizon, for he knew from experience what last throes it was capable of. And in the dark he could hear better too, he could hear the sounds the long day had kept from him, human murmurs for example, and the rain on the water.

Summary
of two preceding chapters

VII

The bog.
The cross.
The ruins.
Mercier and Camier part.
The return.

VIII

The life of afterlife.
Camier alone.
Mercier and Watt.
Mercier, Camier and Watt.
The last policeman.
The last bar.
Mercier and Camier.
Lock Bridge.
The arctic flowers.
Mercier alone.
Dark at its full.

(1946)

Selected Grove Press Paperbacks

E237   ALLEN, DONALD M. (Ed.) / The New American Poetry:
       1945-1960 / $3.95
B181   ANONYMOUS / A Man With A Maid / $1.95
B334   ANONYMOUS / My Secret Life / $2.45
B155   ANONYMOUS / The Pearl / $1.95
B383   ARSAN, EMMANUELLE / Emmanuelle II / $1.95
E425   BARAKA, IMAMU AMIRI (LeRoi Jones) / The Baptism and
       The Toilet / $2.45
E96   BECKETT, SAMUEL / Endgame / $1.95
B78   BECKETT, SAMUEL / Three Novels (Molloy, Malone Dies,
       The Unnamable) / $1.95
E33   BECKETT, SAMUEL / Waiting For Godot / $1.95
B79   BEHAN, BRENDAN / The Quare Fellow and The Hostage:
       Two Plays / $2.45
B186   BERNE, ERIC / Games People Play / $1.50
E300   BERNE, ERIC / Transactional Analysis in
       Psychotherapy / $3.95
E417   BIRCH, CYRIL WITH KEENE, DONALD (Eds.) / Anthology
       of Chinese Literature, Volume 1: From Early Times to the
       Fourteenth Century / $3.95
E584   BIRCH, CYRIL (Ed.) / Anthology of Chinese Literature,
       Volume 2: From the 14th Century to the Present Day / $4.95
E368   BORGES, JORGE LUIS / Ficciones / $2.95
B283   BRAUTIGAN, RICHARD / A Confederate General From Big
       Sur / $1.50 (also available as E478 / $1.95)
B120   BRECHT, BERTOLT / Galileo / $1.95
B108   BRECHT, BERTOLT / Mother Courage and Her
       Children / $1.50
B333   BRECHT, BERTOLT / The Threepenny Opera / $1.45
B115   BURROUGHS, WILLIAM S. / Naked Lunch / $1.95
GT422 CLURMAN, HAROLD (Ed.) / Seven Plays of the Modern
       Theater / $4.95 (Waiting For Godot by Samuel Beckett,
       The Quare Fellow by Brendan Behan, A Taste of Honey by
       Shelagh Delaney, The Connection by Jack Gelber, The
       Balcony by Jean Genet, Rhinoceros by Eugene Ionesco
       and The Birthday Party by Harold Pinter)
E190   CUMMINGS, E. E. / Selected Poems / $1.95
E344   DURRENMATT, FRIEDRICH / The Visit / $2.95
B342   FANON, FRANTZ / The Wretched of the Earth / $1.95
E130   GENET, JEAN / The Balcony / $2.95

E208 GENET, JEAN / The Blacks: A Clown Show / $2.95
B382 GENET, JEAN / Querelle / $1.95
B306 HERNTON, CALVIN C. / Sex and Racism in America / $1.95
E101 IONESCO, EUGENE / Four Plays (The Bald Soprano, The Lesson, The Chairs, and Jack, or The Submission) / $1.95
E259 IONESCO, EUGENE / Rhinoceros and Other Plays / $1.95
E216 KEENE, DONALD (Ed.) / Anthology of Japanese Literature: From the Earliest Era to the Mid-Nineteenth Century / $3.95
E573 KEENE, DONALD (Ed.) / Modern Japanese Literature / $4.95
B300 KEROUAC, JACK / The Subterraneans / $1.50
B9   LAWRENCE, D. H. / Lady Chatterley's Lover / $1.95
B373 LUCAS, GEORGE / American Graffiti / $1.50
B146 MALCOLM X / The Autobiography of Malcolm X / $1.95
B326 MILLER, HENRY / Nexus / $1.95
B100 MILLER, HENRY / Plexus / $1.45
B325 MILLER, HENRY / Sexus / $1.50
B10   MILLER, HENRY / Tropic of Cancer / $1.95
B59   MILLER, HENRY / Tropic of Capricorn / $1.95
E636 NERUDA, PABLO / Five Decades: Poems 1925-1970 / $3.95
E359 PAZ, OCTAVIO / The Labyrinth of Solitude: Life and Thought in Mexico / $3.95
E315 PINTER, HAROLD / The Birthday Party and The Room / $1.95
E411 PINTER, HAROLD / The Homecoming / $1.95
GT614 POPKIN, HENRY (Ed.) / Modern British Drama / $5.95 (A Taste of Honey by Shelagh Delaney, The Hostage by Brendan Behan, Roots by Arnold Wesker, Serjeant Musgrave's Dance by John Arden, One Way Pendulum by N. F. Simpson, The Caretaker by Harold Pinter and essays by major British directors and playwrights.)
B202 REAGE, PAULINE / The Story of O / $1.95
B323 SCHUTZ, WILLIAM C. / Joy / $1.95
B313 SELBY, HUBERT JR. / Last Exit to Brooklyn / $1.95
E618 SNOW, EDGAR / Red Star Over China / $2.95
B319 STOPPARD, TOM / Rosencrantz and Guildenstern Are Dead / $1.95
E219 WATTS, ALAN W. / The Spirit of Zen: A Way of Life, Work, and Art in the Far East / $2.45

GROVE PRESS, INC., 53 East 11th Street, New York, N.Y. 10003